ELECTRICAL SERVICE & REPAIR

1999 Domestic Vehicles

FORD MOTOR CO.

Starting & Charging Systems

Wiring Diagrams

HOW TO FIND
THE INFORMATION

3 Quick Steps

1 On facing page, you'll find the Contents of this manual arranged according to manufacturer. Locate the manufacturer of the vehicle you're working on...notice it has a Black square next to it.

2 **THUMB INDEX RECTANGLE**

Looking along the right-hand edge of the manual, you'll notice additional Black squares. Match the Black square of the appropriate manufacturer with the Black squares in line with it on the manual's edge. Turn directly to the first page (Contents Page) of that manufacturer's "section".

3 Scan the Subjects listed in the Contents page: then turn to the page indicated for the Specific Information you desire.

ELECTRICAL SERVICE & REPAIR

1999 Domestic Vehicles

FORD MOTOR CO.

Starting & Charging Systems

Wiring Diagrams

Mitchell Repair™
Information Company

ACKNOWLEDGMENT | Mitchell Repair Information Company thanks the domestic and import automobile and light truck manufacturers, distributors, and dealers for their generous cooperation and assistance which make this manual possible.

MARKETING
Senior Vice President
David Peterson

Directors
David R. Koontz
Daniel Ramirez

Product Managers
Catherine Smith
Victor Addison
Nick DiVerde
Robert Gardner
Brian Warfield

TECHNICAL LIBRARIAN
Debbie Hickman

EDITORIAL
Director, Annual Data Editorial
Mike Mancini

Director, Special Product Editorial
Ronald E. Garrett

Senior Editors
Chuck Vedra (ASE-Quadruple Master)
Ramiro Gutierrez
John M. Fisher (ASE)
Tom L. Hall (ASE-Quadruple Master)
James A. Hawes (ASE-Quadruple Master)
Eddie Santangelo (ASE)

Technical Editors
Thomas L. Landis
Scott A. Olsen (ASE)
Bob Reel
David W. Himes (ASE)
Alex A. Solis (ASE)
James R. Warren (ASE)
Bobby R. Gifford (ASE)
Linda M. Murphy (ASE)
Donald Lawler (ASE)
Wayne D. Charbonneau (ASE-World Class)
Sal Caloca (ASE)
Bud Gardner (ASE)
Robert L. Eller (ASE-Quadruple Master)
John Schartz (ASE)
Richard C. Hamilton (ASE-Quadruple Master)
Leonid A. Shneyder (ASE)
Brian Yockey (ASE)
John Howard (ASE)
Todd Mercer (ASE)
James Barrow (ASE)
Demian Hurst (ASE)
Jeff Wyatt (ASE)
Patrick Bolton (ASE)
David Steckling (ASE)
Tim Flannery (ASE)
Robert Therieau
Susan Schalk (ASE)
Andrew Smith (ASE)

WIRING DIAGRAMS
Manager
Matthew M. Krimple

PRINT COMPOSITION
Brian Henderson
Julia Gillis (ASE)

TECHNICAL SUPPORT
Bob Pilz

PRODUCT SUPPORT
Product Specialists
James A. Wafford (ASE)
Jeff Hicks
David Block (ASE)
Carol Menickelly
Matt Mathews (ASE)
Bill Belliston (ASE)

GRAPHICS
Manager
Judith A. La Pierre
Supervisor
Ann Klimetz
Graphic Specialists
Sally Muhlbaier
Lynn Plummer
Percella Kuhns
Carmen Rusnak
Deb Eaton
Edder Naguit
Jordan Butcher
Cheryl Griffin
Jean Petaja
Robert Taylor

Published By

MITCHELL REPAIR INFORMATION COMPANY
9889 Willow Creek Road
P.O. Box 26260
San Diego, California 92196-0260

ISBN 0-8470-2215-3

© 1999 Mitchell Repair Information Company, LLC
All Rights Reserved

Printed in U.S.A.

Customer Service Numbers
For Subscription, Billing or Technical Information call:
1-888-724-6742 Toll Free or 858-549-7809
Or Write: P.O. Box 26260, San Diego, CA 92196-0260

Contents

STARTING & CHARGING SYSTEMS

STARTERS

Continental
- Description 2-1
- Component Locations 2-1
- Trouble Shooting 2-1
- On-Vehicle Testing 2-1
- System Tests 2-1
- Bench Testing 2-3
- Removal & Installation 2-3
- Starter Motor Specifications 2-3
- Torque Specifications 2-3
- Wiring Diagrams 2-3

Contour & Mystique
- Description 2-4
- Component Locations 2-4
- Trouble Shooting 2-4
- On-Vehicle Testing 2-4
- System Tests 2-4
- Removal & Installation 2-6
- Starter Motor Specifications 2-6
- Torque Specifications 2-6
- Wiring Diagrams 2-7

Cougar
- Description 2-8
- Component Locations 2-8
- Trouble Shooting 2-8
- System Tests 2-8
- Bench Testing 2-9
- Removal & Installation 2-9
- Starter Motor Specifications 2-10
- Torque Specifications 2-10
- Wiring Diagrams 2-10

Crown Victoria & Grand Marquis
- Description 2-11
- Component Locations 2-11
- Adjustments 2-11
- Trouble Shooting 2-11
- On-Vehicle Testing 2-11
- System Tests 2-12
- Removal & Installation 2-13
- Torque Specifications 2-13
- Wiring Diagrams 2-14

Econoline – Diesel
- Description 2-15
- Component Locations 2-15
- Trouble Shooting 2-15
- On-Vehicle Testing 2-15
- System Tests 2-16
- Removal & Installation 2-16
- Overhaul 2-16
- Starter Motor Specifications 2-16
- Torque Specifications 2-16
- Wiring Diagrams 2-17

STARTING & CHARGING SYSTEMS (Cont.)

STARTERS (Cont.)

Econoline – Except Diesel
- Description 2-18
- Component Locations 2-18
- Adjustments 2-18
- Trouble Shooting 2-18
- On-Vehicle Testing 2-18
- System Tests 2-18
- Bench Testing 2-20
- Removal & Installation 2-20
- Starter Motor Specifications 2-20
- Torque Specifications 2-20
- Wiring Diagrams 2-20

Escort & Tracer
- Description 2-21
- Trouble Shooting 2-21
- On-Vehicle Testing 2-21
- System Tests 2-21
- Removal & Installation 2-22
- Starter Motor Specifications 2-22
- Torque Specifications 2-22
- Wiring Diagrams 2-22

Expedition & Navigator
- Description 2-23
- Component Locations 2-23
- Adjustments 2-23
- Trouble Shooting 2-23
- On-Vehicle Testing 2-23
- System Tests 2-24
- Removal & Installation 2-25
- Torque Specifications 2-25
- Wiring Diagrams 2-25

Explorer & Mountaineer
- Description 2-26
- Component Locations 2-26
- Adjustments 2-26
- Trouble Shooting 2-26
- On-Vehicle Testing 2-26
- System Tests 2-26
- Removal & Installation 2-29
- Starter Motor Specifications 2-29
- Torque Specifications 2-29
- Wiring Diagrams 2-29

Mustang
- Description 2-30
- Component Locations 2-30
- Adjustments 2-30
- Trouble Shooting 2-30
- On-Vehicle Testing 2-30
- System Tests 2-30
- Removal & Installation 2-32
- Starter Motor Specifications 2-32
- Torque Specifications 2-32
- Wiring Diagrams 2-32

STARTING & CHARGING SYSTEMS (Cont.)

STARTERS (Cont.)

F150 & F250 Light-Duty Pickups
Description 2-33
Component Locations 2-33
Adjustments 2-33
Trouble Shooting 2-33
On-Vehicle Testing 2-33
System Tests 2-33
Bench Testing 2-36
Removal & Installation 2-36
Starter Motor Specifications 2-36
Torque Specifications 2-36
Wiring Diagrams 2-36

F250 Super-Duty & F350 Pickups
Description 2-37
Component Locations 2-37
Adjustments 2-37
Trouble Shooting 2-37
On-Vehicle Testing 2-37
Bench Testing 2-40
Removal & Installation 2-40
Overhaul 2-40
Starter Motor Specifications 2-40
Torque Specifications 2-40
Wiring Diagrams 2-41

Ranger
Description 2-42
Component Locations 2-42
Adjustments 2-42
Trouble Shooting 2-42
On-Vehicle Testing 2-42
System Tests 2-42
Removal & Installation 2-44
Starter Specifications 2-45
Torque Specifications 2-45
Wiring Diagrams 2-45

Sable & Taurus
Description 2-46
Component Locations 2-46
Trouble Shooting 2-46
On-Vehicle Testing 2-46
System Tests 2-46
Bench Testing 2-48
Removal & Installation 2-48
Starter Motor Specifications 2-48
Torque Specifications 2-48
Wiring Diagrams 2-48

Town Car
Description 2-49
Component Locations 2-49
Adjustments 2-49
Trouble Shooting 2-49
On-Vehicle Testing 2-49
System Tests 2-50
Removal & Installation 2-51
Torque Specifications 2-51
Wiring Diagrams 2-51

STARTING & CHARGING SYSTEMS (Cont.)

STARTERS (Cont.)

Villager
Description 2-52
Component Locations 2-52
Trouble Shooting 2-52
On-Vehicle Testing 2-52
System Tests 2-52
Removal & Installation 2-54
Torque Specifications 2-54
Wiring Diagrams 2-54

Windstar
Description 2-55
Component Locations 2-55
Adjustments 2-55
Trouble Shooting 2-55
On-Vehicle Testing 2-55
System Tests 2-56
Removal & Installation 2-57
Starter Motor Specifications 2-57
Torque Specifications 2-57
Wiring Diagrams 2-57

GENERATORS

Continental, Crown Victoria, Explorer (4.0L SOHC & 5.0L), Grand Marquis, Mountaineer & Town Car
Description 2-58
Adjustments 2-58
Trouble Shooting 2-58
On-Vehicle Testing 2-58
System Tests 2-58
Removal & Installation 2-59
Torque Specifications 2-60
Wiring Diagrams 2-60

Contour & Mystique
Description 2-61
Adjustments 2-61
Trouble Shooting 2-61
On-Vehicle Testing 2-61
System Tests 2-61
Removal & Installation 2-62
Torque Specifications 2-62
Wiring Diagrams 2-63

Cougar
Description 2-64
Adjustments 2-64
Trouble Shooting 2-64
On-Vehicle Testing 2-64
System Tests 2-64
Removal & Installation 2-64
Torque Specifications 2-65
Wiring Diagrams 2-65

Econoline, Expedition, Explorer (4.0L OHV), Navigator, Pickups (Gasoline) & Ranger
Description 2-66
Adjustments 2-66
Trouble Shooting 2-66
System Tests 2-66
Component Testing 2-68
Removal & Installation 2-68
Torque Specifications 2-69
Wiring Diagrams 2-69

STARTING & CHARGING SYSTEMS (Cont.)

GENERATORS (Cont.)

Escort & Tracer
Description 2-71
Adjustments 2-71
Trouble Shooting 2-71
On-Vehicle Testing 2-71
System Tests 2-71
Removal & Installation 2-72
Torque Specifications 2-72
Wiring Diagrams 2-72

Dual Generators – Diesel
(F250 Super-Duty Pickup & F350 Pickup)
Description 2-73
Adjustments 2-73
Trouble Shooting 2-73
On-Vehicle Testing 2-73
Self-Diagnostic System 2-73
Diagnostic Tests 2-73
System Tests 2-74
Removal & Installation 2-76
Torque Specifications 2-76
Wiring Diagrams 2-76

Single Generator – Diesel
(F250 Super-Duty Pickup & F350 Pickup)
Description 2-78
Adjustments 2-78
Trouble Shooting 2-78
On-Vehicle Testing 2-78
System Tests 2-78
Removal & Installation 2-79
Torque Specifications 2-79
Wiring Diagrams 2-80

Mustang
Description 2-81
Adjustments 2-81
Trouble Shooting 2-81
On-Vehicle Testing 2-81
System Tests 2-81
Removal & Installation 2-82
Torque Specifications 2-82
Wiring Diagrams 2-82

Sable & Taurus
Description 2-83
Adjustments 2-83
Trouble Shooting 2-83
On-Vehicle Testing 2-83
System Tests 2-83
Removal & Installation 2-84
Torque Specifications 2-85
Wiring Diagrams 2-85

STARTING & CHARGING SYSTEMS (Cont.)

GENERATORS (Cont.)

Villager
Description 2-86
Adjustments 2-86
Trouble Shooting 2-86
On-Vehicle Testing 2-86
System Tests 2-86
Removal & Installation 2-87
Torque Specifications 2-87
Wiring Diagrams 2-87

Windstar
Description 2-88
Adjustments 2-88
Trouble Shooting 2-88
On-Vehicle Testing 2-88
Self-Diagnostic System 2-88
System Tests 2-88
Removal & Installation 2-88
Torque Specifications 2-89
Wiring Diagrams 2-89

WIRING DIAGRAMS

DATA LINK CONNECTORS
Wiring Diagrams 3-1

GROUND DISTRIBUTION
Wiring Diagrams 3-8

POWER DISTRIBUTION
Wiring Diagrams 3-58

ELECTRIC COOLING FANS
Wiring Diagrams 3-119

ANTI-LOCK BRAKES
Wiring Diagrams 3-124

ELECTRONIC SUSPENSION
Wiring Diagrams 3-143

ELECTRONIC STEERING
Wiring Diagrams 3-150

ENGINE PERFORMANCE
Wiring Diagrams 3-153

ACCESSORIES & EQUIPMENT
See FORD Supplement 3.

LATEST CHANGES & CORRECTIONS
See FORD Supplement 3.

DESCRIPTION

The starter is a gear-reduction motor with an externally-mounted solenoid. Starting system consists of a starter motor, solenoid, battery, ignition switch, Transmission Range (TR) sensor, starter relay and interconnecting cables and wires.

COMPONENT LOCATIONS

COMPONENT LOCATIONS

Component	Location
Battery Junction Box	In Engine Compartment, Next To Battery
Instrument Panel Fuse Panel	Under Left Side Of Instrument Panel
Inertia Fuel Shutoff Switch	Left Hand Side Of Luggage Compartment
Starter Relay	In Battery Junction Box
Transmission Range Sensor	Top Of Transmission

TROUBLE SHOOTING

- Check battery for state of charge.
- Check cable connections at battery and starter motor.
- Ensure transmission is fully engaged in Park or Neutral.
- Ensure Mega-fuse (175-amp) in engine compartment fuse panel is okay.
- Check fuse No. 4 (40-amp) in engine compartment fuse box.
- Check fuse No. 23 (10-amp) in instrument panel fuse panel.

ON-VEHICLE TESTING

VOLTAGE DROP TEST

NOTE: Make all voltmeter connections at component terminal rather than at cable or wire end.

1) Verify battery condition. Battery voltage should be 12 volts or more. Load test battery at approximately one-half cold cranking amperage rating. See load tester manufacturer's instructions. If battery voltage is less than 12 volts or loaded battery voltage is less than 9.6 volts, service battery or charging system as necessary.
2) Disconnect inertia fuel shutoff switch to disable fuel system. Connect remote starter switch between starter solenoid terminal "S" (White/Pink wire) and positive battery post.
3) Connect positive voltmeter lead to positive battery post, and negative lead to solenoid terminal "M". *See Fig. 1.*

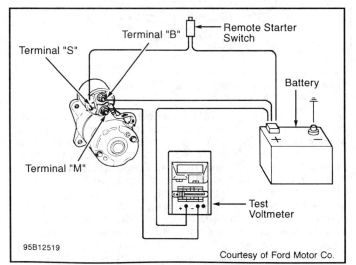

95B12519
Courtesy of Ford Motor Co.

Fig. 1: Testing Voltage Drop

4) Engage remote starter switch. Voltmeter should indicate .5 volt or less. If voltmeter indicates greater than .5 volt, go to next step. If voltmeter indicates .5 volt or less, go to STARTER GROUND CIRCUIT TEST.
5) Move negative voltmeter lead to solenoid terminal "B" (battery cable). Engage remote starter switch. If voltmeter still indicates greater than .5 volt at terminal "B", go to next step. If voltmeter indicates less than .5 volt, solenoid connections or contacts are bad. Clean solenoid terminals "B", "S" and "M". Repeat steps **1)** through **4)**. If voltmeter still indicates greater than .5 volt at terminal "M" and less than .5 volt at terminal "B", solenoid contacts are bad. Replace starter motor See STARTER MOTOR under REMOVAL & INSTALLATION.
6) Clean cables and connections at solenoid and battery. If voltmeter still indicates more than .5 volt at terminal "B", replace battery cable.

NOTE: To locate excessive voltage drop, move voltmeter negative lead toward battery, and check each connection point. When high voltmeter reading disappears, problem is between last connection point and previous connection point.

STARTER GROUND CIRCUIT TEST

NOTE: Make all voltmeter connections at component terminal rather than at cable or wire end.

1) Disconnect inertia fuel shutoff switch to disable fuel system. See COMPONENT LOCATIONS. Connect remote starter switch between starter solenoid terminal "S" (White/Pink wire) and positive battery post.
2) Connect positive voltmeter lead to starter housing, and negative lead to negative battery post. Engage remote starter switch while observing voltmeter. Voltmeter should indicate .2 volt or less. If voltmeter indicates greater than .2 volt, clean negative cable connections at battery and engine.
3) If voltage drop is still excessive, repair or replace negative battery cable and/or engine ground cable as necessary. Repeat starter circuit test after repair to ensure problem has been corrected. If battery and cables test okay and starter motor still cranks slowly, replace starter.

STARTER CIRCUIT CURRENT DRAW TEST

Ensure battery is fully charged. Ensure battery connections are clean and tight. Disconnect inertia fuel shutoff switch to disable fuel pump. Clamp inductive ammeter lead around all wires/cables leading to positive (or negative) battery terminal. *See Fig. 5.* Crank engine for about 5 seconds and check amperage reading while cranking. Normal amperage draw is 130-220 amps. If amperage draw exceeds specification, replace starter.

SYSTEM TESTS

CAUTION: Before testing starter, ensure transmission is in Park or Neutral.

UNUSUAL STARTER NOISE

1) Ensure starter bolts and brackets are secure. Connect a remote starter switch between starter solenoid "B" (battery cable) and "S" (White/Pink wire) terminals. Activate remote starter switch to determine if unusual noise is due to starter operation. If noise is due to starter operation, go to next step. If noise is not due to starter operation, diagnose engine mechanical problem. See appropriate engine article in ENGINES.
2) Remove starter motor. See STARTER MOTOR under REMOVAL & INSTALLATION. Inspect flywheel ring gear for wear or damage. Repair or replace as necessary. If flywheel ring gear is okay, replace starter motor.

STARTER DOES NOT CRANK

1) Verify battery condition. Battery voltage should be 12 volts or more. Load test battery at approximately one-half cold cranking amperage rating. See load tester manufacturer's instructions. If battery voltage is less than 12 volts or loaded battery voltage is less than 9.6 volts, service battery or charging system as necessary.

2) Measure voltage between positive battery post and negative battery cable connection on engine. If battery voltage exists, go to next step. If battery voltage does not exist, replace negative battery cable. Check system operation.

3) Measure voltage between positive battery post and starter motor case. If battery voltage exists, go to next step. If battery voltage does not exist, remove starter and clean starter motor mounting surface. Install starter and check system for normal operation.

4) Measure voltage between starter solenoid "B" (positive battery cable) terminal and ground. If battery voltage exists, go to next step. If battery voltage does not exist, clean terminals or replace battery cable as necessary. Restore electrical connections and check system operation.

5) Connect a remote starter switch between starter solenoid "B" (battery cable) and "S" (White/Pink wire) terminals. Activate remote starter switch. If starter cranks at normal speed, go to next step. If starter motor does not crank, replace starter motor and solenoid. Restore electrical connections and check system operation.

6) Disconnect White/Pink wire from starter solenoid. Hold ignition switch in START position. Measure voltage between ground and terminal "S" (White/Pink) wire at starter solenoid. If battery voltage does not exist, go to next step. If battery voltage exists, ensure terminal "S" connection is clean and tight.

7) Turn ignition off. Remove starter relay. Hold ignition switch in START position. Measure voltage between ground and starter relay harness connector terminal No. 86 (Tan/Red wire). *See Fig. 2.* If battery voltage exists, go to next step. If battery voltage does not exist, go to step 12).

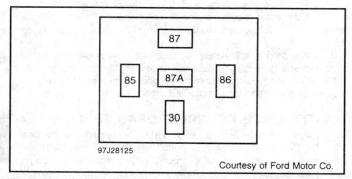

Fig. 2: Identifying Starter Relay Harness Connector Terminals

8) Turn ignition off. Measure voltage between starter relay harness connector terminal No. 30 (Yellow/Light Blue wire). If battery voltage exists, go to next step. If battery voltage does not exist, repair open Yellow/Light Blue wire. Restore electrical connections and check system operation.

9) Measure resistance between starter relay harness connector terminal No. 85 (Black wire) and ground. If resistance is less than 5 ohms, go to next step. If resistance is 5 ohms or greater, repair open Black wire. Restore electrical connections and check system operation.

10) Disconnect White/Pink wire from starter solenoid. Measure resistance between ground and starter relay harness connector terminal No. 87 (White/Pink wire). If resistance is greater than 10,000 ohms, go to next step. If resistance is 10,000 ohms or less, repair short to ground in White/Pink wire. Restore electrical connections and check system operation.

11) Measure resistance wire between starter relay harness connector terminal No. 87 and White/Pink wire at starter solenoid. If resistance is less than 5 ohms, replace starter relay. If resistance is 5 ohms or greater, repair open White/Pink wire. Restore electrical connections and check system operation.

12) Check fuse No. 23 in instrument panel fuse panel. If fuse is okay, go to next step. If fuse is blown, go to step 19).

13) Hold ignition switch in START position. Measure voltage between input side of fuse cavity No. 23 and ground. If battery voltage does not exist, go to next step. If battery voltage exists, go to step 17).

14) Disconnect ignition switch harness connector. Measure voltage between ground and ignition switch harness connector terminal B4 (Black/Orange wire). *See Fig. 3.* If battery voltage exists, go to next step. If battery voltage does not exist, repair open Black/Orange wire. Restore electrical connections and check system operation.

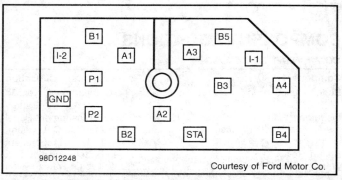

Fig. 3: Identifying Ignition Switch Harness Connector Terminals

15) Measure resistance of Red/Light Blue wire between fuse cavity No. 23 (input side) and ignition switch harness connector terminal STA. *See Fig. 3.* If resistance is less than 5 ohms, go to next step. If resistance is 5 ohms or greater, repair open Red/Light Blue wire. Restore electrical connections and check system operation.

16) Measure resistance between ignition switch harness connector terminal STA and ground. If resistance is less than 10,000 ohms, repair short to ground in Red/Light Blue wire. If resistance is 10,00 ohms or greater, replace ignition switch. Restore electrical connections and check system operation.

17) Disconnect Transmission Range (TR) sensor. Measure resistance of White/Orange wire between TR sensor harness connector terminal No. 10 and fuse cavity No. 23 (output side) in instrument panel fuse panel. *See Fig. 4.* If resistance is less than 5 ohms, go to next step. If resistance is 5 ohms or greater, repair open White/Orange wire. Restore electrical connections and check system operation.

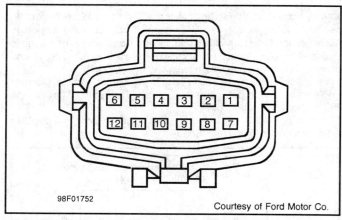

Fig. 4: Identifying Transmission Range Sensor Harness Connector Terminals

18) Measure resistance of Tan/Red wire between TR sensor harness connector terminal No. 12 and starter relay harness connector terminal No. 86. *See Figs. 2 and 4 .* If resistance is greater than 5 ohms, repair open Tan/Red wire. If resistance is 5 ohms or less, check TR sensor adjustment. See ADJUSTMENTS in AUTOMATIC TRANSMISSION article in TRANSMISSION SERVICING in appropriate MITCHELL® manual. If TR sensor adjustment is okay, replace TR sensor. Restore electrical connections and check system operation.

19) Measure resistance of White/Orange wire between ground and fuse cavity No. 23 (output side) in instrument panel fuse panel. If resistance is less than 10,000 ohms, go to next step. If resistance is 10,000 ohms or greater, inspect wires for possible intermittent short to ground. Replace fuse and check system operation.

20) Disconnect TR sensor harness connector. Measure resistance of White/Orange wire between TR sensor harness connector terminal No. 10 and ground. *See Fig. 4.* If resistance is greater than 10,000 ohms, go to next step. If resistance is 10,000 ohms or less, repair short to ground in White/Orange wire. Restore electrical connections and check system operation.

21) Measure resistance of Tan/Red wire between TR sensor harness connector terminal No. 12 and ground. If resistance is greater than 10,000 ohms, check TR sensor adjustment. See ADJUSTMENTS in AUTOMATIC TRANSMISSION article in TRANSMISSION SERVICING in appropriate MITCHELL® manual. If TR sensor adjustment is okay, replace TR sensor. If resistance is 10,000 ohms or less, repair short to ground in Tan/Red wire. Restore electrical connections and check system operation.

STARTER CRANKS SLOWLY OR SOLENOID CLICKS

1) Verify battery condition. Battery voltage should be 12 volts or more. Load test battery at approximately one-half cold cranking amperage rating. See load tester manufacturer's instructions. If battery voltage is less than 12 volts or loaded battery voltage is less than 9.6 volts, service battery or charging system as necessary.

2) Perform VOLTAGE DROP TEST under ON-VEHICLE ADJUSTMENTS. If battery cable voltage drop is .5 volt or less, go to next step. If battery cable voltage drop is greater than .5 volt, repair cable connections or replace cable as necessary. Restore electrical connections and check system operation.

3) Perform STARTER GROUND CIRCUIT TEST under ON-VEHICLE TESTING. If ground circuit voltage drop is .3 volt or less, go to next step. If ground circuit voltage drop is greater than .3 volt, repair starter/engine ground circuit.

4) Perform STARTER CIRCUIT CURRENT DRAW TEST under ON-VEHICLE TESTING. If current draw is within specification, check engine for mechanical concerns. If current draw is excessive, replace starter motor. Restore electrical connections and check system operation.

BENCH TESTING

STARTER NO-LOAD TEST

Remove starter from vehicle. See STARTER MOTOR under REMOVAL & INSTALLATION. Using heavy gauge jumper wires, connect battery to starter "B" and negative to starter frame. *See Fig. 5.* Connect voltmeter, ammeter, and remote starter switch to starter. Engage remote starter switch. Starter should turn smoothly. Ammeter should indicate 60-80 amps. If current is higher than specification, replace or overhaul starter.

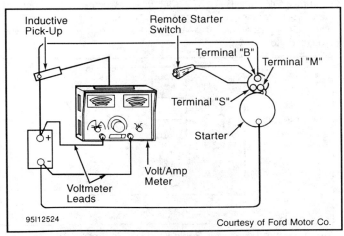

95I12524

Courtesy of Ford Motor Co.

Fig. 5: Testing Starter Draw

REMOVAL & INSTALLATION

STARTER MOTOR

Removal & Installation – Disconnect negative battery cable. Raise vehicle on hoist. Disconnect wiring from starter solenoid. Remove upper and lower starter bolts. Remove starter. To install, reverse removal procedure. Tighten bolts to specification. See TORQUE SPECIFICATIONS.

STARTER MOTOR SPECIFICATIONS

STARTER MOTOR SPECIFICATIONS

Application	Specification
Cranking RPM (Normal Load)	140-220
Current Draw	
Normal Load	130-220 Amps
No Load	60-80 Amps
Starter Circuit Voltage Drop	0.5 Volt

TORQUE SPECIFICATIONS

TORQUE SPECIFICATIONS

Application	Ft. Lbs. (N.m)
Starter Motor Mounting Bolts	16-20 (22-27)

	INCH Lbs. (N.m)
Battery Cable Clamp Bolt	62-89 (7-10)
Solenoid "B" Terminal Nut	61-79 (7-9.0)
Starter Motor Ground Cable Nut	61-79 (7-9.0)

WIRING DIAGRAMS

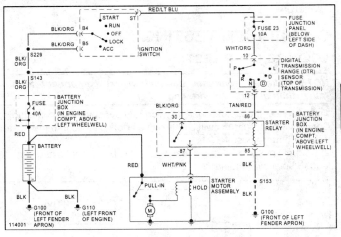

Fig. 6: Starter System Wiring Diagram (Continental)

1999 STARTING & CHARGING SYSTEMS
Starters – Contour & Mystique

DESCRIPTION

The starter motor is equipped with an externally-mounted solenoid. Starting system consists of a starter motor, solenoid, battery, ignition switch, Transmission Range (TR) switch (A/T) or Clutch Pedal Position (CPP) switch (M/T), starter relay, starter relay diode, and interconnecting cables and wires.

COMPONENT LOCATIONS

COMPONENT LOCATIONS

Component	Location
Anti-Theft/Central Lock Module	Base Of Right "A" Pillar
Inertia Fuel Shutoff Switch	Base Of Left "A" Pillar
PATS Module	Base Of Right "A" Pillar
Starter Relay	In Engine Compartment Fuse Box
Starter Relay Diode	In Engine Compartment Fuse Box

TROUBLE SHOOTING

Check the following items before proceeding with testing:
- Check battery for state of charge.
- Check cable connections at battery and starter motor.
- Ensure transmission is fully engaged in Park or Neutral, or clutch pedal is fully depressed.
- Check fuse No. 10 (20-amp) in instrument panel fuse panel.
- On models equipped anti-theft system, ensure anti-theft system is operating properly. See appropriate ANTI-THEFT SYSTEMS – PASSIVE article in ACCESSORIES & EQUIPMENT for additional information.

ON-VEHICLE TESTING

VOLTAGE DROP TEST

NOTE: Make all voltmeter connections at component terminal rather than at cable or wire end.

1) Disconnect inertia fuel shutoff switch to prevent vehicle from starting. Connect remote starter switch between starter solenoid terminal "S" and positive battery post.
2) Connect positive voltmeter lead to positive battery post, and negative lead to solenoid terminal "M". See Fig. 1.

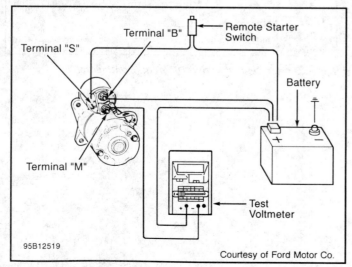

95B12519

Courtesy of Ford Motor Co.

Fig. 1: Testing Voltage Drop

3) Engage remote starter switch. Voltmeter should indicate .5 volt or less. If voltmeter indicates .5 volts or less, system is okay. If voltmeter indicates greater than .5 volt, go to next step.

4) Move negative voltmeter lead to solenoid terminal "B". Engage remote starter switch. If voltmeter indicates less than .5 volt, solenoid connections or contacts are bad. Clean solenoid terminals "B", "S" and "M". Repeat steps 1) through 4).
5) If voltmeter still indicates greater than .5 volt at terminal "M" and less than .5 volt at terminal "B", solenoid contacts are bad. Replace solenoid. If voltmeter indicates greater than .5 volt at terminal "B", clean cables and connections at solenoid.
6) If voltmeter still indicates greater than .5 volt at terminal "B", check for poor positive battery cable connection or bad cable. Repair as necessary.

STARTER NO-LOAD TEST

Connect Starter, Alternator, Battery, and Regulator (SABRE) tester, or equivalent. Follow tester manufacturer's instructions. Engage remote starter switch. Starter should turn smoothly. Voltmeter should indicate 11 volts or greater, and ammeter should indicate 60-80 amps. If voltage is lower or current is higher than specification, replace or overhaul starter.

SYSTEM TESTS

CAUTION: Before testing starter, ensure transmission is in Park or Neutral.

STARTER DOES NOT CRANK BUT RELAY CLICKS

1) Ensure anti-theft system is operating properly, if equipped. See ANTI-THEFT SYSTEMS – PASSIVE article in ACCESSORIES & EQUIPMENT. If anti-theft system is okay, verify battery condition. Battery voltage should be 12 volts or more. Load test battery at approximately one-half cold cranking amperage rating. See load tester manufacturer's instructions. If battery voltage is less than 12 volts or loaded battery voltage is less than 9.6 volts, service battery or charging system as necessary. If battery is okay, go to next step.
2) Disconnect wire from starter solenoid terminal "S" (small gage Black wire). While holding ignition switch in START position, measure voltage between Black wire and ground. If voltage is greater than 10 volts, go to next step. If voltage is 10 volts or less, go to step 5).
3) Turn ignition off. Measure voltage between ground and "B" terminal on starter solenoid (positive battery cable). If voltage is greater than 10 volts, go to next step. If voltage is 10 volts or less, repair positive battery cable. Restore electrical connections and check system operation.
4) Disconnect negative battery cable from starter. Measure resistance of negative battery cable. If resistance is less than 5 ohms, replace starter motor. See STARTER MOTOR under REMOVAL & INSTALLATION. If resistance is 5 ohms or greater, repair or replace negative battery cable. Restore electrical connections and check system operation.
5) Turn ignition off. Remove starter relay. Measure voltage between starter relay harness connector terminal No. 30 and ground. See Fig. 2. If voltage is greater than 10 volts, go to next step. If voltage is 10 volts or less, go to step 22).

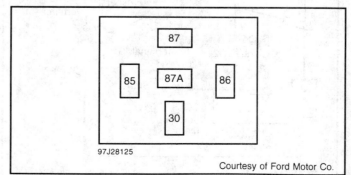

97J28125

Courtesy of Ford Motor Co.

Fig. 2: Identifying Starter Relay Harness Connector Terminals

6) Measure resistance between starter relay connector terminal No. 87 and terminal "S" (Black wire) at starter motor. If resistance is less than 5

ohms, go to next step. If resistance is 5 ohms or greater, go to step **23**). Restore electrical connections and check system operation.

7) While holding ignition switch in START position, measure voltage at starter relay connector terminal No. 85. If voltage is greater than 10 volts, go to step **13**). If voltage is 10 volts or less, go to next step.

8) Turn ignition off. Remove and test fuse No. 10 (20-amp) in engine compartment fuse panel. If fuse is okay, go to next step. Replace fuse if blown. If fuse blows again check circuit for short to ground. See WIRING DIAGRAMS. Restore electrical connections and check system operation.

9) Disconnect ignition switch harness connector (located at ignition switch). Remove fuse No. 10 (20-amp). Measure resistance of Red wire between fuse No. 10 cavity and ignition switch harness connector. If resistance is less than 5 ohms, go to next step. If resistance is 5 ohms or greater, repair open Red wire. Restore electrical connections and check system operation.

10) Hold ignition switch in START position. Measure resistance between ignition switch terminals No. 1 and 5. *See Fig. 3*. If resistance is less than 5 ohms, go to next step. If resistance is 5 ohms or greater, replace ignition switch. Restore electrical connections and check system operation.

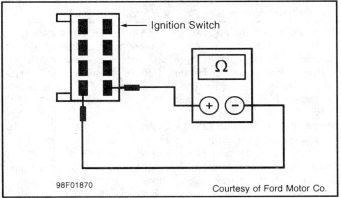

Fig. 3: Testing Ignition Switch

11) Disconnect engine compartment fuse box connector C334 (10-pin connector). Measure resistance of Gray/White wire between engine compartment fuse box connector C334 and ignition switch harness connector terminal. If resistance is less than 5 ohms, go to next step. If resistance is 5 ohms or greater, repair open Gray/White wire. Restore electrical connections and check system operation.

12) Remove starter relay diode from battery junction box. Measure resistance between diode terminals. Continuity should exist in one direction and not in other direction. Replace diode if continuity is not as specified. If continuity is okay, repair open in battery junction box. Restore electrical connections and check system operation.

13) Turn ignition off. Remove starter relay. Connect a jumper wire between positive battery terminal and starter relay terminal No. 86. *See Fig. 4*. Connect another jumper wire between negative battery terminal and starter relay terminal No. 85. Measure resistance between starter relay terminals No. 30 and 87. If resistance is less than 5 ohms, go to next step. If resistance is 5 ohms or greater, replace relay. Restore electrical connections and check system operation.

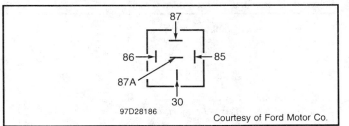

Fig. 4: Identifying Starter Relay Terminals

14) Measure resistance between starter relay harness connector terminal No. 85 and ground. *See Fig. 2*. If resistance is less than 10,000 ohms, repair short to ground in Gray/Black wire. If resistance is 10,000 ohms or greater, go to next step (M/T models) or go to step **16**) (A/T models).

15) Disconnect Clutch Pedal Position (CPP) switch harness connector. Measure resistance of Black/Yellow wire between CPP switch harness connector and starter relay harness connector terminal No. 85. *See Fig. 2*. If resistance is greater than 5 ohms, go to next step. If resistance is 5 ohms or less, go to step **18**).

16) Disconnect Transmission Range (TR) sensor. Measure resistance of Black/Yellow wire between TR sensor harness connector and starter relay harness connector terminal No. 85. If resistance is less than 5 ohms, go to step **19**). If resistance is 5 ohms or greater, go to next step.

17) Disconnect engine compartment fuse box harness connector C334 (10-pin connector). Measure resistance of Black/Yellow wire between C334 and TR sensor harness connector. If resistance is greater than 5 ohms, repair open Black/Yellow wire. If resistance is 5 ohms or less, replace engine compartment fuse panel.

18) Measure resistance between Clutch Pedal Position (CPP) switch terminals while pressing clutch pedal. If resistance is less than 5 ohms, go to step **20**). If resistance is 5 ohms or greater, adjust CPP switch. If problem persists, replace CPP switch. Restore electrical connections and check system operation.

19) Measure resistance between Transmission Range (TR) Sensor harness connector terminals No. 3 (Black/Yellow wire) and 6 (Black/Green) while transmission selector is in Park or Neutral. *See Fig. 5*. If resistance is less than 5 ohms, go to next step. If resistance is 5 ohms or greater, replace TR sensor. Restore electrical connections and check system operation.

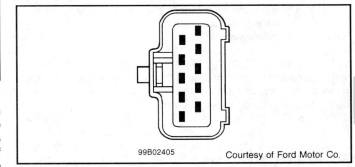

Fig. 5: Identifying Transmission Range (TR) Sensor Terminals

20) If vehicle is equipped with anti-theft system, go to next step. If not equipped with anti-theft system, repair open Black wire between CPP or TR sensor and ground point behind right kick panel.

21) Disconnect PCM 104-pin harness connector. On M/T models, measure resistance of Black or Black/Yellow wire between CPP switch harness connector and PCM harness connector terminal No. 18. On A/T models, measure resistance of Black/Green wire between TR sensor harness connector and PCM harness connector terminal No. 18. On all models, *see Fig. 6*. If resistance is 5 ohms or less, diagnose anti-theft system. See ANTI-THEFT SYSTEMS – PASSIVE article in ACCESSORIES & EQUIPMENT. If resistance is greater than 5 ohms, repair open wire. Restore electrical connections and check system operation.

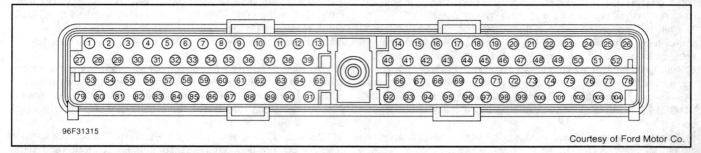

96F31315

Courtesy of Ford Motor Co.

Fig. 6: Identifying Powertrain Control Module (PCM) Terminals

22) Disconnect battery junction box 2-pin connector. Measure voltage between each connector terminal and ground. If voltage is greater than 10 volts at both connector terminals, repair battery junction box and check system operation. If voltage is 10 volts or less on either connector terminal, repair open in appropriate Red wire between battery and battery junction box.

23) Disconnect battery junction box 4 pin connector with Gray/Black wire. Measure resistance of battery junction box between 4-pin connection (corresponding to Gray/Black connector terminal) and starter relay connector terminal 87. If resistance is less than 5 ohms, repair Gray/Black wire between battery junction box and starter solenoid. If resistance is 5 ohms or greater, repair or replace battery junction box. Check system operation.

STARTER CRANKS SLOWLY

1) Verify battery condition. Battery voltage should be 12 volts or more. Load test battery at approximately one-half cold cranking amperage rating. See load tester manufacturer's instructions. If battery voltage is less than 12 volts or loaded battery voltage is less than 9.6 volts, service battery or charging system as necessary. If battery is okay, go to next step.

2) Perform VOLTAGE DROP TEST under ON-VEHICLE TESTING. If voltage drop is okay, go to next step. If voltage drop is excessive, repair cable connections or replace cable as necessary. Restore electrical connections and check system operation.

3) Perform STARTER NO-LOAD TEST under ON-VEHICLE TESTING. If current draw is within specification, check engine for mechanical concerns. If current draw is excessive, repair or replace starter motor. See STARTER MOTOR under REMOVAL & INSTALLATION. Restore electrical connections and check system operation.

UNUSUAL STARTER NOISE

Inspect starter motor mounting. Ensure bolts are tight and starter is properly aligned. If starter motor is mounted properly, remove starter motor and inspect ring gear and starter drive gear for wear or damage. See STARTER MOTOR under REMOVAL & INSTALLATION. Repair as necessary. If ring gear and starter motor drive gear are okay, install new starter motor and check system for normal operation.

REMOVAL & INSTALLATION
STARTER MOTOR

CAUTION: When battery is disconnected, vehicle computer and memory systems may lose memory data. Driveability problems may exist until computer systems have completed a relearn cycle. See COMPUTER RELEARN PROCEDURES article in GENERAL INFORMATION before disconnecting battery. Before testing starter, ensure transmission is in Park or Neutral.

Removal & Installation (2.0L) – Disconnect negative battery cable. Remove air cleaner. Remove upper starter mounting bolts. Raise and support vehicle. Disconnect starter solenoid wire connections. Remove starter motor lower mounting bolt. Remove starter motor. To install, reverse removal procedure. Ensure negative battery cable is installed with starter mounting bolt. Tighten bolts to specification. See TORQUE SPECIFICATIONS table.

Removal & Installation (2.5L) – Disconnect negative battery cable. Remove air cleaner and air cleaner bracket. Disconnect starter solenoid wire connections. Remove starter support bracket. Remove shift cable bracket and disconnect cable. Remove fuel supply line from support bracket. Remove starter bolts. Remove starter. To install, reverse removal procedure. Tighten bolts to specification. See TORQUE SPECIFICATIONS.

STARTER MOTOR SPECIFICATIONS
STARTER MOTOR SPECIFICATIONS

Application	Specification
Current Draw (No Load)	60-80 Amps
Starter Circuit Voltage Drop	0.5 Volt

TORQUE SPECIFICATIONS
TORQUE SPECIFICATIONS

Application	Ft. Lbs. (N.m)
Air Cleaner Bracket Bolts	18 (25)
Starter Motor Bracket & Mounting Bolts	18 (25)
Starter Motor Bracket Nuts	12 (17)

	INCH Lbs. (N.m)
Solenoid "B" & "M" Terminal Nuts	106 (12)
Solenoid "S" Terminal Nut	44 (5)

WIRING DIAGRAMS

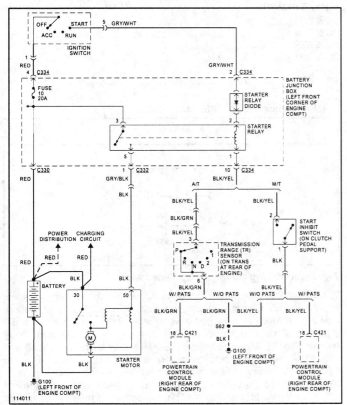

Fig. 7: Starter System Wiring Diagram (Contour & Mystique)

1999 STARTING & CHARGING SYSTEMS
Starters – Cougar

DESCRIPTION

The starter is a gear-reduction motor with an externally-mounted solenoid. Starting system consists of a starter motor, solenoid, battery, ignition switch, Transmission Range (TR) sensor or start inhibit switch, starter relay and interconnecting cables and wires.

COMPONENT LOCATIONS

COMPONENT LOCATIONS

Component	Location
Start Inhibit Switch	On Clutch Pedal Support
Starter Relay & Diode [1]	In Power Distribution Box
Transmission Range Sensor	Top Of Transmission

[1] – See Fig. 3.

TROUBLE SHOOTING

- Check battery for state of charge.
- Check cable connections at battery and starter motor.
- Ensure transmission is fully engaged in Park or Neutral (automatic transmission), or clutch pedal is fully depressed (manual transmission).
- Check fuse No. 10 (20-amp) in engine compartment fuse/relay box.

SYSTEM TESTS

CAUTION: *Before testing starter, ensure transmission is in Park or Neutral.*

STARTER CRANKS SLOWLY OR SOLENOID CLICKS

1) Check starter motor for excessive current draw during operation using ammeter or starting/charging system tester. Refer to tool manufacturer's instructions. If starter current draw is excessive, repair or replace starter motor. If starter current draw is okay, go to next step.

2) To check voltage drop, measure voltage between starter motor battery cable terminal and positive battery terminal with ignition switch in START position. If voltage drop is 0.5 volt or less, go to next step. If voltage drop is 0.5 volt or greater, clean or repair cable connections, or replace cable as necessary. Restore electrical connections and check system operation.

3) To check ground circuit voltage drop, measure voltage between starter motor case and negative battery terminal with ignition switch in START position. If ground circuit voltage drop is 0.5 volt or less, diagnose charging system. See appropriate GENERATORS article. If ground circuit voltage drop is greater than 0.5 volt, clean and tighten starter and engine ground connections. If okay replace negative battery cable.

STARTER DOES NOT CRANK & RELAY CLICKS

1) Verify battery condition. Battery voltage should be 12 volts or more. Load test battery at approximately one-half cold cranking amperage rating. See load tester manufacturer's instructions. If battery is okay, go to next step. If battery voltage is less than 12 volts or loaded battery voltage is less than 9.6 volts, service battery or charging system as necessary.

2) Remove starter relay from power distribution box in engine compartment. Check relay resistance and continuity between relay terminals as specified. See STARTER RELAY SPECIFICATIONS table. See Fig. 1. If relay resistance or continuity is not as specified, replace relay. If relay resistance is as specified, go to next step.

STARTER RELAY SPECIFICATIONS

Relay Terminals	Continuity
85 & 86	[1]
30 & 87a	Yes
30 & 87	No
30 & 86	No
86 & 87a	No
86 & 87	No

[1] – Resistance should be 50-100 ohms.

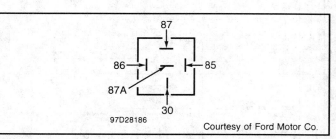

97D28186   Courtesy of Ford Motor Co.

Fig. 1: Identifying Starter Relay Terminals

3) Connect 2 jumper wires from battery positive post to relay terminals No. 30 and 85. Connect jumper from relay terminal No. 86 to ground. See Fig. 1. Measure voltage between relay terminals No. 86 and 87. Battery voltage should be present. Disconnect jumper from relay terminal No. 85. Measure voltage between relay terminals No. 86 and 87a. Battery voltage should be present. If voltage is as specified, go to next step. If battery voltage is not as specified, replace relay.

4) Measure voltage between starter relay harness connector terminal No. 30 and ground. See Fig. 2. If battery voltage is present, go to next step. If battery voltage is not present, verify headlight operation. If headlights operate, replace power distribution center and check system operation. If headlights do not operate, repair Red wire between battery and starter relay harness connector terminal No. 30.

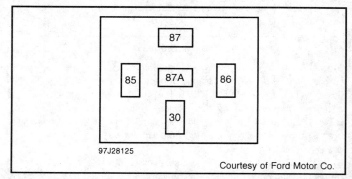

97J28125   Courtesy of Ford Motor Co.

Fig. 2: Identifying Starter Relay Harness Connector Terminals

5) Perform STARTER NO-LOAD TEST under BENCH TESTS. If starter motor tests okay, install original starter motor and go to next step. If starter motor does not test okay, replace starter motor and check system operation.

6) Install starter relay. Connect voltmeter between battery positive terminal and battery cable connection at starter motor. Measure voltage with ignition switch in START position. If voltage is more than .5 volt, replace battery positive cable. If voltage is .5 volt or less, repair Gray/Black wire between starter relay and starter motor.

STARTER DOES NOT CRANK & RELAY DOES NOT CLICK

1) Verify battery condition. Battery voltage should be 12 volts or more. Load test battery at approximately one-half cold cranking amperage rating. See load tester manufacturer's instructions. If battery voltage is less than 12 volts or loaded battery voltage is less than 9.6 volts, service battery or charging system as necessary.

2) Remove starter relay from power distribution box in engine compartment. Measure voltage between starter relay harness connector terminal No. 86 and ground with ignition switch in START position. If battery voltage is present, go to next step. If battery voltage is not present, go to step **4)**.

3) Measure resistance between starter relay harness connector terminal No. 85 and ground with ignition switch in START position. If resistance is less than 5 ohms, install new starter relay and check system operation. If resistance is 5 ohms or greater, go to step **6)** for models with manual transmission or step **9)** for models with automatic transmission.

4) Remove starter diode from power distribution box. *See Fig. 3.* Measure voltage between ground and both diode connector terminals and ground with ignition switch in START position. If battery voltage is present at either terminal, install new diode and check system operation. If battery voltage is not present, go to next step.

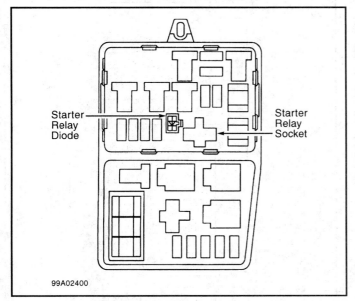

Fig. 3: Locating Starter Relay & Diode

5) Measure resistance between ignition switch connector terminal (Gray/White wire) and both diode connector terminals in power distribution box. See WIRING DIAGRAMS. If resistance is less than 5 ohms on one terminal, replace ignition switch. See appropriate STEERING COLUMN SWITCHES article. If resistance is greater than 5 ohms on both terminals, repair open Gray/White wire between ignition switch and power distribution box.

6) Install starter relay. Disconnect start inhibit switch, located on clutch pedal bracket. Measure voltage between start inhibit switch harness connector Black/Yellow wire and ground with ignition switch in START position. If battery voltage is present, go to next step. If battery voltage is not present, repair Black/Yellow wire and check system operation.

7) Measure resistance between start inhibit switch terminals. Resistance should be less than 5 ohms with clutch pedal depressed, and greater than 100,000 ohms with clutch pedal released. If resistance is as specified, go to next step. If resistance is not as specified, adjust start inhibit switch and retest. If resistance is still not as specified, replace start inhibit switch.

8) Disconnect PCM harness connector located underneath center console. Measure resistance between PCM harness connector terminal 18 and start inhibit switch terminal No. 1 (Black/Yellow wire). *See Fig. 4.* If resistance is less than 5 ohms, reconnect start inhibit switch and go to step **12)**. If resistance is 5 ohms or greater, repair Black wire between PCM connector and start inhibit switch connector.

9) Install starter relay. Disconnect Transmission Range (TR) sensor. Measure voltage between TR sensor connector terminal (Black/Yellow wire) and ground with ignition switch in START position. If battery voltage is present, go to next step. If battery voltage is not present, repair Black/Yellow wire and check system operation.

10) Disconnect PCM 104-pin connector. Measure resistance of Black/Green wire between PCM connector terminal No. 18 and TR sensor connector terminal. *See Fig. 4.* If resistance is less than 5 ohms, go to next step. If resistance is 5 ohms or greater, repair Black/Green wire and check system operation.

11) Measure resistance between TR sensor terminal 4 (terminal corresponds to connector Black/Yellow wire) and terminal 9 (terminal corresponds to connector Black/Green wire). If resistance is less than 5 ohms, reconnect TR sensor harness connector and go to next step. If resistance is greater than 5 ohms, adjust TR sensor using sensor alignment tool (T94P-70010-AH). Recheck resistance. If resistance is still not as specified, replace TR sensor.

12) Install EEC-V PCM breakout box. Connect a jumper wire between breakout box pins No. 18 and No. 77. Momentarily turn ignition switch to START position. If starter motor does not activate, go to STARTER DOES NOT CRANK & RELAY CLICKS. If starter motor activates, and vehicle is equipped with anti-theft system, go to appropriate ANTI-THEFT SYSTEMS article. If starter motor activates, and vehicle is not equipped with anti-theft system, replace PCM and check system operation.

UNUSUAL STARTER NOISE OR STARTER SPINS BUT ENGINE DOES NOT TURN OVER

Inspect starter mounting. Ensure bolts are tight and starter is aligned properly. Repair as necessary and check starter operation. If starter is mounted properly, remove starter and inspect flywheel ring gear for wear or damage. See STARTER under REMOVAL & INSTALLATION. If ring gear is okay, replace starter motor.

BENCH TESTING

STARTER NO-LOAD TEST

Remove starter from vehicle. See STARTER MOTOR under REMOVAL & INSTALLATION. Using heavy gauge jumper wires, connect battery to starter "B" terminal and negative to starter frame. *See Fig. 5.* Connect voltmeter, ammeter, and remote starter switch to starter. Engage remote starter switch. Starter should turn smoothly. Ammeter should indicate 60-80 amps. If current is higher than specification, replace or overhaul starter.

REMOVAL & INSTALLATION

STARTER MOTOR

Removal & Installation (2.0L) – Disconnect negative battery cable. Remove air cleaner. Remove 2 upper starter bolts, noting location of negative battery cable at starter. Cut cable ties. Raise vehicle on hoist. Disconnect wiring from starter solenoid. Remove lower starter bolt. Remove starter. To install, reverse removal procedure. Tighten bolts to specification. See TORQUE SPECIFICATIONS.

Removal & Installation (2.5L) – **1)** Disconnect negative battery cable. Remove air cleaner and air cleaner bracket. Disconnect starter motor electrical connectors. Remove shift cable bracket bolts, and disconnect shift cable.

CAUTION: In the following test step, ensure fuel pressure test adaptor relief valve is fully closed before installing tool.

---

2) Remove starter motor support bracket nuts and bolt. Remove bracket. Remove fuel line Shrader valve cap. Using fuel pressure Test Adaptor (310-042), relieve fuel pressure. Using Spring Lock Disconnect Tool (310-D005 or 310-D004), disconnect fuel supply line. Remove 2 starter mounting bolts. Remove starter motor. To install, reverse removal procedure. Tighten bolts to specification. See TORQUE SPECIFICATIONS.

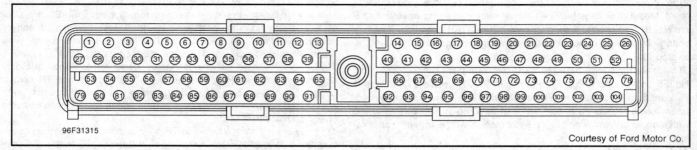

96F31315

Courtesy of Ford Motor Co.

Fig. 4: Identifying Powertrain Control Module (PCM) Connector Terminals

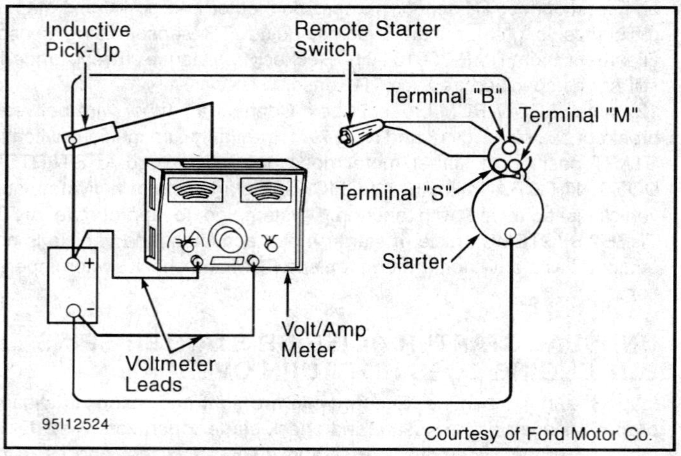

95I12524

Courtesy of Ford Motor Co.

Fig. 5: Testing Starter Draw

STARTER MOTOR SPECIFICATIONS

STARTER MOTOR SPECIFICATIONS

Application	Specification
Current Draw (No Load)	60-80 Amps
Starter Circuit Voltage Drop	0.5 Volt

TORQUE SPECIFICATIONS

TORQUE SPECIFICATIONS

Application	Ft. Lbs. (N.m)
Air Cleaner Bracket Bolts	18 (25)
Starter Motor Bracket Bolts	18 (25)
Starter Motor Bracket Nuts	13 (17)
Starter Motor Mounting Bolts	18 (25)

	INCH Lbs. (N.m)
Starter Battery Cable Terminal Nut	
2.0L	72 (8)
2.5L	106 (12)

WIRING DIAGRAMS

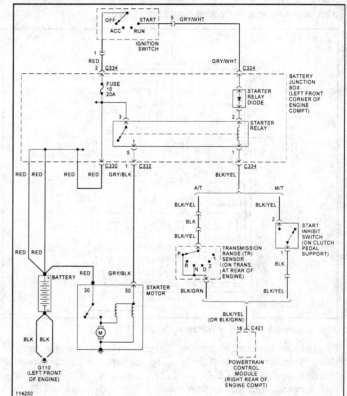

114250

Fig. 6: Starter System Wiring Diagram (Cougar)

Starters – Crown Victoria & Grand Marquis

DESCRIPTION

The starter is a gear-reduction motor with an externally-mounted solenoid. Starting system consists of a starter motor, solenoid, battery, ignition switch, Transmission Range (TR) sensor, starter relay and interconnecting cables and wires.

COMPONENT LOCATIONS

COMPONENT LOCATIONS

Component	Location
Inertia Fuel Shutoff Switch	Left Rear Of Trunk Compartment
Starter Relay	In High Current Relay Center
Transmission Range (TR) Sensor	Left Side Of Transmission

ADJUSTMENTS

SHIFT LINKAGE

1) Place transmission selector in Drive position. Hang a 3-pound weight from end of selector lever. Raise vehicle on hoist. Disconnect shift cable from manual control lever on transmission. Verify manual control lever is in Drive position. Reconnect shift cable. Tighten nut to specification. See TORQUE SPECIFICATIONS table.

2) Lower vehicle and remove weight from selector lever. Verify adjustment. Vehicle should start only in Park or Neutral. Reverse lights should illuminate with transmission selector in Reverse position. If results are not as specified, adjust TR sensor. See TRANSMISSION RANGE (TR) SENSOR.

TRANSMISSION RANGE (TR) SENSOR

CAUTION: When battery is disconnected, vehicle computer and memory systems may lose memory data. Driveability problems may exist until computer systems have completed a relearn cycle. See COMPUTER RELEARN PROCEDURES article in GENERAL INFORMATION before disconnecting battery.

1) Place transmission in Neutral. Turn rear air suspension switch off, if equipped. Switch is located on left side of cargo area. Disconnect battery negative cable. Raise vehicle on hoist.

2) Disconnect manual shift lever cable and electrical connector from TR sensor. Loosen 2 TR sensor bolts. Install TR Sensor Alignment Tool (T97L-70010-A). Tighten TR sensor bolts to specification. See TORQUE SPECIFICATIONS.

3) Connect shift lever cable with TR sensor in Overdrive. Tighten nut to specification. See TORQUE SPECIFICATIONS. Connect TR sensor electrical connector. Lower vehicle and connect negative battery cable. Turn air suspension switch on, if equipped.

TROUBLE SHOOTING

Check the following items before proceeding with testing:
- Check battery for state of charge.
- Check cable connections at battery and starter motor for looseness or corrosion.
- Ensure transmission is fully engaged in Park or Neutral.
- Check fuse No. 2 (30-amp) in battery junction box.

ON-VEHICLE TESTING

STARTER GROUND CIRCUIT TEST

NOTE: Make all voltmeter connections at component terminal rather than at cable or wire end.

1) Disconnect inertia fuel shutoff switch. See COMPONENT LOCATIONS. Connect remote starter switch between starter solenoid terminal "S" (Yellow/Light Blue wire) and positive battery post. See Fig. 1.

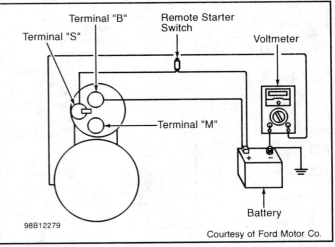

98B12279   Courtesy of Ford Motor Co.

Fig. 1: Testing Ground Voltage Drop

2) Using a digital voltmeter set at lowest voltage scale, connect positive voltmeter lead to starter housing, and negative lead to negative battery post. *See Fig. 1.*

3) Engage remote starter switch while observing voltmeter. If voltmeter indicates .2 volt or less, circuit is okay. If voltmeter indicates more than .2 volt, clean negative cable connections at battery and engine.

4) If voltage drop is still excessive, repair or replace negative battery cable and/or engine ground cable as necessary. Repeat starter circuit test after repair to ensure problem has been corrected.

5) If battery and cables test okay and starter motor still cranks slowly or not at all, install new starter motor.

VOLTAGE DROP TEST

NOTE: Make all voltmeter connections at component terminal rather than at cable or wire end.

1) Verify battery condition. Battery voltage should be 12 volts or more. Load test battery at approximately one-half cold cranking amperage rating. See load tester manufacturer's instructions. If battery voltage is less than 12 volts or loaded battery voltage is less than 9.6 volts, service battery or charging system as necessary. If battery is okay, go to next step.

2) Disconnect inertia fuel shutoff switch. See COMPONENT LOCATIONS. Connect remote starter switch between starter solenoid terminal "S" and positive battery post.

3) Using a digital voltmeter set at lowest voltage scale, connect positive voltmeter lead to positive battery post, and negative lead to solenoid terminal "M". *See Fig. 2.*

4) Engage remote starter switch. Voltmeter should indicate .5 volt or less. If voltmeter indicates more than .5 volt, go to next step. If voltmeter indicates .5 volt or less, go to STARTER GROUND CIRCUIT TEST.

5) Move negative voltmeter lead to solenoid terminal "B". Engage remote starter switch. If voltmeter indicates more than .5 volts, go to next step. If voltmeter indicates less than .5 volt, solenoid connections or contacts are bad. Clean solenoid terminals "B", "S" and "M". Repeat steps **2)** through **5)**. If voltmeter still indicates more than .5 volt at terminal "M" and less than .5 volt at terminal "B", solenoid contacts are bad. Install new starter motor.

6) Clean cables and connections at solenoid. If voltmeter still indicates more than .5 volt at terminal "B", check for poor positive battery cable connection or bad cable. To locate excessive voltage drop, move voltmeter negative lead toward battery, and check each connection point. When high voltmeter reading disappears, last connection point checked is cause of problem. Repair or replace as necessary.

FORD
2-12

1999 STARTING & CHARGING SYSTEMS
Starters – Crown Victoria & Grand Marquis (Cont.)

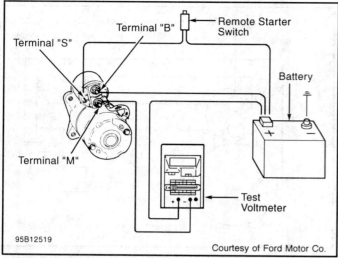

95B12519

Courtesy of Ford Motor Co.

Fig. 2: Testing Voltage Drop

SYSTEM TESTS

CAUTION: Before testing starter, ensure transmission is in Park or Neutral.

STARTER CRANKS IN REVERSE OR FORWARD GEARS

Check shift linkage adjustment. See SHIFT LINKAGE under ADJUSTMENTS. Adjust as necessary. Check adjustment of Transmission Range (TR) sensor. Adjust as necessary. See TRANSMISSION RANGE (TR) SENSOR under ADJUSTMENTS. If problem persists, install new TR sensor and check system for normal operation.

STARTER CRANKS SLOWLY

Perform VOLTAGE DROP TEST under ON-VEHICLE TESTING.

STARTER DOES NOT CRANK

1) Verify battery condition. Battery voltage should be 12 volts or more. Load test battery at approximately one-half cold cranking amperage rating. See load tester manufacturer's instructions. If battery voltage is less than 12 volts or loaded battery voltage is less than 9.6 volts, service battery or charging system as necessary. If battery is okay, go to next step.

2) Measure voltage between positive battery terminal and negative cable connection at engine block. If battery voltage is present, go to next step. If battery voltage is not present, replace ground cable or repair ground connections.

3) Measure voltage between positive battery terminal and starter motor case. If battery voltage is present, go to next step. If battery voltage is not present, remove starter motor and clean mounting surface. See STARTER MOTOR under REMOVAL & INSTALLATION. Install starter and check system for normal operation.

4) Turn ignition off. Measure voltage between starter solenoid terminal "B" (battery cable) and ground. If battery voltage is present, go to next step. If battery voltage is not present, replace battery positive cable and check system for normal operation.

5) Momentarily connect jumper wire between starter solenoid terminal "B" (battery cable) and terminal "S" (Yellow/Light Blue wire). If starter motor cranks engine, go to next step. If starter motor does not crank engine, replace starter motor. See STARTER MOTOR under REMOVAL & INSTALLATION.

6) Disconnect harness connector from starter solenoid terminal "S" (Yellow/Light Blue wire). Measure voltage between starter solenoid connector (Yellow/Light Blue wire) and ground with ignition switch in START position. If battery voltage is not present, go to next step. If battery voltage is present, clean starter solenoid "S" terminal and

connector. Check for loose or intermittent connection. Repair as necessary and check system for normal operation.

7) Turn ignition off. Remove starter relay. Measure voltage between starter relay harness connector terminal No. 86 and ground with ignition in START position. *See Fig. 3.* If battery voltage is present, go to next step. If battery voltage is not present, go to step **12)**.

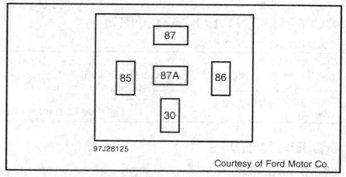

97J28125

Courtesy of Ford Motor Co.

Fig. 3: Identifying Starter Relay Harness Connector Terminals

8) Turn ignition off. Measure voltage between starter relay connector terminal No. 30 and ground. If battery voltage is present, go to next step. If battery voltage is not present, check battery junction box fuse No. 2 (30-amp). If fuse is okay, repair Yellow wire between relay and fuse. Check system for normal operation. See WIRING DIAGRAMS.

9) Measure resistance between starter relay connector terminal No. 85 and ground. If resistance is less than 5 ohms, go to next step. If resistance is 5 ohms or greater, repair Black ground wire between relay connector and ground connection on right fender, near battery. Check system for normal operation.

10) Disconnect starter solenoid "S" terminal connector (Yellow/Light Blue wire). Measure resistance between starter relay connector terminal No. 87 and ground. If resistance is greater than 10,000 ohms, go to next step. If resistance is 10,000 ohms or less, repair short to ground in Yellow/Light Blue wire. Check system for normal operation.

11) Measure resistance between starter relay connector terminal No. 87 and starter solenoid terminal "S" (Yellow/Light Blue wire). If resistance is less than 5 ohms, install new starter relay and check system for normal operation. If resistance is 5 ohms or greater, repair open in Yellow/Light Blue wire between starter and relay. See WIRING DIAGRAMS.

12) Measure voltage at both sides of battery junction box fuse No. 2 (30-amp) and ground. If battery voltage is present at both sides of fuse and ground, go to step **14)**. If battery voltage is not present between both sides of fuse and ground, go to next step.

13) Remove and inspect battery junction box fuse No. 2 (30-amp). If fuse is okay, go to step **15)**. If fuse is blown, measure resistance between fuse No. 2 input cavity and ground. If resistance is more than 10,000 ohms, install new fuse and check for normal system operation. If resistance is 10,000 ohms or less, check for short to ground in Red wire or Gray wire between battery and battery junction box. Also check Gray fusible links. Repair as necessary and check system for normal operation.

14) Disconnect ignition switch harness connector. Measure voltage between ignition switch harness connector terminal B4 and ground. *See Fig. 4.* If battery voltage is present, go to step **16)**. If battery voltage is not present, repair Yellow wire between fuse and ignition switch. See WIRING DIAGRAMS.

15) Check for open in Red or Gray wires between battery and battery junction box, or Gray fusible links. Repair as necessary and check system for normal operation.

16) Reconnect ignition switch harness connector. With voltmeter positive lead, backprobe harness connector terminal STA. Measure voltage between ignition switch harness connector terminal STA and ground with ignition switch in START position. *See Fig. 4.* If battery voltage is present, go to next step. If battery voltage is not present, inspect connector and ignition switch terminals for looseness or corrosion and repair as necessary. If connections are okay, test ignition switch. See appropriate STEERING COLUMN SWITCHES article.

1999 STARTING & CHARGING SYSTEMS
Starters – Crown Victoria & Grand Marquis (Cont.)

FORD
2-13

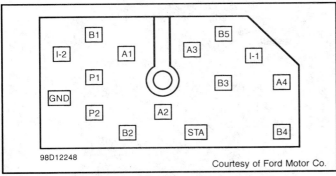

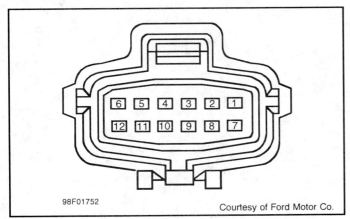

98D12248   Courtesy of Ford Motor Co.

Fig. 4: Identifying Ignition Switch Connector Terminals

17) Disconnect Transmission Range (TR) sensor harness connector. Measure voltage between ground and TR sensor harness connector terminal No. 12 with ignition switch in START position. *See Fig. 5*. If battery voltage is present, go to next step. If battery voltage is not present, repair White/Pink wire between ignition switch and TR sensor. See WIRING DIAGRAMS.

98F01752   Courtesy of Ford Motor Co.

Fig. 5: Identifying Transmission Range Sensor Terminals

18) Reconnect TR sensor connector. Ensure transmission is in Park or Neutral. With voltmeter positive lead, backprobe TR sensor connector terminal No. 10. Measure voltage between connector terminal No. 10 and ground with ignition in START position. If battery voltage is present, go to next step. If battery voltage is not present, inspect connector and sensor for loose or corroded connections. If connections are okay, check shift linkage adjustment. See SHIFT LINKAGE under ADJUSTMENTS. If shift linkage is okay, check TR sensor adjustment. See TRANSMISSION RANGE (TR) SENSOR under ADJUSTMENTS. If TR sensor adjustment is okay, replace TR sensor and check system for normal operation.

19) Disconnect TR sensor connector. Measure resistance of Red/Light Blue wire between TR sensor connector terminal No. 10 and starter relay connector terminal No. 86 in high current relay center. *See Fig. 3 and 5*. If resistance is 5 ohms or greater, repair Red/Light Blue wire. See WIRING DIAGRAMS. If resistance is less than 5 ohms, go to next step.

20) Disconnect TR sensor connector. Measure resistance between TR sensor connector terminal No. 10 and ground. *See Fig. 5*. If resistance is less than 10,000 ohms, repair short to ground in Red/Light Blue wire. If resistance is 10,000 ohms or greater, problem is intermittent. Reconnect all connectors and check system for normal operation.

UNUSUAL STARTER NOISE

1) Verify starter is installed properly. Ensure bolts are tight. Repair as necessary and check system for normal operation. If starter is mounted properly, go to next step.

2) Connect remote starter switch between starter solenoid terminal "B" (positive battery cable connection) and terminal "S" (Yellow/Light Blue wire). Engage starter motor and verify noise is coming from starter motor. If noise is coming from starter motor, go to next step. If noise is not coming from starter motor, diagnose engine mechanical concern. See appropriate engine article in ENGINES.

3) Remove starter motor. See STARTER MOTOR under REMOVAL & INSTALLATION. Inspect flywheel ring gear for wear or damage. If ring gear is okay, replace starter motor. If ring gear is worn or damaged, replace ring gear and inspect starter drive gear. If ring gear is replaced and starter drive gear is also damaged, replace starter motor.

STARTER SPINS BUT ENGINE DOES NOT CRANK

Inspect starter motor mounting. Ensure bolts are tight and starter is properly aligned. If starter motor is mounted properly, remove starter motor and inspect ring gear and starter drive gear for wear or damage. See STARTER MOTOR under REMOVAL & INSTALLATION. Repair as necessary. If ring gear and starter motor drive gear are okay, install new starter motor and check system for normal operation.

REMOVAL & INSTALLATION

STARTER MOTOR

CAUTION: When battery is disconnected, vehicle computer and memory systems may lose memory data. Driveability problems may exist until computer systems have completed a relearn cycle. See COMPUTER RELEARN PROCEDURES article in GENERAL INFORMATION before disconnecting battery.

Removal & Installation – Disconnect negative battery cable. Raise vehicle on hoist. Remove transmission cooler line bracket bolt. Position bracket and transmission cooler lines out of the way. Disconnect wiring from starter solenoid. Remove 3 starter mounting bolts. Remove starter. To install, reverse removal procedure. Tighten bolts to specification. See TORQUE SPECIFICATIONS table.

TORQUE SPECIFICATIONS

TORQUE SPECIFICATIONS

Application	Ft. Lbs. (N.m)
Shift Cable Mounting Nut	22 (30)
Starter Motor Mounting Bolts	17-20 (22-27)
Sift Cable-To-Transmission Range (TR) Sensor Nut	14-19 (19-26)
	INCH Lbs. (N.m)
Solenoid Terminal Nuts	45-61 (5-7)
Starter Motor Ground Cable Nut	97-123 (11-14)
Transmission Cooler Line Bracket Bolt	89 (10)
Transmission Range (TR) Sensor Bolts	62-89 (7-10)

FORD
2-14

1999 STARTING & CHARGING SYSTEMS
Starters – Crown Victoria & Grand Marquis (Cont.)

WIRING DIAGRAMS

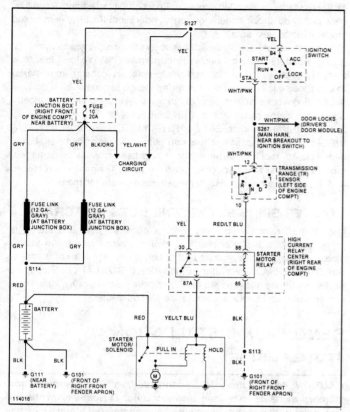

Fig. 6: Starter System Wiring Diagram
(Crown Victoria & Grand Marquis)

NOTE: This article includes Cutaway and RV Cutaway.

DESCRIPTION

The starter used on the 7.3L turbo diesel engine uses internal gear reduction and an externally mounted solenoid. System consists of a ignition switch, starter relay, 2 batteries and wiring.

COMPONENT LOCATIONS

COMPONENT LOCATIONS

Component	Location
Fuse Links "A" & "B"	Near Starter Relay
Starter Relay	Right Front Of Engine Compartment
Transmission Range Sensor	Left Side Of Transmission

TROUBLE SHOOTING

Check the following items before proceeding with testing:
- Check battery for state of charge.
- Check cable connections at battery and starter motor.
- Ensure transmission is fully engaged in Park or Neutral position.
- Ensure fuse links "A" and "B" are okay.
- Check fuse No. 23 (60-amp) engine battery junction box and fuse No. 34 (10-amp) in central junction box.

ON-VEHICLE TESTING

VOLTAGE DROP TEST

NOTE: Make all voltmeter connections at component terminal rather than at cable or wire end.

1) Remove fuse No. 17 from engine compartment fuse box to disable fuel system. Connect remote starter switch between starter solenoid terminal "S" and positive battery post.
2) Connect positive voltmeter lead to positive battery post, and negative lead to solenoid terminal "M". *See Fig. 1.*

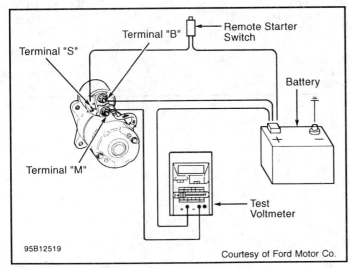

95B12519   Courtesy of Ford Motor Co.

Fig. 1: Testing Voltage Drop

3) Engage remote starter switch. Voltmeter should indicate .5 volt or less. If voltmeter indicates more than .5 volt, move negative voltmeter lead to solenoid terminal "B". If voltmeter indicates .5 volt or less, go to STARTER GROUND CIRCUIT TEST.
4) Engage remote starter switch. If voltmeter indicates less than .5 volt, solenoid connections or contacts are bad. Clean solenoid terminals "B", "S" and "M". Repeat steps 1) through 4). If voltmeter still indicates more

than .5 volt at terminal "M" and less than .5 volt at terminal "B", solenoid contacts are bad. Remove and repair or replace solenoid.
5) If voltmeter indicates more than .5 volt at terminal "B", clean cables and connections at solenoid. If voltmeter still indicates more than .5 volt at terminal "B", replace battery cable.
6) To locate excessive voltage drop, move voltmeter negative lead toward battery, and check each connection point. When high voltmeter reading disappears, problem is between last connection point and previous connection point.

STARTER GROUND CIRCUIT TEST

NOTE: Make all voltmeter connections at component terminal rather than at cable or wire end.

1) Remove fuse No. 17 from engine compartment fuse box to disable fuel system. Connect remote starter switch between starter solenoid terminal "S" and positive battery post. *See Fig. 2.*

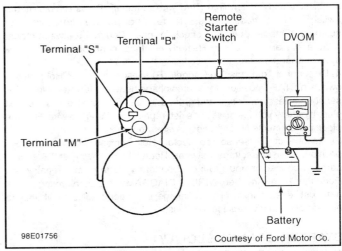

98E01756   Courtesy of Ford Motor Co.

Fig. 2: Testing Starter Ground Circuit

2) Connect positive voltmeter lead to starter housing, and negative lead to negative battery post. Engage remote starter switch while observing voltmeter. Voltmeter should indicate .2 volt or less. If voltmeter indicates more than .2 volt, clean negative cable connections at battery and engine.
3) If voltage drop is still excessive, repair or replace negative battery cable and/or engine ground cable as necessary. Repeat starter circuit test after repair to ensure problem has been corrected.

STARTER CURRENT DRAW TEST

Ensure battery is fully charged. Set parking brake and place transmission in Neutral. Ensure battery connections are clean and tight. Remove fuse No. 17 from engine compartment fuse box to disable fuel system. Clamp inductive ammeter lead around all positive battery cable leading to starter. Crank engine for about 5 seconds and check amperage reading while cranking. Normal amperage draw is 230-630 amps. If amperage draw exceeds specification, replace starter.

STARTER NO-LOAD TEST

Remove starter from vehicle. See STARTER MOTOR under REMOVAL & INSTALLATION. Using heavy gauge jumper wires, connect battery positive to starter terminal "B" and negative to starter frame. Connect voltmeter to battery. Clamp inductive ammeter lead around positive cable. Connect remote starter switch between starter solenoid "S" terminal and positive battery. Engage remote starter switch. Starter should turn smoothly. Voltmeter should indicate 11 volts or more, and ammeter should indicate no more than 170 amps. If voltage is lower or current is higher than specification, replace or overhaul starter.

SYSTEM TESTS

CAUTION: Before testing starter, ensure transmission is in Park or Neutral.

STARTER DOES NOT CRANK

1) Set parking brake and place transmission in neutral. Connect a remote starter switch between positive battery terminal and starter relay terminal (Red/Light Blue wire terminal). Press remote starter switch. If starter cranks engine, go to step **4)**. If starter does not crank engine, and starter relay did not close, go to next step. If starter did not crank engine, but starter relay closed, go to step **3)**.

2) Measure resistance between starter relay case and ground. If resistance is less than 5 ohms, replace relay. Check system operation. If resistance is more than 5 ohms, clean starter relay mounting surface and fasteners. Check system operation.

3) Connect a remote starter between positive battery cable and starter motor solenoid "S" terminal (Red wire terminal). Press remote starter switch. If starter does not operate, repair or replace starter motor or solenoid. If starter operates, check for open Red wire between starter relay and starter solenoid. Restore electrical connections and check system operation.

4) Disconnect Transmission Range (TR) sensor connector. Hold ignition switch in START position. Measure voltage between Tan/Red wire at TR sensor harness connector and ground. If battery voltage exists, go next step. If battery voltage does not exist, repair open Tan/Red wire. Restore electrical connections and check system operation.

5) Reconnect TR sensor connector. Hold ignition switch in START position. Measure voltage between Red/Light Blue wire at TR sensor harness connector and ground. If battery voltage exists, repair open Red/Light Blue wire. See WIRING DIAGRAMS. If battery voltage does not exist, ensure transmission linkage is properly adjusted. If linkage adjustment is okay, replace TR sensor.

STARTER CRANKS SLOWLY

1) Perform STARTER CURRENT DRAW TEST under ON-VEHICLE TESTING. If starter passes current draw test, go to next step. If starter fails current draw verify battery condition. Battery voltage should be 12 volts or more. Load test battery at approximately one-half cold cranking amperage rating. See load tester manufacturer's instructions. If battery voltage is less than 12 volts or loaded battery voltage is less than 9.6 volts, service battery or charging system as necessary.

2) Perform VOLTAGE DROP TEST under ON-VEHICLE TESTING. Repair or replace as necessary. If battery cable voltage drop is .5 volt or less, go to next step.

3) Perform STARTER GROUND CIRCUIT TEST under ON-VEHICLE TESTING. Repair or replace as necessary. If ground circuit voltage drop is .2 volt or less, go to next step.

4) Perform STARTER NO-LOAD TEST under ON-VEHICLE TESTING. If current draw is as specified, check engine for mechanical concerns. If current draw is excessive, replace starter motor. Restore electrical connections and check system operation.

UNUSUAL STARTER NOISE

1) Verify starter is installed properly. Check brackets for cracks. Ensure bolts are tight. Repair or replace as necessary. Check system for normal operation. If noise is still present, go to next step.

2) Remove starter motor. See STARTER MOTOR under REMOVAL & INSTALLATION. Inspect starter motor and flywheel ring gear for wear or damage. If ring gear is worn or damaged, replace ring gear and inspect starter drive gear. If drive gear is also damaged, replace starter motor. If ring gear and starter motor are okay, perform STARTER NO-LOAD TEST under ON-VEHICLE TESTING.

REMOVAL & INSTALLATION

STARTER MOTOR

Removal & Installation – Disconnect negative battery cable. Raise vehicle on hoist. Remove starter solenoid terminal cover. Remove starter ground cable nut. Remove lower starter bolts. Remove starter. To install, reverse removal procedure. Tighten bolts to specification. See TORQUE SPECIFICATIONS.

OVERHAUL

Use illustration for exploded view of starter motor assembly. *See Fig. 3.*

STARTER MOTOR SPECIFICATIONS

STARTER MOTOR SPECIFICATIONS

Application	Specification
Cranking RPM (Normal Load)	150-200
Current Draw	
(Normal Load)	230-630 Amps
(No Load)	170 Amps
Starter Circuit Voltage Drop	0.5 Volt

TORQUE SPECIFICATIONS

TORQUE SPECIFICATIONS

Application	Ft. Lbs. (N.m)
Starter Motor Mounting Bolts	17-21 (22-28)
Starter Motor Ground Cable Nut	13-17 (17-23)

	INCH Lbs. (N.m)
Starter Relay Mounting Screws	62-80 (7-9)
Starter Relay Terminal Nuts	44-97 (5-11)
Solenoid "B" Terminal Nut	80-124 (9-14)

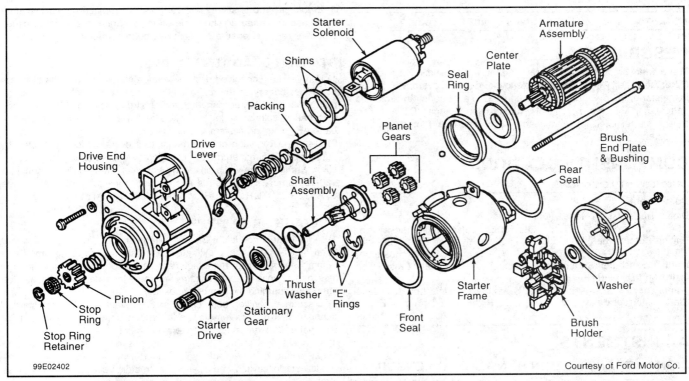

Fig. 3: Exploded View Of Starter Motor Assembly

WIRING DIAGRAMS

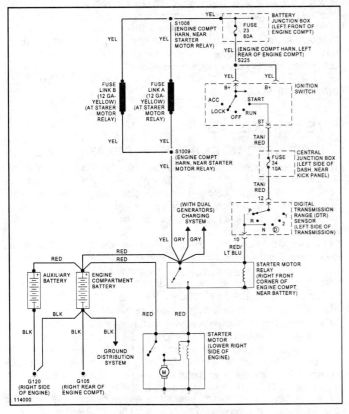

Fig. 4: Starter System Wiring Diagram (Econoline – Diesel)

NOTE: This article includes Cutaway and RV Cutaway.

DESCRIPTION

The starter motor is a permanent magnet, gear reduction, 12-volt DC motor, equipped with an integral solenoid and has an overrunning clutch in the starter drive. Starting system consists of a starter motor, solenoid, battery, ignition switch, Digital Transmission Range (DTR) sensor switch, starter interrupt relay, starter relay diode, and interconnecting cables and wires.

COMPONENT LOCATIONS

COMPONENT LOCATIONS

Component	Location
Digital Transmission Range (DTR) Sensor	Left Side Of Transmission
Engine Compartment Fuse Box	Left Front Of Engine Compartment
Inertia Fuel Shutoff Switch	Behind Right Kick Panel
Instrument Panel (I/P) Fuse Panel	Near Left Kick Panel
Starter Interrupt Relay	Right Front Corner Of Engine Compartment

ADJUSTMENTS

DIGITAL TRANSMISSION RANGE (DTR) SENSOR

1) Place transmission in Neutral. Raise and support vehicle. Disconnect manual shift control cable. Disconnect DTR electrical connector. Loosen DTR sensor bolts. Using DTR Sensor Alignment Tool (T97L-70010-A), align DTR sensor slots.
2) Tighten DTR sensor bolts to specification. See TORQUE SPECIFICATIONS table. Reconnect shift lever control cable. Connect DTR electrical connector. Lower vehicle and check system operation.

TROUBLE SHOOTING

Check the following items before proceeding with testing:
- Check battery for state of charge.
- Check cable connections at battery and starter motor.
- Ensure transmission is fully engaged in Park or Neutral position.
- Check fuse No. 23 (60-amp) in battery junction box.
- Check fuse No. 34 (10-amp) in central junction box.

ON-VEHICLE TESTING

CAUTION: When battery is disconnected, vehicle computer and memory systems may lose memory data. Driveability problems may exist until computer systems have completed a relearn cycle. See COMPUTER RELEARN PROCEDURES article in GENERAL INFORMATION before disconnecting battery. Before testing starter, ensure transmission is in Park or Neutral.

STARTER GROUND CIRCUIT TEST

NOTE: Make all voltmeter connections at component terminal rather than at cable or wire end.

1) Disconnect ignition coil connector from ignition coil to prevent vehicle from starting. Connect remote starter switch between starter solenoid "S" terminal and positive battery post. *See Fig. 1.* Connect positive voltmeter lead to starter housing, and negative lead to negative battery post.
2) Engage remote starter switch while observing voltmeter. Voltmeter should indicate .2 volt or less. If voltmeter indicates more than .2 volt, clean negative cable connections at battery and chassis. Also clean engine ground cable connections at front cover and engine mount bracket.

3) If voltage drop is still excessive, repair or replace negative battery cable and/or engine ground cable as necessary. Repeat starter circuit test after repair to ensure problem has been corrected.

STARTER LOAD TEST

1) Verify battery condition. Battery voltage should be 12 volts or more. Load test battery at approximately one-half cold cranking amperage rating. See load tester manufacturer's instructions. If battery voltage is less than 12 volts or loaded battery voltage is less than 9.6 volts, service battery or charging system as necessary.
2) Disconnect ignition coil connector to prevent vehicle from starting during test. Connect ammeter according to tool manufacturer's instructions. Crank engine while observing ammeter. Current draw should be 130-190 amps. If draw is not as specified, replace starter motor. See STARTER MOTOR under REMOVAL & INSTALLATION.

VOLTAGE DROP TEST

1) Verify battery condition. Battery voltage should be 12 volts or more. Load test battery at approximately one-half cold cranking amperage rating. See load tester manufacturer's instructions. If battery voltage is less than 12 volts or loaded battery voltage is less than 9.6 volts, service battery or charging system as necessary.
2) Disconnect ignition coil connector to prevent vehicle from starting during test. Connect remote starter switch between positive battery terminal and starter motor relay terminal (Red/Light Blue wire).
3) Connect positive voltmeter lead to positive battery terminal and negative lead to starter motor solenoid terminal "M". *See Fig. 1.* Engage remote starter switch and observe voltmeter. Voltage should be less than .5 volt.
4) If voltage is greater than .5 volt, move positive voltmeter lead to starter motor solenoid terminal "B". *See Fig. 1.* If voltage is now less than .5 volt, go to next step. If voltage is still greater than .5 volt, repair poor positive battery cable connections at battery or starter motor solenoid. If connections are okay, replace positive battery cable.
5) Remove and clean all connections at starter motor solenoid. Repeat test. If voltage is still More than .5 volt at terminal "M" and less than .5 volt at terminal "B", starter motor solenoid is faulty. Remove and repair or replace starter motor. See STARTER MOTOR under REMOVAL & INSTALLATION.

SYSTEM TESTS

ENGINE DOES NOT CRANK OR RELAY CLICKS

1) Ensure starter motor is tightly mounted. Verify battery condition. Battery voltage should be 12 volts or more. Load test battery at approximately one-half cold cranking amperage rating. See load tester manufacturer's instructions. If battery voltage is less than 12 volts or loaded battery voltage is less than 9.6 volts, service battery or charging system as necessary.
2) Inspect battery ground cable connection on starter motor. Repair as necessary. If battery ground cable is okay, measure voltage between positive battery cable connection at starter motor and ground. If battery voltage is present, go to next step. If battery voltage is not present, perform VOLTAGE DROP TEST under ON-VEHICLE TESTING. Repair or replace positive cable or connections as necessary.
3) Measure voltage between starter motor solenoid terminal "S" and ground with ignition in START position. *See Fig. 1.* If battery voltage is not present, go to next step. If battery voltage is present, clean and tighten Red wire connections at starter motor and relay and check system operation. If starter motor still does not crank, replace starter motor. See STARTER MOTOR under REMOVAL & INSTALLATION.
4) Measure voltage between each Red starter motor relay wire and ground. Battery voltage should be present at one Red wire with ignition off. Battery voltage should be present at both Red wires with ignition switch in START position. If voltage is as specified, repair open in Red wire between starter motor relay and starter motor. See WIRING DIAGRAMS. If battery voltage is present on only one Red wire with ignition switch in both OFF and START positions, go to next step. If

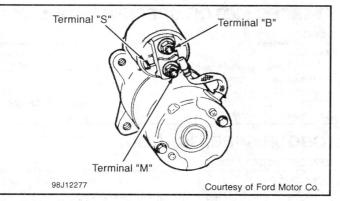

Fig. 1: Identifying Starter Motor Solenoid Terminals

battery voltage is not present at either Red wire, repair open in Red wire between battery positive terminal and starter motor relay. See WIRING DIAGRAMS.

5) Measure voltage between starter motor relay terminal (Red/Light Blue wire) and ground with ignition switch in START position. If battery voltage is not present, go to next step. If battery voltage is present, check starter motor relay mounting bolts and surfaces for looseness or corrosion. Repair as necessary. If relay is tight and mounting surface is free of corrosion, replace starter relay and check system operation.

6) Disconnect Digital Transmission Range (DTR) sensor connector. Measure voltage between DTR sensor connector terminal No. 12 (Tan/Red wire) and ground with ignition switch in START position. See Fig. 2. If battery voltage is present, go to next step. If battery voltage is not present, go to step **9)**.

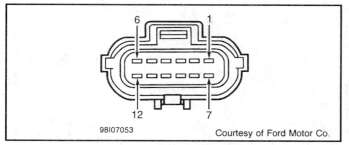

Fig. 2: Identifying Digital Transmission Range (DTR) Sensor Terminals

7) Measure resistance of Red/Light Blue wire between DTR sensor connector terminal No. 10 and starter motor relay. See Fig. 2. If resistance is less than 5 ohms, go to next step. If resistance is greater than 5 ohms, repair open in Red/Light Blue wire and check system operation.

8) Check connections for looseness or corrosion. If connections are okay, adjust DTR sensor, reconnect all connectors and check system operation. See DIGITAL TRANSMISSION RANGE (DTR) SENSOR under ADJUSTMENTS. If starter still does not crank, replace DTR sensor and check system operation.

9) Reconnect DTR sensor connector. Remove and inspect central junction box fuse No. 34 (10-amp). If fuse is okay, go to step **11)**. If fuse is blown, install new fuse and check system operation. If fuse blows again, check for short to ground between fuse No. 34 cavity (output side) and starter motor relay. Disconnect Red/Light Blue wire from starter motor relay and check resistance between fuse No. 34 cavity (output side) and ground. If resistance is greater than 10,000 ohms, replace shorted starter motor relay. If resistance is still less than 10,000 ohms, go to next step.

10) Disconnect DTR sensor connector and check resistance between fuse No. 34 cavity (output side) and ground. If resistance is less than 10,000 ohms, repair short in Tan/Red wire. See WIRING DIAGRAMS. If resistance is greater than 10,000 ohms, measure resistance between DTR sensor connector terminal No. 10 and ground. See Fig. 2. If

resistance is less than 10,000 ohms, repair short to ground in Red/Light Blue wire. See WIRING DIAGRAMS. If resistance is greater than 10,000 ohms, install new DTR sensor and check system operation.

11) Measure voltage between fuse No. 34 cavity (input side) and ground with ignition switch in START position. If battery voltage is not present, go to next step. If battery voltage is present, repair or replace central junction box or open Tan/Red wire between central junction box and DTR sensor connector.

12) Disconnect ignition switch harness connector. Measure voltage between each ignition switch connector terminal BATT (Yellow wires) and ground. If battery voltage is not present, go to step **14)**. If battery voltage is present, go to next step.

13) Measure resistance of ignition switch between terminals BATT (either one) and ST with ignition switch in START position. See Fig. 3. If resistance is greater than 5 ohms, replace igniton switch and check system operation. If resistance is 5 ohms or less, check connectors for looseness or corrosion. If connections are okay, check for open in White/Pink wire between igniton switch connector and central junction box. If wire is okay, repair or replace central junction box.

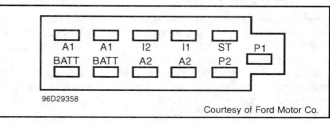

Fig. 3: Identifying Ignition Switch Terminals

14) Reconnect ignition switch connector. Remove and inspect battery junction box fuse No. 23 (60-amp). If fuse is okay, go to step **16)**. If fuse is blown, replace fuse and check system operation. If fuse blows again, short to ground is present between battery junction box fuse No. 23 and central junction box fuse No. 34, (resistance to ground is less than 10,000 ohms). Disconnect ignition switch connector and recheck resistance. If resistance is greater than 10,000 ohms, go to next step. If resistance is still less than 10,000 ohms, repair short to ground in appropriate Yellow wire. For power distribution wiring diagrams, see appropriate wiring diagram in POWER DISTRIBUTION article in WIRING DIAGRAMS.

15) Measure resistance of ignition switch between each BATT terminal and ground in every switch position. See Fig. 3. If resistance is less than 10,000 ohms in any switch position, replace ignition switch and check system operation. If resistance is greater than 10,000 ohms, repair short to ground in White/Pink wire between ignition switch and central junction box.

16) Repair open in power distribution circuit. See appropriate wiring diagram in POWER DISTRIBUTION article in WIRING DIAGRAMS. Check system operation.

ENGINE CRANKS SLOWLY

1) Verify battery condition. Battery voltage should be 12 volts or more. Load test battery at approximately one-half cold cranking amperage rating. See load tester manufacturer's instructions. If battery voltage is less than 12 volts or loaded battery voltage is less than 9.6 volts, service battery or charging system as necessary.

2) Turn ignition switch to OFF position. Using DVOM, check voltage between starter motor solenoid terminal "B" and ground. See Fig. 1. If voltage is greater than 12.5 volts, go to next step. If voltage is 12.5 volts or less, repair or replace positive battery cable or connections between battery and starter solenoid. Recheck system operation.

3) Perform starter ground circuit test. See STARTER GROUND CIRCUIT TEST under ON-VEHICLE TESTING. If ground is okay, replace starter motor. Recheck system operation. If ground circuit is not okay, repair ground circuit as necessary. Recheck system operation.

1999 STARTING & CHARGING SYSTEMS
Starters – Econoline – Except Diesel (Cont.)

UNUSUAL STARTER NOISE

1) Verify starter is installed properly. Ensure bolts are tight. Repair as necessary and check system for normal operation. If starter is mounted properly, go to next step.

2) Connect remote starter switch between positive battery terminal and starter motor relay terminal Red/Light Blue wire. Engage starter motor and verify noise is coming from starter motor. If noise is coming from starter motor, go to next step. If noise is not coming from starter motor, diagnose engine mechanical concern. See appropriate engine article in ENGINES.

3) Remove starter motor. See STARTER MOTOR under REMOVAL & INSTALLATION. Inspect flywheel ring gear for wear or damage. If ring gear is okay, replace starter motor. If ring gear is worn or damaged, replace ring gear and inspect starter drive gear. If drive gear is also damaged, replace starter motor.

BENCH TESTING

STARTER DRIVE TEST

1) Remove starter motor. See STARTER MOTOR under REMOVAL & INSTALLATION. Secure motor in vise. Using fully charged battery, connect jumper from negative battery terminal to starter motor case. Momentarily connect second jumper from positive battery terminal to starter motor Solenoid "S" terminal. See Fig. 1. Verify starter drive ejects. Remove positive jumper from starter motor. Starter drive should return to original position. If starter drive does not eject and return to original position, replace starter motor.

2) Check starter drive. It should turn freely in one direction, and positively engage to armature when rotated in opposite direction. If starter drive does not move as specified, replace starter motor.

STARTER NO-LOAD TEST

1) Remove starter motor. See STARTER MOTOR under REMOVAL & INSTALLATION. Connect remote starter switch between positive battery terminal and starter motor solenoid terminal "S". See Fig. 1. Jumper starter motor "B" terminal to positive battery post. Connect charging/starting system tester according to manufacturer's instructions. Ensure battery and starter motor are grounded.

2) Engage remote starter switch. Starter should eject starter drive and turn smoothly. Voltmeter should indicate 11 volts or more, and ammeter should indicate 60-80 amps. If voltage is lower or current is higher than specification, replace starter motor. See STARTER MOTOR under REMOVAL & INSTALLATION.

REMOVAL & INSTALLATION

STARTER MOTOR

CAUTION: When battery is disconnected, vehicle computer and memory systems may lose memory data. Driveability problems may exist until computer systems have completed a relearn cycle. See COMPUTER RELEARN PROCEDURES article in GENERAL INFORMATION before disconnecting battery. Before testing starter, ensure transmission is in Park or Neutral.

Removal & Installation – Disconnect negative battery cable. Raise and support vehicle. Remove starter solenoid terminal cover. Disconnect starter solenoid wire connections. Remove starter motor mounting nut and ground cable. Remove starter motor mounting bolts. Remove starter motor. To install, reverse removal procedure. Ensure negative battery cable is reinstalled to starter mounting bolt. Tighten bolts to specification. See TORQUE SPECIFICATIONS table.

STARTER MOTOR SPECIFICATIONS

STARTER MOTOR SPECIFICATIONS

Application	Specification
Cranking RPM (Normal Load)	140-220
Current Draw	
Normal Load	130-190 Amps
No Load	60-80 Amps
Starter Circuit Voltage Drop	0.5 Volt

TORQUE SPECIFICATIONS

TORQUE SPECIFICATIONS

Application	Ft. Lbs. (N.m)
Starter Motor Ground Cable Nut	13-17 (17-23)
Starter Motor Mounting Bolts	16-20 (22-28)

	INCH Lbs. (N.m)
Digital Transmission Range Sensor Bolts	71-88 (8-10)
Solenoid "B" Terminal Nut	84-120 (10-14)
Solenoid "S" Terminal Nut	53 (6)
Solenoid Relay Mounting Bolts	61-79 (7-9)

WIRING DIAGRAMS

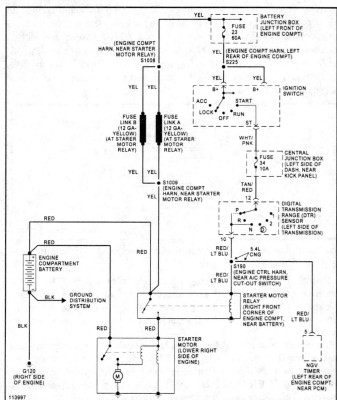

Fig. 4: Starter System Wiring Diagram (Econoline – Gasoline)

DESCRIPTION

The starter is a gear-reduction motor with an externally-mounted solenoid. Starting system consists of a starter motor with integral solenoid, battery, ignition switch, Transmission Range (TR) sensor or Clutch Pedal Position (CPP) switch and interconnecting cables and wires.

TROUBLE SHOOTING

Check the following items before proceeding with testing:
- Check battery for state of charge.
- Check cable connections at battery and starter motor.
- Ensure transmission is fully engaged in Park or Neutral, or clutch pedal is fully depressed.
- Ensure MAIN fuse (100-amp) in battery junction box.

ON-VEHICLE TESTING

VOLTAGE DROP TEST

NOTE: Make all voltmeter connections at component terminal rather than at cable or wire end.

1) Verify battery condition. Battery voltage should be 12 volts or more. Load test battery at approximately at one-half cold cranking amperage rating. See load tester manufacturer's instructions. If battery voltage is less than 12 volts or loaded battery voltage is less than 9.6 volts, service battery or charging system as necessary.
2) Disconnect ignition coil connector to prevent vehicle from starting during testing. Connect remote starter switch between starter solenoid terminal "S" and positive battery post. *See Fig. 1.*

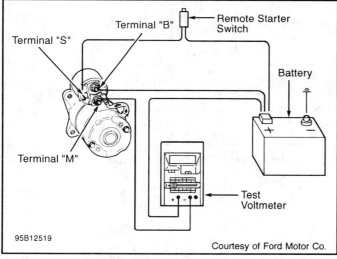

95B12519

Courtesy of Ford Motor Co.

Fig. 1: Testing Voltage Drop

3) Connect positive voltmeter lead to positive battery post, and negative lead to solenoid terminal "M". *See Fig. 1.* Engage remote starter switch. Voltmeter should indicate .5 volt or less. If voltmeter indicates more than .5 volt, go to next step. If voltmeter indicates .5 volt or less, go to STARTER GROUND CIRCUIT TEST.
4) Move negative voltmeter lead to solenoid terminal "B". Engage remote starter switch. *See Fig. 1.* If voltmeter still indicates more than .5 volt at terminal "B", go to next step. If voltmeter indicates less than .5 volt, solenoid connections or contacts are bad. Clean solenoid terminals "B", "S" and "M". Repeat steps **2)** through **4)**. If voltmeter still indicates more than .5 volt at terminal "M" and less than .5 volt at terminal "B", solenoid contacts are bad. Replace entire starter motor assembly. See STARTER MOTOR under REMOVAL & INSTALLATION.
5) Clean cables and connections at solenoid and battery. If voltmeter still indicates more than .5 volt at terminal "B", replace battery cable.

STARTER GROUND CIRCUIT TEST

NOTE: Make all voltmeter connections at component terminal rather than at cable or wire end.

1) Disconnect low voltage wires at coil pack to prevent vehicle from starting during testing. Connect remote starter switch between starter solenoid terminal "S" and positive battery post.
2) Connect positive voltmeter lead to starter housing, and negative lead to negative battery post. Engage remote starter switch while observing voltmeter. Voltmeter should indicate .2 volt or less. If voltmeter indicates more than .2 volt, clean negative cable connections at battery and engine.
3) If voltage drop is still excessive, repair or replace negative battery cable and/or engine ground cable as necessary. Repeat starter circuit test after repair to ensure problem has been corrected. If battery and cables test okay and starter motor still cranks slowly, replace starter. See STARTER MOTOR under REMOVAL & INSTALLATION.

SYSTEM TESTS

CAUTION: Before testing starter, ensure transmission is in Park or Neutral.

STARTER DOES NOT CRANK OR RELAY CLICKS

1) Inspect battery terminals for loose or corroded terminals. Repair as necessary. If battery terminals are okay, go to next step.
2) Load test battery for 15 seconds at approximately one-half cold cranking amperage rating. Voltage should remain at more than 9.6 volts at 72 °F (22 °C). If battery voltage is as specified, go to next step. If battery voltage is not as specified, recharge battery and perform load test. If battery voltage is still not as specified, replace battery and check system operation.
3) Turn ignition off. Disconnect starter 1-pin terminal "S" connector (Black/Red wire). On vehicles equipped with automatic transmission, place transmission in Park or Neutral. On vehicles equipped with manual transmission, fully depress clutch pedal. Turn ignition switch to START position while measuring voltage between starter terminal "S" connector and ground. If battery voltage is present, go to next step. On vehicles equipped with automatic transmission, if battery voltage is not present, go to step **5)**. On vehicles equipped with manual transmission, if battery voltage is not present, go to step **9)**.
4) Perform STARTER GROUND CIRCUIT TEST under ON-VEHICLE TESTING. If ground circuit does not check okay, repair or replace ground cable or connections and check system operation. If ground circuit checks okay, perform VOLTAGE DROP TEST under ON-VEHICLE TESTING.
5) Inspect Transmission Range (TR) sensor and transmission shift linkage adjustment and adjust if necessary. See ADJUSTMENTS in AUTOMATIC TRANSMISSION article in TRANSMISSION SERVICING in appropriate MITCHELL® manual. Adjust as necessary. If adjustment is okay, go to next step.
6) Turn ignition off. Disconnect TR sensor connector. Turn ignition switch to START position while measuring voltage between TR sensor harness connector terminal No. 9 (Red wire) and ground. If battery voltage is present, go to next step. If battery voltage is not present, check circuit between ignition switch and TR sensor for open or high resistance. See WIRING DIAGRAMS. Repair wiring as necessary. If circuit is okay, test ignition switch. See appropriate STEERING COLUMN SWITCHES article in ACCESSORIES & EQUIPMENT.
7) Measure resistance between TR sensor connector terminal No. 6 (Black/Red wire) and ground. If resistance is less than 5 ohms, replace TR sensor and check system operation. If resistance is 5 ohms or more, go to next step.
8) Disconnect starter motor terminal "S" connector (Black/Red wire). Measure resistance between Black wire at terminal "S" connector and ground. If resistance is less than 5 ohms, repair short to ground in Black/Red wire between connector and TR sensor. See WIRING

1999 STARTING & CHARGING SYSTEMS
Starters – Escort & Tracer (Cont.)

DIAGRAMS. If resistance is 5 ohms or more, replace starter motor. See STARTER MOTOR under REMOVAL & INSTALLATION. Check system operation.

9) Turn ignition off. Disconnect clutch start switch connector, (located at top of clutch pedal). Measure voltage between clutch star switch connector terminal (Red/White wire) and ground with ignition in START position. If battery voltage is present, go to next step. If battery voltage is not present, repair open or high resistance in circuit between clutch start switch and ignition switch. See WIRING DIAGRAMS. Check system operation.

10) Measure resistance between clutch start switch terminals while fully depressing clutch pedal. If resistance is less than 5 ohms, go to next step. If resistance is 5 ohms or more, replace clutch start switch and check system operation.

11) Disconnect starter motor terminal "S" connector (Black/Red wire). Measure resistance between Black wire at terminal "S" connector and ground. If resistance is less than 5 ohms, repair short to ground in Black/Red wire between terminal "S" connector and clutch start switch. See WIRING DIAGRAMS. If resistance is 5 ohms or more, replace starter motor. See STARTER MOTOR under REMOVAL & INSTALLATION. Check system operation.

REMOVAL & INSTALLATION

CAUTION: When battery is disconnected, vehicle computer and memory systems may lose memory data. Driveability problems may exist until computer systems have completed a relearn cycle. See COMPUTER RELEARN PROCEDURES article in GENERAL INFORMATION before disconnecting battery. Before testing starter, ensure transmission is in Park or Neutral.

STARTER MOTOR

Removal & Installation (2.0L SOHC Engine) – Disconnect negative battery cable. Remove air cleaner outlet tube. Remove top 2 starter bolts. Raise vehicle on hoist. Remove solenoid wiring protective cap. Disconnect wiring from starter solenoid. Remove lower starter bolt. Remove starter. To install, reverse removal procedure. Tighten bolts to specification. See TORQUE SPECIFICATIONS.

Removal & Installation (2.0L DOHC Engine) – Disconnect negative battery cable. Remove air cleaner outlet tube. Raise vehicle on hoist. Remove lower bolt. Lower vehicle and remove remaining bolts. Raise vehicle on hoist and pull starter motor away from mounting surface to access electrical connections. Remove integral connector nuts and disconnect integral connector from starter. Remove starter. To install, reverse removal procedure. Tighten bolts to specification. See TORQUE SPECIFICATIONS.

STARTER MOTOR SPECIFICATIONS

STARTER MOTOR SPECIFICATIONS

Application	Specification
Cranking RPM (Normal Load)	200-250
Current Draw	
Normal Load	130-190 Amps
No Load	60-80 Amps
Starter Circuit Voltage Drop	0.5 Volt

TORQUE SPECIFICATIONS

TORQUE SPECIFICATIONS

Application	Ft. Lbs. (N.m)
Starter Motor Mounting Bolts	
SOHC	18-20 (25-27)
DOHC	15-20 (20-27)
	INCH Lbs. (N.m)
Solenoid "B" Terminal Nut (SOHC)	80-115 (9-13)
Solenoid Integral Connector Nuts (DOHC)	61 (7)

WIRING DIAGRAMS

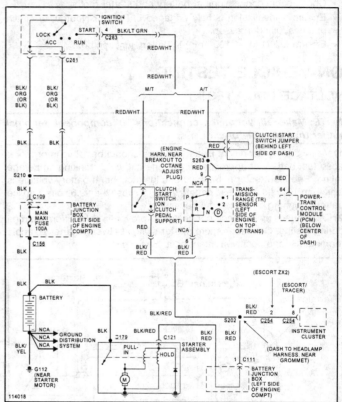

Fig. 2: Starter System Wiring Diagram (Escort & Tracer)

DESCRIPTION

A gear reduction starter with permanent-magnet fields is used. An internal planetary gear reduction unit provides increased cranking torque. The starting system includes a starter motor with solenoid-actuated drive, battery, starter/ignition switch, transmission range sensor, starter relay and associated circuitry.

Power to ignition switch is provided from fuse No. 111 (50-amp) in battery junction box in engine compartment. Power from ignition switch to starter is routed through fuse No. 21 (15-amp) in central junction box and through transmission range switch.

COMPONENT LOCATIONS

COMPONENT LOCATIONS

Component	Location
Battery Junction Box	Left Side Of Engine Compartment
Central Junction Box	Under Left Side Of Instrument Panel
Digital Transmission Range (DTR) Sensor	Left Side Of Transmission
Inertia Fuel Shutoff Switch	Behind Right Side Of Instrument Panel
Starter Relay	Right Rear Of Engine Compartment

ADJUSTMENTS

DIGITAL TRANSMISSION RANGE (DTR) SENSOR

1) Place transmission in Neutral. Raise vehicle on hoist. Disconnect manual shift cable from DTR sensor control lever. Loosen 2 DTR sensor bolts. Install DTR sensor alignment tool (T97L-70010-A).
2) Tighten DTR sensor bolts to specification. See TORQUE SPECIFICATIONS. Connect shift cable. Lower vehicle and check system operation.

TROUBLE SHOOTING

NOTE: See TROUBLE SHOOTING article in GENERAL INFORMATION.

Check the following items before proceeding with testing:
- Check battery for state of charge.
- Check cable connections at battery and starter motor.
- Ensure transmission is fully engaged in Park or Neutral.
- Check battery junction box fuse No. 111 (50-amp) and central junction box fuse No. 21 (15-amp).
- On models equipped anti-theft system, ensure anti-theft system is operating properly. See appropriate ANTI-THEFT SYSTEMS article for additional information.

ON-VEHICLE TESTING

CAUTION: When battery is disconnected, vehicle computer and memory systems may lose memory data. Driveability problems may exist until computer systems have completed a relearn cycle. See COMPUTER RELEARN PROCEDURES article in GENERAL INFORMATION before disconnecting battery.

VOLTAGE DROP TEST

NOTE: Make all voltmeter connections at component terminal rather than at cable or wire end. Clean all connections at starter and battery before beginning this test.

1) Verify battery condition. Battery voltage should be 12 volts or more. Load test battery at approximately one-half cold cranking amperage rating. See load tester manufacturer's instructions. If battery voltage is

less than 12 volts or loaded battery voltage is less than 9.6 volts, service battery or charging system as necessary. If battery is okay, go to next step.
2) Disconnect inertia fuel shutoff switch connector located behind right side of instrument panel.. Connect remote starter switch between starter solenoid terminal "S" and positive battery post.
3) Using a digital voltmeter set at lowest voltage scale, connect positive voltmeter lead to positive battery post, and negative lead to solenoid terminal "M". *See Fig. 1.*

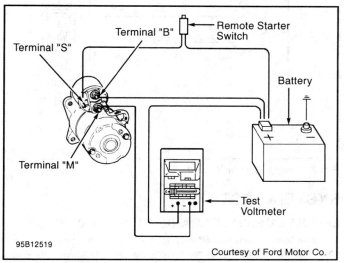

Fig. 1: Testing Voltage Drop

4) Engage remote starter switch. Voltmeter should indicate .5 volt or less. If voltmeter indicates greater than .5 volt, go to next step. If voltmeter indicates .5 volt or less, go to STARTER GROUND CIRCUIT TEST.
5) Move negative voltmeter lead to solenoid terminal "B". Engage remote starter switch. If voltmeter indicates greater than .5 volts, go to next step. If voltmeter indicates .5 volt or less, solenoid connections or contacts are bad. Clean solenoid terminals "B", "S" and "M". Repeat steps 2) through 5). If voltmeter still indicates greater than .5 volt at terminal "M" and .5 volt or less at terminal "B", solenoid contacts are bad. Install new starter motor. See STARTER MOTOR under REMOVAL & INSTALLATION.
6) Clean cables and connections at solenoid. If voltmeter still indicates greater than .5 volt at terminal "B", check for poor positive battery cable connection or bad cable. To locate excessive voltage drop, move voltmeter negative lead toward battery, and check each connection point. When high voltmeter reading disappears, last connection point checked is cause of problem. Repair or replace as necessary.

STARTER GROUND CIRCUIT TEST

NOTE: Make all voltmeter connections at component terminal rather than at cable or wire end.

1) Disconnect inertia fuel shutoff switch connector located behind right side of instrument panel. Connect remote starter switch between starter solenoid terminal "S" and positive battery post. Using a voltmeter, connect positive voltmeter lead to starter housing, and negative lead to negative battery post. *See Fig. 2.* Engage remote starter switch while observing voltmeter. If voltage is greater than .2 volt, leave test equipment attached and go to next step. If voltage is .2 volt or less, starter ground circuit is okay at this time.
2) Clean negative cable connections at battery and chassis. Engage remote starter switch while observing voltmeter. If voltage is greater than .2 volt, leave test equipment attached and go to next step. If voltage is .2 volt or less, starter ground circuit is okay at this time.
3) Connect voltmeter between negative battery post and engine ground where negative battery cable connects. Engage remote starter switch while observing voltmeter. If voltage is greater than .2 volt, replace

1999 STARTING & CHARGING SYSTEMS
Starters – Expedition & Navigator (Cont.)

negative battery cable. If voltage is .2 volt or less, replace starter motor. See STARTER MOTOR under REMOVAL & INSTALLATION.

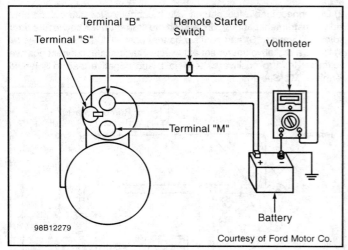

Fig. 2: Testing Ground Circuit

SYSTEM TESTS

ENGINE DOES NOT CRANK OR RELAY CLICKS

1) Check battery condition. Battery voltage should be 12 volts or more. Load test battery at approximately one-half cold cranking amperage rating. See load tester manufacturer's instructions. If battery voltage is less than 12 volts or loaded battery voltage is less than 9.6 volts, service battery or charging system as necessary. If battery is okay, go to next step.

2) Measure voltage between positive battery post and negative battery cable connection at engine block. If battery voltage exists, go to next step. If battery voltage does not exist, perform STARTER GROUND CIRCUIT TEST under ON-VEHICLE TESTING.

3) Measure voltage between positive battery post and starter motor case. If battery voltage exists, go to next step. If battery voltage does not exist, clean starter motor mounting flange and ensure starter motor is properly installed.

4) Turn ignition off. Measure voltage between starter solenoid terminal "B" and ground. *See Fig. 3.* If battery voltage exists, go to next step. If battery voltage does not exist, perform VOLTAGE DROP TEST under ON-VEHICLE TESTING.

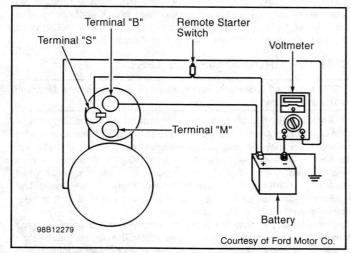

Fig. 3: Identifying Starter Motor Solenoid Terminals

5) Connect a remote starter switch between terminal "B" and "S" at starter solenoid. *See Fig. 3.* Engage remote starter switch. If starter engages and cranks engine, go to next step. If starter motor does not engage and crank engine, replace starter motor. See STARTER MOTOR under REMOVAL & INSTALLATION.

6) Disconnect Red wire from starter solenoid terminal "S". *See Fig. 3.* Measure voltage between starter solenoid terminal "S" connector (Red wire) and ground with ignition switch in START position. If battery voltage does not exist, go to next step. If battery voltage exists, repair poor connection at terminal "S" at starter and check system operation.

7) Turn ignition off. Disconnect Tan/Red wire from starter relay. Starter relay is located in right rear corner of engine compartment. Measure voltage at Tan/Red wire with ignition switch in START position. If battery voltage exists, go to next step. If battery voltage does not exist, go to step **10)**.

8) Turn ignition off. Measure voltage between ground and each Red wire at starter relay. If battery voltage exists at one Red wire, go to next step. If battery voltage does not exist at either Red wire, inspect Gray fusible links near battery. If fusible links are okay, repair open circuit between starter relay at battery. See WIRING DIAGRAMS.

9) Connect Tan/Red wire to starter relay. Measure voltage between ground and each Red wire at starter relay with ignition switch in START position. Battery voltage should exist at both Red wires. If battery voltage does not exist at one Red wire, replace starter relay. If battery voltage exists at both Red wires, repair open circuit between starter relay and starter solenoid terminal "S".

10) Turn ignition off. Remove and inspect central junction box fuse No. 21 (15-amp). If fuse is blown, go to next step. If fuse is okay, go to step **15)**.

11) Remove central junction box fuse No. 20 (5-amp). Measure resistance between central junction box fuse No. 21 output cavity and ground. If resistance is 100 ohms or less, go to next step. If resistance is greater than 100 ohms, install new fuse and check system operation.

12) Disconnect Digital Transmission Range (DTR) sensor harness connector. Measure resistance between central junction box fuse No. 21 output cavity and ground. If resistance is greater than 100 ohms, go to next step. If resistance is 100 ohms or less, repair short to ground in central junction box or Dark Blue/Orange wire between fuse cavity and DTR sensor.

13) Measure resistance between DTR sensor connector terminal No. 12 (Tan/Red wire) and ground. *See Fig. 4.* If resistance is 100 ohms or less, go to next step. If resistance is greater than 100 ohms, check DTR sensor adjustment and adjust as necessary. See DIGITAL TRANSMISSION RANGE (DTR) SENSOR under ADJUSTMENTS. If adjustment is okay, replace transmission range sensor.

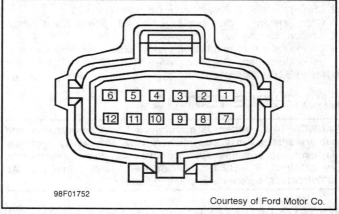

Fig. 4: Identifying Transmission Range Sensor Harness Connector Terminals

14) Disconnect Tan/Red wire from starter relay. Measure resistance between DTR sensor connector terminal No. 12 (Tan/Red wire) and ground. If resistance is 100 ohms or less, repair short to ground in Tan/Red wire between DTR sensor and starter solenoid. If resistance is greater than 100 ohms, replace starter relay.

15) Measure voltage between central junction box fuse No. 21 input cavity and ground with ignition switch in START position. If battery voltage is not present, go to next step. If battery voltage is present, go to step **18**).

16) Disconnect ignition switch harness connector. Measure voltage between ignition switch connector terminal B4 (Light Green/Purple wire) and ground. *See Fig. 5.* If battery voltage is present, go to next step. If battery voltage is not present, repair open circuit in battery junction box or Light Green/Purple wire between ignition switch and fuse No. 111. See appropriate wiring diagram in POWER DISTRIBUTION article in WIRING DIAGRAMS.

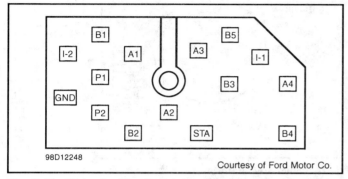

98D12248

Courtesy of Ford Motor Co.

Fig. 5: Identifying Ignition Switch Harness Connector Terminals

17) Measure resistance of Red/Light Blue wire between central junction box fuse No. 21 input cavity and ignition switch connector terminal STA. *See Fig. 5.* If resistance is 5 ohms or less, replace ignition switch. If resistance is greater than 5 ohms, repair open in Red/Light Blue wire between ignition switch and instrument panel fuse box. See WIRING DIAGRAMS.

18) Install central junction box fuse No. 21. Disconnect Digital Transmission Range (DTR) sensor connector. Measure voltage between DTR sensor connector terminal No. 10 (Dark Blue/Orange wire) and ground with ignition switch in START position. *See Fig. 4.* If battery voltage exists, go to next step. If battery voltage does not exist, repair open in Dark Blue/Orange wire between DTR sensor and instrument panel fuse box.

19) Disconnect Tan/Red wire from starter relay. Measure resistance of Tan/Red wire between starter relay connector terminal and DTR sensor connector terminal No. 12. If resistance is greater than 5 ohms, repair open in Tan/Red wire between starter relay and DTR sensor. If resistance is 5 ohms or less, check DTR sensor adjustment and adjust as necessary. See DIGITAL TRANSMISSION RANGE (DTR) SENSOR under ADJUSTMENTS. Restore connections and check system operation. If starter does not crank, replace DTR sensor.

UNUSUAL STARTER NOISE

1) Verify starter is installed properly. Ensure bolts are tight. Repair as necessary and check system for normal operation. If starter is mounted properly, go to next step.

2) Connect remote starter switch between starter solenoid terminal "B" (positive battery cable connection) and terminal "S" (Yellow/Light Blue wire). *See Fig. 3.* Engage starter motor and verify noise is coming from starter motor. If noise is coming from starter motor, go to next step. If noise is not coming from starter motor, diagnose engine mechanical concern. See appropriate engine article in ENGINES.

3) Remove starter motor. See STARTER MOTOR under REMOVAL & INSTALLATION. Inspect flywheel ring gear for wear or damage. If ring gear is okay, replace starter motor. If ring gear is worn or damaged, replace ring gear and inspect starter drive gear. If drive gear is also damaged, replace starter motor.

REMOVAL & INSTALLATION
STARTER MOTOR

CAUTION: When battery is disconnected, vehicle computer and memory systems may lose memory data. Driveability problems may exist until computer systems have completed a relearn cycle. See COMPUTER RELEARN PROCEDURES article in GENERAL INFORMATION before disconnecting battery.

Removal & Installation – Remove starter solenoid protective cover. Disconnect electrical connections. Note location of ground cable at starter. Remove nut and ground cable from starter mounting bolt. Remove 3 bolts and remove starter motor. To install, reverse removal procedure. Torque fasteners to specification. See TORQUE SPECIFICATIONS.

TORQUE SPECIFICATIONS
TORQUE SPECIFICATIONS

Application	Ft. Lbs. (N.m)
Starter Ground Cable Nut	13-16 (17-23)
Starter Motor Bolts	17-20 (22-27)
	INCH Lbs. (N.m)
Starter Relay Bolts	62-79 (7-9)

WIRING DIAGRAMS

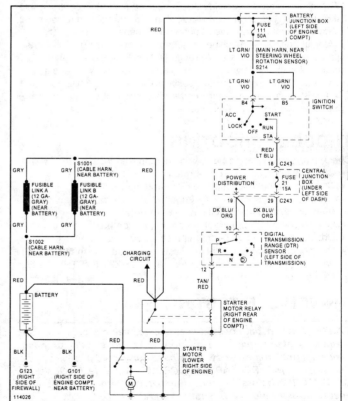

Fig. 6: Starter System Wiring Diagram (Expedition & Navigator)

DESCRIPTION

The starter motor is equipped with an externally mounted solenoid. Starting system consists of a starter motor, solenoid, battery, ignition switch, Digital Transmission Range (DTR) sensor (A/T) or Clutch Pedal Position (CPP) switch (M/T), starter relay and interconnecting cables and wires.

COMPONENT LOCATIONS

COMPONENT LOCATIONS

Component	Location
Digital Transmission Range (DTR) Sensor	Left Side Of Transmission
Fuse Junction Panel	Behind Left Side Of Instrument Panel
Inertia Fuel Shutoff Switch	In Dash Below Radio
PATS Module	Behind Right Side Of Instrument Panel
Battery Junction Box	Left Side Of Engine Compartment
Starter Relay	In Battery Junction Box
Starter Relay Diode	In Battery Junction Box

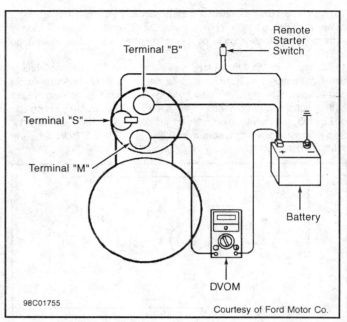

98C01755   Courtesy of Ford Motor Co.

Fig. 1: Testing Voltage Drop

ADJUSTMENTS

DIGITAL TRANSMISSION RANGE (DTR) SENSOR

1) Raise and support vehicle. Disconnect manual shift control cable. Disconnect DTR electrical connector. Remove manual control lever nut. Remove manual control lever. Loosen DTR sensor bolts.
2) Manual shift lever must be in neutral position. Using DTR Sensor Alignment Tool (T97L-70010-A), align DTR sensor slots. Tighten DTR sensor bolts. Install manual control lever. Install NEW manual shaft outer nut. Tighten fasteners to specification. See TORQUE SPECIFICATIONS. With manual lever in overdrive, connect shift lever control cable. Connect DTR electrical connector.

TROUBLE SHOOTING

Check the following items before proceeding with testing:
- Check battery for state of charge.
- Check cable connections at battery and starter motor.
- Ensure transmission is fully engaged in Park or Neutral position (A/T) or clutch pedal is fully depressed (M/T).
- Check fuse No. 5 (50-amp) in battery junction box.
- Check fuse No. 24 (7.5-amp) in fuse junction panel.
- On models equipped with anti-theft system, ensure anti-theft system is operating properly. See appropriate ANTI-THEFT SYSTEMS article for additional information.

ON-VEHICLE TESTING

CAUTION: When battery is disconnected, vehicle computer and memory systems may lose memory data. Driveability problems may exist until computer systems have completed a relearn cycle. See COMPUTER RELEARN PROCEDURES article in GENERAL INFORMATION before disconnecting battery. Before testing starter, ensure transmission is in Park or Neutral.

VOLTAGE DROP TEST

NOTE: Make all voltmeter connections at component terminal rather than at cable or wire end.

1) Ensure battery is fully charged. Disconnect inertia fuel shutoff switch to prevent vehicle from starting. Connect remote starter switch between starter solenoid terminal "S" and positive battery post. Connect positive voltmeter lead to positive battery post, and negative lead to solenoid terminal "M". *See Fig. 1.*

2) Engage remote starter switch. If voltmeter indicates .5 volt or less, go to STARTER GROUND CIRCUIT TEST. If voltmeter indicates greater than .5 volt, go to next step.
3) Move negative voltmeter lead to solenoid terminal "B". Engage remote starter switch. If voltmeter indicates less than .5 volt, solenoid connections or contacts are bad. Clean solenoid terminals "B", "S" and "M". Repeat steps 1) through 3).
4) If voltmeter still indicates more than .5 volt at terminal "M" and less than .5 volt at terminal "B", solenoid contacts are bad. Replace starter motor. See STARTER MOTOR under REMOVAL & INSTALLATION. If voltmeter indicates greater than .5 volt at terminal "B", clean cables and connections at solenoid.
5) If voltmeter still indicates greater than .5 volt at terminal "B", check for poor positive battery cable connection or bad cable. Repair or replace as necessary.

STARTER GROUND CIRCUIT TEST

NOTE: Make all voltmeter connections at component terminal rather than at cable or wire end.

1) Disconnect inertia fuel shutoff switch to prevent vehicle from starting. Connect remote starter switch between starter solenoid terminal "S" and positive battery post. *See Fig. 2.* Connect positive voltmeter lead to starter housing, and negative lead to negative battery post.
2) Engage remote starter switch while observing voltmeter. Voltmeter should indicate .2 volt or less. If voltmeter indicates greater than .2 volt, clean negative cable connections at battery and engine.
3) If voltage drop is still excessive, repair or replace negative battery cable and/or engine ground cable as necessary. Repeat starter circuit test after repair to ensure problem has been corrected.
4) If battery and cables test okay and starter motor still cranks slowly or not at all, replace starter motor. See STARTER MOTOR under REMOVAL & INSTALLATION.

SYSTEM TESTS

ENGINE DOES NOT CRANK OR RELAY CLICKS

1) Ensure battery is fully charged and has sufficient capacity. Replace battery as necessary. If battery is okay, go to next step.
2) Measure voltage between positive battery post and battery ground cable connection at engine block. If battery voltage is present, go to next step. If battery voltage is not present, replace battery ground cable. Check system operation.

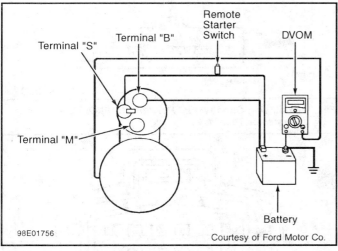

Fig. 2: Starter Ground Circuit Test

3) Using DVOM, check voltage between positive battery post and starter motor case. If battery voltage is present, go to next step. If battery voltage is not present, clean starter motor mounting flange and ensure starter motor is properly mounted. Check system operation.

4) Turn ignition off. Check voltage at starter motor terminal "B" (Red wire). See Fig. 3. If battery voltage is present, go to next step. If battery voltage is not present, replace positive battery cable. Check system operation.

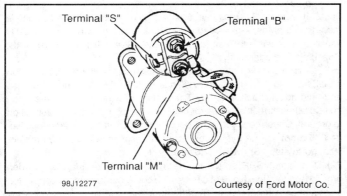

Fig. 3: Identifying Starter Motor Terminals

5) Momentarily connect a jumper wire between starter motor terminal "B" (Red wire) and starter motor solenoid terminal "S" (Yellow/Light Blue wire). See Fig. 3. If starter motor engages and cranks engine, go to next step. If starter motor does not engage and crank engine, replace starter motor. See STARTER MOTOR under REMOVAL & INSTALLATION.

6) Disconnect starter motor solenoid "S" connector. Hold ignition switch in START position. Check voltage at starter motor solenoid terminal "S" (Yellow/Light Blue) harness connector. If battery voltage is not present, go to next step. If battery voltage is present, clean starter solenoid terminal "S" and connector. Check wiring and starter motor for loose or intermittent connection. Check system operation.

7) Turn ignition off. Remove starter relay. Hold ignition switch in START position. Depress and hold clutch pedal down (M/T). On all models, check voltage between ground and starter relay connector terminal No. 86 (Tan/Red wire). See Fig. 4. If battery voltage is present, go to next step. If battery voltage is not present, go to step 11).

8) Turn ignition off. Check voltage between starter relay connector terminal No. 30 (Yellow wire) and ground. If battery voltage is present, go to next step. If battery voltage is not present, repair open in Yellow wire between starter relay connector and battery junction box. Check system operation. See WIRING DIAGRAMS.

9) Disconnect starter solenoid "S" terminal connector. Using DVOM, measure resistance between starter relay harness connector terminal

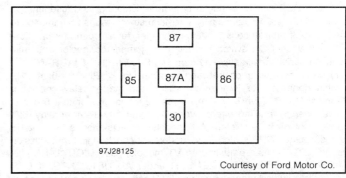

Fig. 4: Identifying Starter Relay Harness Connector Terminals

No. 87 (Yellow/Light Blue wire) and ground. If resistance is greater than 10,000 ohms, go to next step. If resistance is 10,000 ohms or less, repair short to ground in Yellow/Light Blue wire between starter motor relay and starter motor. See WIRING DIAGRAMS.

10) Using DVOM, measure resistance between starter relay connector terminal No. 87 (Yellow/Light Blue wire) and starter solenoid "S" connector (Yellow/Light Blue wire). If resistance is less than 5 ohms, replace starter relay. If resistance is 5 ohms or greater, repair open in Yellow/Light Blue wire between starter relay harness connector starter solenoid "S" connector. See WIRING DIAGRAMS. Check system operation.

11) Turn ignition off. Remove fuse No. 24 (7.5-amp). Check fuse for continuity. If fuse is okay, go to next step. If fuse is not okay, go to step 21).

12) Hold ignition switch to START position. Using DVOM, check voltage at fuse junction panel, fuse No. 24 input cavity. See Fig. 6. If battery voltage is not present, go to next step. If battery voltage is present, go to step 16) (without center console) or step 20) (with center console).

13) Disconnect ignition switch connector. Check voltage between ignition switch connector terminal B4 (Yellow wire) and ground. See Fig. 5. If battery voltage is present, go to next step. If battery voltage is not present, repair open in Yellow wire between battery junction box and starter motor relay. See WIRING DIAGRAMS. Check system operation.

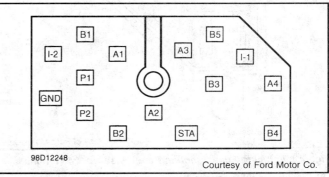

Fig. 5: Identifying Ignition Switch Connector Terminals

14) Using DVOM, measure resistance between ignition switch connector terminal No. STA (Red/Light Blue wire) and fuse junction panel, fuse No. 24 input cavity. See Figs. 5 and 6. If resistance is less than 5 ohms, go to next step. If resistance is 5 ohms or greater, repair open in Red/Light Blue wire between ignition switch connector and battery junction box. Check system operation. See WIRING DIAGRAMS.

15) Using DVOM, measure resistance between ignition switch connector terminal STA (Red/Light Blue wire) and ground. If resistance is less than 10,000 ohms, repair short to ground in Red/Light Blue wire between ignition switch connector and battery junction box. Check system operation. See WIRING DIAGRAMS. If resistance is 10,000 ohms or greater, replace ignition switch.

16) Disconnect clutch pedal position (CPP) switch or disconnect jumper connector Black 6-pin connector. Measure resistance of White/Pink wire

1999 STARTING & CHARGING SYSTEMS
Starters – Explorer & Mountaineer (Cont.)

between CCP switch connector or jumper connector and fuse junction panel, fuse No. 24 output cavity. If resistance is less than 5 ohms, go to next step. If resistance is 5 ohms or greater, repair open in White/Pink wire between CCP switch connector or jumper connector and fuse junction panel. Check system operation. See WIRING DIAGRAMS.

17) Measure resistance between terminal No. 5 (Pink wire) at CPP switch connector or jumper connector and starter relay connector terminal No. 86 (Tan/Red wire). If resistance is greater that 5 ohms, repair open in Tan/Red wire between CPP switch and starter relay (M/T models) or go to next step (A/T models). If resistance is less than 5 ohms, replace CPP switch (M/T models) or check digital transmission range (DTR) sensor adjustment (A/T models). See DIGITAL TRANSMISSION RANGE (DTR) SENSOR under ADJUSTMENTS. If DTR sensor is adjusted properly, replace DTR sensor. Check system operation.

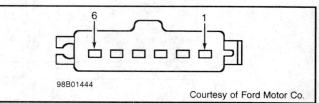

98B01444

Courtesy of Ford Motor Co.

Fig. 7: Identifying Clutch Pedal Position (CPP) Or CPP Jumper Connector Terminals

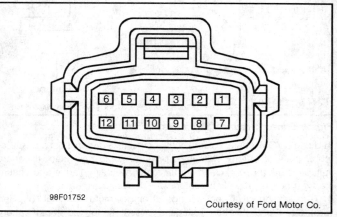

98F01752

Courtesy of Ford Motor Co.

Fig. 8: Identifying Digital Transmission Range (DTR) Sensor Connector Terminals

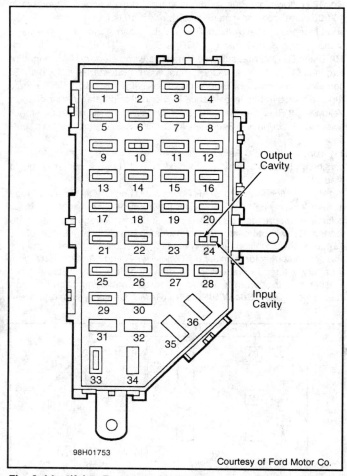

98H01753

Courtesy of Ford Motor Co.

Fig. 6: Identifying Fuse Junction Panel Fuse No. 24 Terminals

18) Disconnect DTR sensor 12-pin connector. Measure resistance of Pink wire between DTR sensor connector terminal No. 12 and CPP jumper connector terminal No. 5. *See Figs. 7 and 8*. If resistance is less than 5 ohms, go to next step. If resistance is 5 ohms or greater, repair open in Pink wire between DTR sensor switch and CPP jumper. See WIRING DIAGRAMS. Check system operation.

19) Measure resistance of Tan/Red wire between starter relay connector terminal 86 and DTR sensor connector terminal No. 10. If resistance is greater than 5 ohms, repair open in Tan/Red wire between DTR sensor connector and starter relay connector. See WIRING DIAGRAMS. If resistance is 5 ohms or less, check DTR sensor adjustment. See DIGITAL TRANSMISSION RANGE (DTR) SENSOR under ADJUSTMENTS. If DTR sensor adjustment is okay, replace DTR sensor. Check system operation.

20) Disconnect DTR sensor 12-pin connector. Measure resistance between DTR sensor connector terminal No. 12 (Pink wire) and fuse

junction panel, fuse No. 24 output cavity (White/Pink wire). *See Figs. 6 and 8*. If resistance is less than 5 ohms, go to next step. If resistance is more than 5 ohms, repair open in Pink or White/Pink wire between DTR sensor connector and fuse junction panel. See WIRING DIAGRAMS. Check system operation.

21) Remove starter relay. Measure resistance between fuse junction panel, fuse No. 24 output cavity (White/Pink wire) and ground. Depress and hold down clutch pedal (M/T models). If resistance is greater than 10,000 ohms, check all wires for chafed wires or intermittent connection to ground. Check connectors for poor terminal contact. Replace fuse No. 24 (7.5-amp). Check system operation. If resistance is 10,000 ohms or less, go to step 25) (M/T models) or go to next step (A/T models).

22) Disconnect CPP switch connector. Measure resistance between ground and terminal No. 6 at CPP switch connector or jumper connector. If resistance is greater than 10,000 ohms, repair short to ground in Pink wire between CPP switch and starter relay (M/T models) or go to next step (A/T models). If resistance is 10,000 ohms or greater, repair White/Pink wire between fuse junction panel and CPP switch. See WIRING DIAGRAMS. Check system operation.

23) Disconnect DTR sensor connector. Measure resistance between ground and terminal No. 5 (Pink wire) at CPP switch connector or jumper connector. If resistance is greater than 10,000 ohms, go to next step. If resistance is 10,000 ohms or less, repair short to ground in Pink wire between CPP switch or jumper connector and DTR sensor.

24) Measure resistance between DTR sensor switch connector terminal No. 10 (Tan/Red wire) and ground. If resistance is greater than 10,000 ohms, check DTR sensor adjustment. See DIGITAL TRANSMISSION RANGE (DTR) SENSOR under ADJUSTMENTS. If DTR sensor adjustment is okay, replace DTR sensor. Check system operation. If resistance is 10,000 ohms or less, repair short to ground in Tan/Red wire between DTR sensor and starter relay. See WIRING DIAGRAMS.

25) With DTR sensor connector and CPP connector disconnected, and starter relay removed, measure resistance between fuse junction panel fuse No. 24 output cavity and ground. *See Fig. 6*. If resistance is greater than 10,000 ohms, go to step 24). If resistance is 10,000 ohms or less, repair short to ground in Pink wire between CPP switch and DTR sensor. See WIRING DIAGRAMS.

UNUSUAL STARTER NOISE

1) Verify starter is installed properly. Ensure bolts are tight. Repair as necessary and check system for normal operation. If starter is mounted properly, go to next step.

2) Connect remote starter switch between positive battery terminal and starter motor relay terminal "S" (Red/Light Blue wire). Engage starter motor and verify noise is coming from starter motor. If noise is coming from starter motor, go to next step. If noise is not coming from starter motor, diagnose engine mechanical concern. See appropriate engine article in ENGINES.

3) Remove starter motor. See STARTER MOTOR under REMOVAL & INSTALLATION. Inspect flywheel ring gear for wear or damage. If ring gear is okay, replace starter motor. If ring gear is worn or damaged, replace ring gear and inspect starter drive gear. If drive gear is also damaged, replace starter motor.

REMOVAL & INSTALLATION

CAUTION: When battery is disconnected, vehicle computer and memory systems may lose memory data. Driveability problems may exist until computer systems have completed a relearn cycle. See COMPUTER RELEARN PROCEDURES article in GENERAL INFORMATION before disconnecting battery. Before testing starter, ensure transmission is in Park or Neutral.

STARTER MOTOR

Removal & Installation (4.0L) – Disconnect negative battery cable. Raise and support vehicle. Remove starter solenoid terminal cover. Disconnect starter solenoid wire connections. Remove starter motor lower mounting nut and ground cable. Remove starter motor mounting bolts. Remove starter motor. To install, reverse removal procedure. Ensure negative battery cable is reinstalled to starter mounting bolt. Tighten bolts to specification. See TORQUE SPECIFICATIONS.

Removal & Installation (5.0L) – Disconnect negative battery cable. Raise and support vehicle. remove starter motor solenoid terminal cover. Disconnect starter solenoid wire connections. Remove starter motor bolts and starter. To install, reverse removal procedure. Tighten bolts to specification. See TORQUE SPECIFICATIONS.

STARTER MOTOR SPECIFICATIONS

STARTER MOTOR SPECIFICATIONS

Application	Specification
Cranking RPM (Normal Load)	140-220
Current Draw	
Normal Load	130-220 Amps
No Load	60-80 Amps
Starter Circuit Voltage Drop	0.5 Volt

TORQUE SPECIFICATIONS

TORQUE SPECIFICATIONS

Application	Ft. Lbs. (N.m)
Starter Motor Ground Cable Nut	14-19 (20-25)
Starter Motor Mounting Bolts	16-20 (22-28)

	INCH Lbs. (N.m)
Solenoid "B" Terminal Nut	88-133 (10-15)
Solenoid "S" Terminal Nut	44-62 (5-7)
Solenoid Relay Switch Terminal Nuts	44-97 (5-11)

WIRING DIAGRAMS

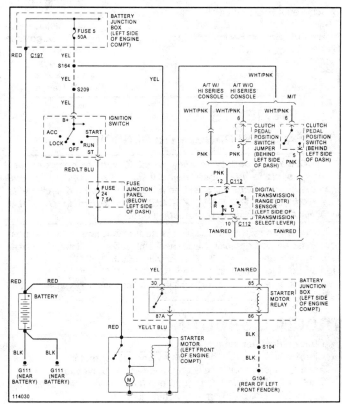

Fig. 9: Starter System Wiring Diagram (Explorer & Mountaineer)

DESCRIPTION

The starter is a gear-reduction motor with an externally-mounted solenoid. Starting system consists of a starter motor, solenoid, battery, ignition switch, Transmission Range (TR) sensor or Clutch Pedal Position (CCP) switch, starter relay and interconnecting cables and wires.

COMPONENT LOCATIONS

COMPONENT LOCATIONS

Component	Location
Central Junction Box	Behind Instrument Panel, Left Of Steering Column
Clutch Pedal Position (CPP) Switch	Top Of Clutch Pedal
Inertia Fuel Shutoff Switch	Left Rear Of Cargo Area
Starter Relay	In Underhood Battery Junction Box
Transmission Range (TR) Sensor	Left Rear Side Of Transmission

ADJUSTMENTS

TRANSMISSION RANGE (TR) SENSOR

CAUTION: When battery is disconnected, vehicle computer and memory systems may lose memory data. Driveability problems may exist until computer systems have completed a relearn cycle. See COMPUTER RELEARN PROCEDURES article in GENERAL INFORMATION before disconnecting battery.

Disconnect battery negative cable. Place transmission in Neutral position. Raise vehicle on hoist. Disconnect shift cable at TR sensor, loosen sensor bolts and install TR Sensor Alignment Tool (T97L-70010-A). Tighten bolts to specification. See TORQUE SPECIFICATIONS table. Reconnect shift cable, lower vehicle and reconnect negative battery cable.

TROUBLE SHOOTING

- Check battery for state of charge.
- Check cable connections at battery and starter motor.
- Ensure transmission is fully engaged in Park or Neutral.
- Check IGN SW fuse (40-amp) in engine battery junction box.
- Check fuse No. 6 (20-amp) in central junction box.

ON-VEHICLE TESTING

CAUTION: Before testing starter, ensure transmission is in Park or Neutral.

VOLTAGE DROP TEST

NOTE: Make all voltmeter connections at component terminal rather than at cable or wire end.

1) Verify battery condition. Battery voltage should be 12 volts or more. Load test battery at approximately one-half cold cranking amperage rating. See load tester manufacturer's instructions. If battery voltage is less than 12 volts or loaded battery voltage is less than 9.6 volts, service battery or charging system as necessary.
2) Disconnect inertia fuel shutoff switch to disable fuel system. Connect remote starter switch between starter solenoid terminal "S" (White/Pink wire) and positive battery post.
3) Connect positive voltmeter lead to positive battery post, and negative lead to solenoid terminal "M" (solenoid-to-motor connection). *See Fig. 1.*
4) Engage remote starter switch. Voltmeter should indicate .5 volt or less. If voltmeter indicates more than .5 volt, go to next step. If voltmeter indicates .5 volt or less, go to STARTER GROUND CIRCUIT TEST.

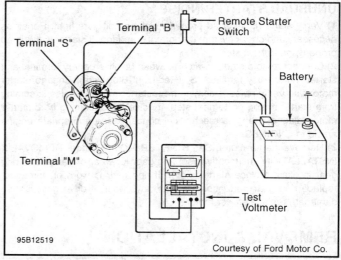

95B12519   Courtesy of Ford Motor Co.

Fig. 1: Testing Voltage Drop

5) Move negative voltmeter lead to solenoid terminal "B". Engage remote starter switch. If voltmeter still indicates more than .5 volt at terminal "B", go to next step. If voltmeter indicates less than .5 volt, solenoid connections or contacts are bad. Clean solenoid terminals "B", "S" and "M". Repeat steps **2)** through **5)**. If voltmeter still indicates more than .5 volt at terminal "M" and less than .5 volt at terminal "B", solenoid contacts are bad. Replace starter motor. See STARTER MOTOR under REMOVAL & INSTALLATION.
6) Clean cables and connections at solenoid and battery. If voltmeter still indicates more than .5 volt at terminal "B", replace battery cable.

NOTE: To locate excessive voltage drop, move voltmeter negative lead toward battery, and check each connection point. When high voltmeter reading disappears, problem is between last connection point and previous connection point.

SYSTEM TESTS

STARTER GROUND CIRCUIT TEST

NOTE: Make all voltmeter connections at component terminal rather than at cable or wire end.

1) Disconnect Inertia Fuel Shutoff (IFS) switch connector to disable fuel pump. IFS switch is located in left side of trunk compartment. Connect remote starter switch between starter solenoid terminal "S" (White/Pink wire) and positive battery post. *See Fig. 2.* Using a digital voltmeter set at lowest voltage scale, connect positive voltmeter lead to starter housing, and negative lead to negative battery post.
2) Engage remote starter switch while observing voltmeter. Voltmeter should indicate .2 volt or less. If voltmeter indicates more than .2 volt, clean negative cable connections at battery and chassis. Also clean engine ground cable connections at front cover and engine mount bracket. If voltage drop is still excessive, repair or replace negative battery cable and/or engine ground cable as necessary. Repeat starter circuit test after repair to ensure problem has been corrected. If battery and cables test okay and starter motor still cranks slowly or not at all, replace starter motor. See STARTER MOTOR under REMOVAL & INSTALLATION.

STARTER CRANKS SLOWLY OR SOLENOID CLICKS

See VOLTAGE DROP TEST under ON-VEHICLE TESTING.

STARTER DOES NOT CRANK

1) Verify battery condition. Battery voltage should be 12 volts or more. Load test battery at approximately one-half cold cranking amperage rating. See load tester manufacturer's instructions. If battery is okay, go

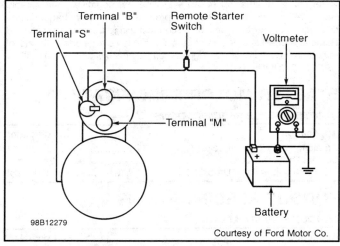

Fig. 2: Testing Ground Circuit

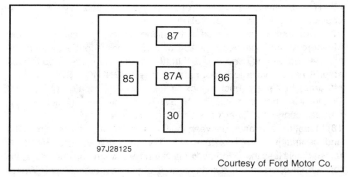

Fig. 3: Identifying Starter Relay Connector Terminals

to next step. If battery voltage is less than 12 volts or loaded battery voltage is less than 9.6 volts, service battery or charging system as necessary.

2) Measure voltage between positive battery terminal and battery ground cable connection on engine. If battery voltage is present, go to next step. If battery voltage is not present, replace battery ground cable and check for normal system operation.

3) Measure voltage between battery positive terminal and starter motor housing. If battery voltage is present, go to next step. If battery voltage is not present, verify starter is correctly and tightly installed. If starter installation is okay, remove starter motor and clean mounting surfaces. See STARTER MOTOR under REMOVAL & INSTALLATION. Install starter motor and check system for normal operation.

4) Measure voltage between starter motor battery cable terminal and ground. If battery voltage is present, go to next step. If battery voltage is not present, replace battery positive cable and check for normal system operation.

5) Momentarily jumper starter positive battery cable terminal and start terminal (White/Pink wire). If starter motor operates properly, go to next step. If starter motor does not operate properly, replace starter motor and check system for normal operation. See STARTER MOTOR under REMOVAL & INSTALLATION.

6) Disconnect starter electrical connector (White/Pink wire). Place transmission in Park or Neutral (A/T), or depress clutch pedal (M/T). Measure voltage between connector terminal (White/Pink wire) and ground with ignition switch in START position. If battery voltage is not present, go to next step. If battery voltage is present, clean starter motor and connector terminals. Check for loose or intermittent connection. Check system for normal operation.

7) Turn ignition off. Remove starter relay from battery junction box. Place transmission in Park or Neutral (A/T), or depress clutch pedal (M/T). Measure voltage between starter relay connector terminal No. 85 and ground with ignition switch in START position. *See Fig. 3.* If battery voltage is present, go to next step. If battery voltage is not present, go to step **12)**.

8) Turn ignition off. Measure voltage between starter relay connector terminal No. 30 and ground. If battery voltage is present, go to next step. If battery voltage is not present, check IGNITION SWITCH fuse (40-amp) in battery junction box. If fuse is okay, repair Light Green/Purple wire between fuse and starter relay connector and check system for normal operation.

9) Measure resistance between starter relay terminal No. 86 and ground. If resistance is less than 5 ohms, go to next step. If resistance is 5 ohms or greater, repair Black wire between starter relay connector and ground and check system for normal operation.

10) Measure resistance between starter relay connector terminal No. 87 (Brown/Pink wire) and ground. If resistance is greater than 10,000

ohms, go to next step. If resistance is 10,000 ohms or less, repair short to ground in Brown/Pink wire and check system for normal operation.

11) Measure resistance between starter relay connector terminal No. 87 (Brown/Pink wire) and starter motor connector (White/Pink wire). If resistance is less than 5 ohms, install new starter relay and check system for normal operation. If resistance is greater than 5 ohms, repair open in Brown/Pink wire and starter motor. See WIRING DIAGRAMS.

12) On M/T models, disconnect Clutch Pedal Position (CPP) switch connector. On A/T models, disconnect CPP jumper connector located left of clutch pedal assembly. To identify harness, see WIRING DIAGRAMS. On all models, measure voltage between CPP connector (or jumper connector) Red/Light Blue wire and ground with ignition switch in START position. If battery voltage is present, go to step **14)**. If battery voltage is not present, go to next step.

13) Measure voltage between central junction box fuse No. 6 (20-amp) input side and ground with ignition switch in START position. If battery voltage is not present, go to step **17)**. If battery voltage is present, check fuse No. 6. If fuse is okay, repair Red/Light Blue wire between fuse and CPP connector, (or CPP jumper connector), and check system for normal operation.

14) Measure resistance between CCP connector (or CPP jumper connector) White/Pink wire and starter relay connector terminal No. 85. If resistance is less than 5 ohms, replace CPP switch (or CPP jumper and check system for normal operation. If resistance is greater than 5 ohms, go to next step (A/T) or repair wire between CPP switch and starter relay connector (M/T). Check system for normal operation. See WIRING DIAGRAMS.

15) Disconnect Transmission Range (TR) sensor. Measure resistance between CPP jumper harness connector (White/Pink wire) and TR sensor connector terminal No. 10 (Red/Light Blue wire). *See Fig. 4.* If resistance is 5 ohms or less, go to next step. If resistance is greater than 5 ohms, repair open White/Pink wire or Red/Light Green wire between CPP jumper connector and TR sensor connector. Check system for normal operation. See WIRING DIAGRAMS.

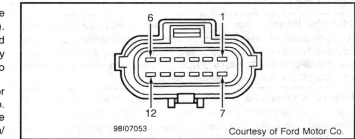

Fig. 4: Identifying Transmission Range (TR) Sensor Terminals

16) Measure resistance of White/Pink wire between starter relay connector terminal No. 85 and TR sensor connector terminal No. 12. If resistance is greater than 5 ohms, repair open White/Pink wire between starter relay connector and TR sensor connector and check system for normal operation. If resistance is 5 ohms or less, adjust TR sensor and recheck. See TRANSMISSION RANGE (TR) SENSOR under ADJUST-

MENTS. If resistance is still 5 ohms or less, replace TR sensor and check system for normal operation.

17) Turn ignition off. Disconnect ignition switch harness connector. Measure voltage between ignition switch harness connector terminal No. B4 and ground. *See Fig. 5.* If battery voltage is present, go to next step. If battery voltage is not present, check IGNITION SWITCH fuse (40-amp) in battery junction box. If fuse is okay, repair Light Green/Purple wire between IGNITION SWITCH fuse and ignition switch harness connector. Check system for normal operation.

18) Measure resistance between ignition switch connector terminal STA and central junction box fuse No. 6 input terminal. *See Fig. 5.* If resistance is less than 5 ohms, replace ignition switch and check system for normal operation. If resistance is 5 ohms or greater, repair White/Pink wire between ignition switch and fuse. Check system for normal operation.

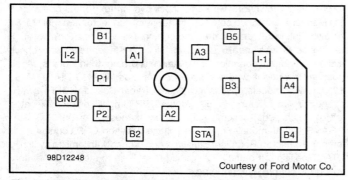

Fig. 5: Identifying Ignition Switch Connector Terminals

UNUSUAL STARTER NOISE

1) Ensure starter mounting bolts are tight and installed properly. Correct as necessary. If starter is mounted correctly, go to next step.

2) Turn ignition off. Connect remote starter switch between starter terminals "B" (battery cable) and "S" (White/Pink wire). Ensure transmission is in Park or Neutral and ignition is off. Engage starter motor and verify noise is from starter. If noise is from starter, go to next step. If noise is not from starter, check for engine mechanical concerns. See appropriate engine article in ENGINES.

3) Remove starter motor. See STARTER MOTOR under REMOVAL & INSTALLATION. Inspect flywheel ring gear for wear or damage. Inspect starter drive gear for wear or damage. Replace ring gear, starter or both as necessary. If no wear or damage is found, replace starter motor and check for normal system operation.

REMOVAL & INSTALLATION

STARTER MOTOR

CAUTION: When battery is disconnected, vehicle computer and memory systems may lose memory data. Driveability problems may exist until computer systems have completed a relearn cycle. See COMPUTER RELEARN PROCEDURES article in GENERAL INFORMATION before disconnecting battery.

Removal & Installation (3.8L) – Disconnect negative battery cable. Raise vehicle on hoist. Remove engine block ground cable nut and remove ground cable from stud. Remove protective cap from battery cable connection at starter solenoid. Remove positive battery cable-to-starter solenoid nut and disconnect cable. Remove upper and lower starter bolts. Remove starter. To install, reverse removal procedure. Tighten bolts to specification. See TORQUE SPECIFICATIONS.

Removal & Installation (4.6L) – Disconnect negative battery cable. Raise vehicle on hoist. Remove protective cap from battery cable connection at starter solenoid. Disconnect wiring from starter solenoid. Remove upper and lower starter bolts. Remove starter. To install, reverse removal procedure. Tighten bolts to specification. See TORQUE SPECIFICATIONS.

STARTER MOTOR SPECIFICATIONS

STARTER MOTOR SPECIFICATIONS

Application	Specification
Cranking RPM (Normal Load)	140-220
Current Draw (No Load)	60-80 Amps
Starter Circuit Voltage Drop	0.5 Volt

TORQUE SPECIFICATIONS

TORQUE SPECIFICATIONS

Application	Ft. Lbs. (N.m)
Starter Motor Ground Cable Nut (3.8L)	17 (23)
Starter Motor Mounting Bolts	17 (23)
	INCH Lbs. (N.m)
Battery Cable Retaining Nut	70-130
	(8.0-14.7)
Solenoid "B" Terminal Nut	106 (12)

WIRING DIAGRAMS

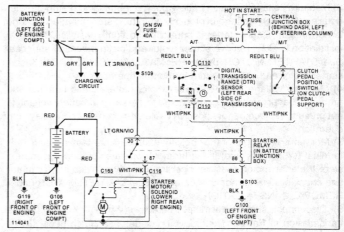

Fig. 6: Starter System Wiring Diagram (Mustang)

DESCRIPTION

The starter motor is a permanent magnet, gear reduction, 12 volt DC motor, equipped with an integral solenoid. Starting system consists of a starter motor, solenoid, battery, ignition switch, Digital Transmission Range (DTR) sensor switch (A/T), or Clutch Pedal Position (CPP) switch (M/T), starter relay, and interconnecting cables and wires.

COMPONENT LOCATIONS

COMPONENT LOCATIONS

Component	Location
Battery Junction Box	Left Side Of Engine Compartment
Central Junction Box	Under Left Of Instrument Panel
Digital Transmission Range Sensor	Left Side Of Transmission
Inertia Fuel Shutoff Switch	Behind Right Side Of Instrument Panel
Starter Relay	Right Rear Of Engine Compartment

ADJUSTMENTS

DIGITAL TRANSMISSION RANGE (DTR) SENSOR

1) Raise and support vehicle. Disconnect manual shift control cable. Disconnect DTR electrical connector. Remove manual control lever nut. Remove manual control lever. Loosen DTR sensor bolts.
2) Manual shift lever must be in Neutral position. Using DTR Sensor Alignment Tool (T97L-70010-A), align DTR sensor slots. Tighten DTR sensor bolts. Install manual control lever. Install NEW manual shaft outer nut. Tighten fasteners to specification. See TORQUE SPECIFICATIONS. With manual lever in overdrive, connect shift lever control cable. Connect DTR electrical connector.

TROUBLE SHOOTING

Check the following items before proceeding with testing:
- Check battery for state of charge.
- Check cable connections at battery and starter motor.
- Ensure transmission is fully engaged in Park or Neutral position or clutch pedal is fully depressed.
- Check fuse No. 111 (50-amp) in power distribution box.
- Check fuse No. 21 (15-amp) in junction box fuse/relay panel.
- On models equipped with anti-theft system, ensure anti-theft system is operating properly. See appropriate ANTI-THEFT SYSTEMS article for additional information.

ON-VEHICLE TESTING

CAUTION: *When battery is disconnected, vehicle computer and memory systems may lose memory data. Driveability problems may exist until computer systems have completed a relearn cycle. See COMPUTER RELEARN PROCEDURES article in GENERAL INFORMATION before disconnecting battery. Before testing starter, ensure transmission is in Park or Neutral.*

VOLTAGE DROP TEST

NOTE: *Make all voltmeter connections at component terminal rather than at cable or wire end.*

1) Ensure battery is fully charged. Disconnect ignition coil connector from ignition coil to prevent vehicle from starting. Connect remote starter switch between starter solenoid terminal "S" and positive battery post. Connect positive voltmeter lead to positive battery post, and negative lead to solenoid terminal "M". See Fig. 1.

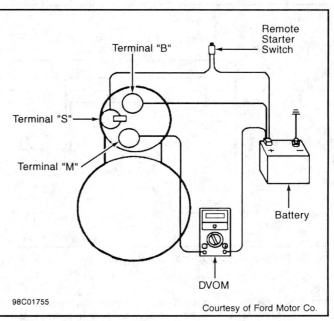

98C01755   Courtesy of Ford Motor Co.

Fig. 1: Testing Voltage Drop

2) Engage remote starter switch. Voltmeter should indicate .5 volt or less. If voltmeter indicates .5 volt or less, go to STARTER GROUND CIRCUIT TEST. If voltmeter indicates greater than .5 volt, go to next step.
3) Move negative voltmeter lead to solenoid terminal "B". Engage remote starter switch. If voltmeter indicates less than .5 volt, solenoid connections or contacts are bad. Clean solenoid terminals "B", "S" and "M". Repeat steps 1) through 3).
4) If voltmeter still indicates greater than .5 volt at terminal "M" and less than .5 volt at terminal "B", solenoid contacts are bad. Replace starter motor. See STARTER MOTOR under REMOVAL & INSTALLATION. If voltmeter indicates greater than .5 volt at terminal "B", clean cables and connections at solenoid.
5) If voltmeter still indicates greater than .5 volt at terminal "B", check for poor positive battery cable connection or bad cable. Repair as necessary.

STARTER GROUND CIRCUIT TEST

NOTE: *Make all voltmeter connections at component terminal rather than at cable or wire end.*

1) Disconnect ignition coil connector from ignition coil to prevent vehicle from starting. Connect remote starter switch between starter solenoid terminal "S" and positive battery post. Connect positive voltmeter lead to starter housing, and negative lead to negative battery post. See Fig. 2.
2) Engage remote starter switch while observing voltmeter. Voltmeter should indicate .2 volt or less. If voltmeter indicates greater than .2 volt, clean negative cable connections at battery and engine.
3) If voltage drop is still excessive, repair or replace negative battery cable and/or engine ground cable as necessary. Repeat starter circuit test after repair to ensure problem has been corrected.
4) If battery and cables test okay and starter motor still cranks slowly or not at all, replace starter motor. See STARTER MOTOR under REMOVAL & INSTALLATION.

SYSTEM TESTS

ENGINE DOES NOT CRANK OR RELAY CLICKS

1) Verify battery condition. If battery is okay, measure voltage between each Red wire at starter relay and ground. Battery voltage should be present at one Red wire only. If battery voltage is present on one Red wire, go to next step. If battery voltage is not present on either Red wire, repair or replace Red wire between battery and starter relay cable. Check system operation.

FORD
2-34

1999 STARTING & CHARGING SYSTEMS
Starters – F150 & F250 Light-Duty Pickups (Cont.)

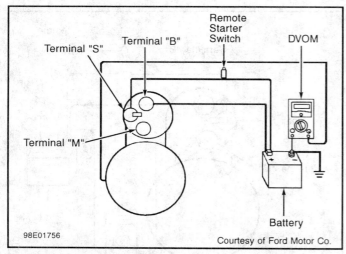

98E01756   Courtesy of Ford Motor Co.

Fig. 2: Testing Starter Ground Circuit

2) Measure voltage between starter motor solenoid "B" terminal and ground. *See Fig. 3*. If battery voltage is present, go to next step. If battery voltage is not present, clean and tighten battery and solenoid terminal connections. If battery voltage is still not present, replace positive battery cable. Check system operation.

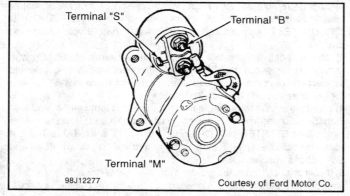

98J12277   Courtesy of Ford Motor Co.

Fig. 3: Identifying Starter Solenoid Terminals (Typical)

3) Using jumper wire, connect one end to positive battery terminal and with other end, momentarily touch starter solenoid "S" terminal. *See Fig. 3*. If solenoid engages, go to next step. If solenoid does not engage, replace starter motor. See STARTER MOTOR under REMOVAL & INSTALLATION. Check system operation.
4) Using jumper wire, connect one end to positive battery terminal and with other end, momentarily touch starter solenoid "M" terminal. *See Fig. 3*. If starter spins, go to next step. If starter does not spin, replace starter motor. See STARTER MOTOR under REMOVAL & INSTALLATION. Check system operation.
5) Disconnect starter relay connectors. Disconnect starter motor solenoid connectors. Measure resistance of Red wire between starter relay and starter solenoid. If resistance is less than 5 ohms, replace starter relay. If resistance is 5 ohms or greater, repair or replace Red wire between starter relay and starter solenoid. Check system operation.

ENGINE DOES NOT CRANK & RELAY DOES NOT CLICK

1) Remove fuse No. 111 (50-amp), located in battery junction box. Check continuity of fuse No. 111 (50-amp). If fuse No. 111 is okay, reinstall fuse and go to next step. If fuse No. 111 is open, install new fuse and go to step **15**).
2) Remove fuse No. 21 (15-amp), located in central junction box. Check for continuity of fuse No. 21 (15-amp). If fuse No. 21 is okay, reinstall fuse and go to next step. If fuse No. 21 is open, install new fuse, and go to step **18**).

3) Measure voltage between central junction box fuse No. 21 and ground while holding ignition switch in START position. If battery voltage is present, go to step **6**). If battery voltage is not present, go to next step.
4) Disconnect ignition switch 15-pin connector. Measure resistance between central junction box fuse No. 21 (15-amp) and ignition switch connector terminal STA (Red/Light Blue wire). *See Fig. 4*. If resistance is less than 5 ohms, go to next step. If resistance is 5 ohms or greater, repair poor connection or open in Red/Light Blue wire between ignition switch connector and central junction box. See WIRING DIAGRAMS. Check system operation. Check system operation.

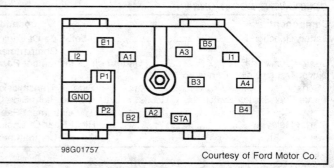

98G01757   Courtesy of Ford Motor Co.

Fig. 4: Identifying Ignition Switch Connector Terminals

5) Remove battery junction box fuse No. 111 (50-amp). Measure resistance of Light Green/Purple wire between ignition switch harness connector terminal No. B4 and battery junction box fuse No. 111 (50-amp) output cavity. *See Fig. 4*. If resistance is less than 5 ohms, replace ignition switch. See appropriate STEERING COLUMN SWITCHES article in ACCESSORIES & EQUIPMENT. If resistance is 5 ohms or greater, repair poor connection or open in Light Green/Purple wire between ignition switch harness connector and output cavity of fuse No. 111 (50-amp). See WIRING DIAGRAMS. Check system operation.
6) Turn ignition off. Disconnect starter relay connector (Tan/Red wire). Measure voltage between starter relay connector terminal (Tan/Red wire) and ground while momentarily turning ignition switch to START position. If battery voltage is present, replace starter relay. Check system operation. If battery voltage is not present, go to next step (A/T models) or go to step **12**) (M/T models).
7) Disconnect Digital Transmission Range (DTR) sensor 12-pin connector. Measure resistance of Tan/Red wire between DTR sensor connector terminal No. 12 and starter relay connector. *See Fig. 5*. If resistance is less than 5 ohms, go to next step. If resistance is 5 ohms or greater, repair Tan/Red wire between DTR sensor connector and starter relay connector. See WIRING DIAGRAMS. Check system operation.

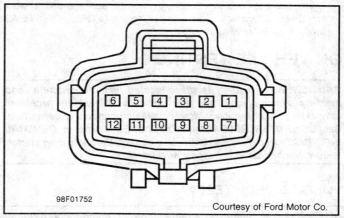

98F01752   Courtesy of Ford Motor Co.

Fig. 5: Identifying Digital Transmission Range Sensor Connector Terminals

8) Perform DTR sensor adjustment. See DIGITAL TRANSMISSION RANGE (DTR) SENSOR under ADJUSTMENTS. Adjust as necessary. Check system operation. If DTR sensor is adjusted properly, go to next step.

1999 STARTING & CHARGING SYSTEMS
Starters – F150 & F250 Light-Duty Pickups (Cont.)

FORD
2-35

9) Connect a jumper wire between DTR sensor connector terminals No. 12 (Tan/Red wire) and No. 10 (Dark Blue/Orange wire). *See Fig. 5.* Attempt to start vehicle. If vehicle starts, replace DTR sensor. Check system operation. If vehicle does not start, go to next step.

10) Disconnect Clutch Pedal Position (CPP) jumper 6-pin connector. Measure resistance of Dark Blue/Orange wire between DTR connector terminal No. 10 and CPP jumper connector terminal No. 2. *See Figs. 5 and 6.* If resistance is less than 5 ohms, go to next step. If resistance is 5 ohms or greater, repair Dark Blue/Orange wire between DTR sensor connector and CPP switch. See WIRING DIAGRAMS. Check system operation.

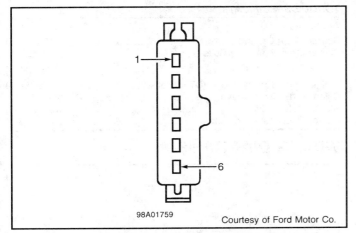

Fig. 6: Identifying Clutch Pedal Position (CPP) Switch Or Jumper Connector Terminals

98A01759   Courtesy of Ford Motor Co.

11) Measure resistance between CPP jumper terminals No. 1 and 2. If resistance is greater than 5 ohms, replace CPP jumper. If resistance is 5 ohms or less, go to step **14)**. Check system operation.

12) Disconnect starter relay connector. Disconnect CPP switch connector. Measure resistance between starter relay connector terminal (Tan/Red wire) and CPP switch connector terminal No. 2 (Dark Blue/Orange wire). *See Fig. 6.* If resistance is less than 5 ohms, reconnect starter relay, go to next step. If resistance is 5 ohms or greater, repair open in Tan/Red wire or Dark Blue/Orange wire between CPP and starter relay. See WIRING DIAGRAMS. Check system operation.

13) Disconnect CPP switch 6-pin connector. Connect a jumper wire between CPP switch connector terminals No. 5 (White/Pink wire) and No. 6 (Gray/Yellow wire). Connect another jumper wire between CPP switch connector terminals No. 1 (White/Pink wire) and No. 2 (Dark Blue/Orange wire). *See Fig. 6.* Attempt to start vehicle. If vehicle starts, replace CPP switch. If vehicle does not start, go to next step. Check system operation.

14) Disconnect central junction box black 34-pin connector. Measure resistance of White/Pink wire between connector terminal No. 29 and CCP switch connector terminal No. 1. If resistance is less than 5 ohms, replace central junction box. If resistance is 5 ohms or greater, repair open in White/Pink wire between central junction box connector and CPP switch connector. Check system operation.

15) Momentarily turn ignition switch to START position. Turn ignition off. Remove fuse No. 111 (50-amp) from battery junction box. Check fuse for open. If fuse is okay, system is okay at this time. If fuse is open, go to next step.

16) Disconnect ignition switch connector. Measure resistance between ignition switch connector terminal B5 (Light Green/Purple wire) and ground. *See Fig. 4.* If resistance is greater than 10,000 ohms, go to next step. If resistance is 10,000 ohms or less, repair short to ground in Light Green/Purple wire between ignition switch connector and power distribution box. See WIRING DIAGRAMS.

17) Remove fuse No. 21 (15-amp) from central junction box. Measure resistance between ignition switch connector terminal STA and ground. *See Fig. 4.* If resistance is greater than 10,000 ohms, replace ignition switch. Check system operation. If resistance is 10,000 ohms or less,

repair short to ground in Red/Light Blue wire between ignition switch and central junction box. See WIRING DIAGRAMS.

18) Turn ignition switch to START position momentarily. Turn ignition off. Remove and recheck fuse No. 21 (15-amp). If fuse is not open, no problem is indicated at this time. If fuse is open, install new fuse and go to next step.

19) Disconnect starter relay connectors. Momentarily turn ignition switch to START position. Turn ignition switch off. Recheck fuse No. 21 (15-amp). If fuse is okay, replace starter relay. Check system operation. If fuse is open, install new fuse and go to next step.

20) Disconnect CPP switch or CPP jumper connector. Measure resistance between CPP switch or CPP jumper connector terminal No. 1 (White/Pink wire) and ground. *See Fig. 6.* If resistance is greater than 10,000 ohms, go to next step (A/T models) or go to step **24)** (M/T models). If resistance is less than 10,000 ohms, repair short to ground in White/Pink wire between CPP switch or CPP jumper and central junction box. See WIRING DIAGRAMS. Check system operation.

21) Place transmission in PARK position. Measure resistance between starter relay connector terminal (Tan/Red wire) and ground. If resistance is greater than 10,000 ohms, replace CPP jumper. Check system operation. If resistance is 10,000 ohms or less, go to next step.

22) Disconnect DTR sensor connector. Measure resistance between DTR sensor connector terminal No. 10 (Dark Blue/Orange wire) and ground. *See Fig. 5.* If resistance is greater than 10,000 ohms, go to next step. If resistance is 10,000 ohms or less, repair short to ground in Dark Blue/Orange wire between DTR sensor and CPP jumper. See WIRING DIAGRAMS. Check system operation.

23) Measure resistance between DTR sensor connector terminal No. 12 (Tan/Red wire) and ground. If resistance is greater than 10,000 ohms, replace DTR sensor. Check system operation. If resistance is 10,000 ohms or less, repair short to ground in Tan/Red wire between DTR sensor and starter relay. See WIRING DIAGRAMS. Check system operation.

24) Disconnect starter relay connectors. Measure resistance between CPP switch connector terminal No. 2 (Dark Blue/Orange wire) and ground. If resistance is greater than 10,000 ohms, replace CPP switch. Check system operation. If resistance is 10,000 ohms or less, repair short to ground in Tan/Red wire between CPP switch and starter relay. See WIRING DIAGRAMS. Check system operation.

ENGINE CRANKS SLOWLY

1) Turn ignition switch to OFF position. Check voltage between starter motor solenoid positive terminal "B" and ground. If battery voltage is present, go to next step. If battery voltage is not present, clean and tighten connections. If battery voltage is still not present, repair or replace positive battery cable. Check system operation.

2) Perform starter ground circuit test. See STARTER GROUND CIRCUIT TEST under ON-VEHICLE TESTING. If ground is okay, replace starter motor. See STARTER MOTOR under REMOVAL & INSTALLATION. Check system operation. If ground is not okay, repair ground circuit as necessary. Check system operation.

UNUSUAL STARTER NOISE

1) Verify starter is installed properly. Check brackets for cracks. Ensure bolts are tight. Repair or replace as necessary. Check system for normal operation. If noise is still present, go to next step.

2) Remove starter motor. See STARTER MOTOR under REMOVAL & INSTALLATION. Inspect starter motor and flywheel ring gear for wear or damage. If ring gear is worn or damaged, replace ring gear and inspect starter drive gear. If drive gear is also damaged, replace starter motor. If ring gear and starter motor are okay, perform STARTER NO-LOAD TEST under ON-VEHICLE TESTING.

1999 STARTING & CHARGING SYSTEMS
Starters – F150 & F250 Light-Duty Pickups (Cont.)

BENCH TESTING

STARTER DRIVE TEST

NOTE: Make all voltmeter connections at component terminal rather than at cable or wire end.

1) Remove starter motor. See STARTER MOTOR under REMOVAL & INSTALLATION. Secure motor in vise. Using fully charged battery, connect negative battery terminal to starter motor case. Momentarily connect positive battery terminal to "S" terminal. Verify starter drive ejects. Remove positive lead from starter motor. Starter drive should return to original position. If starter drive does not eject and return to original position, install new starter motor.
2) Check starter drive. It should turn freely in one direction, and positively engage to armature when rotated in opposite direction. If starter drive does not move as specified, replace starter motor.

STARTER NO-LOAD TEST

NOTE: Make all voltmeter connections at component terminal rather than at cable or wire end.

1) Remove starter motor. See STARTER MOTOR under REMOVAL & INSTALLATION. Place starter motor securely in a vise. Connect remote starter switch between positive battery terminal and starter motor "S" terminal. Connect starter motor "B" terminal to positive battery post. Connect Alternator, Regulator, Battery and Starter Tester (ARBST), or equivalent, according to tool manufacturer's instructions.
2) Ensure starter motor is grounded. Engage remote starter switch. Starter should eject starter drive and turn smoothly and quietly. Voltmeter should indicate 11 volts or more, and ammeter should indicate 60-80 amps. If voltage is lower or current is higher than specification, or unusual noise is present, install new starter motor.

REMOVAL & INSTALLATION

STARTER MOTOR

CAUTION: When battery is disconnected, vehicle computer and memory systems may lose memory data. Driveability problems may exist until computer systems have completed a relearn cycle. See COMPUTER RELEARN PROCEDURES article in GENERAL INFORMATION before disconnecting battery.

Removal & Installation – Disconnect negative battery cable. Raise and support vehicle. Remove starter solenoid terminal cover. Disconnect starter solenoid wire connections. On 4.2L engines, remove starter motor mounting nut and ground cable. On all engines, remove starter motor mounting bolts. Remove starter motor. To install, reverse removal procedure. Ensure negative battery cable is installed in proper location. Tighten fasteners to specification. See TORQUE SPECIFICATIONS.

STARTER MOTOR SPECIFICATIONS

STARTER MOTOR SPECIFICATIONS

Application	Specification
Cranking RPM (Normal Load)	140-220
Current Draw	
Normal Load	130-220 Amps
No Load	60-80 Amps
Starter Circuit Voltage Drop	0.5 Volt

TORQUE SPECIFICATIONS

TORQUE SPECIFICATIONS

Application	Ft. Lbs. (N.m)
Starter Motor Ground Cable Nut	15-18 (20-25)
Starter Motor Mounting Bolts	16-20 (22-28)

	INCH Lbs. (N.m)
Digital Transmission Range (DTR) Bolts	71-88 (8-10)
Solenoid "B" Terminal Nut	88-1240 (10-14)
Starter Relay Bolts	61-79 (7-9)
Starter Relay Terminal Nuts	44-61 (5-7)

WIRING DIAGRAMS

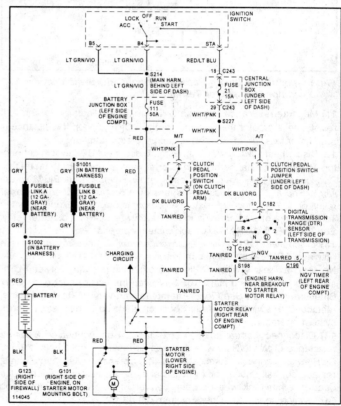
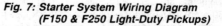

Fig. 7: Starter System Wiring Diagram (F150 & F250 Light-Duty Pickups)

Starters – F250 Super-Duty & F350 Pickups

NOTE: References to Pickup include Cab & Chassis.

DESCRIPTION

The starter motor is a permanent magnet, gear reduction, 12-volt DC motor, equipped with an integral solenoid. Starting system consists of a starter motor, solenoid, battery, ignition switch, Digital Transmission Range (DTR) sensor (A/T) or Clutch Pedal Position (CPP) switch (M/T), starter relay, and interconnecting cables and wires.

COMPONENT LOCATIONS

COMPONENT LOCATIONS

Component	Location
Power Distribution Box	Left Side Of Engine Compartment
Junction Box Fuse/Relay Panel	Under Left Side Of I/P
Digital Transmission Range Sensor	Left Side Of Transmission
Inertia Fuel Shutoff Switch (Gasoline)	Behind Right Side Of I/P
Starter Relay	Right Rear Of Engine Compartment

ADJUSTMENTS

DIGITAL TRANSMISSION RANGE (DTR) SENSOR

1) Raise and support vehicle. Disconnect manual shift control cable from DTR sensor. Disconnect DTR sensor electrical connector. Place DTR sensor control lever in neutral position. Remove nut retaining manual control lever to DTR sensor and remove manual control lever. Loosen DTR sensor bolts.

2) Using DTR Sensor Alignment Tool (T97L-70010-A), align DTR sensor slots. Tighten DTR sensor bolts. Install manual control lever. Install NEW nut. Tighten fasteners to specification. See TORQUE SPECIFICATIONS. Place DTR sensor control lever in overdrive position and connect shift lever control cable. Connect DTR electrical connector.

TROUBLE SHOOTING

Check the following items before proceeding with testing:
- Check battery for state of charge.
- Check cable connections at batteries and starter motor.
- Ensure transmission is fully engaged in Park or Neutral position (A/T) or clutch pedal is fully depressed (M/T).
- Check fuse No. 20 (50-amp) in power distribution box.
- Check fuse No. 20 (15-amp) in junction box fuse/relay panel.

ON-VEHICLE TESTING

CAUTION: When battery is disconnected, vehicle computer and memory systems may lose memory data. Driveability problems may exist until computer systems have completed a relearn cycle. See COMPUTER RELEARN PROCEDURES article in GENERAL INFORMATION before disconnecting battery. Before testing starter, ensure transmission is in Park or Neutral.

ENGINE DOES NOT CRANK & RELAY CLICKS

1) Verify battery condition. If battery is okay, measure voltage between Red wire at starter relay and ground. If battery voltage is present, go to next step. If battery voltage is not present, repair or replace Red wire between battery and starter relay cable. Check system operation.

2) Measure voltage between starter motor solenoid "B" terminal and ground. *See Fig. 1.* If battery voltage is present, go to next step. If battery voltage is not present, clean and tighten battery and solenoid terminal connections. If battery voltage is still not present, replace positive battery cable. Check system operation.

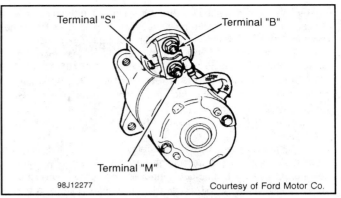

Fig. 1: Identifying Starter Solenoid Terminals (Typical)

3) Using jumper wire, connect one end to positive battery terminal and with other end, momentarily touch starter solenoid "S" terminal. *See Fig. 1.* If solenoid engages, go to next step. If solenoid does not engage, replace starter motor. See STARTER MOTOR under REMOVAL & INSTALLATION. Check system operation.

4) Using jumper wire, connect one end to positive battery terminal and with other end, momentarily touch starter solenoid "M" terminal. *See Fig. 1.* If starter spins, go to next step. If starter does not spin, replace starter motor. See STARTER MOTOR under REMOVAL & INSTALLATION. Check system operation.

5) Disconnect starter relay connectors. Disconnect starter motor solenoid connectors. Measure resistance of Yellow/Light Blue wire between starter relay and starter solenoid. If resistance is less than 5 ohms, replace starter relay. If resistance is greater than 5 ohms, repair or replace Yellow/Light Blue wire between starter relay and starter solenoid. Check system operation.

ENGINE DOES NOT CRANK & RELAY DOES NOT CLICK

1) Remove fuse No. 20 (50-amp), located in power distribution box. Check continuity of fuse No. 20 (50-amp). If fuse is okay, reinstall fuse and go to next step. If fuse is open, install new fuse and go to step **15)**.

2) Remove fuse No. 20 (15-amp), located in junction box fuse/relay panel. Check for continuity of fuse No. 20 (15-amp). If fuse No. 20 is okay, reinstall fuse and go to next step. If fuse No. 20 is open, install new fuse, and go to step **18)**.

3) Measure voltage between junction box fuse/relay panel fuse No. 20 and ground while holding ignition key in START position. If battery voltage is present, go to step **6)**. If battery voltage is not present, go to next step.

4) Disconnect ignition switch 15-pin connector. Measure resistance between junction box fuse/relay panel fuse No. 20 (15-amp) and ignition switch connector terminal STA (Red/Light Blue wire). *See Fig. 2.* If resistance is less than 5 ohms, go to next step. If resistance is greater than 5 ohms, repair poor connection or open in Red/Light Blue wire between ignition switch connector and junction box fuse/relay panel. See WIRING DIAGRAMS. Check system operation. Check system operation.

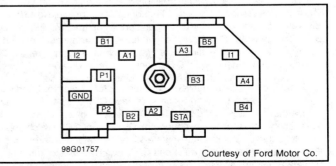

Fig. 2: Identifying Ignition Switch Connector Terminals

FORD
2-38

1999 STARTING & CHARGING SYSTEMS
Starters – F250 Super-Duty & F350 Pickups (Cont.)

5) Remove power distribution box fuse No. 20 (50-amp). Measure resistance of Light Green/Purple wire between ignition switch harness connector terminal No. B4 and power distribution box fuse No. 20 (50-amp) output cavity. See Fig. 2. If resistance is less than 5 ohms, replace ignition switch. See appropriate STEERING COLUMN SWITCHES article in ACCESSORIES & EQUIPMENT. If resistance is greater than 5 ohms, repair poor connection or open in Light Green/Purple wire between ignition switch harness connector and output cavity of fuse No. 20 (50-amp). See WIRING DIAGRAMS. Check system operation.

6) Turn ignition off. Disconnect starter relay connector (Tan/Red or Dark Blue/Orange wire). Measure voltage between starter relay connector terminal (Tan/Red or Dark Blue/Orange wire) and ground while momentarily turning ignition to START position. If battery voltage is present, replace starter relay. Check system operation. If battery voltage is not present, and vehicle is equipped with automatic transmission, go to next step. If battery voltage is not present, and vehicle is equipped with manual transmission go to step **12)**.

7) Disconnect Digital Transmission Range (DTR) sensor 12-pin connector. Measure resistance between DTR sensor connector terminal No. 12 (Tan/Red wire) and starter relay connector terminal (Tan/Red wire). See Fig. 3. If resistance is less than 5 ohms, go to next step. If resistance is greater than 5 ohms, repair Tan/Red wire between DTR sensor connector and starter relay connector. See WIRING DIAGRAMS. Check system operation.

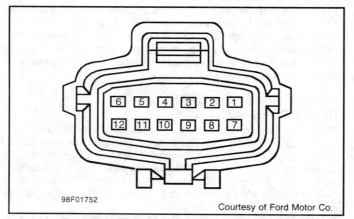

Fig. 3: Identifying Digital Transmission Range Sensor Connector Terminals

8) Perform DTR sensor adjustment. See DIGITAL TRANSMISSION RANGE (DTR) SENSOR under ADJUSTMENTS. Adjust as necessary. Check system operation. If DTR sensor is adjusted properly, go to next step.

9) Restore all connections except DTR sensor. Connect a jumper wire between DTR sensor connector terminals No. 12 (Tan/Red wire) and No. 10 (Dark Blue/Orange wire). See Fig. 3. Attempt to start vehicle. If vehicle starts, replace DTR sensor. Check system operation. If vehicle does not start, go to next step.

10) Disconnect Clutch Pedal Position (CPP) jumper 6-pin connector. Measure resistance between DTR connector terminal No. 10 (Dark Blue/Orange wire) and CPP jumper connector terminal No. 2 (Dark Blue/Orange wire). See Figs. 3 and 4. If resistance is less than 5 ohms, go to next step. If resistance is greater than 5 ohms, repair Dark Blue/Orange wire between DTR sensor connector and CPP switch jumper. See WIRING DIAGRAMS. Check system operation.

11) Measure resistance between CPP jumper terminals No. 1 and No. 2. If resistance is greater than 5 ohms, replace CPP jumper. If resistance is less than 5 ohms, go to step **14)**. Check system operation.

12) Disconnect starter relay connector. Disconnect CPP switch connector. Measure resistance between starter relay connector terminal (Tan/Red or Dark Blue/Orange wire) and CPP switch connector terminal No. 2 (Dark Blue/Orange wire). See Fig. 4. If resistance is less than 5 ohms, reconnect starter relay, go to next step. If resistance is greater than 5

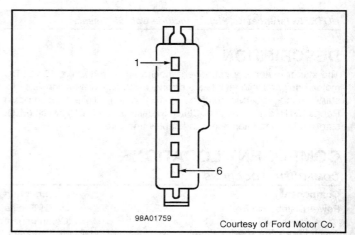

98A01759

Courtesy of Ford Motor Co.

Fig. 4: Identifying Clutch Pedal Position (CPP) Switch Or Jumper Connector Terminals

ohms, repair open in Tan/Red wire or Dark Blue/Orange wire between CPP and starter relay. See WIRING DIAGRAMS. Check system operation.

13) Disconnect CPP switch 6-pin connector. Connect jumper wire between CPP switch connector terminals No. 1 and 2. On models with manual transmission and gasoline engine, connect an additional jumper wire between CPP switch connector terminals No. 5 and 6. See Fig. 4. Attempt to start vehicle. If vehicle starts, replace CPP switch. If vehicle does not start, go to next step. Check system operation.

14) Disconnect junction box fuse/relay panel Black 34-pin connector. Measure resistance between connector terminal (White/Pink wire) and CCP switch connector, terminal No. 1 (White/Pink wire). If resistance is less than 5 ohms, replace junction box fuse/relay panel. If resistance is greater than 5 ohms, repair open in White/Pink wire between junction box fuse/relay panel connector and CPP switch connector. Check system operation.

15) Momentarily turn ignition switch to START position. Turn ignition off. Remove fuse No. 20 (50-amp) from power distribution box. Check fuse for open. If fuse is okay, system is okay at this time. If fuse is open, go to next step.

16) Disconnect ignition switch connector. Measure resistance between ignition switch connector terminal B4 (Light Green/Purple wire) and ground. See Fig. 2. If resistance is greater than 10 k/ohms, go to next step. If resistance is less than 10 k/ohms, repair short to ground in Light Green/Purple wire between ignition switch connector and power distribution box. See WIRING DIAGRAMS.

17) Remove fuse No. 20 (15-amp) from junction box fuse/relay panel. Measure resistance between ignition switch connector terminal STA and ground. See Fig. 2. If resistance is greater than 10 k/ohms, replace ignition switch. Check system operation. If resistance is less than 10 k/ohms, repair short to ground in Red/Light Blue wire between ignition switch and junction box fuse/relay panel. See WIRING DIAGRAMS.

18) Turn ignition switch to START position momentarily. Turn ignition off. Remove and recheck fuse No. 20 (15-amp). If fuse is okay, system is okay at this time. If fuse is open, install new fuse and go to next step.

19) Disconnect starter relay connectors. Momentarily turn ignition switch to START position. Turn ignition switch off. Recheck fuse No. 20 (15-amp). If fuse is okay, replace starter relay. Check system operation. If fuse is open, install new fuse and go to next step.

20) Disconnect CPP switch or CPP jumper connector. Measure resistance between CPP switch or CPP jumper connector terminal No. 1 (White/Pink wire) and ground. See Fig. 4. If resistance is greater than 10 k/ohms and vehicle is equipped with automatic transmission, go to next step. If resistance is greater than 10 k/ohms and vehicle is equipped with manual transmission, go to step **23)**. If resistance is less than 10 k/ohms, repair short to ground in White/Pink wire between CPP switch or CPP jumper and junction box fuse/relay panel. See WIRING DIAGRAMS. Check system operation.

1999 STARTING & CHARGING SYSTEMS
Starters – F250 Super-Duty & F350 Pickups (Cont.)

FORD
2-39

21) Disconnect DTR sensor connector. Measure resistance between DTR sensor connector terminal No. 10 (Dark Blue/Orange wire) and ground. *See Fig. 3.* If resistance is greater than 10 k/ohms, go to next step. If resistance is less than 10 k/ohms, repair short to ground in Dark Blue/Orange wire between DTR sensor and CPP jumper. See WIRING DIAGRAMS. Check system operation.

22) Measure resistance between DTR sensor connector terminal No. 12 (Tan/Red wire) and ground. If resistance is greater than 10 k/ohms, replace DTR sensor. Check system operation. If resistance is less than 10 k/ohms, repair short to ground in Tan/Red wire between DTR sensor and starter relay. See WIRING DIAGRAMS. Check system operation.

23) Disconnect starter relay connectors. Measure resistance between CPP switch connector terminal No. 2 (Dark Blue/Orange wire) and ground. If resistance is greater than 10 k/ohms, replace CPP switch. Check system operation. If resistance is less than 10 k/ohms, repair short to ground in Tan/Red or Dark Blue/Orange wire between CPP switch and starter relay. See WIRING DIAGRAMS. Check system operation.

ENGINE CRANKS SLOWLY

1) Turn ignition off. Check voltage between starter motor solenoid positive terminal "B" and ground. *See Fig. 1.* If battery voltage is present, go to next step. If battery voltage is not present, clean and tighten connections. If battery voltage is still not present, repair or replace positive battery cable. Check system operation.

2) Perform starter ground circuit test. See STARTER GROUND CIRCUIT TEST. If ground is okay, replace starter motor. See STARTER MOTOR under REMOVAL & INSTALLATION. Check system operation. If ground is not okay, repair ground circuit as necessary. Check system operation.

UNUSUAL STARTER NOISE

1) Verify starter is installed properly. Check starter mounting brackets for cracks. Ensure starter bolts are tight. Repair or replace as necessary. Check system for normal operation. If noise is still present, go to next step.

2) Remove starter motor. See STARTER MOTOR under REMOVAL & INSTALLATION. Inspect starter motor and flywheel ring gear for wear or damage. If ring gear is worn or damaged, replace ring gear and inspect starter drive gear. If drive gear is also damaged, replace starter motor. If ring gear and starter motor are okay, perform STARTER NO-LOAD TEST.

VOLTAGE DROP TEST

NOTE: Make all voltmeter connections at component terminal rather than at cable or wire end.

1) Ensure battery is fully charged. To prevent vehicle from starting, on gasoline engines disconnect ignition coil connector from ignition coil. On diesel engines, remove power distribution box fuse No. 17. On all models, connect remote starter switch between starter solenoid terminal "S" and positive battery post. Connect positive voltmeter lead to positive battery post, and negative lead to solenoid terminal "M". *See Fig. 5.*

2) Engage remote starter switch. Voltmeter should indicate .5 volt or less. If voltmeter indicates .5 volt or less, go to STARTER GROUND CIRCUIT TEST. If voltmeter indicates more than .5 volt, go to next step.

3) Move negative voltmeter lead to solenoid terminal "B". Engage remote starter switch. If voltmeter indicates less than .5 volt, solenoid connections or contacts are bad. Clean solenoid terminals "B", "S" and "M". Repeat steps **1)** through **3)** then go to next step.

4) If voltmeter still indicates more than .5 volt at terminal "M" and less than .5 volt at terminal "B", solenoid contacts are bad. Replace starter motor. See STARTER MOTOR under REMOVAL & INSTALLATION. If voltmeter indicates more than .5 volt at terminal "B", clean cables and connections at solenoid. Go to next step.

5) If voltmeter still indicates more than .5 volt at terminal "B", check for poor positive battery cable connection or bad cable. Repair as necessary.

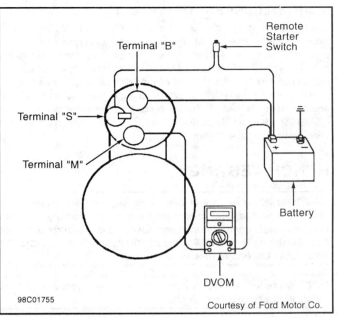

98C01755   Courtesy of Ford Motor Co.

Fig. 5: Testing Voltage Drop

STARTER GROUND CIRCUIT TEST

NOTE: Make all voltmeter connections at component terminal rather than at cable or wire end.

1) To prevent vehicle from starting, on gasoline engines disconnect ignition coil connector from ignition coil. On diesel engines, remove power distribution box fuse No. 17. On all models, connect remote starter switch between starter solenoid terminal "S" and positive battery post. Connect positive voltmeter lead to starter housing, and negative lead to negative battery post. *See Fig. 6.*

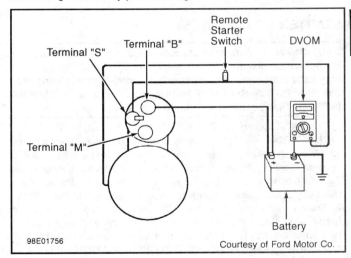

98E01756   Courtesy of Ford Motor Co.

Fig. 6: Testing Starter Ground Circuit

2) Engage remote starter switch while observing voltmeter. Voltmeter should indicate .2 volt or less. If voltmeter indicates more than .2 volt, clean negative cable connections at battery and chassis. Also clean engine ground cable connections at front cover and engine mount bracket.

3) If voltage drop is still excessive, repair or replace negative battery cable and/or engine ground cable as necessary. Repeat starter circuit test after repair to ensure problem has been corrected.

4) If battery and cables test okay and starter motor still cranks slowly or not at all, replace starter motor. See STARTER MOTOR under REMOVAL & INSTALLATION.

FORD
2-40

1999 STARTING & CHARGING SYSTEMS
Starters – F250 Super-Duty & F350 Pickups (Cont.)

STARTER CURRENT DRAW TEST

Ensure battery is fully charged. Set parking brake and place transmission in neutral. Ensure battery connections are clean and tight. To prevent vehicle from starting, on gasoline engines disconnect ignition coil connector from ignition coil. On diesel engines, remove power distribution box fuse No. 17. On all models, clamp inductive ammeter lead around all positive battery cable leading to starter. Crank engine for about 5 seconds and check amperage reading while cranking. See STARTER MOTOR SPECIFICATIONS. If amperage draw exceeds specification, replace starter.

BENCH TESTING

CAUTION: When battery is disconnected, vehicle computer and memory systems may lose memory data. Driveability problems may exist until computer systems have completed a relearn cycle. See COMPUTER RELEARN PROCEDURES article in GENERAL INFORMATION before disconnecting battery.

NOTE: Make all voltmeter connections at component terminal rather than at cable or wire end.

STARTER DRIVE TEST

1) Remove starter motor. See STARTER MOTOR under REMOVAL & INSTALLATION. Secure motor in vise. Using fully charged battery, connect negative battery terminal to starter motor case. Momentarily connect positive battery terminal to "S" terminal. See Fig. 1. Verify starter drive ejects. Remove positive lead from starter motor. Starter drive should return to original position. If starter drive does not eject and return to original position, install new starter motor.
2) Check starter drive. It should turn freely in one direction, and positively engage to armature when rotated in opposite direction. If starter drive does not move as specified, replace starter motor.

STARTER NO-LOAD TEST

CAUTION: When battery is disconnected, vehicle computer and memory systems may lose memory data. Driveability problems may exist until computer systems have completed a relearn cycle. See COMPUTER RELEARN PROCEDURES article in GENERAL INFORMATION before disconnecting battery.

1) Remove starter motor. See STARTER MOTOR under REMOVAL & INSTALLATION. Place starter motor securely in a vise. Connect remote starter switch between positive battery terminal and starter motor "S" terminal. Connect starter motor "B" terminal to positive battery post. See Fig. 1. Connect Alternator, Regulator, Battery and Starter Tester (ARBST), or equivalent, according to tool manufacturers instructions.
2) Ensure starter motor is grounded. Engage remote starter switch. Starter should eject starter drive and turn smoothly and quietly. Voltmeter should indicate 11 volts or more. Amperage draw should be within specification. See STARTER MOTOR SPECIFICATIONS. If voltage is lower or current is higher than specification, or unusual noise is present, install new starter motor.

REMOVAL & INSTALLATION
STARTER MOTOR

Removal & Installation – Disconnect negative battery cable. Raise and support vehicle. Remove starter solenoid terminal cover. Disconnect starter solenoid wire connections. On diesel engines, remove nut and starter ground cable from starter mounting bolt. Remove starter motor mounting bolts. Remove starter motor. To install, reverse removal procedure. Tighten bolts to specification. See TORQUE SPECIFICATIONS.

OVERHAUL

Use illustration for exploded view of starter motor assembly. See Fig. 7.

STARTER MOTOR SPECIFICATIONS

STARTER MOTOR SPECIFICATIONS

Application	Specification
Current Draw	
Gasoline	
Normal Load	130-190 Amps
No Load	60-80 Amps
Diesel	
Normal Load	230-630 Amps
No Load	170 Amps
Starter Circuit Voltage Drop	0.5 Volt

TORQUE SPECIFICATIONS

TORQUE SPECIFICATIONS

Application	Ft. Lbs. (N.m)
Solenoid "B" Terminal Nut	7-10 (10-14)
Starter Ground Cable Nut (Diesel)	13-17 (17-23)
Starter Motor Mounting Bolts	17-20 (22-28)

	INCH Lbs. (N.m)
Digital Transmission Range (DTR) Sensor	71-88 (8-10)
Solenoid "B" Terminal Nut	84-120 (10-14)
Solenoid "S" Terminal Nut	36-53 (4-6)
Starter Relay Bolts	62-79 (7-9)

1999 STARTING & CHARGING SYSTEMS
Starters – F250 Super-Duty & F350 Pickups (Cont.)

FORD
2-41

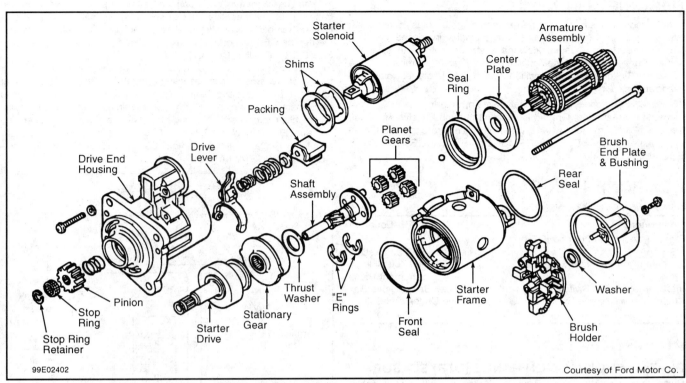

Fig. 7: Exploded View Of Starter Motor Assembly (Diesel Shown)

WIRING DIAGRAMS

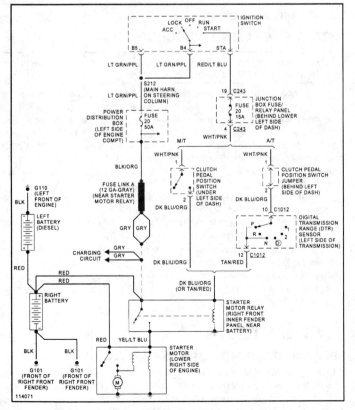

**Fig. 8: Starter System Wiring Diagram
(F250 Super-Duty & F350 Pickups)**

1999 STARTING & CHARGING SYSTEMS
Starters – Ranger

DESCRIPTION

A gear reduction starter with permanent magnet fields is used. An internal planetary gear reduction unit provides increased cranking torque. The starting system includes a starter motor with solenoid-actuated drive, battery, starter/ignition switch, digital transmission range sensor (A/T), clutch pedal position switch (M/T), starter relay and associated circuitry.

If vehicle is equipped with anti-theft system, starter relay coil is not permanently grounded. Ground is supplied through Passive Anti-Theft System (PATS) module when system conditions are satisfied. See appropriate ANTI-THEFT SYSTEMS article in ACCESSORIES & EQUIPMENT for additional information.

COMPONENT LOCATIONS

COMPONENT LOCATIONS

Component	Location
Digital Transmission Range (DTR)	
Sensor	Left Side Of Transmission
Fuse Junction Panel	Behind Left Side Of Instrument Panel
Inertia Fuel Shutoff Switch	Below Glove Box
Starter Motor Relay	In Underhood Battery Junction Box

ADJUSTMENTS

DIGITAL TRANSMISSION RANGE (DTR) SENSOR

Raise and support vehicle. Disconnect manual shift control cable. Disconnect DTR electrical connector. Loosen DTR sensor bolts. Manual shift lever must be in neutral position. Using DTR Sensor Alignment Tool (T97L-70010-A), align DTR sensor slots. Tighten DTR sensor bolts to specification. See TORQUE SPECIFICATIONS table. Reconnect shift lever control cable. Connect DTR electrical connector.

TROUBLE SHOOTING

NOTE: See TROUBLE SHOOTING article in GENERAL INFORMATION.

Check the following items before proceeding with testing:
- Check battery for state of charge.
- Check starter mounting nuts/bolts.
- Check cable connections at battery and starter motor.
- Ensure transmission is fully engaged in Park or Neutral position.
- Check megafuse (175-amp) near battery junction box.
- Check fuse No. 5 (50-amp) in battery junction box.
- Check fuse No. 24 (7.5-amp) in instrument fuse junction panel.
- On models equipped anti-theft system, ensure anti-theft system is operating properly. See appropriate ANTI-THEFT SYSTEMS article in ACCESSORIES & EQUIPMENT for additional information.

ON-VEHICLE TESTING

CAUTION: When battery is disconnected, vehicle computer and memory systems may lose memory data. Driveability problems may exist until computer systems have completed a relearn cycle. See COMPUTER RELEARN PROCEDURES article in GENERAL INFORMATION before disconnecting battery.

VOLTAGE DROP TEST

NOTE: Make all voltmeter connections at component terminal rather than at cable or wire end. Clean all connections at starter and battery before beginning this test.

1) Disconnect inertia fuel shutoff switch connector located below glow box. Connect remote starter switch between starter solenoid terminal "S" and positive battery post. Connect voltmeter positive lead to positive battery post and negative lead to solenoid terminal "M". See Fig. 1. Engage remote starter switch while observing voltmeter. If voltage is greater than .5 volt, go to next step. If voltage is .5 volt or less, perform STARTER GROUND CIRCUIT TEST.

2) Move negative voltmeter lead to solenoid terminal "B". Engage remote starter switch while observing voltmeter. If voltage is greater than .5 volt, replace positive battery cable. If voltage is .5 volt or less, disconnect and clean 'S", "B" and "M" terminals. Reconnect terminals and recheck voltage drop. If voltage is still greater than .5 volt at terminal "M" and .5 volt or less at terminal "B", problem is in starter motor contacts. Replace starter motor. See STARTER MOTOR under REMOVAL & INSTALLATION.

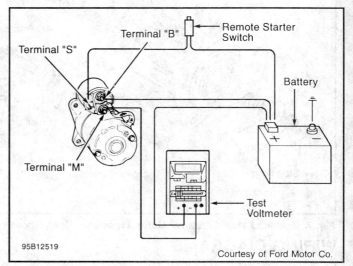

95B12519   Courtesy of Ford Motor Co.

Fig. 1: Testing Voltage Drop

STARTER GROUND CIRCUIT TEST

NOTE: Make all voltmeter connections at component terminal rather than at cable or wire end.

1) Disconnect inertia fuel shutoff switch connector located below glove box. Connect remote starter switch between starter solenoid terminals "S" and battery positive terminal. See Fig. 2. Using a voltmeter, connect positive voltmeter lead to starter housing, and negative lead to negative battery post. Engage remote starter switch while observing voltmeter. If voltage is greater than .2 volt, leave test equipment attached and go to next step. If voltage is .2 volt or less exists, starter ground circuit is okay at this time.

2) Clean negative cable connections at battery and engine. Engage remote starter switch while observing voltmeter. If voltage is greater than .2 volt, leave test equipment attached and go to next step. If voltage is .2 volt or less, starter ground circuit is okay at this time.

3) Connect voltmeter between negative battery post and engine ground where negative battery cable connects. Engage remote starter switch while observing voltmeter. If voltage is greater than .2 volt, replace negative battery cable. If voltage is .2 volt or less, repair or replace starter as necessary.

SYSTEM TESTS

ENGINE DOES NOT CRANK

1) Verify battery condition. Battery voltage should be 12 volts or more. Load test battery at approximately one-half cold cranking amperage rating. See load tester manufacturer's instructions. If battery voltage is less than 12 volts or loaded battery voltage is less than 9.6 volts, service battery or charging system as necessary.

2) Measure voltage between positive battery post and engine block where negative battery cable is connected (on 4.0L negative battery cable grounds to starter mounting stud). If battery voltage exists, go to

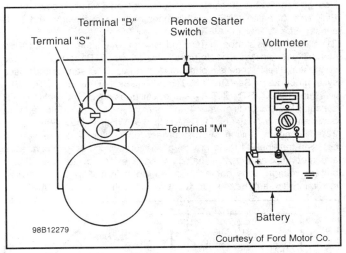

Fig. 2: Testing Ground Circuit

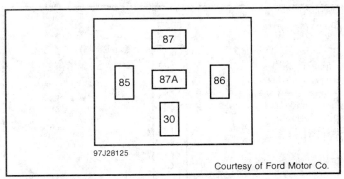

Fig. 4: Identifying Starter Relay Socket Terminals

next step. If battery voltage does not exist, clean and tighten ground cable connections and recheck. If battery voltage still does not exist, replace negative battery cable.

3) Measure voltage between positive battery post and starter motor case. If battery voltage exists, go to next step. If battery voltage does not exist, clean starter motor mounting flange and ensure starter motor is properly installed.

4) Turn ignition switch to LOCK position. Measure voltage at between starter motor solenoid terminal "B" and ground. *See Fig. 3*. If battery voltage exists, go to next step. If battery voltage does not exist, clean and tighten positive cable connections and recheck. If battery voltage still does not exist, replace positive battery cable.

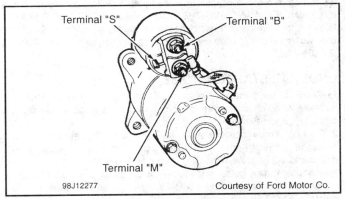

Fig. 3: Identifying Starter Solenoid Terminals

5) Connect remote starter switch between starter motor solenoid terminals "B" and "S". Engage remote starter switch. If starter engages and engine cranks, go to next step. If starter motor does not engage, repair or replace starter motor as necessary. See STARTER MOTOR under REMOVAL & INSTALLATION. If starter motor engages but engine does not crank, check for engine mechanical failure (hydrolock, seized, transmission locked up, etc.). If mechanical failure does not exist, repair replace starter motor as necessary.

6) Disconnect Yellow/Light Blue wire from terminal "S" at starter solenoid. *See Fig. 3*. Measure voltage at Yellow/Light Blue wire with ignition switch in START position. If battery voltage does not exist, go to next step. If battery voltage exists, repair poor connection at terminal "S" at starter solenoid and check system operation.

7) Turn ignition off. Remove starter relay from battery junction box. Measure voltage at terminal No. 86 (Tan/Red wire) at starter relay socket with ignition switch in START position. *See Fig. 4*. If battery voltage exists, go to next step. If battery voltage does not exist, go to step **12**).

8) Turn ignition off. Measure voltage between starter relay socket terminal No. 30 (Yellow wire) and ground. If battery voltage exists, go to next step. If battery voltage does not exist, check fuse No. 5 for open. If fuse is okay, repair open in Yellow wire or battery junction box between starter relay and fuse No. 5. See WIRING DIAGRAMS.

9) Measure resistance between ground and starter relay socket terminal No. 85 (Black wire). If resistance is 5 ohms or less, go to next step. If resistance is greater than 5 ohms, and vehicle is not equipped with anti-theft system, repair open in Black wire between battery junction box and ground. If resistance is greater than 5 ohms, and vehicle is equipped with anti-theft system, check resistance of Dark Blue/Orange wire (or Pink/Orange wire) between battery junction box and PATS module. If resistance is greater than 5 ohms, repair open in Dark Blue/Orange wire (or Pink/Orange wire). See WIRING DIAGRAMS. If resistance is less than 5 ohms, check anti-theft system operation. See appropriate ANTI-THEFT SYSTEMS article in ACCESSORIES & EQUIPMENT.

10) Ensure Yellow/Light Blue wire is disconnected from terminal "S" at starter. Measure resistance between ground and starter relay socket terminal No. 87 (Yellow/Light Blue wire). If resistance is greater than 10,000 ohms, go to next step. If resistance is 10,000 ohms or less, repair short to ground in Yellow/Light Blue wire between battery junction box and starter. See WIRING DIAGRAMS.

11) Measure resistance in Yellow/Light Blue wire between starter motor solenoid terminal "S" connector and starter relay socket terminal No. 87. If resistance is greater than 5 ohms, repair open in Yellow/Light Blue wire between battery junction box and starter. See WIRING DIAGRAMS. If resistance is 5 ohms or less, replace starter relay and check system operation.

NOTE: On vehicles equipped with automatic transmission, Clutch Pedal Position (CPP) switch is substituted with a CPP jumper.

12) Disconnect Clutch Pedal Position (CPP) switch (M/T) or CPP jumper (A/T) harness connector. Both components are located on clutch pedal bracket. Ensure anti-theft system is disabled (if equipped). Measure voltage at terminal No. 6 (White/Pink wire) at CPP switch/jumper harness connector C206 with ignition switch in START position. *See Fig. 5*. If battery voltage does not exist, go to next step. If battery voltage exists, go to step **19**).

13) Turn ignition off. Remove and inspect fuse No. 24 (7.5-amp) in fuse junction panel. If fuse is okay, go to next step. If fuse is blown, go to step **15**).

14) Measure voltage at input side of fuse No. 24 with ignition switch in START position. If battery voltage does not exist, go to step **22**). If battery voltage exists, repair open in White/Pink wire between fuse junction panel and CPP switch/jumper harness connector. See WIRING DIAGRAMS.

15) Measure resistance between ground and terminal No. 6 (White/Pink wire) at CPP switch/jumper harness connector. If resistance is greater than 10,000 ohms, go to next step. If resistance is 10,000 ohms or less, repair short to ground in White/Pink wire between fuse junction panel and CPP switch/jumper harness connector. See WIRING DIAGRAMS.

16) Remove starter relay from battery junction box in engine compartment. Measure resistance between ground and terminal No. 5 (Pink

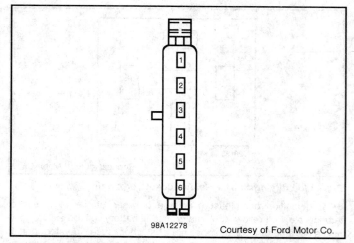

Fig. 5: Identifying Clutch Pedal Position (CPP) Switch/Jumper Harness Connector

wire) at CPP switch/jumper harness connector. If resistance is greater than 10,000 ohms, replace fuse No. 24 and check system operation. If resistance is 10,000 ohms or less, go to next step (A/T models) or repair short to ground in Pink and/or Tan/Red wires between starter relay and CPP switch/jumper harness connector (M/T models). See WIRING DIAGRAMS.

17) Disconnect Digital Transmission Range (DTR) sensor harness connector. Measure resistance between ground and terminal No. 5 (Pink wire) at CPP sensor/jumper harness connector. If resistance is greater than 10,000 ohms, go to next step. If resistance is 10,000 ohms or less, repair short to ground in Pink wire between DTR sensor and CPP switch/jumper harness connector. See WIRING DIAGRAMS.

18) Measure resistance between ground and terminal No. 10 (Tan/Red wire) at DTR sensor harness connector. See Fig. 6. If resistance is greater than 10,000 ohms, adjust DTR sensor and check system operation. See DIGITAL TRANSMISSION RANGE (DTR) SENSOR under ADJUSTMENTS. If starter still does not crank, replace DTR sensor. If resistance is 10,000 ohms or less, repair short to ground in Tan/Red wire between DTR sensor and starter relay. See WIRING DIAGRAMS.

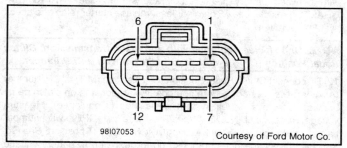

Fig. 6: Identifying Transmission Range Sensor Harness Connector Terminals

19) Remove starter relay from battery junction box in engine compartment. Measure resistance between terminal No. 5 (Pink wire) at CPP switch/jumper harness connector and terminal No. 86 (Tan/Red wire) at starter relay socket. See Figs. 4 and 5. If resistance is 5 ohms or less, replace CPP switch/jumper switch or jumper. If resistance is greater than 5 ohms, go to next step (A/T models) or repair open in Pink and/or Tan/Red wire between CPP switch/jumper harness connector and starter relay (M/T models). See WIRING DIAGRAMS.

20) Disconnect Digital Transmission Range (DTR) sensor harness connector. Measure resistance in Pink wire between terminal No. 5 at CPP switch/jumper harness connector and terminal No. 12 at DTR sensor harness connector. See Figs. 5 and 6. If resistance is 5 ohms or

less, go to next step. If resistance is greater than 5 ohms, repair open in Pink wire between CPP switch/jumper harness connector and DTR sensor. See WIRING DIAGRAMS.

21) Measure resistance in Tan/Red wire between terminal No. 86 at starter relay socket and terminal No. 10 at DTR sensor harness connector. If resistance is 5 ohms or less, adjust DTR sensor and check system operation. See DIGITAL TRANSMISSION RANGE (DTR) SENSOR under ADJUSTMENTS. If starter still does not crank, replace DTR sensor. If resistance is greater than 5 ohms, repair open in Tan/Red wire between starter relay and DTR sensor. See WIRING DIAGRAMS.

22) Disconnect ignition switch harness connector. Measure voltage between terminal B4 (Yellow wire) at ignition switch harness connector and ground. See Fig. 7. If battery voltage exists, go to next step. If battery voltage does not exist, repair open in Yellow wire between ignition switch and battery junction box. See WIRING DIAGRAMS.

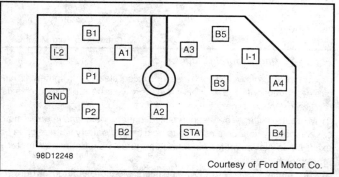

Fig. 7: Identifying Ignition Switch Harness Connector Terminals

23) Remove fuse No. 24 (7.5-amp) from fuse junction panel. Measure resistance in Red/Light Blue wire between output side of fuse No. 24 and terminal STA at ignition switch harness connector. See Fig. 7. If resistance is 5 ohms or less, replace ignition switch. See appropriate STEERING COLUMN SWITCHES article in ACCESSORIES & EQUIPMENT. If resistance is greater than 5 ohms, repair open in Red/Light Blue wire between ignition switch and fuse junction panel. See WIRING DIAGRAMS.

UNUSUAL STARTER NOISE

1) Verify starter is installed properly. Ensure bolts are tight. Repair as necessary and check system for normal operation. If starter is mounted properly, go to next step.

2) Connect remote starter switch between positive battery terminal and starter motor relay terminal "S" (Red/Light Blue wire). Engage starter motor and verify noise is coming from starter motor. If noise is coming from starter motor, go to next step. If noise is not coming from starter motor, diagnose engine mechanical concern. See appropriate engine article in ENGINES article.

3) Remove starter motor. See STARTER MOTOR under REMOVAL & INSTALLATION. Inspect flywheel ring gear for wear or damage. If ring gear is okay, replace starter motor. If ring gear is worn or damaged, replace ring gear and inspect starter drive gear. If drive gear is also damaged, replace starter motor.

REMOVAL & INSTALLATION
STARTER MOTOR

CAUTION: When battery is disconnected, vehicle computer and memory systems may lose memory data. Driveability problems may exist until computer systems have completed a relearn cycle. See COMPUTER RELEARN PROCEDURES article in GENERAL INFORMATION before disconnecting battery. Before testing starter, ensure transmission is in Park or Neutral.

Removal & Installation – Disconnect battery ground cable. On 4.0L engines, remove battery negative cable from starter mounting bolt. On all engines, remove starter mounting nuts or bolts and lower starter.

Remove starter motor solenoid terminal cap. Disconnect wiring and remove starter from vehicle. To install, reverse removal procedure. Tighten fasteners to specification. See TORQUE SPECIFICATIONS.

STARTER SPECIFICATIONS

STARTER MOTOR SPECIFICATIONS

Application	Specification
Cranking RPM (Normal Load)	140-220
Current Draw (No Load)	60-80 Amps
Starter Circuit Voltage Drop	0.5 Volt

TORQUE SPECIFICATIONS

TORQUE SPECIFICATIONS

Application	Ft. Lbs. (N.m)
Starter-To-Engine Nuts/Bolts	17-20 (22-27)
Starter Motor Ground Cable Nut (4.0L)	15-18 (20-25)

	INCH Lbs. (N.m)
Solenoid Terminal "B" Nut	98-115 (11-13)
Solenoid Terminal "S" Nut	45-53 (5-6)

WIRING DIAGRAMS

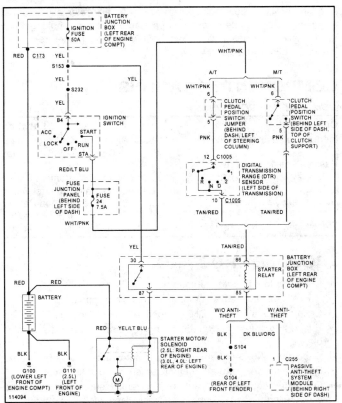

Fig. 8: Starter System Wiring Diagram (Ranger)

1999 STARTING & CHARGING SYSTEMS
Starters – Sable & Taurus

DESCRIPTION

The starter is a gear-reduction motor with an externally-mounted solenoid. Starting system consists of a starter motor, solenoid, battery, ignition switch, Transmission Range (TR) sensor, starter relay and interconnecting cables and wires.

COMPONENT LOCATIONS

COMPONENT LOCATIONS

Component	Location
Inertia Fuel Shutoff Switch	Right Rear Of Cargo Area, Behind Right Wheelwell
Passive Anti-Theft System (PATS) Module	In Center of Instrument Panel, Behind Integrated Control Panel
Starter Relay	In Underhood Battery Junction Box
Transmission Range Sensor	Top Of Transmission

TROUBLE SHOOTING

- Check battery for state of charge.
- Check cable connections at battery and starter motor.
- Ensure transmission is fully engaged in Park or Neutral.
- Ensure Mega-fuse (175-amp) in engine compartment fuse panel is okay.
- Check fuse No. 3 (40-amp) in engine compartment fuse/relay box.
- Check fuse No. 7 (10-amp) in instrument panel fuse panel.
- On models equipped with anti-theft system, ensure anti-theft system is operating properly (horn honks, lights flash, etc.) See appropriate ANTI-THEFT SYSTEMS article in ACCESSORIES & EQUIPMENT for additional information.

ON-VEHICLE TESTING

CAUTION: Before testing starter, ensure transmission is in Park or Neutral.

VOLTAGE DROP TEST

NOTE: Make all voltmeter connections at component terminal rather than at cable or wire end.

1) Verify battery condition. Battery voltage should be 12 volts or more. Load test battery at approximately one-half cold cranking amperage rating. See load tester manufacturer's instructions. If battery voltage is less than 12 volts or loaded battery voltage is less than 9.6 volts, service battery or charging system as necessary.
2) Disconnect low voltage wires at coil pack to prevent vehicle from starting during testing. Connect remote starter switch between starter solenoid terminal "S" and positive battery post. See Fig. 1.
3) Connect positive voltmeter lead to positive battery post, and negative lead to solenoid terminal "M". See Fig. 1.
4) Engage remote starter switch. Voltmeter should indicate .5 volt or less. If voltmeter indicates more than .5 volt, go to next step. If voltmeter indicates .5 volt or less, go to STARTER GROUND CIRCUIT TEST.
5) Move negative voltmeter lead to solenoid terminal "B". Engage remote starter switch. See Fig. 1. If voltmeter still indicates more than .5 volt at terminal "B", go to next step. If voltmeter indicates less than .5 volt, solenoid connections or contacts are bad. Clean solenoid terminals "B", "S" and "M". Repeat steps 2) through 5). If voltmeter still indicates more than .5 volt at terminal "M" and less than .5 volt at terminal "B", solenoid contacts are bad. Replace solenoid or entire starter assembly. See STARTER MOTOR under REMOVAL & INSTALLATION.

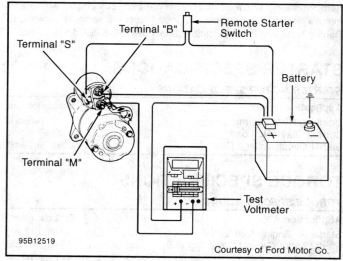

Fig. 1: Testing Voltage Drop

6) Clean cables and connections at solenoid and battery. If voltmeter still indicates more than .5 volt at terminal "B", replace battery cable.

NOTE: To locate excessive voltage drop, move voltmeter negative lead toward battery, and check each connection point. When high voltmeter reading disappears, problem is between last connection point and previous connection point.

STARTER GROUND CIRCUIT TEST

NOTE: Make all voltmeter connections at component terminal rather than at cable or wire end.

1) Disconnect low voltage wires at coil pack to prevent vehicle from starting during testing. Connect remote starter switch between starter solenoid terminal "S" and positive battery post.
2) Connect positive voltmeter lead to starter housing, and negative lead to negative battery post. Engage remote starter switch while observing voltmeter. Voltmeter should indicate .3 volt or less. If voltmeter indicates more than .3 volt, clean negative cable connections at battery and engine.
3) If voltage drop is still excessive, repair or replace negative battery cable and/or engine ground cable as necessary. Repeat starter circuit test after repair to ensure problem has been corrected. If battery and cables test okay and starter motor still cranks slowly, replace starter.

STARTER CIRCUIT CURRENT DRAW TEST

Ensure battery is fully charged. Ensure battery connections are clean and tight. Disconnect low voltage wires at coil pack to prevent vehicle from starting during testing. Disconnect inertia fuel shut off switch. Connect Starter, Alternator, Battery, Regulator Electrical tester (Rotunda 010-00730). Follow tool manufacturer's instructions. If tool is not available, use conventional ammeter. Clamp inductive ammeter lead around all positive (or negative) battery cables. See Fig. 2. Crank engine for about 5 seconds and check amperage reading while cranking. Normal amperage draw is 140-220 amps. If amperage draw exceeds specification, replace starter.

SYSTEM TESTS

STARTER CRANKS SLOWLY OR SOLENOID CLICKS

1) Turn ignition off. Turn headlights on for 10 seconds to remove surface charge. Turn headlights off. Measure voltage between battery terminals. If battery voltage is 12.4 volts or more, go to next step. If battery voltage is less than 12.4 volts, service battery or charging system as necessary.
2) Perform VOLTAGE DROP TEST. If battery cable voltage drop is 0.5 volt or less, go to next step. If battery cable voltage drop is 0.5 volt or

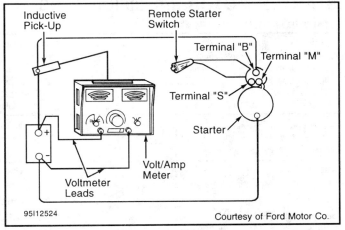

95I12524   Courtesy of Ford Motor Co.

Fig. 2: Testing Starter Draw

greater, repair cable connections or replace cable as necessary. Restore electrical connections and check system operation.

3) Perform STARTER GROUND CIRCUIT TEST. If ground circuit voltage drop is 0.3 volt or less, go to next step. If ground circuit voltage drop is greater than 0.3 volt, repair starter/engine ground circuit.

4) Perform STARTER CIRCUIT CURRENT DRAW TEST under ON-VEHICLE TESTING. If current draw is within specification, check engine for mechanical concerns. If current draw is excessive, replace starter motor. Restore electrical connections and check system operation.

STARTER DOES NOT CRANK

1) If vehicle is equipped with Passive Anti-Theft System (PATS), check system for Diagnostic Trouble Codes (DTCs). See appropriate ANTI-THEFT SYSTEMS article in ACCESSORIES & EQUIPMENT. Repair as necessary.

2) Verify battery condition. Battery voltage should be 12 volts or more. Load test battery at approximately one-half cold cranking amperage rating. See load tester manufacturer's instructions. If battery voltage is less than 12 volts or loaded battery voltage is less than 9.6 volts, service battery or charging system as necessary.

3) Measure voltage between battery positive post and battery ground cable connection at engine. If battery voltage is present, go to next step. If battery voltage is not present, replace battery ground cable and check system operation.

4) Measure voltage between battery positive post and starter motor case. If battery voltage is present, go to next step. If battery voltage is not present, verify starter is mounted correctly. Repair as necessary. If starter is mounted properly, remove starter and clean mounting surfaces. See STARTER MOTOR under REMOVAL & INSTALLATION.

5) Turn ignition off and place transaxle in Park or Neutral. Remove starter solenoid plastic safety cap (install when testing is complete). Measure voltage between starter motor terminal "B" and ground. To identify starter terminals, see Fig. 1. If battery voltage is present, go to next step. If battery voltage is not present, replace battery positive cable and check system operation.

6) Connect one end of a jumper wire to starter "B" terminal. Momentarily touch other end of jumper wire to starter "S" terminal. If starter motor operates, go to next step. If starter motor does not operate, replace starter motor and check system operation. See STARTER MOTOR under REMOVAL & INSTALLATION.

7) Disconnect starter motor electrical connector. Turn ignition switch to START position and measure voltage between starter motor electrical connector White/Pink wire and ground. If battery voltage is present ignition in START position, go to next step. If battery voltage is not present, Clean starter motor terminal "S". Check wires and connections for looseness or corrosion. Repair as necessary. Check system operation.

8) Remove starter relay from engine compartment fuse/relay box. With transaxle in Park or Neutral and ignition switch in START position, measure voltage between starter relay electrical connector terminal No.

86 and ground. *See Fig. 3.* If battery voltage is present, go to next step. If battery voltage is not present, go to step **13**).

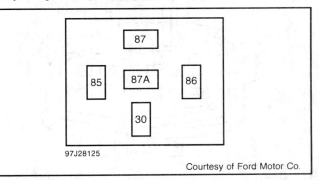

97J28125   Courtesy of Ford Motor Co.

Fig. 3: Identifying Starter Relay Harness Connector Terminals

9) Measure voltage between starter relay connector terminal No. 30 and ground. *See Fig. 3.* If battery voltage is present, go to next step. If battery voltage is not present, check fuse No. 3 (40-amp) in engine compartment fuse/relay box. If fuse is okay, repair open in Light Green/Purple wire. See WIRING DIAGRAMS.

10) Measure resistance of starter relay ground circuit. On models without Passive Anti-Theft System (PATS), measure resistance between starter relay electrical connector terminal No. 85 (Black wire) and ground. If resistance is more than 5 ohms, repair open in Black wire and check system operation. If resistance is less than 5 ohms, go to step **12**). On models with PATS, measure resistance between starter relay electrical connector terminal No. 85 (Pink wire) and ground with ignition switch in START position. If resistance is less than 5 ohms, go to step **12**). If resistance is more than 5 ohms, go to next step.

11) Disconnect PATS module connector. Measure resistance of Pink wire between starter relay connector terminal No. 85 and PATS module connector. If resistance is less than 5 ohms, install new PATS module and check system operation. If resistance is more than 5 ohms, repair Pink wire and check system operation.

12) Measure resistance between starter relay connector terminal No. 87 (White/Pink wire) and starter motor connector terminal "S". If resistance is less than 5 ohms, install new starter relay and check system operation. If resistance is more than 5 ohms, repair White/Pink wire and check system operation.

13) Disconnect ignition switch connector. Measure voltage between connector terminal (Light Green/Purple wire) and ground. If battery voltage is present, go to next step. If battery voltage is not present, inspect fuse No. 3 (40-amp) in engine compartment fuse/relay box. If fuse is okay, repair Light Green/Purple wire.

14) Reconnect ignition switch connector. Remove fuse No. 7 (10-amp) from instrument panel fuse panel. Hold ignition switch in START position and measure voltage between fuse No. 7 input cavity (Red/Light Blue wire) and ground. If battery voltage is present, go to step **16**). If battery voltage is not present, go to next step.

15) Test ignition switch. See STEERING COLUMN SWITCHES – SABLE & TAURUS article in ACCESSORIES & EQUIPMENT. Replace as necessary. If ignition switch is okay, repair open or short in Light Blue wire between ignition switch connector and fuse No. 7.

16) Install fuse No. 7. Disconnect Transmission Range (TR) sensor. Measure voltage between TR sensor electrical connector terminal No. 10 (Brown/Pink wire) and ground with ignition switch in START position. *See Fig. 4.* If battery voltage is present, go to next step. If battery voltage is not present, repair Brown/Pink wire and check system operation.

17) Measure resistance of Tan/Red wire between starter relay connector and TR sensor. If resistance is more than 5 ohms, repair Tan/Red wire and check system operation. If resistance is 5 ohms or more, check TR sensor adjustment. Adjust as necessary, using TR Sensor Alignment Tool (T97L-70010-A). If adjustment is okay, replace TR sensor and check system operation.

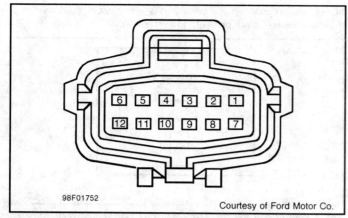

98F01752

Courtesy of Ford Motor Co.

Fig. 4: Identifying Transmission Range Sensor Connector Terminals

BENCH TESTING

STARTER NO-LOAD TEST

Remove starter from vehicle. See STARTER MOTOR under REMOVAL & INSTALLATION. Using heavy gauge jumper wires, connect battery positive to starter terminal "B", and negative battery terminal to starter frame. *See Fig. 2.* Connect voltmeter, ammeter, and remote starter switch to starter. Engage remote starter switch. Starter should turn smoothly. Ammeter should indicate 60-80 amps. If current is higher than specification, replace or overhaul starter.

REMOVAL & INSTALLATION

STARTER MOTOR

CAUTION: When battery is disconnected, vehicle computer and memory systems may lose memory data. Driveability problems may exist until computer systems have completed a relearn cycle. See COMPUTER RELEARN PROCEDURES article in GENERAL INFORMATION before disconnecting battery. Before testing starter, ensure transmission is in Park or Neutral.

Removal & Installation – Disconnect negative battery cable. Raise vehicle on hoist. Disconnect wiring from starter solenoid. Remove upper and lower starter bolts. Remove starter. To install, reverse removal procedure. Tighten bolts to specification. See TORQUE SPECIFICATIONS.

STARTER MOTOR SPECIFICATIONS

STARTER MOTOR SPECIFICATIONS	
Application	Specification
Cranking RPM (Normal Load)	140-220
Current Draw	
Normal Load	130-220 Amps
No Load	60-80 Amps
Starter Circuit Voltage Drop	0.5 Volt

TORQUE SPECIFICATIONS

TORQUE SPECIFICATIONS	
Application	Ft. Lbs. (N.m)
Starter Motor Mounting Bolt/Nut	16-21 (21-29)
	INCH Lbs. (N.m)
Battery Cable Retaining Nut	70-130 (8.0-14.7)
Solenoid "B" & "M" Terminal Nuts	80-123 (9-14)

WIRING DIAGRAMS

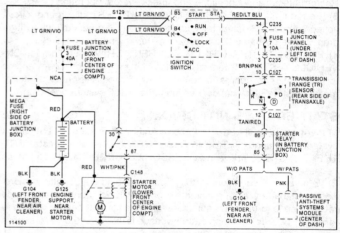

114100

Fig. 5: Starter System Wiring Diagram (Sable & Taurus)

Starters – Town Car

DESCRIPTION

The starter is a gear-reduction motor with an externally-mounted solenoid. Starting system consists of a starter motor, solenoid, battery, ignition switch, Transmission Range (TR) sensor, starter relay and interconnecting cables and wires.

COMPONENT LOCATIONS

COMPONENT LOCATIONS

Component	Location
Inertia Fuel Shutoff Switch	Behind Left Kick Panel
Starter Relay	In Underhood Fuse/Relay Box
Transmission Range Sensor	Side Of Transmission

ADJUSTMENTS

TRANSMISSION RANGE SENSOR

Place transmission in Neutral. Raise and support vehicle. Disconnect manual shift lever control cable. Loosen bolts on Transmission Range (TR) sensor. Ensure manual lever on transmission is in Neutral position. Install TR Sensor Alignment Tool (T97L-70010-A). Tighten TR sensor bolts to specification. See TORQUE SPECIFICATIONS. Reconnect manual shift lever cable. Lower vehicle and check system operation.

TROUBLE SHOOTING

Check the following items before proceeding with testing:

- Check battery for state of charge.
- Check starter for proper mounting.
- Check cable connections at battery and starter motor.
- Ensure transmission is fully engaged in Park or Neutral.
- Check battery junction box fuse No. 1 (50-amp).
- Check battery junction box fuse No. 6 (30-amp).
- Check fuse junction panel fuse No. 26 (5-amp).

ON-VEHICLE TESTING

STARTER GROUND CIRCUIT TEST

NOTE: Make all voltmeter connections at component terminal rather than at cable or wire end.

1) Disconnect inertia fuel shutoff switch located behind left kick panel. Connect remote starter switch between starter solenoid terminal "S" (Yellow/Light Blue wire) and positive battery post. *See Fig. 1.*

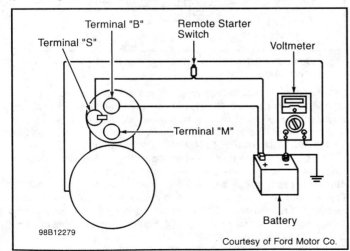

Fig. 1: Testing Ground Voltage Drop

2) Using a digital voltmeter set at lowest voltage scale, connect positive voltmeter lead to starter housing, and negative lead to negative battery post. *See Fig. 1.*
3) Engage remote starter switch while observing voltmeter. If voltmeter indicates .2 volt or less, circuit is okay. If voltmeter indicates more than .2 volt, clean negative cable connections at battery and engine.
4) If voltage drop is still excessive, repair or replace negative battery cable and/or engine ground cable as necessary. Repeat starter circuit test after repair to ensure problem has been corrected.
5) If battery and cables test okay and starter motor still cranks slowly or not at all, replace starter motor.

VOLTAGE DROP TEST

NOTE: Make all voltmeter connections at component terminal rather than at cable or wire end.

1) Verify battery condition. Battery voltage should be 12 volts or more. Load test battery at approximately one-half cold cranking amperage rating. See load tester manufacturer's instructions. If battery voltage is less than 12 volts or loaded battery voltage is less than 9.6 volts, service battery or charging system as necessary. If battery is okay, go to next step.
2) Disconnect inertia fuel shutoff switch. See COMPONENT LOCATIONS. Connect remote starter switch between starter solenoid terminal "S" and positive battery post.
3) Using a digital voltmeter set at lowest voltage scale, connect positive voltmeter lead to positive battery post, and negative lead to solenoid terminal "M". *See Fig. 2.*

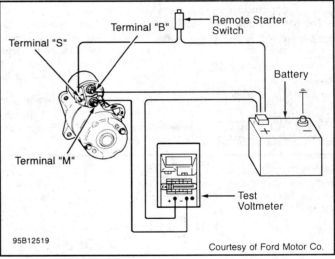

Fig. 2: Testing Voltage Drop

4) Engage remote starter switch. Voltmeter should indicate .5 volt or less. If voltmeter indicates more than .5 volt, go to next step. If voltmeter indicates .5 volt or less, go to STARTER GROUND CIRCUIT TEST.
5) Move negative voltmeter lead to solenoid terminal "B". Engage remote starter switch. If voltmeter indicates more than .5 volt, go to next step. If voltmeter indicates .5 volt or less, solenoid connections or contacts are bad. Clean solenoid terminals "B", "S" and "M". Repeat steps 2) through 5). If voltmeter still indicates .5 volt or less at terminal "B", solenoid contacts are bad. Install new starter motor.
6) Clean cables and connections at solenoid. If voltmeter still indicates more than .5 volt at terminal "B", check for poor positive battery cable connection or bad cable. To locate excessive voltage drop, move voltmeter negative lead toward battery, and check each connection point. When high voltmeter reading disappears, last connection checked is cause of problem. Repair or replace as necessary.

SYSTEM TESTS

CAUTION: Before testing starter, ensure transmission is in Park or Neutral.

STARTER DOES NOT CRANK

1) Verify battery condition. Battery voltage should be 12 volts or more. Load test battery at approximately one-half cold cranking amperage rating. See load tester manufacturer's instructions. If battery voltage is less than 12 volts or loaded battery voltage is less than 9.6 volts, service battery or charging system as necessary. If battery is okay, go to next step.

2) Measure voltage between positive battery terminal and ground cable connection on cylinder block. If voltage is greater than 10 volts, go to next step. If voltage is 10 volts or less, replace negative battery cable. Restore electrical connections and check system operation.

3) Measure voltage between positive battery terminal and starter motor case. If voltage is greater than 10 volts, go to next step. If voltage is 10 volts or less, ensure starter motor is correctly mounted. Restore electrical connections and check system operation.

4) Measure voltage between ground and terminal "B" (battery positive cable connection) on starter solenoid. If voltage is greater than 10 volts, go to next step. If voltage is 10 volts or less, replace positive battery cable. Restore electrical connections and check system operation.

5) Connect a remote starter switch between starter solenoid terminal "B" and terminal "S" (Yellow/Light Blue wire) on starter solenoid. Operate remote starter switch. If starter engages and engine cranks, go to next step. If starter motor does not operate, replace starter motor. Restore electrical connections and check system operation.

6) Disconnect starter solenoid terminal "S" (Yellow/Light Blue wire). Hold ignition switch in START position while measuring voltage at "S" terminal harness connector. If voltage is less than 10 volts, go to next step. If voltage is 10 volts or greater, clean "S" terminal wire connector and check Yellow/Light Blue wire for intermittent open. Restore electrical connections and check system operation.

7) Turn ignition off. Remove starter relay. Hold ignition switch in START position while measuring voltage at starter relay harness connector terminal No. 86. *See Fig. 3.* If voltage is greater than 10 volts, go to next step. If voltage is 10 volts or less, go to step **12**).

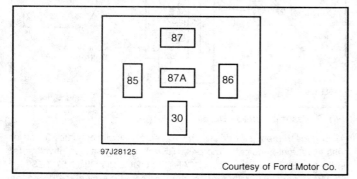

97J28125

Courtesy of Ford Motor Co.

Fig. 3: Identifying Starter Relay Connector Terminals

8) Turn ignition off. Measure voltage at starter relay harness connector terminal No. 30. *See Fig. 3.* If voltage is 10 volts or greater, go to next step. If voltage is less than 10 volts, repair open Black/Yellow wire between power distribution box and starter relay harness connector. Restore electrical connections and check system operation.

9) Measure resistance between starter relay harness connector terminal No. 85 and ground. *See Fig. 3.* If resistance is less than 5 ohms, go to next step. If resistance is 5 ohms or greater, repair open ground (Black) wire. Ground connection point is on left front fender apron, near air cleaner.

10) Measure resistance between starter relay harness connector terminal No. 87 and ground. *See Fig. 3.* If resistance is less than 10,000 ohms, repair Yellow/Light Blue wire for short to ground. If resistance is 10,000 ohms or greater, go to next step. Restore electrical connections and check system operation.

11) Measure resistance between starter relay harness connector terminal No. 87 and starter solenoid "S" terminal wire (Yellow/Light Blue wire). If resistance is 5 ohms or greater, repair open Yellow/Light Blue wire. If resistance is less than 5 ohms, go to next step. Restore electrical connections and check system operation.

12) Test fuse No. 26 (5-amp) in instrument panel fuse panel. If fuse is okay, go to next step. If fuse is blown, go to step **19**).

13) Measure voltage at fuse cavity (input side) while holding ignition switch in START position. If voltage is 10 volts or less, go to next step. If voltage is greater than 10 volts, go to step **17**).

14) Disconnect ignition switch harness connector. Measure voltage at all Yellow wires at ignition switch harness connector. If voltage is greater than 10 volts, go to next step. If voltage is 10 volts or less, repair open Yellow wire. See appropriate wiring diagram in POWER DISTRIBUTION article in WIRING DIAGRAMS.

15) Measure resistance of Red/Light Blue wire between ignition switch harness connector and instrument panel fuse panel cavity No. 26 (input side). If resistance is less than 5 ohms, go to next step. If resistance is 5 ohms or greater, repair open Red/Light Blue wire. Restore electrical connections and check system operation.

16) Measure resistance of Red/Light Blue wire between ignition switch harness connector and ground. If resistance is greater than 10,000 ohms, replace ignition switch. If resistance is 10,000 ohms or less, repair short to ground in Red/Light Blue wire. Restore electrical connections and check system operation.

17) Disconnect Transmission Range (TR) sensor. Measure resistance of Brown/Pink wire between TR sensor harness connector, terminal No. 12 and instrument panel fuse panel cavity No. 26 (output side). *See Fig. 4.* If resistance is less than 5 ohms, go to next step. If resistance is 5 ohms or greater, repair open Brown/Pink wire. Restore electrical connections and check system operation.

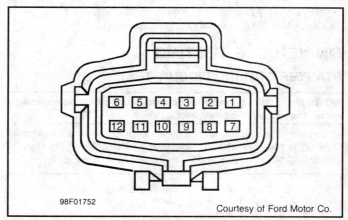

98F01752

Courtesy of Ford Motor Co.

Fig. 4: Identifying Transmission Range Sensor Connector Terminal

18) Disconnect Transmission Range (TR) sensor. Measure resistance of White/Pink wire between TR sensor harness connector, terminal No. 10 and starter relay harness connector terminal No. 86. *See Figs. 3 and 4.* If resistance is less than 5 ohms, check TR sensor adjustment See TRANSMISSION RANGE SENSOR under ADJUSTMENTS. If resistance is 5 ohms or greater, repair open White/Pink wire. Restore electrical connections and check system operation.

19) Measure resistance between instrument panel fuse cavity No. 26 (output side) and ground. If resistance is less than 10,000 ohms, go to next step. If resistance is 10,000 ohms or greater, visually inspect wires for damage that may cause an intermittent short to ground. Replace fuse and check system for normal operation.

20) Disconnect TR sensor harness connector. Measure resistance between TR sensor harness connector terminal No. 12 (Brown/Pink wire) and ground. *See Fig. 4.* If resistance is greater than 10,000 ohms, go to next step. If resistance is 10,000 ohms or less, repair Brown/Pink wire for short to ground.

21) Ensure starter relay is disconnected. Measure resistance of White/Pink wire between TR sensor harness connector terminal No. 10 and ground. *See Fig. 4.* If resistance is greater than 10,000 ohms, replace TR sensor. If resistance is 10,000 ohms or less, repair short to ground in White/Pink wire. Restore electrical connections and check system operation.

UNUSUAL STARTER NOISE

1) Verify starter is installed properly. Ensure bolts are tight. Repair as necessary and check system for normal operation. If starter is mounted properly, go to next step.

2) Connect remote starter switch between starter solenoid terminal "B" (positive battery cable connection) and terminal "S" (Yellow/Light Blue wire). Engage starter motor and verify noise is coming from starter motor. If noise is coming from starter motor, go to next step. If noise is not coming from starter motor, diagnose engine mechanical concern. See appropriate engine article in ENGINES.

3) Remove starter motor. See STARTER MOTOR under REMOVAL & INSTALLATION. Inspect flywheel ring gear for wear or damage. If ring gear is okay, replace starter motor. If ring gear is worn or damaged, replace ring gear and inspect starter drive gear. If drive gear is also damaged, replace starter motor.

STARTER SPINS BUT ENGINE DOES NOT CRANK

Inspect starter motor mounting. Ensure bolts are tight and starter is properly aligned. If starter motor is mounted properly, remove starter motor and inspect ring gear and starter drive gear for wear or damage. See STARTER MOTOR under REMOVAL & INSTALLATION. Repair as necessary. If ring gear and starter motor drive gear are okay, install new starter motor and check system for normal operation.

REMOVAL & INSTALLATION

STARTER MOTOR

CAUTION: When battery is disconnected, vehicle computer and memory systems may lose memory data. Driveability problems may exist until computer systems have completed a relearn cycle. See COMPUTER RELEARN PROCEDURES article in GENERAL INFORMATION before disconnecting battery.

Removal & Installation – Disconnect negative battery cable. Raise vehicle on hoist. Remove transmission cooler line bracket bolt. Position bracket and transmission cooler lines out of the way. Disconnect wiring from starter solenoid. Remove 3 starter mounting bolts. Remove starter. To install, reverse removal procedure. Tighten bolts to specification. See TORQUE SPECIFICATIONS.

TORQUE SPECIFICATIONS

TORQUE SPECIFICATIONS

Application	Ft. Lbs. (N.m)
Starter Motor Mounting Bolts	17-20 (22-27)
	INCH Lbs. (N.m)
Starter Motor Ground Cable Nut	97-123 (11-14)
Solenoid Terminal Nuts	45-61 (5-7)
Transmission Cooler Line Bracket Bolt	89 (10)
Transmission Range (TR) Sensor Bolts	61-89 (7-10)

WIRING DIAGRAMS

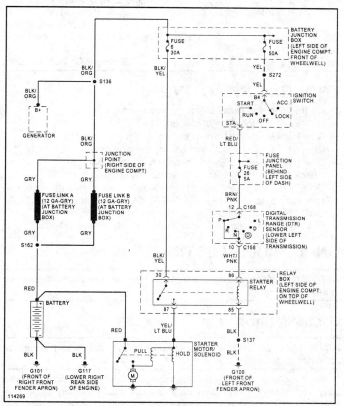

Fig. 5: Starter System Wiring Diagram (Town Car)

DESCRIPTION

The starter is a gear-reduction, permanent-magnet type motor with an externally mounted solenoid. Starting system consists of a starter motor, solenoid, battery, ignition switch, Transmission Range (TR) sensor, starter interrupt relay, anti-theft relay (if equipped with anti-theft system) and interconnecting cables and wires.

COMPONENT LOCATIONS

COMPONENT LOCATIONS

Component	Location
Anti-Theft Relay	Engine Compartment Relay Box
Inertia Fuel Shutoff Switch	Behind Left Side Of Instrument Panel
Start Inhibit Relay	Engine Compartment Relay Box
Transmission Range (TR) Sensor	Front Of Transmission

TROUBLE SHOOTING

Check the following items before proceeding with testing:
* Check battery for state of charge.
* Check cable connections at battery and starter motor.
* Check fuse F23 (30-amp) in battery junction box.
* Check fuse F29 (100-amp) in battery junction box.
* Check fuse F35 (10-amp) in fuse junction panel.
* On models equipped anti-theft system, ensure anti-theft system is operating properly. See ANTI-THEFT SYSTEMS article in ACCESSORIES & EQUIPMENT for additional information.
* Ensure transmission is fully engaged in Park or Neutral position.

ON-VEHICLE TESTING

CAUTION: Before testing starting system, ensure transmission is in Park or Neutral.

VOLTAGE DROP TEST

NOTE: Make all voltmeter connections at component terminal rather than at cable or wire end.

1) Verify battery condition. Battery voltage should be 12 volts or more. Load test battery at approximately one-half cold cranking amperage rating. See load tester manufacturer's instructions. If battery is okay, go to next step. If battery voltage is less than 12 volts or loaded battery voltage is less than 9.6 volts, service battery or charging system as necessary.
2) Disconnect inertia fuel shutoff switch connector. Connect remote starter switch between starter solenoid terminal "S" (Red/White wire) and positive battery terminal. Using a digital voltmeter set at lowest voltage scale, connect positive voltmeter lead to positive battery post, and negative lead to solenoid terminal "M". *See Fig. 1.*
3) Engage remote starter switch. Voltmeter should indicate .5 volt or less. If voltmeter indicates more than .5 volt, move negative voltmeter lead to solenoid terminal "B". If voltmeter indicates .5 volt or less, go to STARTER GROUND CIRCUIT TEST.
4) Engage remote starter switch. If voltmeter indicates less than .5 volt, solenoid connections or contacts are bad. Clean solenoid terminals "B", "S" and "M". Repeat steps **1)** through **4)**. If voltmeter still indicates more than .5 volt at terminal "M" and less than .5 volt at terminal "B", solenoid contacts are bad. Replace starter motor. See STARTER MOTOR under REMOVAL & INSTALLATION.
5) If voltmeter indicates more than .5 volt at terminal "B", clean cables and connections at solenoid. If voltmeter still indicates more than .5 volt at terminal "B", check for poor positive battery cable connection or bad cable. Repair or replace as necessary.
6) To locate excessive voltage drop, move voltmeter negative lead toward battery, and check each connection point. When high voltmeter reading disappears, last connection point checked is cause of problem.

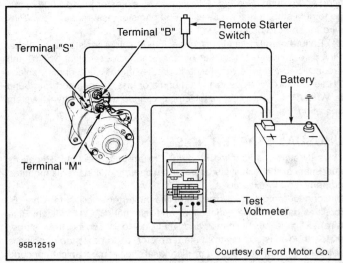

95B12519   Courtesy of Ford Motor Co.

Fig. 1: Testing Voltage Drop

STARTER GROUND CIRCUIT TEST

NOTE: Make all voltmeter connections at component terminal rather than at cable or wire end.

1) Disconnect both connectors from distributor. Connect remote starter switch between starter solenoid terminal "S" and positive battery post. *See Fig. 2.*

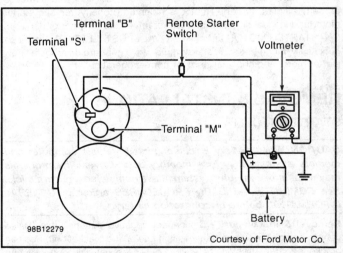

98B12279   Courtesy of Ford Motor Co.

Fig. 2: Testing Ground Circuit

2) Using a digital voltmeter set at lowest voltage scale, connect positive voltmeter lead to starter housing, and negative lead to negative battery post.
3) Engage remote starter switch while observing voltmeter. Voltmeter should indicate .2 volt or less. If voltmeter indicates more than .2 volt, clean negative cable connections at battery and engine.
4) If voltage drop is still excessive, repair or replace negative battery cable and/or engine ground cable as necessary. Repeat starter circuit test after repair to ensure problem has been corrected.
5) If battery and cables test okay and starter motor still cranks slowly or not at all, replace starter motor. See STARTER MOTOR under REMOVAL & INSTALLATION.

SYSTEM TESTS

Identify symptom and perform appropriate system tests.

ENGINE DOES NOT CRANK

1) Observe anti-theft indicator. If anti-theft indicator is off, go to next step. If anti-theft indicator is ON or flashing, see appropriate ANTI-THEFT SYSTEMS article in ACCESSORIES & EQUIPMENT.

2) Verify battery condition. Battery voltage should be 12 volts or more. Load test battery at approximately one-half cold cranking amperage rating. See load tester manufacturer's instructions. If battery is okay, go to next step. If battery voltage is less than 12 volts or loaded battery voltage is less than 9.6 volts, service battery or charging system as necessary.

3) Measure voltage between battery positive terminal and ground cable connection at engine block. If battery voltage is present, go to next step. If battery voltage is not present, clean and tighten ground cable connections and recheck voltage. If battery voltage is still not present, replace battery ground cable and check system operation.

4) Measure voltage between battery positive terminal and starter motor case. If battery voltage is present, go to next step. If battery voltage is not present, clean starter mounting surface and verify proper installation. Check system operation.

5) Measure voltage between starter solenoid terminal "B" and ground. See Fig. 3. If battery voltage is present, go to next step. If battery voltage is not present, clean and tighten positive battery cable connections, and recheck voltage . If battery voltage is still not present, replace positive battery cable.

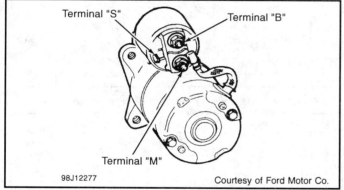

Fig. 3: Identifying Starter Solenoid Terminals (Typical)

6) Disconnect starter solenoid terminal "S". Momentarily connect a 30-amp fused jumper wire between starter solenoid terminals "B" and "S". See Fig. 3. If starter motor operates and engine cranks, go to next step. If starter motor does not engage, or engine does not crank, replace starter motor. See STARTER MOTOR under REMOVAL & INSTALLATION. Check system operation.

7) Measure voltage between starter solenoid terminal "S" connector (Red/White wire) and ground with ignition in START position. If battery voltage is not present, go to next step. If battery voltage is present, check connector for looseness or corrosion. Repair as necessary. Restore connections and check system operation.

8) Turn ignition off. Remove start inhibit relay. Measure voltage between start inhibit relay connector terminal No. 7 (Red wire) and ground with ignition in START position. See Fig. 4. If battery voltage is present, go to next step. If battery voltage is not present, test ignition switch. See STEERING COLUMN SWITCHES – Villager article in ACCESSORIES & EQUIPMENT.

9) Connect a jumper wire between start inhibit relay connector terminals No. 6 and 7. See Fig. 4. Turn ignition switch to START position. If starter motor operates, remove jumper wire and go to next step. If starter motor does not operate, repair engine compartment relay box or Red/White wire between start inhibit relay terminal No. 6 and starter solenoid terminal "S". See WIRING DIAGRAMS.

10) Measure resistance between start inhibit relay connector terminal No. 2 and ground. See Fig. 4. If resistance is 5 ohms or less, go to next step. If resistance is greater than 5 ohms, repair Black wire between relay terminal and ground. See WIRING DIAGRAMS.

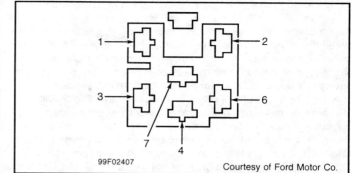

Fig. 4: Identifying Start Inhibit Relay Connector Terminals

11) With ignition switch in START or RUN position, and transmission in Park or Neutral, measure resistance between start inhibit relay terminal No. 1 and ground. If battery voltage is present, replace start inhibit relay and check system operation. If battery voltage is not present, and vehicle is equipped with anti-theft system, go to next step. If battery voltage is not present, and vehicle is not equipped with anti-theft system, go to step **14)**.

12) Remove anti-theft relay. Measure voltage between anti-theft relay connector terminal No. 2 and ground. See Fig. 5. If battery voltage is present, go to next step. If battery voltage is not present, repair Green/Red wire between anti-theft relay connector and battery junction box. See WIRING DIAGRAMS.

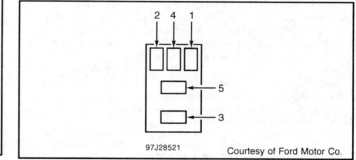

Fig. 5: Identifying Anti-Theft Relay Connector Terminals

13) With ignition switch in START or RUN position, and transmission in Park or Neutral, measure resistance between anti-theft relay connector terminal No. 4 and ground. If battery voltage is present, go to step **16)**. If battery voltage is not present, go to next step.

14) Disconnect Transmission Range (TR) sensor connector. Measure voltage between TR sensor connector terminal No. 3 (Light Green wire) and ground with ignition switch in START or RUN position. See Fig. 6. If battery voltage is present, go to next step. If battery voltage is not present, repair Light Green wire or connections between fuse junction panel and TR sensor. See WIRING DIAGRAMS.

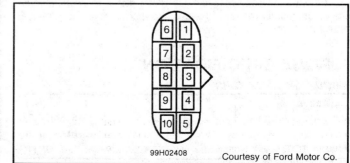

Fig. 6: Identifying Transmission Range (TR) Sensor Connector Terminals

15) Measure resistance of Light Green/Black wire between anti-theft relay terminal No. 4 and TR sensor terminal No. 2. *See Fig. 6.* Resistance should be less than 5 ohms. Measure resistance of Light Green/Black wire between TR sensor connector terminal No. 2 and ground. Resistance should be more than 10 k/ohms. If resistance is as specified for both measurements, replace TR sensor and check system operation. If resistance is not as specified for either measurement, repair open or short in Light Green/Black wire. See WIRING DIAGRAMS.

16) Measure resistance of Blue/White wire between anti-theft relay connector terminal No. 3 and start inhibit relay connector terminal No. 1. *See Figs. 4 and 5.* Resistance should be less than 5 ohms. Measure resistance of Blue/White wire between anti-theft relay connector terminal No. 3 and ground. Resistance should be more than 10 k/ohms. If resistance is as specified for both measurements, fault is in anti-theft system. See ANTI-THEFT SYSTEMS article in ACCESSORIES & ELECTRICAL. If resistance is not as specified for either measurement, repair open or short in Blue/White wire. See WIRING DIAGRAMS.

ENGINE CRANKS SLOWLY

Perform voltage drop test. See VOLTAGE DROP TEST under ON-VEHICLE TESTING. Repair or replace as necessary.

UNUSUAL STARTER NOISE

1) Ensure starter mounting bolts are tight and installed properly. Repair as necessary. If starter is mounted correctly, go to next step.

2) Turn ignition off. Connect remote starter switch between starter solenoid terminals "B" (battery cable) and "S" (Red/White wire). *See Fig. 3.* Ensure transmission is in Park or Neutral and ignition is off. Engage starter motor and verify noise is from starter. If noise is from starter, go to next step. If noise is not from starter, check for engine mechanical concerns. See appropriate article in ENGINES.

3) Remove starter motor. See STARTER MOTOR under REMOVAL & INSTALLATION. Inspect flywheel ring gear for wear or damage. Inspect starter drive gear for wear or damage. Replace ring gear, starter or both as necessary. If no wear or damage is found, replace starter motor and check system operation.

REMOVAL & INSTALLATION

STARTER MOTOR

CAUTION: When battery is disconnected, vehicle computer and memory systems may lose memory data. Driveability problems may exist until computer systems have completed a relearn cycle. See COMPUTER RELEARN PROCEDURES article in GENERAL INFORMATION before disconnecting battery. Before testing starter, ensure transmission is in Park or Neutral.

Removal & Installation – Disconnect negative battery cable. Remove air cleaner assembly. Disconnect starter solenoid wiring. Remove starter motor mounting bolts. Remove starter motor. To install, reverse removal procedure. Tighten all fasteners to specification. See TORQUE SPECIFICATIONS.

TORQUE SPECIFICATIONS

TORQUE SPECIFICATIONS	
Application	Ft. Lbs. (N.m)
Starter Motor Mounting Bolts	15-20 (20-27)
	INCH Lbs. (N.m)
Solenoid "B" Terminal Nuts	98 (11)

WIRING DIAGRAMS

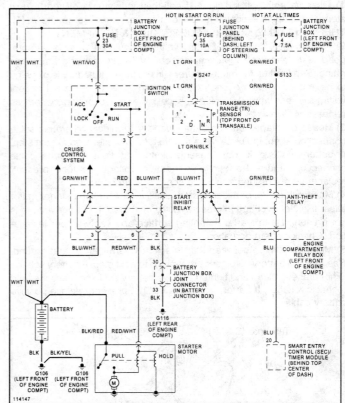

Fig. 7: Starter System Wiring Diagram (Villager W/Anti-Theft)

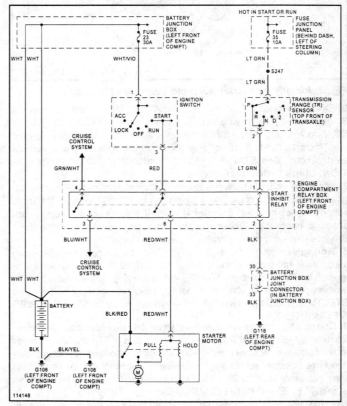

Fig. 8: Starter System Wiring Diagram (Villager W/O Anti-Theft)

Starters – Windstar

DESCRIPTION

The starter is a gear-reduction motor with an externally mounted solenoid. Starting system consists of a starter motor, solenoid, battery, ignition switch, Digital Transmission Range (DTR) sensor, starter interrupt relay and interconnecting cables and wires.

COMPONENT LOCATIONS

COMPONENT LOCATIONS

Component	Location
Inertia Fuel Shutoff Switch	On Left "A" Pillar, Under Instrument Panel
Starter Interrupt Relay	In Fuse Junction Panel
Digital Transmission Range Sensor	Top Of Transmission

ADJUSTMENTS

DIGITAL TRANSMISSION RANGE (DTR) SENSOR

CAUTION: When battery is disconnected, vehicle computer and memory systems may lose memory data. Driveability problems may exist until computer systems have completed a relearn cycle. See COMPUTER RELEARN PROCEDURES article in GENERAL INFORMATION before disconnecting battery.

1) Set parking brake. Place transmission in Neutral. Disconnect negative battery cable. Remove engine air cleaner assembly. Disconnect Digital Transmission Range (DTR) sensor connector. Disconnect shift cable from DTR sensor. Remove nut and manual control lever from DTR sensor.

2) Loosen DTR sensor bolts. Install DTR sensor Alignment Tool (T97L-70010-A). Tighten DTR sensor bolts to specification. Install manual control lever and nut, and torque to specification. See TORQUE SPECIFICATIONS. Reconnect DTR sensor connector, air cleaner assemble, and negative battery cable.

TROUBLE SHOOTING

Check the following items before proceeding with testing:
- Check battery for state of charge.
- Check cable connections at battery and starter motor.
- Ensure transmission is fully engaged in Park or Neutral position.
- Check battery junction box fuses No. 105 (30-amp) and No. 121 (20-amp).
- On models equipped with anti-theft system, ensure anti-theft system is operating properly. Check fuse No. 9 (10-amp) in fuse junction panel. See appropriate ANTI-THEFT SYSTEMS article in ACCESSORIES & EQUIPMENT for additional information.

ON-VEHICLE TESTING

VOLTAGE DROP TEST

NOTE: Make all voltmeter connections at component terminal rather than at cable or wire end.

1) Disconnect inertia fuel shutoff switch. Connect remote starter switch between starter solenoid terminal "S" and positive battery post. Using a digital voltmeter set at lowest voltage scale, connect positive voltmeter lead to positive battery post, and negative lead to solenoid terminal "M". *See Fig. 1.*

2) Engage remote starter switch. If voltmeter indicates greater than .5 volt, go to next step. If voltmeter indicates .5 volt or less, go to STARTER GROUND CIRCUIT TEST.

3) Move negative voltmeter lead to solenoid terminal "B". Engage remote starter switch. If voltmeter indicates more than .5 volt , go to next step. If voltmeter indicates less than .5 volt, solenoid connections or contacts are bad. Clean solenoid terminals "B", "S" and "M". Repeat steps **1)** through **4)**. If voltmeter still indicates greater than .5 volt at

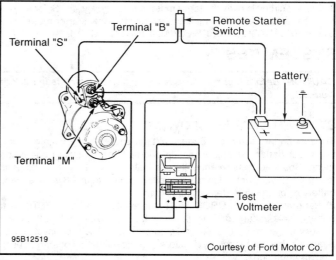

95B12519

Courtesy of Ford Motor Co.

Fig. 1: Testing Voltage Drop

terminal "M" and less than .5 volt at terminal "B", solenoid contacts are bad. Replace starter motor. See STARTER MOTOR under REMOVAL & INSTALLATION.

4) Clean cables and connections at solenoid. If voltmeter still indicates greater than .5 volt at terminal "B", check positive battery cable connections. If connections are okay, replace positive battery cable and check system operation.

STARTER GROUND CIRCUIT TEST

NOTE: Make all voltmeter connections at component terminal rather than at cable or wire end.

1) Disconnect inertia fuel shutoff switch. Connect remote starter switch between starter solenoid terminal "S" and positive battery post. Using a digital voltmeter set at lowest voltage scale, connect positive voltmeter lead to positive battery post, and negative lead to solenoid terminal "M". *See Fig. 2.*

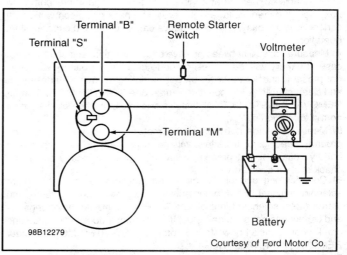

98B12279

Courtesy of Ford Motor Co.

Fig. 2: Testing Ground Circuit

2) Using a digital voltmeter set at lowest voltage scale, connect positive voltmeter lead to starter housing, and negative lead to negative battery post. Engage remote starter switch while observing voltmeter. If voltage is .2 volt or less, go to next step. If voltmeter indicates greater than .2 volt, clean negative cable connections at battery and engine and recheck voltage drop. If voltage is still greater than .2 volt, repair or replace negative battery cable and/or engine ground cable as necessary. Repeat starter circuit test after repair to ensure problem has been corrected.

3) Ground circuit is okay. If starter motor cranks slowly, check for engine mechanical concerns. If engine is okay, install new starter motor. See STARTER MOTOR under REMOVAL & INSTALLATION.

SYSTEM TESTS

CAUTION: Before testing starter, ensure transmission is in Park or Neutral.

STARTER CRANKS SLOWLY

1) Verify battery condition. Battery voltage should be 12 volts or more. Load test battery at approximately one-half cold cranking amperage rating. See load tester manufacturer's instructions. If battery voltage is less than 12 volts or loaded battery voltage is less than 9.6 volts, service battery or charging system as necessary.

2) Perform VOLTAGE DROP TEST under ON-VEHICLE TESTING. If battery cable voltage drop is .5 volt or less, go to next step. If battery cable voltage drop is .5 volt or greater, repair cable connections or replace cable as necessary. Restore electrical connections and check system operation.

3) Perform STARTER GROUND CIRCUIT TEST under ON-VEHICLE TESTING. If ground circuit voltage drop is .2 volt or less, replace starter motor. See STARTER MOTOR under REMOVAL & INSTALLATION. If ground circuit voltage drop is greater than .2 volt, repair starter/engine ground circuit.

STARTER DOES NOT CRANK

1) Perform instrument cluster self-test to check for trouble codes. See appropriate INSTRUMENT PANELS article in ACCESSORIES & EQUIPMENT. If any Passive Anti-Theft System (PATS) codes are present, repair as necessary. See appropriate PASSIVE ANTI-THEFT SYSTEMS article. If no PATS trouble codes are present, go to next step.

2) Verify battery condition. Battery voltage should be 12 volts or more. Load test battery at approximately one-half cold cranking amperage rating. See load tester manufacturer's instructions. If battery voltage is less than 12 volts or loaded battery voltage is less than 9.6 volts, service battery or charging system as necessary.

3) Measure voltage between battery positive terminal and negative battery cable connection at engine. If battery voltage is present, go to next step. If battery voltage is not present, check cable connections. If connections are okay, replace negative battery cable and check system operation.

4) Measure voltage between positive battery terminal and starter motor case. If battery voltage is present, go to next step. If battery voltage is not present, check starter for proper mounting. Remove starter motor and clean starter motor mounting flange. See STARTER MOTOR under REMOVAL & INSTALLATION. Install starter motor and check system for normal operation.

5) Measure voltage between starter motor solenoid terminal "B" and ground. See Fig. 3. If battery voltage is present, go to next step. If battery voltage is not present, install new positive battery cable and check system operation.

6) Connect one end of 30-amp fused jumper wire to starter motor solenoid terminal "B". Momentarily connect other end of jumper to starter motor solenoid terminal "S". See Fig. 3. If starter motor engages and cranks engine, go to next step. If starter motor does not engage and crank engine, install new starter motor. See STARTER MOTOR under REMOVAL & INSTALLATION.

7) Disconnect starter motor solenoid terminal "S" (Yellow/Light Blue wire). Measure voltage between terminal "S" harness connector and ground with ignition switch in START position. If battery voltage is not present, go to next step. If battery voltage is present, clean and tighten terminal "S" connections. Reconnect connector and check system operation.

8) Remove starter interrupt relay from fuse junction panel. Place vehicle in Park or Neutral. Measure voltage between starter interrupt relay socket terminal No. 86 and ground with ignition switch in START position. See Fig. 4. If battery voltage is present, go to next step. If battery voltage is not present, go to step **13**).

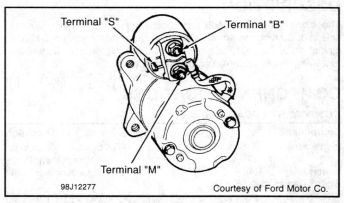

Fig. 3: *Identifying Starter Motor Solenoid Terminals*

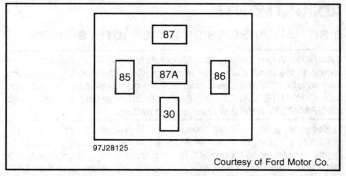

Fig. 4: Identifying Starter Interrupt Relay Harness Connector Terminals

9) Measure voltage between starter interrupt relay socket terminal No. 30 and ground. *See Fig. 4.* If battery voltage is present, go to next step. If battery voltage is not present, inspect battery junction box fuse No. 105 (30-amp) and replace as necessary. If fuse is okay, check Light Green/Purple wire and connections between fuse and relay for open. See WIRING DIAGRAMS. If wire and connections are okay, repair open in battery junction box or fuse junction panel.

10) Measure resistance between starter interrupt relay socket terminal No. 85 and ground with ignition switch in START position. If resistance is greater than 5 ohms, go to next step. If resistance is 5 ohms or less, go to step **12**).

11) Disconnect instrument cluster 22-pin connector C241. Connector C241 is identical to instrument cluster connector C239, and can only be identified by validating wire colors. See appropriate wiring diagram in INSTRUMENT PANELS article. Measure resistance of Light Green/Yellow wire between starter interrupt relay socket terminal No. 85 and instrument cluster connector C241 terminal No. 10. *See Fig. 5.* If resistance is less than 5 ohms, install new instrument cluster and check system operation. If resistance is 5 ohms or greater, repair open in circuit between relay and instrument cluster. See WIRING DIAGRAMS.

12) Measure resistance of Yellow/Light blue wire between starter interrupt relay socket terminal No. 87 and starter motor solenoid connector terminal "S". *See Fig. 4.* If resistance is less than 5 ohms, install new starter interrupt relay and check system operation. If resistance is 5 ohms or greater, repair open circuit between relay socket and starter solenoid connector. See WIRING DIAGRAMS.

13) Remove fuse junction panel fuse No. 19 (10-amp). Measure voltage between fuse input cavity and ground with ignition switch in START position. If battery voltage is present, go to next step. If battery voltage is not present, go to step **16**).

14) Install fuse No. 19. Disconnect Digital Transmission Range (DTR) sensor connector. Measure voltage between DTR connector terminal no. 10 (Red/Light Blue wire) and ground with ignition switch in START position. *See Fig. 6.* If battery voltage is present, go to next step. If battery voltage is not present, repair open in circuit between DTR sensor and fuse junction panel. See WIRING DIAGRAMS.

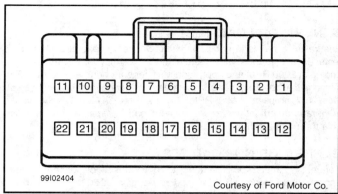

99102404

Courtesy of Ford Motor Co.

Fig. 5: Identifying Instrument Cluster Connector C241 Terminals

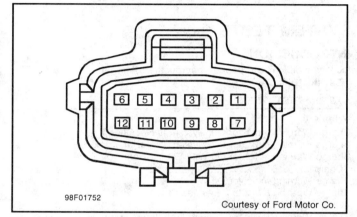

98F01752

Courtesy of Ford Motor Co.

Fig. 6: Identifying Digital Transmission Range (DTR) Sensor Terminals

15) Measure resistance of White/Pink wire between DTR sensor connector terminal No. 12 and starter interrupt relay socket terminal No. 86. *See Figs. 4 and 6.* If resistance is greater than 5 ohms, repair open circuit between relay socket and DTR sensor and check system operation. See WIRING DIAGRAMS. If resistance is 5 ohms or less, check DTR sensor adjustment. See DIGITAL TRANSMISSION RANGE (DTR) SENSOR under ADJUSTMENTS. If sensor is adjusted properly and system still does not function properly, replace DTR sensor and check system operation

16) Disconnect ignition switch connector. Measure voltage between ignition switch connector terminal B4 (Light Green/Purple wire) and ground. If battery voltage is present, go to next step. If battery voltage is not present, repair open circuit between battery junction box fuse No. 105 (30-amp) and ignition switch connector terminal B4. See WIRING DIAGRAMS.

17) Test ignition switch. See appropriate STEERING COLUMN SWITCHES article in ACCESSORIES & EQUIPMENT. Replace ignition switch if necessary. If ignition switch tests okay, repair open circuit between ignition switch connector terminal STA and fuse junction panel fuse No. 19. See appropriate wiring diagram in POWER DISTRIBUTION article in WIRING DIAGRAMS. Recheck system operation.

REMOVAL & INSTALLATION

CAUTION: When battery is disconnected, vehicle computer and memory systems may lose memory data. Driveability problems may exist until computer systems have completed a relearn cycle. See COMPUTER RELEARN PROCEDURES article in GENERAL INFORMATION before disconnecting battery. Before testing starter, ensure transmission is in Park or Neutral.

STARTER MOTOR

Removal & Installation – Disconnect negative battery cable. Remove starter bolts and lower starter. Remove protective caps and disconnect wiring from starter solenoid. Remove starter. To install, reverse removal procedure. Tighten bolts to specification. See TORQUE SPECIFICATIONS.

STARTER MOTOR SPECIFICATIONS

STARTER MOTOR SPECIFICATIONS

Application	Specification
Cranking RPM (Normal Load)	140-220
Current Draw (No Load)	60-80 Amps
Starter Circuit Voltage Drop	.5 Volt

TORQUE SPECIFICATIONS

TORQUE SPECIFICATIONS

Application	Ft. Lbs. (N.m)
Solenoid "B" Terminal Nut	10 (13)
Starter Motor Mounting Bolts	20 (28)
	INCH Lbs. (N.m)
Solenoid "S" Terminal Nut	53 (6)

WIRING DIAGRAMS

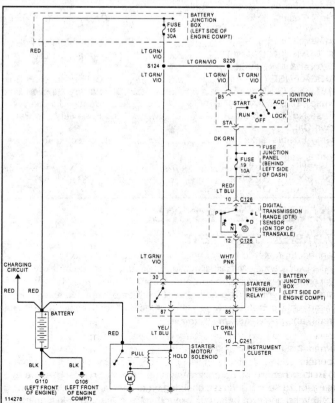

Fig. 7: Starter System Wiring Diagram (Windstar)

1999 STARTING & CHARGING SYSTEMS
Generators – Continental, Crown Victoria, Explorer (4.0L SOHC & 5.0L), Grand Marquis, Mountaineer & Town Car

DESCRIPTION

System consists of a 130-amp generator, voltage regulator, battery, charge warning indicator and related fuses and wiring. Charge warning indicator illuminates with ignition on, engine off as a bulb-check. Voltage regulator is integral type and cannot be serviced separately.

ADJUSTMENTS

BELT TENSION

Vehicles are equipped with automatic drive belt tensioner. Drive belt does not require adjustment. Inspect condition and tension of generator drive belt prior to performing any on-vehicle charging system tests. Replace belt and/or repair tensioner mechanism if necessary.

TROUBLE SHOOTING

NOTE: See TROUBLE SHOOTING article in GENERAL INFORMATION.

PRELIMINARY CHECKS

- Verify battery condition.
- Inspect accessory drive belt and tensioner.
- Check all connections for looseness or corrosion.
- Inspect appropriate fuses and fusible links. See FUSE IDENTIFICATION table.

FUSE IDENTIFICATION

Fuse Identification	Location
Continental	
Mega Fuse (175-Amp)	Battery Junction Box
Fuse No. 2 (20-Amp)	Battery Junction Box
Fuse No. 4 (40-Amp)	Battery Junction Box
Fuse No. 5 (10-Amp)	Fuse Junction Panel
Crown Victoria & Grand Marquis	
Gray Fusible Links	Connected To Battery Junction Box
Fuse No. 2 (30-Amp)	Battery Junction Box
Fuse No. 15 (10-Amp)	Central Junction Box
Explorer & Mountaineer	
MEGA FUSE (175-Amp)	On Battery Junction Box
ALT SYS (30-Amp)	Battery Junction Box
Fuse No. 5 (50-Amp Maxi)	Battery Junction box
Fuse No. 15 (7.5-amp)	Fuse Junction Panel
Town Car	
Gray Fusible Links	Connected To Battery Junction Box
Fuse No. 2 (40-Amp)	Battery Junction Box
Fuse No. 12 (15-Amp)	Fuse Junction Panel
Fuse No. 13 (15-Amp)	Battery Junction Box

ON-VEHICLE TESTING

PARASITIC DRAW TEST

Connect ammeter to battery negative cable according to tool manufacturers instructions. With all accessories off, doors closed and key out of ignition, current drain should be less than 50 milliamps. To locate the cause of current drains greater than 50 milliamps, remove fuses one at a time until current draw is within specification. Repair appropriate circuit, and check system operation.

BATTERY LOAD TEST

Connect battery tester according to tool manufacturers instructions. Load test battery at approximately one-half cold-cranking amperage rating for 15 seconds while observing battery voltage. If voltage reading is 9.6 volts or more, battery is okay. If voltage reading is less than 9.6 volts, charge battery and retest. If loaded battery voltage is still less than 9.6 volts after charging battery, replace battery.

GENERATOR LOAD TEST

Ensure drive belt is in good condition. Connect charging system load tester in accordance with manufacturer's instructions. Start and run engine at 2000 RPM and apply load until generator output levels off. For all models except Explorer & Mountaineer, generator output should be at least 107 amps at 2000 RPM. On Explorer & Mountaineer, verify amperage output increases with system load (no specification is available from manufacturer).

GENERATOR NO-LOAD TEST

Connect voltmeter positive lead to B+ terminal on generator and negative lead to ground. Start and run engine at 2000 RPM with no electrical load (all accessories off). Read voltmeter when voltage stabilizes. Voltage should be 13-15 volts.

SYSTEM TESTS

INTRODUCTION

Identify symptom and perform appropriate system test. See SYSTEM TEST INDEX table.

SYSTEM TEST INDEX

Symptom	Test
Charge Warning Indicator On, System Is Not Charging	A
Charge Warning Indicator Off, System Is Not Charging	B
Charge Warning Indicator On With Engine Running, System Is Charging	C
Charge Warning Indicator Off With Ignition On	D
Charge Warning Indicator Operates Properly, System Is Not Charging	E
Charge Warning Indicator Flickers Or Is Intermittent	G
System Overcharges	H

TEST A

1) With ignition on, engine off, inspect appropriate fuses and/or fusible links. See FUSE IDENTIFICATION table. Replace fuses and/or fusible links as necessary. If okay, go to next step.
2) Measure voltage between generator B+ terminal (Black/Orange wire) and ground. If battery voltage is present, go to next step. If battery voltage is not present, repair Black/Orange wire. See WIRING DIAGRAMS. Check system operation.
3) Disconnect generator 3-pin connector. Measure voltage between generator connector terminal "A" (Yellow/White wire) and ground. If battery voltage is present, go to next step. If battery voltage is not available, repair Yellow/White wire. See WIRING DIAGRAMS. Check system operation.
4) Reconnect generator 3-pin connector. Start engine. Backprobe 3-pin connector terminal "I" (Light Green/Red wire) with voltmeter positive probe. Connect voltmeter negative probe to ground. If voltage is greater than one volt, replace generator. See GENERATOR under REMOVAL & INSTALLATION. If voltage is one volt or less, repair Light Green/Red wire between generator and instrument cluster. See WIRING DIAGRAMS.

TEST B

1) Disconnect generator 3-pin connector. Inspect connector for loose, damaged or corroded terminals. Repair as necessary and check system operation. If connector is okay, go to next step.
2) Ensure battery ground connections are clean and tight. Ensure generator mounting surfaces are clean and fasteners are tight. Clean and tighten as necessary and check system operation. If no problem is indicated, go to next step.
3) Reconnect generator 3-pin connector. Start engine. Backprobe 3-pin connector terminal "I" (Light Green/Red wire) with voltmeter positive probe. Connect voltmeter negative probe to ground. If voltage is greater than one volt, replace generator. See GENERATOR under REMOVAL &

1999 STARTING & CHARGING SYSTEMS

FORD
2-59

Generators – Continental, Crown Victoria, Explorer (4.0L SOHC & 5.0L), Grand Marquis, Mountaineer & Town Car (Cont.)

INSTALLATION. If voltage is one volt or less, repair Light Green/Red wire between generator and instrument cluster. See WIRING DIAGRAMS.

TEST C

1) Disconnect generator 3-pin connector. Inspect connector for loose, damaged or corroded terminals. Ensure generator connector is connected properly. If connector is not okay, repair as necessary and check system operation. If connector is okay, go to next step.
2) With engine running at 2000 RPM, measure voltage between generator terminal B+ (Black/Orange wire) and ground. If voltage is less than 15.5 volts, go to next step. If voltage is 15.5 volts or greater, go to TEST H.
3) Turn ignition off. Disconnect generator 3-pin connector. Start engine and observe charge warning indicator. If indicator does not illuminate, go to TEST D. If indicator illuminates, repair short to ground in Light Green/Red wire and check system operation. See WIRING DIAGRAMS.

TEST D

Disconnect generator 3-pin connector. Jumper connector terminal "I" (Light Green/Red wire) to ground. With ignition on, engine off, observe charge warning indicator. If indicator illuminates, replace generator. See GENERATOR under REMOVAL & INSTALLATION. If indicator does not illuminate, repair open in Light Green/Red wire and check system operation. See WIRING DIAGRAMS.

TEST E

1) With ignition on, engine off, measure voltage between generator terminal B+ (Black/Orange wire) and ground. If battery voltage is present, go to next step. If battery voltage is not present, repair Black/Orange wire and check system operation. See WIRING DIAGRAMS.
2) Disconnect generator 3-pin connector and inspect for damaged, loose or corroded terminals. Repair connector as necessary. If connector is okay, perform GENERATOR LOAD TEST and GENERATOR NO-LOAD TEST under ON-VEHICLE TESTING. Replace as necessary and check system operation.

TEST G

1) With ignition on, engine off, inspect appropriate fuses and/or fusible links. See FUSE IDENTIFICATION table. Replace as necessary. If okay, go to next step.
2) Turn ignition off. Measure voltage between generator test point "F" and ground. *See Fig. 1.* If battery voltage is present, go to next step. If battery voltage is not present, replace generator. See GENERATOR under REMOVAL & INSTALLATION. Check system operation.

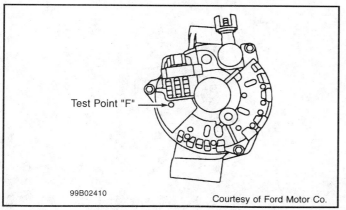

Test Point "F"

99B02410

Courtesy of Ford Motor Co.

Fig. 1: Identifying Generator Test terminal "F"

3) Start engine and run at 2000 RPM. Measure battery voltage and observe charge warning indicator. If battery voltage increases to greater

than 15.5 volts or indicator flickers, replace generator. See GENERATOR under REMOVAL & INSTALLATION. Check system operation. If battery voltage is 15.5 volts or less and indicator does not flicker, repair Yellow/White wire and check system operation. See WIRING DIAGRAMS.

TEST H

1) With ignition on, engine off, measure voltage drop by connecting voltmeter positive probe to generator 3-pin connector terminal "A" (Yellow/White wire) and negative voltmeter probe to battery positive terminal. If voltage is less than .5 volt, go to next step. If voltage is .5 volts or greater, repair Yellow/White wire and check system operation. See WIRING DIAGRAMS.
2) Start engine. Turn off all accessories. Measure battery voltage while increasing engine speed. If battery voltage increases to greater than 15 volts, replace generator. See GENERATOR under REMOVAL & INSTALLATION. Check system operation. If battery voltage is 15 volts or less, go to next step.
3) Turn ignition off. Measure voltage between generator test point "F" and ground. *See Fig. 1.* If battery voltage is present, go to next step. If battery voltage is not present, replace generator. See GENERATOR under REMOVAL & INSTALLATION. Check system operation.
4) Run engine at 2000 RPM. Measure battery voltage and observe charge warning indicator. If battery voltage increases to greater than 15.5 volts or indicator flickers, repair Yellow/White wire or Light Green/Red wire as necessary and check system operation. See WIRING DIAGRAMS. If battery voltage is 15.5 volts or less and indicator does not flicker, replace generator. See GENERATOR under REMOVAL & INSTALLATION. Check system operation.

REMOVAL & INSTALLATION

CAUTION: When battery is are disconnected, vehicle computer and memory systems may lose memory data. Driveability problems may exist until computer systems have completed a relearn cycle. See COMPUTER RELEARN PROCEDURES article in GENERAL INFORMATION before disconnecting battery.

GENERATOR

Removal & Installation (Continental) – 1) Disconnect negative battery cable. Drain radiator until coolant has drained from coolant overflow bottle. Disconnect overflow hose at bottle. Remove 2 top power steering reservoir bolts and position reservoir out of the way. Disconnect coolant level sensor and bottom hose from coolant overflow bottle. Remove retaining nut and bolt and remove bottle.
2) Remove drive belt. Remove 4 fasteners from top generator bracket and remove bracket. Remove attachment bolts and remove generator from vehicle. To install reverse removal procedure. Fill radiator and overflow bottle. Bleed air from cooling system. Tighten fasteners to specification. See TORQUE SPECIFICATIONS.
Removal & Installation (Crown Victoria, Grand Marquis & Town Car) – Disconnect negative battery cable. Remove rear engine cover screw. Pull cover forward to disengage front clips, and remove cover. Disengage push pins and pull harness away from top of generator. Remove 4 bolts and upper generator bracket. Disconnect wiring from generator. Remove drive belt. Remove attachment bolts and remove generator from vehicle. To install reverse removal procedure. Tighten fasteners to specification. See TORQUE SPECIFICATIONS.
Removal & Installation (Explorer & Mountaineer) – Disconnect negative battery cable. Remove air cleaner inlet tube. Remove drive belt. Disconnect wiring from generator. On 5.0L, remove A/C manifold bracket nut and position A/C manifold to one side. On all models, disconnect wiring harness retaining pin from generator. Remove 3 attachment bolts and remove generator from vehicle. To install reverse removal procedure. Tighten fasteners to specification. See TORQUE SPECIFICATIONS.

FORD
2-60

1999 STARTING & CHARGING SYSTEMS
Generators – Continental, Crown Victoria, Explorer (4.0L SOHC & 5.0L), Grand Marquis, Mountaineer & Town Car (Cont.)

TORQUE SPECIFICATIONS

TORQUE SPECIFICATIONS (ALL EXCEPT EXPLORER & MOUNTAINEER)

Application	Ft. Lbs. (N.m)
Generator Mounting Bolts	15-22 (20-30)
	INCH Lbs. (N.m)
Generator Support Bracket	71-106 (8-12)
Generator Terminal B+ Nut	62-79 (7-9)

TORQUE SPECIFICATIONS (EXPLORER & MOUNTAINEER)

Application	Ft. Lbs. (N.m)
A/C Manifold Bracket Nut	11-16 (15-22)
Generator Mounting Bolts	30-40 (40-55)
	INCH Lbs. (N.m)
Generator Terminal B+ Nut	80-106 (9-12)

WIRING DIAGRAMS

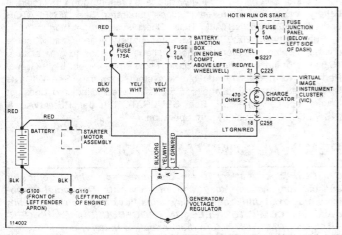

Fig. 2: Charging System Wiring Diagram (Continental)

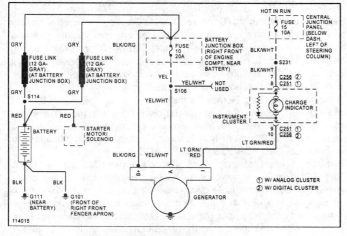

Fig. 3: Charging System Wiring Diagram (Crown Victoria & Grand Marquis)

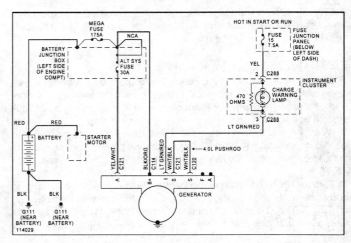

Fig. 4: Charging System Wiring Diagram (Explorer & Mountaineer)

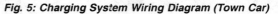
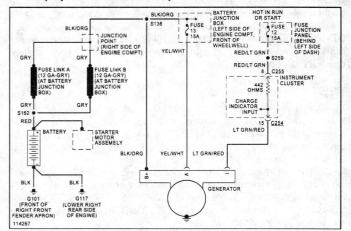

Fig. 5: Charging System Wiring Diagram (Town Car)

DESCRIPTION

System consists of generator, integral voltage regulator, battery, charge warning indicator and related fuses and wiring. Charge warning indicator illuminates with ignition on, engine off as a bulb-check.

ADJUSTMENTS

BELT TENSION

Vehicles are equipped with automatic drive belt tensioner. Drive belt does not require adjustment. Inspect condition and tension of generator drive belt prior to performing any on-vehicle charging system tests. Replace belt and/or repair tensioner mechanism if necessary.

TROUBLE SHOOTING

NOTE: See TROUBLE SHOOTING article in GENERAL INFORMATION.

PRELIMINARY CHECKS

- Verify battery condition.
- Inspect accessory drive belt and tensioner.
- Inspect battery junction box fuse No. 5 (15-amp).
- Inspect central junction box fuse No. 30 (7.5-amp).
- Inspect 175-amp fuse on starter motor.
- Check all connections for looseness or corrosion.

ON-VEHICLE TESTING

GENERATOR LOAD TEST

Ensure drive belt is in good condition and properly tightened. Turn on headlights for 15 seconds to remove surface charge. Turn off headlights. Measure battery voltage and record. Start and run engine at 2000 RPM. Turn on high beams and turn blower to high position. Turn on air conditioning, if equipped. Run engine at 2000 RPM and observe voltmeter. Voltage should increase at least .5 volt over recorded value.

GENERATOR NO-LOAD TEST

Connect voltmeter positive lead to B+ terminal on generator and negative lead to ground. Turn on headlights for 15 seconds to remove surface charge. Turn off headlights. Measure battery voltage and record. Start and run engine at 1500 RPM with no electrical load (all accessories off). Read voltmeter when voltage stabilizes. Voltage should be 14.1-14.7 volts.

SYSTEM TESTS

INTRODUCTION

Identify symptom and perform appropriate system test. See SYSTEM TEST INDEX table.

SYSTEM TEST INDEX

Condition	Test
System Does Not Charge	A
System Overcharges	B
Charge Warning Indicator Stays On	C
Charge Warning Indicator Inoperative	D
Charge System Indicator Flickers Or Operates Intermittently	E

TEST A

1) Turn ignition off. Measure ground circuit voltage drop by touching negative voltmeter probe to battery negative terminal, and voltmeter positive probe to generator case. If voltmeter reads less than .25 volt, go to next step. If voltmeter reads .25 volt or greater, clean or repair ground connections or generator mounting surfaces. Check system operation.

2) Measure voltage between battery terminal B+ (Black wire) and ground. If battery voltage is present, go to next step. If battery voltage is not present, repair circuit between battery and generator. See WIRING DIAGRAMS.

3) Measure voltage between generator terminal "A" screw and ground. See Fig. 1. If battery voltage is present, go to next step. If battery voltage is not present, repair circuit between battery and generator. See WIRING DIAGRAMS. Check system operation.

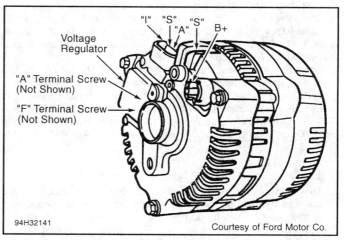

94H32141
Courtesy of Ford Motor Co.

Fig. 1: Identifying Generator Terminals (Typical)

4) Measure voltage drop by connecting voltmeter positive probe to generator terminal "A" screw, and voltmeter negative probe to battery positive terminal. See Fig. 1. If voltmeter reads less than .25 volt, go to next step. If voltmeter reads .25 volt or less, repair high resistance in circuit between battery and generator. See WIRING DIAGRAMS. Check system operation.

5) Turn ignition switch to RUN position. Measure voltage between generator test terminal "F" screw and ground. See Fig. 1. If battery voltage is present, go to next step. if battery voltage is not present, replace generator. See GENERATOR under REMOVAL & INSTALLATION.

6) Measure voltage between generator connector terminal (Green/Black wire) and ground by backprobing connector. Connector must not be disconnected for measurement. If voltage is greater than one volt, go to next step. If voltage is one volt or less, repair circuit between generator and instrument cluster. See WIRING DIAGRAMS. Check system operation.

7) Start engine. Measure voltage between generator terminal "F" screw and ground. If voltage is less than 2 volts, go to next step. If voltage is 2 volts or greater, replace generator. See GENERATOR under REMOVAL & INSTALLATION.

8) Turn headlights on and place blower in high position. With engine running at 2000 RPM, measure voltage drop in B+ circuit by connecting voltmeter positive probe to generator terminal B+ (Black wire), and voltmeter negative probe to battery positive terminal. If voltmeter reads less than .5 volt, go to next step. If voltmeter reads .5 volt or more, repair circuit between battery and generator. See WIRING DIAGRAMS. Check system operation.

9) With all accessories off, run engine at 1500 RPM and record battery voltage. Connect jumper wire between generator terminal "F"screw and battery negative terminal. Run engine at 1500 RPM and compare voltmeter reading with recorded voltage. If voltage is at least .5 volt greater than recorded voltage, replace voltage regulator. See VOLTAGE REGULATOR under REMOVAL & INSTALLATION. If voltage is within .5 volt of recorded voltage, replace generator. See GENERATOR under REMOVAL & INSTALLATION. Check system operation.

TEST B

With ignition in RUN position, measure voltage between generator terminal "F" screw and ground. See Fig. 1. If battery voltage is present, replace voltage regulator. See VOLTAGE REGULATOR under

REMOVAL & INSTALLATION. If battery voltage is not present, repair circuit (Black wire) between battery and generator. See WIRING DIAGRAMS. Check system operation.

TEST C

1) Measure voltage between generator terminal "A" screw and ground. *See Fig. 1.* If battery voltage is present, go to next step. If battery voltage is not present, repair circuit (Black wire) between battery and generator. See WIRING DIAGRAMS. Check system operation.

2) Disconnect generator 3-pin connector. Observe charge warning indicator with ignition in RUN and OFF positions. If indicator is illuminated in either position, go to next step. If indicator is not illuminated in either position, go to TEST A.

3) Disconnect instrument cluster 16-pin connector. Measure resistance between generator 3-pin connector terminal (Green/Black wire) and ground. If resistance is greater than 10 k/ohms, replace instrument cluster. See appropriate INSTRUMENT PANEL article in ACCESSORIES & EQUIPMENT. If resistance is 10 k/ohms or less, repair short in Green/Black wire and check system operation. See WIRING DIAGRAMS.

TEST D

1) Turn ignition off. Disconnect generator 3-pin connector. Connect jumper wire between generator 3-pin connector terminal (Black/Green wire) and ground. Turn ignition switch to RUN position and observe charge warning indicator. If indicator illuminates, go to next step. If indicator does not illuminate, go to step **4)**.

2) Turn ignition off. Measure resistance between generator case and ground. If resistance is less than 5 ohms, go to next step. If resistance is 5 ohms or greater, clean and repair ground connections or generator mounting as necessary. Check system operation.

3) On 2.5L, disconnect generator 1-pin connector (Gray wire). Measure voltage between generator terminal and ground. On 2.0L, disconnect generator 3-pin connector. Measure voltage between middle generator terminal (no wire in corresponding connector terminal) and ground. If voltage is greater than one volt, replace generator. See GENERATOR under REMOVAL & INSTALLATION. Check system operation. If voltage is one volt or less, replace voltage regulator. See VOLTAGE REGULATOR under REMOVAL & INSTALLATION. Check system operation.

4) Turn ignition off. Disconnect instrument cluster 16-pin connector. Measure resistance of Green/Black wire between generator 3-pin connector and instrument cluster 16-pin connector. If resistance is less than 5 ohms, replace instrument cluster. See appropriate INSTRUMENT PANEL article in ACCESSORIES & EQUIPMENT. If resistance is 5 ohms or greater, repair open in Green/Black wire and check system operation.

TEST E

1) Turn ignition off. Measure voltage between generator terminal "F" screw and ground. *See Fig. 1.* If battery voltage is present, go to next step. If battery voltage is not present, go to step **3)**.

2) Start engine. Connect jumper wire between generator terminal "A" screw and battery positive terminal. *See Fig. 1.* Observe charge warning indicator. If indicator flickers, replace voltage regulator. See VOLTAGE REGULATOR under REMOVAL & INSTALLATION. Check system operation. If indicator does not flicker, repair Black wire or connections between generator and battery. See WIRING DIAGRAMS. Check system operation.

3) Remove generator. See GENERATOR under REMOVAL & INSTALLATION. Check brush holder screws (generator terminals "A" and "F"). *See Fig. 1.* Clean and tighten screws as necessary. If screws are okay, go to next step.

4) Remove voltage regulator. See VOLTAGE REGULATOR under REMOVAL & INSTALLATION. Measure resistance between each generator slip ring and ground. *See Fig. 2.* If resistance is 200 ohms or greater, replace voltage regulator. If resistance is less than 200 ohms, clean accumulated grease or dirt from around slip rings and recheck resistance. If resistance is still less than 200 ohms, replace generator.

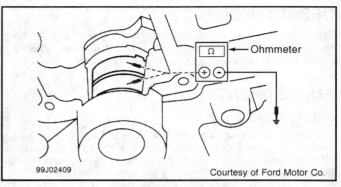

99J02409   Courtesy of Ford Motor Co.

Fig. 2: Checking For Grounded Generator Slip Ring

REMOVAL & INSTALLATION

CAUTION: When batteries are disconnected, vehicle computer and memory systems may lose memory data. Driveability problems may exist until computer systems have completed a relearn cycle. See COMPUTER RELEARN PROCEDURES article in GENERAL INFORMATION before disconnecting battery.

GENERATOR

Removal & Installation (2.0L) – 1) Disconnect negative battery cable. Remove 4 intake air resonator bolts and clamp. Raise resonator and disconnect vacuum line. Remove resonator. Disconnect wiring from generator. Disconnect ground strap from engine lift bracket, near fuel pressure regulator. Raise and support vehicle. Remove radiator splash shield. Remove right front wheel.

2) Remove right wheel housing splash shield. Remove accessory drive belt. Remove lower generator bolts and lower vehicle. Remove upper generator bolt and remove generator. To install, reverse removal procedure. Tighten fasteners to specification. See TORQUE SPECIFICATIONS.

Removal & Installation (2.5L) – 1) Disconnect negative battery cable. Raise and support vehicle. Remove radiator splash shield. Remove right front wheel. Remove right wheel housing splash shield. Remove accessory drive belt. Remove right outer tie rod end cotter pin and loosen nut. Using suitable tie rod end separator, separate tie rod end from steering knuckle.

2) Remove nut and lift tie rod end from steering knuckle. Disconnect wiring from generator. Remove generator rear support bracket bolt from generator. Remove upper generator bolt, then lower generator bolt. Remove generator through wheel housing. To install, reverse removal procedure. Use new cotter pin on outer tie rod end. Tighten fasteners to specification. See TORQUE SPECIFICATIONS.

VOLTAGE REGULATOR

Removal & Installation – Remove generator. See GENERATOR. Remove 4 regulator retaining screws. Remove regulator. To install, reverse removal procedures. New regulators are supplied with retaining pin to hold brushes during installation. After installation, remove retaining pin.

TORQUE SPECIFICATIONS
TORQUE SPECIFICATIONS

Application	Ft. Lbs. (N.m)
Generator Mounting Bolts	33 (45)
Generator Rear Bracket Bolt	18 (25)
Tie Rod End Nut	21 (28)
Wheel Nut	94 (128)

Generators – Contour & Mystique (Cont.)

WIRING DIAGRAMS

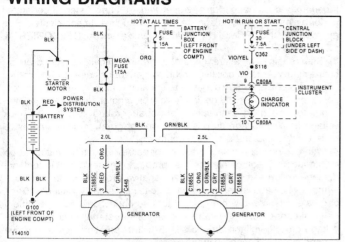

Fig. 3: Charging System Wiring Diagram (Contour & Mystique)

DESCRIPTION

System consists of generator, integral voltage regulator, battery, charge warning indicator and related fuses and wiring. Charge warning indicator illuminates with ignition on, engine off as a bulb-check.

ADJUSTMENTS

BELT TENSION

Vehicles are equipped with automatic drive belt tensioner. Drive belt do not require adjustment. Inspect condition and tension of generator drive belt prior to performing any on-vehicle charging system tests. Replace belt and/or repair tensioner mechanism if necessary.

TROUBLE SHOOTING

NOTE: *See TROUBLE SHOOTING article in GENERAL INFORMATION.*

PRELIMINARY CHECKS

- Verify battery condition.
- Inspect accessory drive belt and tensioner.
- Inspect battery junction box fuse No. 7 (30-amp).
- Inspect central junction box fuse No. 30 (7.5-amp).
- Inspect 175-amp fuse on starter motor.
- Check all connections for looseness or corrosion.

ON-VEHICLE TESTING

GENERATOR LOAD TEST

Ensure drive belt is in good condition. Replace belt as necessary. If belt is okay. turn on headlights for 30 seconds to remove surface charge. Turn off headlights. Measure battery voltage and record. Start and run engine at 2000 RPM. Turn on high beams and turn blower to high position. Turn on air conditioning, if equipped. Run engine at 2000 RPM and observe voltmeter. Voltage should increase at least .5 volt over recorded value.

GENERATOR NO-LOAD TEST

Connect voltmeter positive lead to B+ terminal on generator and negative lead to ground. Turn on headlights for 30 seconds to remove surface charge. Turn off headlights. Measure battery voltage and record. Start and run engine at 1500 RPM with no electrical load (all accessories off). Read voltmeter when voltage stabilizes. Voltage should be at least 2.5 volts higher than recorded reading.

SYSTEM TESTS

INTRODUCTION

Identify symptom and perform appropriate system test. See SYSTEM TEST INDEX table.

SYSTEM TEST INDEX

Symptom	Test
Charge Warning Indicator On, Flickers Or Is Intermittent With Engine Running	A
System Overcharges	1

1 – Replace generator and check system operation. See GENERATOR under REMOVAL & INSTALLATION.

TEST A

1) Connect battery load tester according to manufacturer's instructions. Load battery at approximately one-half battery cold-cranking amperage rating for fifteen seconds. If battery voltage remains greater than 9.6 volts, go to next step. If battery voltage drops to less than 9.6 volts, charge battery and retest. If recharged battery tests okay, go to next step. If voltage still drops to less than 9.6 volts, replace battery and check system operation.

2) Perform GENERATOR LOAD TEST under ON-VEHICLE TESTING. If generator does not perform as specified, go to next step. If generator performs as specified, diagnose problem in instrument cluster. See appropriate INSTRUMENT PANELS article in ACCESSORIES & EQUIPMENT.

3) Start engine. Measure generator ground circuit voltage drop by connecting voltmeter positive probe to generator case and voltmeter negative probe to battery negative terminal. If voltage is less than .5 volt, go to next step. If voltage is .5 volt or greater, clean and tighten generator mounting, and clean or repair ground cables. Recheck voltage drop. If voltage drop is still .5 volt or greater, replace negative battery cable and check system operation.

4) With engine still running, measure generator B+ circuit voltage drop by connecting voltmeter positive probe to generator B+ terminal (Orange/Yellow wire) and voltmeter negative probe to battery positive terminal. If voltage is less than .5 volt, go to next step. If voltage is .5 volt or greater, clean and tighten generator B+ connections, positive battery terminal connections and cable connections at starter motor. Recheck voltage drop. If voltage drop is still .5 volt or greater, replace positive battery cable and check system operation.

5) Measure voltage between generator terminal B+ (Orange/Yellow wire) and ground. If battery voltage is present, go to next step. If battery voltage is not present, inspect 175-amp fuse at starter motor. Replace as necessary. If fuse is okay, repair circuit between battery, starter motor and generator. See WIRING DIAGRAMS.

6) Disconnect generator 3-pin connector. Measure voltage between generator 3-pin connector terminal No. 3 (Red wire) and ground. If voltage is 10 volts or less, inspect fuse No. 7 in battery junction box and replace as necessary. If fuse is okay, repair circuit. See WIRING DIAGRAMS. On 2.5L, if voltage is greater than 10 volts, go to next step. On 2.0L, if voltage is greater than 10 volts, replace generator and check system operation. See GENERATOR under REMOVAL & INSTALLATION.

7) Disconnect generator 1-pin connector (Gray wire). Measure resistance of Gray wire between generator 3-pin connector terminal No. 2 and generator 1-pin connector terminal. If resistance is less than 5 ohms, replace generator. See GENERATOR under REMOVAL & INSTALLATION. If resistance is 5 ohms or greater, repair open in Gray wire. See WIRING DIAGRAMS.

REMOVAL & INSTALLATION

CAUTION: *When batteries are disconnected, vehicle computer and memory systems may lose memory data. Driveability problems may exist until computer systems have completed a relearn cycle. See COMPUTER RELEARN PROCEDURES article in GENERAL INFORMATION before disconnecting battery.*

GENERATOR

Removal & Installation (2.0L) – **1)** Disconnect negative battery cable. Remove 4 intake air resonator bolts and clamp. Raise resonator and disconnect vacuum line. Remove resonator. Detach coolant hose from retaining clip and position to one side. Disconnect wiring from generator. Disconnect ground strap from engine lift bracket, near fuel pressure regulator. Raise and support vehicle.

2) Remove right front wheel. Remove right wheel housing splash shield. Remove accessory drive belt. Remove lower generator bolts and lower vehicle. Remove upper generator bolt. Remove generator from top, taking care not to overstress hoses and cables. To install, reverse removal procedure. Tighten fasteners to specification. See TORQUE SPECIFICATIONS.

Removal & Installation (2.5L) – **1)** Disconnect negative battery cable. Raise and support vehicle. Remove radiator splash shield. Remove right front wheel. Remove right wheel housing splash shield. Remove accessory drive belt. Loosen right outer tie rod end nut. Using suitable tie rod end separator, separate tie rod end from steering knuckle. Remove nut and lift tie rod end from steering knuckle.

2) Disconnect wiring from generator. Remove generator rear support bracket bolt from generator. Remove upper generator bolt, then lower generator bolt. Remove generator through wheel housing. To install, reverse removal procedures. Tighten fasteners to specification. See TORQUE SPECIFICATIONS.

VOLTAGE REGULATOR

Removal & Installation – Remove generator. See GENERATOR. Remove 4 regulator retaining screws. Remove regulator. To install, reverse removal procedures. New regulators are supplied with retaining pin to hold brushes during installation. After installation, remove retaining pin.

TORQUE SPECIFICATIONS

TORQUE SPECIFICATIONS

Application	Ft. Lbs. (N.m)
Generator Mounting Bolts	33 (45)
Generator Rear Bracket Bolt	18 (25)
Tie Rod End Nut	21 (28)
Wheel Nut	94 (128)

WIRING DIAGRAMS

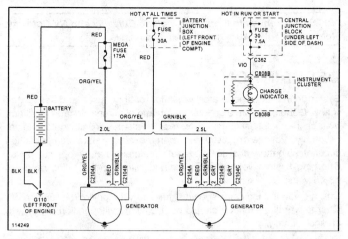

Fig. 1: Charging System Wiring Diagram (Cougar)

1999 STARTING & CHARGING SYSTEMS
Generators – Econoline, Expedition, Explorer (4.0L OHV), Navigator, Pickups (Gasoline) & Ranger

NOTE: References to Econoline include Cutaway and RV Cutaway. References to Pickup include Cab & Chassis.

NOTE: Testing information is not available for Econoline models with Mitsubishi 215-amp generators, or dual Motorcraft 110-amp generators.

DESCRIPTION

System consists of generator, regulator, battery, fuses and associated wiring. Generators have an internal fan and electronic voltage regulator. Voltage regulator is fastened to rear of alternator with brush holder assembly. Voltage regulator incorporates temperature compensation circuitry, so battery charging voltage is maintained at the optimum level. Charging system voltage is maintained within an operating range of 13-15 volts.

Charge warning indicator should illuminate with ignition on, engine off. Charge warning indicator should not illuminate with ignition off, or with engine running.

ADJUSTMENTS

BELT TENSION

Vehicles are equipped with automatic drive belt tensioner. Drive belt does not require adjustment. Inspect condition and tension of generator drive belt prior to performing any on-vehicle charging system tests. Replace belt and/or repair tensioner mechanism if necessary.

TROUBLE SHOOTING

NOTE: See TROUBLE SHOOTING article in GENERAL INFORMATION.

PRELIMINARY INSPECTION

Ensure battery posts and cables are clean and tight. Inspect drive belt. Ensure connections at generator, regulator and engine ground are clean and tight. Check fuses or fusible links and replace as necessary.

Turn ignition on and ensure charge warning light operates. Check bulb and circuit, if necessary. Start engine and verify charge warning light goes out.

SYSTEM TESTS

CAUTION: When battery is disconnected, vehicle computer and memory systems may lose memory data. Driveability problems may exist until computer systems have completed a relearn cycle. See COMPUTER RELEARN PROCEDURES article in GENERAL INFORMATION before disconnecting battery.

INTRODUCTION

Identify symptom and perform appropriate system test. See SYSTEM TEST INDEX table.

SYSTEM TEST INDEX

Symptom	Test
Warning Indicator Is ON With Engine Running, System Is Not Charging	A
Warning Indicator Is OFF With Ignition On, System Is Not Charging	B
Warning Indicator Is ON With Engine Running, System Is Charging	C
Warning Indicator Is OFF With Engine Running, System Is Charging	D
Warning Indicator Operates Properly, System Is Not Charging	E
Warning Indicator Flickers Or Operates Intermittently	F
System Overcharges	G

TEST A

1) Check appropriate generator fuse. See CHARGING SYSTEM FUSE APPLICATION table. Replace fuse as necessary. If fuse is okay, go to next step.

CHARGING SYSTEM FUSE APPLICATION

Application	Fuse
Econoline	Starter Relay Fuse Links A, B & C
Expedition & Navigator	Battery Junction Box Fuse No. 11 (20-Amp)
Explorer, Mountaineer & Ranger	Battery Junction Box 175-Amp Mega Fuse & ALTSYS (30-Amp)
Pickup	
F150 & F250 Light-Duty Pickups	Battery Junction Box Fuse No. 11 (20-Amp)
F250 Super-Duty & F350 Pickups	Starter Relay Fuse Links B & C

2) Measure voltage between generator terminal B+ Black/Orange wire (Yellow/White wire on F250 Super-Duty and F350 Pickups) and ground. See Fig. 1. If battery voltage is present, go to next step. If battery voltage is not present, repair Black/Orange wire or Yellow/White wire between generator and appropriate fuse. See WIRING DIAGRAMS.

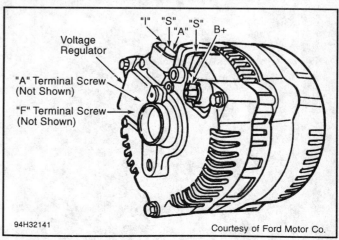

94H32141

Courtesy of Ford Motor Co.

Fig. 1: Identifying Generator Terminals

1999 STARTING & CHARGING SYSTEMS

FORD 2-67

Generators – Econoline, Expedition, Explorer (4.0L OHV), Navigator, Pickups (Gasoline) & Ranger (Cont.)

3) Disconnect generator 3-pin electrical connector. Measure voltage between generator connector terminal "A" and ground. *See Fig. 2.* If battery voltage is present, go to next step. If battery voltage is not present, repair wire between battery junction box and generator connector. See WIRING DIAGRAMS.

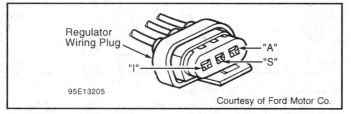

95E13205   Courtesy of Ford Motor Co.

Fig. 2: Identifying Generator 3-Pin Connector Terminals

4) Reconnect generator 3-pin connector. Turn ignition on. Measure voltage between connector terminal "I" (Light Green/Red wire) and ground by backprobing generator connector. *See Fig. 2.* If voltage is greater than one volt, go to next step. If voltage is not greater than one volt, repair Light Green/Red wire between generator connector and instrument cluster. See WIRING DIAGRAMS.

5) Start engine. Connect jumper wire between generator terminal "F" screw and ground. *See Fig. 3.* Charging system warning indicator should turn off, and battery voltage should increase. If system reacts as specified, replace voltage regulator. See VOLTAGE REGULATOR under REMOVAL & INSTALLATION. If system does not react as specified, replace generator. See GENERATOR under REMOVAL & INSTALLATION.

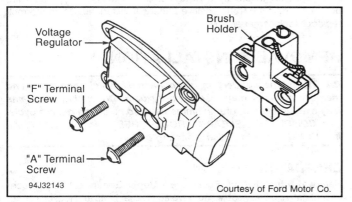

94J32143   Courtesy of Ford Motor Co.

Fig. 3: Exploded View Of Voltage Regulator & Brush Holder

TEST B

1) Disconnect generator 3-pin electrical connector. Check for bent or damaged pins. Repair as necessary and check system operation. If connector is okay, go to next step.

2) Check generator and regulator grounds (mounting surfaces and fasteners). Check battery ground. Repair as necessary and check system operation. If all grounds are okay, go to next step.

3) Reconnect generator 3-pin connector. Turn ignition on. Measure voltage between generator connector terminal "I" (Light Green/Red wire) and ground by backprobing generator connector. *See Fig. 2.* If voltage is greater than one volt, replace voltage regulator. See VOLTAGE REGULATOR under REMOVAL & INSTALLATION. If voltage is not greater than one volt, repair Light Green/Red wire between generator connector and instrument cluster. See WIRING DIAGRAMS.

TEST C

1) Ensure good connection at generator 3-pin electrical connector. Repair as necessary and check system operation. If connection is okay, go to next step.

2) With engine at 2000 RPM, measure voltage between generator terminal B+, Black/Orange wire (Yellow/White wire on F250 Super-Duty

and F350 Pickups) and ground. *See Fig. 1.* If voltage is less than 16 volts, go to next step. If voltage is 16 volts or more, go to TEST G.

3) With engine running at 2000 RPM, measure voltage between generator 1-pin connector terminal "S" (White/Black wire) and ground. *See Fig. 1.* If voltage is 5 volts or greater, go to next step. If voltage is less than 5 volts, replace voltage regulator. See VOLTAGE REGULATOR under REMOVAL & INSTALLATION.

4) Turn ignition off. Disconnect generator 1-pin connector terminal "S" (White/Black wire). *See Fig. 1.* Start vehicle. With engine running, measure voltage between generator terminal "S" and ground. If voltage is 5 volts or greater, repair White/Black wire between generator 1-pin connector and generator 3-pin connector. See WIRING DIAGRAMS. If voltage is less than 5 volts, replace generator. See GENERATOR under REMOVAL & INSTALLATION.

TEST D

1) Turn ignition on. Disconnect generator 3-pin connector. Connect a jumper wire between generator connector terminal "I" (Light Green/Red wire) and ground. *See Fig. 2.* If charge indicator warning light is on, restore connection and go to next step. If charge indicator warning light is not on, repair Light Green/Red wire or connector. See WIRING DIAGRAMS.

2) Turn ignition on. Disconnect generator 1-pin connector (White/Black wire). If charge indicator warning light is on, replace generator. See GENERATOR under REMOVAL & INSTALLATION. If charge indicator warning light is not on, replace voltage regulator. See VOLTAGE REGULATOR under REMOVAL & INSTALLATION.

TEST E

1) With ignition on and engine off, measure voltage between generator terminal B+, Black/Orange wire (Yellow/White wire on F250 Super-Duty and F350 Pickups) and ground. *See Fig. 1.* If battery voltage is present, go to next step. If battery voltage is not present, repair Black/Orange wire or Yellow/White wire. See WIRING DIAGRAMS.

2) Inspect generator for clean and tight connections. Repair or service connections as necessary. If connections are okay, test generator. See AMPERAGE OUTPUT TEST and VOLTAGE OUTPUT TEST under ON-VEHICLE TESTING.

TEST F

1) Inspect appropriate fuses. See CHARGING SYSTEM FUSE APPLICATION table. Replace as necessary. If fuses are okay, go to next step.

2) Measure voltage between generator terminal "F" screw and ground. *See Fig. 3.* If battery voltage is not present, go to next step . If battery voltage is present, go to step **4)**.

3) Disconnect generator 3-pin and 1-pin connectors. Remove voltage regulator and brush holder. See VOLTAGE REGULATOR under REMOVAL & INSTALLATION. Measure resistance between each generator slip ring and ground. *See Fig. 4.* If resistance is greater than 1000 ohms between both slip rings and ground, replace voltage regulator. If resistance between one or both slip rings and ground is less than 1000 ohms, replace generator. See GENERATOR under REMOVAL & INSTALLATION.

4) Start engine. Measure voltage between generator terminal B+ and ground. Increase engine speed while observing charge indicator light and voltmeter. If voltage is greater than 15 volts or indicator flickers, repair generator circuits "A" or "I". See WIRING DIAGRAMS. If voltage is 15 volts or less and indicator does not flicker, replace generator. See GENERATOR under REMOVAL & INSTALLATION.

TEST G

1) Turn ignition switch to RUN position and measure voltage drop in voltage sensing circuit "A" by connecting voltmeter positive lead to battery positive terminal. Connect voltmeter negative lead to generator terminal "A" screw. *See Fig. 3.* If voltage is less than .5 volt, go to next step. If voltage is .5 volt or greater, voltage drop is excessive. Repair circuit "A" and check system operation. See WIRING DIAGRAMS.

1999 STARTING & CHARGING SYSTEMS
Generators – Econoline, Expedition, Explorer (4.0L OHV), Navigator, Pickups (Gasoline) & Ranger (Cont.)

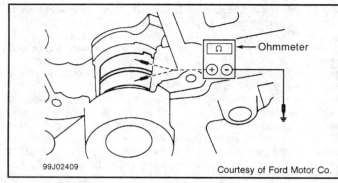

Fig. 4: Checking For Grounded Generator Slip Ring

2) Start engine and turn off all accessories. Increase engine speed while measuring voltage between battery terminals. If battery voltage stays at or less than 15 volts, go to next step. If battery voltage increases to greater than 15 volts, go to step 6).

3) Turn ignition off. Measure voltage between generator terminal "F" screw and ground. See Fig. 3. If battery voltage is present, go to step 5). If battery voltage is not present, go to next step.

4) Disconnect generator 3-pin and 1-pin connectors. Remove voltage regulator and brush holder. See VOLTAGE REGULATOR under REMOVAL & INSTALLATION. Measure resistance between each generator slip ring and ground. See Fig. 4. If resistance is greater than 1000 ohms between both slip rings and ground, replace voltage regulator. If resistance between one or both slip rings and ground is less than 1000 ohms, replace generator. See GENERATOR under REMOVAL & INSTALLATION.

5) Start engine. Measure battery voltage and observe charge indicator while increasing engine speed. If battery voltage increases to greater than 15 volts, or indicator light flickers, repair "A" or "I" circuits from generator. See WIRING DIAGRAMS. If battery voltage is 15 volts or less and indicator light does not flicker, replace generator. See GENERATOR under REMOVAL & INSTALLATION.

6) Measure voltage between generator terminal "F" screw and ground while increasing engine speed. If voltage increases with engine speed, replace generator. See GENERATOR under REMOVAL & INSTALLATION. If voltage does not increase with engine speed, replace voltage regulator. See VOLTAGE REGULATOR under REMOVAL & INSTALLATION.

COMPONENT TESTING

NOTE: Testing information is not available for Econoline models with Mitsubishi 215-amp generators, or dual Motorcraft 110-amp generators.

AMPERAGE OUTPUT TEST

1) Ensure drive belt is in good condition. Replace belt as necessary. If belt is okay, connect charging system load tester in accordance with manufacturer's instructions. Start and run engine at 2000-3000 RPM and apply load until generator output levels off.

2) Record maximum generator output current. See GENERATOR AMPERAGE RATING SPECIFICATIONS table for output values. If generator output is 10-20 percent of rated amperage, generator output is okay. If generator does not produce rated output, go to VOLTAGE OUTPUT TEST.

GENERATOR OUTPUT SPECIFICATIONS

Application	Maximum Amperage Output Rating
Econoline & Pickup	95 (130-Amp Optional)
Expedition/Navigator	130
Explorer/Mountaineer	
35/90 Generator	45
45/110	60
58/120	65
Ranger	
Except 4.0L A/T	95
4.0L A/T	130

VOLTAGE OUTPUT TEST

1) Ensure battery is fully charged and all accessories are off. Turn ignition switch to RUN position with engine off. Battery voltage should be present at terminals B+ and "A" at generator connector. See Fig. 1. Approximately one volt should be present at generator terminal "I". If voltages are correct, go to next step. If voltages are not correct, go to step 3).

2) Start engine and run at 2000 RPM. With generator connected, check voltage at generator terminals B+, "A" and "I". At generator terminals B+ and "A", 14.1-14.7 volts should be present. At generator terminal "I", 13-14 volts should be present (engine running). If voltages are not as specified, go to next step. If voltages are as specified, go to step 4).

3) Check all fuses and fusible links. If fuses are okay, test B+, "A" and "I" circuits for open, short and excessive resistance. Repair as necessary. If circuits are okay, go to next step.

4) Perform voltage drop test on B+ circuit (between positive battery and terminal B+ on generator). If voltage drop is .5 volt or more, repair wire between terminal B+ and positive battery. If voltage is still not correct, repair or replace generator.

REMOVAL & INSTALLATION

CAUTION: When battery is disconnected, vehicle computer and memory systems may lose memory data. Driveability problems may exist until computer systems have completed a relearn cycle. See COMPUTER RELEARN PROCEDURES article in GENERAL INFORMATION before disconnecting battery.

GENERATOR

Removal & Installation (Econoline – Upper Generator) – 1) Disconnect negative battery cable. Remove air cleaner bolts and loosen clamp. Position air cleaner assembly to one side. Disconnect MAF electrical connector (except on dual generator models). On 4.6L, remove spark plug wire routing clips from generator. On all models, remove plenum-to-generator bracket bolts, if equipped.

2) Remove drive belt from generator pulley. Disconnect generator electrical connectors. Remove mounting bolts and generator from vehicle. To install, reverse removal procedure. Tighten fasteners to specification. See TORQUE SPECIFICATIONS.

Removal & Installation (Econoline – Optional Lower Generator) – Disconnect negative battery cable. Remove air cleaner bolts and loosen clamp. Position air cleaner assembly to one side. Disengage drive belt from generator pulley. Raise vehicle on hoist. Disconnect generator harness connector. Remove 3 mounting bolts and move generator to access generator B+ terminal. Disconnect B+ terminal and remove generator from vehicle. To install, reverse removal procedure. Tighten fasteners to specification. See TORQUE SPECIFICATIONS.

Removal & Installation (Explorer & Ranger) – Disconnect negative battery cable. On all except 2.5L, remove air cleaner tube. Remove drive belt from generator pulley. On 5.0L, position air conditioning manifold and tube bracket to one side. On all models, disconnect generator electrical connectors. Remove mounting bolts and generator from vehicle. To install, reverse removal procedure. Tighten fasteners to specification. See TORQUE SPECIFICATIONS.

1999 STARTING & CHARGING SYSTEMS
Generators – Econoline, Expedition, Explorer (4.0L OHV), Navigator, Pickups (Gasoline) & Ranger (Cont.)

FORD
2-69

Removal & Installation (Expedition, Navigator & Pickup) – Disconnect negative battery cable. On 5.4L DOHC, remove air cleaner tube, radiator shroud and cooling fan. On all models, remove drive belt from generator pulley. Remove rear generator bracket bolts, if equipped. Disconnect generator electrical connectors. Remove generator mounting bolts and remove generator from vehicle. To install, reverse removal procedure. Tighten fasteners to specification. See TORQUE SPECIFICATIONS.

VOLTAGE REGULATOR

Removal & Installation – 1) Remove generator. See GENERATOR. Remove 4 screws front regulator and remove regulator and brush holder assembly from generator. Remove 2 screws and separate regulator from brush holder. *See Fig. 3.*

2) To install, attach brush holder to regulator. Manually depress brushes, and install wire in hole to retain brushes during installation. Install regulator and brush assembly onto generator and remove retaining wire. Tighten fasteners to specification. See TORQUE SPECIFICATIONS. Install generator in vehicle.

TORQUE SPECIFICATIONS

TORQUE SPECIFICATIONS

Application	Ft. Lbs. (N.m)
Generator Mounting Bolts	
Econoline	
4.2L	30-40 (41-54)
Except 4.2L	16-21 (22-28)
Expedition, Explorer, Mountaineer & Navigator	16-21 (22-28)
Pickup	
4.2L	30-40 (41-54)
Except 4.2L	16-21 (22-28)
Ranger	30-40 (41-54)
	INCH Lbs. (N.m)
Brush Holder-To-Regulator Screws	25-35 (2.8-4)
Generator Rear Bracket Bolts (If Equipped)	80-106 (9-12)
Regulator Assembly Mounting Screw	20-30 (2.3-3.4)

WIRING DIAGRAMS

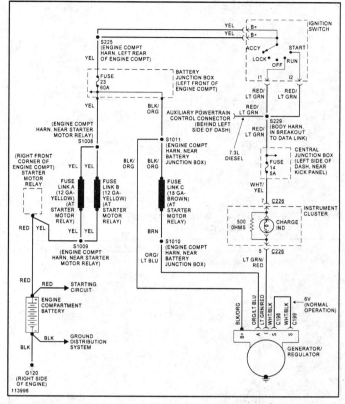

Fig. 5: Charging System Wiring Diagram (Econoline)

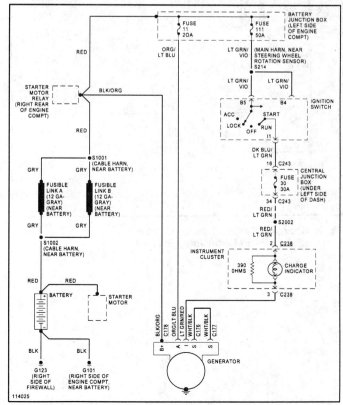

Fig. 6: Charging System Wiring Diagram (Expedition & Navigator)

1999 STARTING & CHARGING SYSTEMS
Generators – Econoline, Expedition, Explorer (4.0L OHV), Navigator, Pickups (Gasoline) & Ranger (Cont.)

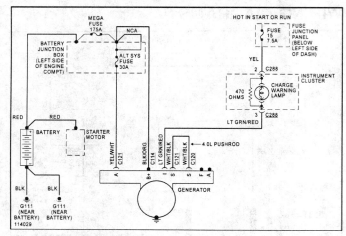

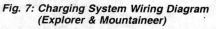

Fig. 7: Charging System Wiring Diagram (Explorer & Mountaineer)

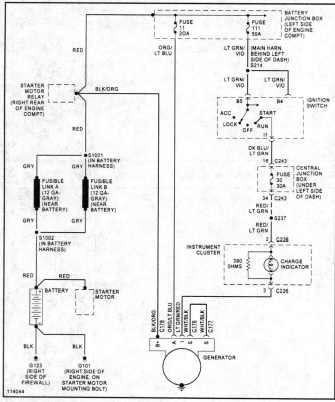

Fig. 8: Charging System Wiring Diagram (F150 & F250 Light-Duty Pickups)

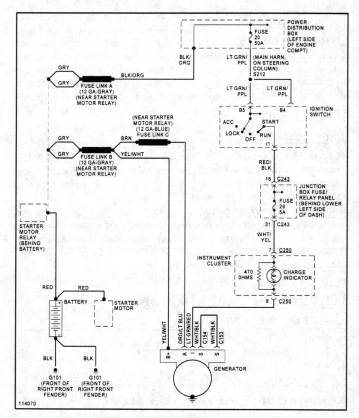

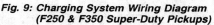

Fig. 9: Charging System Wiring Diagram (F250 & F350 Super-Duty Pickups)

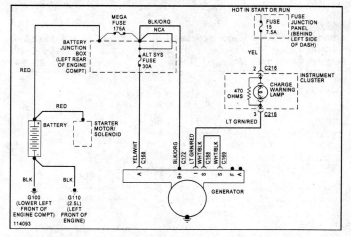

Fig. 10: Charging System Wiring Diagram (Ranger)

DESCRIPTION

System consists of generator , integral voltage regulator, battery, charge warning indicator and related fuses and wiring. Generator output is rated at 95-amps for Coupe models, and 75-amps for Sedan and Wagon models. Charge warning indicator illuminates with key on, engine off as a bulb-check.

ADJUSTMENTS

BELT TENSION

Vehicles are equipped with automatic drive belt tensioner. Drive belt does not require adjustment. Inspect condition and tension of generator drive belt prior to performing any on-vehicle charging system tests. Replace belt and/or repair tensioner mechanism if necessary.

TROUBLE SHOOTING

NOTE: See TROUBLE SHOOTING article in GENERAL INFORMATION.

PRELIMINARY CHECKS

- Verify battery condition.
- Inspect accessory drive belt and tensioner.
- Inspect battery junction box MAIN fuse (100-amp).
- Inspect battery junction box FUEL INJECTOR fuse (30-amp).
- Inspect central junction box METER fuse (10-amp).
- Check all connections for looseness or corrosion.

ON-VEHICLE TESTING

GENERATOR LOAD TEST (VOLTAGE)

Ensure drive belt is in good condition. Replace belt as necessary. If belt is okay, turn on headlights for 15 seconds to remove surface charge. Turn off headlights. Measure battery voltage and record. Start and run engine at 2000 RPM. Turn on high beams and turn blower to high position. Turn on air conditioning, if equipped. Run engine at 2000 RPM and observe voltmeter. Voltage should increase at least .5 volt over recorded value.

GENERATOR LOAD TEST (AMPERAGE)

Ensure drive belt is in good condition. Replace belt as necessary. If belt is okay, connect charging system tester with ammeter according to tool manufacturers instructions. With system loaded and engine at 2000 RPM, generator output should exceed 76 amps for 95-amp generators or 60 amps for 75-amp models.

GENERATOR NO-LOAD TEST

Connect voltmeter positive lead to B+ terminal on generator and negative lead to ground. Turn on headlights for 15 seconds to remove surface charge. Turn off headlights. Measure battery voltage and record. Start and run engine at 1500 RPM with no electrical load (all accessories off). Read voltmeter when voltage stabilizes. Voltage should be at least 2.5 volts higher than recorded reading.

SYSTEM TESTS

INTRODUCTION

Identify symptom and perform appropriate system test. See SYSTEM TEST INDEX table.

SYSTEM TEST INDEX

Symptom	Test
System Overcharges	A
Charge Warning Indicator On With Engine Running	B
Charge Warning Indicator Flickers Or Is Intermittent	C
System Does Not Charge	D

TEST A

1) With ignition on, engine off, measure voltage between generator terminal "A" screw and ground. *See Fig. 1.* If voltage is less than .25 volt, go to next step. If voltage is .25 volt or greater, repair open White/Green wire or battery junction box. See WIRING DIAGRAMS.

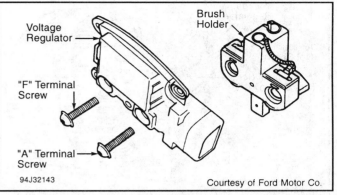

Fig. 1: Identifying Generator Test Points

Courtesy of Ford Motor Co.

2) Turn ignition off. Disconnect generator 3-pin connector and generator 1-pin connector. Measure resistance of Orange wire between 3-pin connector terminal and 1-pin connector terminal. If resistance is less than 5 ohms, go to next step. If resistance is 5 ohms or greater, repair open in Orange wire or poor connections. See WIRING DIAGRAMS. Check system operation.

3) Check for loose fasteners or dirty mating surfaces between regulator and generator and between generator and engine. Also check battery ground cable between battery and engine for poor connection. Repair as necessary and check system operation. If all connections are clean and tight, and symptoms remain, replace voltage regulator. See VOLTAGE REGULATOR under REMOVAL & INSTALLATION.

TEST B

1) Perform GENERATOR NO-LOAD TEST under ON-VEHICLE TESTING. If voltage is less than specified, go to next step. If voltage is as specified, repair short to ground in White/Blue wire, battery junction box or instrument cluster. See WIRING DIAGRAMS. Check system operation.

2) Turn ignition off. Measure voltage between generator terminal "A" screw and ground. *See Fig. 1.* If battery voltage is present, go to next step. If battery voltage is not present, repair White/Green wire or battery junction box. See WIRING DIAGRAMS. Check system operation.

3) Disconnect generator 3-pin connector. Observe charge warning indicator with ignition on, engine off. If indicator does not illuminate, go to next step. If indicator illuminates, repair short to ground in White/Blue wire, battery junction box or instrument cluster. See WIRING DIAGRAMS. Check system operation.

4) Turn ignition off. Reconnect generator 3-pin connector. Disconnect generator 1-pin connector (Orange wire). Install a jumper wire between 1-pin connector terminal and ground. Observe charge warning indicator with ignition on, engine off. If indicator illuminates, go to next step. If indicator does not illuminate, go to step **6)**.

5) Turn ignition off. Disconnect generator 3-pin connector. Measure resistance of Orange wire between generator 3-pin connector terminal and generator 1-pin connector terminal. If resistance is less than 5 ohms, replace voltage regulator and check system operation. See VOLTAGE REGULATOR under REMOVAL & INSTALLATION. If resistance is 5 ohms or greater, repair high resistance or open on Orange wire. See WIRING DIAGRAMS. Check system operation.

6) Start engine and measure voltage between generator "S" terminal and ground. *See Fig. 2.* If voltage is one-half battery voltage or greater, go to next step. If voltage is less than one-half battery voltage, system is okay at this time. Restore connections and check system operation.

7) Run engine at 1500 RPM with all accessories off. Measure voltage between generator terminal B+ and ground. *See Fig. 2.* If voltage is 14.1

volts or greater, go to TEST A. If voltage is less than 14.1 volts, replace voltage regulator. See VOLTAGE REGULATOR under REMOVAL & INSTALLATION.

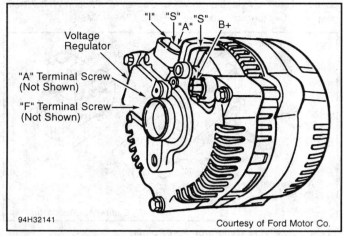

94H32141

Courtesy of Ford Motor Co.

Fig. 2: Identifying Generator Terminals

TEST C

1) Turn ignition off. Inspect generator connections, battery junction box connections and battery cable connections for looseness, damage or corrosion. Repair as necessary and check system operation. If all connections are okay, go to next step.

2) Ensure voltage regulator brush holder screws (terminal "A" and "F" screws) are secure. *See Fig. 1.* If screws are secure, go to next step. If screws are not secure, tighten as necessary and check system operation.

3) Disconnect generator 3-pin connector. Remove voltage regulator. See VOLTAGE REGULATOR under REMOVAL & INSTALLATION. Measure resistance between each generator slip ring and ground. *See Fig. 3.* If resistance is greater than 200 ohms between both slip rings and ground, install new voltage regulator. If resistance between one or both slip rings and ground is 200 ohms or less, clean slip rings and retest. If resistance is still 200 ohms or less, replace generator. See GENERATOR under REMOVAL & INSTALLATION. Check system operation.

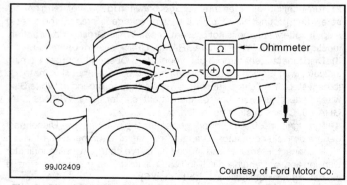

99J02409

Courtesy of Ford Motor Co.

Fig. 3: Checking For Grounded Generator Slip Ring

TEST D

1) Inspect drive belt condition and tension. If belt or tension are not okay, repair or replace as necessary and check system operation. If belt and tension are okay, go to next step.

2) Perform GENERATOR NO-LOAD TEST under ON-VEHICLE TESTING. If voltage is less than specified, go to PINPOINT TEST B. If voltage is as specified, check system for parasitic drain and repair as necessary.

REMOVAL & INSTALLATION

CAUTION: When batteries are disconnected, vehicle computer and memory systems may lose memory data. Driveability problems may exist until computer systems have completed a relearn cycle. See COMPUTER RELEARN PROCEDURES article in GENERAL INFORMATION before disconnecting battery.

GENERATOR

Removal & Installation (Coupe) – Disconnect negative battery cable. Remove accessory drive belt. Remove coolant reservoir tank. Disconnect wiring from generator. Remove 3 generator bolts. Remove generator from vehicle. To install, reverse removal procedures. Tighten fasteners to specification. See TORQUE SPECIFICATIONS.

Removal & Installation (Sedan & Wagon) – Disconnect negative battery cable. Release tension on accessory drive belt and remove belt from pulley. Disconnect oxygen sensor harness clip from generator bracket. remove A/C line bracket bolt, 3 power steering pressure line bracket bolts and 2 generator bracket bolts. Position generator bracket to one side. Remove 2 generator mounting bolts. remove generator enough to access electrical connections. Disconnect wiring from generator. Remove generator. To install, reverse removal procedures. Tighten fasteners to specification. See TORQUE SPECIFICATIONS.

VOLTAGE REGULATOR

Removal & Installation – Remove generator. See GENERATOR. Remove 4 regulator retaining screws. Remove regulator. Before mounting new regulator, depress brushes and insert wire into hole on outside of regulator to retain brushes. Install regulator and tighten screw to specification. See TORQUE SPECIFICATIONS. After installation, remove retaining pin.

TORQUE SPECIFICATIONS

TORQUE SPECIFICATIONS

Application	Ft. Lbs. (N.m)
Generator Bracket Bolts	15 (20)
Generator Mounting Bolts (Coupe)	29-40 (40-55)
Generator Lower Bolt (Sedan & Wagon)	15-22 (20-30)
Generator Upper Bolt (Sedan & Wagon)	29-40 (40-55)
Power Steering Pressure Line Bracket Bolts	15 (20)
	INCH Lbs. (N.m)
Voltage Regulator Screws	26-41 (3.0-4.6)

WIRING DIAGRAMS

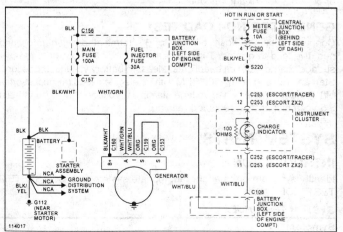

114017

Fig. 4: Charging System Wiring Diagram (Escort & Tracer)

Dual Generators – Diesel

F250 Super-Duty Pickup, F350 Pickup

NOTE: This article includes Cab & Chassis.

DESCRIPTION

System consists of dual 110-amp generators with internal voltage regulators, 2 batteries, PCM, warning indicator and wiring. Generators operate independently through internal voltage regulation. PCM monitors both generators and is able to set trouble codes and control charge warning indicator operation. PCM generator control is limited to disabling lower generator during glow plug operation to avoid over-voltage damage to glow plug circuit. Generators have different size pulleys, and are not interchangeable.

Charge warning indicator should illuminate with ignition on, engine off. Charge warning indicator should not illuminate with ignition off, or with engine running.

NOTE: Generator and regulator cannot be serviced separately, and must be replaced as an assembly.

ADJUSTMENTS

BELT TENSION

Vehicles are equipped with automatic drive belt tensioner. Drive belt does not require adjustment. Inspect condition and tension of generator drive belt prior to performing any on-vehicle charging system tests. Replace belt and/or tensioner mechanism if necessary.

TROUBLE SHOOTING

NOTE: See TROUBLE SHOOTING article in GENERAL INFORMATION.

PRELIMINARY CHECKS

- Verify battery condition.
- Inspect accessory drive belt and tensioner.
- Inspect Gray fusible links at starter relay.
- Inspect power distribution box fuse No. 5 (5-amp), fuse No. 6 (10-amp) and fuse No. 7 (5-amp).
- Check all connections for looseness or corrosion.

ON-VEHICLE TESTING

CAUTION: When battery is disconnected, vehicle computer and memory systems may lose memory data. Driveability problems may exist until computer systems have completed a relearn cycle. See COMPUTER RELEARN PROCEDURES article in GENERAL INFORMATION before disconnecting battery.

NO-LOAD TEST

Connect voltmeter positive lead to B+ terminal on generator and negative lead to ground. Start engine and bring to normal operating temperature, (it takes at least 2 minutes for glow plugs to time-out). Run engine at 2000 RPM with all accessories off. Read voltmeter when voltage stabilizes. This may require waiting a few minutes. Voltage should be 13-15 volts.

LOAD TEST

1) Ensure drive belt is in good condition. Replace belt as necessary. If belt is okay, connect charging system load tester in accordance with manufacturer's instructions. Start engine and bring to normal operating temperature, (it takes at least 2 minutes for glow plugs to time-out). Run engine at 2000 RPM and apply load until generator output amperage levels off.

2) Record maximum generator amperage output. See GENERATOR OUTPUT SPECIFICATIONS table for output values. Generator amperage should be as specified with voltage between 12.5 and 14.5 volts.

GENERATOR OUTPUT SPECIFICATIONS

RPM	Amps Rating (Approximate)
500	28
1000	63
1500	82
2000	89
2500	95

SELF-DIAGNOSTIC SYSTEM

RETRIEVING DIAGNOSTIC TROUBLE CODES

Connect New Generation Star (NGS) tester to Data Link Connector (DLC) and retrieve any charging system Diagnostic Trouble Codes (DTCs). Perform appropriate diagnostic test. See CHARGING SYSTEM DIAGNOSTIC TROUBLE CODES table. After repair is complete, clear DTCs. See CLEARING DIAGNOSTIC TROUBLE CODES. If no DTCs are present, diagnose by symptom. See SYSTEM TESTS.

CHARGING SYSTEM DIAGNOSTIC TROUBLE CODES

DTC	[1] Go To Test
P1105	CM
P1106	CN
P1107	CP
P1108	CQ

[1] – Perform appropriate test under DIAGNOSTIC TESTS.

CLEARING DIAGNOSTIC TROUBLE CODES

Connect New Generation Star (NGS) tester to Data Link Connector (DLC). Using NGS tester manufacturer's instructions, clear DTCs.

DIAGNOSTIC TESTS

TEST CM

1) With ignition off, disconnect upper generator 3-pin connector. Inspect connector for damage or loose connections. If connector is okay, restore connection and go to next step. If connector is not okay, repair as necessary and clear DTC. Check system operation.

2) Measure voltage between generator B+ connector (Black/Orange wire) and ground. If battery voltage is present, go to next step. If battery voltage is not present, repair open in Black/Orange wire, fuse link "B", or Red wire between batteries and starter relay. See WIRING DIAGRAMS.

3) Disconnect upper generator 3-pin connector. Measure voltage between generator 3-pin connector terminal "A" (Orange/Light Blue wire) and ground. If battery voltage is present, go to next step. If battery voltage is not present, repair open in circuit, fuses or fuse links between starter relay and generator connector. See WIRING DIAGRAMS.

4) Turn ignition switch to RUN position. With engine off, measure voltage between generator 3-pin connector terminal "I" (Light Green/Red wire) and ground. If battery voltage is present, go to step **6)**. If battery voltage is not present, go to next step.

5) Turn ignition off. Disconnect PCM 104-pin connector. Measure resistance between generator 3-pin connector terminal "I" (Light Green/Red wire) and PCM 104-pin connector terminal No. 35 (Light Blue/Black wire). *See Fig. 1.* If resistance is less than 5 ohms, replace PCM and check system operation. If resistance is 5 ohms or greater, repair wire between generator and PCM. See WIRING DIAGRAMS.

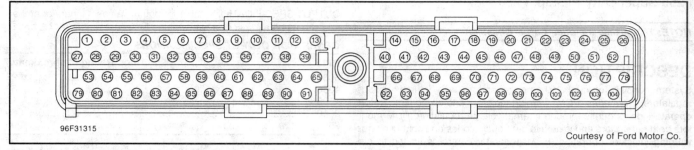

96F31315

Courtesy of Ford Motor Co.

Fig. 1: Identifying PCM Connector Terminals

6) Restore upper generator connections. Disconnect lower generator connector. Start engine and allow to run at least 2 minutes (until glow plugs turn off). Measure battery voltage. If voltage is greater than 13 volts, go to next step. If voltage is 13 volts or less, replace upper generator. See UPPER GENERATOR under REMOVAL & INSTALLATION. Check system operation.

7) With lower generator disconnected, test upper generator. See NO-LOAD TEST and LOAD TEST under ON-VEHICLE TESTING. If generator does not test okay, replace generator. See UPPER GENERATOR under REMOVAL & INSTALLATION. Clear DTC and check system operation. If generator tests okay, problem is not present at this time. Restore all connections and check system operation.

TEST CN

1) Turn ignition off. Disconnect lower generator 3-pin connector. Inspect connector for damage or loose connections. If connector is okay, restore connection and go to next step. If connector is not okay, repair as necessary and clear DTC. Check system operation.

2) Measure voltage between generator B+ connector (Yellow/White wire) and ground. If battery voltage is present, go to next step. If battery voltage is not present, repair open in Yellow/White wire, fuse link "B", or Red wire between batteries and starter relay. See WIRING DIAGRAMS.

3) Disconnect upper generator 3-pin connector. Measure voltage between generator 3-pin connector terminal "A" (Orange/Light Blue wire) and ground. If battery voltage is present, go to next step. If battery voltage is not present, repair open in circuit, fuse or fuse link between starter relay and generator connector. See WIRING DIAGRAMS.

4) Turn ignition switch to RUN position. With engine off, measure voltage between generator 3-pin connector terminal "I" (Yellow wire) and ground. If battery voltage is present, go to step 6). If battery voltage is not present, go to next step.

5) Turn ignition off. Disconnect PCM 104-pin connector. Measure resistance of Yellow wire between generator 3-pin connector terminal "I" and PCM 104-pin connector terminal No. 60. See Fig. 1. If resistance is less than 5 ohms, replace PCM and check system operation. If resistance is 5 ohms or greater, repair wire between generator and PCM. See WIRING DIAGRAMS.

6) Restore lower generator connections. Disconnect upper generator connector. Start engine and allow to run at least 2 minutes (until glow plugs turn off). Measure battery voltage. If voltage is greater than 13 volts, go to next step. If voltage is 13 volts or less, replace lower generator. See LOWER GENERATOR under REMOVAL & INSTALLATION. Check system operation.

7) With upper generator disconnected, test lower generator. See NO-LOAD TEST and LOAD TEST under ON-VEHICLE TESTING. If generator does not test okay, replace generator. See LOWER GENERATOR under REMOVAL & INSTALLATION. Clear DTC and check system operation. If generator tests okay, problem is not present at this time. Restore all connections and check system operation.

TEST CP

1) Turn ignition off. Disconnect lower generator connector. Turn ignition switch to RUN position. Measure voltage between connector male pin (Yellow wire) and ground. If no voltage is present, go to next step. If

voltage is present, replace lower generator. See LOWER GENERATOR under REMOVAL & INSTALLATION. Clear DTC and check system operation.

2) Turn ignition off. Disconnect PCM 104-pin connector. Turn ignition switch to RUN position. Measure voltage between PCM connector terminal No. 60 (Yellow wire) and ground. See Fig. 1. If no voltage is present. go to next step. If voltage is present, repair short to power in Yellow wire. Clear DTC and check system operation.

3) Turn ignition off. Reconnect PCM 104-pin connector. Turn ignition switch to RUN position. Perform glow plug test using New Generation Start (NGS) tester. While test is in progress, measure voltage between generator connector terminal (Yellow wire) and ground. If voltage is present replace PCM and check system operation. If voltage is not present, system is okay at this time. Clear DTC and check circuit for intermittent short to power.

TEST CQ

1) Turn ignition off. Inspect junction box fuse/relay panel fuse No. 29 (5-amp). If fuse is okay, go to next step. If fuse is not okay, install new fuse, clear DTC and check system operation.

2) Disconnect PCM 104-pin connector. With ignition on, engine off, measure voltage between PCM connector terminal No. 67 (Light Green/Red wire) and ground. See Fig. 1. If battery voltage is present, go to next step. If battery voltage is not present, repair circuit between fuse No. 29 (5-amp), instrument cluster and PCM connector. See WIRING DIAGRAMS.

3) Turn ignition off. Measure voltage between PCM connector terminal No. 67 (Light Green/Red wire) and ground. See Fig. 1. If battery voltage is present, repair short to power in circuit between fuse No. 29 (5-amp), instrument cluster and PCM connector. See WIRING DIAGRAMS. If battery voltage is not present, check PCM connector for loose connection. If PCM connector is okay, check circuit for intermittent connections. Repair as necessary and check system operation.

SYSTEM TESTS

INTRODUCTION

Identify symptom and perform appropriate system test. See SYSTEM TEST INDEX table.

SYSTEM TEST INDEX

Symptom	[1] Test
Warning Indicator Is ON With Engine Running, System Is Not Charging	CA
Warning Indicator Is OFF With Ignition On	CB
Warning Indicator Is ON With Engine Running, System Is Charging	CC
Warning Indicator Operates Properly, System Is Not Charging	CD
Warning Indicator Flickers	CF
System Overcharges (Greater Than 15.5 Volts)	CG

[1] – Perform appropriate SYSTEM TEST.

TEST CA

1) Connect New Generation Star (NGS) tester. Check for Key On, Engine Off (KOEO) codes. If generator codes are present, perform

appropriate diagnostic test. See SELF-DIAGNOSTIC SYSTEM. If no generator codes are present, go to next step.

2) Turn ignition off and disconnect NGS tester. Disconnect upper generator 3-pin connector. With key on, engine off, measure voltage between 3-pin connector terminal "I" (Light Green/Red wire) and ground. If voltage is greater than 12 volts, go to step **4)**. If voltage is 12 volts or less, go to next step.

3) Turn ignition off. Disconnect PCM 104-pin connector. Measure resistance between generator 3-pin connector terminal "I" (Light Green/Red wire) and PCM 104-pin connector terminal No. 35 (Light Blue/Black wire). *See Fig. 1.* If resistance is less than 5 ohms, go to step **5)**. If resistance is 5 ohms or greater, repair open circuit between PCM and upper generator. See WIRING DIAGRAMS.

4) Connect upper generator connector. Disconnect lower generator connector. Measure resistance of Yellow wire between lower generator connector terminal "I"and PCM 104-pin connector terminal No. 60. *See Fig. 1.* If resistance is less than 5 ohms, go to next step. If resistance is 5 ohms or greater, repair open Yellow wire between PCM and lower generator.

5) Turn ignition off. Reconnect PCM 104-pin connector. Test upper generator. See LOAD TEST under ON-VEHICLE TESTING. If generator is okay, go to next step. If generator is not okay, replace generator. See UPPER GENERATOR under REMOVAL & INSTALLATION. Check system operation.

6) Turn ignition off. Reconnect lower generator connector. Disconnect upper generator 3-pin connector. Test upper generator. See LOAD TEST under ON-VEHICLE TESTING. If generator is okay, replace PCM and check system operation. If generator is not okay, replace generator. See LOWER GENERATOR under REMOVAL & INSTALLATION. Check system operation.

TEST CB

1) Connect New Generation Star (NGS) tester. Check for Key On, Engine Off (KOEO) codes. If generator codes are present, perform appropriate diagnostic test. See SELF-DIAGNOSTIC SYSTEM. If no generator codes are present, go to next step.

2) Turn ignition off and disconnect NGS tester. Disconnect PCM 104-pin connector. Jumper PCM connector terminal No. 67 (Light Green/Red wire) to negative battery terminal. *See Fig. 1.* If charge warning indicator illuminates, replace PCM and check system operation. If charge warning indicator does not illuminate, check indicator bulb and Light Green/Red wire between PCM connector and instrument cluster. See WIRING DIAGRAMS.

TEST CC

1) Connect New Generation Star (NGS) tester. Check for Key On, Engine Off (KOEO) codes. If generator codes are present, perform appropriate diagnostic test. See SELF-DIAGNOSTIC SYSTEM. If no generator codes are present, go to next step.

2) Turn ignition off and disconnect NGS tester. Start engine and turn off all accessories. While varying engine speed, measure voltage at primary battery. If voltage is greater than 15.5 volts, go to TEST CG. If voltage is 15.5 volts or less, go to next step.

3) Turn engine off. Disconnect upper generator 3-pin connector. With key on, engine off, measure voltage between 3-pin connector terminal "A" (Orange/Light Blue wire) and ground. If battery voltage is present, go to next step. If battery voltage is not present, repair Orange/Light Blue wire between upper generator and power distribution box. See WIRING DIAGRAMS.

4) Turn ignition off. Reconnect upper generator 3-pin connector. Disconnect lower generator connector. With key on, engine off, measure voltage between connector terminal "A" (Orange/Light Blue wire) and ground. If battery voltage is present, go to next step. If battery voltage is not present, repair Orange/Light Blue wire between lower generator and power distribution box. See WIRING DIAGRAMS.

5) Turn ignition off. Reconnect lower generator connector. Disconnect PCM 104-pin connector. With key on, engine off, observe charge warning indicator. If light is not illuminated, go to next step. If light is

illuminated, repair short to ground in Light Green/Red wire between PCM and instrument cluster. See WIRING DIAGRAMS.

6) Turn ignition off. Reconnect PCM 104-pin connector. Disconnect lower generator connector. Test upper generator. See LOAD TEST under ON-VEHICLE TESTING. If upper generator is okay, go to next step. If upper generator is not okay, replace generator. See UPPER GENERATOR under REMOVAL & INSTALLATION. Check system operation.

7) Reconnect lower generator connector. Disconnect upper generator 3-pin connector. Test lower generator. See LOAD TEST under ON-VEHICLE TESTING. If lower generator is okay, replace PCM and check system operation. If lower generator is not okay, replace generator. See LOWER GENERATOR under REMOVAL & INSTALLATION. Check system operation.

TEST CD

1) Connect New Generation Star (NGS) tester. Check for Key On, Engine Off (KOEO) codes. If generator codes are present, perform appropriate diagnostic test. See SELF-DIAGNOSTIC SYSTEM. If no generator codes are present, go to next step.

2) Turn ignition off and disconnect NGS tester. Check all battery and generator connections for corrosion, damage or looseness. Repair as necessary. If connections are okay, go to next step.

3) Measure voltage between upper generator terminal B+ (Black/Orange wire) and ground. If battery voltage is present, go to next step. If battery voltage is not present, repair Black/Orange wire or fusible links between starter relay and upper generator. See WIRING DIAGRAMS. Check system operation.

4) Measure voltage between lower generator terminal B+ (Yellow/White wire) and ground. If battery voltage is present, go to next step. If battery voltage is not present, repair Yellow/White wire or fusible links between starter relay and lower generator. See WIRING DIAGRAMS. Check system operation.

5) Connect load tester to either battery according to tool manufacturers instructions. Load test at one-half battery amperage rating for 15 seconds. If battery voltage drops to less than 9.6 volts, charge battery and retest. Replace battery if loaded voltage is still less than 9.6 volts. Repeat test on remaining battery. If both batteries are okay, go to next step.

6) Disconnect lower generator connector. Test upper generator output. See LOAD TEST and NO-LOAD TEST under ON-VEHICLE TESTING. If upper generator is okay, go to next step. If upper generator is not okay, replace generator and check system operation. See UPPER GENERATOR under REMOVAL & INSTALLATION.

7) Reconnect lower generator connector. Disconnect upper generator connector. Test lower generator output. See LOAD TEST and NO-LOAD TEST under ON-VEHICLE TESTING. If lower generator is okay, system is okay at this time. Restore connections and check system operation. If lower generator is not okay, replace generator and check system operation. See LOWER GENERATOR under REMOVAL & INSTALLATION.

TEST CF

1) Connect New Generation Star (NGS) tester. Check for Key On, Engine Off (KOEO) codes. If generator codes are present, perform appropriate diagnostic test. See SELF-DIAGNOSTIC SYSTEM. If no generator codes are present, go to next step.

2) Turn ignition off and disconnect NGS tester. Inspect "A" and "I" circuits for both upper and lower generators for intermittent opens or shorts. See WIRING DIAGRAMS. Inspect all related fuses. Repair or replace as necessary. If all circuits are okay, go to next step.

3) Disconnect and inspect all generator connectors for corrosion, damage or looseness. Repair as necessary. If all connections are okay, restore connections and go to next step.

4) Start engine and measure battery voltage while varying engine speed. If voltage is greater than 15.5 volts, go to TEST CG. If voltage is 15.5 volts or less, go to next step.

5) Turn ignition off. Disconnect PCM 104-pin connector. Jumper PCM connector terminal No. 67 (Light Green/Red wire) to ground. Observe charge warning indicator. If indicator illuminates, go to next step. If indicator does not illuminate, repair open in Light Green/Red wire and check system operation. See WIRING DIAGRAMS.

6) Turn ignition off. Reconnect PCM 104-pin connector. With ignition on, engine off, observe charge warning indicator. If indicator illuminates, system is operating properly. Check generators and all circuits for intermittent open or short. See WIRING DIAGRAMS. If indicator does not illuminate, replace PCM and check system for normal operation.

TEST CG

1) Connect New Generation Star (NGS) tester. Check for Key On, Engine Off (KOEO) codes. If generator codes are present, perform appropriate diagnostic test. See SELF-DIAGNOSTIC SYSTEM. If no generator codes are present, go to next step.

2) Turn ignition off and disconnect NGS tester. Start engine and measure battery voltage at either battery while varying engine speed. If voltage is greater than 15.5 volts, go to step **4)**. If voltage is 15.5 volts or less, go to next step.

3) Vary engine speed and observe instrument cluster voltage gauge. If voltage gauge reads 15.5 volts or less, go to next step. If voltage gauge reads above 15.5 volts, gauge is inaccurate. For repair, see appropriate INSTRUMENT PANELS article in ACCESSORIES & EQUIPMENT.

4) Turn ignition off. Disconnect lower generator connector. Start engine and wait 2 minutes. Turn all accessories off. Measure voltage at either battery while varying engine speed. If voltage is greater than 15.5 volts, go to next step. If voltage is 15.5 volts or less, go to step **6)**.

5) Turn ignition off. Reconnect lower generator connector. Disconnect upper generator 3-pin connector. With key on, engine off, measure voltage between upper generator connector terminal "A" (Orange/Light Blue wire) and ground. If voltage is within .5 volt of battery voltage, replace upper generator. See UPPER GENERATOR under REMOVAL & INSTALLATION. If not within .5 volt of battery voltage, repair high resistance in Orange/Light Blue wire and check system operation. See WIRING DIAGRAMS.

6) Turn ignition off. Disconnect upper generator 3-pin connector. Start engine and wait at least 2 minutes. Turn off all accessories. Measure battery voltage at either battery while varying engine speed. If voltage increases to greater than 15.5 volts, go to next step. If voltage is 15.5 volts or less, check upper and lower generator "A" circuits (Orange/Light Blue wire) for intermittent open or short. Check system operation.

7) Turn ignition off. Reconnect upper generator 3-pin connector. Disconnect lower generator connector. With key on, engine off, measure voltage between lower generator connector terminal "A" (Orange/Light Blue wire) and ground. If voltage is within .5 volt of battery voltage, replace lower generator. See LOWER GENERATOR under REMOVAL & INSTALLATION. If voltage is not within .5 volt of battery voltage, repair high resistance in Orange/Light Blue wire and check system operation. See WIRING DIAGRAMS.

REMOVAL & INSTALLATION

CAUTION: When battery is disconnected, vehicle computer and memory systems may lose memory data. Driveability problems may exist until computer systems have completed a relearn cycle. See COMPUTER RELEARN PROCEDURES article in GENERAL INFORMATION before disconnecting battery.

UPPER GENERATOR

Removal & Installation – Disconnect negative battery cable. Remove drive belt from pulley. Disconnect wiring from generator. Remove 3 generator mounting bolts. Remove generator. To install, reverse removal procedure. Tighten fasteners to specification. See TORQUE SPECIFICATIONS.

LOWER GENERATOR

Removal & Installation – Disconnect negative battery cable. Remove drive belt from pulley. Raise and support vehicle. Disconnect wiring from generator. Remove 3 generator mounting bolts. Remove generator. To install, reverse removal procedure. Tighten fasteners to specification. See TORQUE SPECIFICATIONS.

TORQUE SPECIFICATIONS

TORQUE SPECIFICATIONS

Application	Ft. Lbs. (N.m)
Generator Mounting Bolts	31-39 (41-54)
	INCH Lbs. (N.m)
Generator B+ Terminal Nut	62-79 (7-9)

WIRING DIAGRAMS

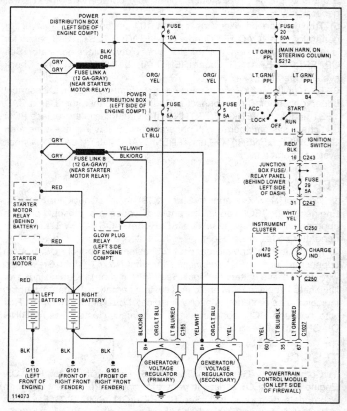

Fig. 2: Dual Generator System Wiring Diagram (F250 & F350 Super-Duty Pickups – Diesel)

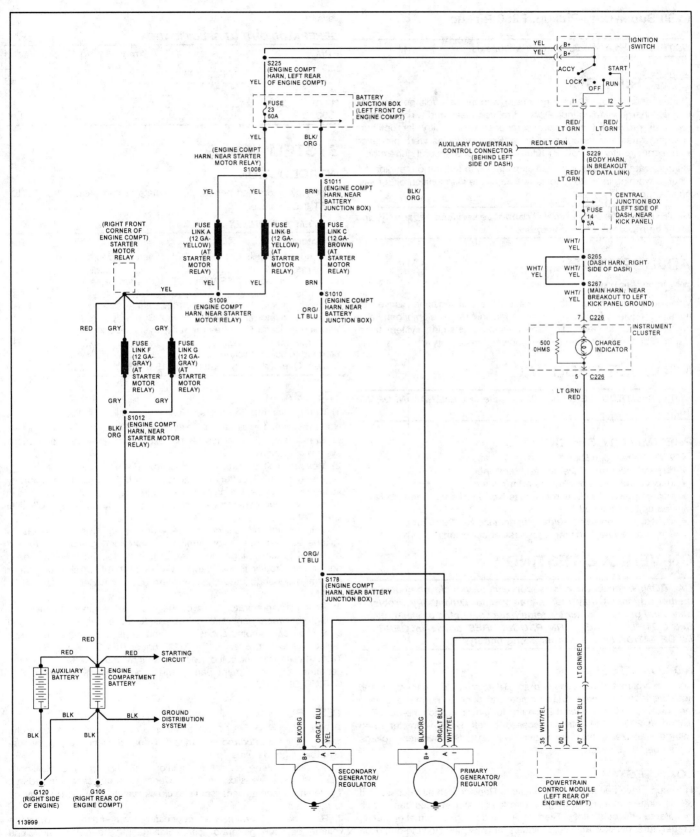

Fig. 3: Dual Generator System Wiring Diagram (Econoline Super-Duty – Diesel)

1999 STARTING & CHARGING SYSTEMS
Single Generator – Diesel

F250 Super-Duty Pickup, F350 Pickup

NOTE: This article includes Cab & Chassis.

DESCRIPTION

System consists of 110-amp generator with internal voltage regulator, battery, charge warning indicator and related fuses and wiring. Internal regulator provides temperature compensation circuitry for optimum charging rates in different conditions. Some vehicles were produced with extra circuitry to allow for future addition of a second generator.

Charge warning indicator should illuminate with ignition on, engine off. Charge warning indicator should not illuminate with ignition off, or with engine running.

NOTE: Generator and regulator cannot be serviced separately, and must be replaced as an assembly.

ADJUSTMENTS

BELT TENSION

Vehicles are equipped with automatic drive belt tensioner. Drive belt does not require adjustment. Inspect condition and tension of generator drive belt prior to performing any on-vehicle charging system tests. Replace belt and/or tensioner mechanism if necessary.

TROUBLE SHOOTING

NOTE: See TROUBLE SHOOTING article in GENERAL INFORMATION.

PRELIMINARY CHECKS

- Verify battery condition.
- Inspect accessory drive belt and tensioner.
- Inspect Gray fusible links at starter relay.
- Inspect power distribution box fuse No. 6 (10-amp) and fuse No. 7 (5-amp), if equipped.
- Inspect junction box fuse/relay panel fuse No. 29 (5-amp).
- Check all connections for looseness or corrosion.

ON-VEHICLE TESTING

CAUTION: When battery is disconnected, vehicle computer and memory systems may lose memory data. Driveability problems may exist until computer systems have completed a relearn cycle. See COMPUTER RELEARN PROCEDURES article in GENERAL INFORMATION before disconnecting battery.

NO-LOAD TEST

Connect voltmeter positive lead to B+ terminal on generator and negative lead to ground. Start engine and bring to normal operating temperature, (it takes at least 2 minutes for glow plugs to time-out). Run engine at 2000 RPM with all accessories off. Read voltmeter when voltage stabilizes. This may require waiting a few minutes. Voltage should be 13-15 volts.

LOAD TEST

1) Ensure drive belt is in good condition. Replace belt as necessary. If belt is okay, connect charging system load tester in accordance with manufacturer's instructions. Start engine and bring to normal operating temperature, (it takes at least 2 minutes for glow plugs to time-out). Run engine at 2000 RPM and apply load until generator output amperage levels off.

2) Record maximum generator amperage output. See GENERATOR OUTPUT SPECIFICATIONS table for output values. Generator amperage should be within specification with voltage between 12.5 and 14.5 volts.

GENERATOR OUTPUT SPECIFICATIONS

RPM	Amps Rating (Approximate)
500	28
1000	63
1500	82
2000	89
2500	95

SYSTEM TESTS

INTRODUCTION

Identify symptom and perform appropriate system test. See SYSTEM TEST INDEX table.

SYSTEM TEST INDEX

Symptom	Test
Warning Indicator Is ON With KOER, System Does Not Charge	BA
Warning Indicator Is OFF With KOEO, System Does Not Charge	BB
Warning Indicator Is ON With KOER, System Charges	BC
Warning Indicator Is OFF With KOEO, System Charges	BD
Warning Indicator Operates Properly, System Does Not Charge	BE
Warning Indicator Flickers	BG
System Overcharges (Greater Than 15.5 Volts)	BH

TEST BA

1) Turn ignition off. Remove and inspect fuse No. 6 (10-amp) and fuse No. 7 (5-amp), if equipped, in power distribution box. If fuses are okay, go to next step. If either fuse is not okay, install new fuse and check system operation.

2) Measure voltage between generator "B+" terminal (Black/Orange wire) and ground. If battery voltage is present, go to next step. If battery voltage is not present, repair Black/Orange wire or fusible links between starter relay and generator and check system operation. See WIRING DIAGRAMS.

3) With ignition off, disconnect generator 3-pin connector. Measure voltage between connector terminal "A" (Orange/Light Blue wire) and ground. If battery voltage is present, go to next step. If battery voltage is not present, repair Black/Orange wire or fusible link between starter relay and generator and check system operation. See WIRING DIAGRAMS.

4) Reconnect generator 3-pin connector. Start engine and measure voltage between generator connector (Light Green/Red wire) and ground by backprobing connector. If voltage is greater than one volt, replace generator. See GENERATOR under REMOVAL & INSTALLATION. If voltage is one volt or less, repair Light Green/Red wire between generator and instrument panel, and check system operation. See WIRING DIAGRAMS.

TEST BB

1) Disconnect generator 3-pin connector. Inspect connector for bent, damaged, loose or corroded terminals. Repair as necessary. If connector is okay, go to next step.

2) Inspect battery ground connections. Verify generator is tightly mounted and there is continuity between generator case and ground. Tighten and clean as necessary and check system operation. If okay, go to next step.

3) Reconnect generator 3-pin connector. Start engine and measure voltage between generator connector (Light Green/Red wire) and ground by backprobing connector. If voltage is greater than one volt, replace generator. See GENERATOR under REMOVAL & INSTALLATION. If voltage is one volt or less, repair Light Green/Red wire between generator and instrument panel, and check system operation. See WIRING DIAGRAMS.

TEST BC

1) Inspect generator 3-pin connector for damaged, loose or corroded terminals. Repair as necessary and check system operation. If connector is okay, go to next step.

2) Run engine at 2000 RPM and measure voltage between generator B+ terminal (Black/Orange wire) and ground. If voltage is less than 15 volts, go to next step. If voltage is 15 volts or greater, go to TEST BH.

3) Turn ignition off. Disconnect generator 3-pin connector. Start engine and observe charge warning indicator. If indicator does not illuminate, go to TEST BD. If indicator illuminates, repair circuit between generator connector terminal "I" and fuse No. 29 (5-amp) in junction box fuse/relay panel. See WIRING DIAGRAMS.

TEST BD

Disconnect generator 3-pin connector. With ignition on, engine off, connect a jumper wire between generator 3-pin connector terminal "I" (Light Green/Red wire) and ground. If charge warning indicator illuminates, replace generator and check system operation. See GENERATOR under REMOVAL & INSTALLATION. If charge warning indicator does not illuminate, repair circuit between generator connector terminal "I" and instrument cluster. See WIRING DIAGRAMS

TEST BE

1) With ignition on, engine off, measure voltage between generator terminal B+ (Black/Orange wire) and ground. If battery voltage is present, go to next step. If battery voltage is not present, repair circuit between generator terminal B+ and starter relay, (including fusible link). See WIRING DIAGRAMS.

2) Disconnect and inspect generator 3-pin connector. Check for damaged, loose or corroded terminals. repair as necessary and check system operation. If connector is okay, check generator output. See LOAD TEST and NO-LOAD TEST under ON-VEHICLE TESTING. Replace generator as necessary.

TEST BG

1) With key on, engine off, measure voltage at both side of fuse No. 6 (10-amp) in power distribution box, and fuse No. 29 (5-amp) in junction box fuse/relay panel. If equipped, also check fuse No. 7 (5-amp) in power distribution box. If voltage is not present at both sides of all fuses, repair wiring. See POWER DISTRIBUTION article in WIRING DIAGRAMS. If voltage is present on only one side of any fuse, replace fuse and check system operation. If fuses are okay, go to next step.

2) Turn ignition off. Using an insulated probe, measure voltage between generator test point "F" and ground. *See Fig. 1.* If battery voltage is present, go to next step. If battery voltage is not present, replace generator and check system operation. See GENERATOR under REMOVAL & INSTALLATION.

3) Start engine and increase engine speed to 2000 RPM. Observe charge warning indicator, and measure battery voltage. If voltage increases to greater than 15 volts or indicators flickers, repair circuits between generator connector terminal "A" (Orange/Light Blue wire) and starter relay or between generator connector terminal "I" (Light Green/Red wire) and instrument cluster. See WIRING DIAGRAMS. If neither of the above conditions are observed, replace generator. See GENERATOR under REMOVAL & INSTALLATION.

TEST BH

1) With key on, engine off, check circuit "A" for voltage drop. Backprobe generator 3-pin connector terminal "A" (Orange/Light Blue wire). If voltage is less than .5 volt, go to next step. If voltage is .5 volt or greater, repair high resistance in Orange/Light Blue wire. See WIRING DIAGRAMS.

2) Start engine and increase engine speed to 2000 RPM. Measure battery voltage. If voltage is 15.5 volts or less, go to next step. If voltage increases to greater than 15.5 volts, replace generator. See GENERATOR under REMOVAL & INSTALLATION.

3) Turn ignition off. Using an insulated probe, measure voltage between generator test point "F" and ground. *See Fig. 1.* If battery voltage is present, go to next step. If battery voltage is not present, replace generator and check system operation. See GENERATOR under REMOVAL & INSTALLATION.

4) Start engine and increase engine speed to 2000 RPM. Observe charge warning indicator, and measure battery voltage. If voltage increases to greater than 15.5 volts or indicators flickers, repair circuits between generator connector terminal "A" and starter relay, or between generator connector terminal "I" and instrument cluster. See WIRING DIAGRAMS. If neither of the above conditions are observed, replace generator. See GENERATOR under REMOVAL & INSTALLATION.

REMOVAL & INSTALLATION

CAUTION: When battery is disconnected, vehicle computer and memory systems may lose memory data. Driveability problems may exist until computer systems have completed a relearn cycle. See COMPUTER RELEARN PROCEDURES article in GENERAL INFORMATION before disconnecting battery.

GENERATOR

Removal & Installation – Disconnect negative battery cable. Disengage drive belt from pulley. Disconnect wiring from generator. Remove 3 generator mounting bolts. Remove generator. To install, reverse removal procedure. Tighten fasteners to specification. See TORQUE SPECIFICATIONS.

TORQUE SPECIFICATIONS

TORQUE SPECIFICATIONS

Application	Ft. Lbs. (N.m)
Generator Mounting Bolts	31-39 (41-54)
	INCH Lbs. (N.m)
Generator B+ Terminal Nut	62-79 (7-9)

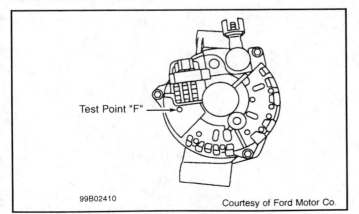

99B02410

Courtesy of Ford Motor Co.

Fig. 1: Identifying Generator Test Point "F"

WIRING DIAGRAMS

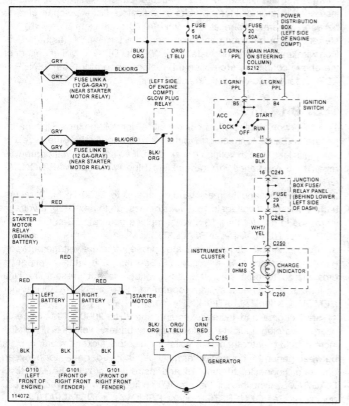

Fig. 2: Single Generator System Wiring Diagram
(Pickup – Diesel)

Generators – Mustang

DESCRIPTION

System consists of generator, integral voltage regulator, battery, charge warning indicator and related fuses and wiring. Charge warning indicator illuminates with ignition on, engine off as a bulb-check. Generator maximum rated output is 115-amps on 3.8L engines, 110-amps on 4.6L 2-valve engines and 120-amps on 4.6L 4-valve engines. Voltage regulator is mounted internally on 4.6L models. Generator and regulator cannot be serviced separately. On 3.8L models, voltage regulator is mounted to rear of generator and can be replaced.

ADJUSTMENTS

BELT TENSION

Vehicles are equipped with automatic drive belt tensioner. Drive belt does not require adjustment. Inspect condition and tension of generator drive belt prior to performing any on-vehicle charging system tests. Replace belt and/or repair tensioner mechanism if necessary.

TROUBLE SHOOTING

NOTE: Also see TROUBLE SHOOTING article in GENERAL INFORMATION.

PRELIMINARY CHECKS

- Verify battery condition.
- Inspect accessory drive belt and tensioner.
- Inspect Gray fusible links "A" and "B", (in harness, near battery junction box).
- Inspect battery junction box ALT fuse (20-amp).
- Inspect central junction box fuse No. 5 (15-amp).
- Check all connections for looseness or corrosion.

ON-VEHICLE TESTING

GENERATOR LOAD TEST

Ensure drive belt is in good condition. Replace belt as necessary. If belt is okay, connect charging system load tester in accordance with manufacturer's instructions. Start and run engine at 2000 RPM and apply load until generator output levels off. Generator output should be at least 89 amps at 2000 RPM.

GENERATOR NO-LOAD TEST

Connect voltmeter positive lead to B+ terminal on generator and negative lead to ground. Start and run engine at 2000 RPM with no electrical load (all accessories off). Read voltmeter when voltage stabilizes. Voltage should be 13-15 volts.

SYSTEM TESTS

INTRODUCTION

Identify symptom and perform appropriate system test. See SYSTEM TEST INDEX table.

SYSTEM TEST INDEX

Symptom	Test
System Does Not Charge	A
System Overcharges	B
Charge Warning Indicator On With Engine Running	C
Charge Warning Indicator Inoperative	D
Charge Warning Indicator Flickers Or Is Intermittent	E

TEST A

1) Measure voltage between generator terminal B+ (Black/Orange wire) and ground. If battery voltage is present, go to next step. If battery voltage is not present, repair open in Black/Orange wire between generator terminal and fusible links "A" and "B" in harness near battery junction box. See WIRING DIAGRAMS.

2) Disconnect generator 3-pin connector. Measure voltage between generator connector terminal "A" (Yellow/White wire) and ground. If battery voltage is present, go to next step. If battery voltage is not present, check ALT fuse (20-amp) in battery junction box. If fuse is okay, repair open in Yellow/White wire or Gray wire. See WIRING DIAGRAMS. If fuse is not okay, install new fuse and check system operation. If new fuse blows, repair short to ground in Yellow/White wire or Gray wire.

3) Reconnect generator 3-pin connector. With ignition on, engine off, measure voltage between 3-pin connector terminal "I" (Light Green/Red wire) and ground by backprobing connector. If battery voltage is present, go to next step. If battery voltage is not present, repair open or high resistance in circuit between generator and charge warning indicator in instrument cluster. See WIRING DIAGRAMS.

4) Measure voltage drop in circuit B+ by connecting voltmeter positive probe to generator terminal B+ (Black/Orange wire). Connect voltmeter negative probe to battery positive terminal. If voltage is .5 volt or greater, repair high resistance in circuit and check system operation. See WIRING DIAGRAMS. On 3.8L engines, if voltage is less than .5 volt, go to next step. On 4.6L engines, if voltage is less than .5 volts, replace generator. See GENERATOR under REMOVAL & INSTALLATION.

5) Restore connections. Start engine. Measure battery voltage and record value. Connect jumper wire between generator terminal "F" screw and ground. *See Fig. 1.* Measure battery voltage and compare to recorded value. If battery voltage increased, replace voltage regulator and check system operation. See VOLTAGE REGULATOR under REMOVAL & INSTALLATION. If battery voltage did not increase, replace generator and check system operation. See GENERATOR under REMOVAL & INSTALLATION.

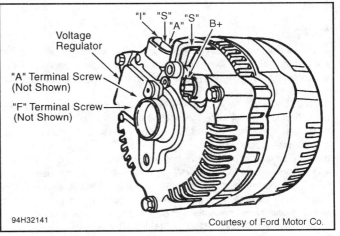

94H32141   Courtesy of Ford Motor Co.

Fig. 1: Identifying Generator Terminals

TEST B

1) Disconnect generator 3-pin connector. With key on, engine off, measure voltage drop in circuit "A" by connecting voltmeter positive probe to generator 3-pin connector terminal "A" (Yellow/White wire). Connect voltmeter negative probe to positive battery terminal. If voltage is less than .25 volt, go to next step. If voltage is .25 volt or greater, check fuses and circuit between battery and generator connector terminal "A". Repair as necessary. See WIRING DIAGRAMS.

2) Inspect ground connections between battery and engine. Ensure generator mounting surfaces are clean and bolts are secure. On 3.8L, also ensure voltage regulator mounting surfaces are clean and screws are secure. On all models, if all grounds or mounting surfaces are not okay, repair as necessary and check system operation. If grounds and mounting are okay, replace generator and check system operation. See GENERATOR under REMOVAL & INSTALLATION.

TEST C

1) Disconnect generator 3-pin connector. Observe charge warning indicator with ignition on, engine off. If indicator illuminates, repair short to ground in Light Green/Red wire. See WIRING DIAGRAMS. Check system operation. On 3.8L, if indicator does not illuminate, go to next step. On 4.6L, if indicator does not illuminate, replace generator. See GENERATOR under REMOVAL & INSTALLATION. Check system operation.

2) Inspect generator 1-pin and 3-pin connector terminals for looseness, corrosion or damage. Repair as necessary and check system operation. If connector terminals are okay, go to next step.

3) Reconnect generator 3-pin connector and disconnect generator 1-pin connector (White/Black wire). Start engine and run at 2000 RPM. Measure voltage between generator 1-pin connector White/Black wire and ground. If voltage is greater than 5 volts, replace voltage regulator and check system operation. See VOLTAGE REGULATOR under REMOVAL & INSTALLATION. If voltage is 5 volts or less, replace generator and check system operation. See GENERATOR under REMOVAL & INSTALLATION.

TEST D

1) Disconnect generator 3-pin connector. With ignition on, engine off, connect a 15-amp fused jumper wire between generator 3-pin connector terminal "I" (Light Green/Red wire) and ground. If charge warning indicator does not illuminate, diagnose instrument cluster. See appropriate INSTRUMENT PANELS article in ACCESSORIES & EQUIPMENT. Check system operation.

2) On 3.8L engines, if indicator illuminates, replace voltage regulator and check system operation. See VOLTAGE REGULATOR under REMOVAL & INSTALLATION. On 4.6L engines, if indicator illuminates, replace generator. See GENERATOR under REMOVAL & INSTALLATION.

TEST E

1) Inspect battery, battery junction box, central junction box and generator connectors for loose, corroded or damaged connections. Repair as necessary and check system operation. If all connections are okay, go to next step.

2) Start engine. Wiggle appropriate fuses and fusible links while observing charge warning indicator. If indicator does not flicker, go to next step. If indicator flickers, repair appropriate loose connection and check system operation.

3) With generator connectors connected, backprobe generator 3-pin connector terminal "A" (Yellow/White wire) with a 20-amp fused jumper wire. Connect other end of jumper to battery positive terminal. Start engine and observe charge warning indicator. If indicator does not flicker, repair loose connections in circuit between battery and generator 3-pin connector. See WIRING DIAGRAMS. Check system operation. On 3.8L, if indicator flickers, go to next step. On 4.6L, if indicator flickers, replace generator. See GENERATOR under REMOVAL & INSTALLATION.

4) Disconnect generator 1-pin connector. Inspect connector for looseness, corrosion or damage. If connector is okay, go to next step. If connector is not okay, repair as necessary and check system operation.

5) Remove generator. See GENERATOR under REMOVAL & INSTALLATION. Measure resistance between generator terminal "A" and generator terminal "F" screw. See Fig. 1. If resistance is 5 ohms or greater, go to next step. If resistance is less than 5 ohms, install new generator and check system operation.

6) Remove voltage regulator to expose generator slip rings. See VOLTAGE REGULATOR under REMOVAL & INSTALLATION. Measure resistance between each slip ring and ground. If resistance between either slip ring and ground is greater than 1000 ohms, replace generator and check system operation. If resistance is 1000 ohms or less, replace voltage regulator and check system operation.

REMOVAL & INSTALLATION

CAUTION: When battery is disconnected, vehicle computer and memory systems may lose memory data. Driveability problems may exist until computer systems have completed a relearn cycle. See COMPUTER RELEARN PROCEDURES article in GENERAL INFORMATION before disconnecting battery.

GENERATOR

Removal & Installation (3.8L) – Disconnect negative battery cable. Remove accessory drive belt. Disconnect wiring from generator. Remove 2 generator bolts and remove generator from vehicle. To install, reverse removal procedure. Tighten fasteners to specification. See TORQUE SPECIFICATIONS.

Removal & Installation (4.6L) – Disconnect negative battery cable. Remove accessory drive belt. Remove 4 upper generator bracket bolts, and remove bracket. Disconnect wiring from generator. Remove 2 lower generator bolts and remove generator from vehicle. To install, reverse removal procedure. Tighten fasteners to specification. See TORQUE SPECIFICATIONS.

VOLTAGE REGULATOR

Removal & Installation (3.8L Only) – Remove generator. See GENERATOR. Remove 4 voltage regulator screws. Remove voltage regulator and brush assembly. Before installation, insert wire or paper clip in hole on front of regulator while depressing brushes. Install regulator and 4 screws. Tighten fasteners to specification. See TORQUE SPECIFICATIONS. Remove wire or paper clip and install generator on vehicle.

TORQUE SPECIFICATIONS

TORQUE SPECIFICATIONS

Application	Ft. Lbs. (N.m)
Generator Mounting Bolts (Except 3.8L Lower Bolt)	18 (25)
Generator Lower Mounting Bolt (3.8L)	35 (47)
	INCH Lbs. (N.m)
Generator Terminal B+ Nut	71 (8)
Upper Generator Bracket Bolts	89 (10)
Voltage Regulator Screws	27 (3)

WIRING DIAGRAMS

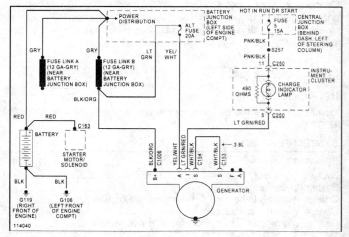

Fig. 2: Charging System Wiring Diagram (Mustang)

DESCRIPTION

System consists of a 130-amp generator, voltage regulator, battery, charge warning indicator and related fuses and wiring. Charge warning indicator illuminates with ignition on, engine off as a bulb-check. Voltage regulator is mounted to rear of generator on 3.0L 2-valve models (including Flex Fuel Vehicles). Voltage regulator is mounted internally on all 3.0L 4-valve and 3.4L SHO models. Internal regulators cannot be serviced separately.

ADJUSTMENTS

BELT TENSION

Vehicles are equipped with automatic drive belt tensioner. Drive belt does not require adjustment. Inspect condition and tension of generator drive belt prior to performing any on-vehicle charging system tests. Replace belt and/or repair tensioner mechanism if necessary.

TROUBLE SHOOTING

NOTE: Also see TROUBLE SHOOTING article in GENERAL INFORMATION.

PRELIMINARY CHECKS
- Verify battery condition.
- Inspect accessory drive belt and tensioner.
- Inspect battery junction box MEGA FUSE (175-amp).
- Inspect battery junction box fuse No. 26 (30-amp).
- Inspect fuse junction panel fuse No. 11 (5-amp).
- Check all connections for looseness or corrosion.

ON-VEHICLE TESTING

PARASITIC DRAW TEST

Connect ammeter to battery negative cable according to tool manufacturer's instructions. With all accessories off, doors closed and key out of ignition, current drain should be less than 50 milliamps. To locate the cause of current drains greater than 50 milliamps, remove fuses one at a time until current draw is within specification. Repair appropriate circuit, and check system operation.

BATTERY LOAD TEST

Connect battery tester according to tool manufacturer's instructions. Load test battery at approximately one-half cold-cranking amperage rating for 15 seconds while observing battery voltage. Compare readings to BATTERY LOAD TEST SPECIFICATIONS table. If voltage readings are within specification, battery is okay. If voltage readings are not within specification, charge battery and retest. If loaded battery voltage is still not within specification after charging, replace battery.

BATTERY LOAD TEST SPECIFICATIONS

Approximate Battery Temperature °F (°C)	Min. Voltage Under Load
80 (27) Or Greater	9.6
70 (21)	9.6
60 (16)	9.5
50 (10)	9.4
40 (4)	9.3
30 (-1)	9.1
20 (-7)	8.9
10 (-12)	8.7

GENERATOR LOAD TEST

Ensure drive belt is in good condition. Replace belt as necessary. If belt is okay, connect charging system load tester in accordance with manufacturer's instructions. Start and run engine at 2000 RPM and apply load until generator output levels off. Generator output should be at least 87 amps at 2000 RPM.

GENERATOR NO-LOAD TEST

Connect voltmeter positive lead to B+ terminal on generator and negative lead to ground. Start and run engine at 2000 RPM with no electrical load (all accessories off). Read voltmeter when voltage stabilizes. Voltage should be 13-15 volts.

SYSTEM TESTS

INTRODUCTION

Identify symptom and perform appropriate system test. See SYSTEM TEST INDEX table.

SYSTEM TEST INDEX

Symptom	Test
System Does Not Charge	A
System Overcharges	B
Charge Warning Indicator On With Engine Running	C
Charge Warning Indicator Inoperative	D

TEST A

1) Inspect accessory drive belt and tensioner. Repair or replace as necessary and check system operation. If drive belt and tensioner are okay, go to next step.
2) Inspect battery terminals. If battery terminal connections are loose or corroded, repair or replace as necessary and check system operation. If battery terminal connections are okay, go to next step.
3) Inspect battery posts for looseness. If either battery post is loose, replace battery and check system operation. If battery posts are okay, go to next step.
4) Remove battery retaining hardware. Inspect battery case for damage. Replace battery as necessary. If battery is okay, go to next step.
5) Perform PARASITIC DRAW TEST under ON-VEHICLE TESTING.. If key-off draw is within specification, go to next step. If key-off draw is not within specification, repair circuit or component causing excessive drain. Check system operation.
6) Perform BATTERY LOAD TEST under ON-VEHICLE TESTING. Replace battery as necessary. If battery tests okay, go to next step.
7) Measure voltage between generator terminal B+ (Yellow/White wire) and ground. If battery voltage is present, go to next step. If battery voltage is not present, repair open in Yellow/White wire between generator terminal and MEGA FUSE (175-amp) in battery junction box. See WIRING DIAGRAMS.
8) Disconnect generator 3-pin connector. Measure voltage between connector terminal "A" (Orange/Light Blue wire) and ground. If battery voltage is present, go to next step. If battery voltage is not present, check fuse No. 26 (30-amp) in battery junction box. If fuse is okay, repair open in Orange/Light Blue wire between generator and battery junction box. See WIRING DIAGRAMS. If fuse is not okay, replace fuse and check system operation. If new fuse blows, repair short to ground in Orange/Light Blue wire.
9) Reconnect generator 3-pin connector. With ignition on, engine off, measure voltage between 3-pin connector terminal "I" (Light Green/Red wire) and ground by backprobing connector. If voltage is greater than one volt, go to next step. If voltage is one volt or less, repair open or high resistance in circuit between generator and charge warning indicator in instrument cluster. See WIRING DIAGRAMS.
10) Disconnect generator 3-pin connector. Measure voltage drop in circuit "A" by connecting voltmeter positive probe to generator connector terminal "A" (Orange/Light Blue wire). Connect voltmeter negative probe to battery positive terminal. If voltage is less than .25 volt, go to next step. If voltage is .25 volt or greater, repair high resistance in circuit. Also inspect fuse No. 26 (30-amp) in battery junction box for high resistance. See WIRING DIAGRAMS.
11) Restore connections. Start engine. Turn on headlights and set blower motor to high position. Run engine at 2000 RPM and measure voltage drop in B+ circuit by connecting voltmeter positive lead to generator terminal B+ (Yellow/White wire) and negative lead to battery positive terminal. If voltage is less than .5 volt, go to next step. If voltage

is .5 volt or greater, repair high resistance in circuit between battery and generator. See WIRING DIAGRAMS.

12) On 3.0L 4-valve and 3.4L engines, replace generator. See GENERATOR under REMOVAL & INSTALLATION. Check system operation. On 3.0L 2-valve engines, remove voltage regulator to expose generator slip rings. See VOLTAGE REGULATOR under REMOVAL & INSTALLATION. Measure resistance between slip rings. If resistance is greater than 10 ohms or less than one ohm, replace generator and check system operation. If resistance is 1-10 ohms, replace voltage regulator and check system operation.

TEST B

1) Disconnect generator 3-pin connector. With ignition on, engine off, measure voltage drop in circuit "A" by connecting voltmeter positive probe to generator 3-pin connector terminal "A" (Orange/Light Blue wire). Connect voltmeter negative probe to positive battery terminal. If voltage is less than .25 volt, go to next step. If voltage is .25 volt or greater, check fuses and circuit between battery and generator connector terminal "A". Repair as necessary. See WIRING DIAGRAMS.

2) Reconnect generator 3-pin connector. Backprobe 3-pin connector terminal "I" (Light Green/Red wire) with voltmeter positive probe. Connect voltmeter negative probe to ground. If voltage is greater than one volt, go to next step. If voltage is one volt or less, repair high resistance in Light Green/Red wire between generator and instrument cluster. See WIRING DIAGRAMS.

3) Inspect ground connections between battery and engine. Ensure generator mounting surfaces are clean and bolts are secure. On 3.0L 2-valve engines, also ensure voltage regulator mounting surfaces are clean and screws are secure. On all models, if all grounds or mounting surfaces are not okay, repair as necessary and check system operation. If grounds and mounting are okay, replace generator and check system operation. See GENERATOR under REMOVAL & INSTALLATION.

TEST C

1) Disconnect generator 3-pin connector. Measure voltage between connector terminal "A" (Orange/Light Blue wire) and ground. If battery voltage is present, go to next step. If battery voltage is not present, check battery junction box fuse No. 26 (30-amp). Replace fuse as necessary. If fuse is okay, repair open in Orange/Light Blue wire. See WIRING DIAGRAMS. Check system operation.

2) Leave generator 3-pin connector disconnected. Observe charge warning indicator with ignition on, engine off. If indicator does not illuminate, go to next step. If indicator illuminates, repair short to ground in Light Green/Red wire. See WIRING DIAGRAMS. Check system operation.

3) Restore connections and turn off all accessories. Start engine and run at 2000 RPM. Measure voltage between generator terminal B+ (Yellow/White wire) and ground. If voltage is greater than 15.5 volts, go to TEST B. If voltage is 15.5 volts or less, replace voltage regulator and check system operation. See VOLTAGE REGULATOR under REMOVAL & INSTALLATION.

TEST D

1) Observe all instrument cluster warning indicators as ignition switch is turned from OFF to RUN position. If other warning indicators illuminate, (even temporarily), go to next step. If no other indicators illuminate, diagnose instrument cluster. See appropriate INSTRUMENT PANELS article in ACCESSORIES & EQUIPMENT.

2) Disconnect generator 3-pin connector. With ignition on, engine off, measure voltage between generator 3-pin connector terminal "I" (Light Green/Red wire) and ground. If battery voltage is present, go to next step. If battery voltage is not present, repair open circuit. See WIRING DIAGRAMS. Check system operation.

3) Connect jumper wire between generator 3-pin connector terminal "I" (Light Green/Red wire) and ground while observing charge warning indicator. If indicator illuminates, remove jumper and go to next step. If indicator does not illuminate, check indicator bulb and replace as necessary. If bulb is okay, repair high resistance in bulb socket or Light Green/Red wire. See WIRING DIAGRAMS. Check system operation.

4) Inspect ground connections between battery and engine. Ensure generator mounting surfaces are clean and bolts are secure. On 3.0L 2-valve engines, also ensure voltage regulator mounting surfaces are clean and screws are secure. On all models, if any grounds or mounting surfaces are not okay, repair as necessary and check system operation. If grounds and mounting are okay, replace generator and check system operation. See GENERATOR under REMOVAL & INSTALLATION. Check system operation.

REMOVAL & INSTALLATION

CAUTION: When battery is disconnected, vehicle computer and memory systems may lose memory data. Driveability problems may exist until computer systems have completed a relearn cycle. See COMPUTER RELEARN PROCEDURES article in GENERAL INFORMATION before disconnecting battery.

GENERATOR

Removal & Installation (3.0L 2-Valve) – Disconnect negative battery cable. Disconnect wiring from generator. Loosen generator pivot bolt and remove mounting brace bolt. Remove accessory drive belt. Remove nut and 2 small bolts, and remove generator brace. Remove generator pivot bolt and remove generator from vehicle. To install reverse removal procedure. Tighten fasteners to specification. See TORQUE SPECIFICATIONS.

Removal & Installation (3.0L 4-Valve) – Disconnect negative battery cable. Remove nut and position engine control sensor and hose bracket to one side. Remove inboard upper generator bolt. Loosen outboard upper generator bolt. Remove accessory drive belt. Disconnect wiring from generator. Raise vehicle on hoist. Remove right front wheel and splash shield. Remove outboard upper generator bolt. Remove lower generator bolt and remove generator. To install reverse removal procedure. Tighten fasteners to specification. See TORQUE SPECIFICATIONS.

Removal & Installation (3.4L) – Disconnect negative battery cable. Remove right side cowl vent screen. Raise vehicle on hoist. Remove right front wheel. Using suitable tie rod end separator tool, separate right outer tie rod end from steering knuckle. Remove accessory drive belt. Disconnect wiring from generator. Remove nut and position engine control sensor wiring harness to one side. Remove 3 generator mounting bolts and remove generator from vehicle. To install reverse removal procedure. Tighten fasteners to specification. See TORQUE SPECIFICATIONS.

VOLTAGE REGULATOR

Removal & Installation (3.0L 2-Valve) – Remove generator. See GENERATOR. Remove four voltage regulator screws. Remove voltage regulator and brush assembly. Before installation, insert wire or paper clip in hole on front of regulator while depressing brushes. Install regulator and 4 screws. Tighten fasteners to specification. See TORQUE SPECIFICATIONS. Remove wire or paper clip and install generator on vehicle.

TORQUE SPECIFICATIONS

TORQUE SPECIFICATIONS (3.0L 2-Valve)

Application	Ft. Lbs. (N.m)
Mounting Brace Bolt (Large) & Nut	15-22 (20-30)
Pivot Bolt	30-40 (40-55)
	INCH Lbs. (N.m)
Mounting Brace Bolts (Small)	76-97 (8.5-11)
Voltage Regulator Screws	21-30 (2.3-3.4)

TORQUE SPECIFICATIONS (3.0L 4-Valve & 3.4L)

Application	Ft. Lbs. (N.m)
Engine Control Sensor Harness Nut	11-14 (15-20)
Generator Mounting Bolts	15-22 (20-30)
	INCH Lbs. (N.m)
Generator Terminal B+ Nut	80-106 (9-12)

WIRING DIAGRAMS

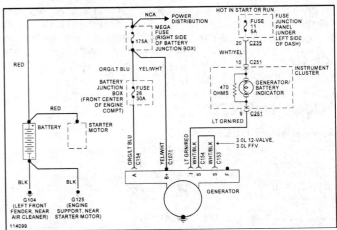

Fig. 1: Charging System Wiring Diagram (Sable & Taurus)

DESCRIPTION

System consists of 125-amp generator, internal voltage regulator, battery, charge warning indicator, bulb check relay and related fuses and wiring. Charge warning indicator should illuminate with ignition on, engine off. Charge warning indicator should not illuminate with ignition off, or with engine running. Generator and regulator cannot be serviced separately, and must be replaced as an assembly.

ADJUSTMENTS

GENERATOR BELT

Tension Adjustment – Raise and support vehicle. Remove engine splash shield. Install suitable tension gauge. Loosen generator-to-bracket mounting bolts. Tighten adjusting bolt while observing tension gauge. See DRIVE BELT TENSION SPECIFICATIONS table. Tighten all fasteners.

DRIVE BELT TENSION SPECIFICATIONS

Application	Tension Lbs. (kg)
New Belt	151-170 (68-77)
Used Belt	125-144 (57-65)

Deflection Adjustment – Allow engine to cool at least 30 minutes before checking adjustment. Apply 22 lbs. (10 kg) force to generator belt midway between generator pulley and crankshaft pulley. With force applied, deflection should be within specification. See DRIVE BELT DEFLECTION SPECIFICATIONS table.

DRIVE BELT DEFLECTION SPECIFICATIONS

Application	In. (mm)
New Belt	.26-.30 (6.5-7.5)
Used Belt	.30-.34 (7.5-8.5)

TROUBLE SHOOTING

NOTE: See TROUBLE SHOOTING article in GENERAL INFORMATION.

PRELIMINARY CHECKS

- Verify battery condition.
- Inspect accessory drive belt and tensioner.
- Inspect battery junction box fuse No. 9 (10-amp) and fuse No. 28 (140-amp).
- Inspect fuse junction panel fuse No. 37 (10-amp)
- Check all connections for looseness or corrosion.

ON-VEHICLE TESTING

GENERATOR LOAD TEST

Ensure drive belt is in good condition. Replace belt as necessary. If belt is okay, connect charging system load tester and ammeter in accordance with tool manufacturer's instructions. Start engine and run at specified RPM while loading system. Compare readings with GENERATOR OUTPUT SPECIFICATIONS table.

GENERATOR OUTPUT SPECIFICATIONS

RPM	Min. Amperage Output
1300	35
2500	92
5000	118

GENERATOR NO-LOAD TEST

Connect voltmeter positive lead to B+ terminal on generator and negative lead to ground. Start and run engine at 2000 RPM with no electrical load (all accessories off). Read voltmeter when voltage stabilizes. Voltage should be 14.1-15.1 volts.

SYSTEM TESTS

INTRODUCTION

Identify symptom and perform appropriate system test. See SYSTEM TEST INDEX table.

SYSTEM TEST INDEX

Symptom	Test
System Overcharges (More Than 15 Volts)	A
System Is Not Charging, Charge Warning Indicator Operates Properly	B
Charge Warning Indicator On With Engine Running, System Is Charging	C
Charge System Indicator Flickers Or Operates Intermittently	D

TEST A

1) Turn ignition off. Disconnect generator 2-pin connector. Remove battery junction box fuse No. 9 (10-amp). Measure resistance of Blue wire between generator connector terminal and fuse No. 9 output terminal. If resistance is less than 5 ohms, go to next step. If resistance is 5 ohms or greater, repair open circuit in Blue wire. See WIRING DIAGRAMS.

2) Measure resistance between generator connector terminal (Blue wire) and ground. If resistance is greater than 10 k/ohms, replace generator. See GENERATOR under REMOVAL & INSTALLATION. If resistance is 10 k/ohms or less, repair short to ground in Blue wire between generator and battery junction box fuse No. 9. See WIRING DIAGRAMS.

TEST B

1) Perform NO-LOAD TEST under ON-VEHICLE TESTING. If generator output is lower than specified, go to next step. If generator output is as specified, check battery state of charge and perform battery load test according to load tester manufacturer's instructions.

2) Turn ignition off. Inspect drive belt condition and tension. See ADJUSTMENTS. Adjust, repair or replace belt as necessary and check system operation. If drive belt is okay, disconnect generator terminal B+ (Black wire) connector. Measure voltage between generator B+ connector terminal and ground. If battery voltage is present, go to next step. If battery voltage is not present, repair circuit and check system operation. See WIRING DIAGRAMS.

3) Disconnect generator 2-pin connector. Measure voltage between generator connector terminal (Blue wire) and ground. If battery voltage is present, go to next step. If battery voltage is not present, repair circuit and check system operation. See WIRING DIAGRAMS.

4) Disconnect generator ground connector (smaller gauge Black wire). Measure resistance between generator connector Black wire and ground. If resistance is greater than 5 ohms, repair ground wire or ground connection, and check system operation. If resistance is 5 ohms or less, replace generator. See GENERATOR under REMOVAL & INSTALLATION.

TEST C

1) Turn ignition off. Disconnect generator 2-pin connector. Start engine and observe charge warning indicator. If indicator illuminates, go to next step. If indicator does not illuminate, replace generator. See GENERATOR under REMOVAL & INSTALLATION.

2) Turn ignition off. Disconnect 33-pin in-line connector located behind top left side of instrument panel. Start engine and observe charge warning indicator. If warning indicator illuminates, repair Yellow/Blue wire between in-line connector and instrument cluster. If warning indicator does not illuminate, repair Yellow/Black wire between in-line connector and generator. See WIRING DIAGRAMS. Check system operation.

TEST D

1) Turn ignition off. Inspect generator and battery junction box connections for loose, damaged or corroded terminals. Repair as necessary and check system operation. If all connections are okay, go to next step.

2) Inspect accessory drive belt for condition and proper tension. Replace as necessary and check system operation. If belt is okay, replace generator. See GENERATOR under REMOVAL & INSTALLATION.

REMOVAL & INSTALLATION

CAUTION: When batteries are disconnected, vehicle computer and memory systems may lose memory data. Driveability problems may exist until computer systems have completed a relearn cycle. See COMPUTER RELEARN PROCEDURES article in GENERAL INFORMATION before disconnecting battery.

GENERATOR

Removal & Installation – Disconnect negative battery cable. Raise and support vehicle. Remove engine splash shield. Remove generator adjuster bolt. Remove 2 generator mounting bolts and support generator. Rotate generator to access electrical connections. Disconnect electrical connections and remove generator from vehicle. To install reverse removal procedures. Tighten fasteners to specification. See TORQUE SPECIFICATIONS.

TORQUE SPECIFICATIONS

TORQUE SPECIFICATIONS

Application	Ft. Lbs. (N.m)
Generator Mounting Bolts	19 (25)
Generator Adjuster Bolt	14 (19)

WIRING DIAGRAMS

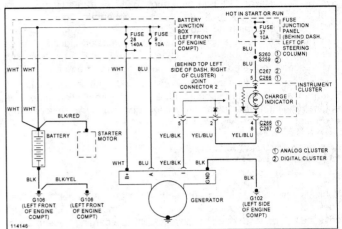

Fig. 1: Charging System Wiring Diagram (Villager)

1999 STARTING & CHARGING SYSTEMS
Generators – Windstar

DESCRIPTION

System consists of 110-amp generator (3.0L) or 125-amp generator (3.8L), internal voltage regulator, battery, Powertrain Control Module (PCM), charge warning indicator and related fuses and wiring. PCM and generator communicate using pulse-width modulated signals. A dedicated line communicates desired charging rate from PCM to generator and a second dedicated line communicates load from generator to PCM.

Charge warning indicator should illuminate with ignition on, engine off. Charge warning indicator should not illuminate with ignition off, or with engine running. Generator and regulator cannot be serviced separately, and must be replaced as an assembly.

ADJUSTMENTS

BELT TENSION

Vehicles are equipped with automatic drive belt tensioner. Drive belt does not require adjustment. Inspect condition and tension of generator drive belt prior to performing any on-vehicle charging system tests. Replace belt and/or repair tensioner mechanism if necessary.

TROUBLE SHOOTING

NOTE: See TROUBLE SHOOTING article in GENERAL INFORMATION.

PRELIMINARY CHECKS

- Verify battery condition.
- Inspect accessory drive belt and tensioner.
- Inspect Gray fusible links "A", "B" and "C" at battery junction box.
- Inspect battery junction box fuse No. 20 (15-amp).
- Check all connections for looseness or corrosion.

ON-VEHICLE TESTING

LOAD TEST

Verify battery condition. Charge or replace as necessary. Connect load tester and ammeter according to tool manufacturer's instructions. With engine running at 2000 RPM and all accessories off, load system until amperage output peaks. Generator should produce at least 89 amps at 2000 RPM. Replace generator if output is not as specified. See GENERATOR under REMOVAL & INSTALLATION.

NO-LOAD TEST

Verify battery condition. Charge or replace battery as necessary. Connect voltmeter positive lead to B+ terminal on generator and negative lead to ground. Start and run engine at 2000 RPM with no electrical load (accessories off). Read voltmeter when voltage stabilizes. Voltage should be 13-15 volts. If voltage is not as specified, replace generator. See GENERATOR under REMOVAL & INSTALLATION.

SELF-DIAGNOSTIC SYSTEM

RETRIEVING DIAGNOSTIC TROUBLE CODES

Connect New Generation Star (NGS) tester to Data Link Connector (DLC) and retrieve charging system Diagnostic Trouble Codes (DTCs). If DTC P1246 is present, go to TEST A under SYSTEM TESTS. If any other DTCs are present, see SELF-DIAGNOSTICS – EEC-V article in ENGINE PERFORMANCE in appropriate MITCHELL® manual to diagnose fault. After repair is complete, clear DTCs. See CLEARING DIAGNOSTIC TROUBLE CODES. If no DTCs are present, diagnose by symptom. See SYSTEM TEST INDEX table under SYSTEM TESTS.

CLEARING DIAGNOSTIC TROUBLE CODES

Connect New Generation Star (NGS) tester to Data Link Connector (DLC). Using NGS tester manufacturer's instructions, clear DTCs.

SYSTEM TESTS

INTRODUCTION

Identify symptom and perform appropriate system test. See SYSTEM TEST INDEX table.

SYSTEM TEST INDEX

Symptom	Test
Charging System Malfunction	A
Charge Warning Indicator Malfunction	B

TEST A

1) Start engine and measure battery voltage. If battery voltage is 13-15 volts, problem is intermittent. Check for loose connections. If battery voltage is not 13-15 volts, go to next step.
2) Turn engine off and inspect accessory drive belt condition. Replace drive belt as necessary and check system operation. If belt is okay, go to next step.
3) Inspect generator connectors and generator mounting for looseness or corrosion. Repair as necessary and check system operation. If connections and mounting are okay, go to next step.
4) Inspect battery cables for clean an tight connections at battery. Repair as necessary and check system operation. If connections are okay, go to next step.
5) Verify battery condition. Load test battery at one-half rated amperage for 15 seconds. If battery is okay, go to next step. If battery voltage drops to less than 9.6 volts, charge and retest. If battery voltage still drops to less than 9.6 volts, replace battery and check system operation.
6) Turn ignition off. Disconnect generator 3-pin connector. Measure voltage between 3-pin connector terminal (Orange/Light Blue wire) and ground. If battery voltage is present, go to next step. If battery voltage is not present, inspect circuit for open, (including fusible links). See WIRING DIAGRAMS.
7) Reconnect generator 3-pin connector. Measure voltage between generator terminal B+ (Yellow/White wire) and ground. If battery voltage is present, go to next step. If battery voltage is not present, inspect circuit for open, (including fusible links). See WIRING DIAGRAMS.
8) Check generator output. Perform LOAD TEST and NO-LOAD TEST under ON-VEHICLE TESTING. If generator is okay, check system for intermittent failure. If generator is not okay, continue diagnosis of PCM controlled charging system DTC P1246. See SELF-DIAGNOSTICS – EEC-V article in ENGINE PERFORMANCE in appropriate MITCHELL® manual.

TEST B

Start engine and measure voltage between generator terminal B+ (Yellow/White wire) and ground. If voltage is less than 13 volts or more than 15 volts, go to TEST A. If voltage is 13-15 volts, diagnose warning indicator. See appropriate INSTRUMENT PANELS article in ACCESSORIES & EQUIPMENT.

REMOVAL & INSTALLATION

CAUTION: When batteries are disconnected, vehicle computer and memory systems may lose memory data. Driveability problems may exist until computer systems have completed a relearn cycle. See COMPUTER RELEARN PROCEDURES article in GENERAL INFORMATION before disconnecting battery.

GENERATOR

Removal & Installation – Disconnect negative battery cable. Remove drive belt from pulley. Disconnect wiring from generator. Remove 3 mounting bolts and generator. To install reverse removal procedure. Tighten fasteners to specification. See TORQUE SPECIFICATIONS.

TORQUE SPECIFICATIONS

TORQUE SPECIFICATIONS

Application	Ft. Lbs. (N.m)
Generator Mounting Bolts	18 (25)
	INCH Lbs. (N.m)
Generator Terminal B+ Nut	89 (10)

WIRING DIAGRAMS

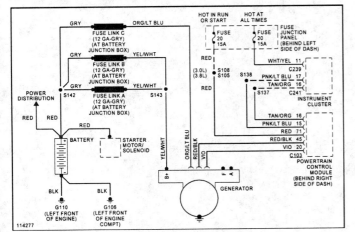

Fig. 1: Charging System Wiring Diagram (Windstar)

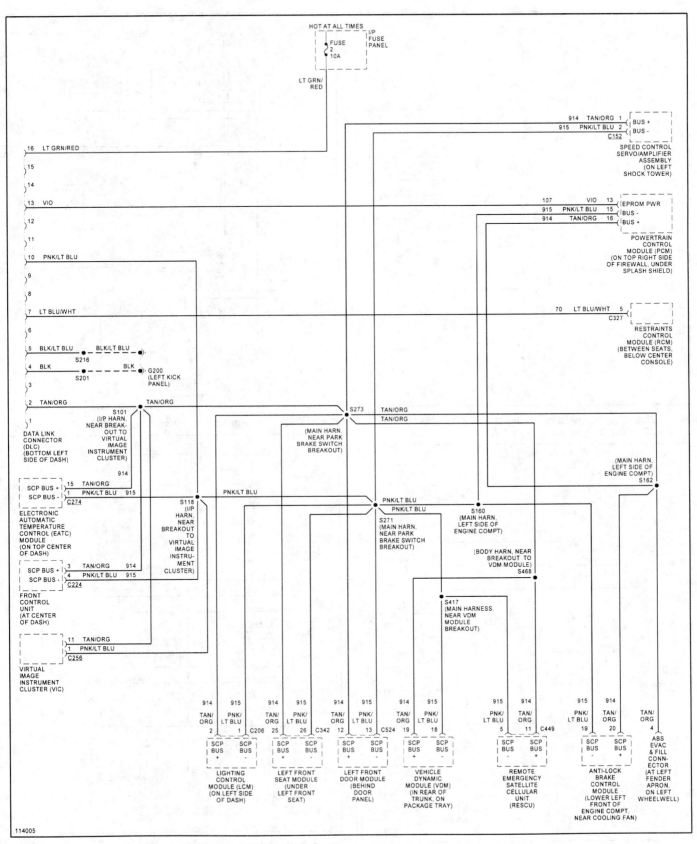

Fig. 1: Data Link Connectors Wiring Diagram (Continental)

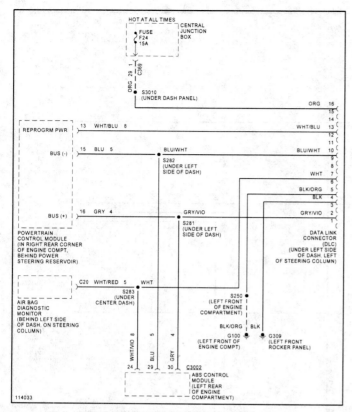

Fig. 2: Data Link Connectors Wiring Diagram (Contour & Mystique – With ABS)

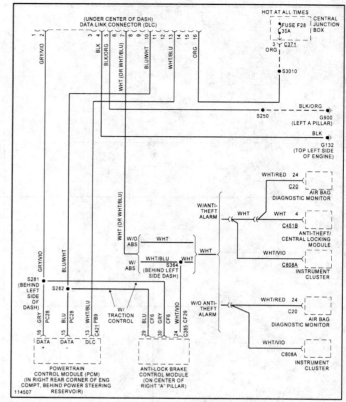

Fig. 4: Data Link Connectors Wiring Diagram (Cougar)

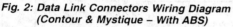

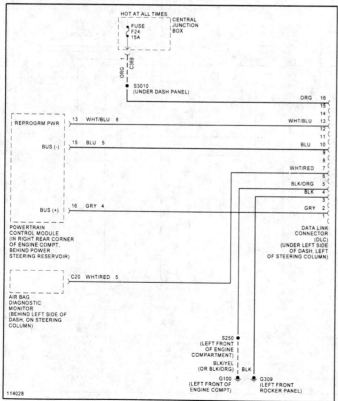

Fig. 3: Data Link Connectors Wiring Diagram (Contour & Mystique – Without ABS)

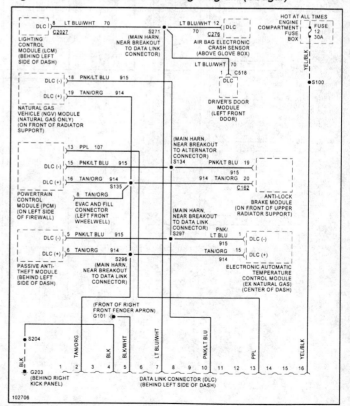

Fig. 5: Data Link Connectors Wiring Diagram (Crown Victoria & Grand Marquis)

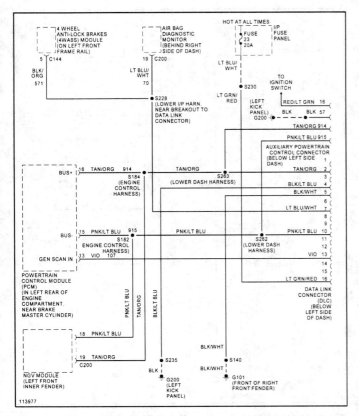

Fig. 6: Data Link Connectors Wiring Diagram (Econoline)

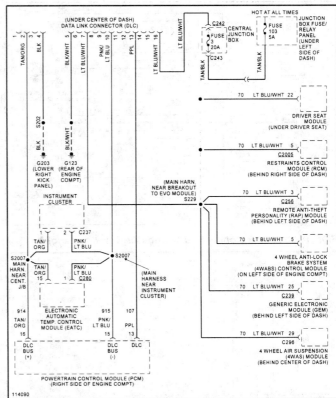

Fig. 8: Data Link Connectors Wiring Diagram (Expedition & Navigator)

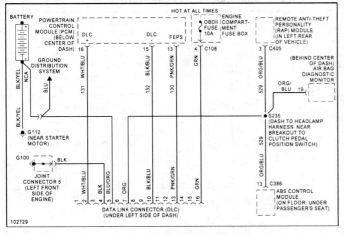

Fig. 7: Data Link Connectors Wiring Diagram (Escort & Tracer)

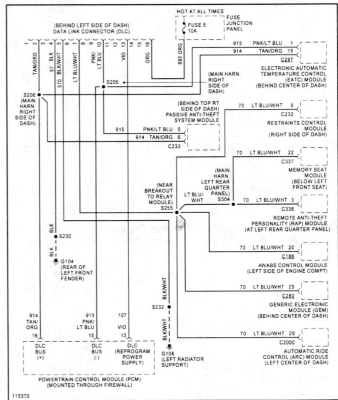

Fig. 9: Data Link Connectors Wiring Diagram (Explorer & Mountaineer)

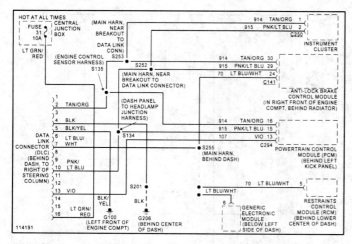

Fig. 10: Data Link Connectors Wiring Diagram (Mustang)

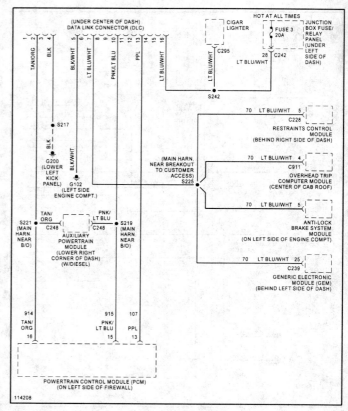

Fig. 12: Data Link Connectors Wiring Diagram (F250 Super-Duty & F350 Pickups)

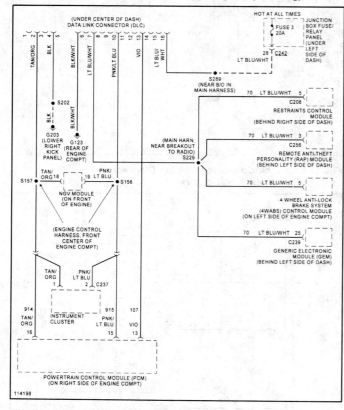

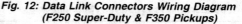

Fig. 11: Data Link Connectors Wiring Diagram (F150 & F250 Light-Duty Pickups)

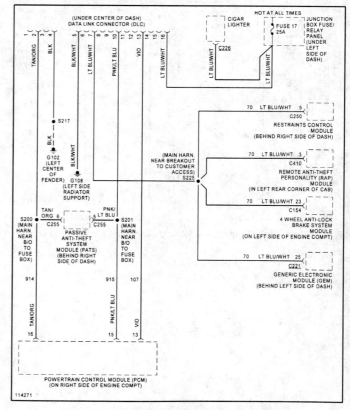

Fig. 13: Data Link Connectors Wiring Diagram (Ranger)

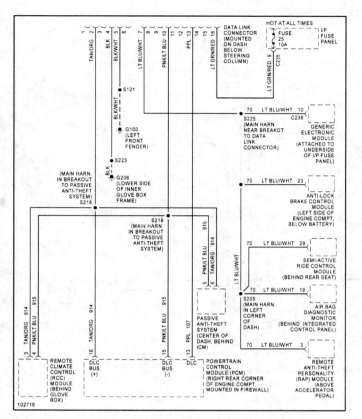

Fig. 14: Data Link Connectors Wiring Diagram (Sable & Taurus)

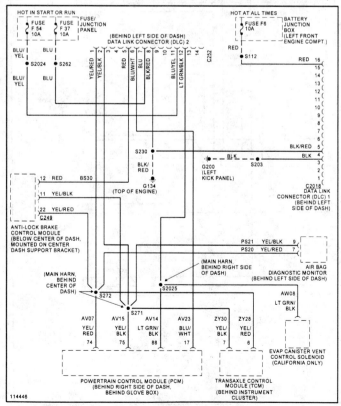

Fig. 15: Data Link Connectors Wiring Diagram (Villager)

1999 WIRING DIAGRAMS
Data Link Connectors (Cont.)

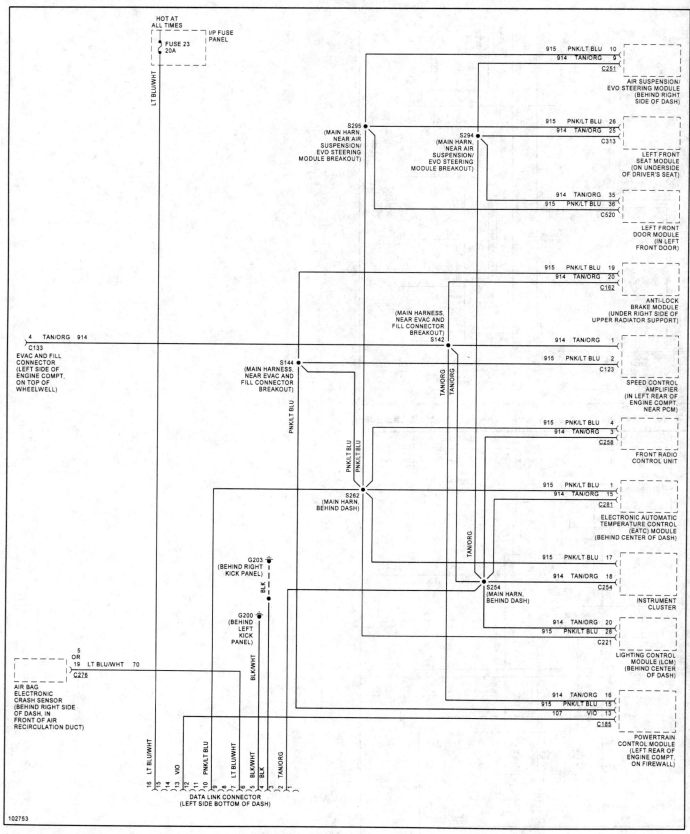

Fig. 16: Data Link Connectors Wiring Diagram (Town Car)

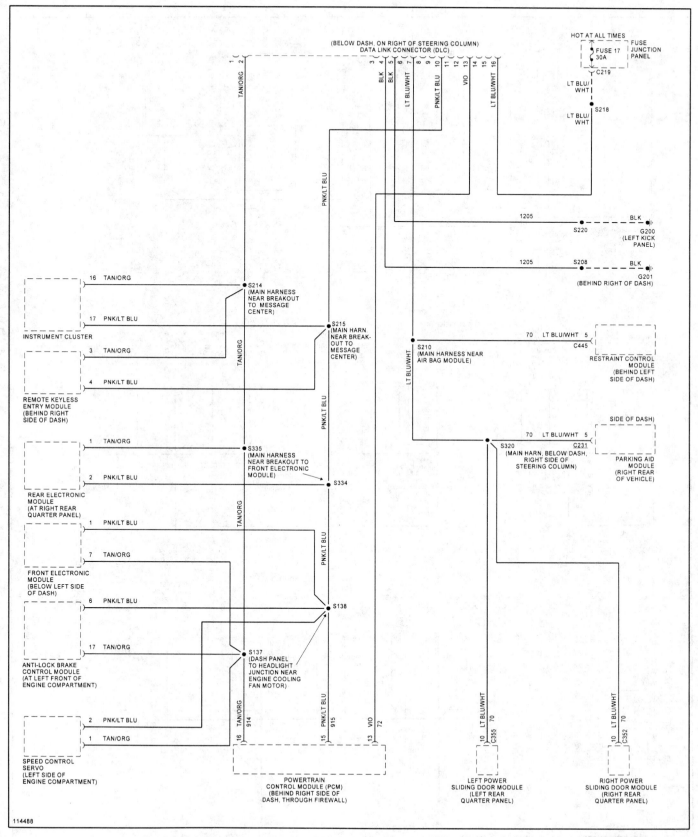

Fig. 17: Data Link Connectors Wiring Diagram (Windstar)

114488

1999 WIRING DIAGRAMS
Ground Distribution

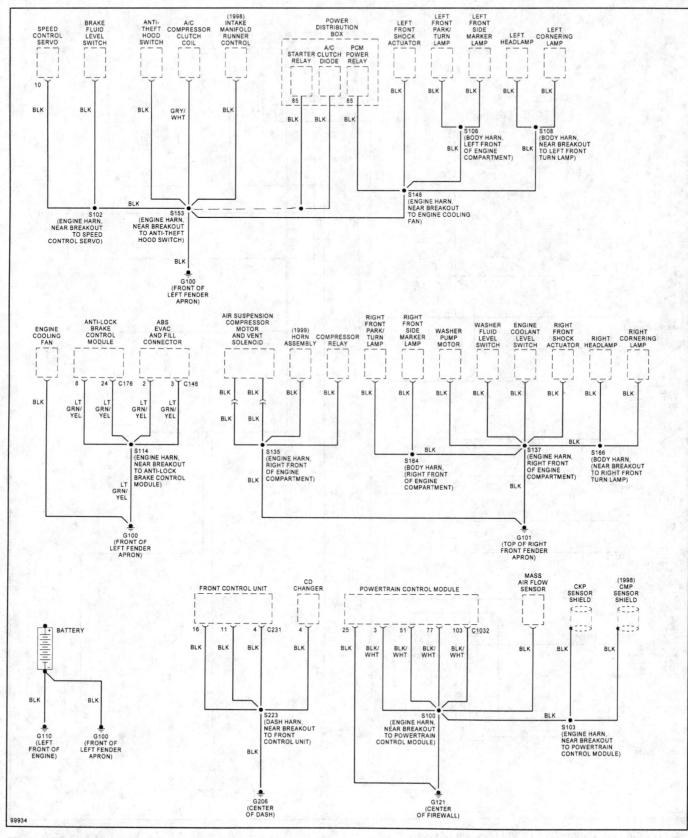

Fig. 1: Ground Distribution Wiring Diagram (Continental – 1 Of 3)

99934

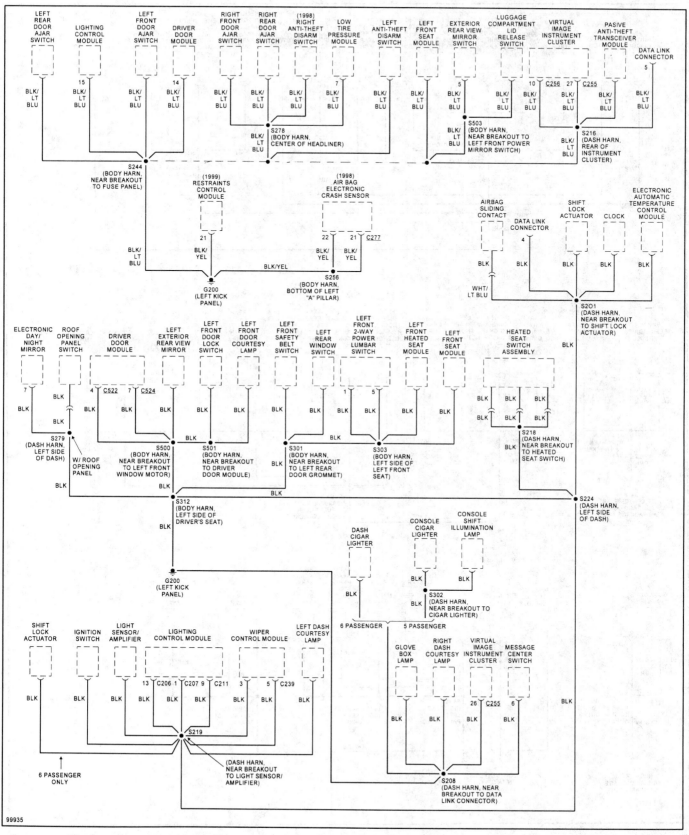

Fig. 2: Ground Distribution Wiring Diagram (Continental – 2 Of 3)

99935

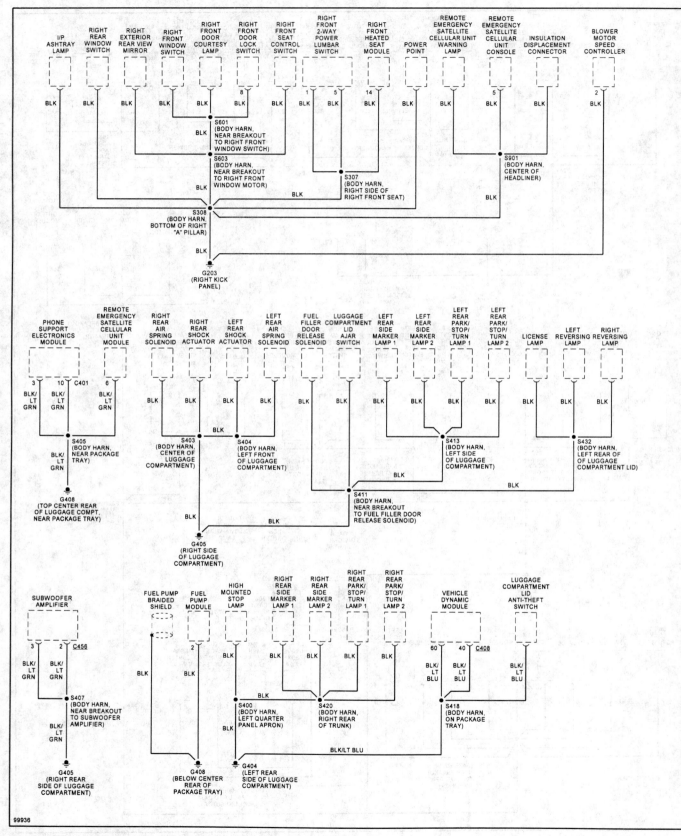

Fig. 3: Ground Distribution Wiring Diagram (Continental – 3 Of 3)

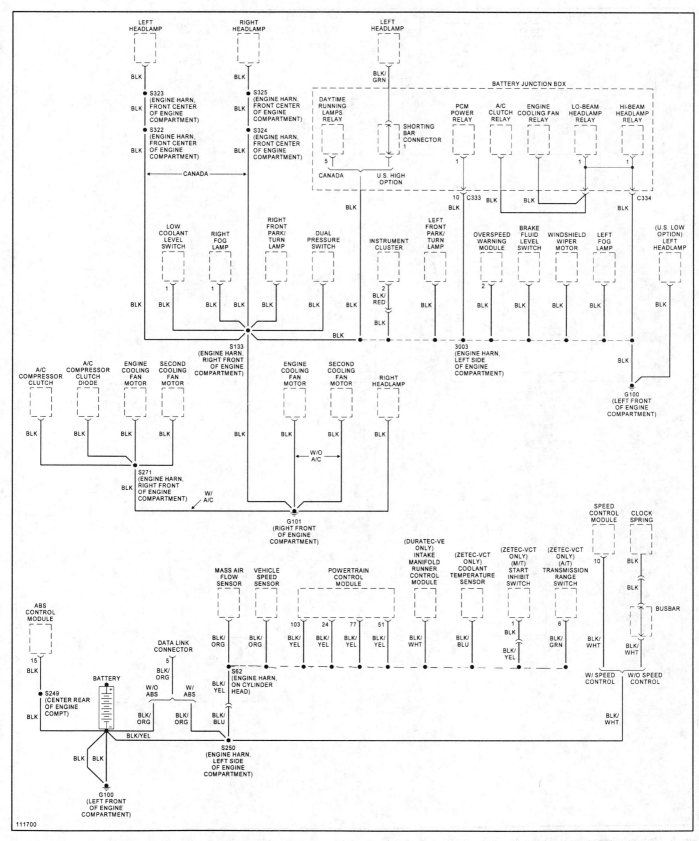

Fig. 4: Ground Distribution Wiring Diagram (Contour & Mystique – 1 Of 3)

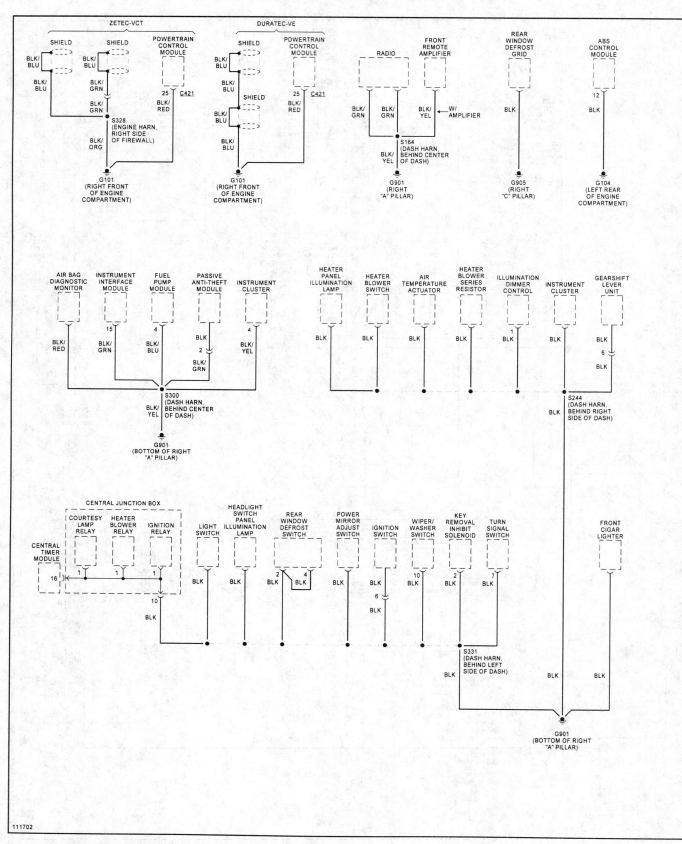

Fig. 5: Ground Distribution Wiring Diagram (Contour & Mystique – 2 Of 3)

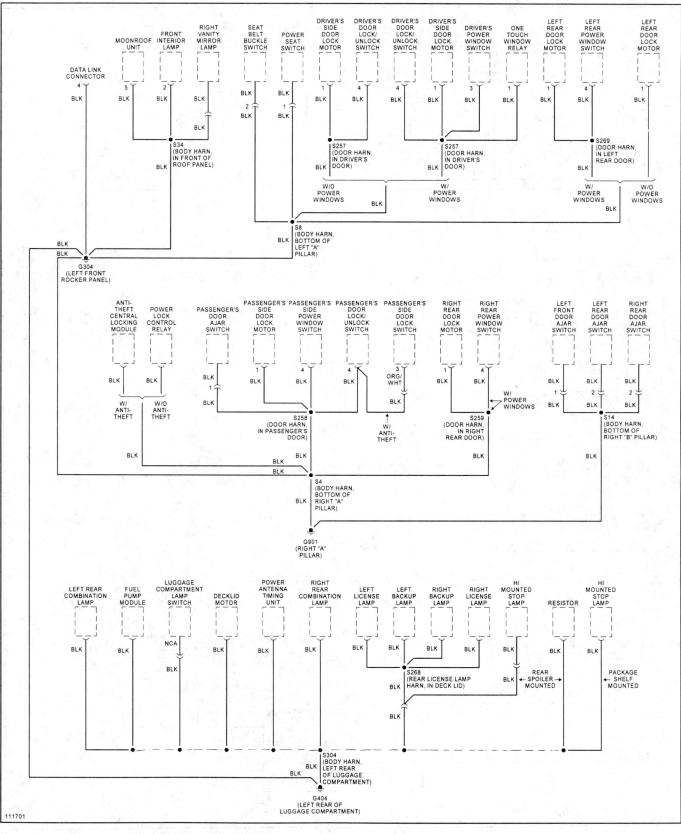

Fig. 6: Ground Distribution Wiring Diagram (Contour & Mystique – 3 Of 3)

111701

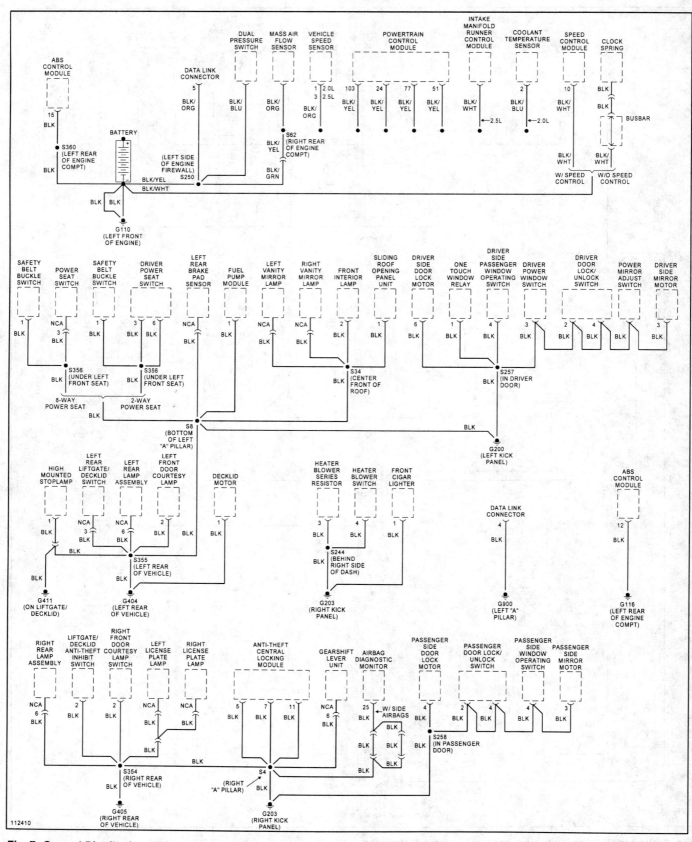

Fig. 7: Ground Distribution Wiring Diagram (Cougar – 1 Of 3)

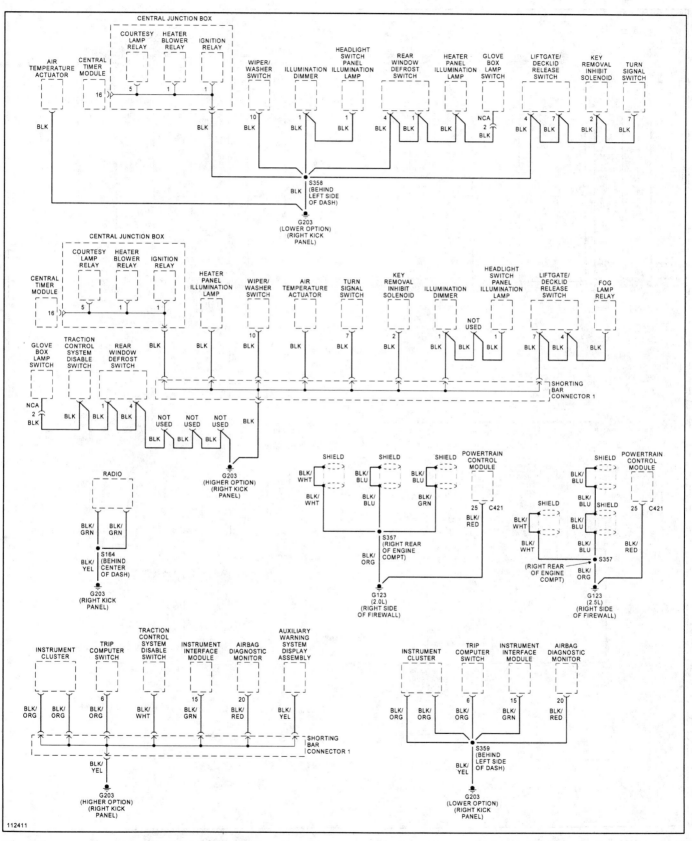

Fig. 8: Ground Distribution Wiring Diagram (Cougar – 2 Of 3)

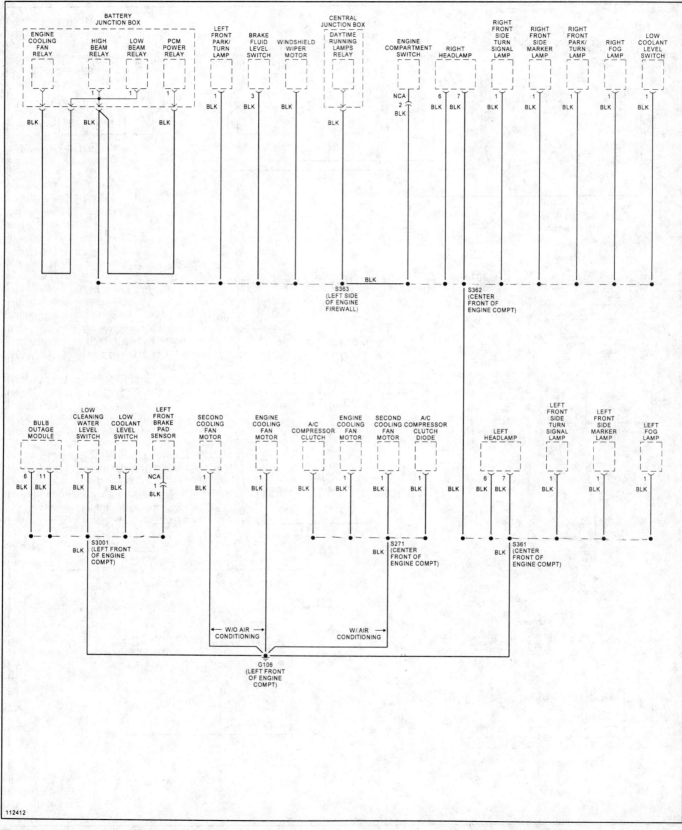

Fig. 9: Ground Distribution Wiring Diagram (Cougar – 3 Of 3)

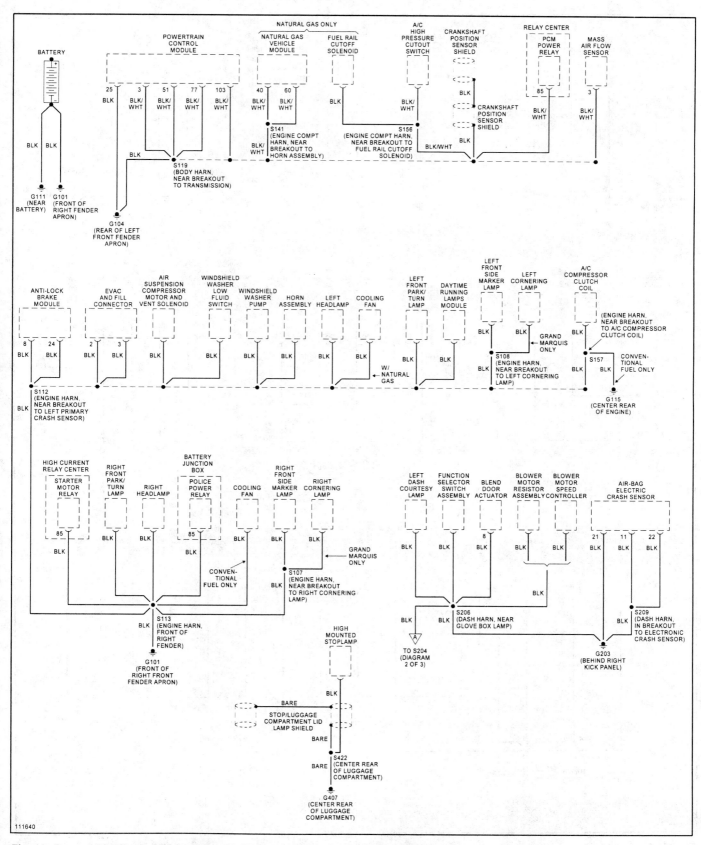

Fig. 10: Ground Distribution Wiring Diagram (Crown Victoria & Grand Marquis – 1 Of 3)

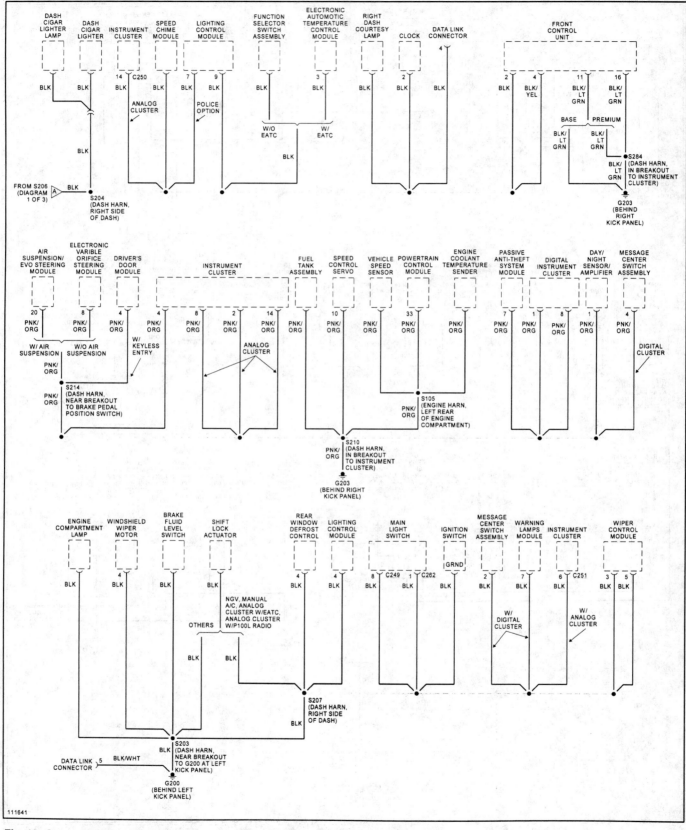

Fig. 11: Ground Distribution Wiring Diagram (Crown Victoria & Grand Marquis – 2 Of 3)

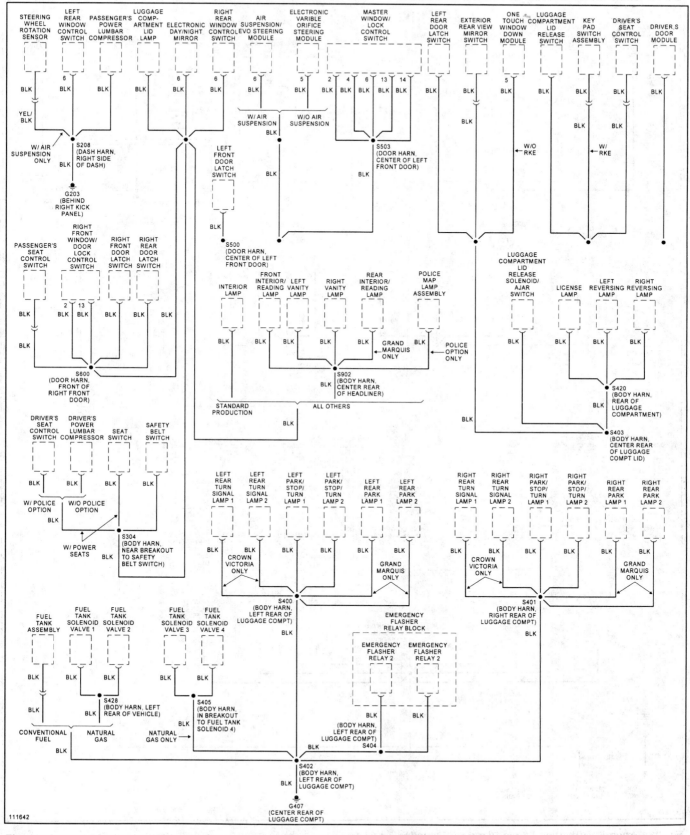

Fig. 12: Ground Distribution Wiring Diagram (Crown Victoria & Grand Marquis – 3 Of 3)

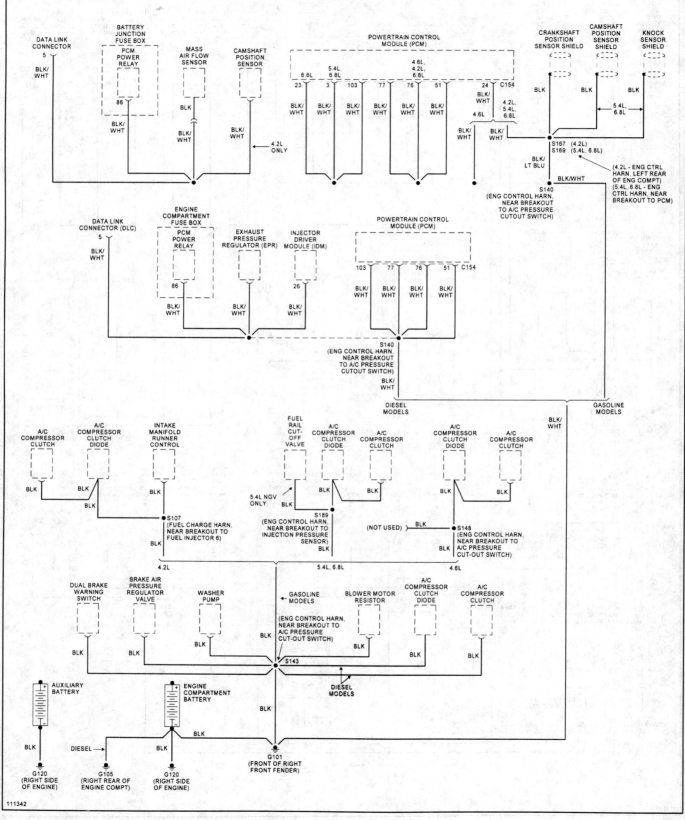

Fig. 13: Ground Distribution Wiring Diagram (Econoline – 1 Of 4)

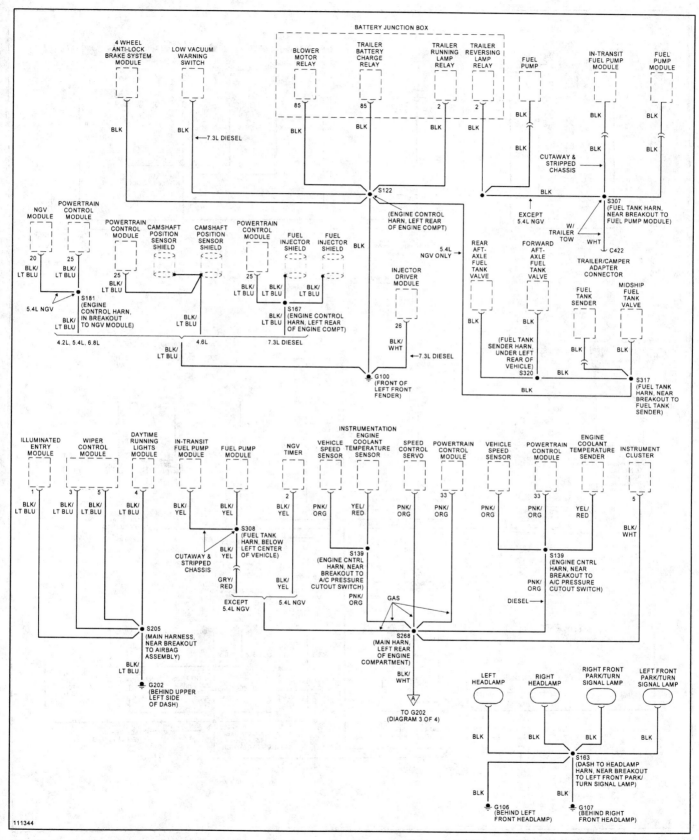

Fig. 14: Ground Distribution Wiring Diagram (Econoline – 2 Of 4)

111344

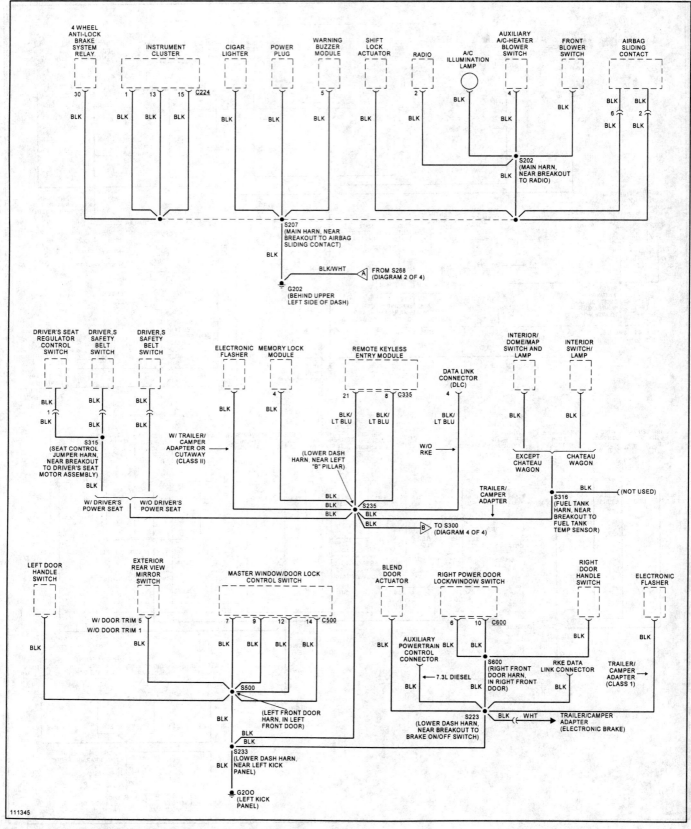

Fig. 15: Ground Distribution Wiring Diagram (Econoline – 3 Of 4)

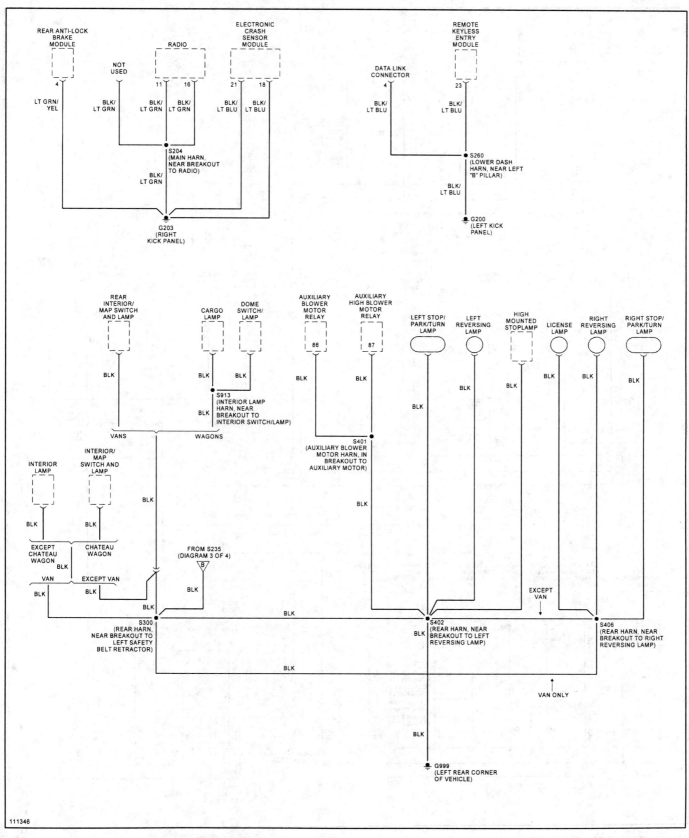

Fig. 16: Ground Distribution Wiring Diagram (Econoline – 4 Of 4)

111346

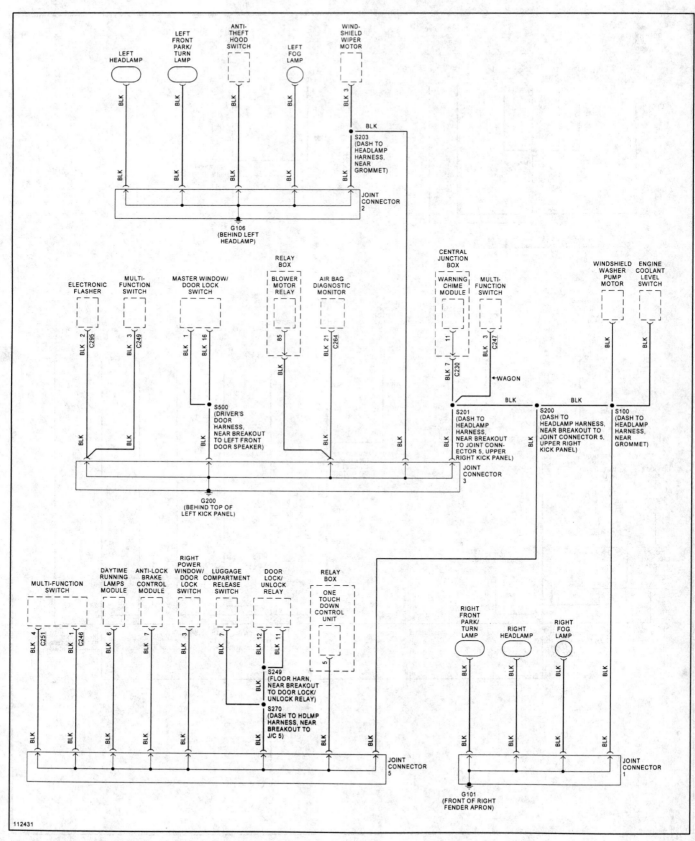

Fig. 17: Ground Distribution Wiring Diagram (Escort & Tracer – 1 Of 3)

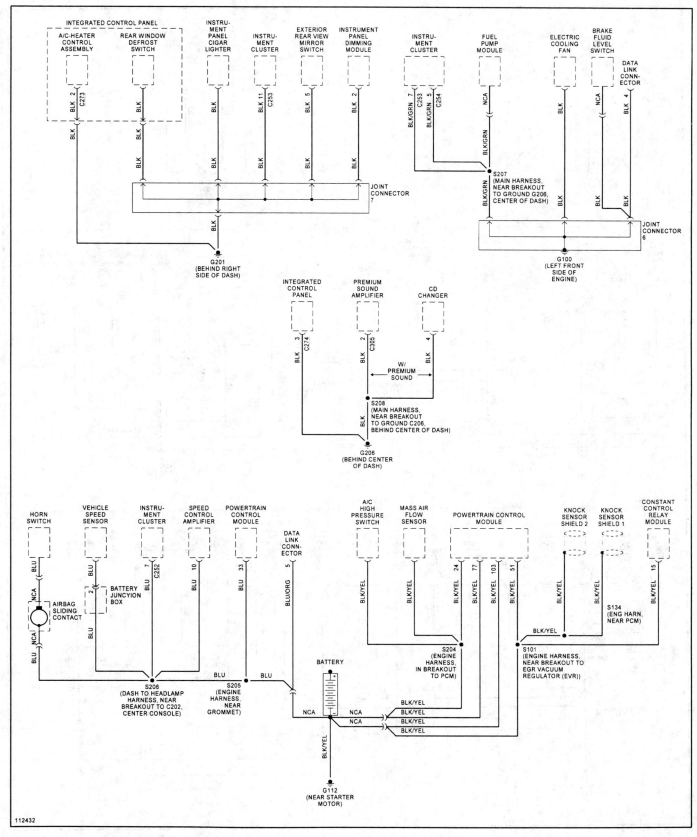

Fig. 18: Ground Distribution Wiring Diagram (Escort & Tracer – 2 Of 3)

1999 WIRING DIAGRAMS
Ground Distribution (Cont.)

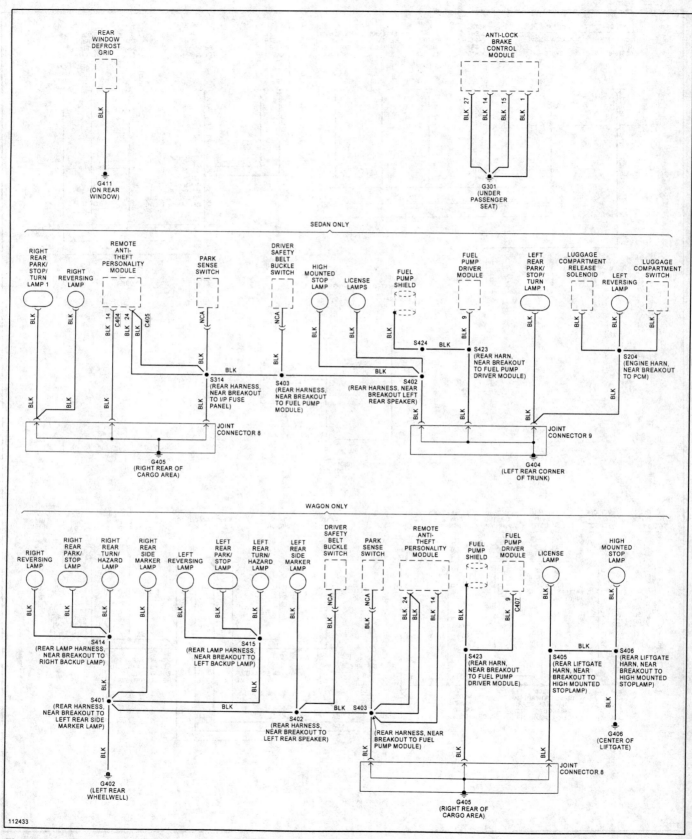

Fig. 19: Ground Distribution Wiring Diagram (Escort & Tracer – 3 Of 3)

112433

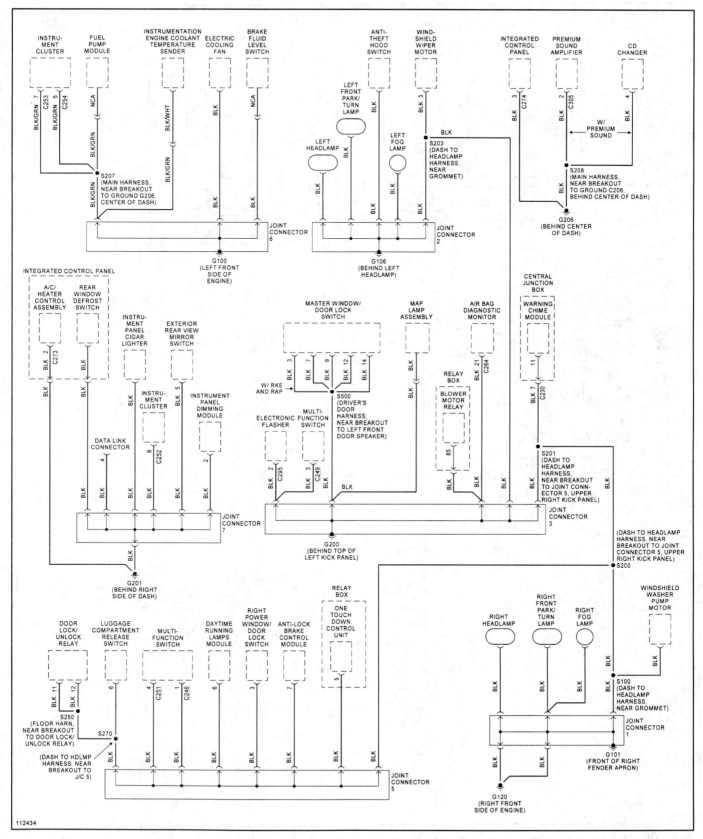

Fig. 20: Ground Distribution Wiring Diagram (Escort ZX2 – 1 Of 2)

112434

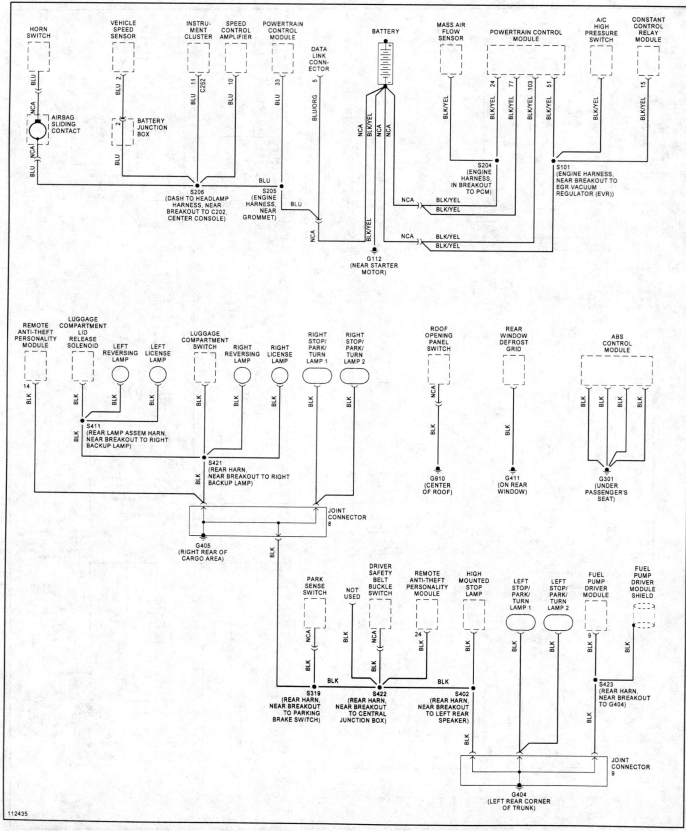

Fig. 21: Ground Distribution Wiring Diagram (Escort ZX2 – 2 Of 2)

112435

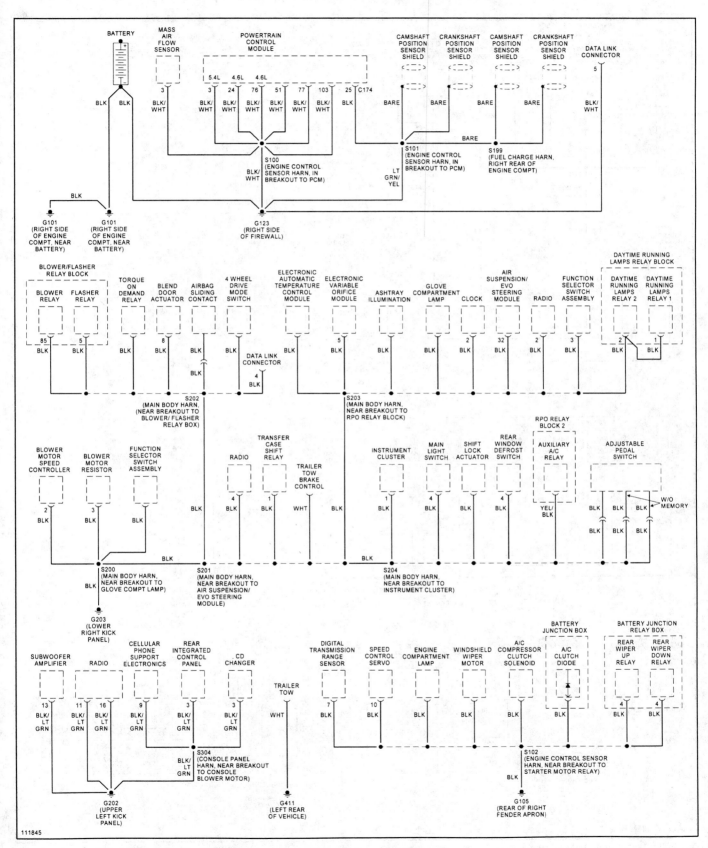

Fig. 22: Ground Distribution Wiring Diagram (Expedition & Navigator – 1 Of 4)

1999 WIRING DIAGRAMS
Ground Distribution (Cont.)

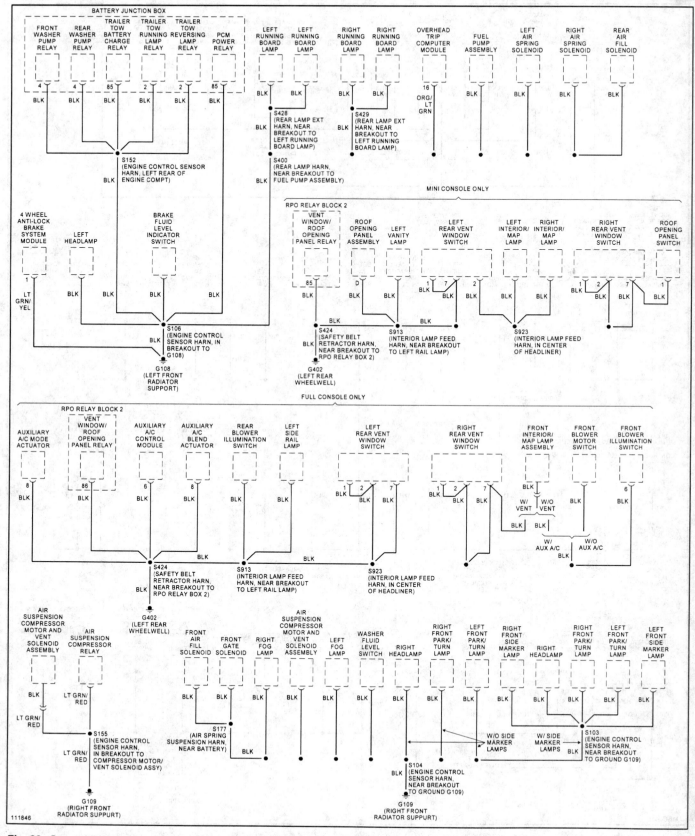

Fig. 23: Ground Distribution Wiring Diagram (Expedition & Navigator – 2 Of 4)

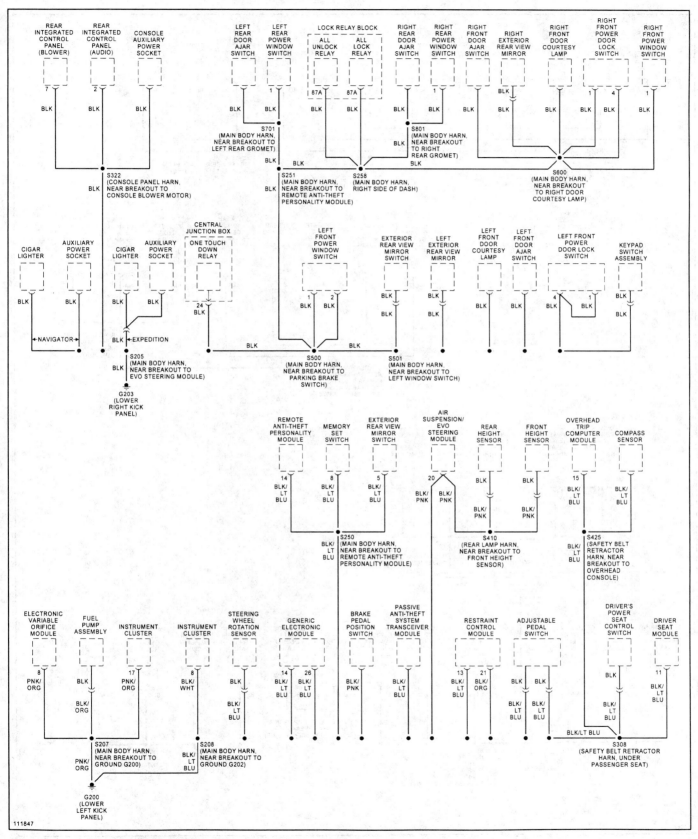

Fig. 24: Ground Distribution Wiring Diagram (Expedition & Navigator – 3 Of 4)

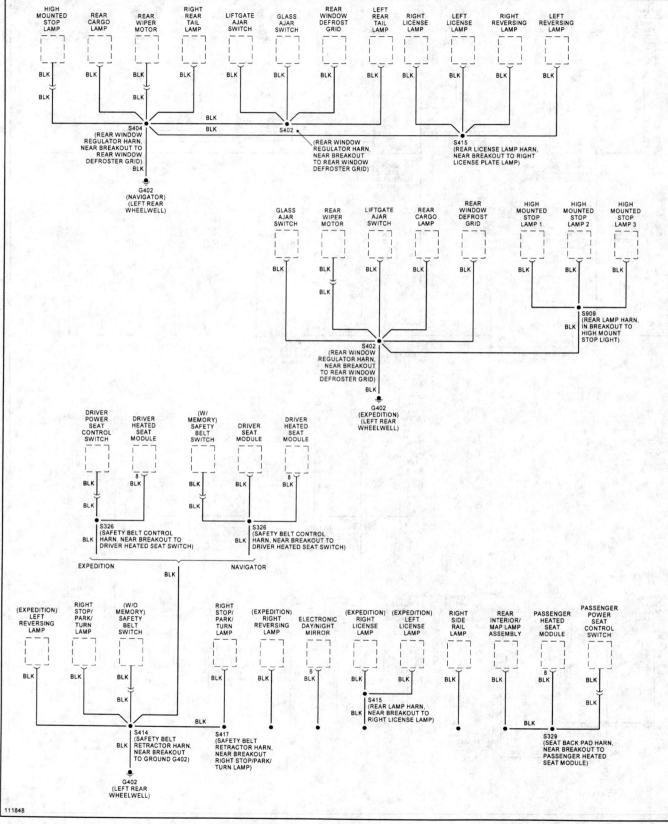

Fig. 25: Ground Distribution Wiring Diagram (Expedition & Navigator – 4 Of 4)

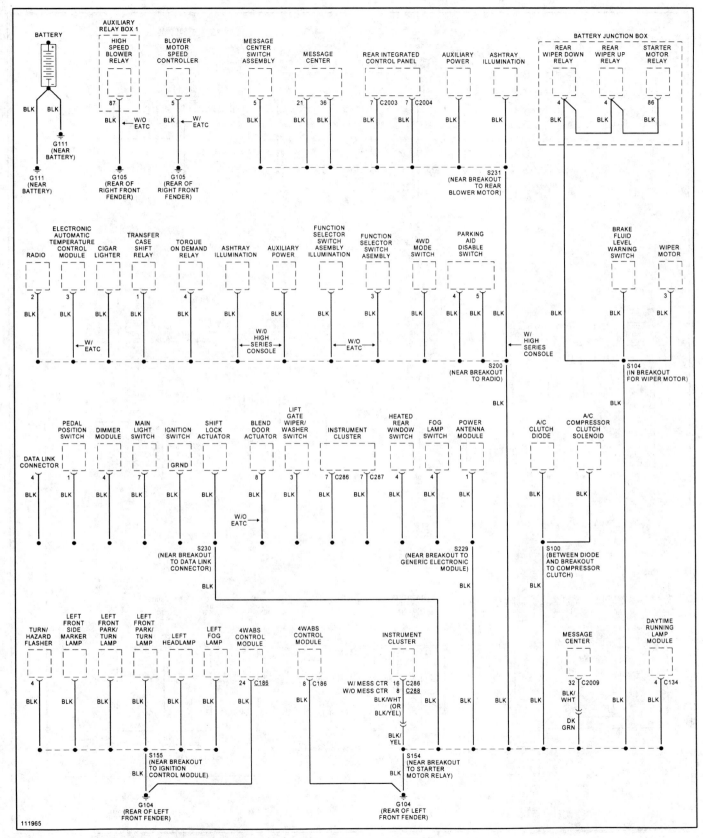

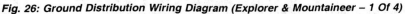

Fig. 26: Ground Distribution Wiring Diagram (Explorer & Mountaineer – 1 Of 4)

1999 WIRING DIAGRAMS
Ground Distribution (Cont.)

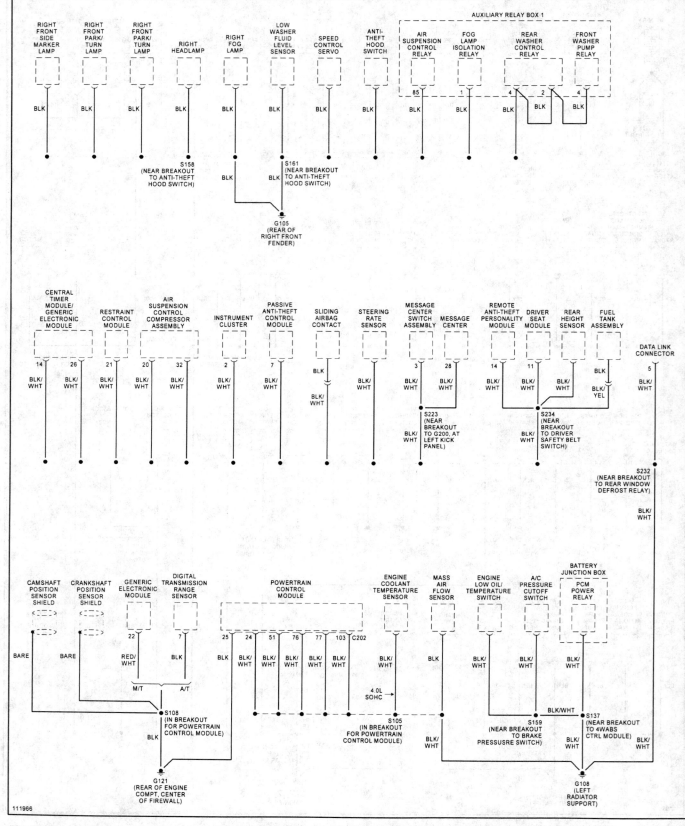

Fig. 27: Ground Distribution Wiring Diagram (Explorer & Mountaineer – 2 Of 4)

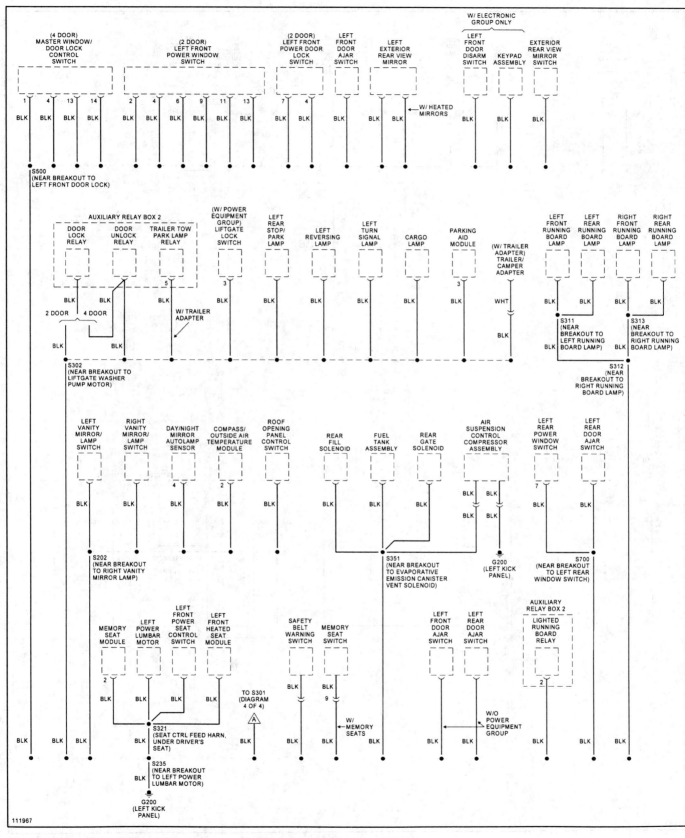

Fig. 28: Ground Distribution Wiring Diagram (Explorer & Mountaineer – 3 Of 4)

1999 WIRING DIAGRAMS
Ground Distribution (Cont.)

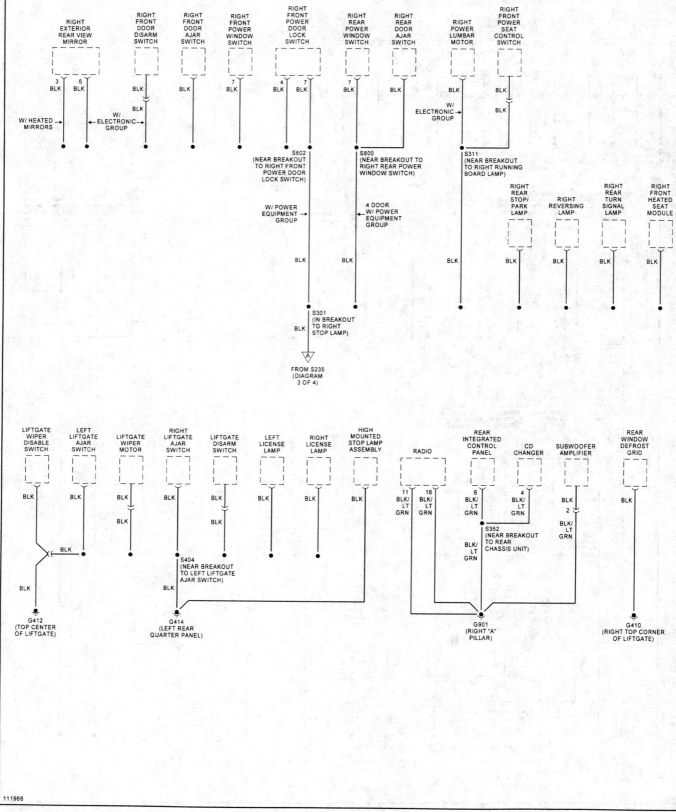

Fig. 29: Ground Distribution Wiring Diagram (Explorer & Mountaineer – 4 Of 4)

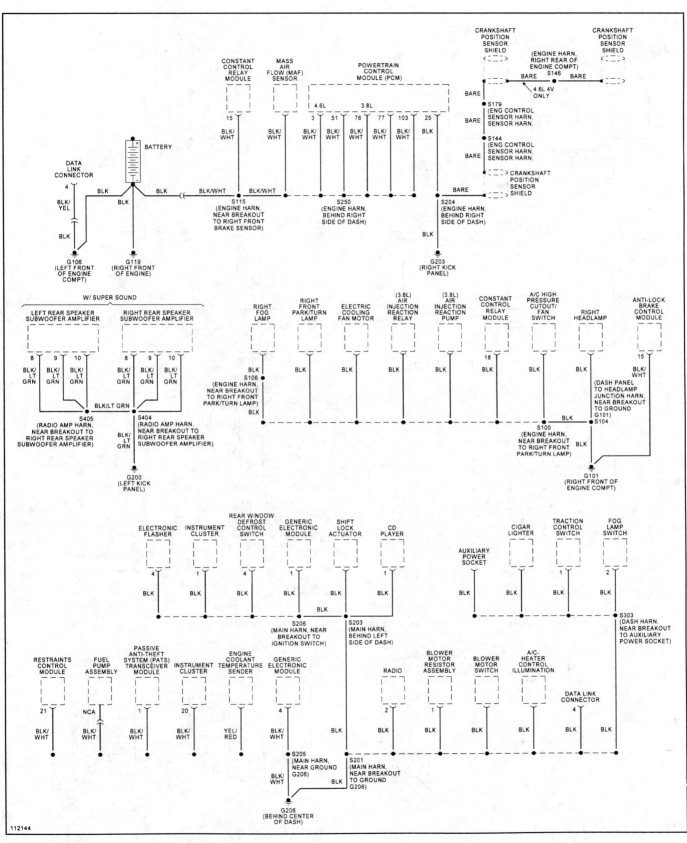

Fig. 30: Ground Distribution Wiring Diagram (Mustang – 1 Of 2)

112144

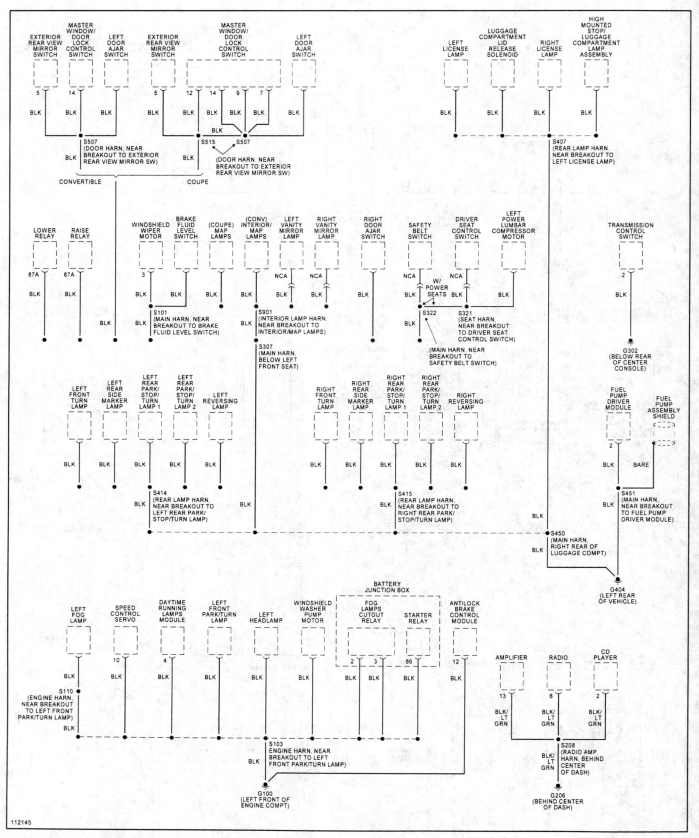

Fig. 31: Ground Distribution Wiring Diagram (Mustang – 2 Of 2)

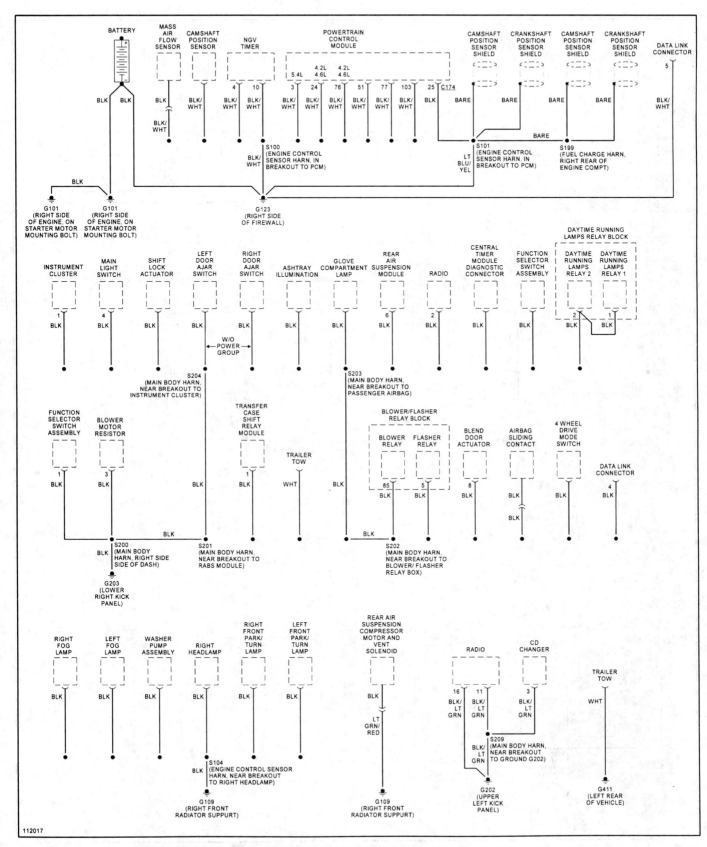

Fig. 32: Ground Distribution Wiring Diagram (F150 & F250 Light-Duty Pickups – 1 Of 3)

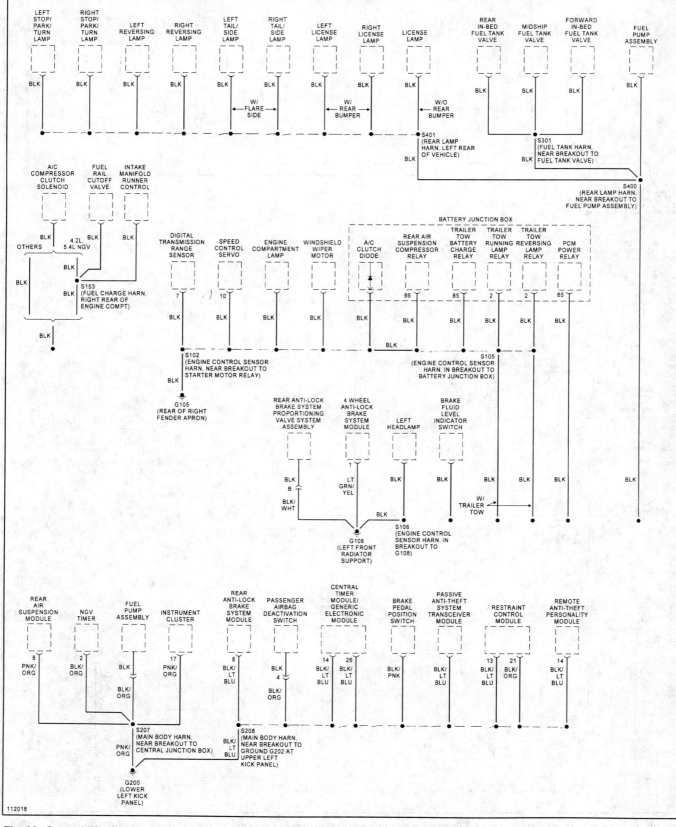

Fig. 33: Ground Distribution Wiring Diagram (F150 & F250 Light-Duty Pickups – 2 Of 3)

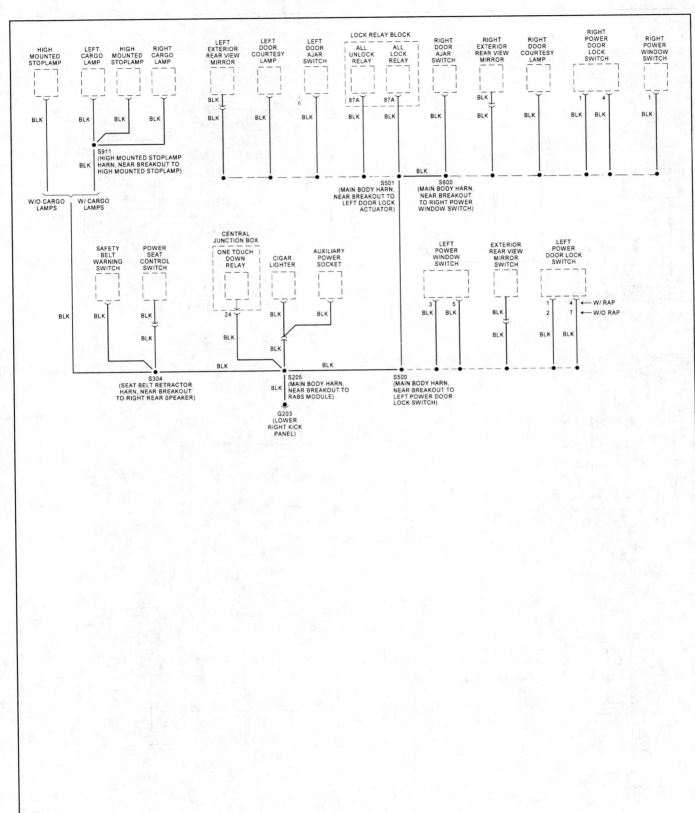

Fig. 34: Ground Distribution Wiring Diagram (F150 & F250 Light-Duty Pickups – 3 Of 3)

112019

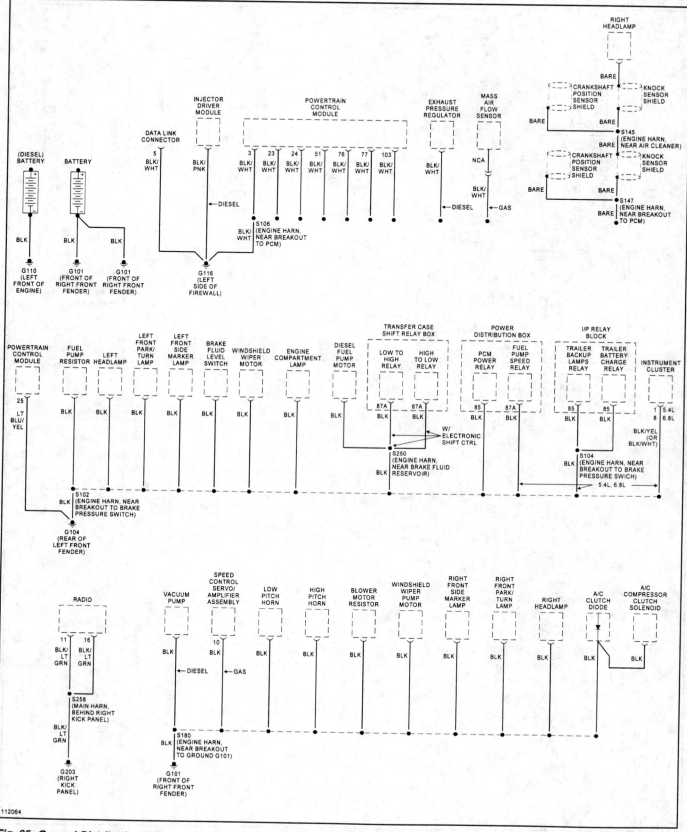

Fig. 35: Ground Distribution Wiring Diagram (F250 Super-Duty & F350 Pickups – 1 Of 3)

112064

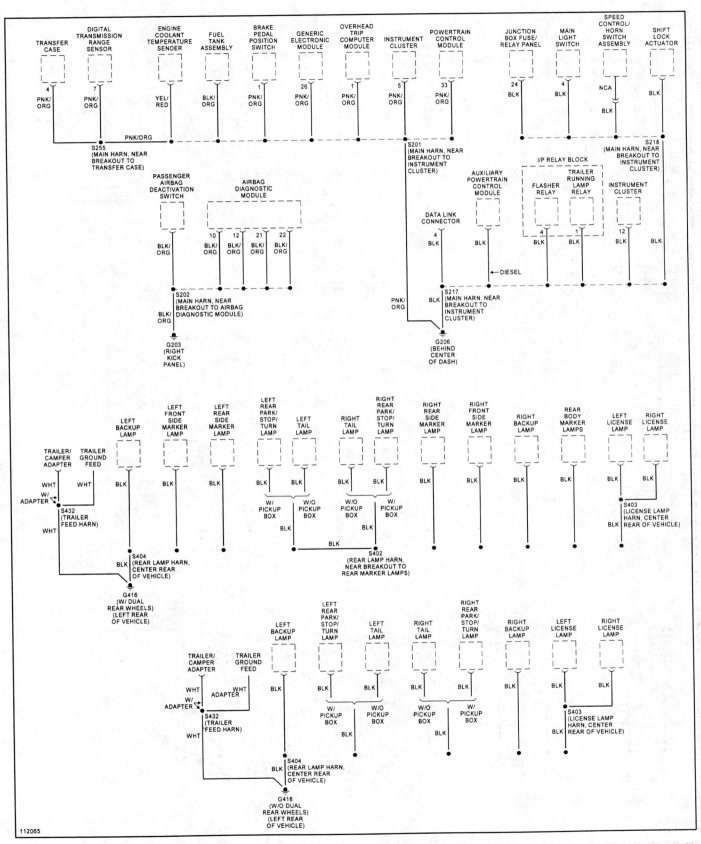

Fig. 36: Ground Distribution Wiring Diagram (F250 Super-Duty & F350 Pickups – 2 Of 3)

1999 WIRING DIAGRAMS
Ground Distribution (Cont.)

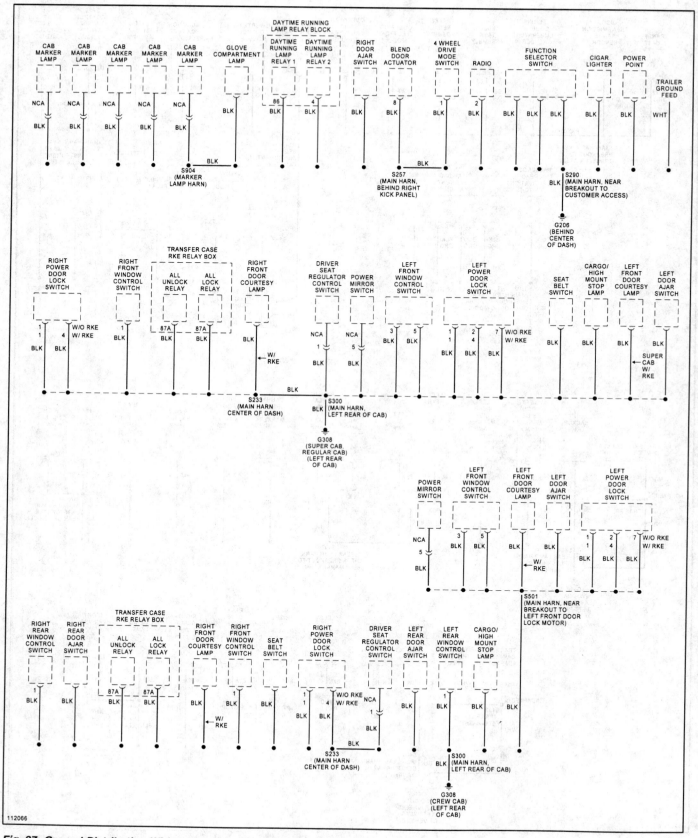

Fig. 37: Ground Distribution Wiring Diagram (F250 Super-Duty & F350 Pickups – 3 Of 3)

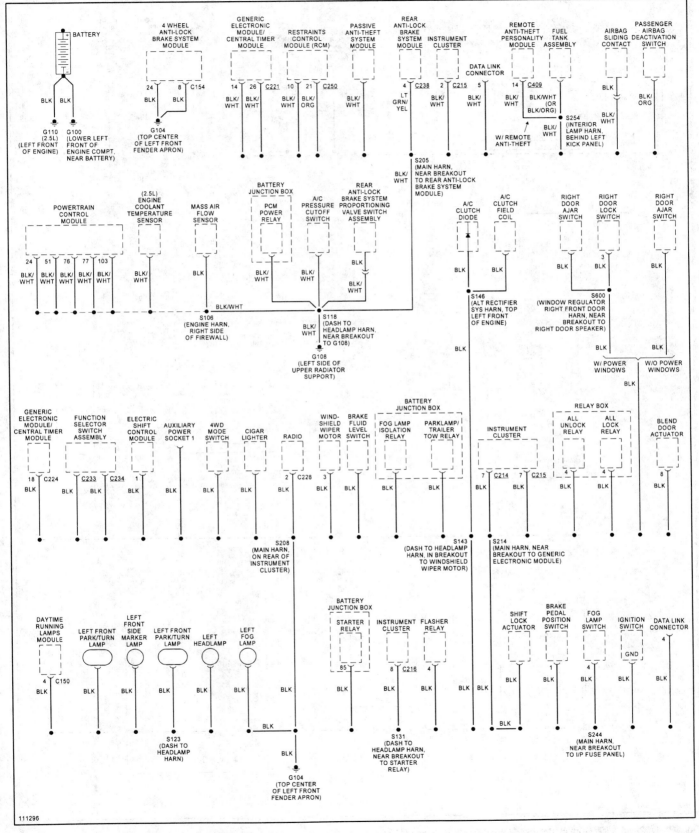

Fig. 38: Ground Distribution Wiring Diagram (Ranger – 1 Of 2)

1999 WIRING DIAGRAMS
Ground Distribution (Cont.)

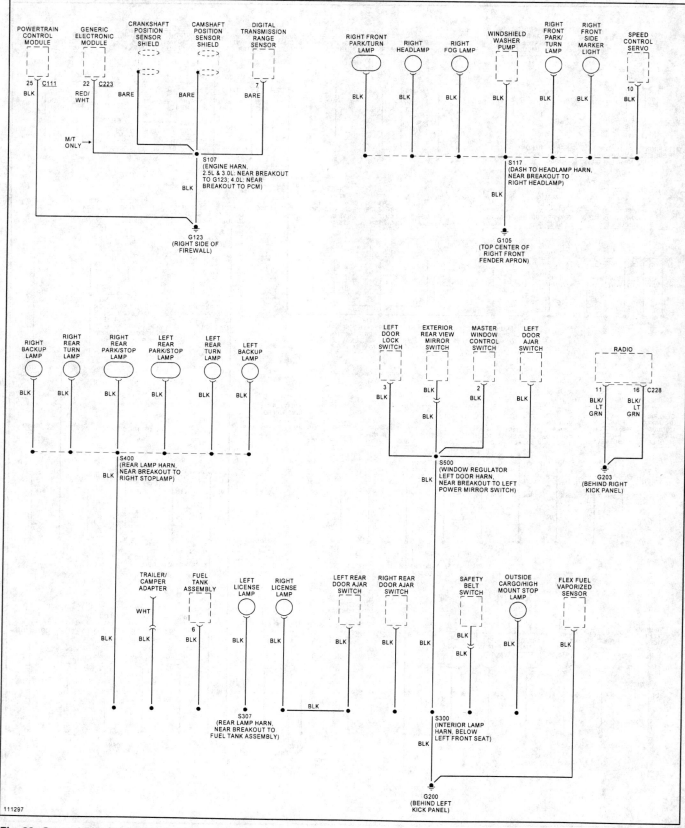

Fig. 39: Ground Distribution Wiring Diagram (Ranger – 2 Of 2)

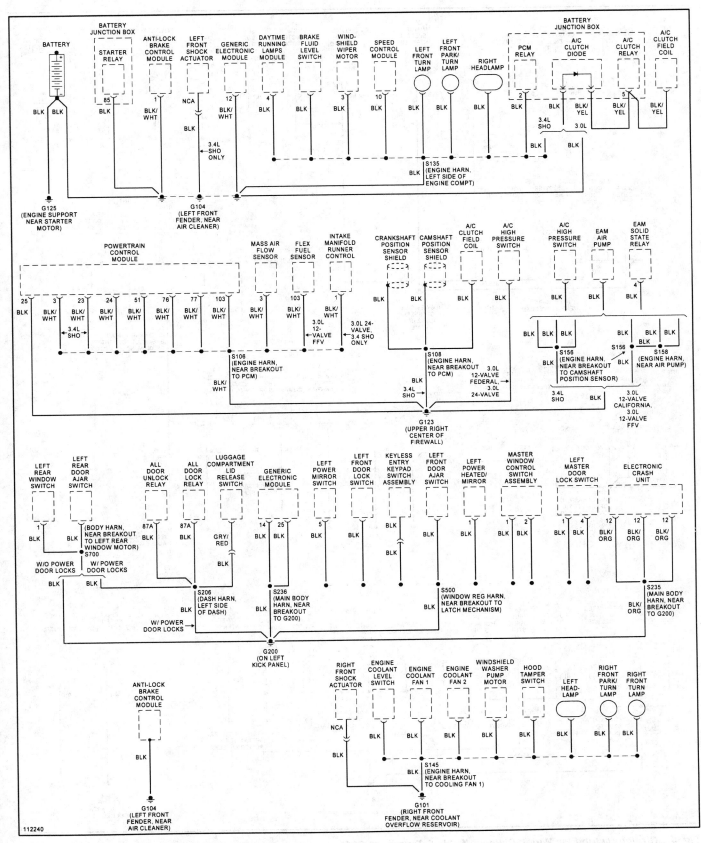

Fig. 40: Ground Distribution Wiring Diagram (Sable & Taurus – 1 Of 3)

112240

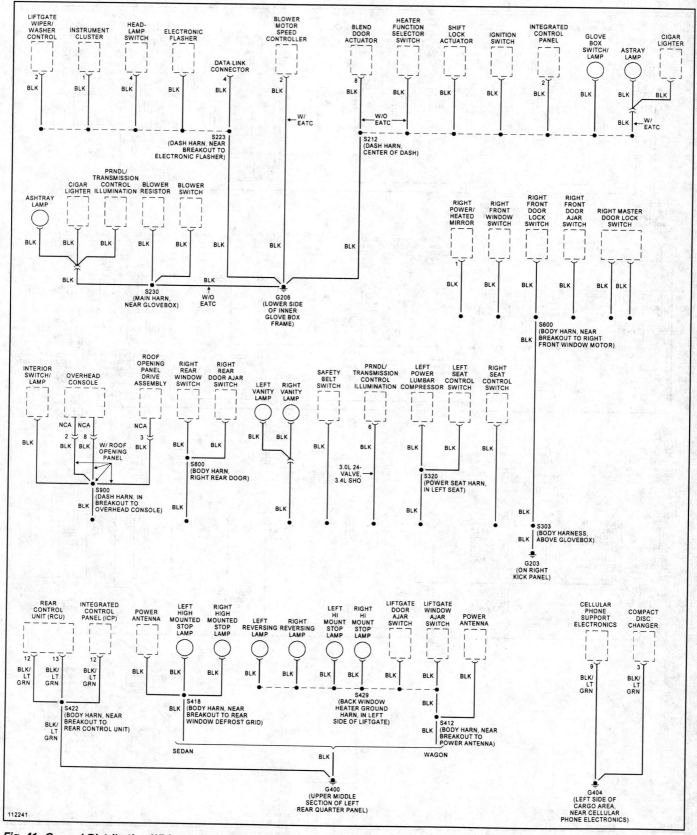

Fig. 41: Ground Distribution Wiring Diagram (Sable & Taurus – 2 Of 3)

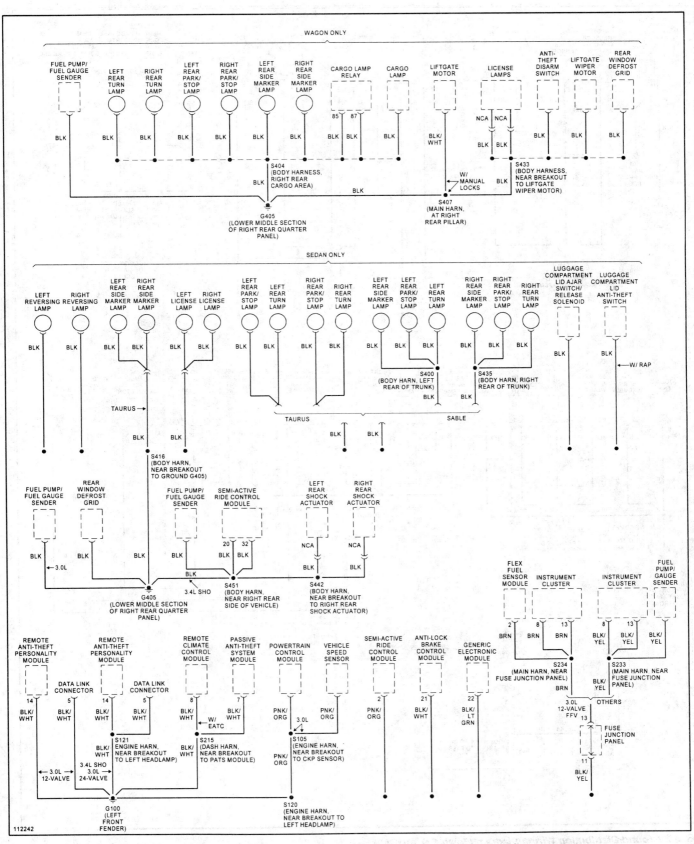

Fig. 42: Ground Distribution Wiring Diagram (Sable & Taurus – 3 Of 3)

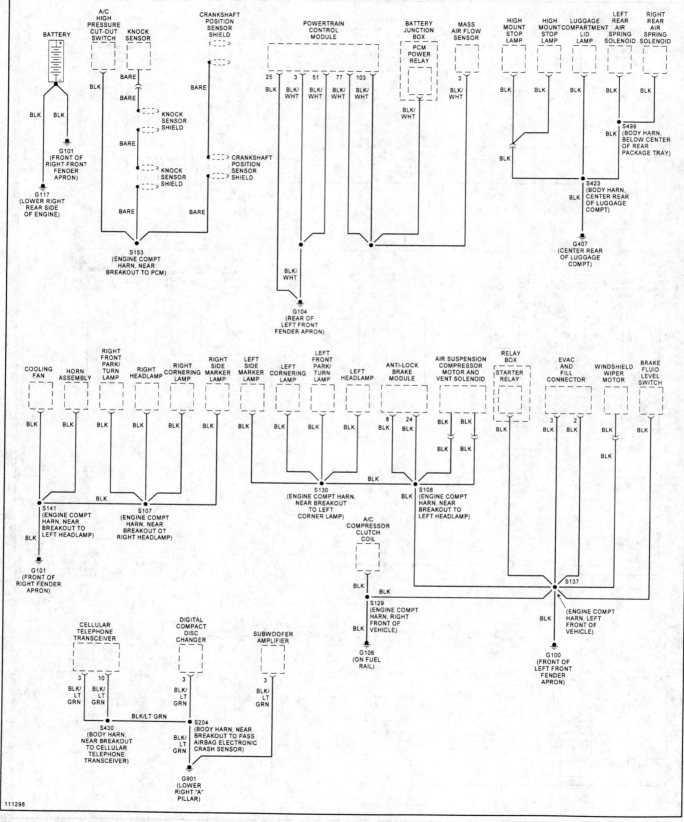

Fig. 43: Ground Distribution Wiring Diagram (Town Car – 1 Of 3)

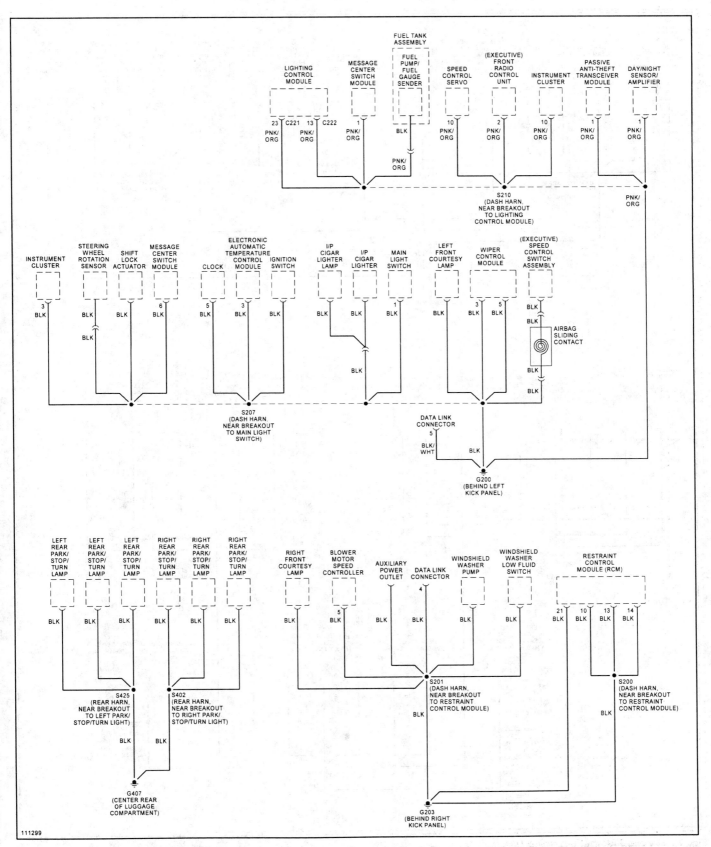

Fig. 44: Ground Distribution Wiring Diagram (Town Car – 2 Of 3)

111299

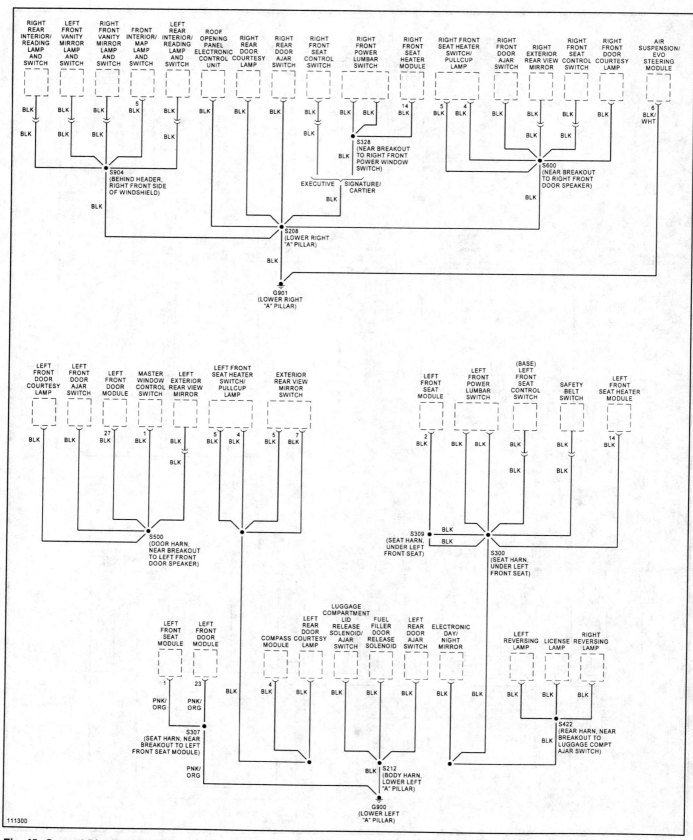

Fig. 45: Ground Distribution Wiring Diagram (Town Car – 3 Of 3)

111300

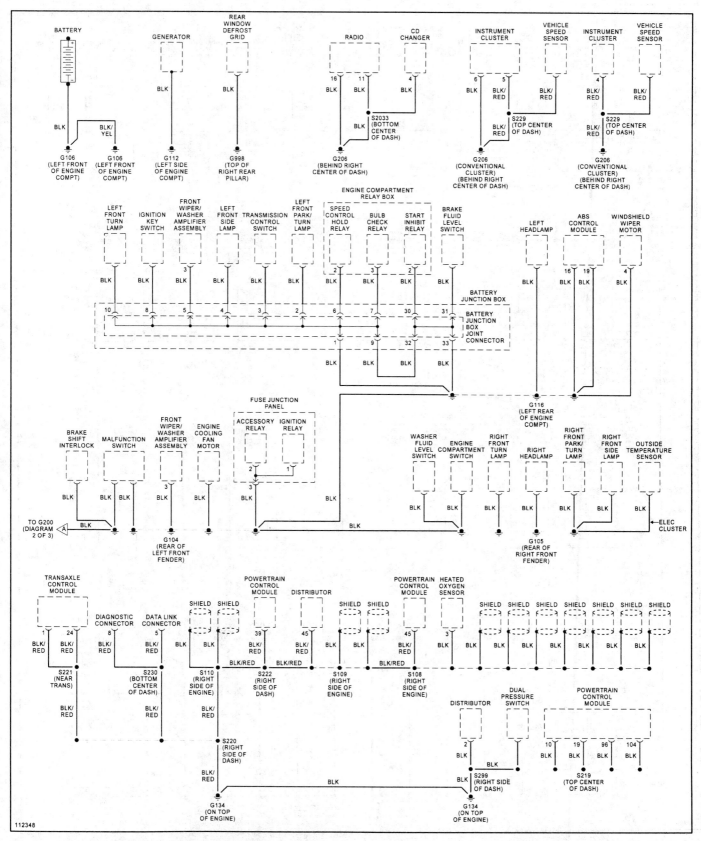

Fig. 46: Ground Distribution Wiring Diagram (Villager – 1 Of 3)

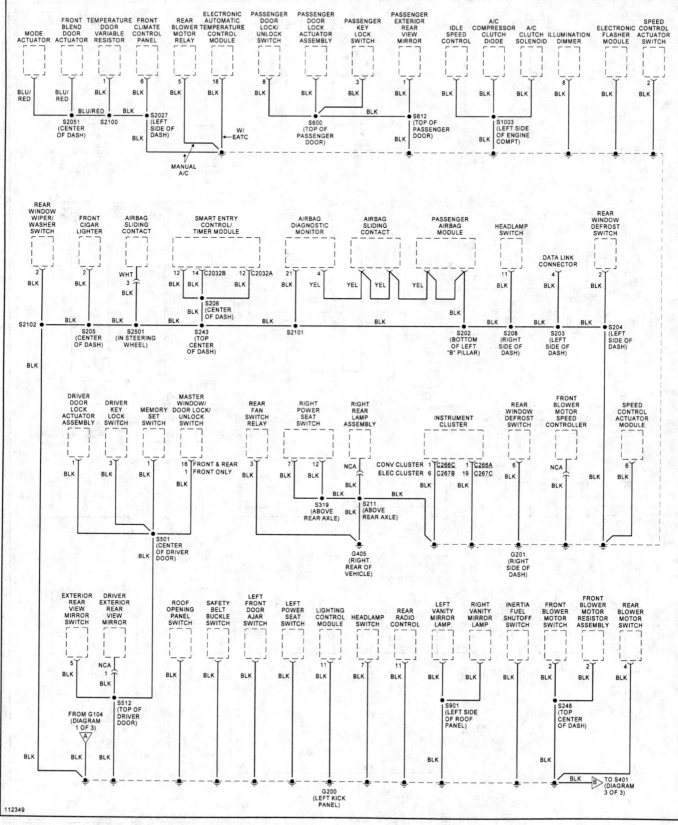

Fig. 47: Ground Distribution Wiring Diagram (Villager – 2 Of 3)

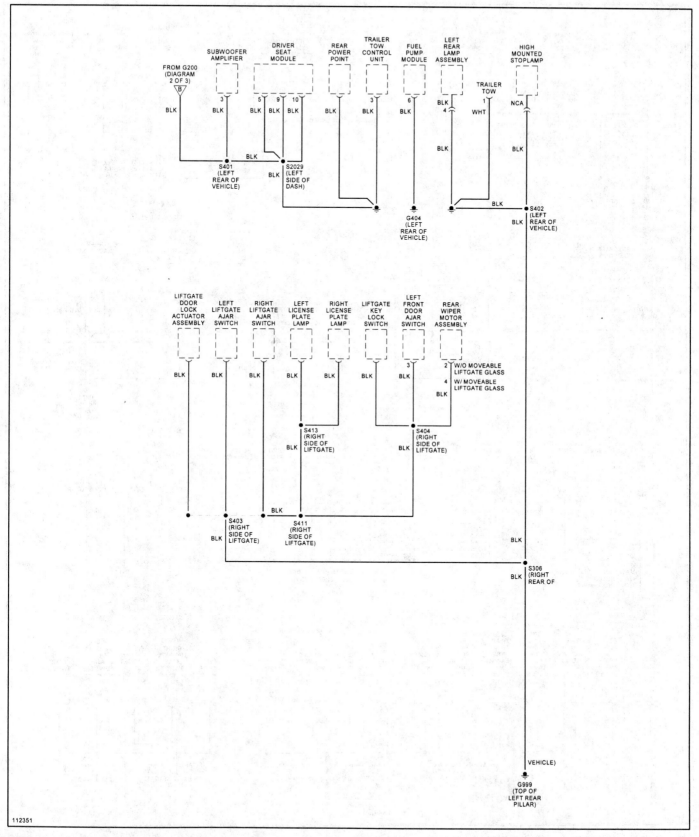

Fig. 48: Ground Distribution Wiring Diagram (Villager – 3 Of 3)

112351

1999 WIRING DIAGRAMS
Ground Distribution (Cont.)

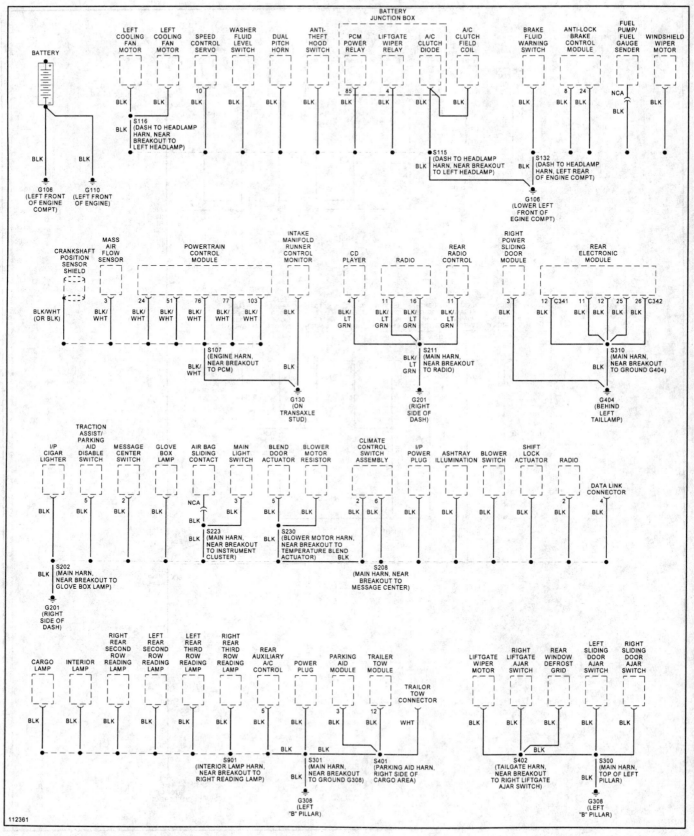

Fig. 49: Ground Distribution Wiring Diagram (Windstar – 1 Of 2)

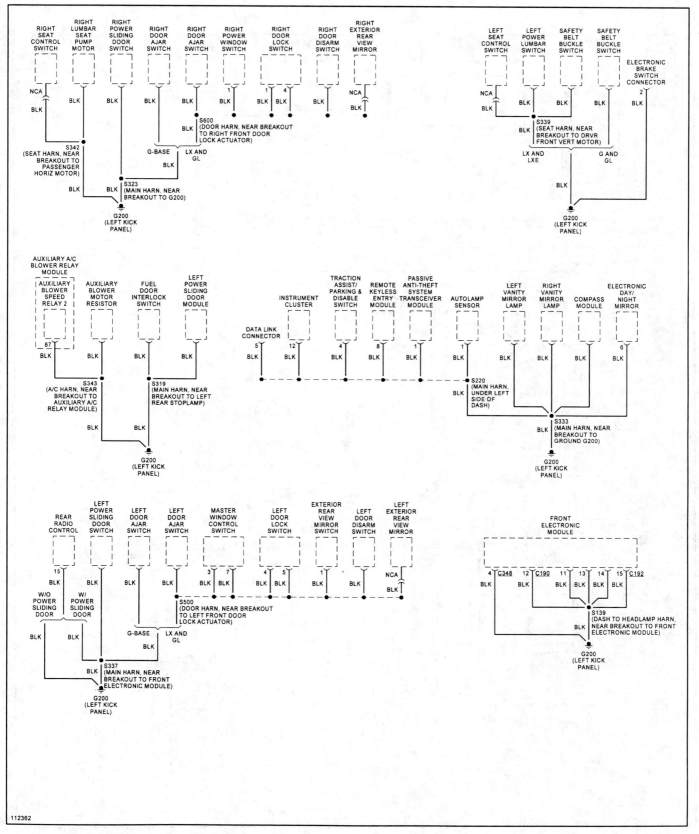

Fig. 50: Ground Distribution Wiring Diagram (Windstar – 2 Of 2)

112362

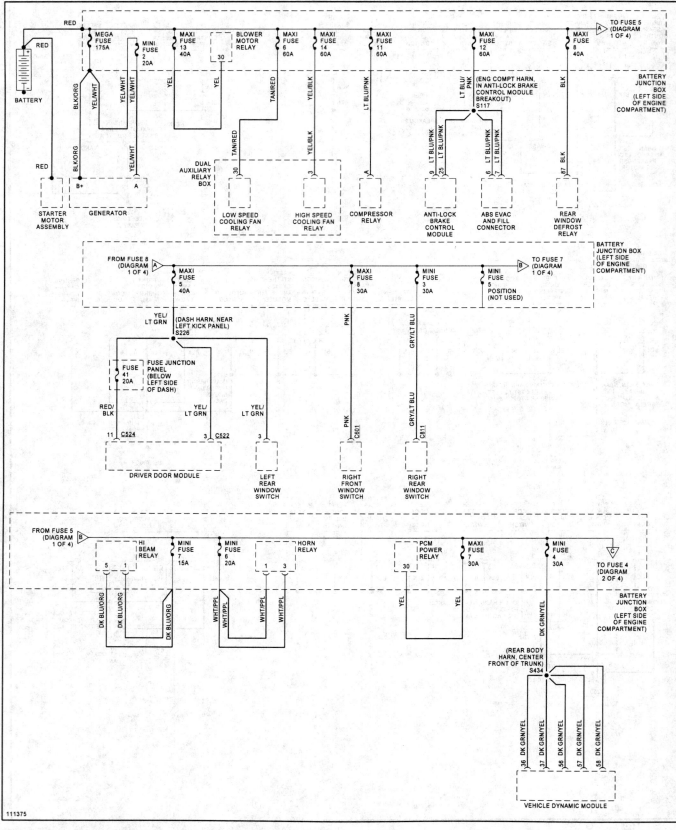

Fig. 1: Power Distribution Wiring Diagram (Continental – 1 Of 4)

111375

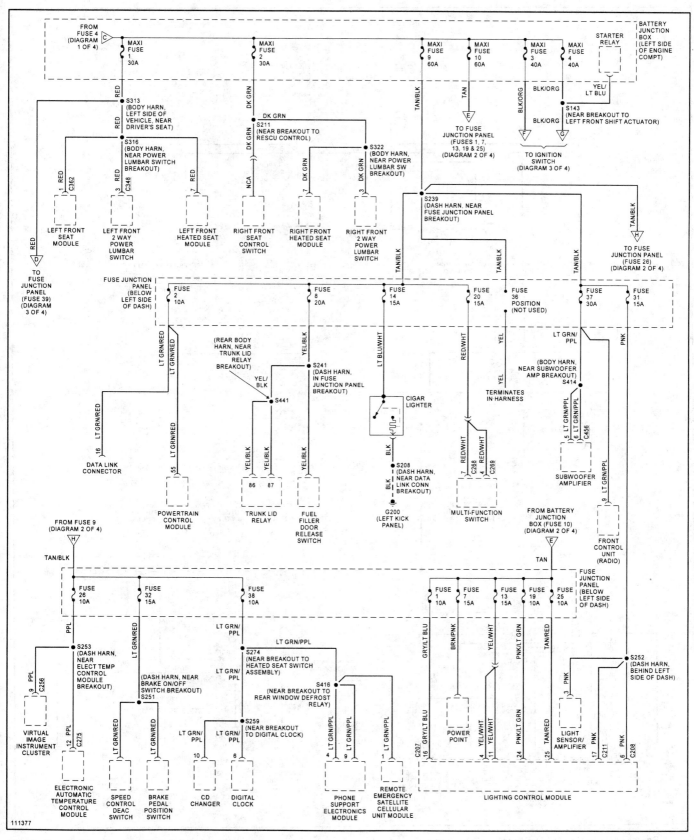

Fig. 2: Power Distribution Wiring Diagram (Continental – 2 Of 4)

111377

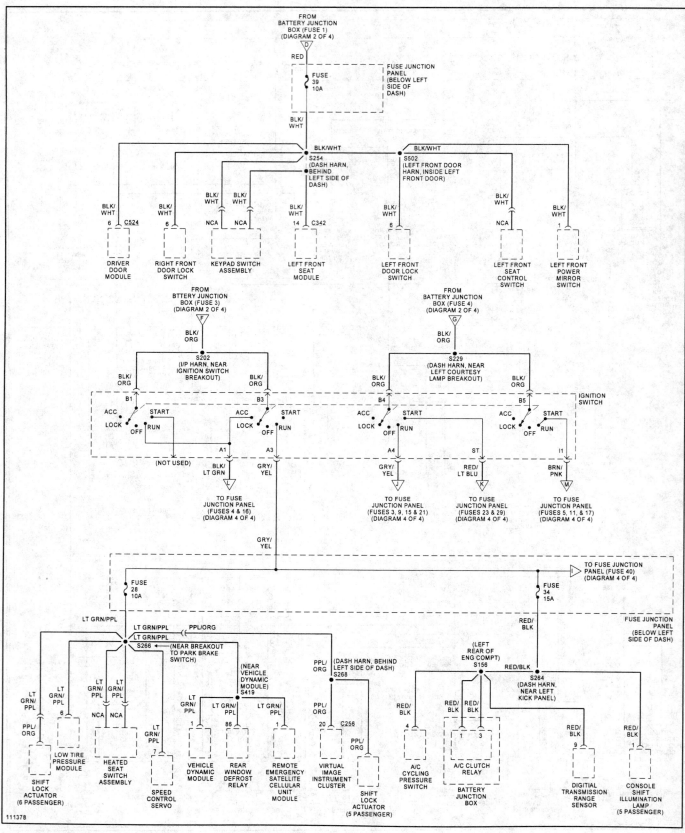

Fig. 3: Power Distribution Wiring Diagram (Continental – 3 Of 4)

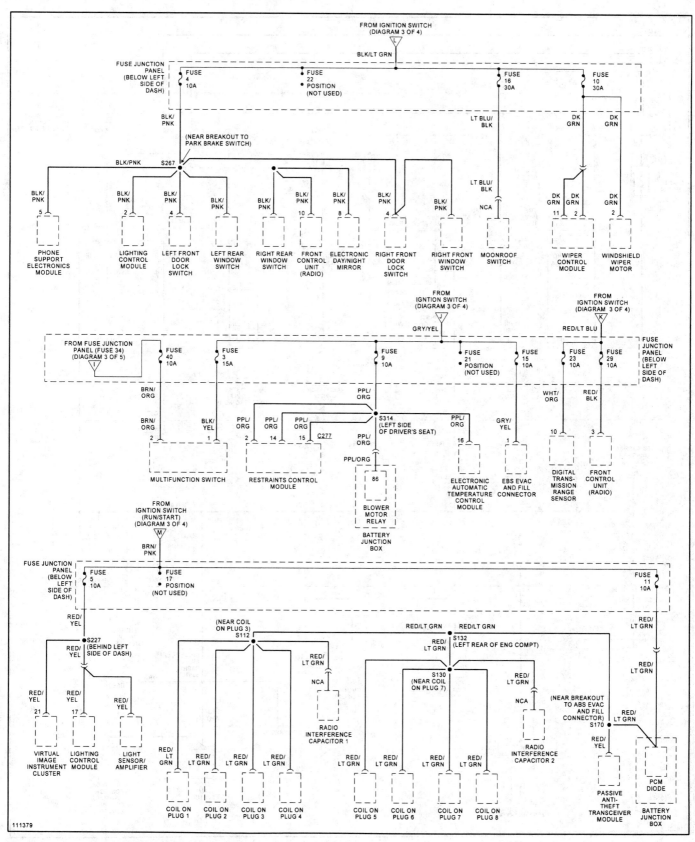

Fig. 4: Power Distribution Wiring Diagram (Continental – 4 Of 4)

111379

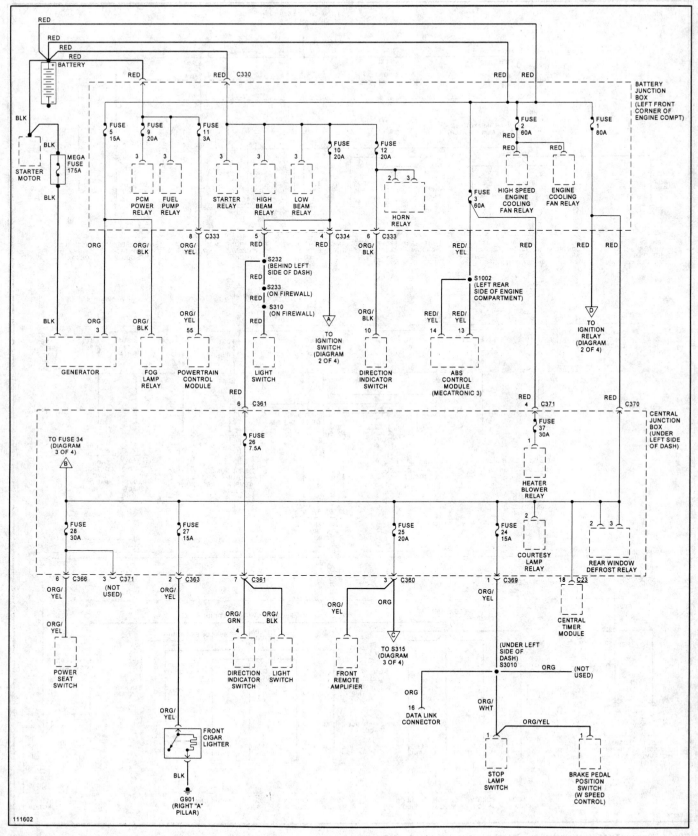

Fig. 5: Power Distribution Wiring Diagram (Contour & Mystique – 1 Of 4)

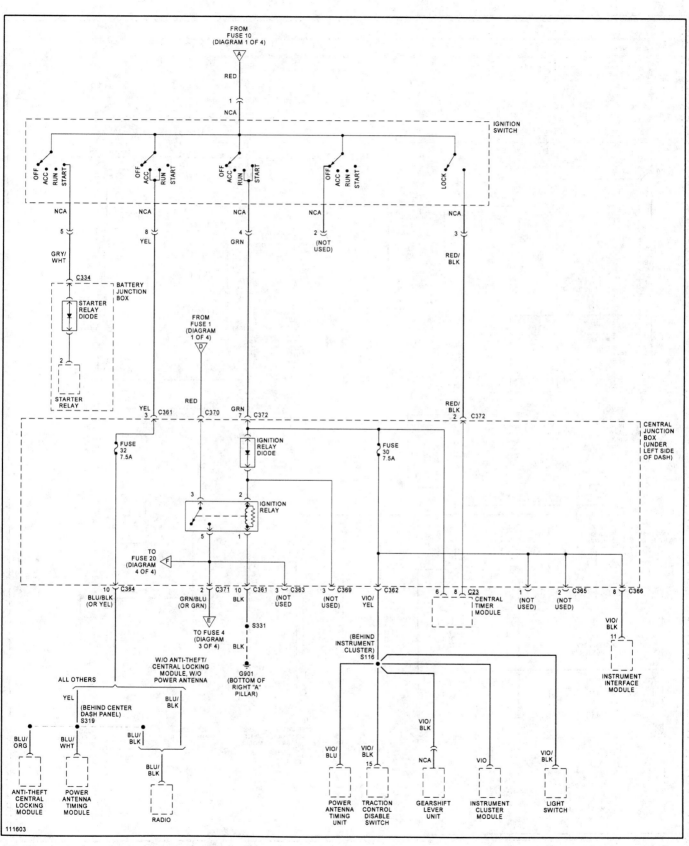

Fig. 6: Power Distribution Wiring Diagram (Contour & Mystique – 2 Of 4)

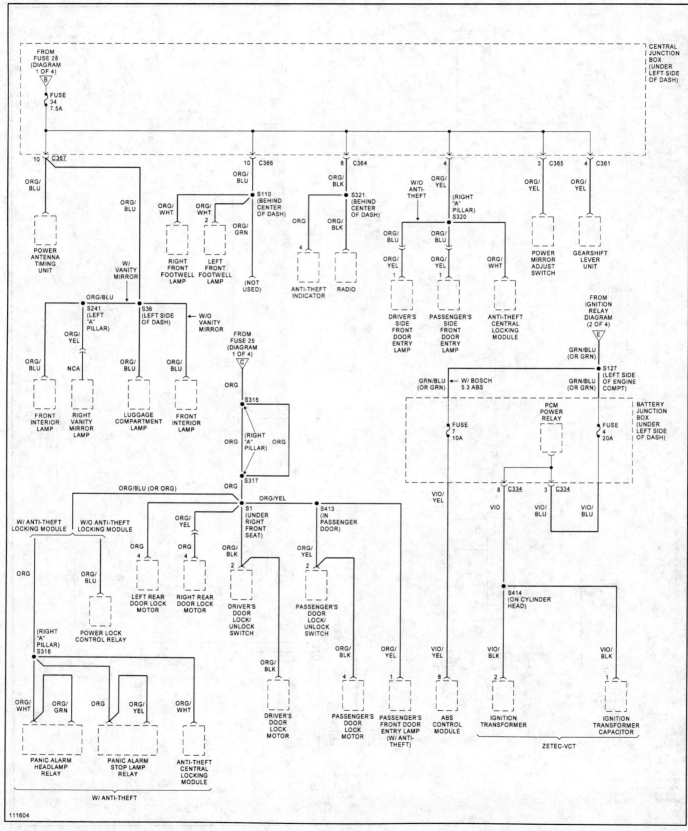

Fig. 7: Power Distribution Wiring Diagram (Contour & Mystique – 3 Of 4)

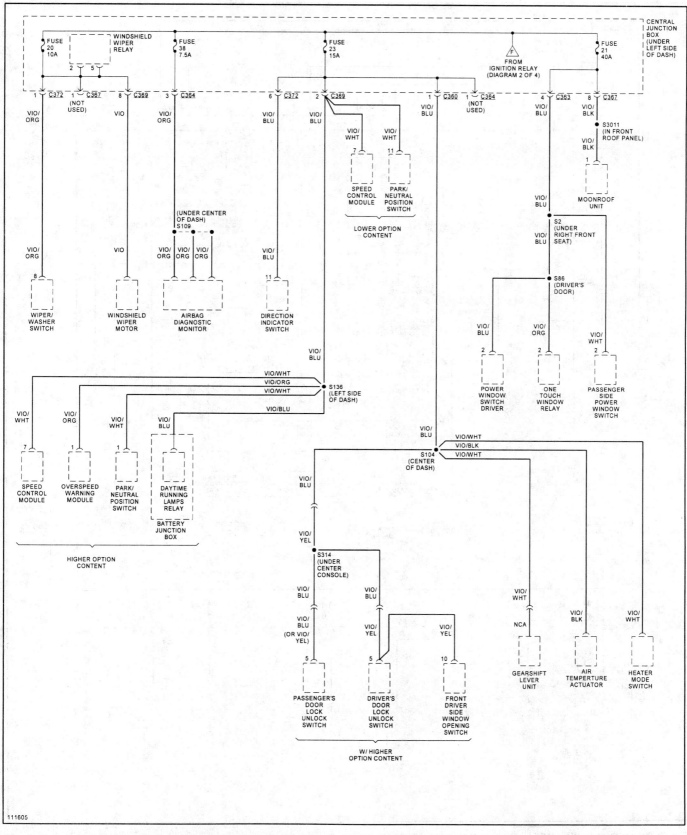

Fig. 8: Power Distribution Wiring Diagram (Contour & Mystique – 4 Of 4)

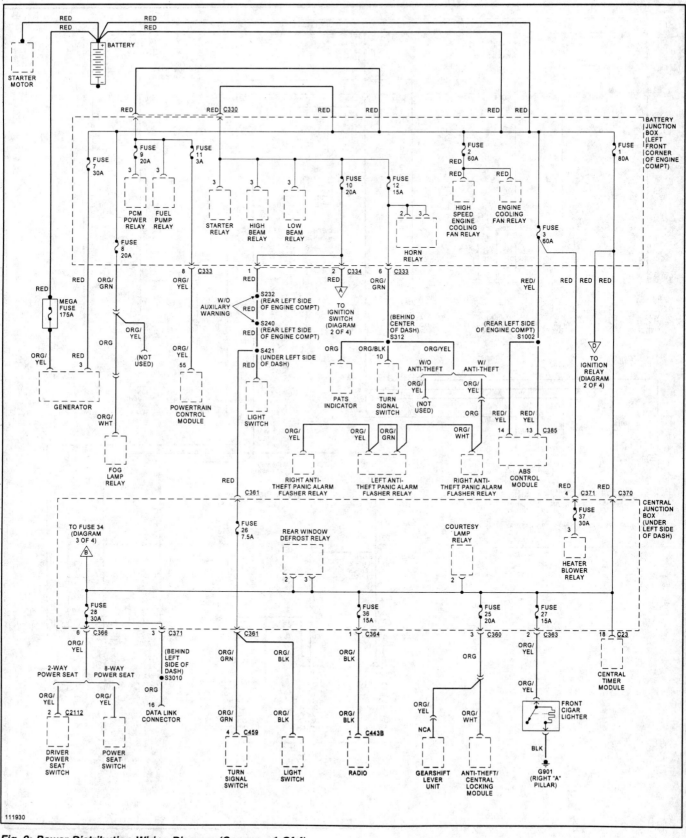

Fig. 9: Power Distribution Wiring Diagram (Cougar – 1 Of 4)

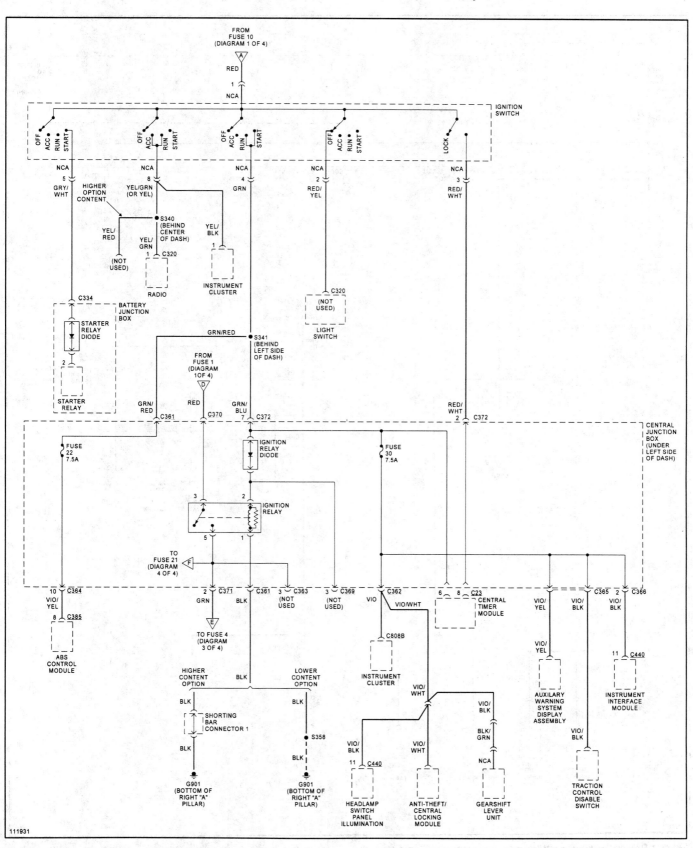

Fig. 10: Power Distribution Wiring Diagram (Cougar – 2 Of 4)

111931

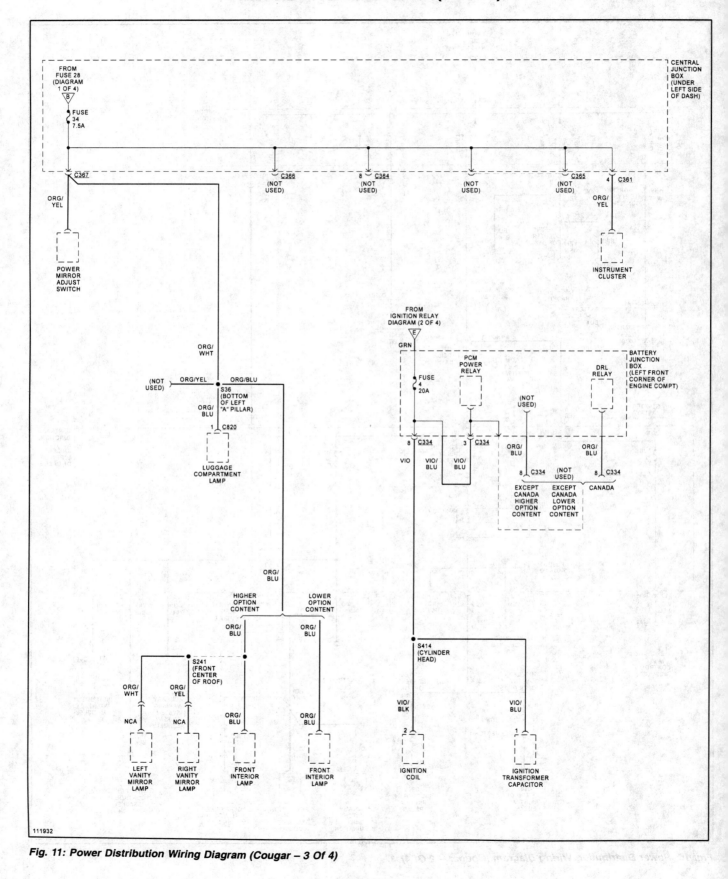

Fig. 11: Power Distribution Wiring Diagram (Cougar – 3 Of 4)

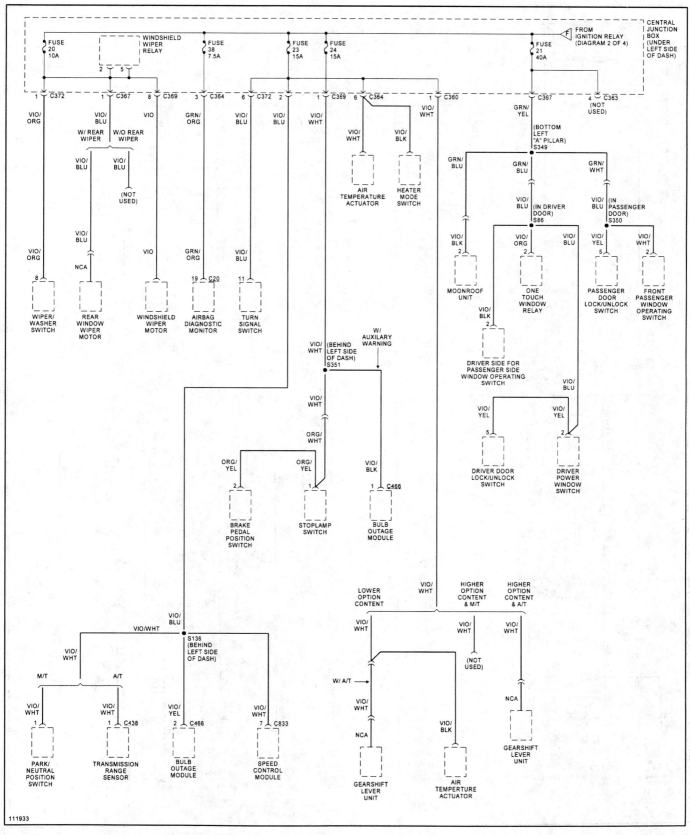

Fig. 12: Power Distribution Wiring Diagram (Cougar – 4 Of 4)

111933

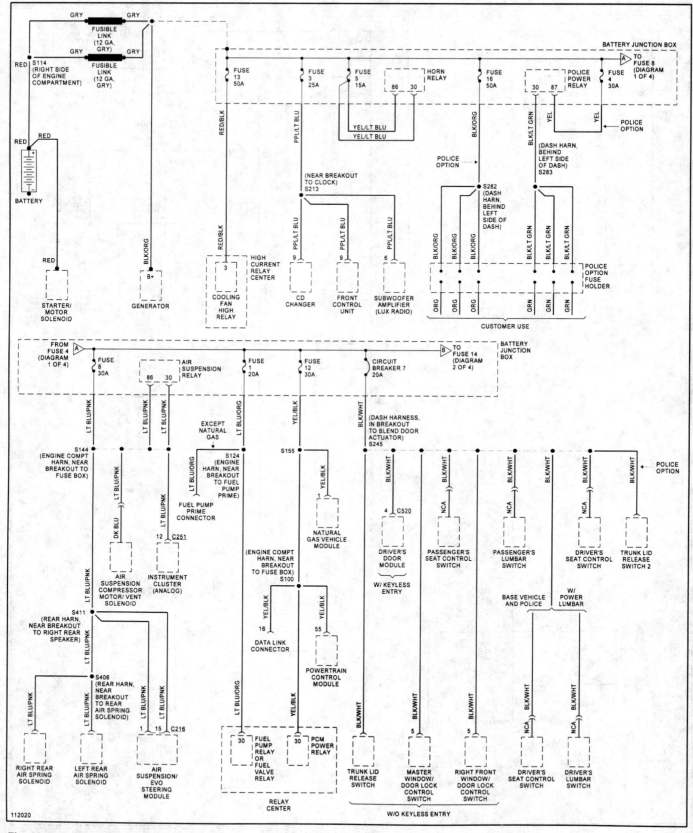

Fig. 13: Power Distribution Wiring Diagram (Crown Victoria & Grand Marquis – 1 Of 4)

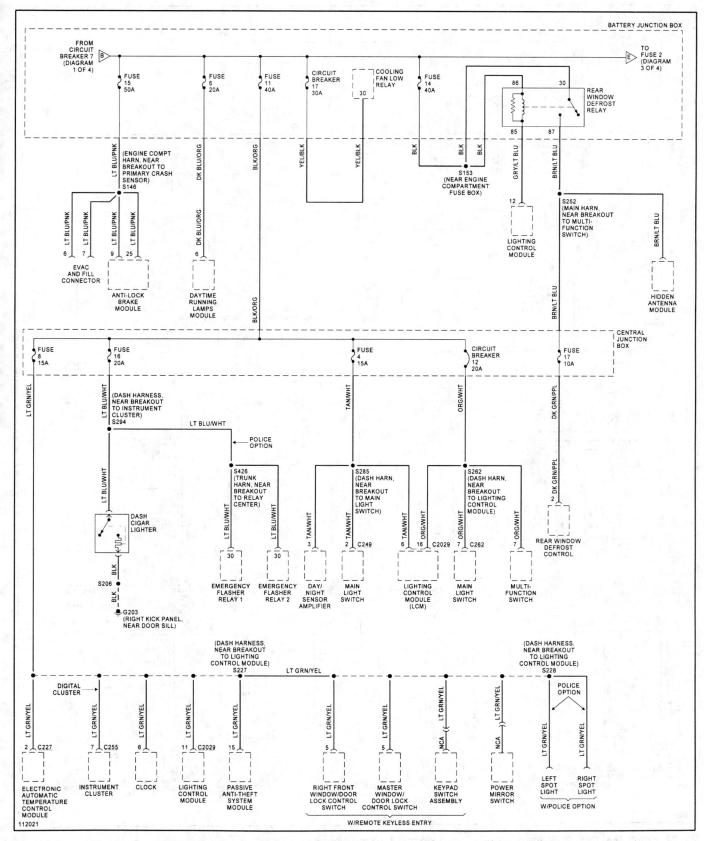

Fig. 14: Power Distribution Wiring Diagram (Crown Victoria & Grand Marquis – 2 Of 4)

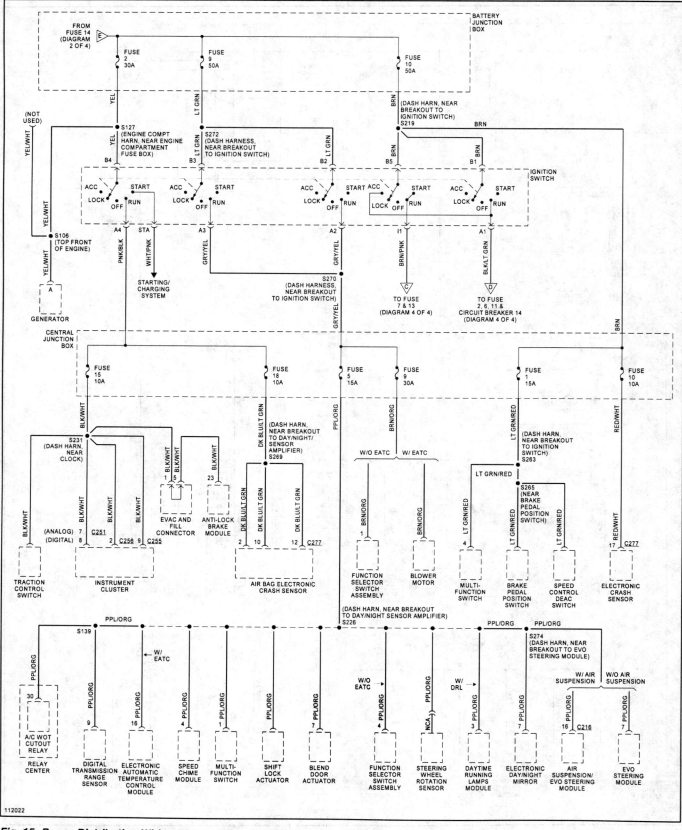

Fig. 15: Power Distribution Wiring Diagram (Crown Victoria & Grand Marquis – 3 Of 4)

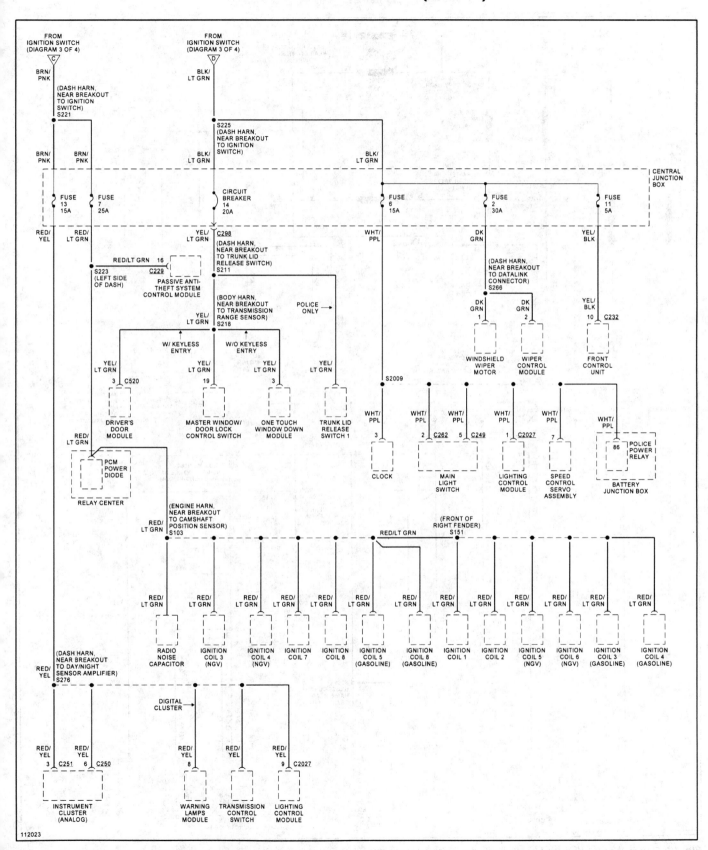

Fig. 16: Power Distribution Wiring Diagram (Crown Victoria & Grand Marquis – 4 Of 4)

1999 WIRING DIAGRAMS
Power Distribution (Cont.)

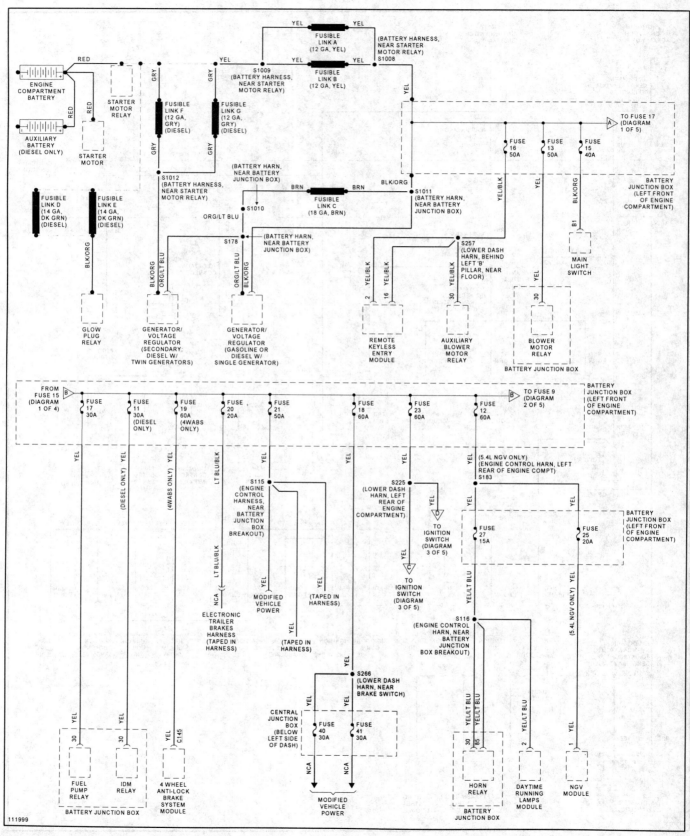

Fig. 17: Power Distribution Wiring Diagram (Econoline – 1 Of 5)

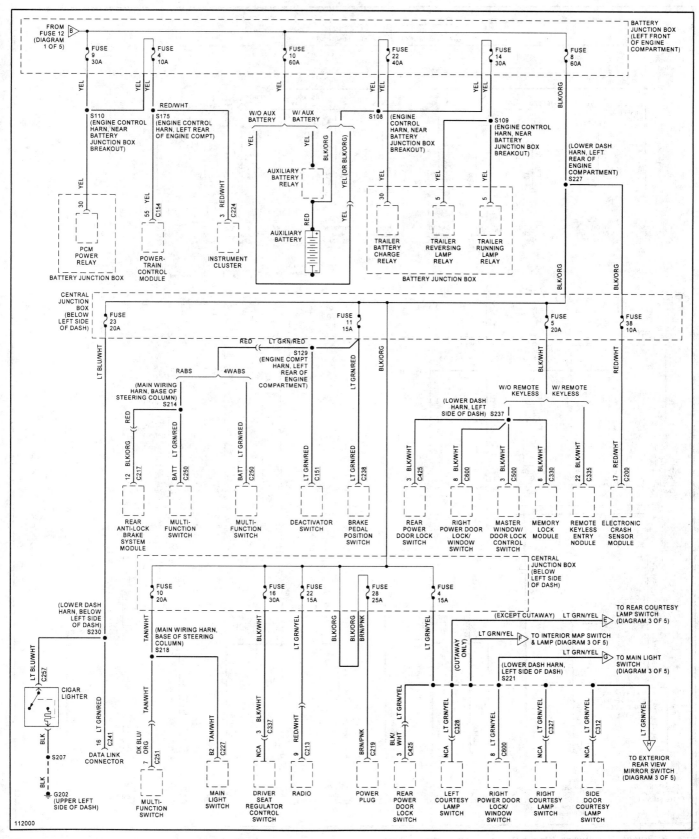

Fig. 18: Power Distribution Wiring Diagram (Econoline – 2 Of 5)

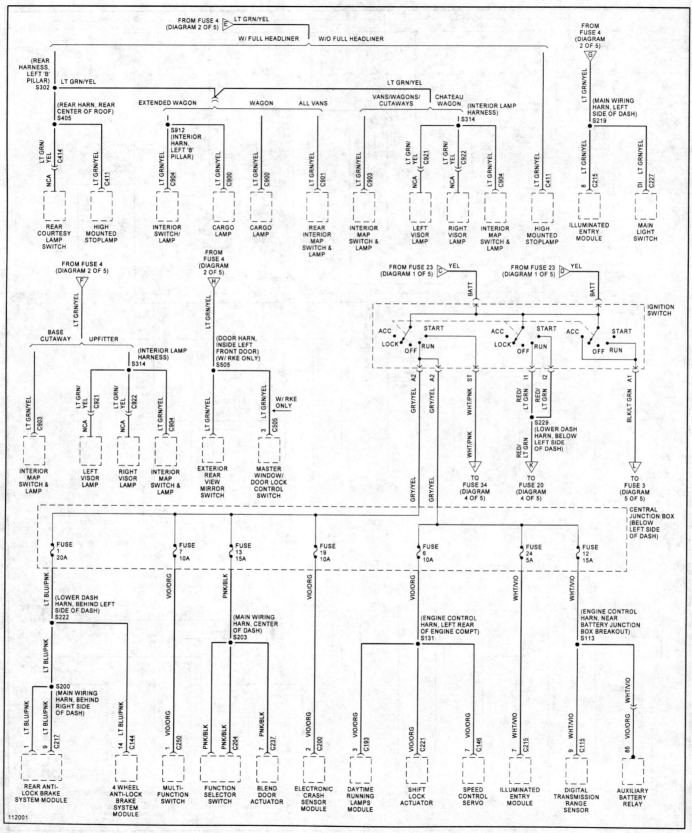

Fig. 19: Power Distribution Wiring Diagram (Econoline – 3 Of 5)

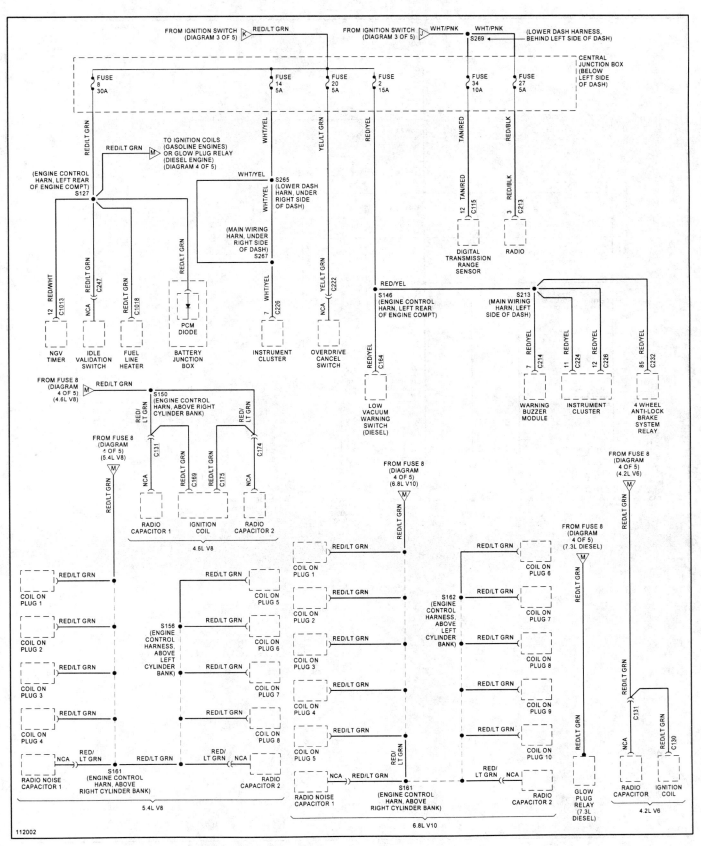

Fig. 20: Power Distribution Wiring Diagram (Econoline – 4 Of 5)

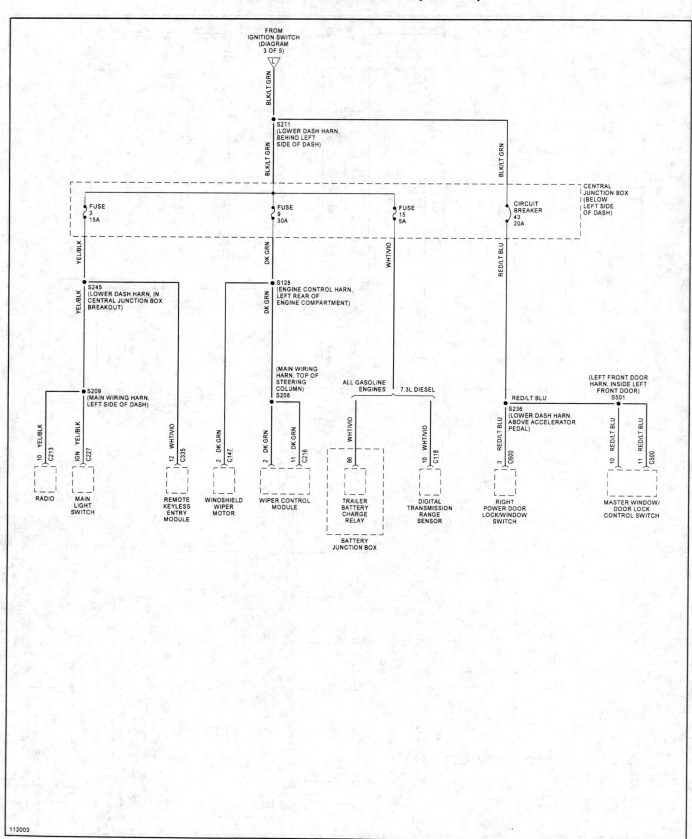

Fig. 21: Power Distribution Wiring Diagram (Econoline – 5 Of 5)

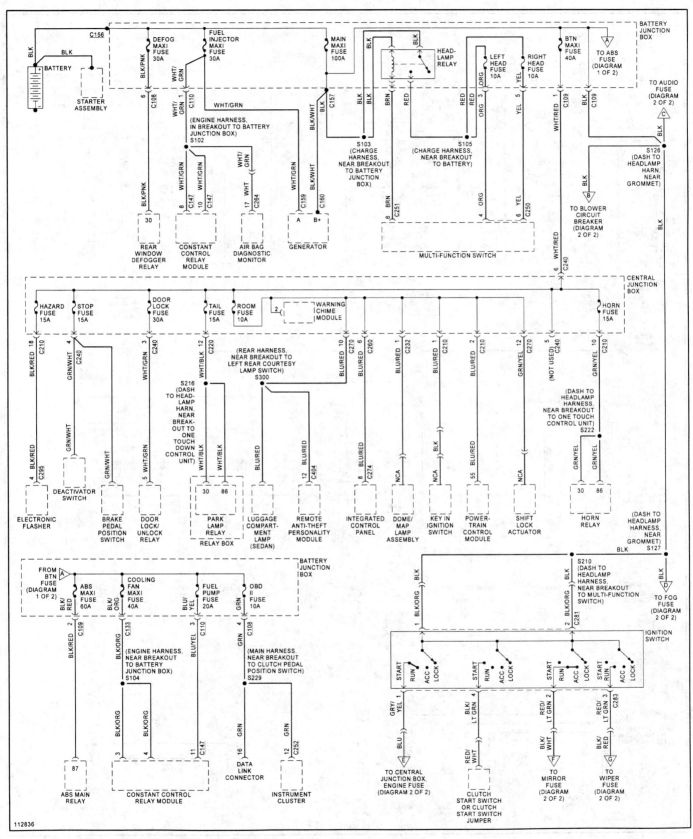

Fig. 22: Power Distribution Wiring Diagram (Escort & Tracer – 1 Of 2)

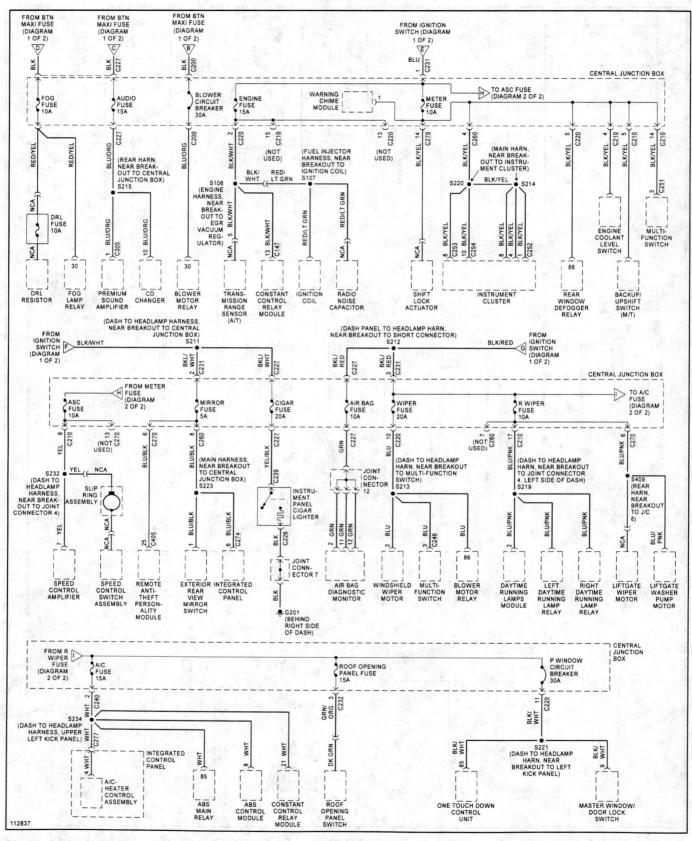

Fig. 23: Power Distribution Wiring Diagram (Escort & Tracer – 2 Of 2)

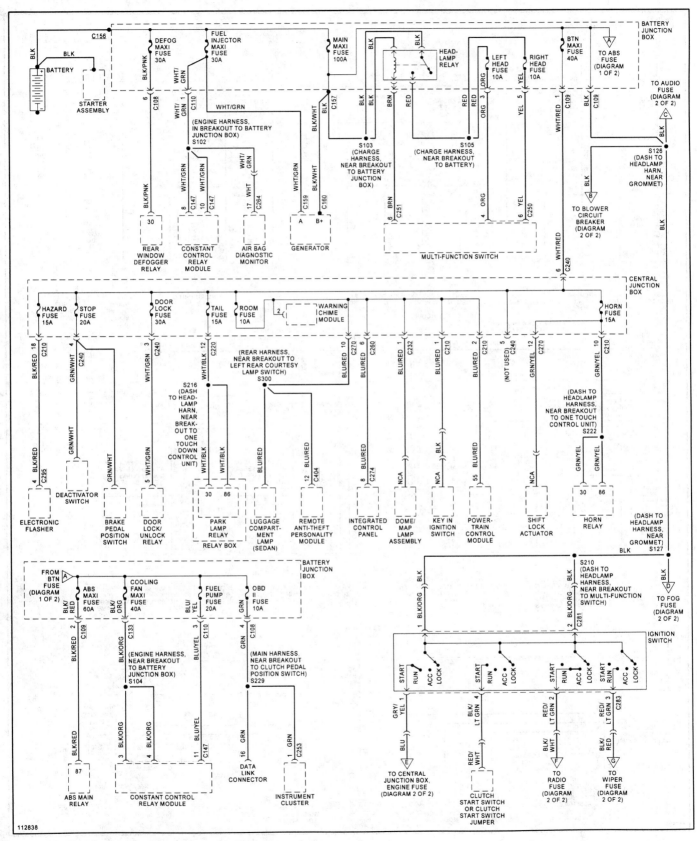

Fig. 24: Power Distribution Wiring Diagram (Escort ZX2 – 1 Of 2)

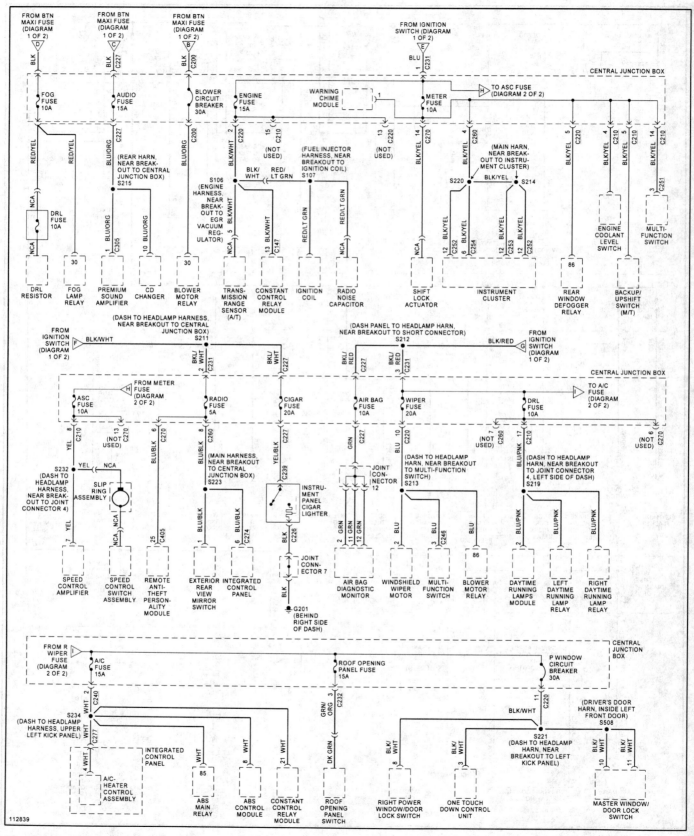

Fig. 25: Power Distribution Wiring Diagram (Escort ZX2 – 2 Of 2)

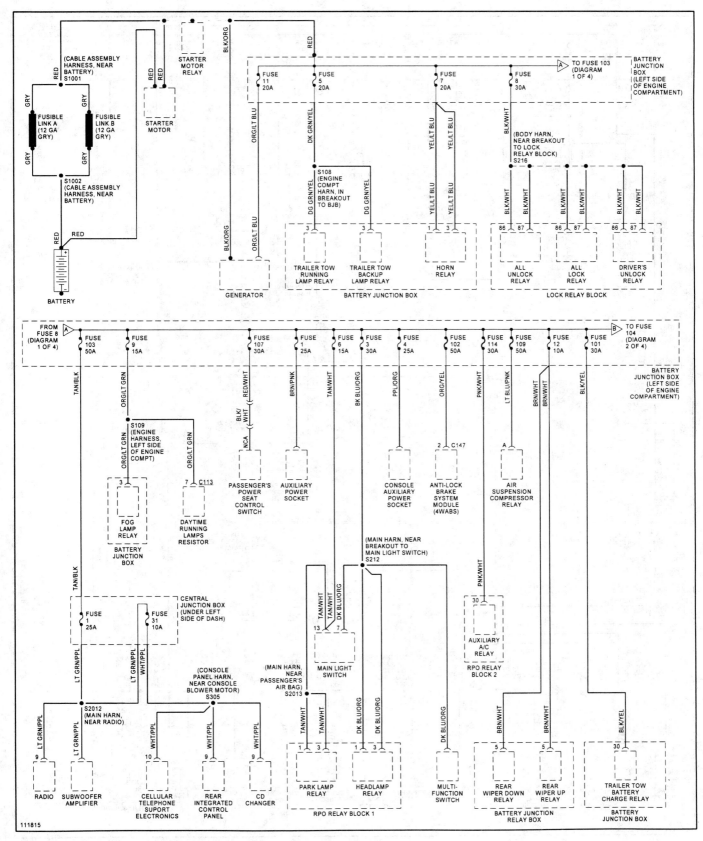

Fig. 26: Power Distribution Wiring Diagram (Expedition & Navigator – 1 Of 4)

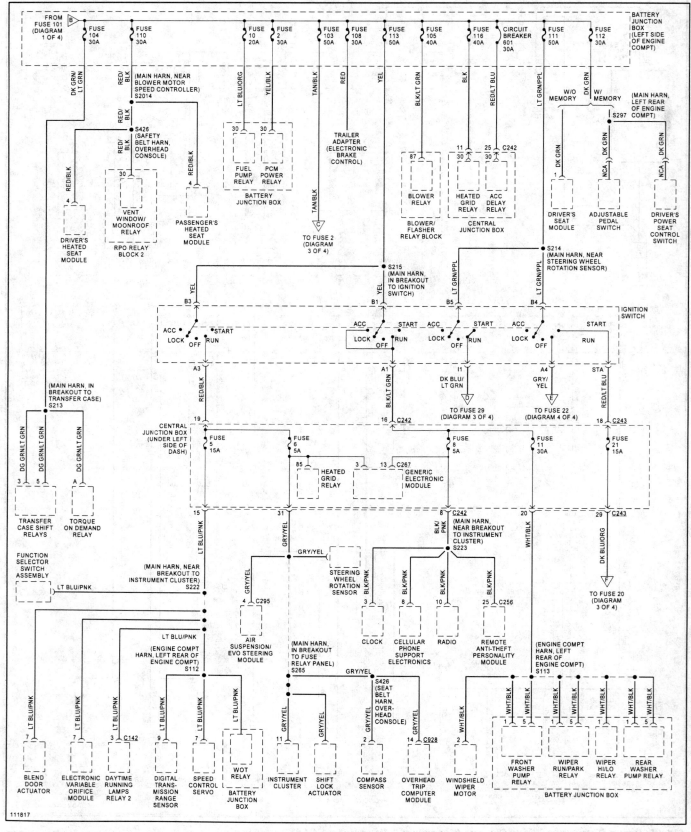

Fig. 27: Power Distribution Wiring Diagram (Expedition & Navigator – 2 Of 4)

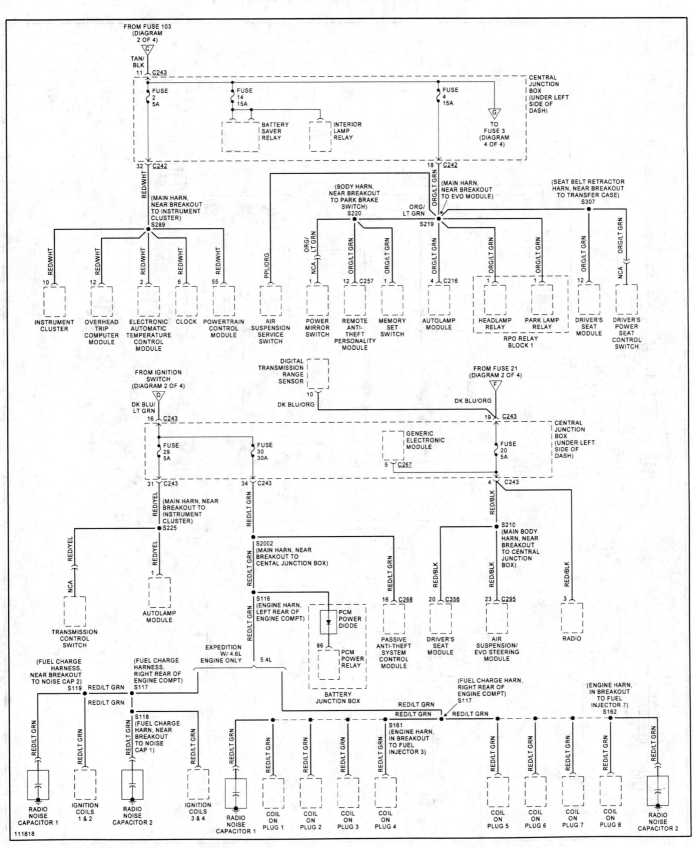

Fig. 28: Power Distribution Wiring Diagram (Expedition & Navigator – 3 Of 4)

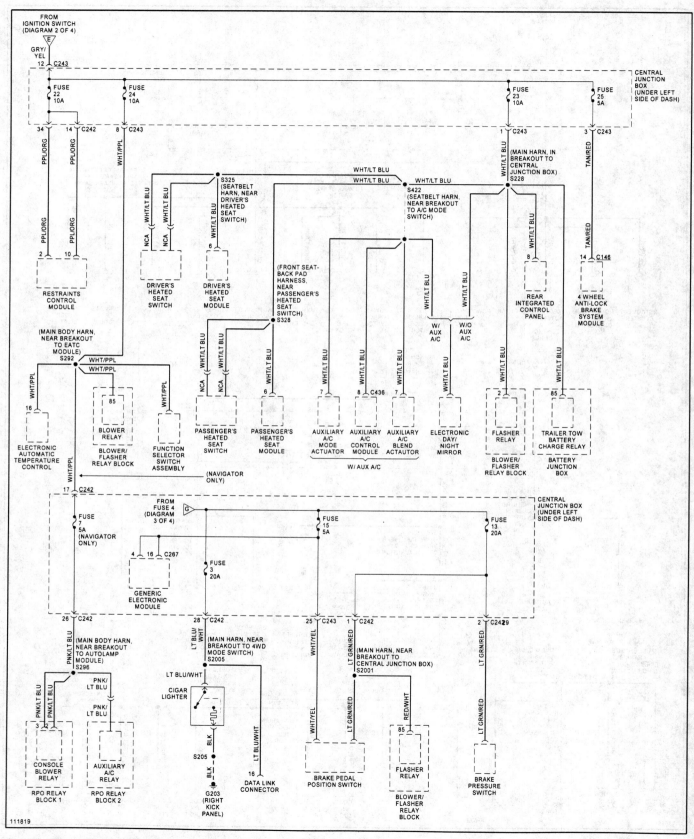

Fig. 29: Power Distribution Wiring Diagram (Expedition & Navigator – 4 Of 4)

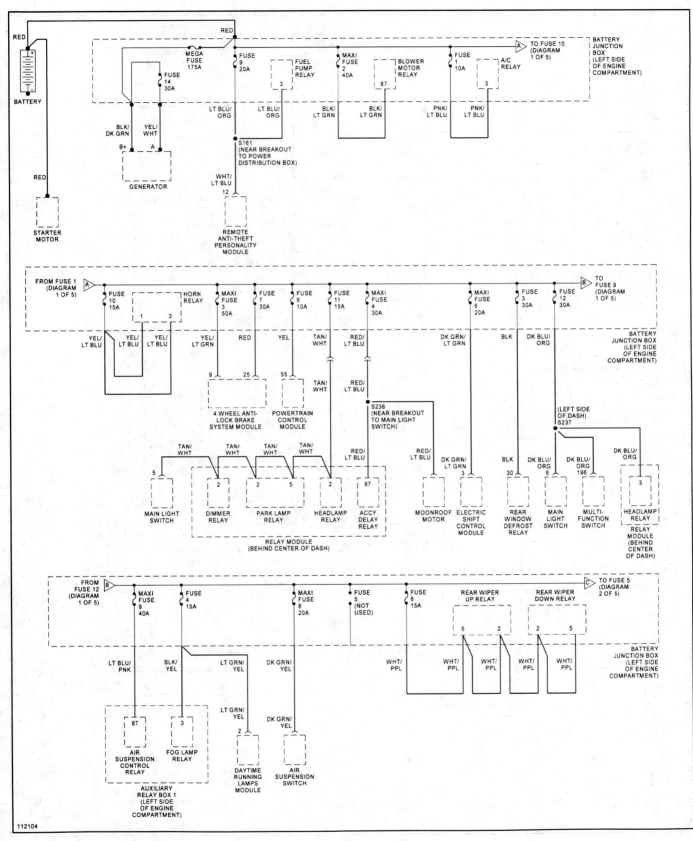

Fig. 30: Power Distribution Wiring Diagram (Explorer & Mountaineer – 1 Of 5)

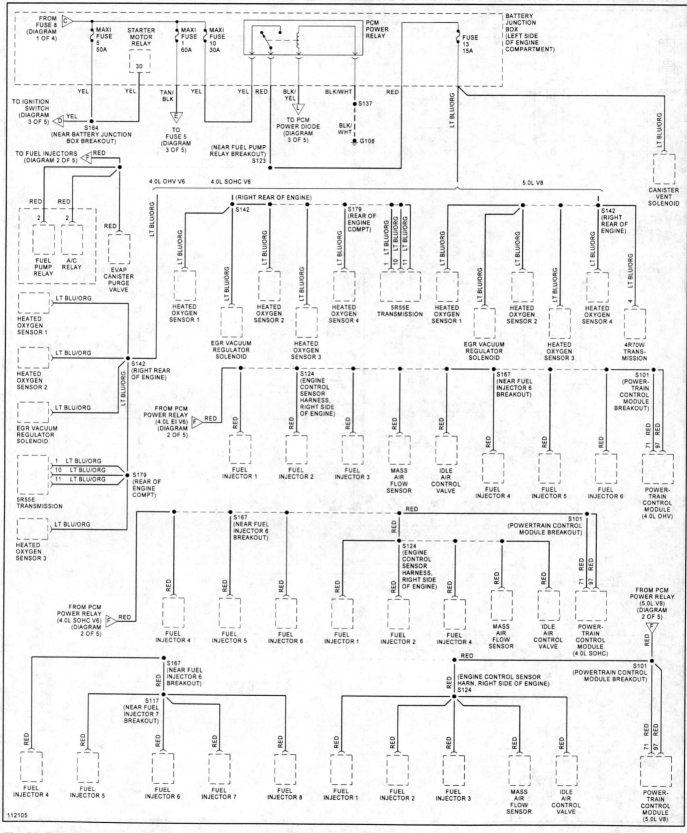

Fig. 31: Power Distribution Wiring Diagram (Explorer & Mountaineer – 2 Of 5)

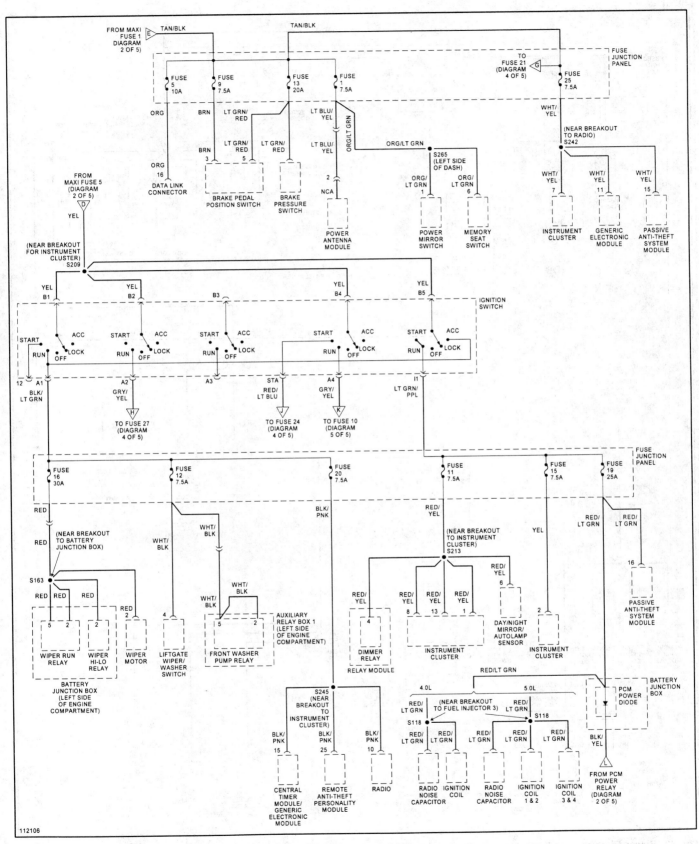

Fig. 32: Power Distribution Wiring Diagram (Explorer & Mountaineer – 3 Of 5)

112106

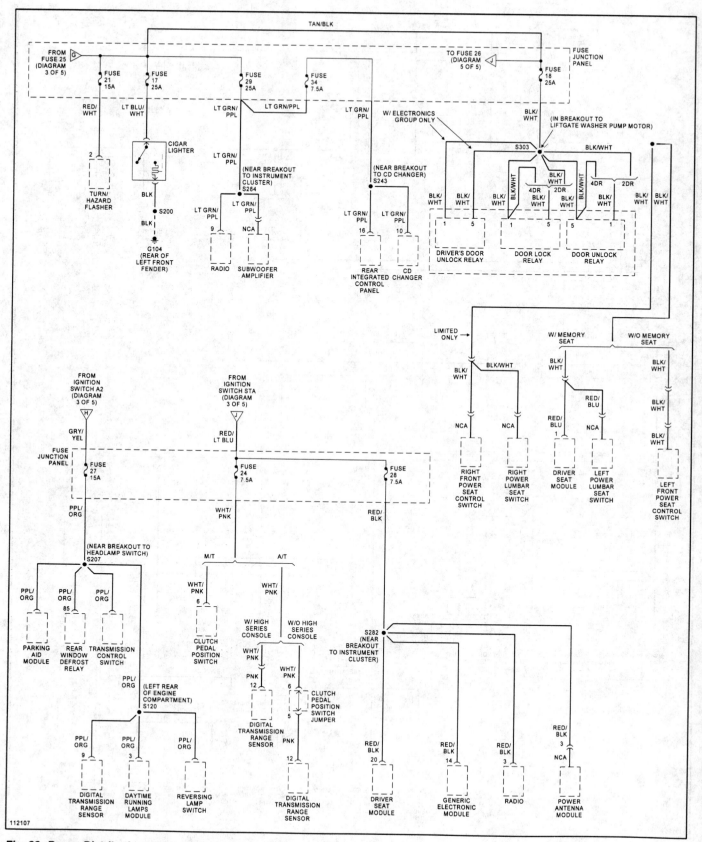

Fig. 33: Power Distribution Wiring Diagram (Explorer & Mountaineer – 4 Of 5)

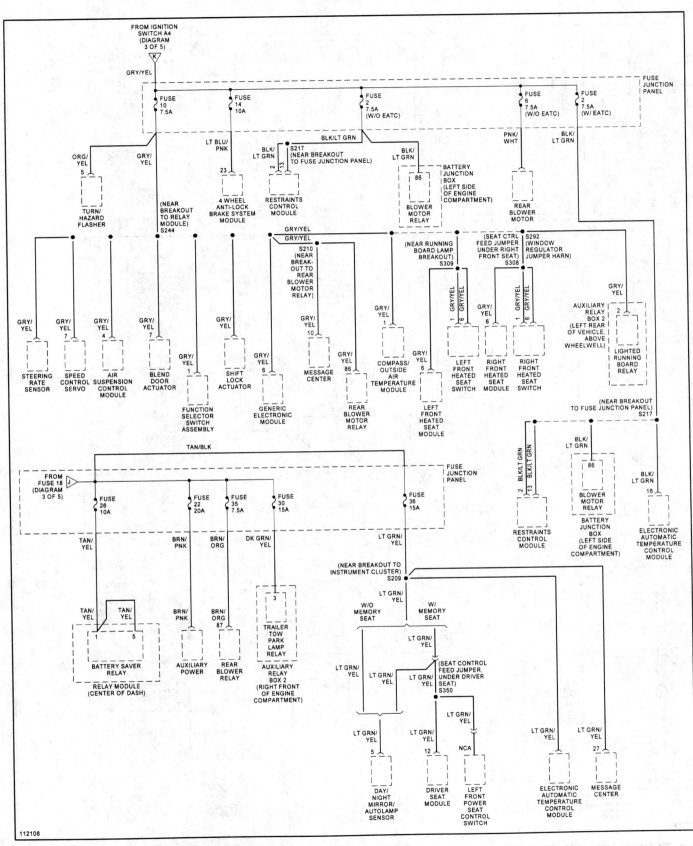

Fig. 34: Power Distribution Wiring Diagram (Explorer & Mountaineer – 5 Of 5)

112108

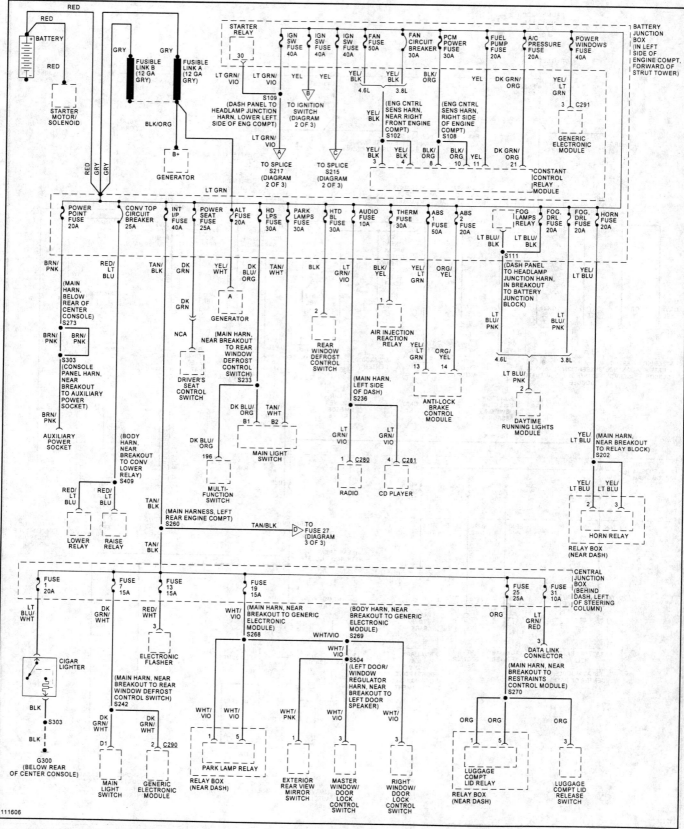

Fig. 35: Power Distribution Wiring Diagram (Mustang – 1 Of 3)

111606

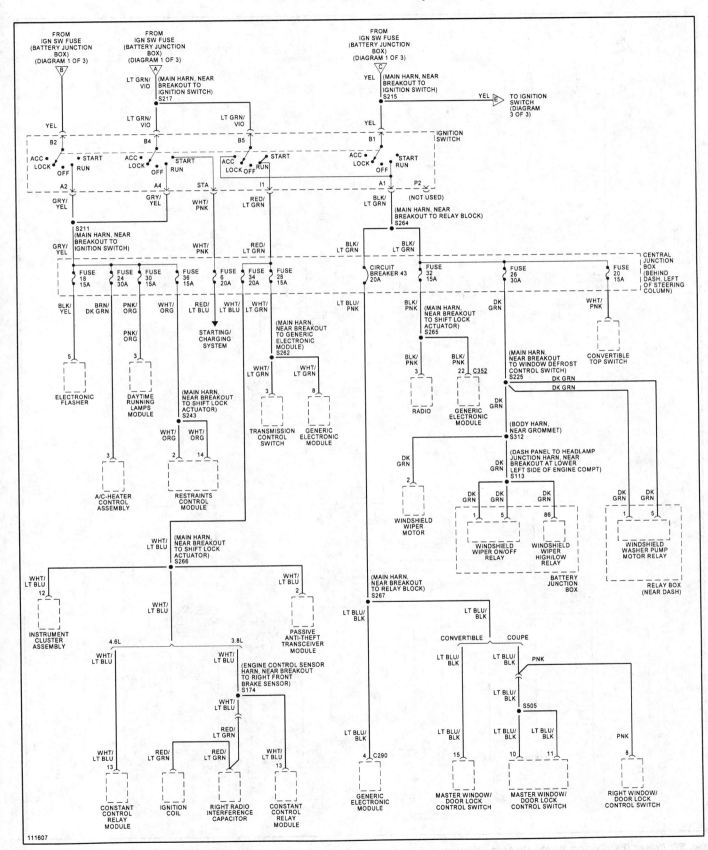

Fig. 36: Power Distribution Wiring Diagram (Mustang – 2 Of 3)

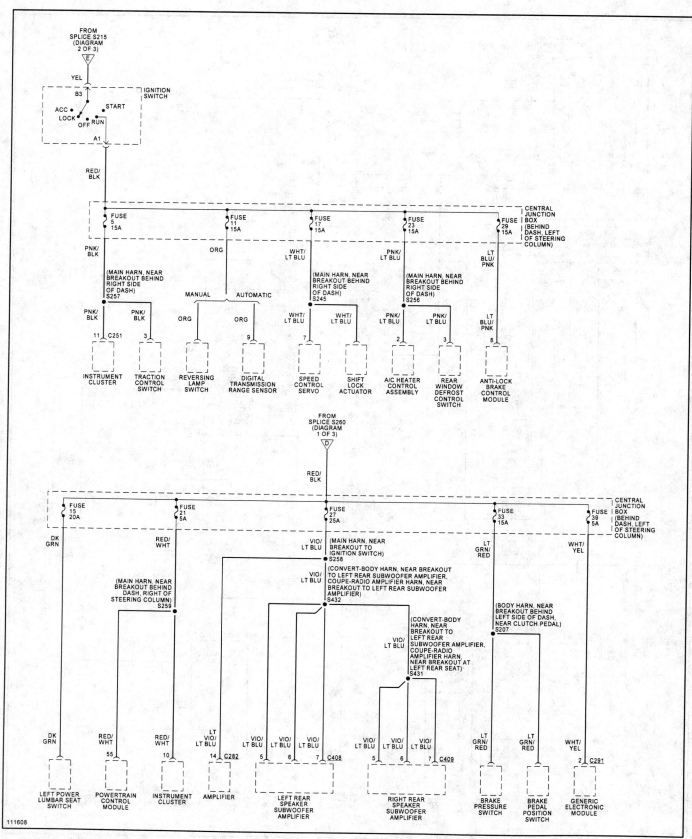

Fig. 37: Power Distribution Wiring Diagram (Mustang – 3 Of 3)

111608

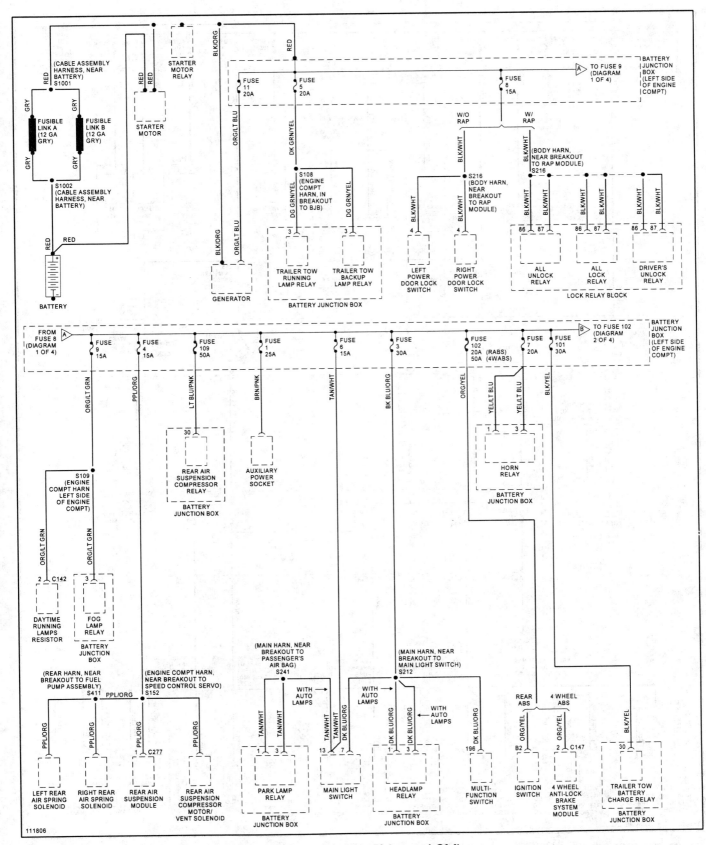

Fig. 38: Power Distribution Wiring Diagram (F150 & F250 Light-Duty Pickups – 1 Of 4)

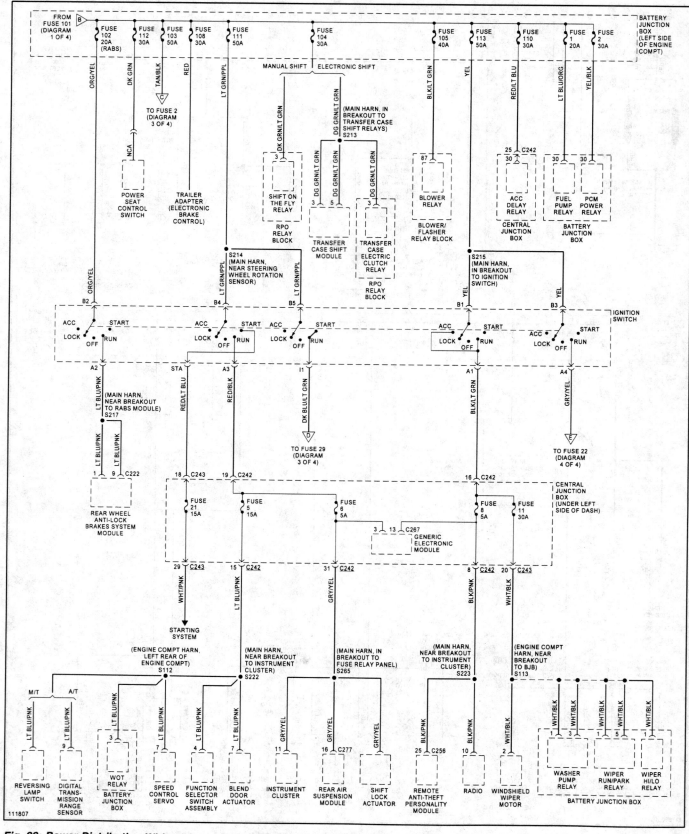

Fig. 39: Power Distribution Wiring Diagram (F150 & F250 Light-Duty Pickups – 2 Of 4)

111807

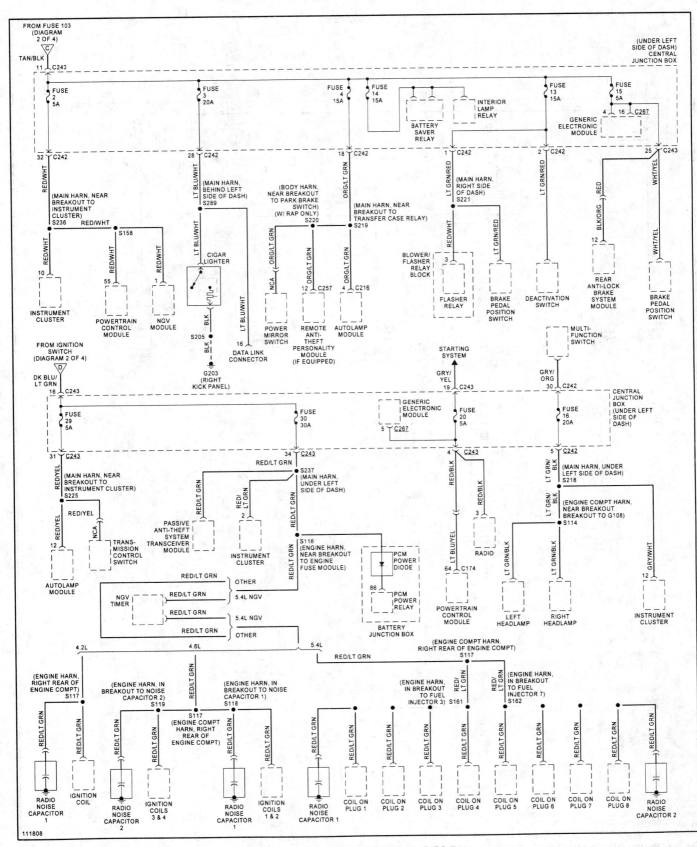

Fig. 40: Power Distribution Wiring Diagram (F150 & F250 Light-Duty Pickups – 3 Of 4)

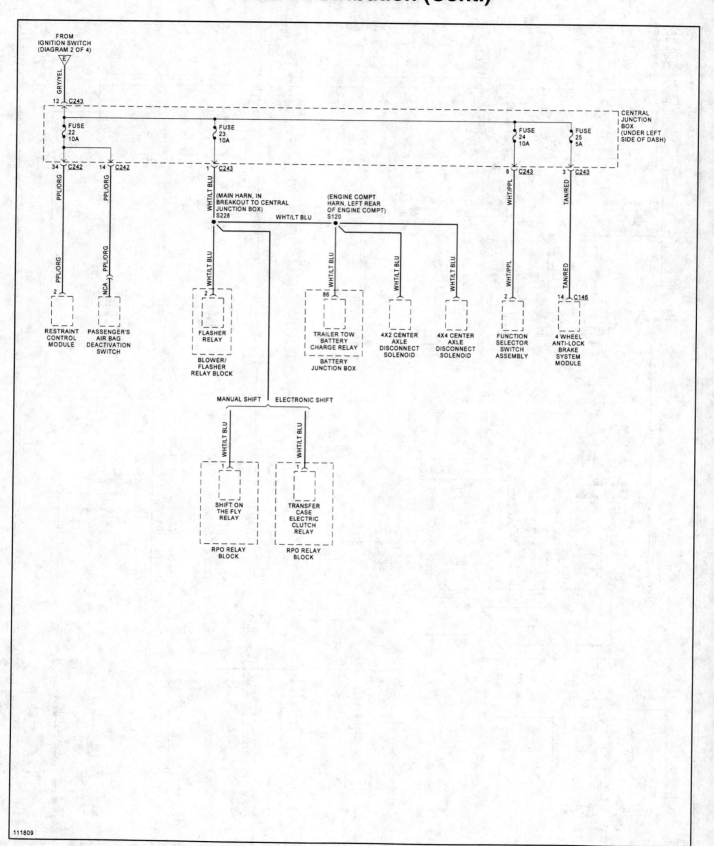

Fig. 41: Power Distribution Wiring Diagram (F150 & F250 Light-Duty Pickups – 4 Of 4)

111809

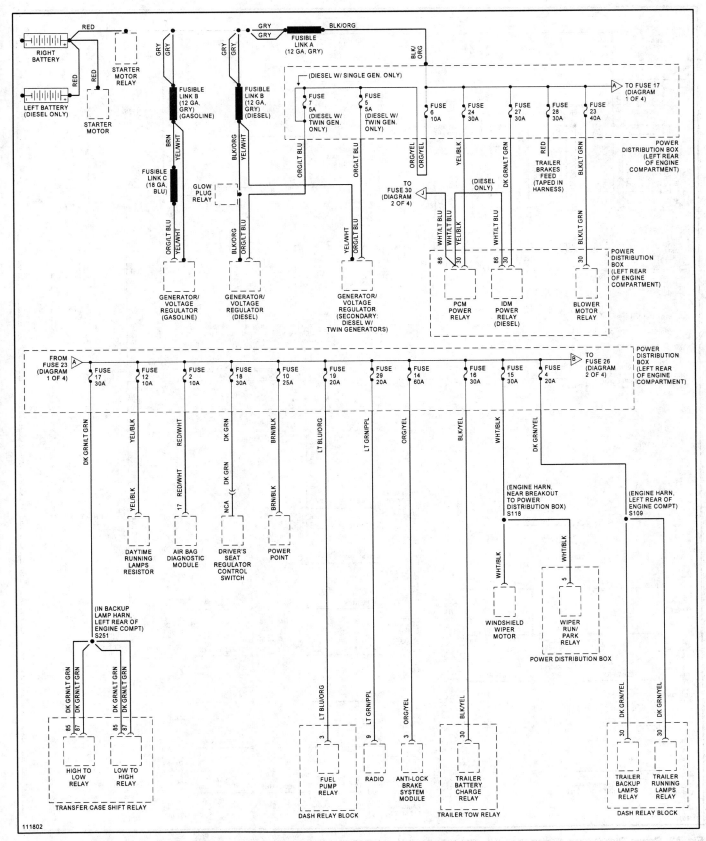

Fig. 42: Power Distribution Wiring Diagram (F250 Super-Duty & F350 Pickups – 1 Of 4)

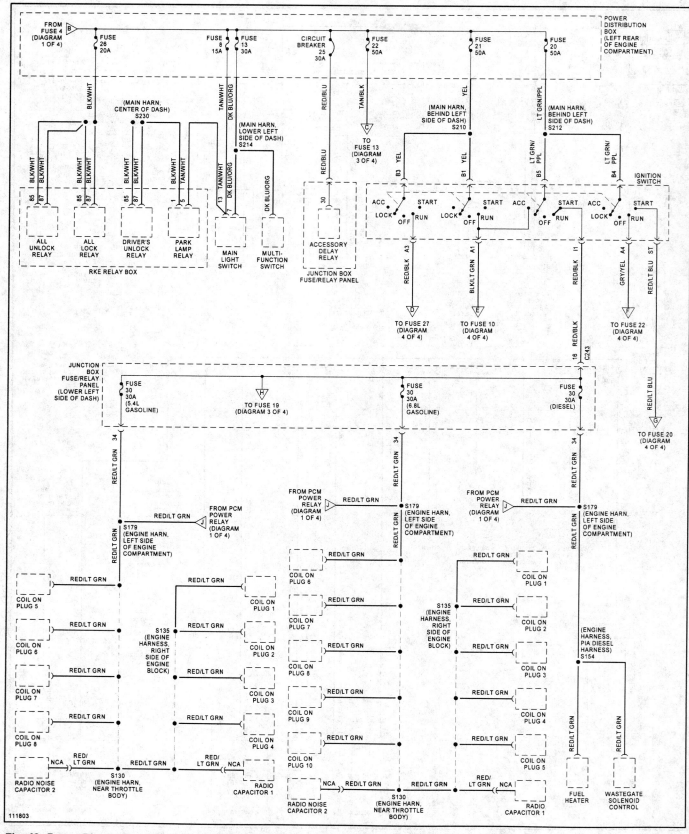

Fig. 43: Power Distribution Wiring Diagram (F250 Super-Duty & F350 Pickups – 2 Of 4)

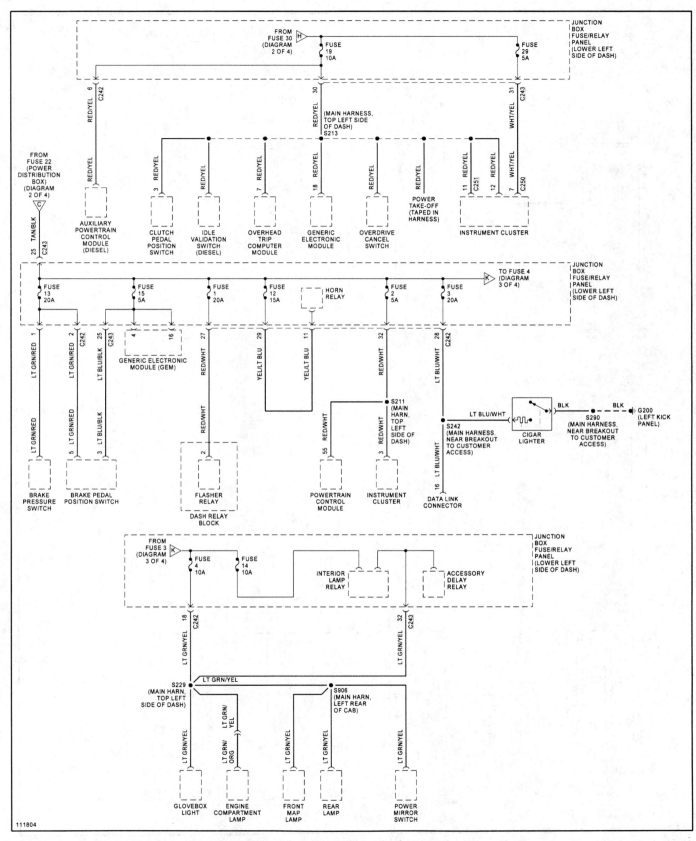

Fig. 44: Power Distribution Wiring Diagram (F250 Super-Duty & F350 Pickups – 3 Of 4)

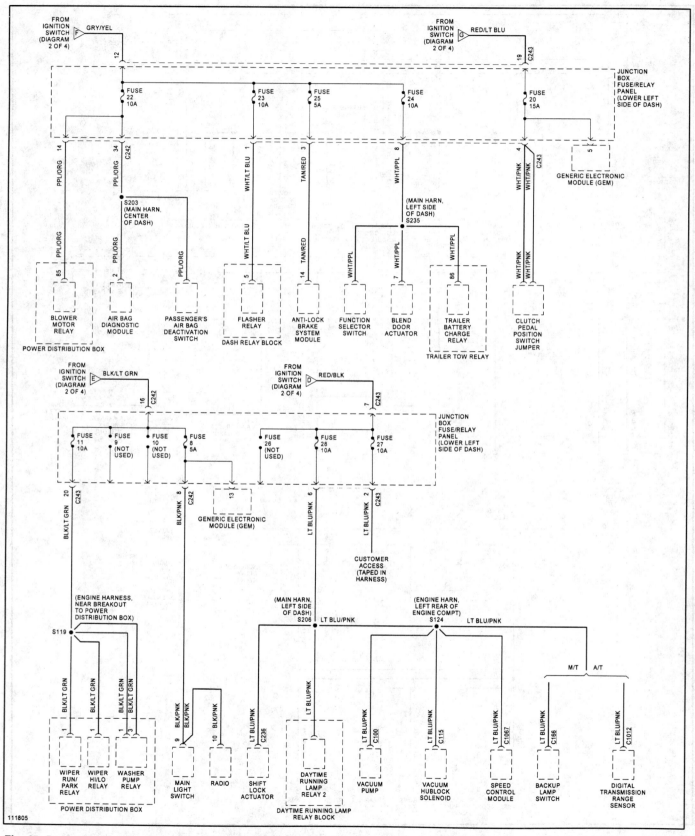

Fig. 45: Power Distribution Wiring Diagram (F250 Super-Duty & F350 Pickups – 4 Of 4)

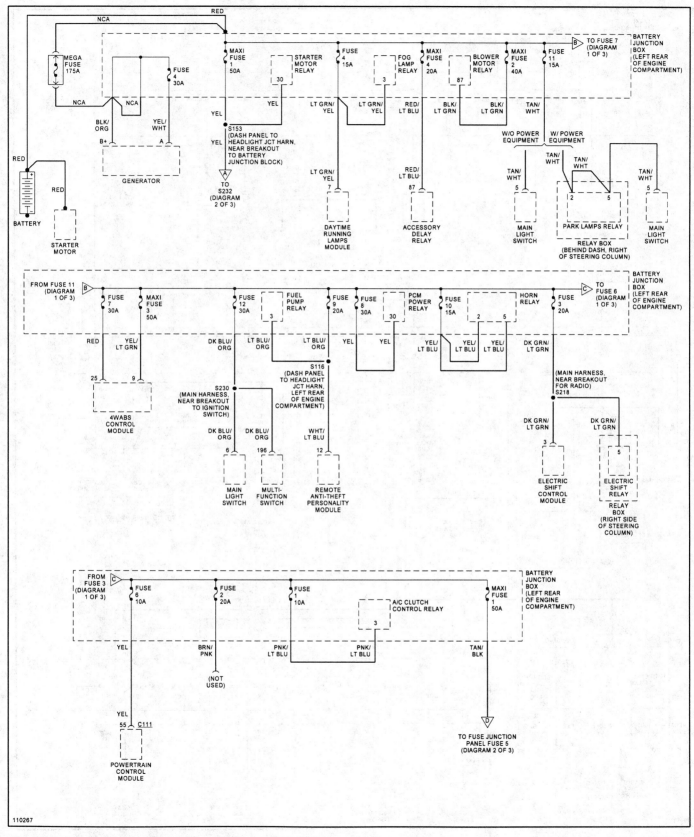

Fig. 46: Power Distribution Wiring Diagram (Ranger – 1 Of 3)

110267

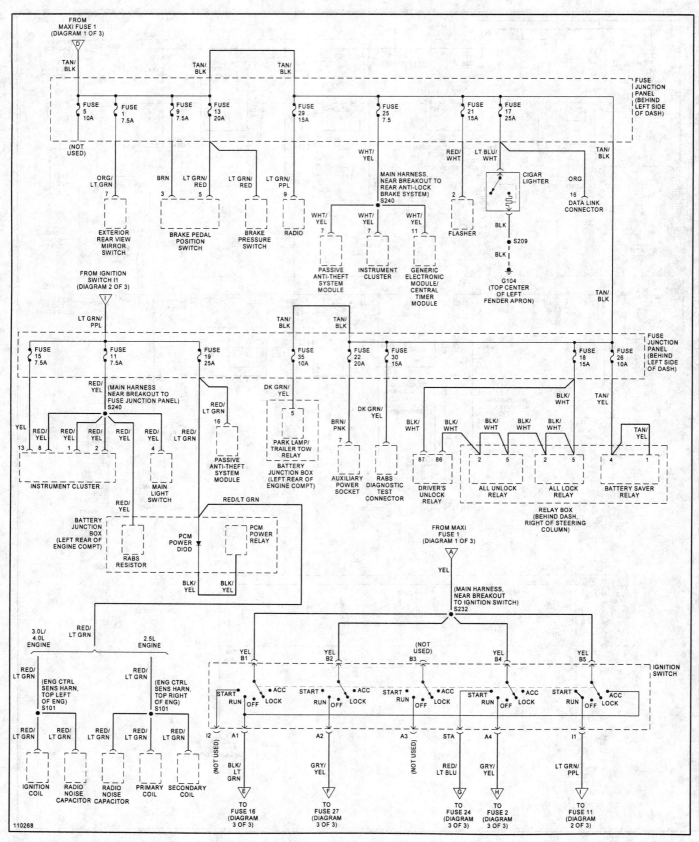

Fig. 47: Power Distribution Wiring Diagram (Ranger – 2 Of 3)

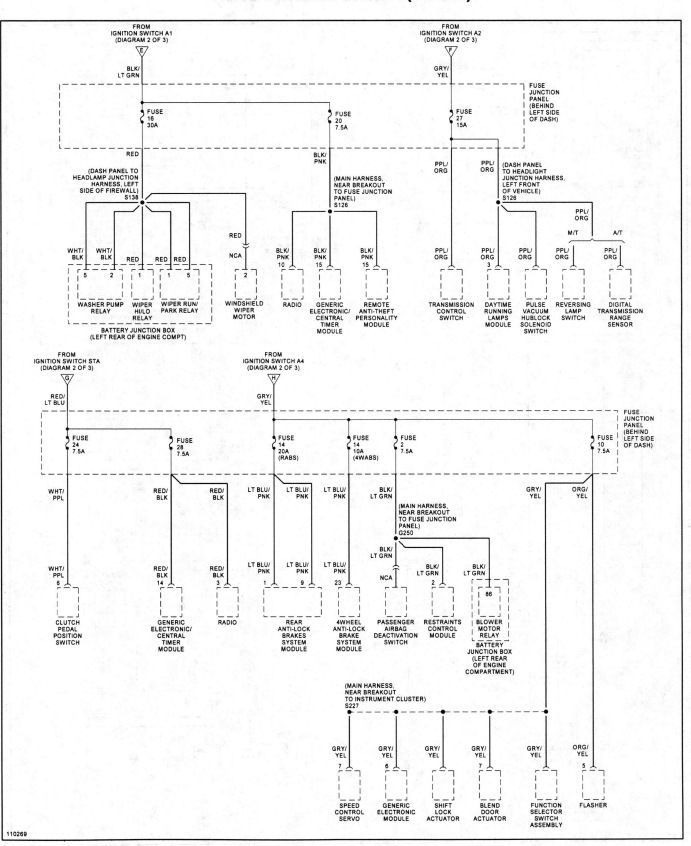

Fig. 48: Power Distribution Wiring Diagram (Ranger – 3 Of 3)

110269

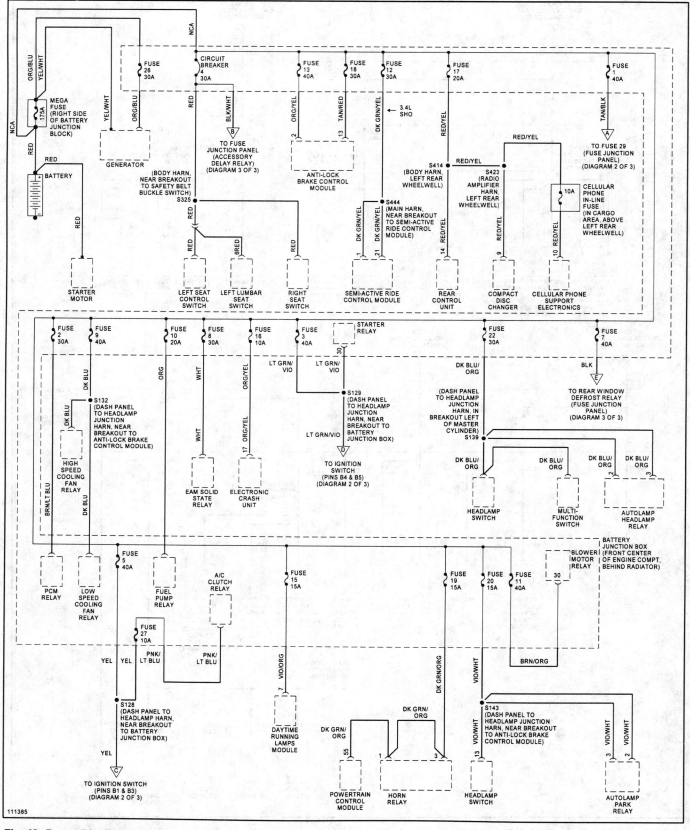

Fig. 49: Power Distribution Wiring Diagram (Sable & Taurus – 1 Of 3)

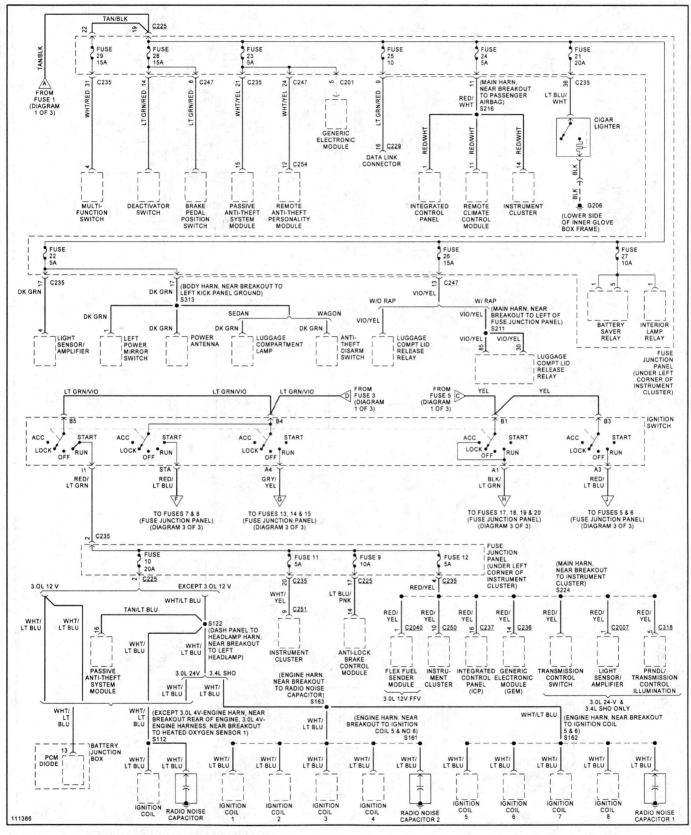

Fig. 50: Power Distribution Wiring Diagram (Sable & Taurus – 2 Of 3)

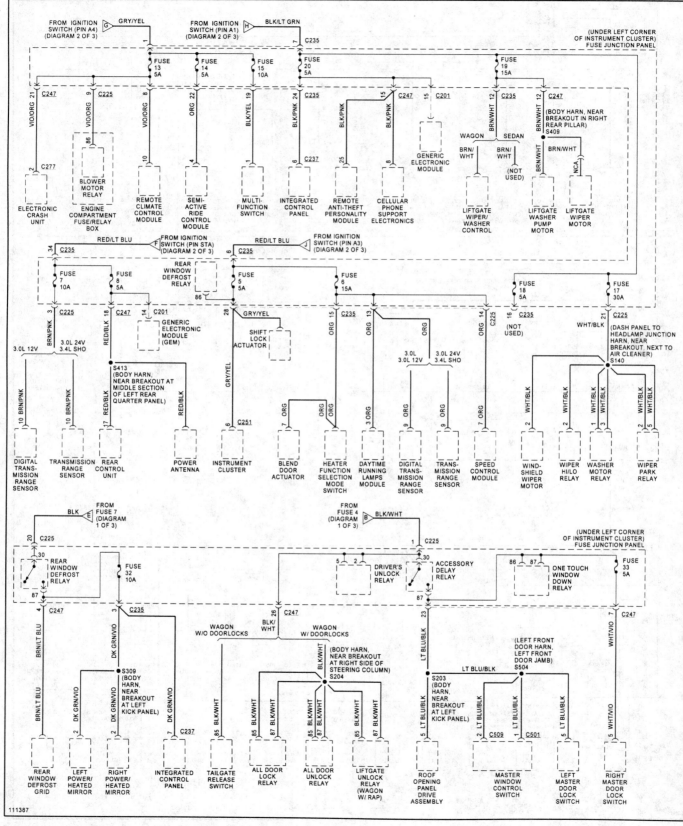

Fig. 51: Power Distribution Wiring Diagram (Sable & Taurus – 3 Of 3)

111387

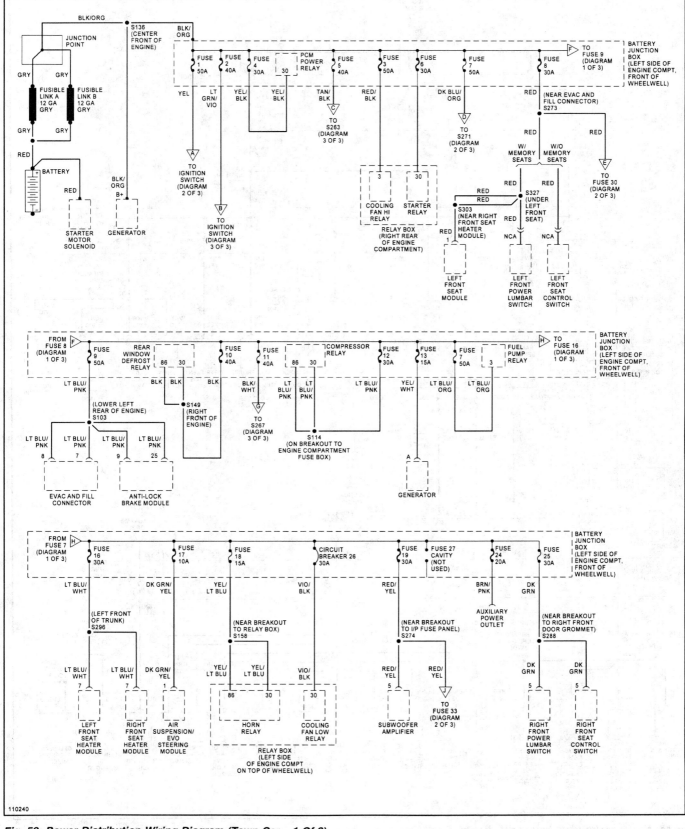

Fig. 52: Power Distribution Wiring Diagram (Town Car – 1 Of 3)

110240

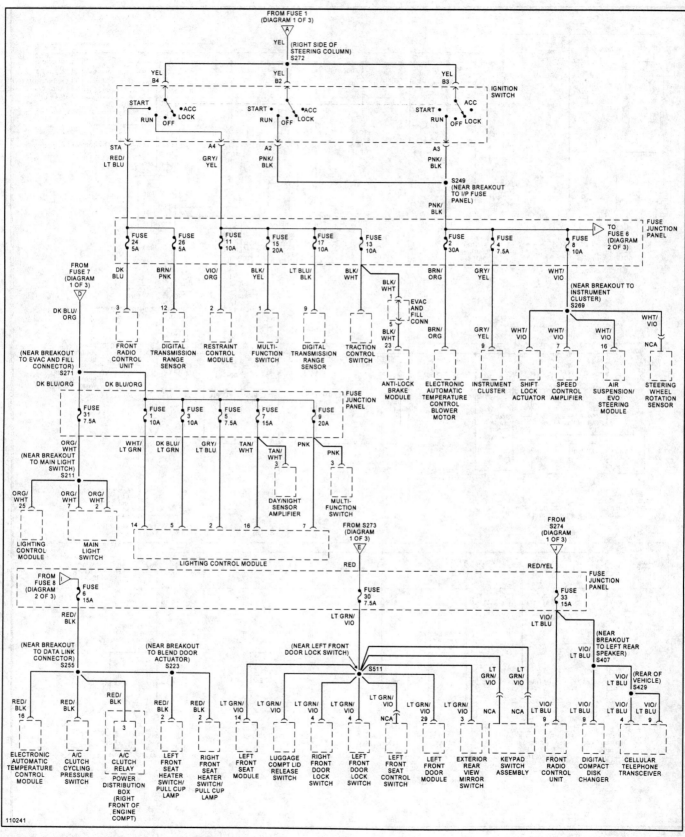

Fig. 53: Power Distribution Wiring Diagram (Town Car – 2 Of 3)

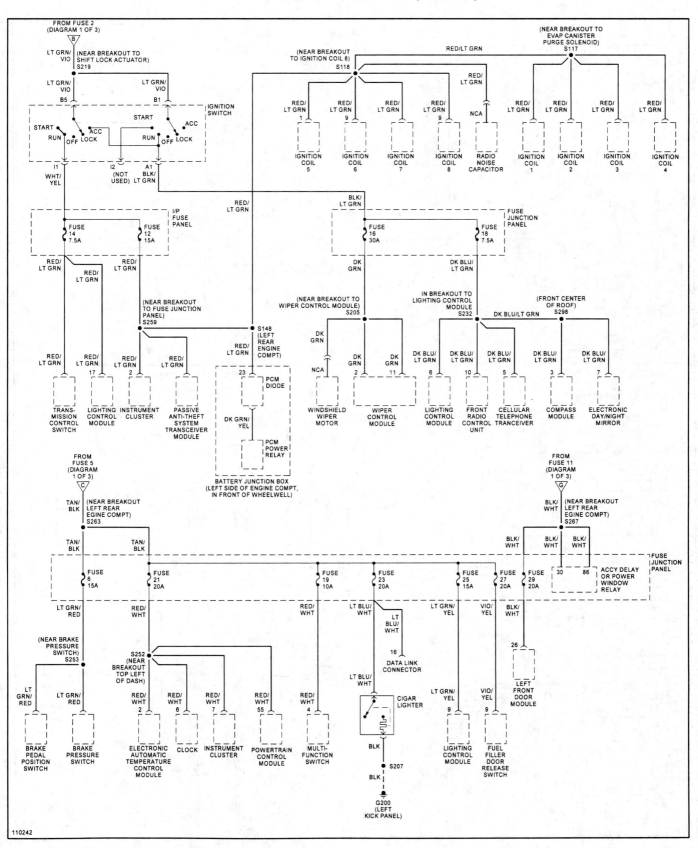

Fig. 54: Power Distribution Wiring Diagram (Town Car – 3 Of 3)

110242

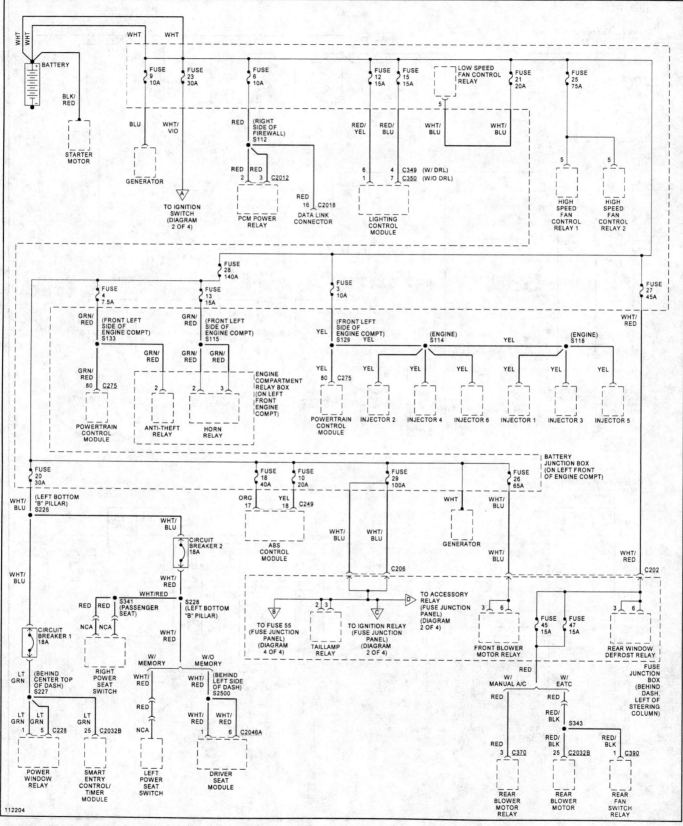

Fig. 55: Power Distribution Wiring Diagram (Villager – 1 Of 4)

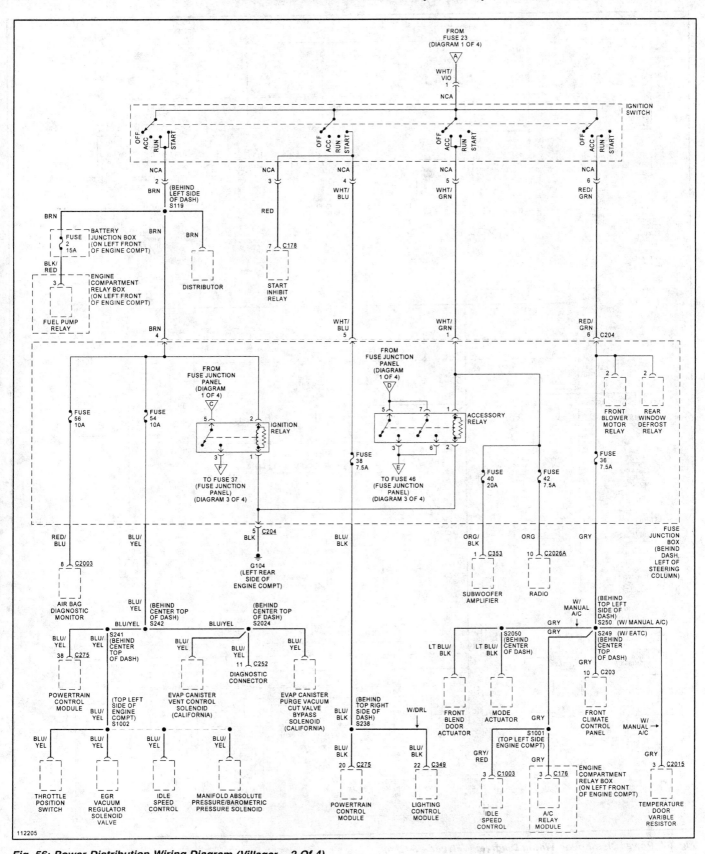

Fig. 56: Power Distribution Wiring Diagram (Villager – 2 Of 4)

112205

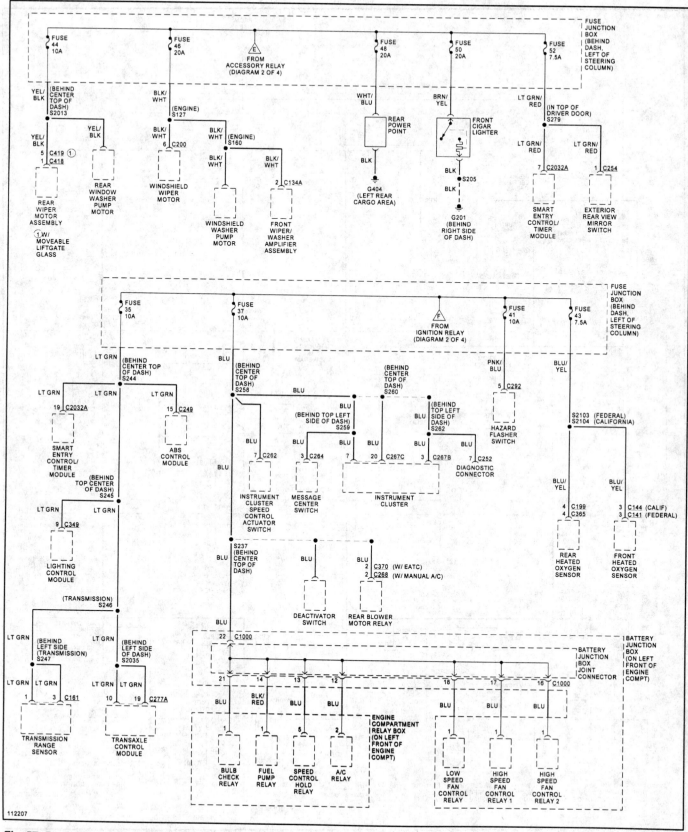

Fig. 57: Power Distribution Wiring Diagram (Villager – 3 Of 4)

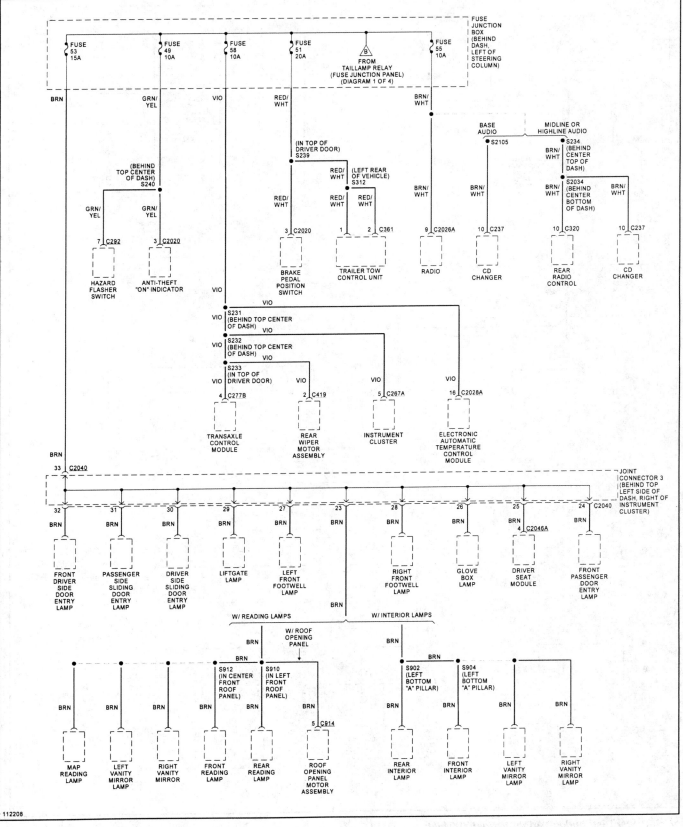

Fig. 58: Power Distribution Wiring Diagram (Villager – 4 Of 4)

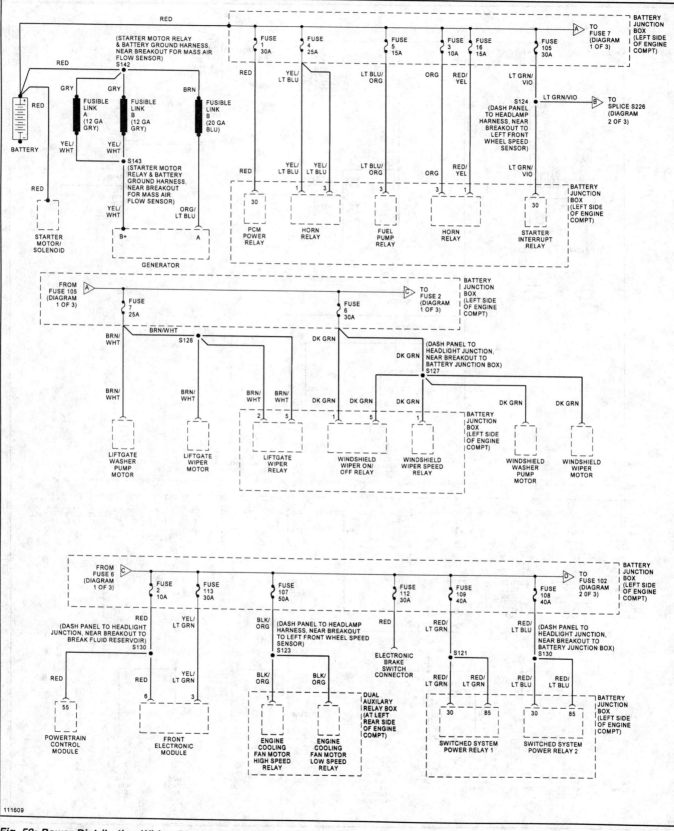

Fig. 59: Power Distribution Wiring Diagram (Windstar – 1 Of 3)

111609

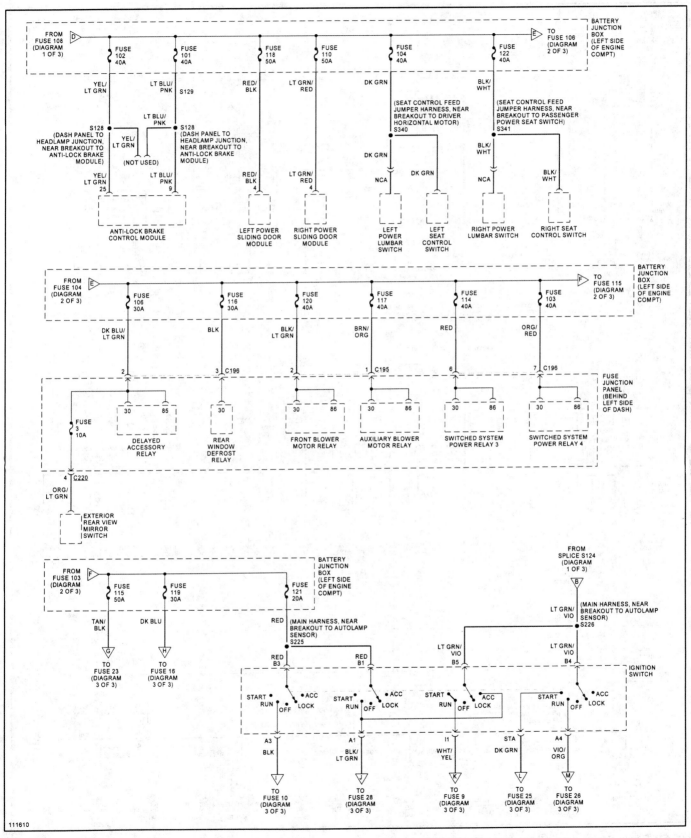

Fig. 60: Power Distribution Wiring Diagram (Windstar – 2 Of 3)

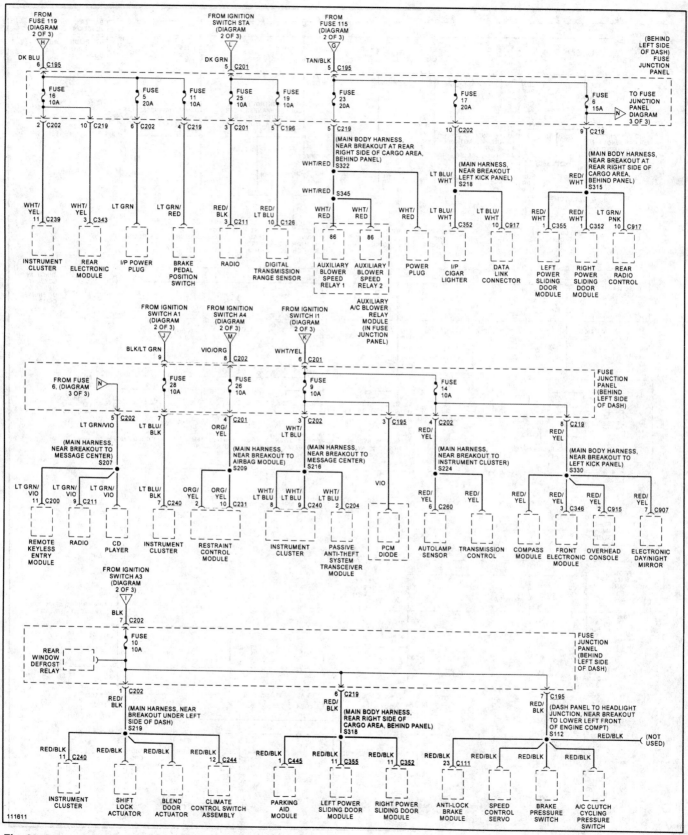

Fig. 61: Power Distribution Wiring Diagram (Windstar – 3 Of 3)

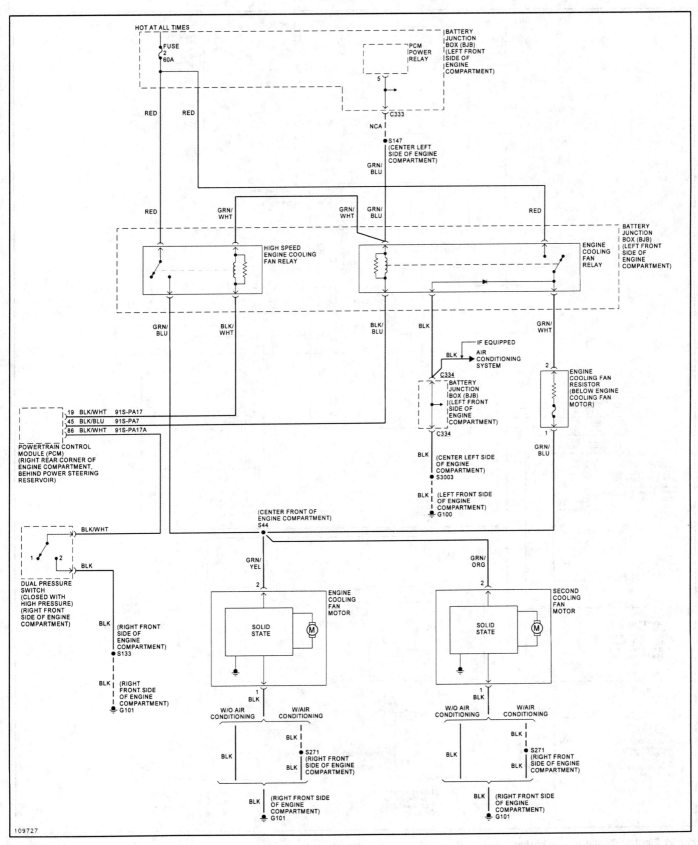

Fig. 1: Electric Cooling Fans Wiring Diagram (Contour & Mystique)

109727

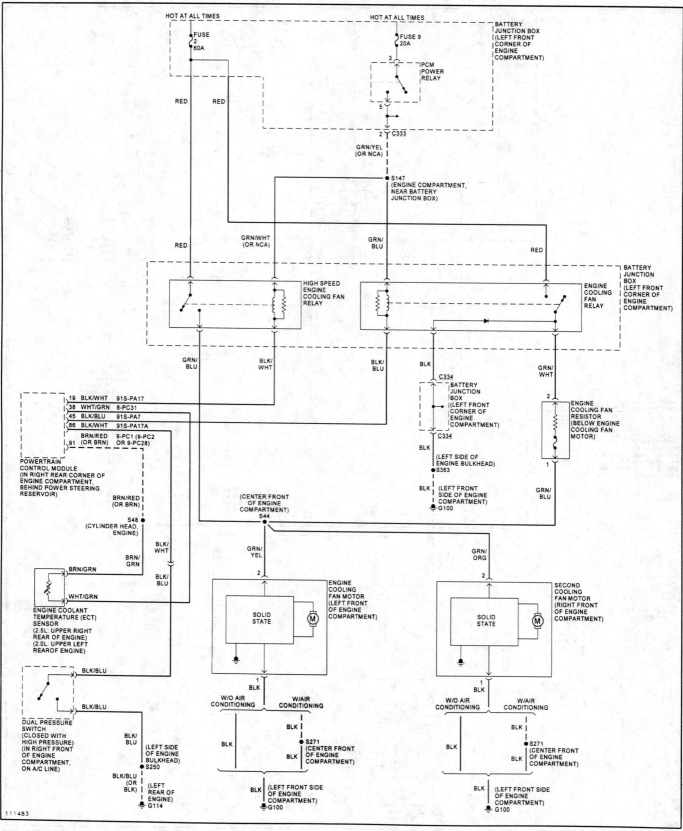

Fig. 2: Electric Cooling Fans Wiring Diagram (Cougar)

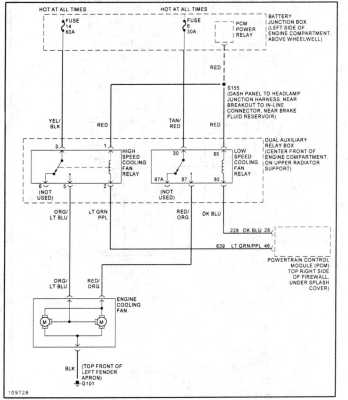

Fig. 3: Electric Cooling Fans Wiring Diagram (Continental)

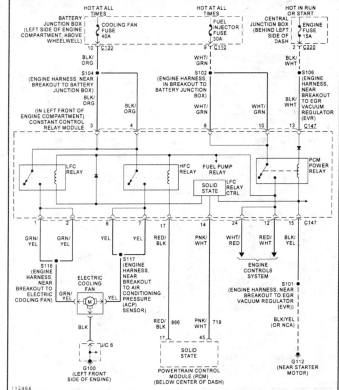

Fig. 5: Electric Cooling Fans Wiring Diagram (Escort & Tracer)

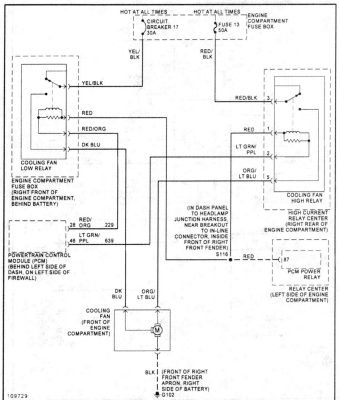

Fig. 4: Electric Cooling Fans Wiring Diagram
(Crown Victoria & Grand Marquis)

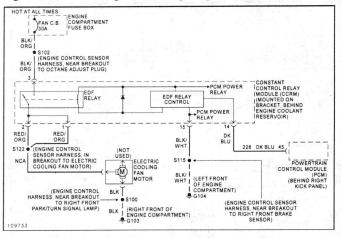

Fig. 6: Electric Cooling Fans Wiring Diagram (Mustang – 3.8L)

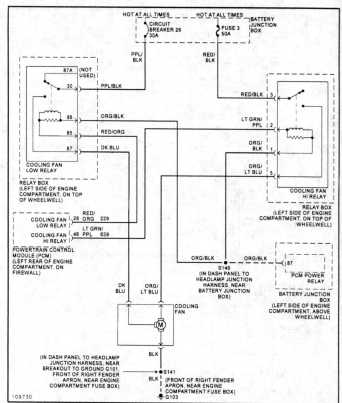

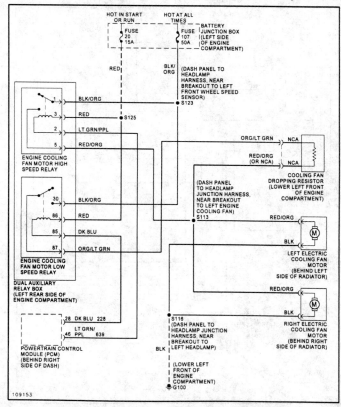

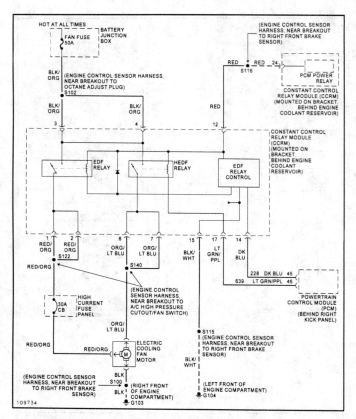

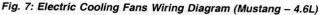

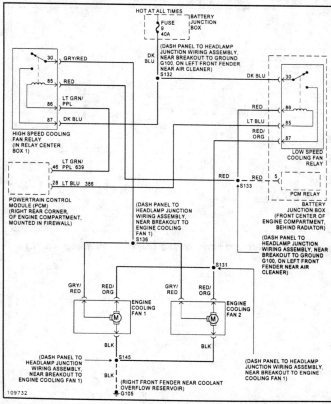

Fig. 7: Electric Cooling Fans Wiring Diagram (Mustang – 4.6L)

Fig. 9: Electric Cooling Fans Wiring Diagram (Town Car)

Fig. 8: Electric Cooling Fans Wiring Diagram (Sable & Taurus)

Fig. 10: Electric Cooling Fans Wiring Diagram (Windstar)

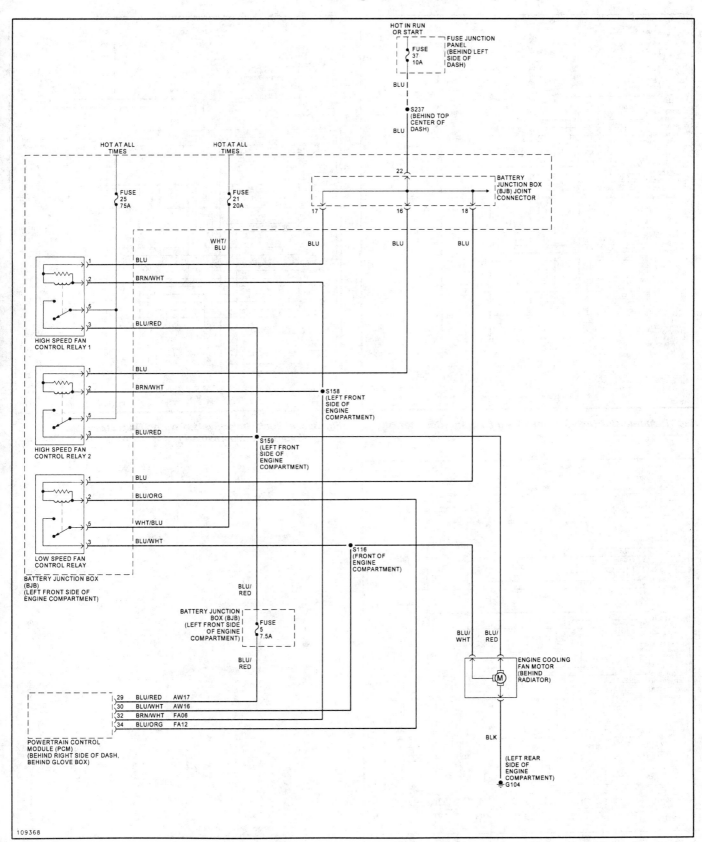

Fig. 11: Electric Cooling Fans Wiring Diagram (Villager)

109368

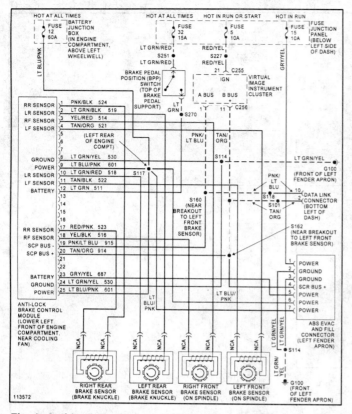

Fig. 1: Anti-Lock Brake System Wiring Diagram (Continental)

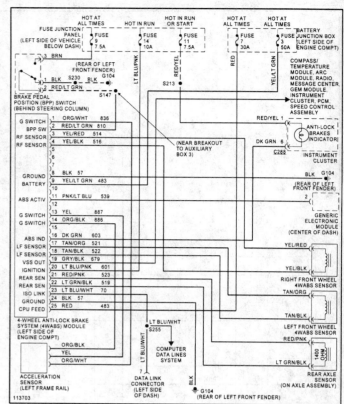

Fig. 3: Anti-Lock Brake System Wiring Diagram (Explorer & Mountaineer)

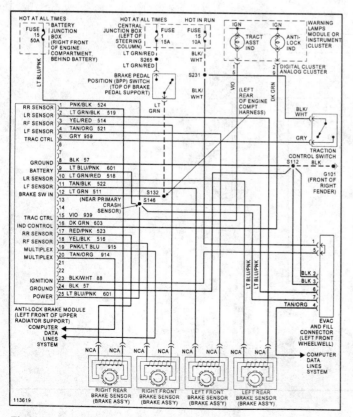

Fig. 2: Anti-Lock Brake System Wiring Diagram (Crown Victoria & Grand Marquis)

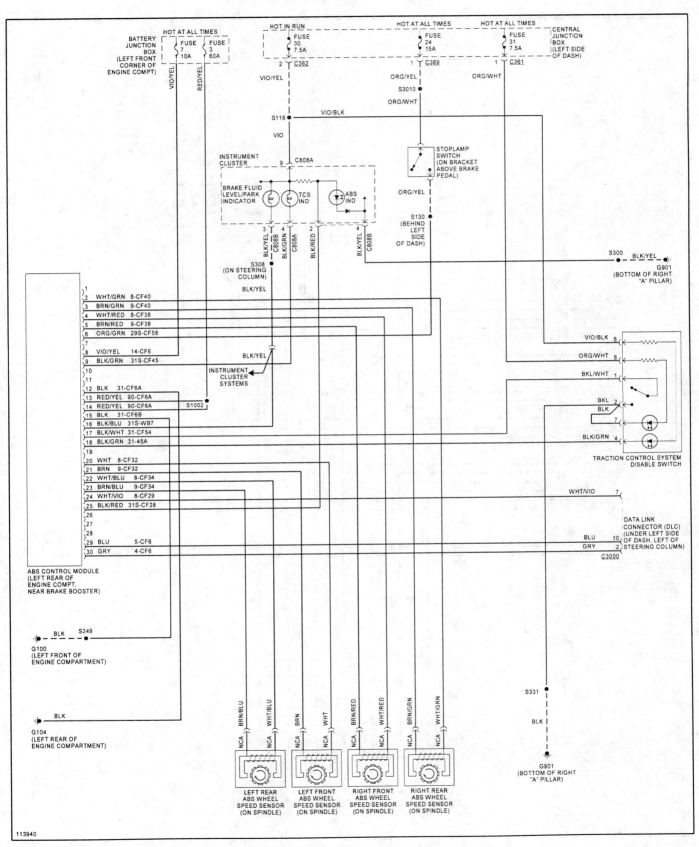

Fig. 4: Anti-Lock Brake System Wiring Diagram (Contour & Mystique – With Traction Control)

113940

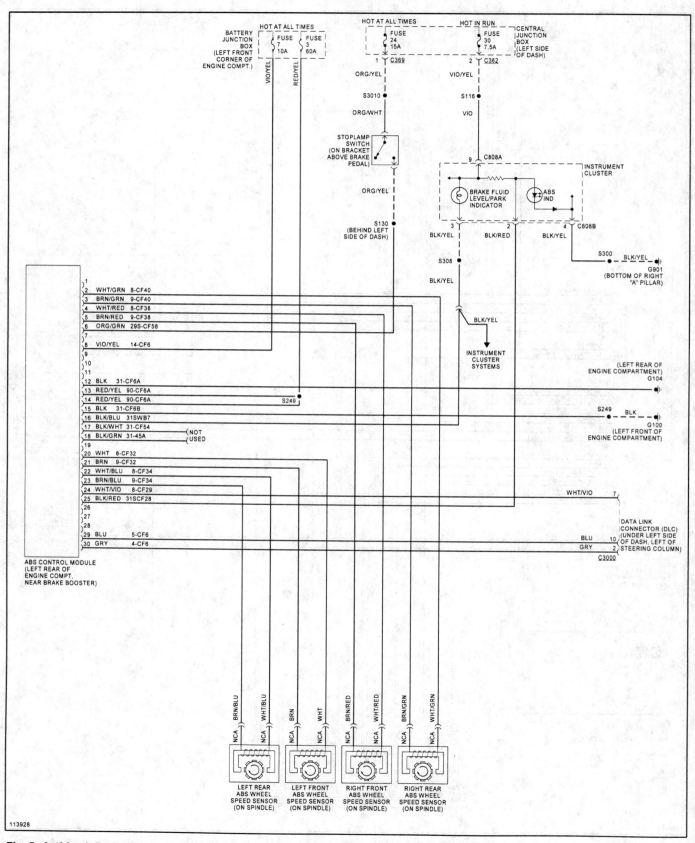

Fig. 5: Anti-Lock Brake System Wiring Diagram (Contour & Mystique – Without Traction Control)

113928

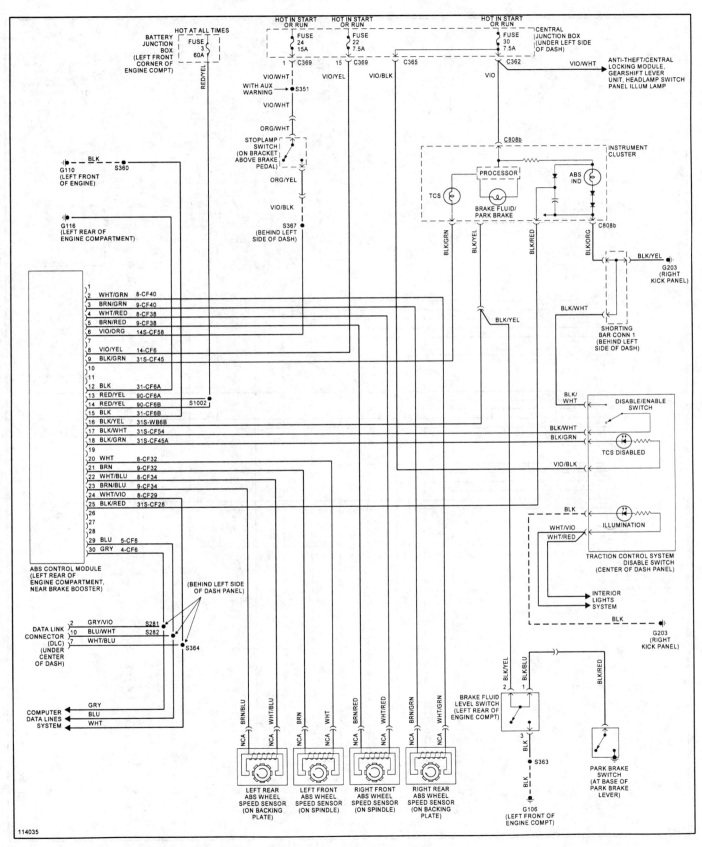

Fig. 6: Anti-Lock Brake System Wiring Diagram (Cougar – With Traction Control)

114035

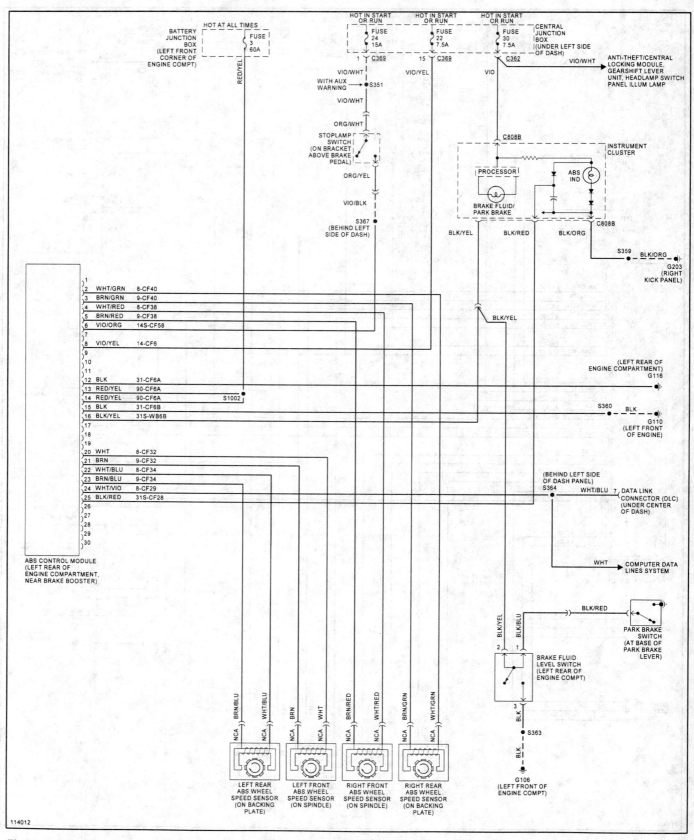

Fig. 7: Anti-Lock Brake System Wiring Diagram (Cougar – Without Traction Control)

114012

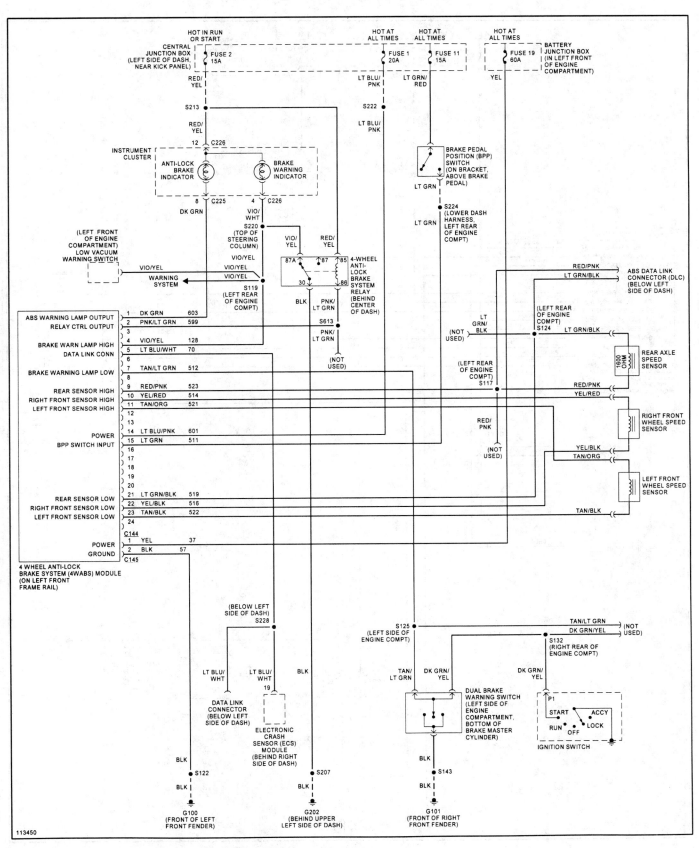

Fig. 8: Anti-Lock Brake System Wiring Diagram (Econoline – All-Wheel)

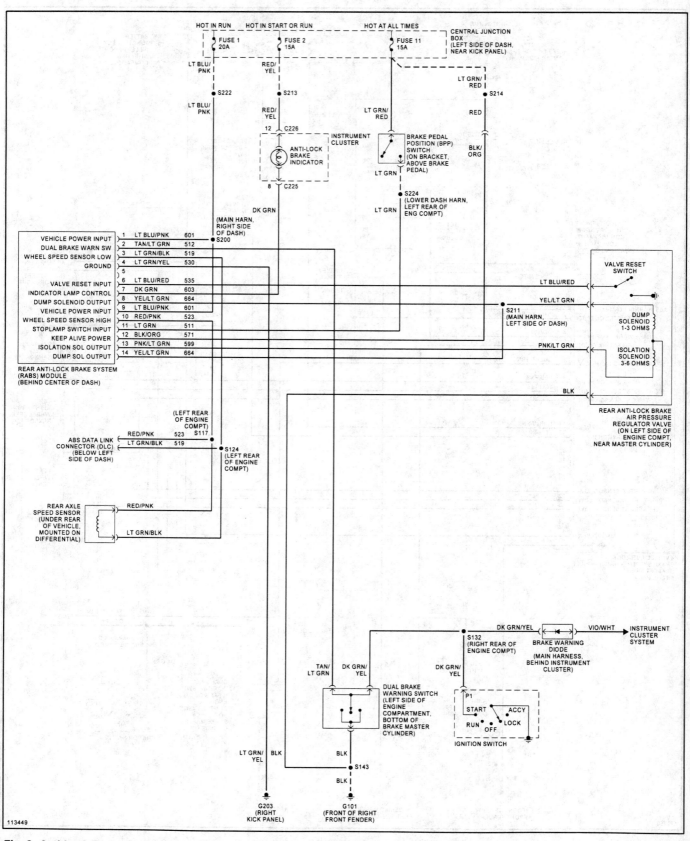

Fig. 9: Anti-Lock Brake System Wiring Diagram (Econoline – Rear Wheel)

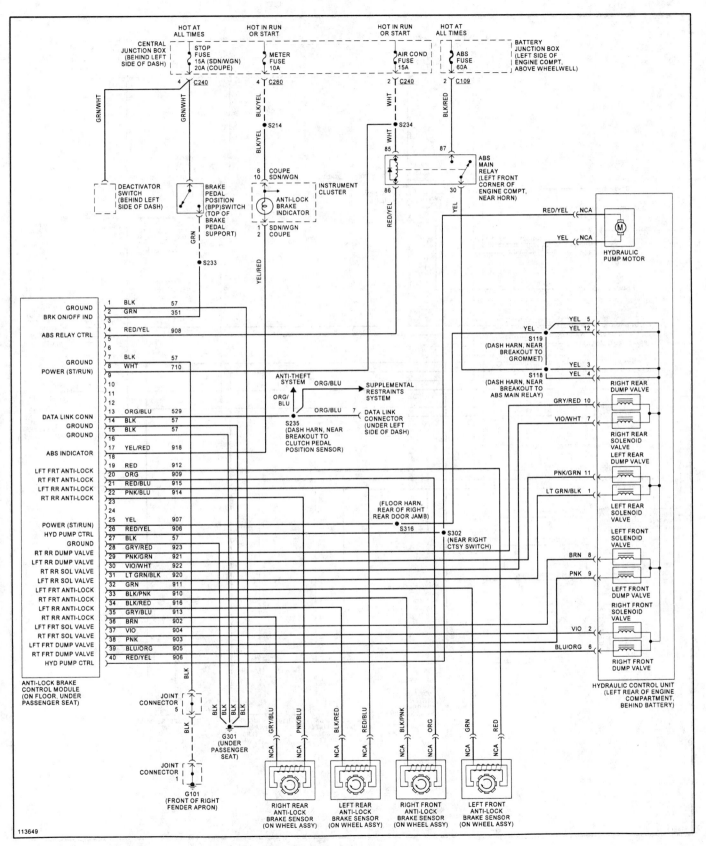

Fig. 10: Anti-Lock Brake System Wiring Diagram (Escort & Tracer)

113649

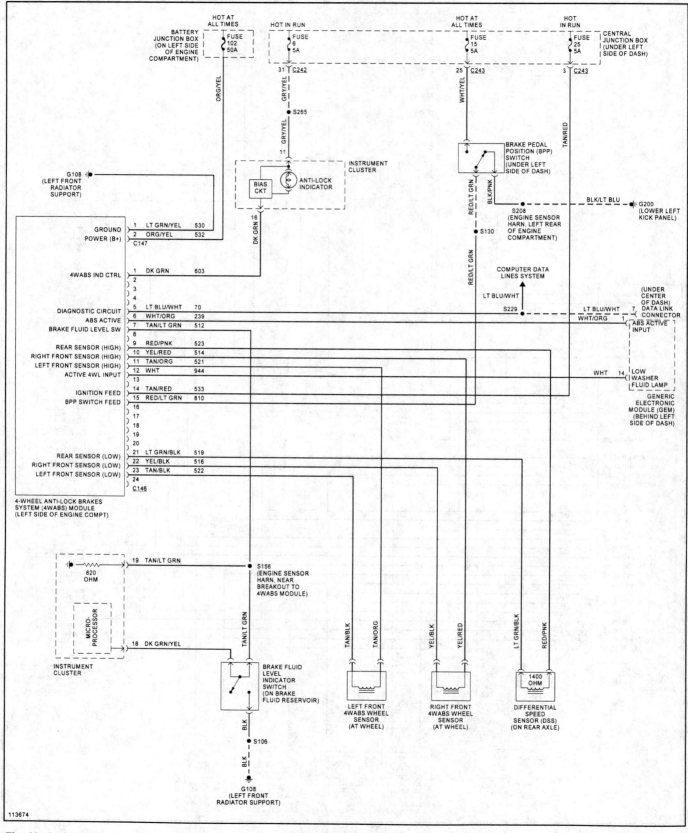

Fig. 11: Anti-Lock Brake System Wiring Diagram (Expedition & Navigator)

113674

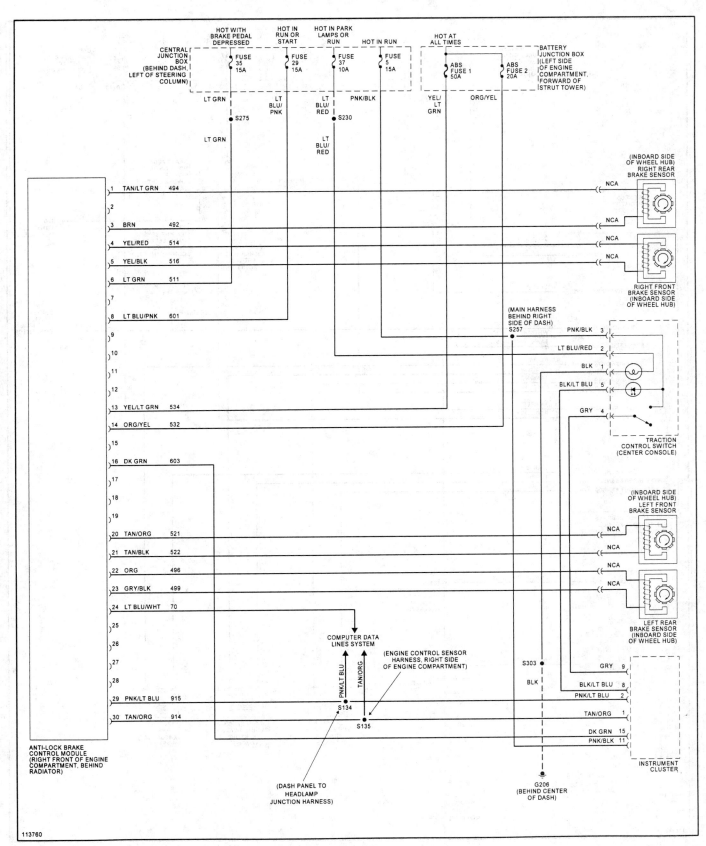

Fig. 12: Anti-Lock Brake System Wiring Diagram (Mustang)

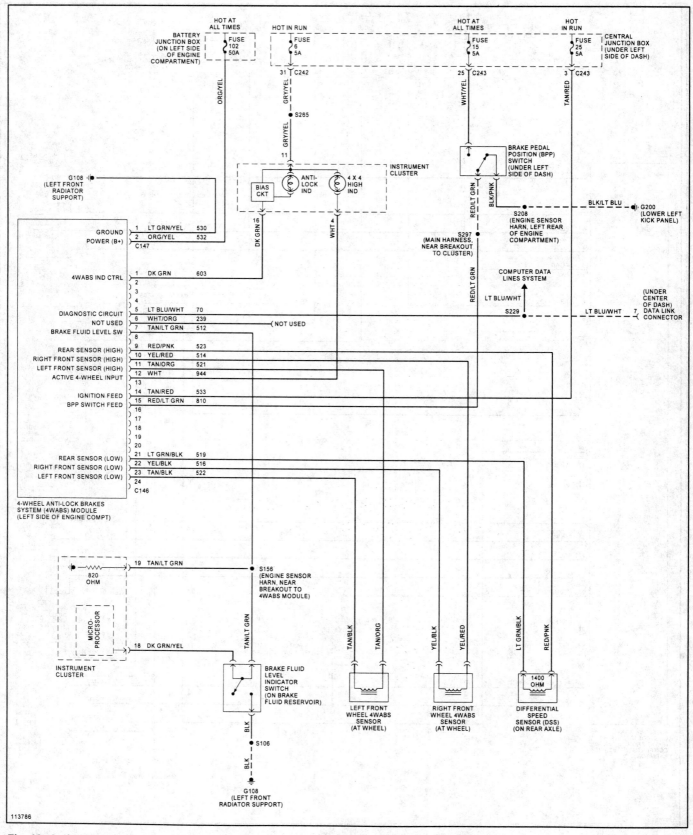

Fig. 13: Anti-Lock Brake System Wiring Diagram (F150 & F250 Light-Duty Pickups – All-Wheel)

113786

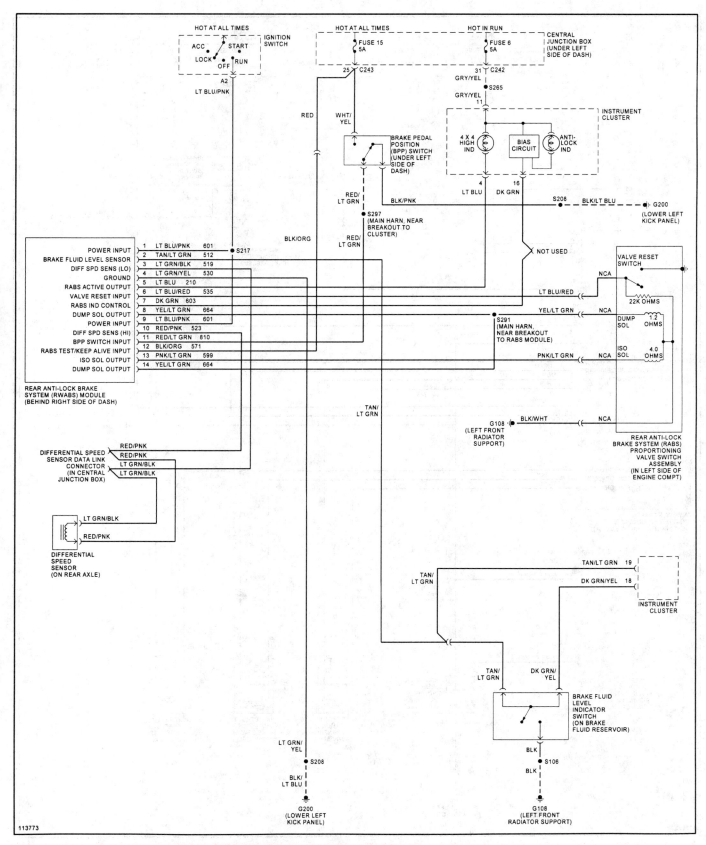

Fig. 14: Anti-Lock Brake System Wiring Diagram (F150 & F250 Light-Duty Pickups – Rear Wheel)

113773

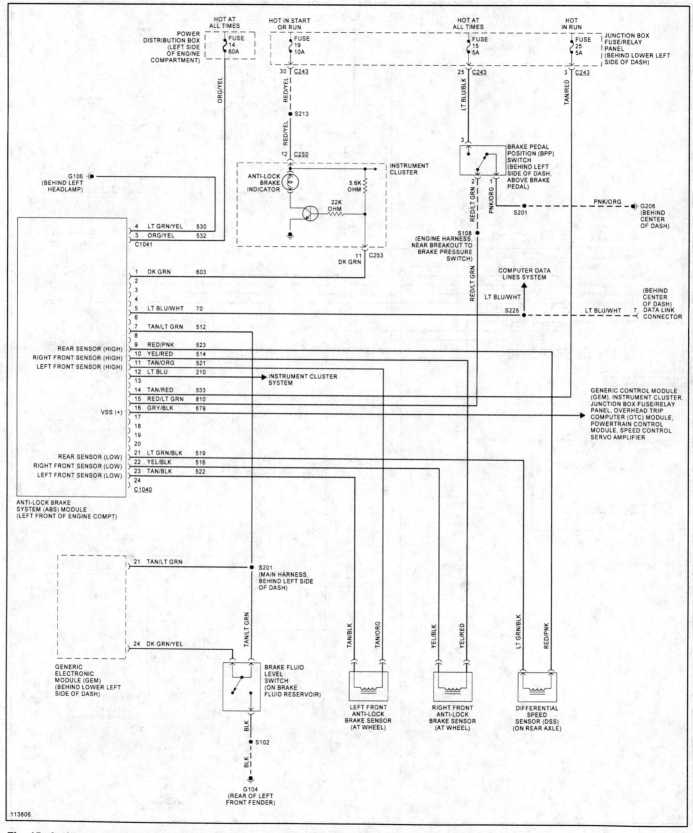

Fig. 15: Anti-Lock Brake System Wiring Diagram (F250 Super-Duty & F350 Pickups)

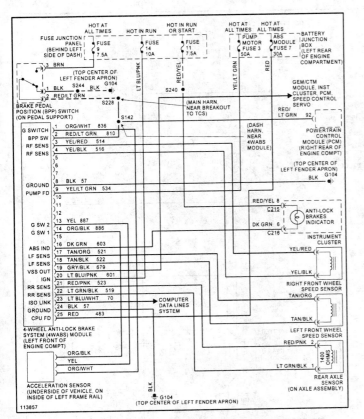

Fig. 16: Anti-Lock Brake System Wiring Diagram
(Ranger – All-Wheel)

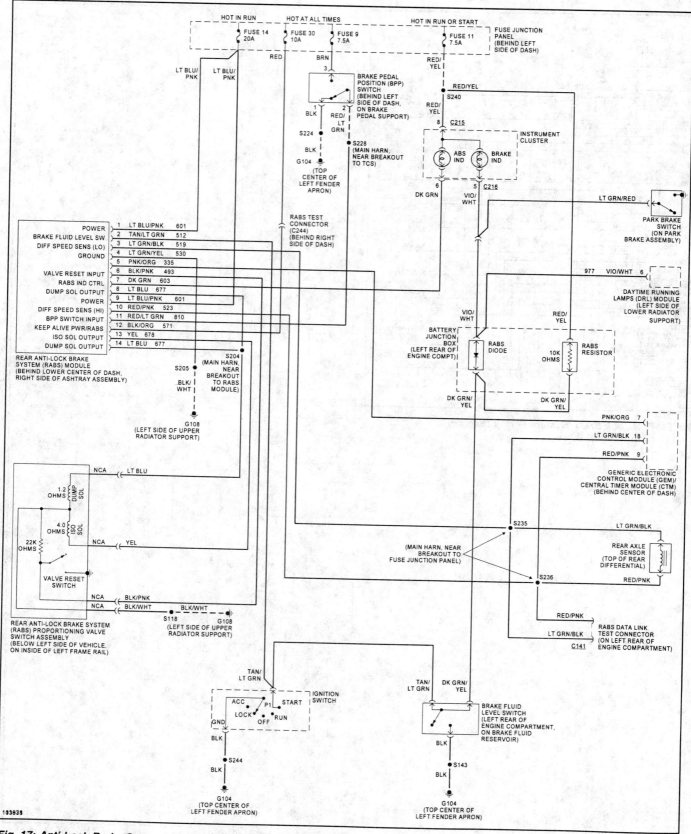

Fig. 17: Anti-Lock Brake System Wiring Diagram (Ranger – Rear Wheel)

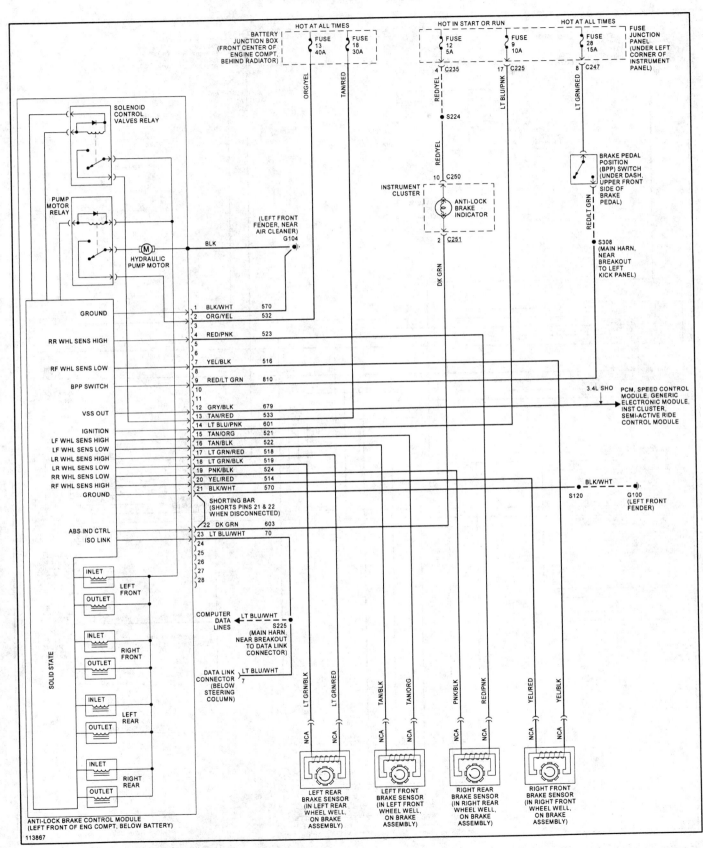

Fig. 18: Anti-Lock Brake System Wiring Diagram (Sable & Taurus)

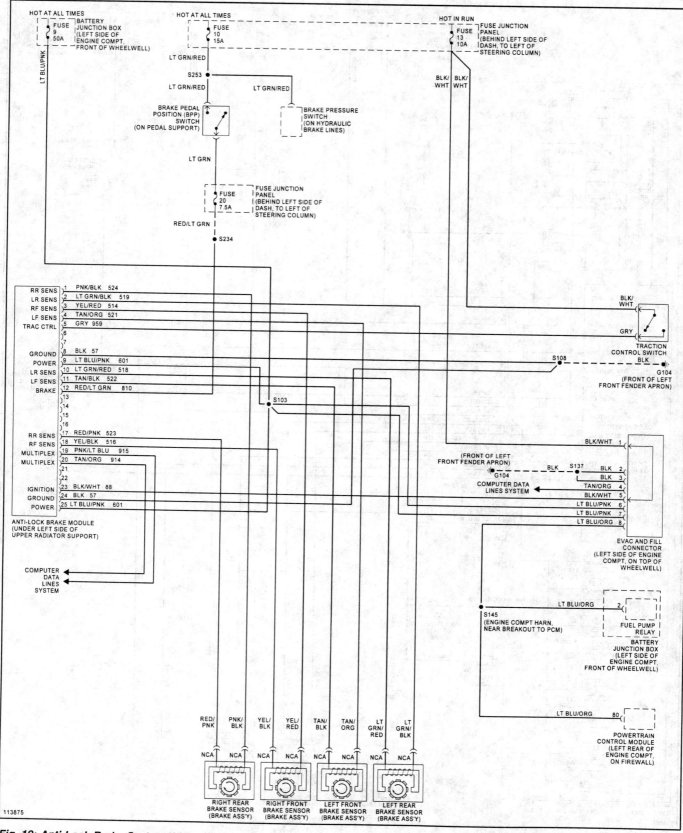

Fig. 19: Anti-Lock Brake System Wiring Diagram (Town Car)

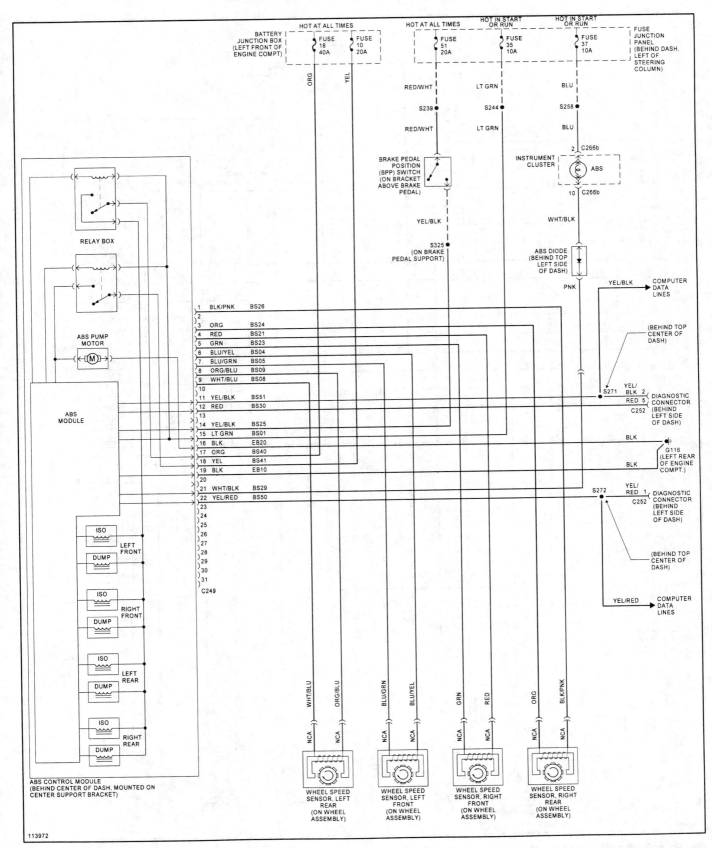

Fig. 20: Anti-Lock Brake System Wiring Diagram (Villager)

113972

1999 WIRING DIAGRAMS
Anti-Lock Brakes (Cont.)

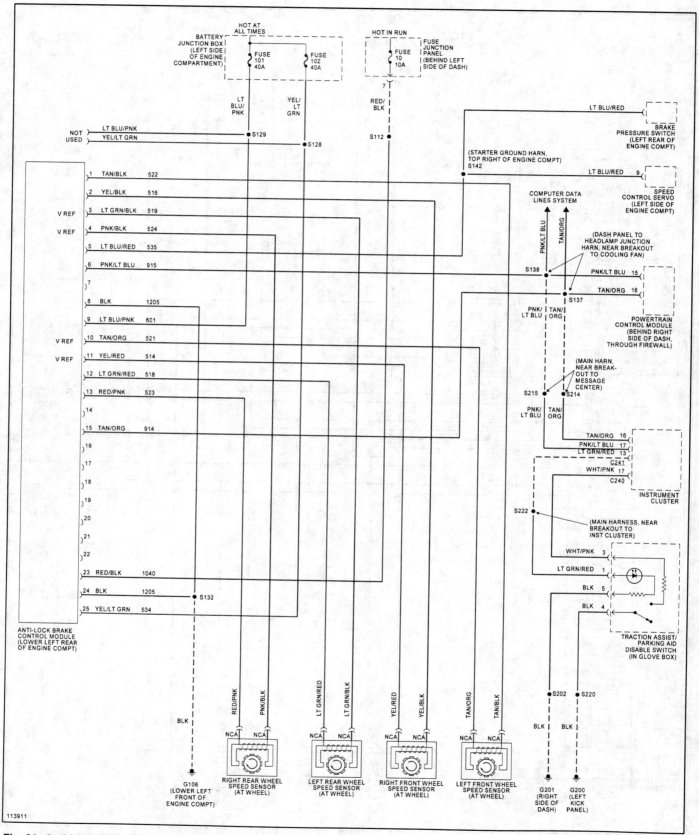

Fig. 21: Anti-Lock Brake System Wiring Diagram (Windstar)

Electronic Suspension

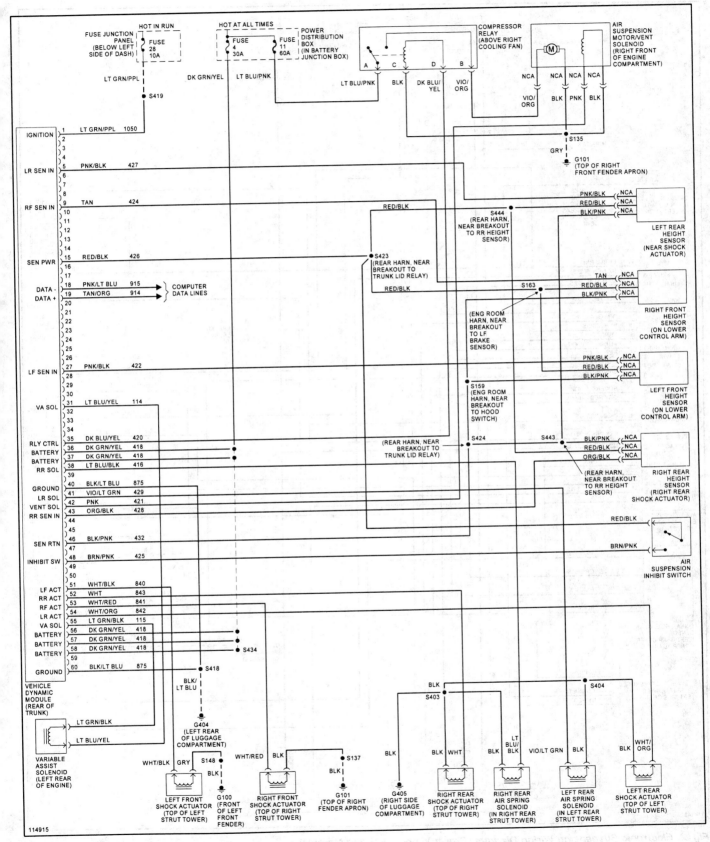

Fig. 1: Electronic Suspension Wiring Diagram (Continental)

114915

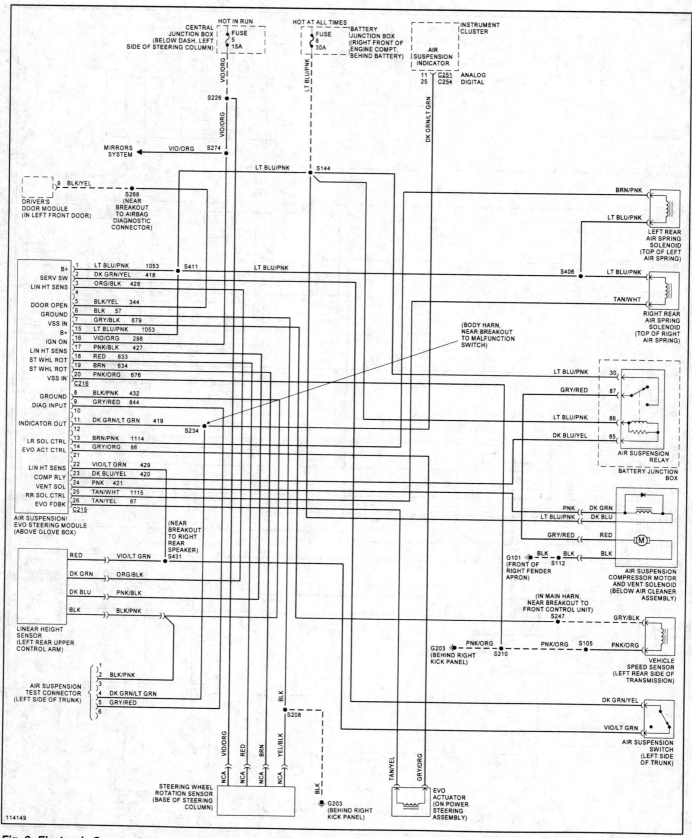

Fig. 2: Electronic Suspension Wiring Diagram (Crown Victoria & Grand Marquis)

114149

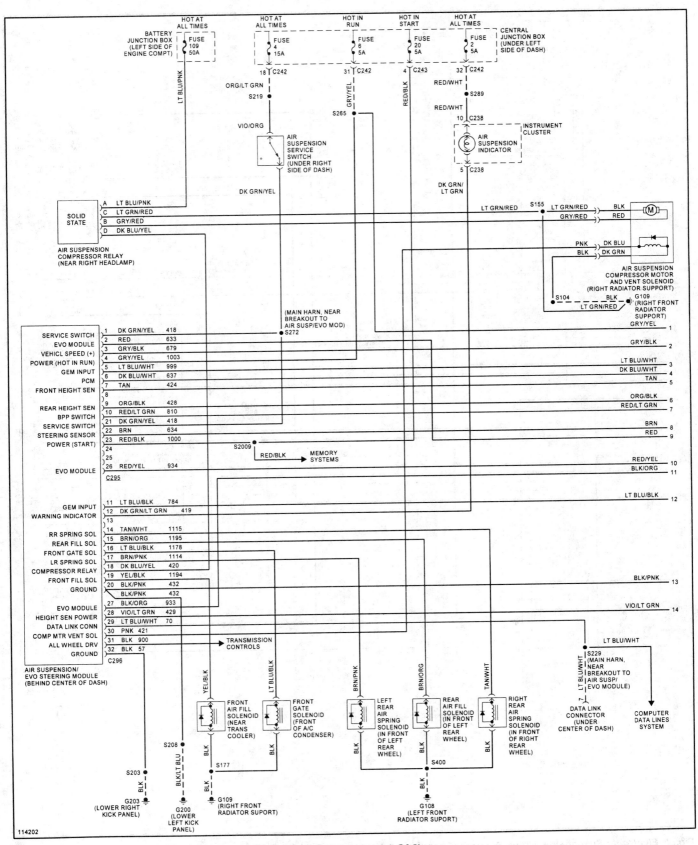

Fig. 3: Electronic Suspension Wiring Diagram (Expedition & Navigator – 1 Of 2)

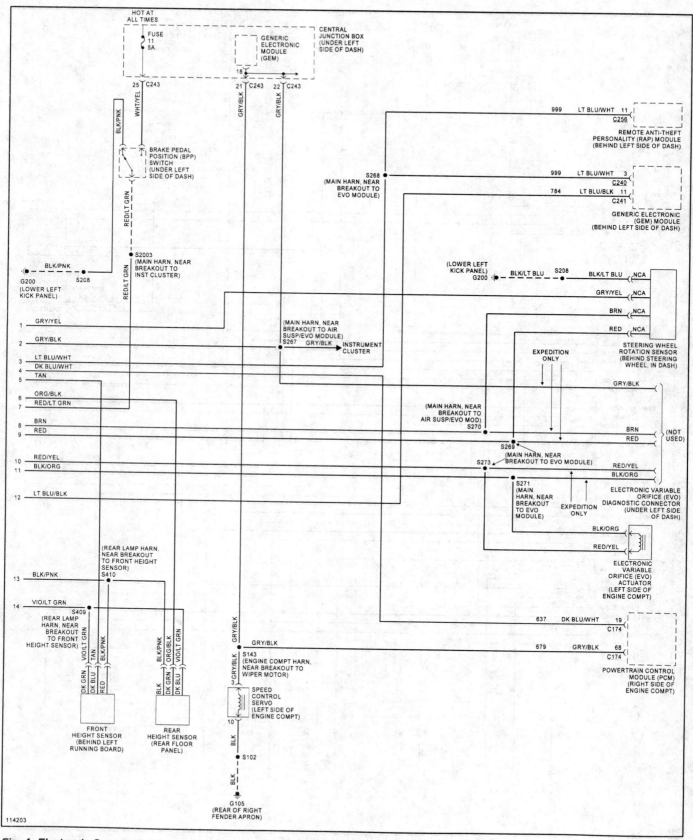

Fig. 4: Electronic Suspension Wiring Diagram (Expedition & Navigator – 2 Of 2)

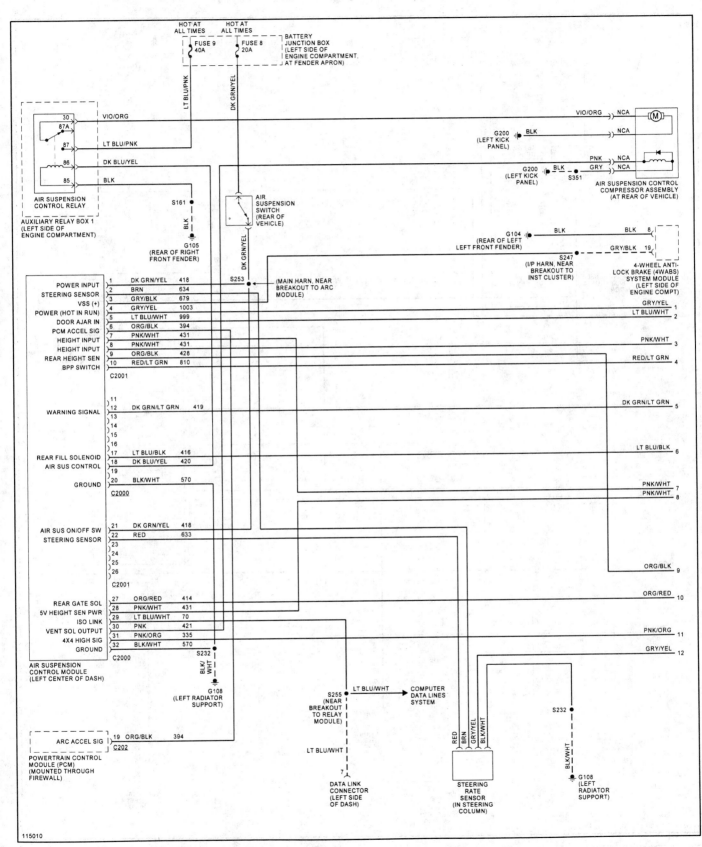

Fig. 5: Electronic Suspension Wiring Diagram (Explorer & Mountaineer – 1 Of 2)

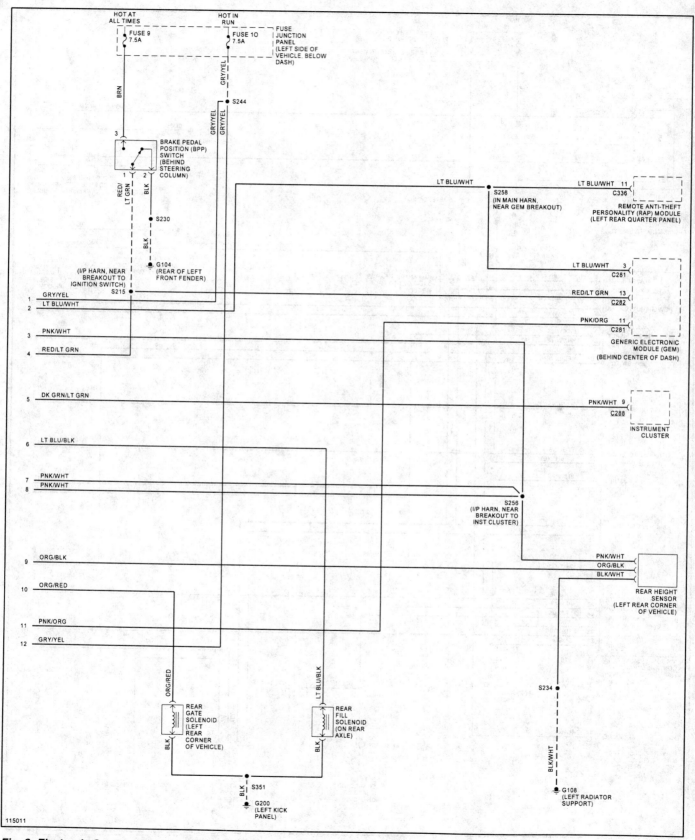

Fig. 6: Electronic Suspension Wiring Diagram (Explorer & Mountaineer – 2 Of 2)

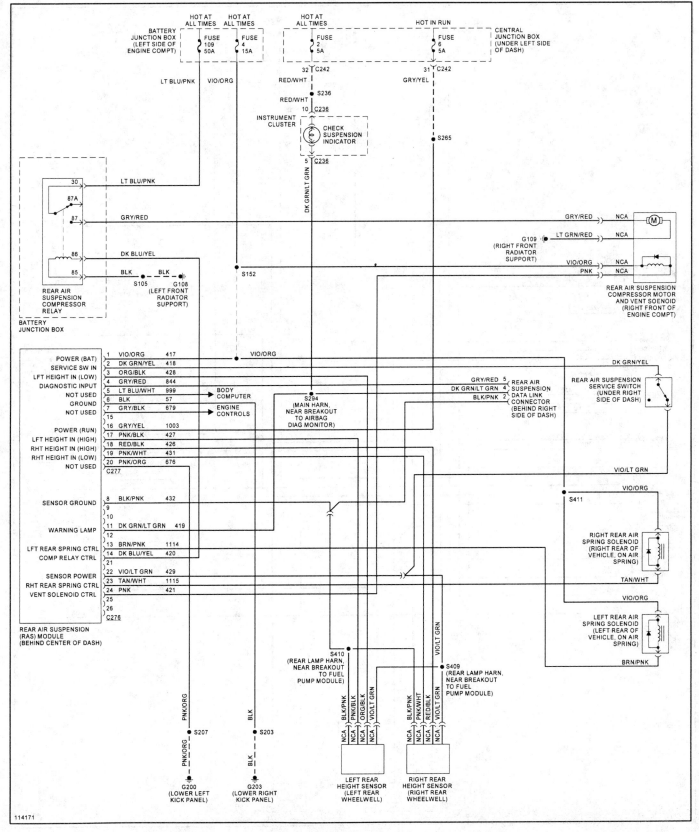

Fig. 7: Electronic Suspension Wiring Diagram (F150 & F250 Light-Duty Pickups)

114171

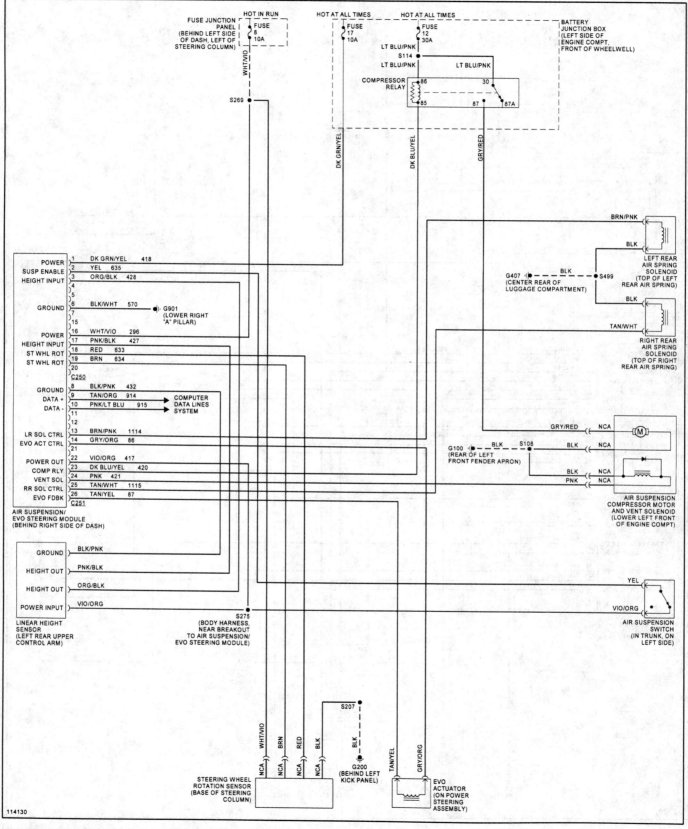

Fig. 8: Electronic Suspension Wiring Diagram (Town Car)

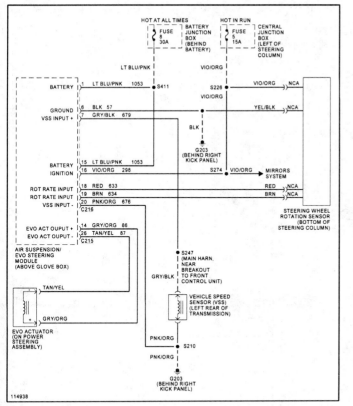

Fig. 1: Electronic Steering Wiring Diagram (Crown Victoria & Grand Marquis – With Air Suspension)

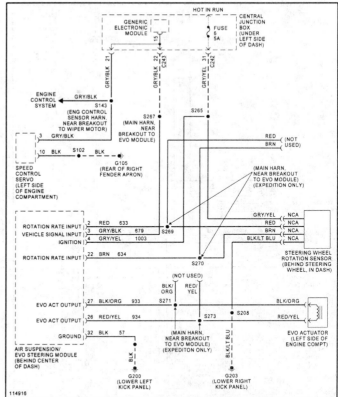

Fig. 3: Electronic Steering Wiring Diagram (Expedition & Navigator – With Air Suspension)

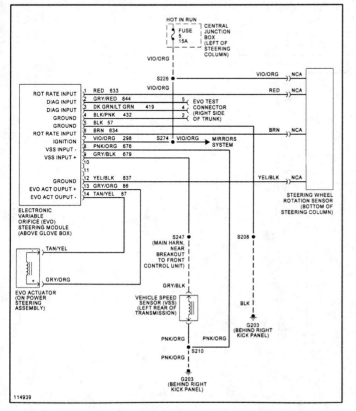

Fig. 2: Electronic Steering Wiring Diagram (Crown Victoria & Grand Marquis – Without Air Suspension)

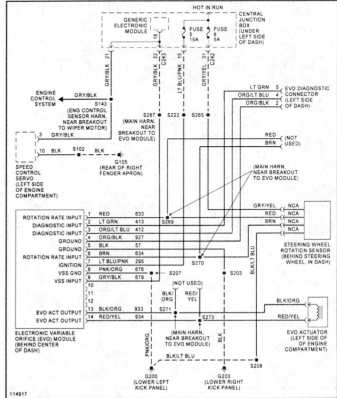

Fig. 4: Electronic Steering Wiring Diagram (Expedition & Navigator – Without Air Suspension)

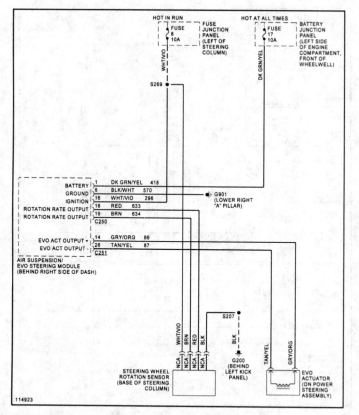

Fig. 5: Electronic Steering Wiring Diagram (Town Car)

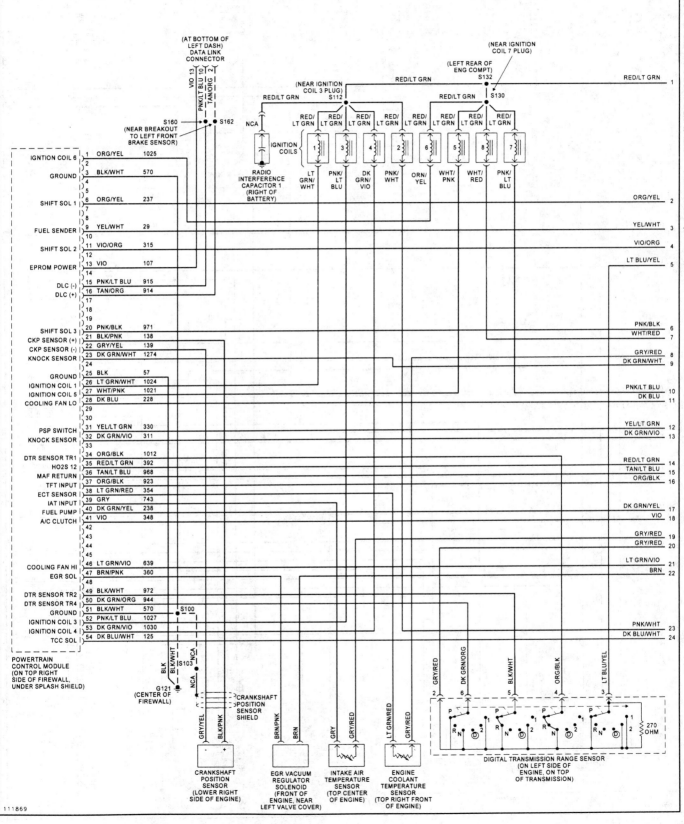

Fig. 1: Continental (4.6L – 1 Of 4)

111869

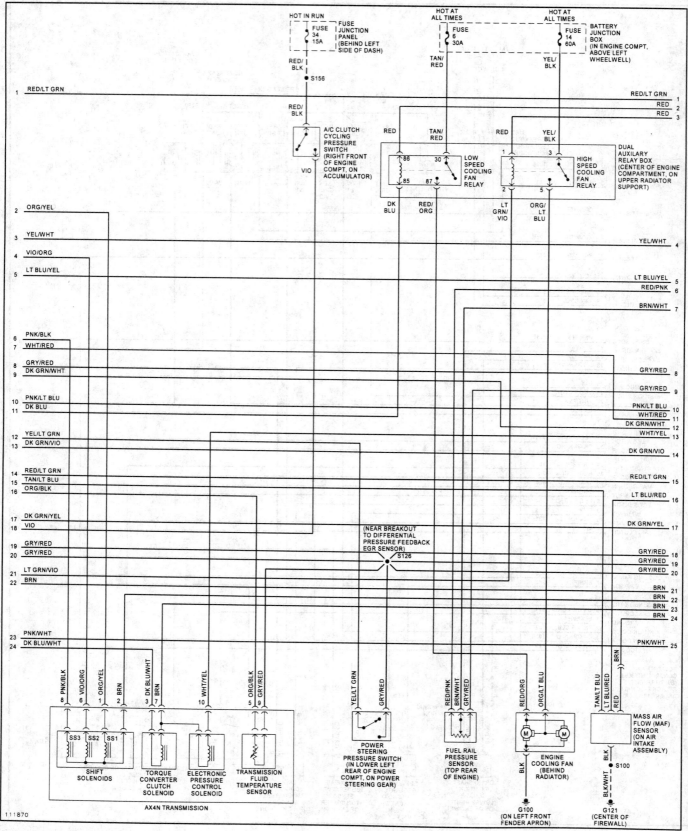

Fig. 2: Continental (4.6L – 2 Of 4)

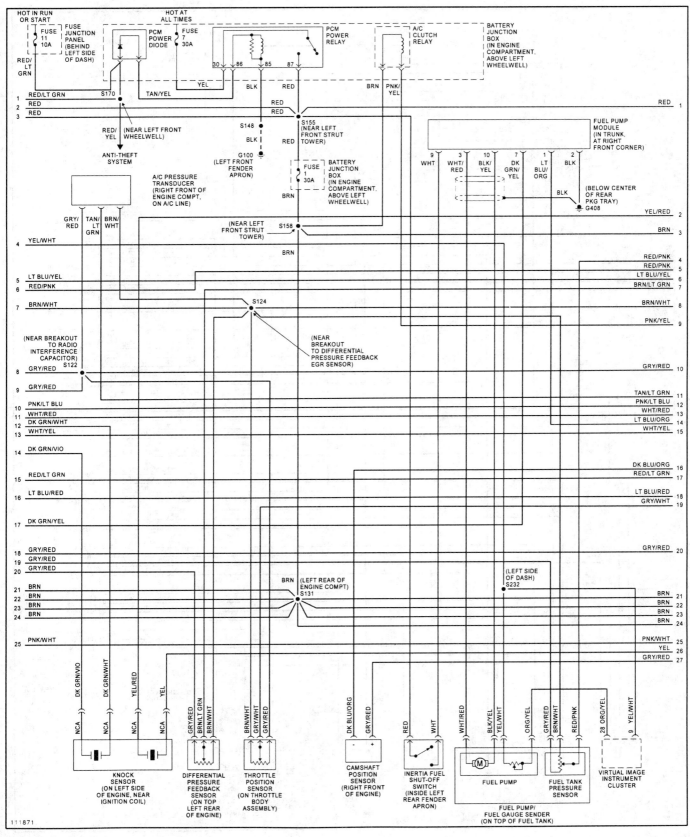

Fig. 3: Continental (4.6L – 3 Of 4)

111871

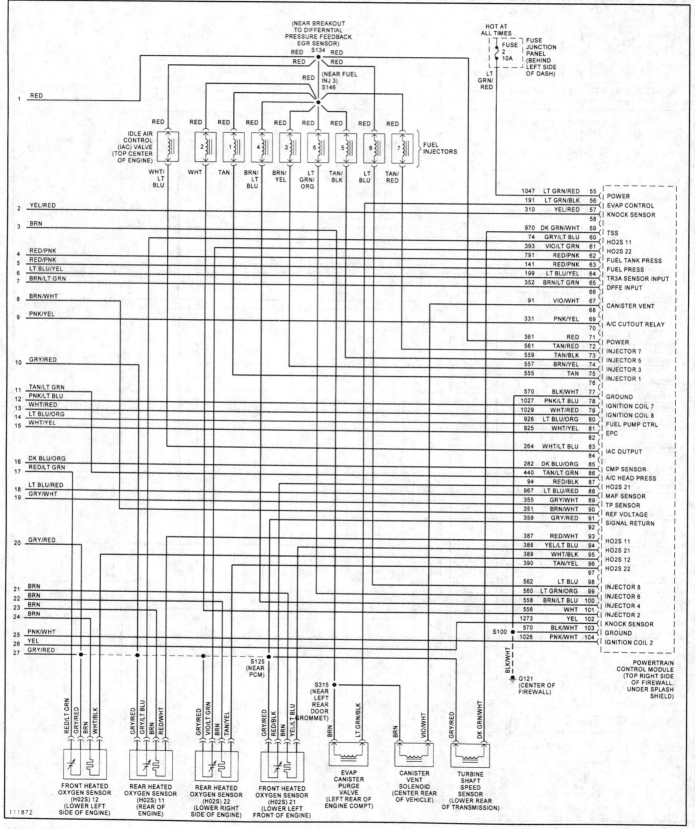

Fig. 4: Continental (4.6L – 4 Of 4)

111872

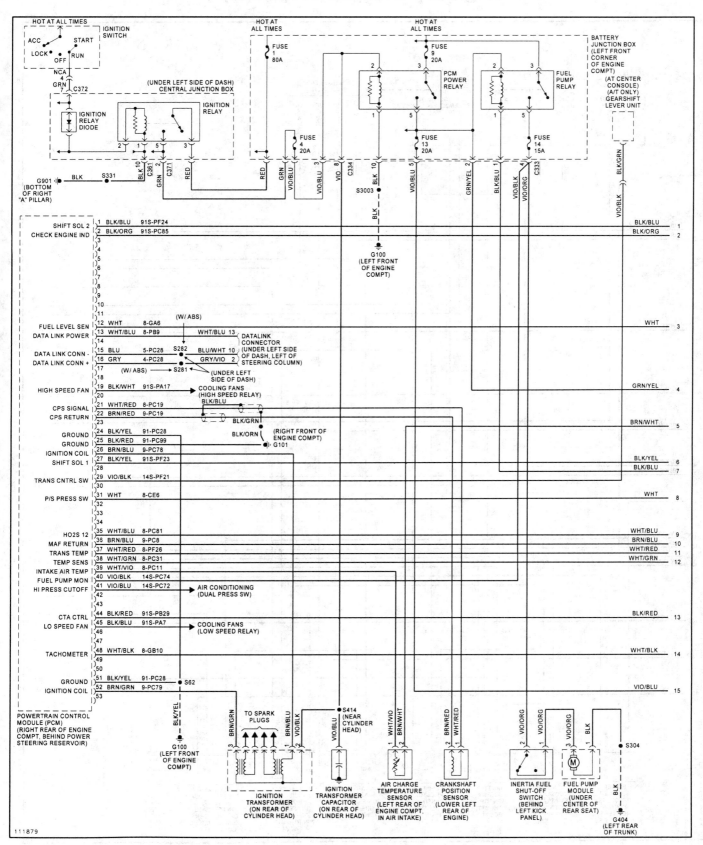

Fig. 5: Contour & Mystique (2.0L – 1 Of 3)

111879

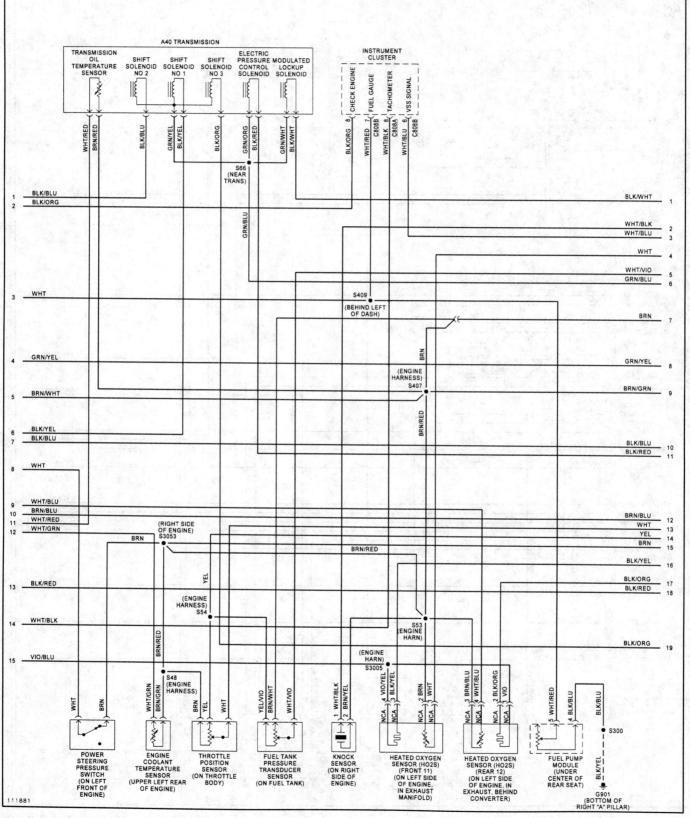

Fig. 6: Contour & Mystique (2.0L – 2 Of 3)

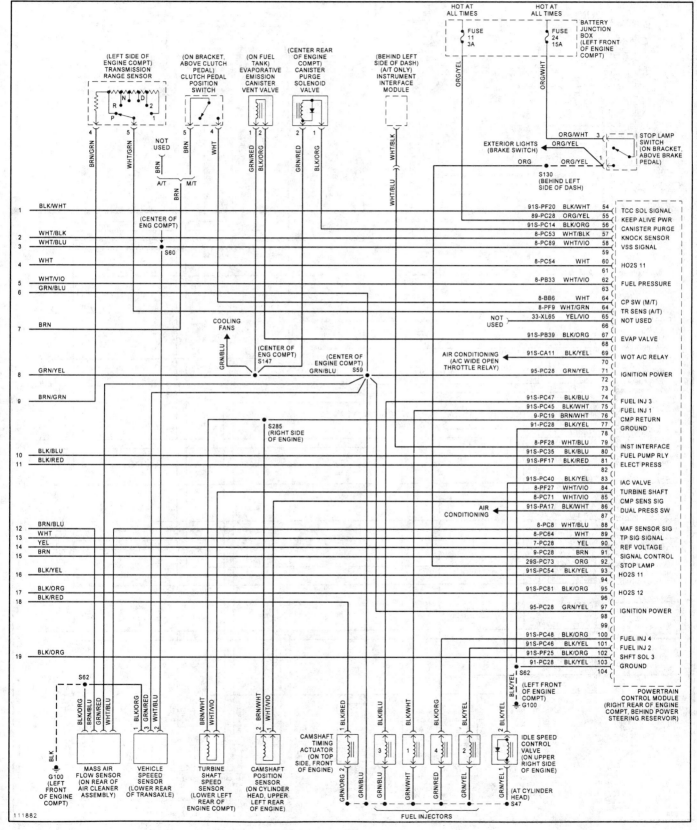

Fig. 7: Contour & Mystique (2.0L – 3 Of 3)

111882

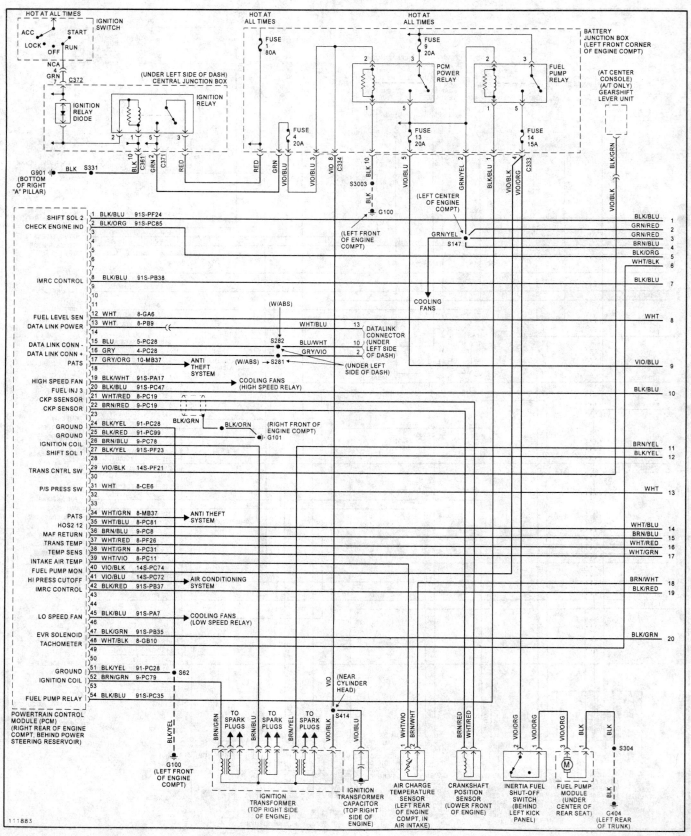

Fig. 8: Contour & Mystique (2.5L – 1 Of 3)

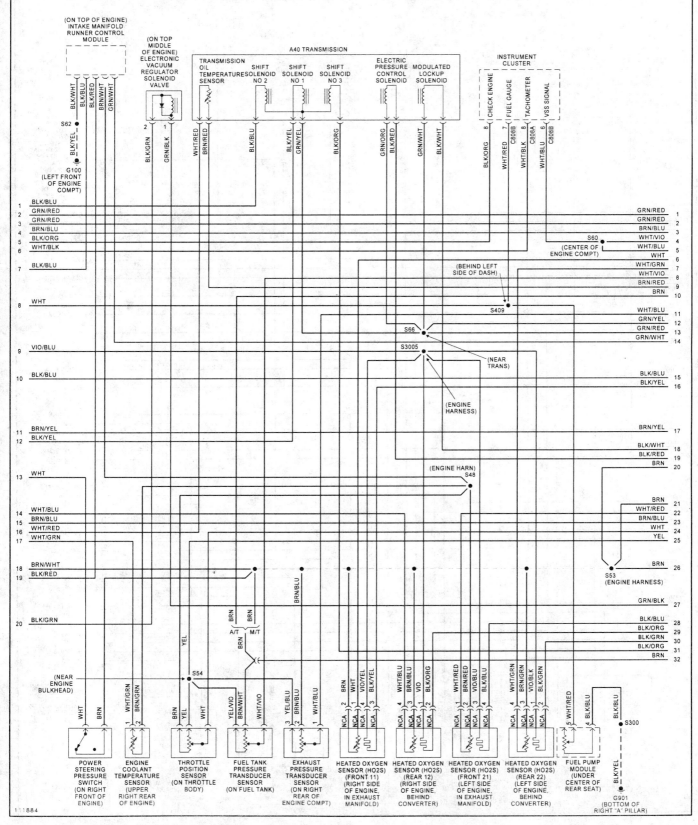

Fig. 9: Contour & Mystique (2.5L – 2 Of 3)

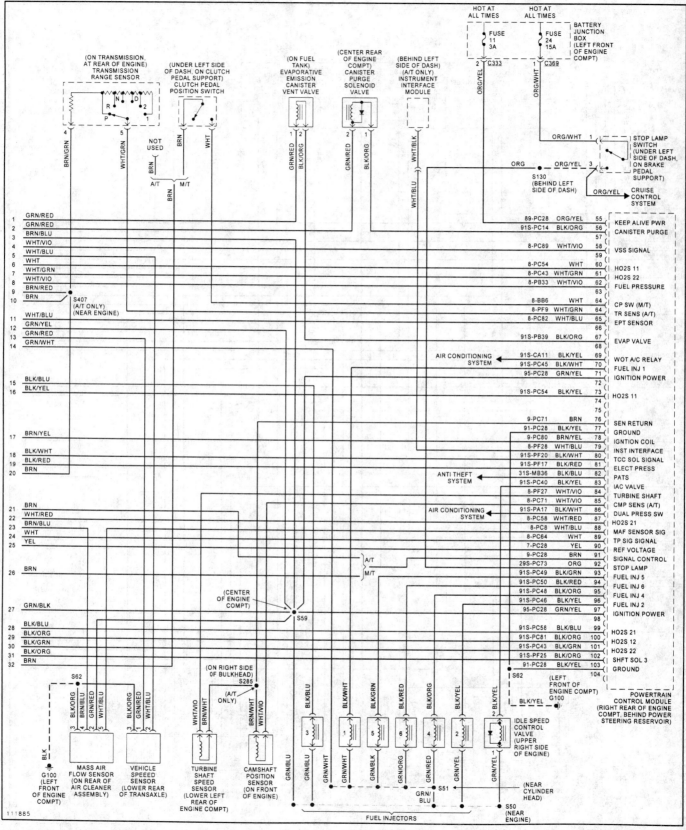

Fig. 10: Contour & Mystique (2.5L – 3 Of 3)

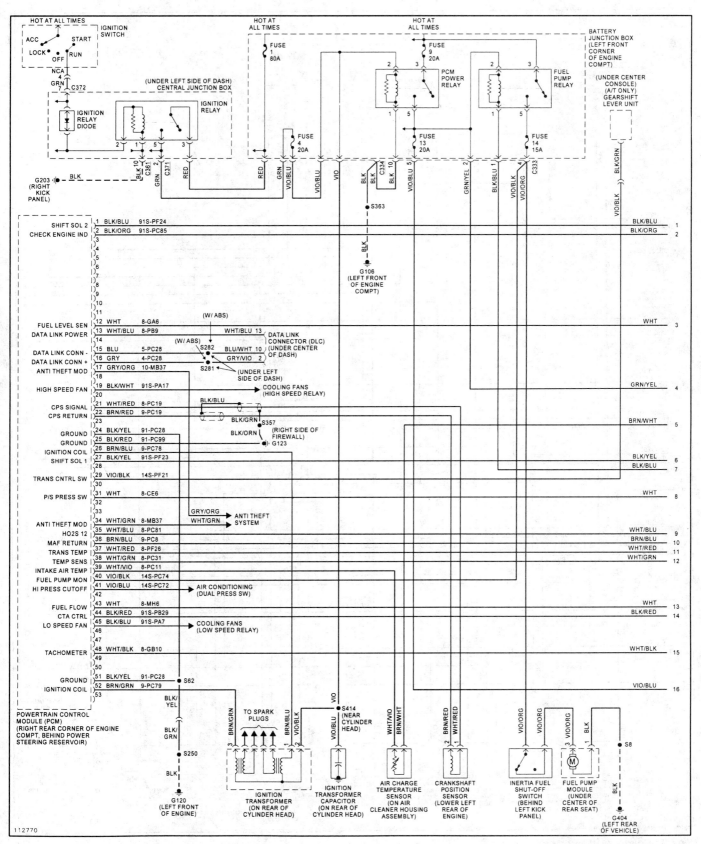

Fig. 11: Cougar (2.0L – 1 Of 3)

112770

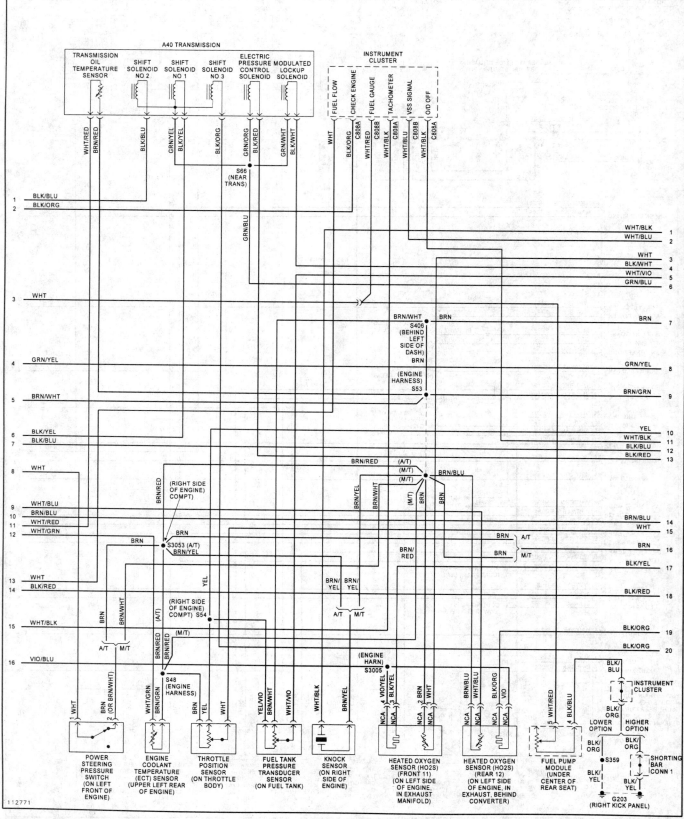

Fig. 12: Cougar (2.0L – 2 Of 3)

112771

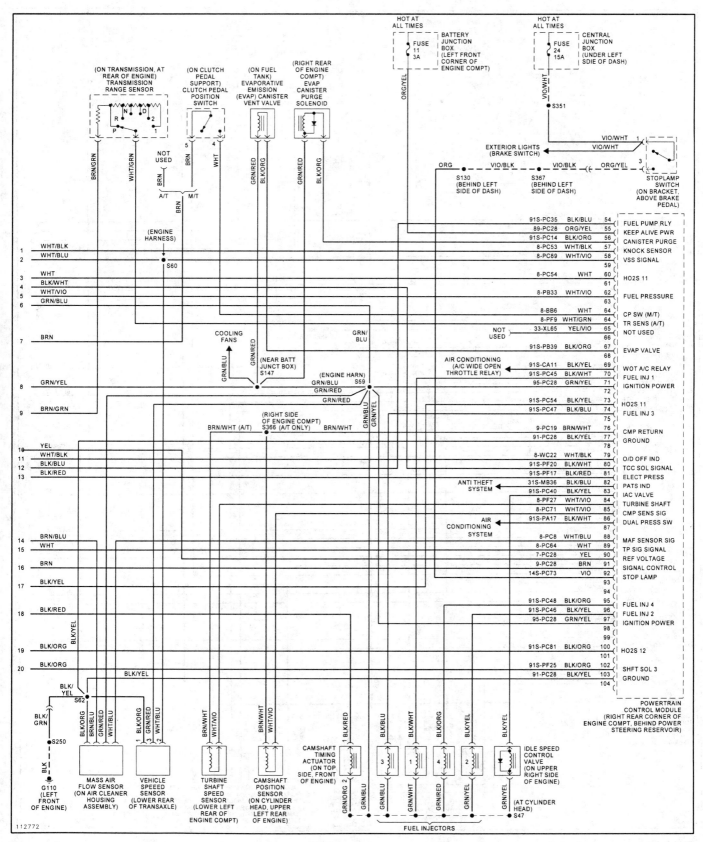

Fig. 13: Cougar (2.0L – 3 Of 3)

112772

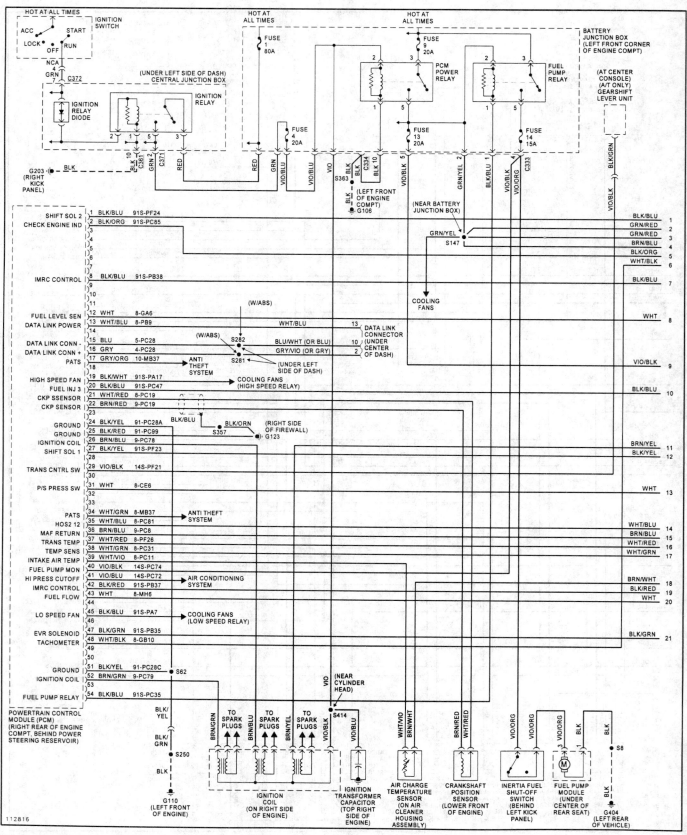

Fig. 14: Cougar (2.5L – 1 Of 3)

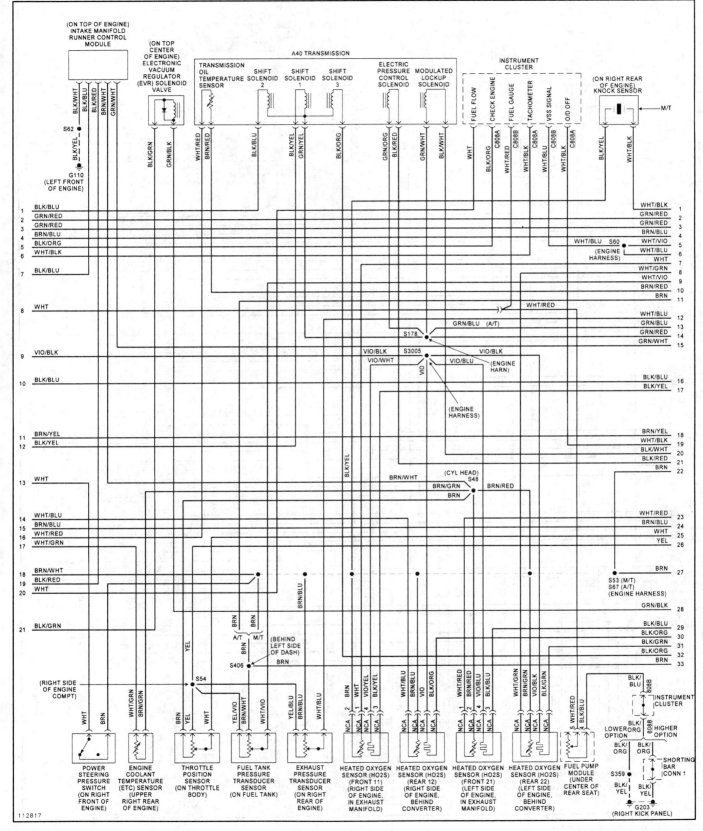

Fig. 15: Cougar (2.5L – 2 Of 3)

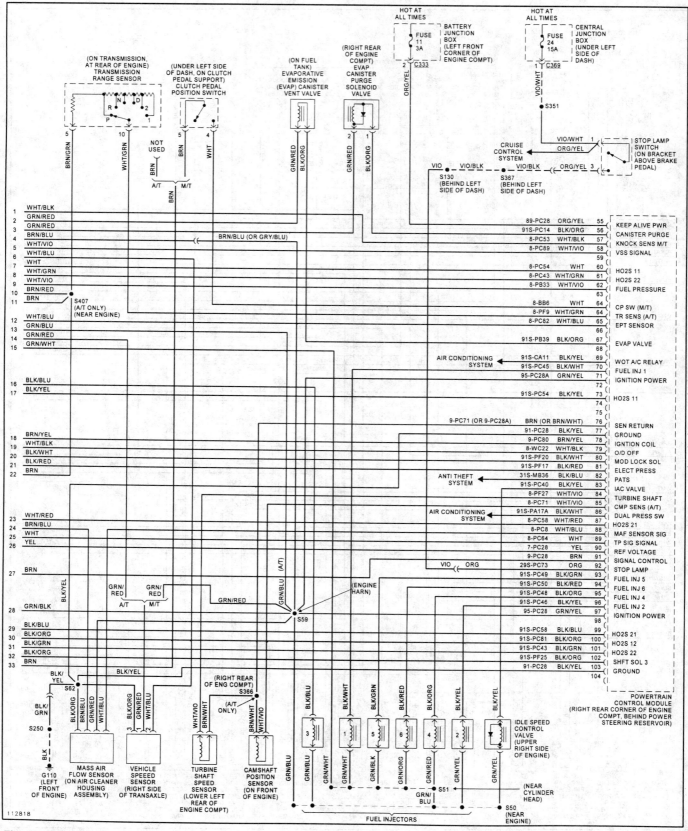

Fig. 16: Cougar (2.5L – 3 Of 3)

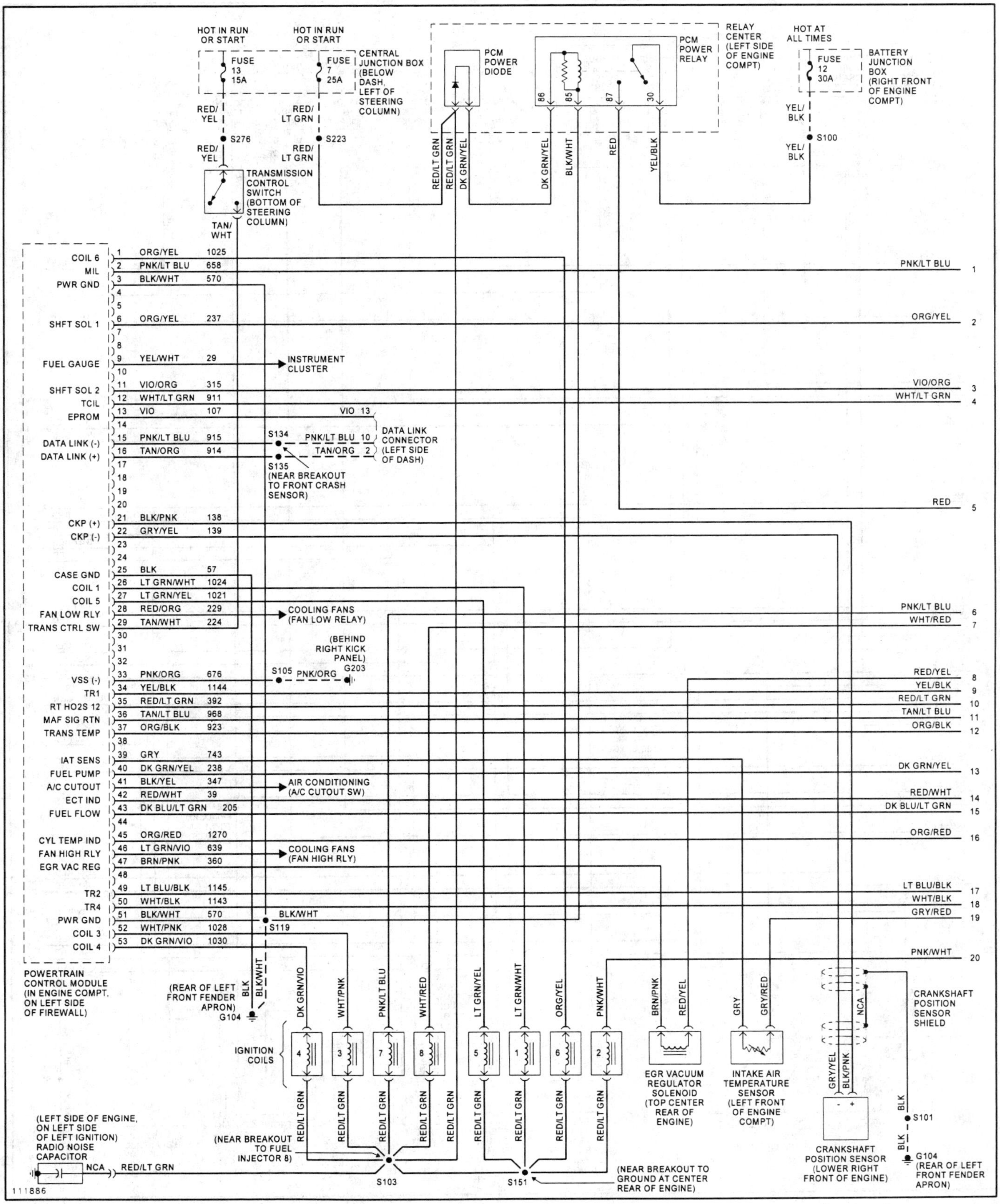

HOT IN RUN OR START — FUSE 13 15A — RED/YEL — S276 — RED/YEL

HOT IN RUN OR START — FUSE 7 25A — RED/LT GRN — S223 — RED/LT GRN

CENTRAL JUNCTION BOX (BELOW DASH, LEFT OF STEERING COLUMN)

TRANSMISSION CONTROL SWITCH (BOTTOM OF STEERING COLUMN)
TAN/WHT

PCM POWER DIODE — RED/LT GRN — RED/LT GRN — DK GRN/YEL

PCM POWER RELAY — 86 85 87 30 — DK GRN/YEL — BLK/WHT — RED — YEL/BLK

RELAY CENTER (LEFT SIDE OF ENGINE COMPT)

HOT AT ALL TIMES — FUSE 12 30A — YEL/BLK — S100 — YEL/BLK

BATTERY JUNCTION BOX (RIGHT FRONT OF ENGINE COMPT)

Pin	Label	Color	Num
1	COIL 6	ORG/YEL	1025
2	MIL	PNK/LT BLU	658
3	PWR GND	BLK/WHT	570
4			
5			
6	SHFT SOL 1	ORG/YEL	237
7			
8			
9	FUEL GAUGE	YEL/WHT	29
10			
11	SHFT SOL 2	VIO/ORG	315
12	TCIL	WHT/LT GRN	911
13	EPROM	VIO	107
14			
15	DATA LINK (-)	PNK/LT BLU	915
16	DATA LINK (+)	TAN/ORG	914
17			
18			
19			
20			
21	CKP (+)	BLK/PNK	138
22	CKP (-)	GRY/YEL	139
23			
24			
25	CASE GND	BLK	57
26	COIL 1	LT GRN/WHT	1024
27	COIL 5	LT GRN/YEL	1021
28	FAN LOW RLY	RED/ORG	229
29	TRANS CTRL SW	TAN/WHT	224
30			
31			
32			
33	VSS (-)	PNK/ORG	676
34	TR1	YEL/BLK	1144
35	RT HO2S 12	RED/LT GRN	392
36	MAF SIG RTN	TAN/LT BLU	968
37	TRANS TEMP	ORG/BLK	923
38			
39	IAT SENS	GRY	743
40	FUEL PUMP	DK GRN/YEL	238
41	A/C CUTOUT	BLK/YEL	347
42	ECT IND	RED/WHT	39
43	FUEL FLOW	DK BLU/LT GRN	205
44			
45	CYL TEMP IND	ORG/RED	1270
46	FAN HIGH RLY	LT GRN/VIO	639
47	EGR VAC REG	BRN/PNK	360
48			
49	TR2	LT BLU/BLK	1145
50	TR4	WHT/BLK	1143
51	PWR GND	BLK/WHT	570
52	COIL 3	WHT/PNK	1028
53	COIL 4	DK GRN/VIO	1030

INSTRUMENT CLUSTER

S134 — PNK/LT BLU 10 — TAN/ORG 2 — DATA LINK CONNECTOR (LEFT SIDE OF DASH)
VIO 13
S135 (NEAR BREAKOUT TO FRONT CRASH SENSOR)

COOLING FANS (FAN LOW RELAY)
(BEHIND RIGHT KICK PANEL)

S105 — PNK/ORG — G203

AIR CONDITIONING (A/C CUTOUT SW)

COOLING FANS (FAN HIGH RLY)

BLK/WHT — S119

Right side connectors:
- PNK/LT BLU — 1
- ORG/YEL — 2
- VIO/ORG — 3
- WHT/LT GRN — 4
- RED — 5
- PNK/LT BLU — 6
- WHT/RED — 7
- RED/YEL — 8
- YEL/BLK — 9
- RED/LT GRN — 10
- TAN/LT BLU — 11
- ORG/BLK — 12
- DK GRN/YEL — 13
- RED/WHT — 14
- DK BLU/LT GRN — 15
- ORG/RED — 16
- LT BLU/BLK — 17
- WHT/BLK — 18
- GRY/RED — 19
- PNK/WHT — 20

POWERTRAIN CONTROL MODULE (IN ENGINE COMPT, ON LEFT SIDE OF FIREWALL)

(REAR OF LEFT FRONT FENDER APRON) G104
BLK / BLK/WHT

IGNITION COILS — 4 3 7 8 5 1 6 2
DK GRN/VIO — WHT/PNK — PNK/LT BLU — WHT/RED — LT GRN/YEL — LT GRN/WHT — ORG/YEL — PNK/WHT
RED/LT GRN (each coil)
(NEAR BREAKOUT TO FUEL INJECTOR 8)
S103

EGR VACUUM REGULATOR SOLENOID (TOP CENTER REAR OF ENGINE)
BRN/PNK — RED/YEL

INTAKE AIR TEMPERATURE SENSOR (LEFT FRONT OF ENGINE COMPT)
GRY — GRY/RED

S151
(NEAR BREAKOUT TO GROUND AT CENTER REAR OF ENGINE)

CRANKSHAFT POSITION SENSOR SHIELD
GRY/YEL — BLK/PNK — NCA

CRANKSHAFT POSITION SENSOR (LOWER RIGHT FRONT OF ENGINE)
BLK — S101
BLK — G104 (REAR OF LEFT FRONT FENDER APRON)

(LEFT SIDE OF ENGINE, ON LEFT SIDE OF LEFT IGNITION) RADIO NOISE CAPACITOR
NCA — RED/LT GRN

111886

Fig. 17: Crown Victoria & Grand Marquis (4.6L Gasoline – 1 Of 4)

4R7OW TRANSMISSION

TRANSMISSION FLUID TEMPERATURE SENSOR

SHIFT SOLENOIDS
SS1   SS2

ELECTRONIC PRESSURE CONTROL SOLENOID

TORQUE CONVERTER CLUTCH SOLENOID

INSTRUMENT CLUSTER

MALFUNCTION INDICATOR INPUT	TRANSMISSION CONTROL INDICATOR INPUT	FUEL FLOW RATE INPUT	CYLINDER HEAD TEMP INPUT	ENGINE COOLANT TEMP INPUT	(SPEEDOMETER/ ODOMETER) VEHICLE SPEED INPUT	
9 C256	14 C255	11 C255	18 C255	4 C255	12 C255	← DIGITAL
4 C251	3 C250		12 C250	5 C250	16 C251	← ANALOG

ORG/BLK 5
GRY/RED 2
ORG/YEL 7
VIO/ORG 8
RED 4
WHT/YEL 6
VIO/YEL 3

PNK/LT BLU
WHT/LT GRN
DK BLU/LT GRN
ORG/RED
RED/WHT
GRY/BLK

1 PNK/LT BLU
2 ORG/YEL
3 VIO/ORG
4 WHT/LT GRN
5 RED
6 PNK/LT BLU
7 WHT/RED
8 RED/YEL
9 YEL/BLK
10 RED/LT GRN
11 TAN/LT BLU
12 ORG/BLK
13 DK GRN/YEL
14 RED/WHT
15 DK BLU/LT GRN
16 ORG/RED
17 LT BLU/BLK
18 WHT/BLK
19 GRY/RED
20 PNK/WHT

GRY/BLK 1
VIO/YEL 2
LT GRN/BLK 3
LT BLU/YEL 4
BRN/LT GRN 5
RED 6
RED/YEL   RED 7
RED 8
GRY/RED 9
GRY/RED 10
PNK/LT BLU 11
WHT/RED 12
WHT/YEL 13
RED/YEL 14
RED/YEL 15
RED/LT GRN 16
LT BLU/RED 17
GRY/WHT 18
DK GRN/YEL 19
GRY/RED 20
GRY/RED 21
GRY/RED 22
RED 23
PNK/WHT 24
BRN/WHT 25

S150
(NEAR BREAKOUT TO RIGHT HEATED OXYGEN SENSOR 11)

S222
(NEAR BREAKOUT TO INST CLUSTER)

WHT/BLK   6
LT BLU/BLK 5
YEL/BLK   4
LT BLU/YEL 3
GRY/RED   2

P R N D 2 (×5)

DIGITAL TRANSMISSION RANGE SENSOR (DTR SENSOR) (LEFT SIDE OF TRANSMISSION)

RED/YEL
LT GRN/BLK

EVAP CANISTER PURGE VALVE (REAR CENTER OF ENGINE COMPT)

GRY/RED
BRN/LT GRN
BRN/WHT

DIFFERENTIAL PRESSURE FEEDBACK EGR SENSOR (RIGHT SIDE OF INTAKE MANIFOLD)

BRN/WHT
GRY/WHT
GRY/RED

S126
(NEAR BREAKOUT TO RIGHT HTD OXY SENS 11)

THROTTLE POSITION SENSOR (LEFT SIDE OF THROTTLE BODY)

PNK/ORG
PNK/ORG   S105

G203 (BEHIND RIGHT KICK PANEL)

PNK/ORG
RED/WHT

ENGINE COOLANT TEMPERATURE SENSOR (TOP RIGHT FRONT OF ENGINE)

TAN/LT BLU
RED
LT BLU/RED
4 2 5 3

MASS AIR FLOW SENSOR (BEHIND AIR CLEANER ASSEMBLY)

BLK/WHT
S119

BLK/WHT
G104 (REAR OF LEFT FRONT FENDER APRON)

111887

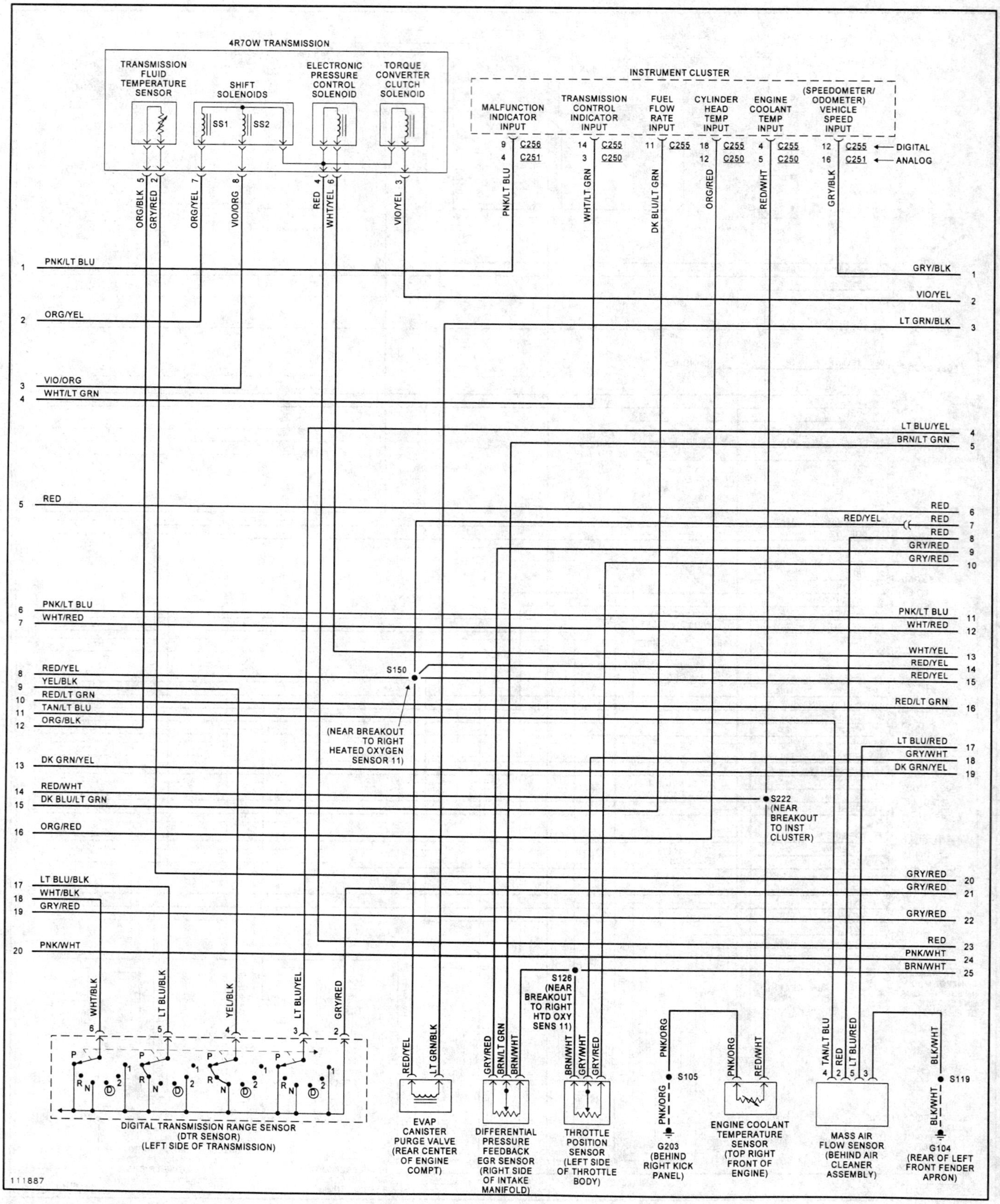

Fig. 18: Crown Victoria & Grand Marquis (4.6L Gasoline – 2 Of 4)

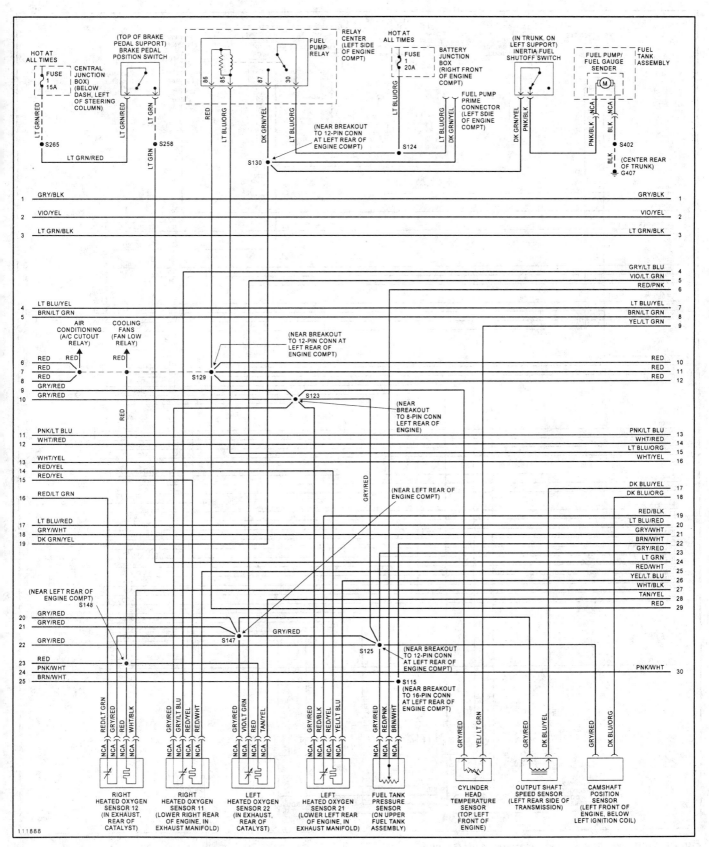

Fig. 19: Crown Victoria & Grand Marquis (4.6L Gasoline – 3 Of 4)

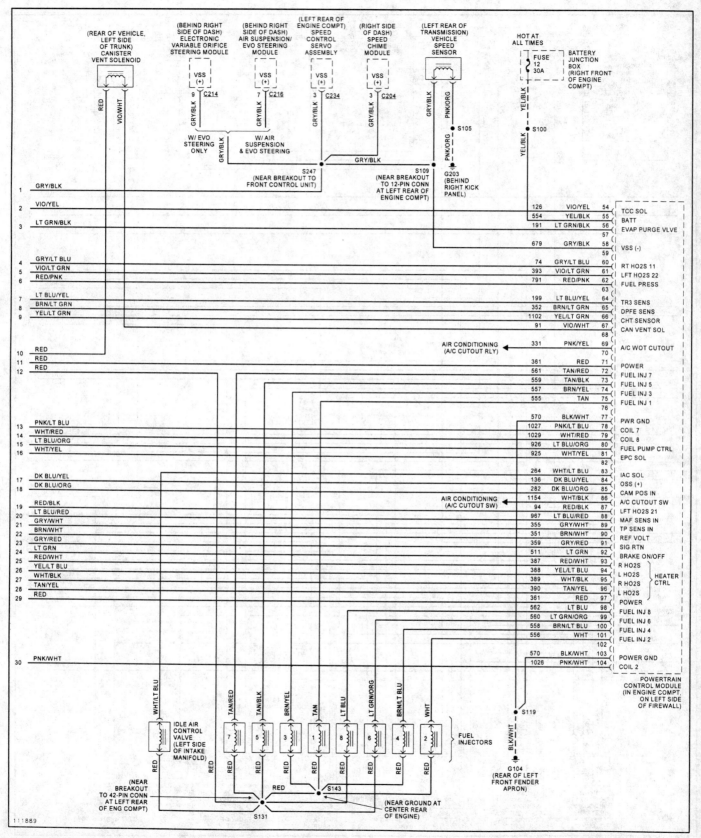

Fig. 20: Crown Victoria & Grand Marquis (4.6L Gasoline – 4 Of 4)

HOT IN RUN OR START

HOT IN RUN OR START

FUSE 13 15A

FUSE 7 25A

CENTRAL JUNCTION BOX (BELOW DASH, LEFT OF STEERING COLUMN)

PCM POWER DIODE

PCM POWER RELAY

RELAY CENTER (LEFT SIDE OF ENGINE COMPT)

HOT AT ALL TIMES

FUSE 12 30A

BATTERY JUNCTION BOX (RIGHT FRONT OF ENGINE COMPT)

RED/YEL

RED/LT GRN

S276

S223

RED/YEL

RED/LT GRN

86 85 87 30

YEL/BLK

TRANSMISSION CONTROL SWITCH (BOTTOM OF STEERING COLUMN)

TAN/WHT

RED/LT GRN

RED/LT GRN

DK GRN/YEL

DK GRN/YEL

BLK/WHT

RED

YEL/BLK

YEL/BLK

S100

S155

Pin	Label	Color	Number
1	COIL 6	ORG/YEL	1025
2	MIL	PNK/LT BLU	658
3	PWR GND	BLK/WHT	570
4			
5			
6	SHFT SOL 1	ORG/YEL	237
7			
8			
9			
10			
11	SHFT SOL 2	VIO/ORG	315
12	TCIL	WHT/LT GRN	911
13	EPROM	VIO	107
14			
15	DATA LINK (-)	PNK/LT BLU	915
16	DATA LINK (+)	TAN/ORG	914
17			
18			
19			
20			
21	CKP (+)	BLK/PNK	138
22	CKP (-)	GRY/YEL	139
23			
24			
25	CASE GND	BLK	57
26	COIL 1	LT GRN/WHT	1024
27	COIL 5	LT GRN/YEL	1021
28	FAN LOW RLY	RED/ORG	229
29	TRANS CTRL SW	TAN/WHT	224
30			
31			
32			
33	VSS (+)	PNK/ORG	676
34	TR1	YEL/BLK	1144
35	RT HO2S 12	RED/LT GRN	392
36	MAF SIG RTN	TAN/LT BLU	968
37	TRANS TEMP	ORG/BLK	923
38			
39	IAT SENS	GRY	743
40	FUEL SOL VLV	DK GRN/YEL	238
41	A/C CYCLING	BLK/YEL	347
42	ECT IND	RED/WHT	39
43			
44			
45	CYL TEMP IND	ORG/RED	1270
46	FAN HIGH RLY	LT GRN/VIO	639
47	EGR VAC REG	BRN/PNK	360
48			
49	TR2	LT BLU/BLK	1145
50	TR4	WHT/BLK	1143
51	PWR GND	BLK/WHT	570
52	COIL 3	WHT/PNK	1028
53	COIL 4	DK GRN/VIO	1030

PNK/LT BLU 1
ORG/YEL 2
VIO/ORG 3
WHT/LT GRN 4
TAN/ORG 5
PNK/LT BLU 6
RED 7
PNK/WHT 8
PNK/LT BLU 9
WHT/RED 10
RED 11
YEL/BLK 12
RED/LT GRN 13
TAN/LT BLU 14
ORG/BLK 15
DK GRN/YEL 16
BLK/YEL 17
RED/WHT 18
ORG/RED 19
LT BLU/BLK 20
WHT/BLK 21
GRY/RED 22
YEL/BLK 23

VIO 13

S134

PNK/LT BLU 10

TAN/ORG 2

S135

DATA LINK CONNECTOR (LEFT SIDE OF DASH)

(NEAR BREAKOUT TO FRONT CRASH SENSOR)

COOLING FANS (FAN LOW RELAY)

(BEHIND RIGHT KICK PANEL)

S105 PNK/ORG G203

COOLING FANS (FAN HIGH RLY)

BLK/WHT S119

POWERTRAIN CONTROL MODULE (BEHIND LEFT SIDE OF DASH, ON LEFT SIDE OF FIREWALL)

(REAR OF LEFT FRONT FENDER APRON) G104

BLK BLK/WHT

DK GRN/VIO

WHT/PNK

PNK/LT BLU

WHT/RED

LT GRN/YEL

LT GRN/WHT

ORG/YEL

PNK/WHT

BRN/PNK

RED

GRY

GRY/RED

NCA

GRY/YEL BLK/PNK

BLK

IGNITION COILS

4 3 7 8 5 1 6 2

RED/LT GRN

EGR VACUUM REGULATOR SOLENOID (TOP CENTER REAR OF ENGINE)

INTAKE AIR TEMPERATURE SENSOR (LEFT FRONT OF ENGINE COMPT)

CRANKSHAFT POSITION SENSOR SHIELD

CRANKSHAFT POSITION SENSOR (LOWER RIGHT FRONT OF ENGINE)

S101

G104 (REAR OF LEFT FRONT FENDER APRON)

(LEFT FRONT OF ENGINE, ON LEFT SIDE OF LEFT IGNITION) RADIO NOISE CAPACITOR

NCA RED/LT GRN

(NEAR BREAKOUT TO FUEL INJECTOR 8)

RED/LT GRN

S103

S151

(NEAR GROUND AT CENTER REAR OF ENGINE)

111892

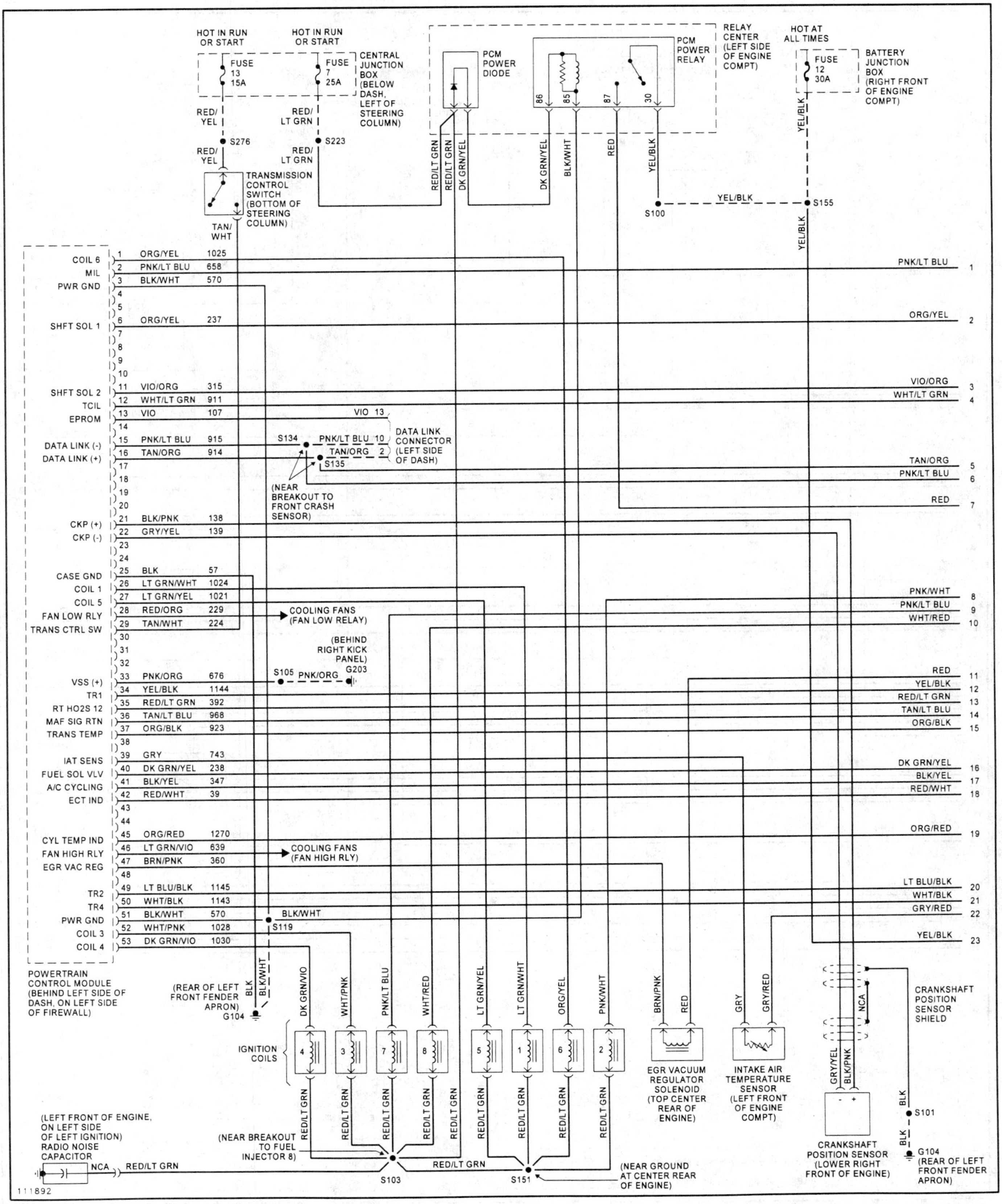

Fig. 21: Crown Victoria (4.6L CNG – 1 Of 5)

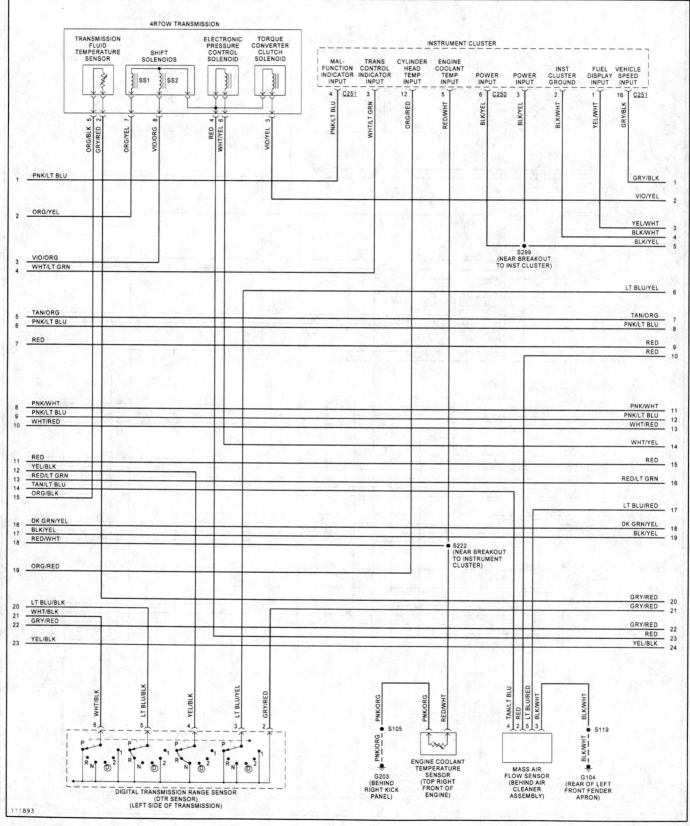

Fig. 22: Crown Victoria (4.6L CNG - 2 Of 5)

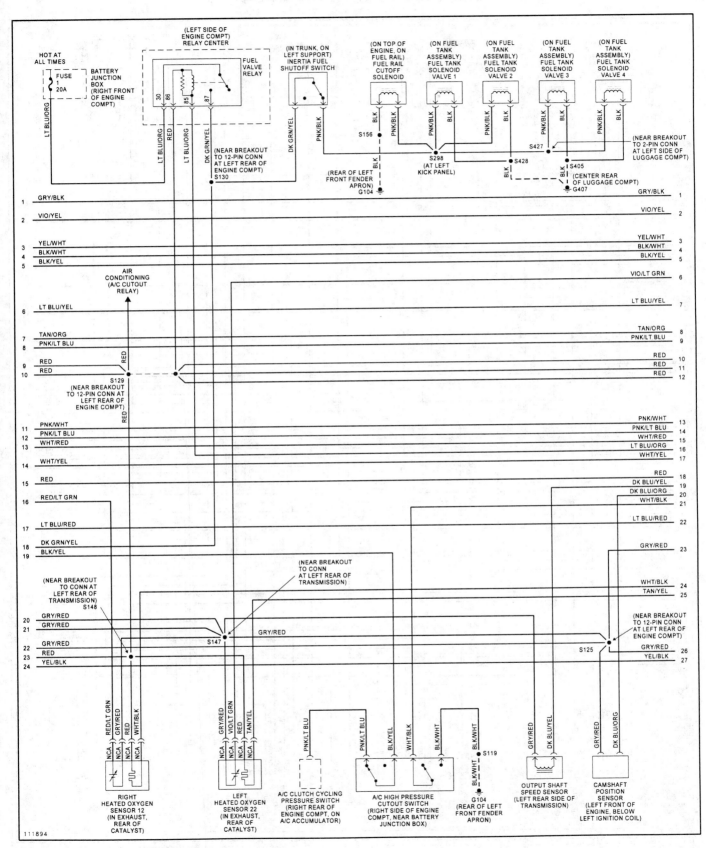

Fig. 23: Crown Victoria (4.6L CNG – 3 Of 5)

111894

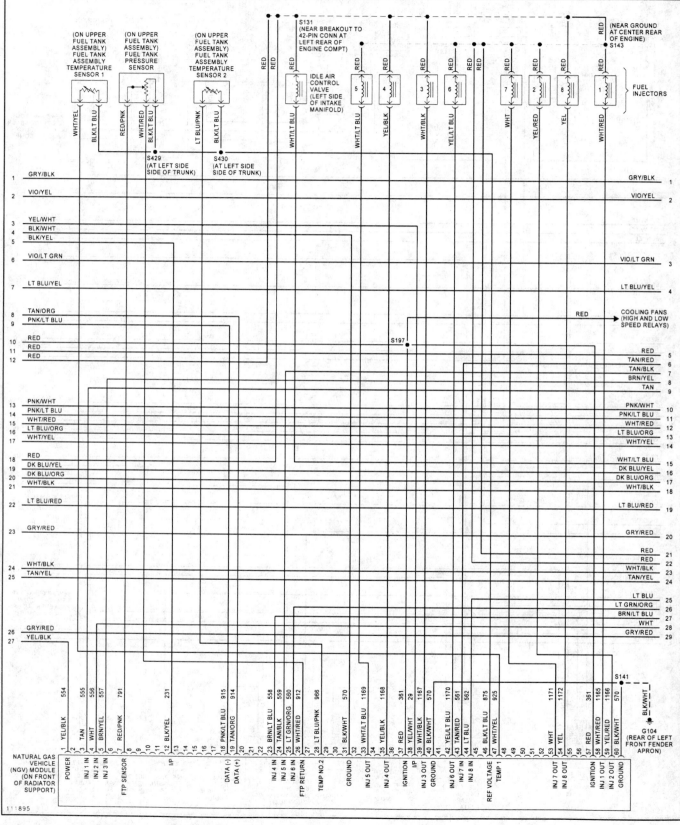

Fig. 24: Crown Victoria (4.6L CNG – 4 Of 5)

HOT AT ALL TIMES — CENTRAL JUNCTION BOX (BELOW DASH, LEFT OF STEERING COLUMN) — FUSE 1 15A

(TOP OF BRAKE PEDAL SUPPORT) BRAKE PEDAL POSITION SWITCH

(BEHIND RIGHT SIDE OF DASH) ELECTRONIC VARIABLE ORIFICE STEERING MODULE — VSS (+) 9 C214

(BEHIND RIGHT SIDE OF DASH) AIR SUSPENSION/ EVO STEERING MODULE — VSS (+) 7 C216

(LEFT REAR OF ENGINE COMPT) SPEED CONTROL SERVO ASSEMBLY — VSS (+) 3 C234

(RIGHT SIDE OF DASH) SPEED CHIME MODULE — VSS (+) 3 C204

(LEFT REAR OF TRANSMISSION) VEHICLE SPEED SENSOR

HOT AT ALL TIMES — FUSE 12 30A — BATTERY JUNCTION BOX (RIGHT FRONT OF ENGINE COMPT)

- S265 (LT GRN/RED)
- S258 (NEAR BREAKOUT TO BRAKE PEDAL PRESSURE SWITCH)
- W/ EVO STEERING ONLY (GRY/BLK)
- W/ AIR SUSPENSION & EVO STEERING
- S247 (NEAR BREAKOUT TO FRONT CONTROL UNIT)
- S109 (NEAR BREAKOUT TO 12-PIN CONN AT LEFT REAR OF ENGINE COMPT)
- S105 (PNK/ORG)
- S100 (YEL/BLK)
- G203 (BEHIND RIGHT KICK PANEL)

POWERTRAIN CONTROL MODULE (BEHIND LEFT SIDE OF DASH, ON LEFT SIDE OF FIREWALL)

#	Wire	Circuit	Pin	Label
1	GRY/BLK			
2	VIO/YEL	126 VIO/YEL	54	TCC SOL
		554 YEL/BLK	55	BATT
			56	
			57	
		679 GRY/BLK	58	VSS (-)
			59	
		74 GRY/LT BLU	60	RT HO2S 11
3	VIO/LT GRN	393 VIO/LT GRN	61	LFT HO2S 22
		225 BLK/YEL	62	FUEL TEMP
		141 RED/PNK	63	IP SENSOR
4	LT BLU/YEL	199 LT BLU/YEL	64	DTR SENS
		352 BRN/LT GRN	65	DPFE SENS
		1102 YEL/LT GRN	66	CHT SENSOR
			67	
			68	
	AIR CONDITIONING (A/C CUTOUT RLY)	331 PNK/YEL	69	A/C WOT CUTOUT
			70	
5	RED	361 RED	71	POWER
6	TAN/RED	561 TAN/RED	72	FUEL INJ 7
7	TAN/BLK	559 TAN/BLK	73	FUEL INJ 5
8	BRN/YEL	557 BRN/YEL	74	FUEL INJ 3
9	TAN	555 TAN	75	FUEL INJ 1
			76	
10	PNK/WHT	570 BLK/WHT	77	PWR GND
11	PNK/LT BLU	1027 PNK/LT BLU	78	COIL 7
12	WHT/RED	1029 WHT/RED	79	COIL 8
13	LT BLU/ORG	926 LT BLU/ORG	80	FUEL PUMP CTRL
14	WHT/YEL	925 WHT/YEL	81	EPC SOL
			82	
15	WHT/LT BLU	264 WHT/LT BLU	83	IAC SOL
16	DK BLU/YEL	136 DK BLU/YEL	84	OSS (+)
17	DK BLU/ORG	282 DK BLU/ORG	85	CAM POS IN
18	WHT/BLK	1154 WHT/BLK	86	FAN RLY FEED
		94 RED/BLK	87	LFT HO2S 21
19	LT BLU/RED	967 LT BLU/RED	88	MAF SENS IN
		355 GRY/WHT	89	TP SENS IN
		351 BRN/WHT	90	REF VOLT
20	GRY/RED	359 GRY/RED	91	SIG RTN
		511 LT GRN	92	BRAKE ON/OFF
21	RED	387 RED/WHT	93	R HO2S
22	RED	388 YEL/LT BLU	94	L HO2S
23	WHT/BLK	389 WHT/BLK	95	R HO2S
24	TAN/YEL	390 TAN/YEL	96	L HO2S
			97	
25	LT BLU	562 LT BLU	98	FUEL INJ 8
26	LT GRN/ORG	560 LT GRN/ORG	99	FUEL INJ 6
27	BRN/LT BLU	558 BRN/LT BLU	100	FUEL INJ 4
28	WHT	556 WHT	101	FUEL INJ 2
29	GRY/RED		102	
		570 BLK/WHT	103	POWER GND
		1026 PNK/WHT	104	COIL 2

HEATER CTRL (brackets R HO2S / L HO2S / R HO2S / L HO2S)

- S123 (AT LOWER LEFT REAR OF ENGINE)
- S126 (NEAR BREAKOUT TO RIGHT H2OS 11)
- S119
- G104 (REAR OF LEFT FRONT FENDER APRON)

Sensors / wires:
- GRY/RED, BLK/YEL — ENGINE FUEL TEMPERATURE SENSOR (ON TOP OF ENGINE)
- GRY/RED, YEL/LT GRN — CYLINDER HEAD TEMPERATURE SENSOR (TOP LEFT FRONT OF ENGINE)
- GRY/RED, RED/PNK, BRN/WHT — INJECTION PRESSURE SENSOR (ON TOP OF ENGINE)
- GRY/RED, BRN/LT GRN, BRN/WHT — DIFFERENTIAL PRESSURE FEEDBACK EGR SENSOR (RIGHT SIDE OF INTAKE MANIFOLD)
- GRY/RED, GRY/WHT, BRN/WHT — THROTTLE POSITION SENSOR (LEFT SIDE OF THROTTLE BODY)
- NCA, GRY/RED, GRY/LT BLU, RED, RED/WHT — RIGHT HEATED OXYGEN SENSOR 11 (LOWER RIGHT REAR OF ENGINE, IN EXHAUST MANIFOLD)
- NCA, GRY/RED, RED/BLK, RED, YEL/LT BLU — LEFT HEATED OXYGEN SENSOR 21 (LOWER LEFT REAR OF ENGINE, IN EXHAUST MANIFOLD)
- BLK/WHT

111896

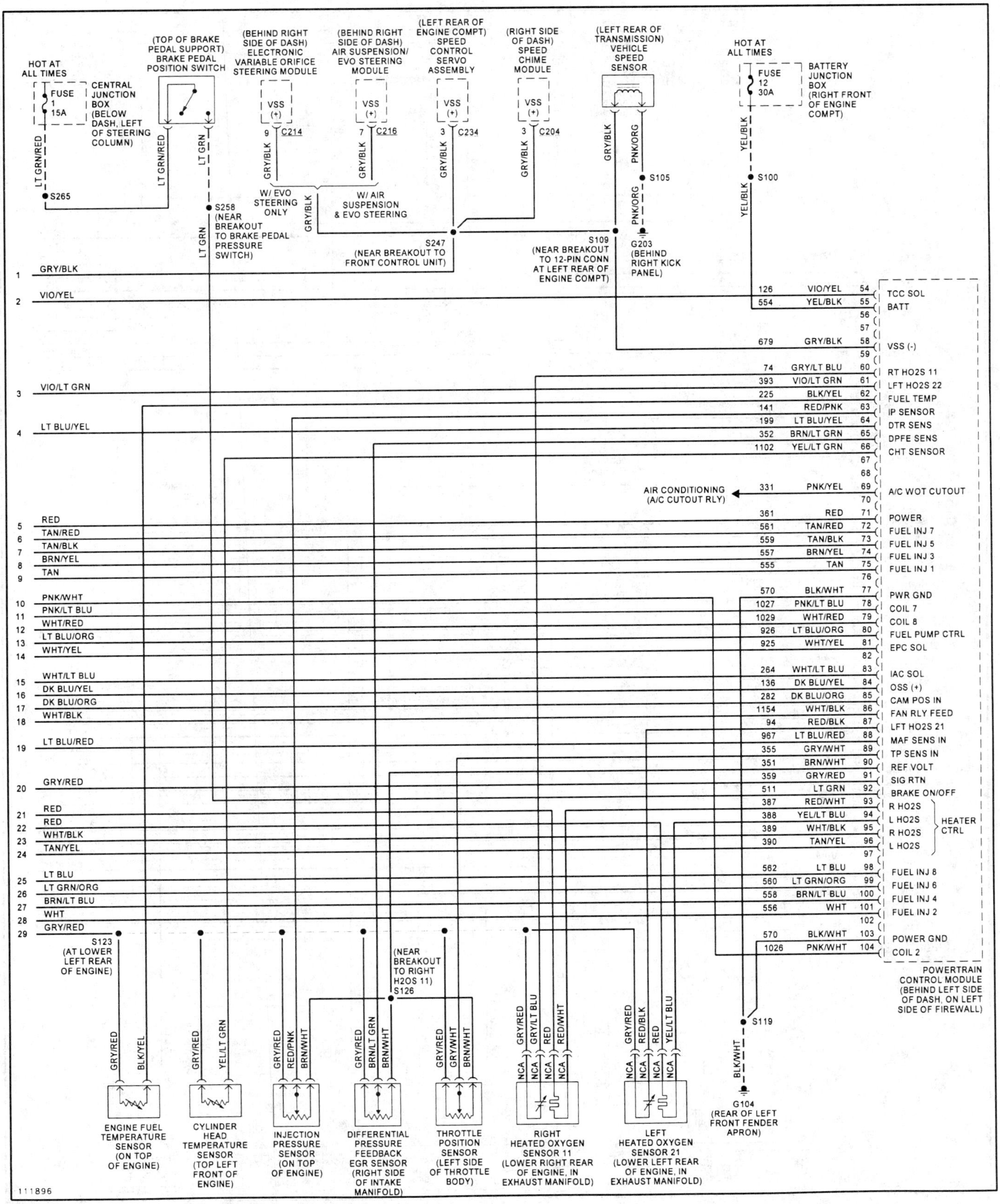

Fig. 25: Crown Victoria (4.6L CNG – 5 Of 5)

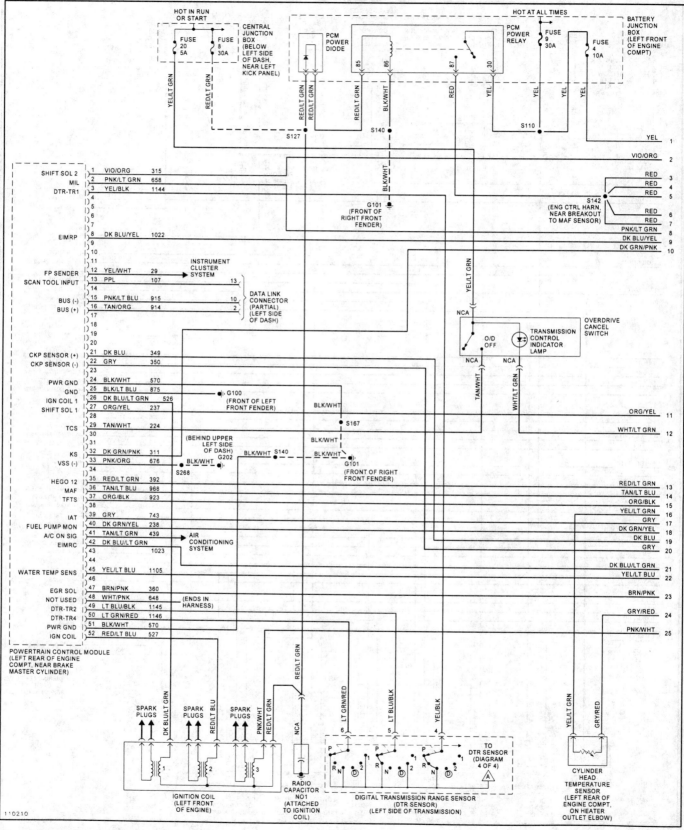

Fig. 26: Econoline – E150 & E250 (4.2L – 1 Of 4)

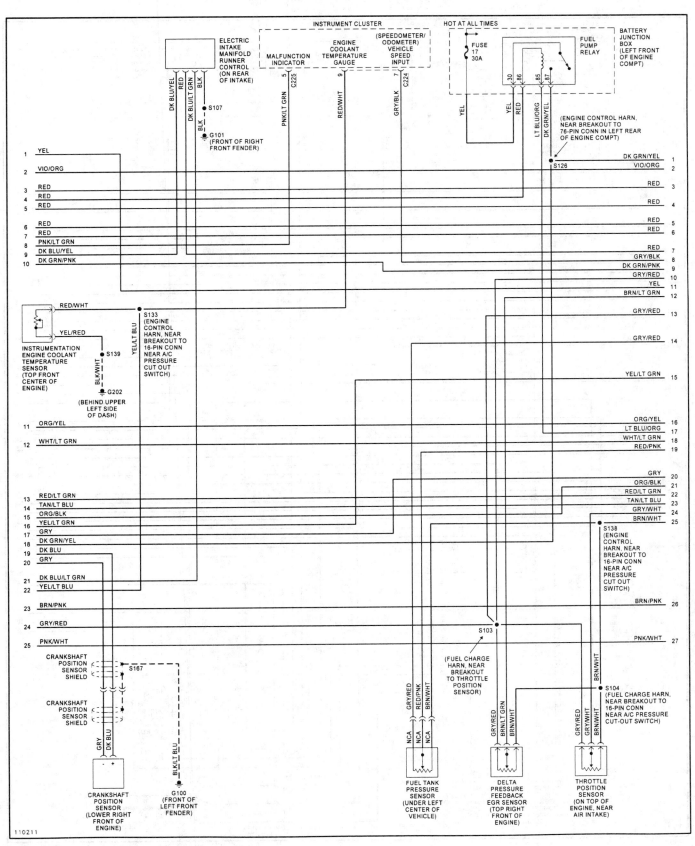

Fig. 27: Econoline – E150 & E250 (4.2L – 2 Of 4)

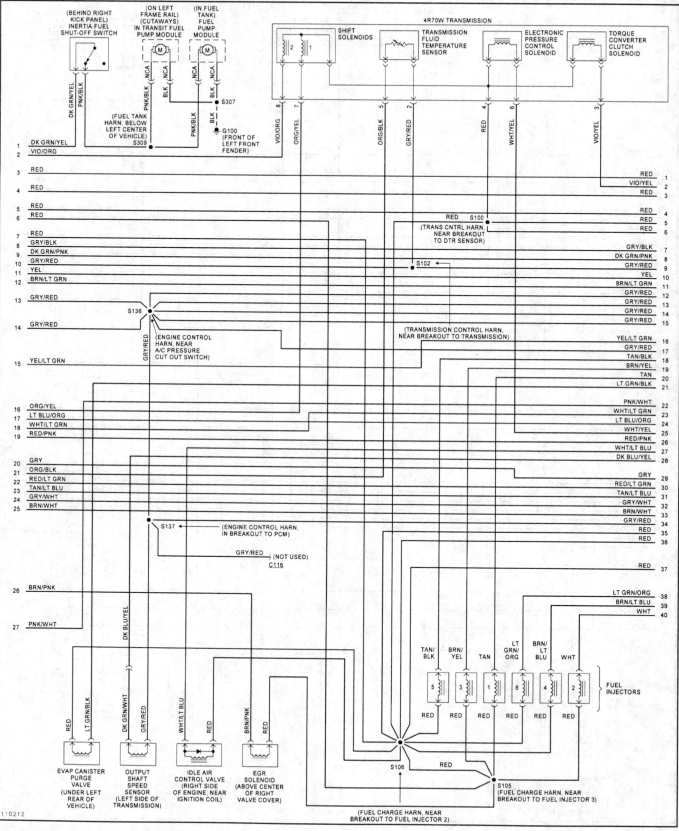

Fig. 28: Econoline – E150 & E250 (4.2L – 3 Of 4)

(UNDER VEHICLE, LEFT SIDE OF TRANSMISSION) VEHICLE SPEED SENSOR

(NEAR BRAKE MASTER CYLINDER) SPEED CONTROL SERVO

VSS INPUT

(UNDER LEFT REAR OF VEHICLE) EVAPORATIVE EMISSIONS CANISTER PURGE VALVE

(RIGHT REAR SIDE OF ENGINE) KNOCK SENSOR

HOT AT ALL TIMES

FUSE 11 15A

CENTRAL JUNCTION BOX (BELOW LEFT SIDE OF DASH, NEAR LEFT KICK PANEL)

BRAKE PEDAL POSITION SWITCH

FROM DTR SENSOR (DIAGRAM 1 OF 4)

GRY/RED 2

240 OHMS

LT BLU/YEL 3

DIGITAL TRANSMISSION RANGE SENSOR (DTR SENSOR) (LEFT SIDE OF TRANSMISSION)

S134 (ENGINE CONTROL HARN, NEAR A/C PRESSURE CUT OUT SWITCH)

S268
S135 (ENGINE CONTROL HARN, NEAR A/C PRESSURE CUT OUT SWITCH)

(UPPER LEFT SIDE OF DASH)
G202

#	Wire		Pin	Circuit	Function
1	RED		53		
2	VIO/YEL	480	54	VIO/YEL	TCC SOL
3	RED	37	55	YEL	KAP B(+)
		191	56	LT GRN/BLK	EVAP VALVE
4	RED	310	57	YEL/RED	KNOCK SENSOR
5	RED	679	58	GRY/BLK	VSS (+)
6	RED		59		
		74	60	GRY/LT BLU	HEGO 11
7	GRY/BLK	393	61	VIO/LT GRN	HEGO 22
8	DK GRN/PNK	791	62	RED/PNK	FUEL TANK PRESS
9	GRY/RED		63		
10	YEL	199	64	LT BLU/YEL	DTR-TR3A
11	BRN/LT GRN	352	65	BRN/LT GRN	DPFE SENS
12	GRY/RED	1102	66	YEL/LT GRN	CHT SENSOR
13	GRY/RED	91	67	VIO/WHT	EVAP PURGE VALV
14	GRY/RED		68		
15	GRY/RED	883	69	BLK/LT BLU	A/C RLY CNTRL
			70		
16	YEL/LT GRN	361	71	RED	VPWR
17	GRY/RED		72		
18	TAN/BLK	559	73	TAN/BLK	FUEL INJ 5
19	BRN/YEL	557	74	BRN/YEL	FUEL INJ 3
20	TAN	555	75	TAN	FUEL INJ 1
21	LT GRN/BLK	570	76	BLK/WHT	PWR GND
		570	77	BLK/WHT	PWR GND
22	PNK/WHT	528	78	PNK/WHT	IGN COIL
23	WHT/LT GRN	911	79	WHT/LT GRN	TRANS CTRL IND
24	LT BLU/ORG	926	80	LT BLU/ORG	FUEL PUMP CTRL
25	WHT/YEL	925	81	WHT/YEL	EPC SOL
26	RED/PNK		82		
27	WHT/LT BLU	264	83	WHT/LT BLU	IAC VALVE
28	DK BLU/YEL	136	84	DK BLU/WHT	OSS (+)
		795	85	DK GRN	CMP SENSOR
29	GRY		86		
30	RED/LT GRN	94	87	RED/BLK	HEGO 21
31	TAN/LT BLU	967	88	LT BLU/RED	MAF SENS IN
32	GRY/WHT	355	89	GRY/WHT	TP SENS IN
33	BRN/WHT	351	90	BRN/WHT	REF OUTPUT VOLT
34	GRY/RED	359	91	GRY/RED	SIG RTN
35	RED	511	92	LT GRN	BRAKE ON/OFF
36	RED	387	93	RED/WHT	HEGO 11
		388	94	YEL/LT BLU	HEGO 21 (HEATER CTRL)
		389	95	WHT/BLK	HEGO 12
37	RED	390	96	TAN/YEL	HEGO 22
		560	99	LT GRN/ORG	FUEL INJ 6
38	LT GRN/ORG	558	100	BRN/LT BLU	FUEL INJ 4
39	BRN/LT BLU	556	101	WHT	FUEL INJ 2
40	WHT		102		
		570	103	BLK/WHT	PWR GND
			104		

POWERTRAIN CONTROL MODULE (LEFT REAR OF ENGINE COMPT, NEAR MASTER CYLINDER)

AIR COND SYSTEM

S167
BLK/LT BLU
CAMSHAFT POSITION SENSOR SHIELD
G100 (FRONT OF LEFT FRONT FENDER)

S140
BLK/WHT
G101 (FRONT OF RIGHT FRONT FENDER)

CAMSHAFT POSITION SENSOR (ON FRONT CENTER OF ENGINE)

MASS AIR FLOW SENSOR (ON TOP (CENTER OF ENGINE COMPT)

HEATED OXYGEN SENSOR 12 (HO2S) (RIGHT SIDE OF TRANSMISSION)

HEATED OXYGEN SENSOR 11 (HO2S) (LOWER RIGHT REAR OF ENGINE)

HEATED OXYGEN SENSOR 22 (HO2S) (UNDER CENTER OF VEHICLE)

HEATED OXYGEN SENSOR 21 (HO2S) (LEFT REAR OF ENGINE)

S140
G101 (FRONT OF RIGHT FRONT FENDER)

110213

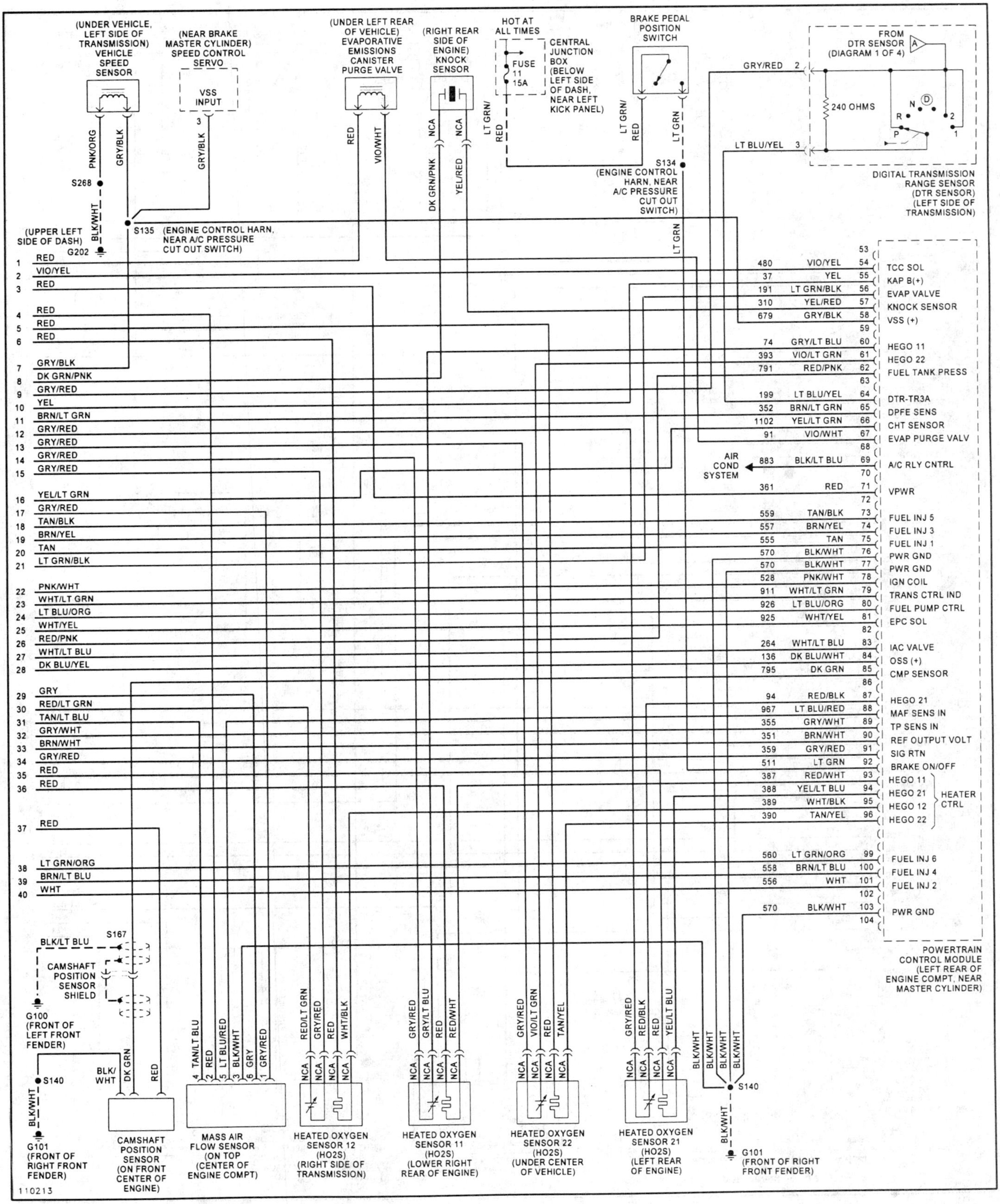

Fig. 29: Econoline – E150 & E250 (4.2L – 4 Of 4)

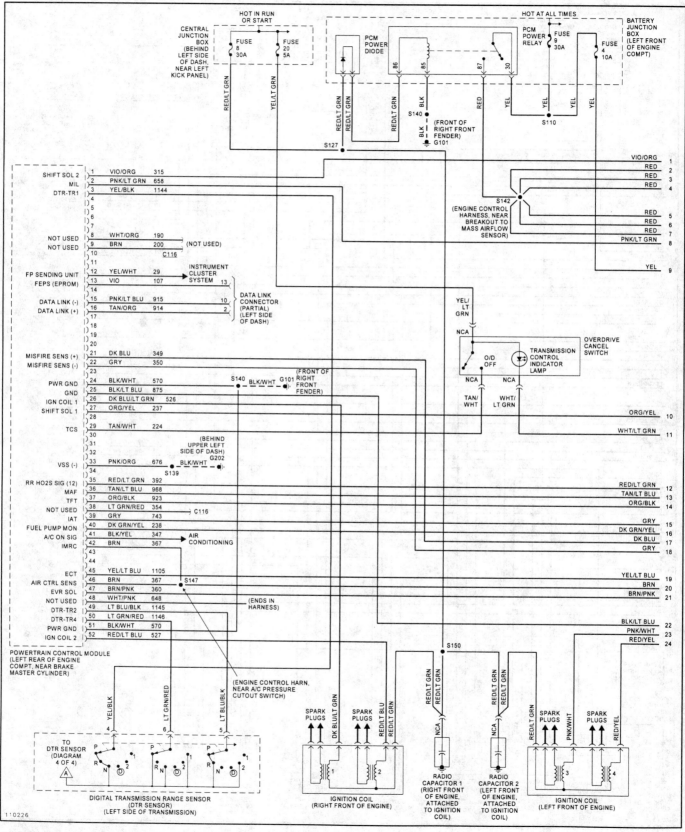

Fig. 30: Econoline – E150 & E250 (4.6L – 1 Of 4)

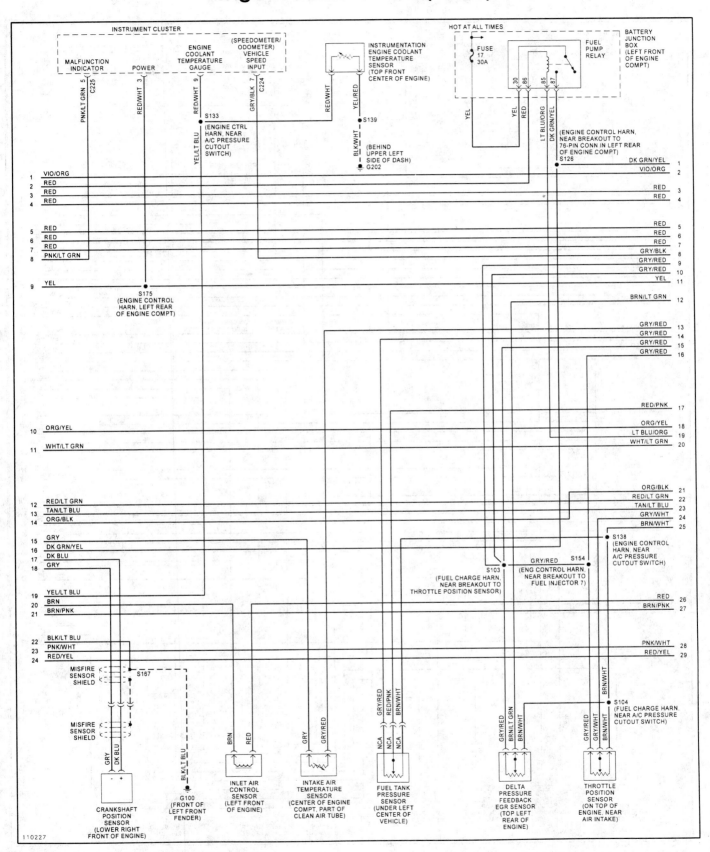

Fig. 31: Econoline – E150 & E250 (4.6L – 2 Of 4)

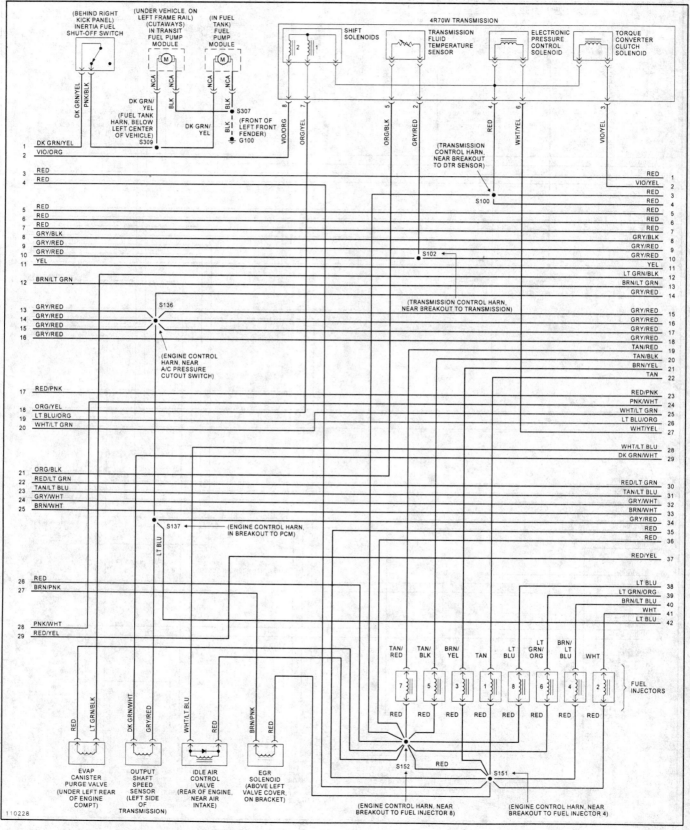

Fig. 32: Econoline – E150 & E250 (4.6L – 3 Of 4)

110228

(LEFT SIDE OF TRANSMISSION) VEHICLE SPEED SENSOR

(LEFT SIDE OF ENGINE COMPT) SPEED CONTROL SERVO — VSS INPUT — 3

(TOP OF LEFT CYL HEAD) CYLINDER HEAD TEMPERATURE SENSOR

(UNDER LEFT REAR OF VEHICLE) EVAPORATIVE EMISSIONS CANISTER PURGE VALVE

(TOP RIGHT REAR SIDE OF ENGINE) KNOCK SENSOR

HOT AT ALL TIMES — FUSE 11 15A — CENTRAL JUNCTION BOX (BEHIND LEFT SIDE OF DASH, NEAR LEFT KICK PANEL)

(ENGINE CONTROL HARN, NEAR A/C PRESSURE CUTOUT SWITCH)

BRAKE PEDAL POSITION SWITCH

FROM DTR SENSOR (DIAGRAM 1 OF 4) — A

240 OHMS

N D R P 2 1

DIGITAL TRANSMISSION RANGE SENSOR (DTR SENSOR) (LEFT SIDE OF TRANSMISSION)

PNK/ORG, GRY/BLK — S139 — BLK/WHT — (BEHIND UPPER LEFT SIDE OF DASH) G202 — S135 (ENGINE CONTROL HARN, NEAR A/C PRESSURE CUTOUT SWITCH)

GRY/BLK (3) GRY/RED, YEL/LT GRN, RED, VIO/WHT, GRY/RED, YEL/RED (NCA), LT GRN/RED, GRY/RED, LT GRN, S134, LT GRN, GRY/RED (2), LT BLU/YEL (3)

Pin	Wire		Code	Wire	Pin	Signal
1	RED				53	
2	VIO/YEL		480	VIO/YEL	54	TCC SOL
3	RED		37	YEL	55	KAP B(+)
4	RED		191	LT GRN/BLK	56	VAPOR VALVE
5	RED		310	YEL/RED	57	KNOCK SENSOR
6	RED		679	GRY/BLK	58	VSS (+)
7	RED				59	
8	GRY/BLK		74	GRY/LT BLU	60	RF HO2S SIG (11)
9	GRY/RED		393	VIO/LT GRN	61	LR HO2S SIG (22)
10	GRY/RED		791	RED/PNK	62	FUEL TANK PRESS
11	YEL				63	
12	LT GRN/BLK		199	LT BLU/YEL	64	DTR-TR3A
13	BRN/LT GRN		352	BRN/LT GRN	65	DPFE SENS
14	GRY/RED		1102	YEL/LT GRN	66	CYL HEAD TEMP
			91	VIO/WHT	67	EVAP SOL
15	GRY/RED				68	
16	GRY/RED				69	
17	GRY/RED				70	
18	GRY/RED		361	RED	71	VPWR
19	TAN/RED		561	TAN/RED	72	FUEL INJ 7
20	TAN/BLK		559	TAN/BLK	73	FUEL INJ 5
21	BRN/YEL		557	BRN/YEL	74	FUEL INJ 3
22	TAN		555	TAN	75	FUEL INJ 1
			570	BLK/WHT	76	PWR GND
			570	BLK/WHT	77	PWR GND
23	RED/PNK		528	PNK/WHT	78	IGN COIL 3
24	PNK/WHT		911	WHT/LT GRN	79	TRANS CTRL IND
25	WHT/LT GRN		926	LT BLU/ORG	80	FUEL PUMP CTRL
26	LT BLU/ORG		925	WHT/YEL	81	EPC SOL
27	WHT/YEL				82	
			264	WHT/LT BLU	83	IAC SOL
28	WHT/LT BLU		970	DK GRN/WHT	84	OSS (+)
29	DK GRN/WHT		795	DK GRN	85	CYLINDER ID
					86	
			94	RED/BLK	87	LF HO2S SIG (21)
30	RED/LT GRN		967	LT BLU/RED	88	MAF SENS IN
31	TAN/LT BLU		355	GRY/WHT	89	TP SENS IN
32	GRY/WHT		351	BRN/WHT	90	5V REF
33	BRN/WHT		359	GRY/RED	91	SIG RTN
34	GRY/RED		511	LT GRN	92	BRAKE ON/OFF
35	RED		387	RED/WHT	93	RF HO2S
36	RED		388	YEL/LT BLU	94	LF HO2S
			389	WHT/BLK	95	RR HO2S (HEATER CTRL)
37	RED/YEL		390	TAN/YEL	96	LR HO2S
			361	RED	97	VPWR
			562	LT BLU	98	FUEL INJ 8
38	LT BLU		560	LT GRN/ORG	99	FUEL INJ 6
39	LT GRN/ORG		558	BRN/LT BLU	100	FUEL INJ 4
40	BRN/LT BLU		556	WHT	101	FUEL INJ 2
41	WHT				102	
42	LT BLU		570	BLK/WHT	103	PWR GND
			529	RED/YEL	104	IGN COIL 4

POWERTRAIN CONTROL MODULE (LEFT REAR OF ENGINE COMPT, NEAR BRAKE MASTER CYLINDER)

S167

BLK/LT BLU

CAMSHAFT POSITION SENSOR SHIELD

BLK/LT BLU

G100 (FRONT OF LEFT FRONT FENDER)

LT BLU, DK GRN — CAMSHAFT POSITION SENSOR (FRONT OF LEFT CYLINDER HEAD)

TAN/LT BLU, RED, LT BLU/RED, BLK/WHT (NCA) — MASS AIR FLOW SENSOR (TOP CENTER OF ENGINE COMPT)

RED/LT GRN, GRY/RED, RED, WHT/BLK (NCA) — HEATED OXYGEN SENSOR (HO2S) 12 (RIGHT SIDE OF TRANSMISSION)

GRY/RED, GRY/LT BLU, RED, RED/WHT (NCA) — HEATED OXYGEN SENSOR (HO2S) 11 (LOWER RIGHT REAR OF ENGINE)

GRY/RED, PPL/LT GRN, RED, TAN/YEL (NCA) — HEATED OXYGEN SENSOR (HO2S) 22 (UNDER CENTER OF VEHICLE)

GRY/RED, RED/BLK, RED, YEL/LT BLU (NCA) — HEATED OXYGEN SENSOR (HO2S) 21 (LOWER LEFT REAR OF ENGINE)

BLK/WHT, BLK/WHT, BLK/WHT — S140 — BLK/WHT — G101 (FRONT OF RIGHT FRONT FENDER)

110229

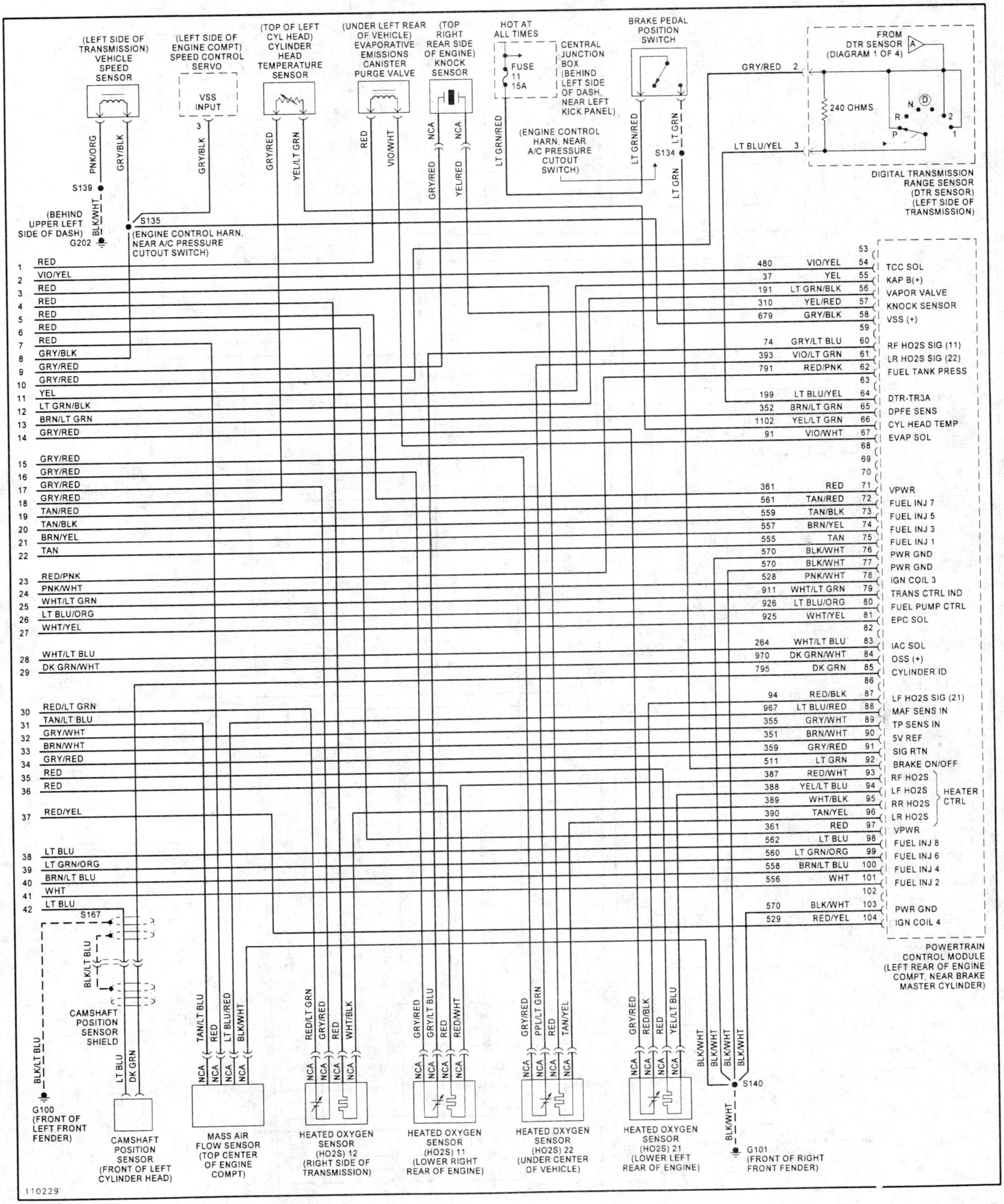

Fig. 33: Econoline – E150 & E250 (4.6L – 4 Of 4)

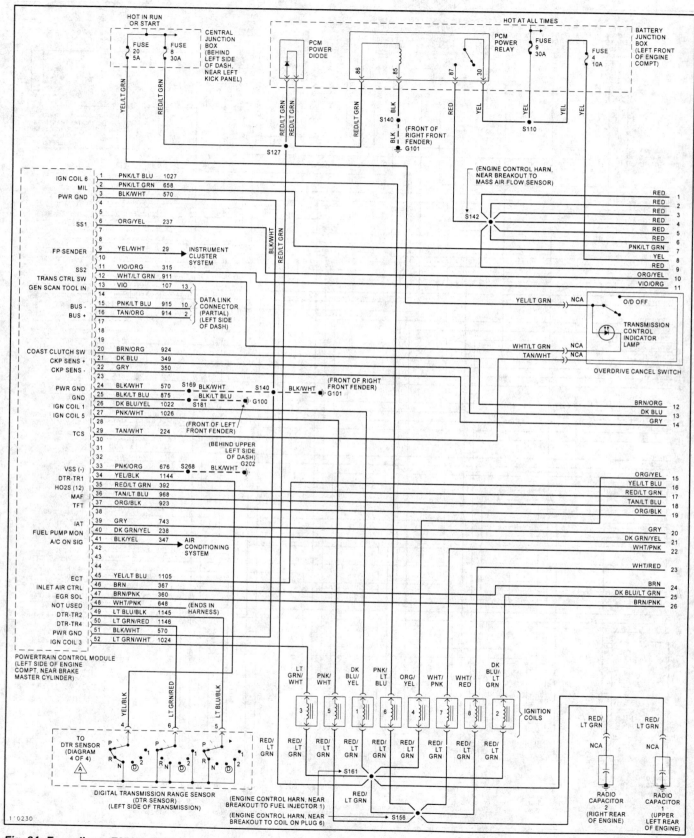

Fig. 34: Econoline – E250 & E350 Super Duty (5.4L Gasoline – 1 Of 4)

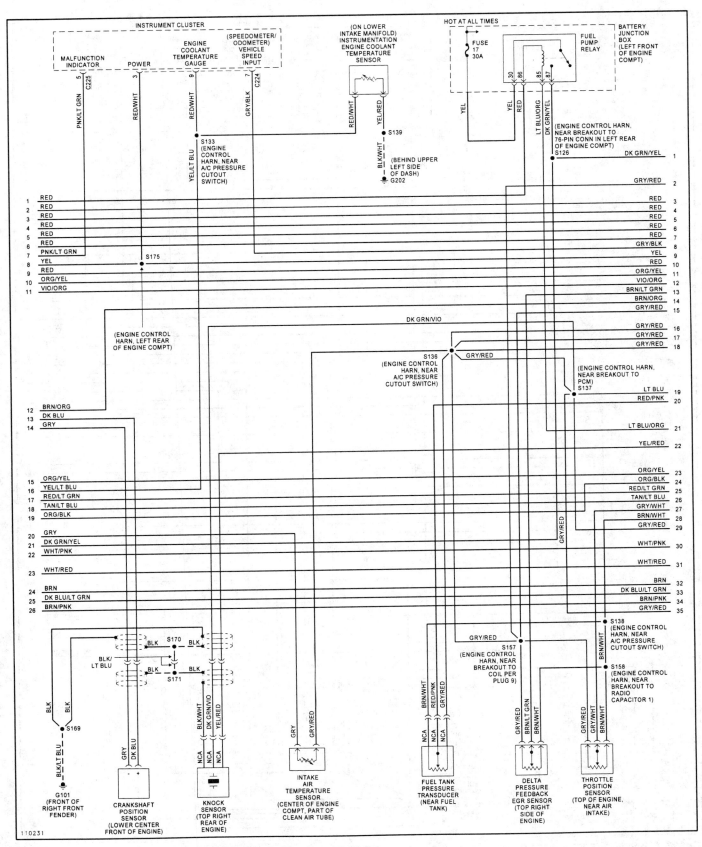

Fig. 35: Econoline – E250 & E350 Super Duty (5.4L Gasoline – 2 Of 4)

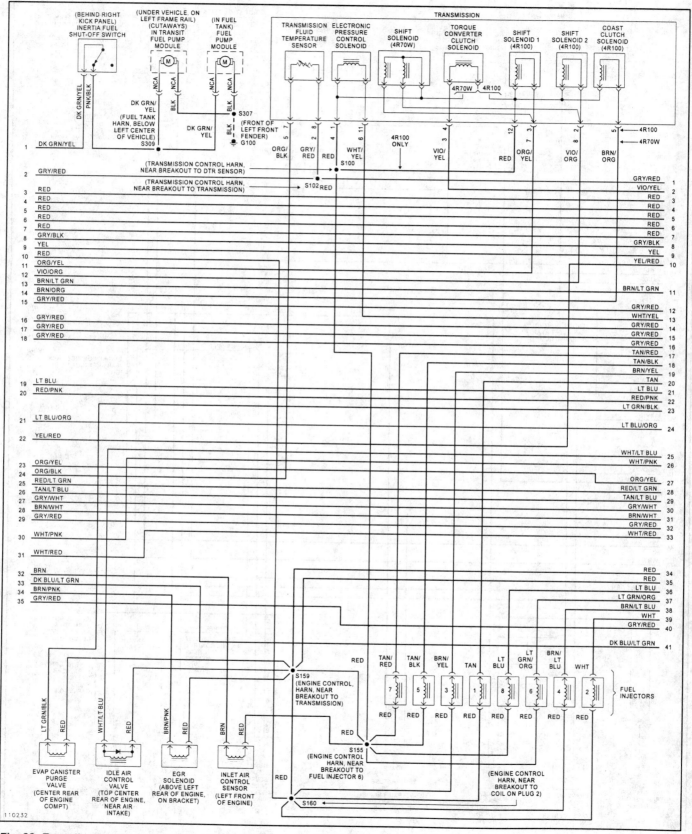

Fig. 36: Econoline – E250 & E350 Super Duty (5.4L Gasoline – 3 Of 4)

110232

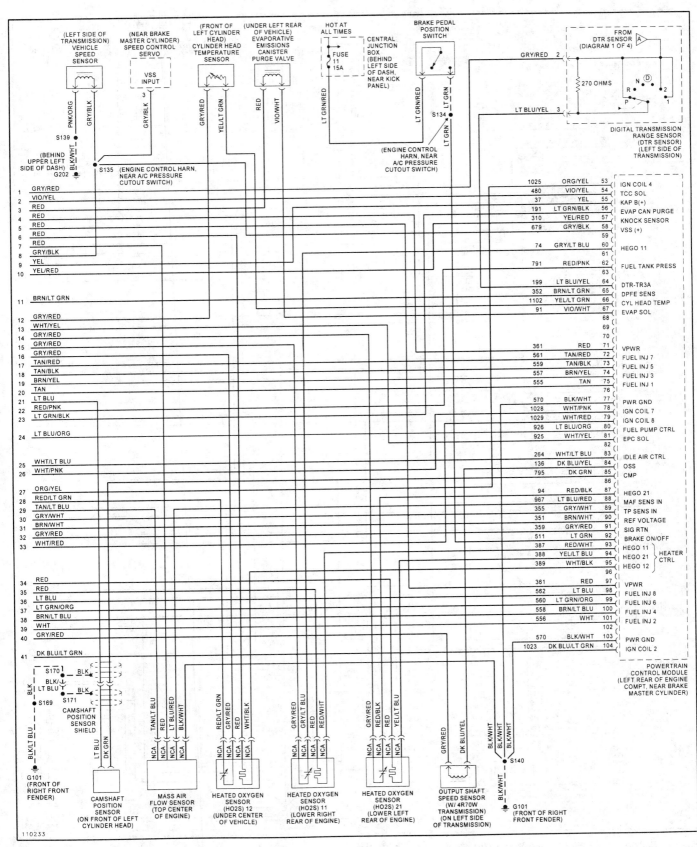

Fig. 37: Econoline – E250 & E350 Super Duty (5.4L Gasoline – 4 Of 4)

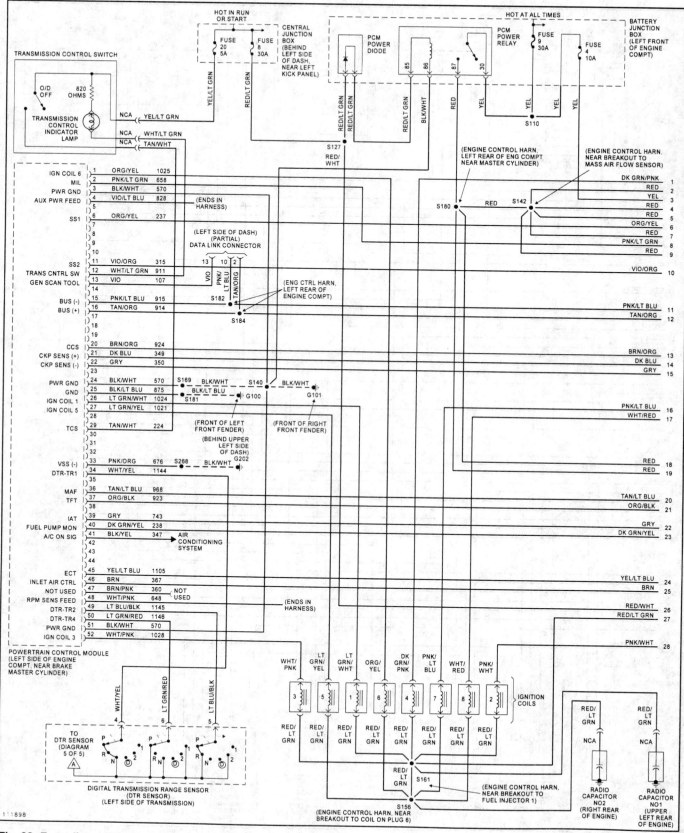

Fig. 38: Econoline – E250 & E350 Super Duty (5.4L CNG – 1 Of 5)

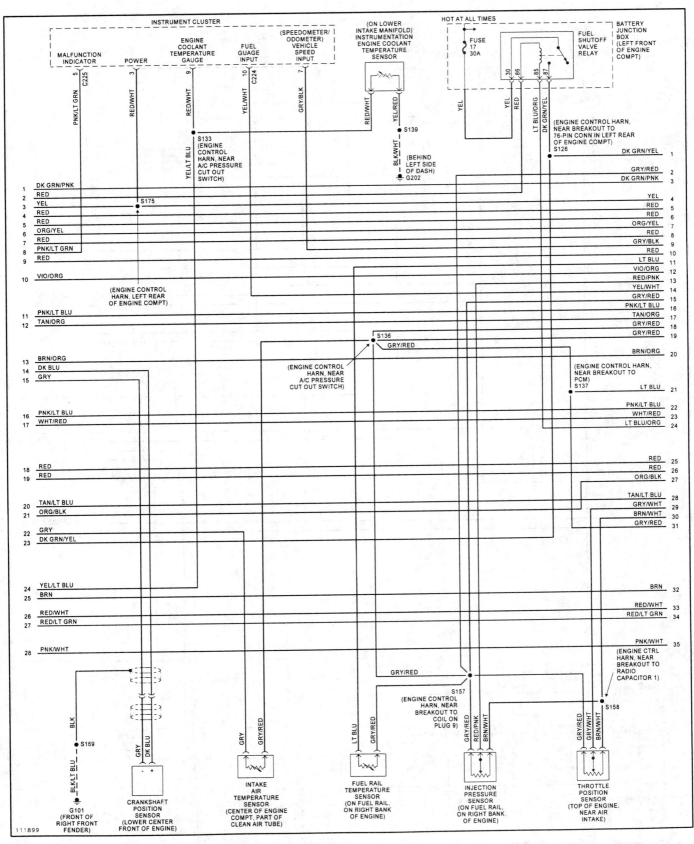

Fig. 39: Econoline – E250 & E350 Super Duty (5.4L CNG – 2 Of 5)

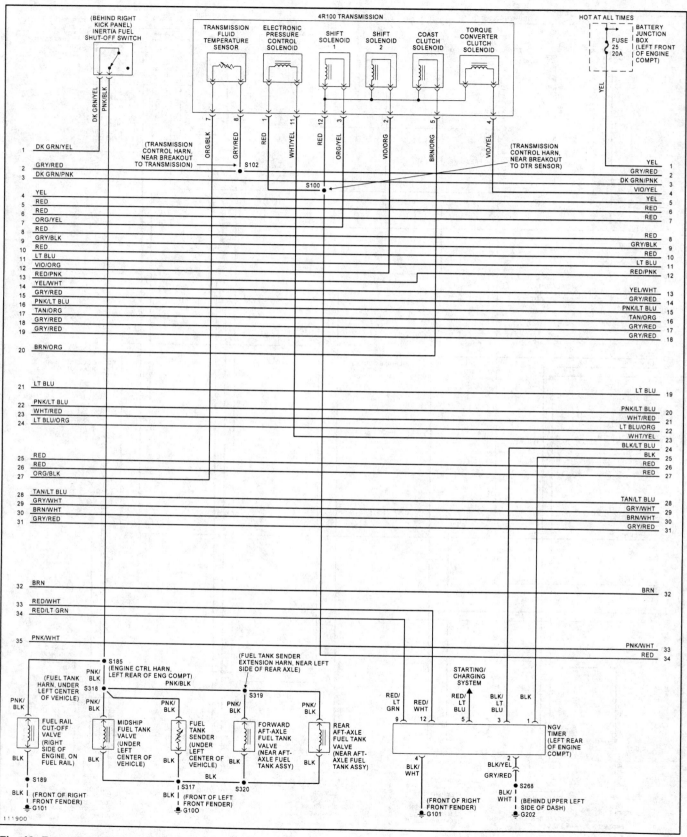

Fig. 40: Econoline – E250 & E350 Super Duty (5.4L CNG – 3 Of 5)

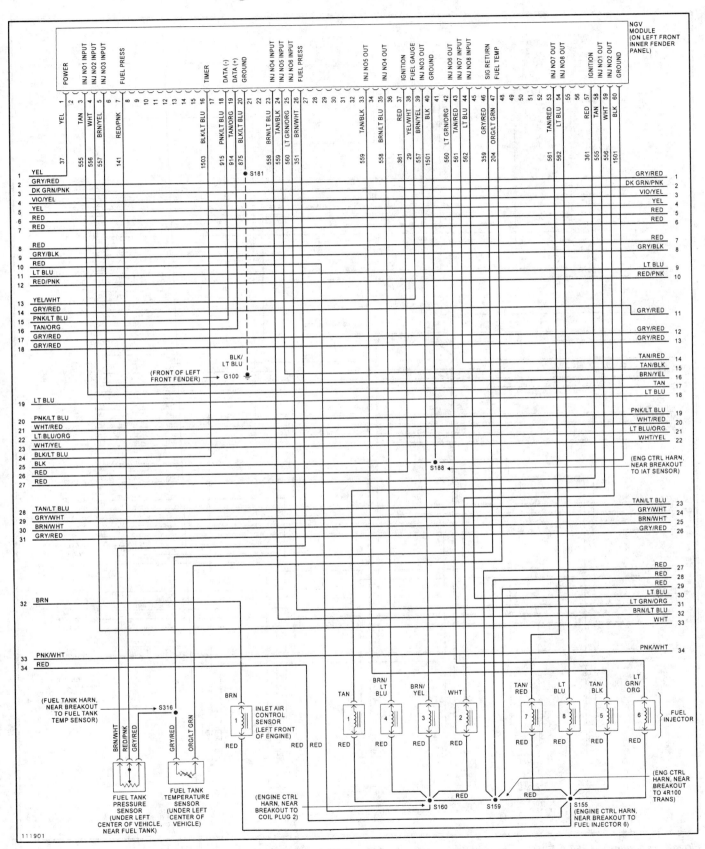

Fig. 41: Econoline – E250 & E350 Super Duty (5.4L CNG – 4 Of 5)

(LEFT SIDE OF TRANSMISSION) VEHICLE SPEED SENSOR

(NEAR BRAKE MASTER CYLINDER) SPEED CONTROL SERVO

VSS INPUT 3

(TOP FRONT OF LEFT CYLINDER HEAD) CYLINDER HEAD TEMPERATURE SENSOR

HOT AT ALL TIMES
FUSE 11 15A

CENTRAL JUNCTION BOX (BEHIND LEFT SIDE OF DASH, NEAR LEFT KICK PANEL)

BRAKE PEDAL POSITION SWITCH

FROM DTR SENSOR (DIAGRAM 1 OF 5)

270 OHMS

DIGITAL TRANSMISSION RANGE SENSOR (DTR SENSOR) (LEFT SIDE OF TRANSMISSION)

PNK/ORG   GRY/BLK   GRY/BLK   GRY/RED   YEL/LT GRN   LT GRN/RED   LT GRN/RED   LT GRN   GRY/RED 2   LT BLU/YEL 3

S139

(BEHIND UPPER LEFT SIDE OF DASH) BLK/WHT
G202

S134

(ENGINE CONTROL HARN. NEAR A/C PRESSURE CUTOUT SWITCH)

S135

Pin	Circuit	No.	Circuit	Pin	Function
1	GRY/RED				
2	DK GRN/PNK	1030	DK GRN/PNK	53	IGN COIL 4
3	VIO/YEL	480	VIO/YEL	54	TCC SOL
4	YEL	37	YEL	55	KAP B(+)
5	RED			56	
6	RED	NOT USED 310	YEL/RED	57	NOT USED
7	RED	679	GRY/BLK	58	VSS (+)
8	GRY/BLK			59	
9	LT BLU	74	GRY/LT BLU	60	HEGO 11
10	RED/PNK			61	
		1164	LT BLU	62	FUEL TEMP
		141	RED/PNK	63	INJ PRESS
		199	LT BLU/YEL	64	DTR-TR3A
11	GRY/RED	NOT USED 352	BRN/LT GRN	65	NOT USED
		1102	YEL/LT GRN	66	CYL HEAD TEMP
12	GRY/RED			67	
13	GRY/RED			68	
				69	
				70	
14	TAN/RED	361	RED	71	VPWR
15	TAN/BLK	561	TAN/RED	72	FUEL INJ 7
16	BRN/YEL	559	TAN/BLK	73	FUEL INJ 5
17	TAN	557	BRN/YEL	74	FUEL INJ 3
18	LT BLU	555	TAN	75	FUEL INJ 1
				76	
19	PNK/LT BLU	570	BLK/WHT	77	PWR GND
20	WHT/RED	1027	PNK/LT BLU	78	IGN COIL 7
21	LT BLU/ORG	1029	WHT/RED	79	IGN COIL 8
22	WHT/YEL	926	LT BLU/ORG	80	FUEL SHUT OFF
		925	WHT/YEL	81	EPC SOL
				82	
		264	WHT/LT BLU	83	IDLE AIR CTRL
				84	
		795	DK GRN	85	CYL IDENT SENS
				86	
23	TAN/LT BLU	94	RED/BLK	87	HEGO 21
24	GRY/WHT	967	LT BLU/RED	88	MAF SENS IN
25	BRN/WHT	355	GRY/WHT	89	TP SENS IN
26	GRY/RED	351	BRN/WHT	90	REF VOLTAGE
		359	GRY/RED	91	SIG RTN
		511	LT GRN	92	BRAKE ON/OFF
		387	RED/WHT	93	HEGO 11
		388	YEL/LT BLU	94	HEGO 21
27	RED			95	
28	RED			96	
29	RED	361	RED	97	VPWR
30	LT BLU	562	LT BLU	98	FUEL INJ 8
31	LT GRN/ORG	560	LT GRN/ORG	99	FUEL INJ 6
32	BRN/LT BLU	558	BRN/LT BLU	100	FUEL INJ 4
33	WHT	556	WHT	101	FUEL INJ 2
				102	
34	PNK/WHT	570	BLK/WHT	103	PWR GND
		1026	PNK/WHT	104	IGN COIL 2

POWERTRAIN CONTROL MODULE (LEFT REAR OF ENGINE COMPT, NEAR BRAKE MASTER CYLINDER)

S170   BLK   BLK/ LT BLU   BLK   S171
S169   CAMSHAFT POSITION SENSOR SHIELD
BLK   BLK/LT BLU

BLK/LT BLU
G101 (FRONT OF RIGHT FRONT FENDER)

LT BLU   DK GRN
CAMSHAFT POSITION SENSOR (ON FRONT OF LEFT CYLINDER HEAD)

RED   WHT/LT BLU
IDLE AIR CONTROL VALVE (TOP CENTER REAR OF ENGINE, NEAR AIR INTAKE)

TAN/LT BLU   RED   LT BLU/RED   BLK/WHT
MASS AIR FLOW SENSOR (TOP CENTER OF ENGINE)

GRY/RED   GRY/LT BLU   RED   RED/WHT
HEATED OXYGEN SENSOR (HO2S) 11 (LOWER RIGHT REAR OF ENGINE)

GRY/RED   RED/BLK   RED   YEL/LT BLU
HEATED OXYGEN SENSOR (HO2S) 21 (LOWER LEFT REAR OF ENGINE)

BLK/WHT   BLK/WHT   BLK/WHT
BLK/WHT
S140
G101 (FRONT OF RIGHT FRONT FENDER)

111902

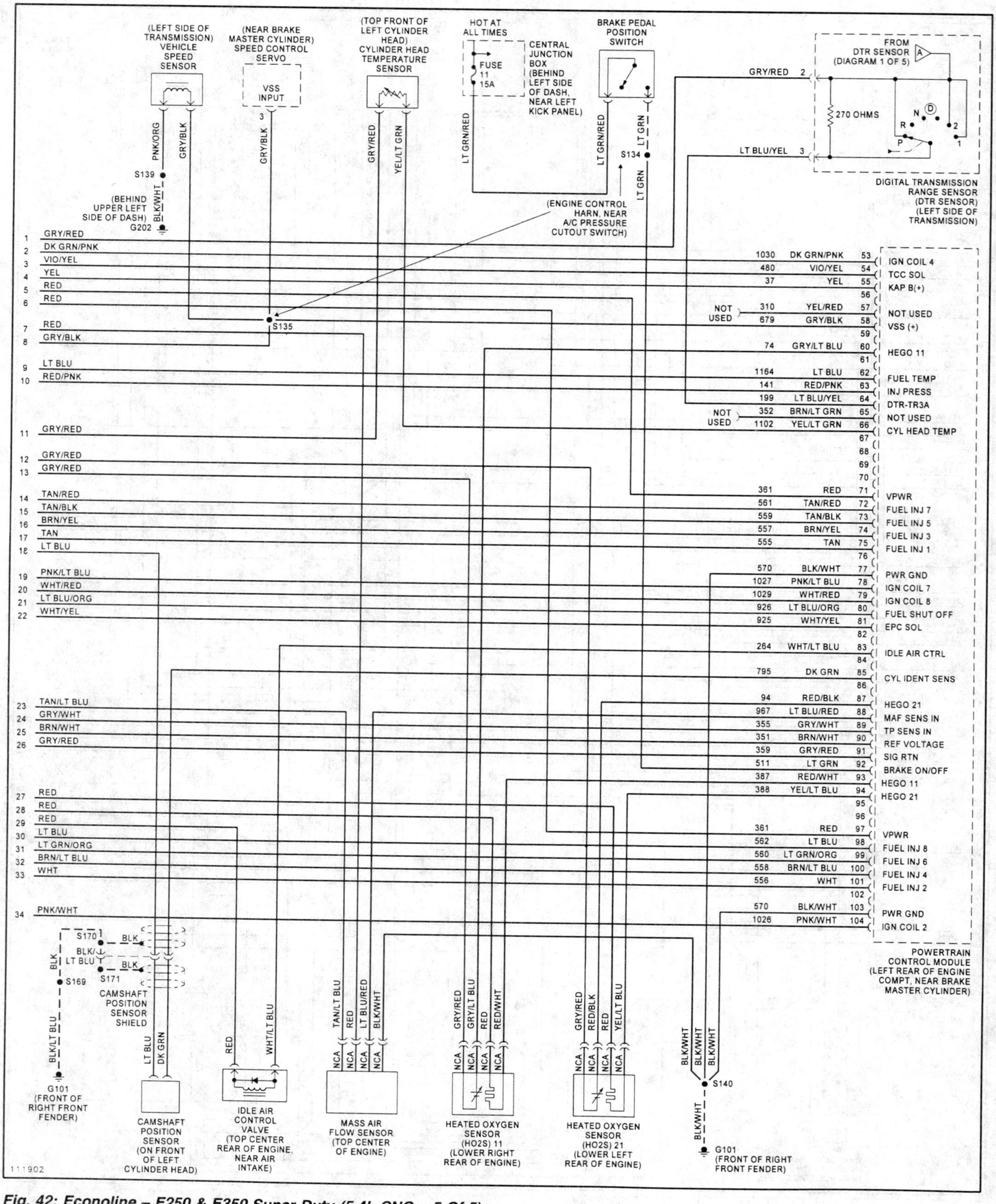

Fig. 42: Econoline – E250 & E350 Super Duty (5.4L CNG – 5 Of 5)

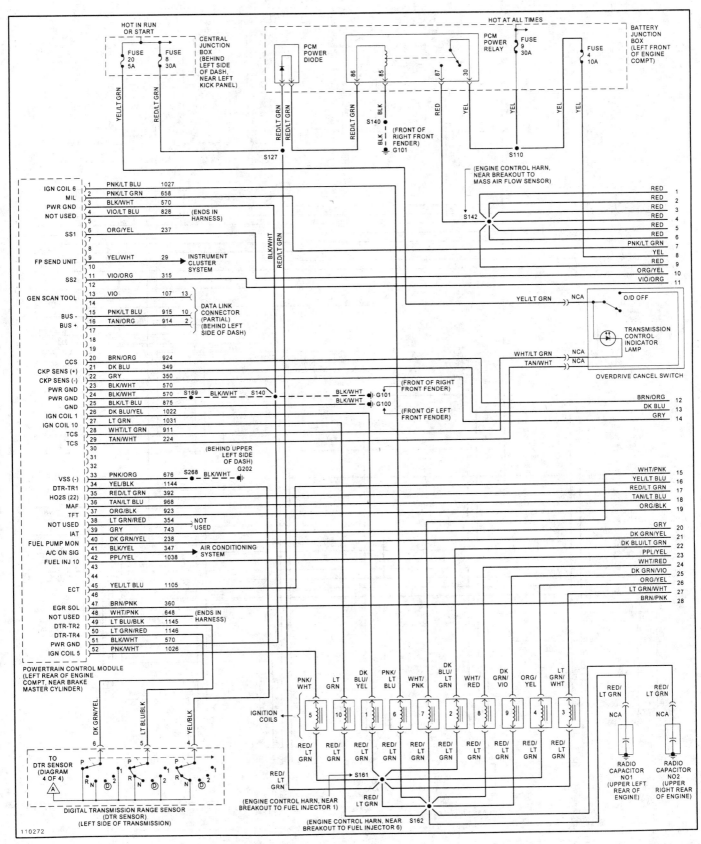

Fig. 43: Econoline – E250 & E350 Super Duty (6.8L – 1 Of 4)

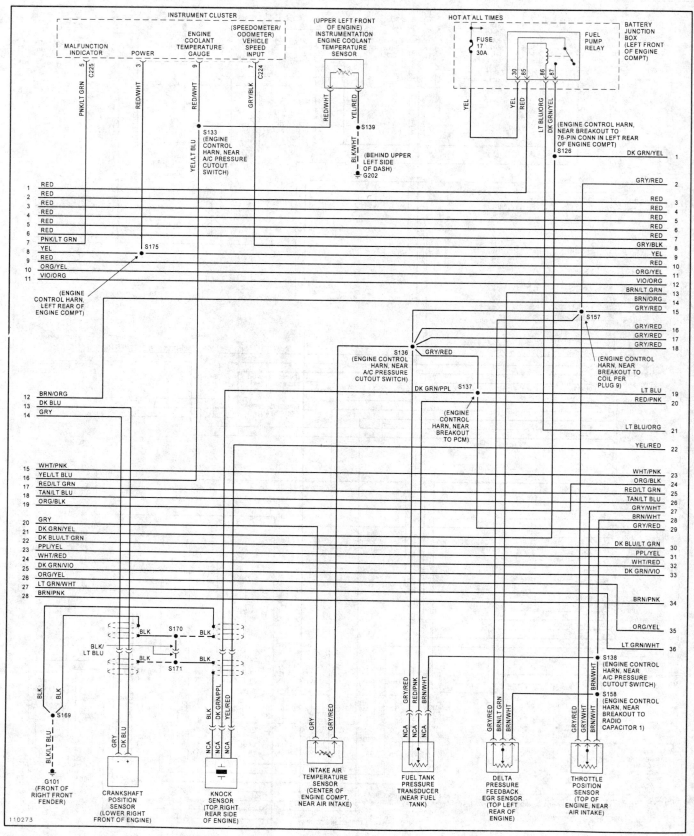

Fig. 44: Econoline – E250 & E350 Super Duty (6.8L – 2 Of 4)

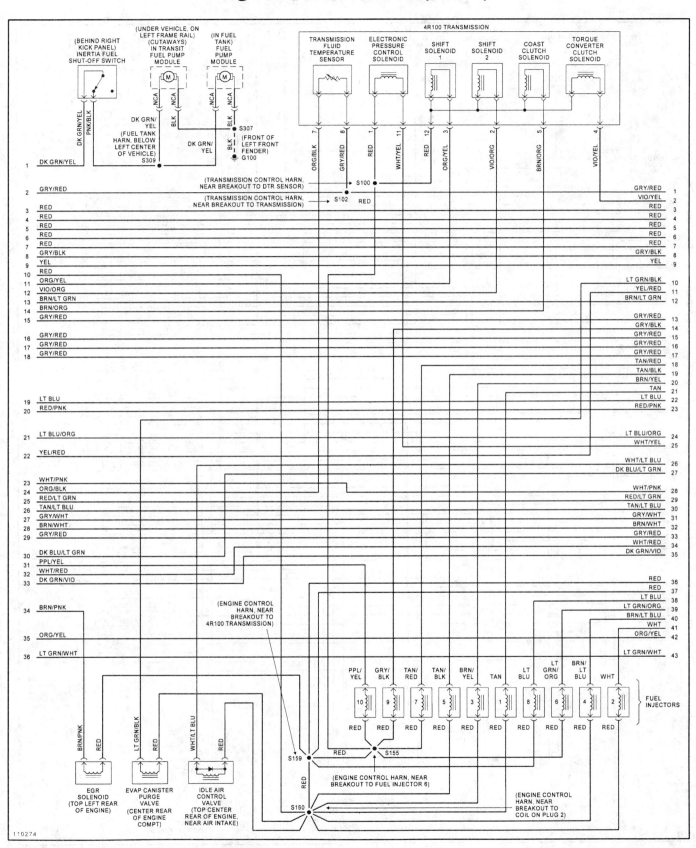

Fig. 45: Econoline – E250 & E350 Super Duty (6.8L – 3 Of 4)

110274

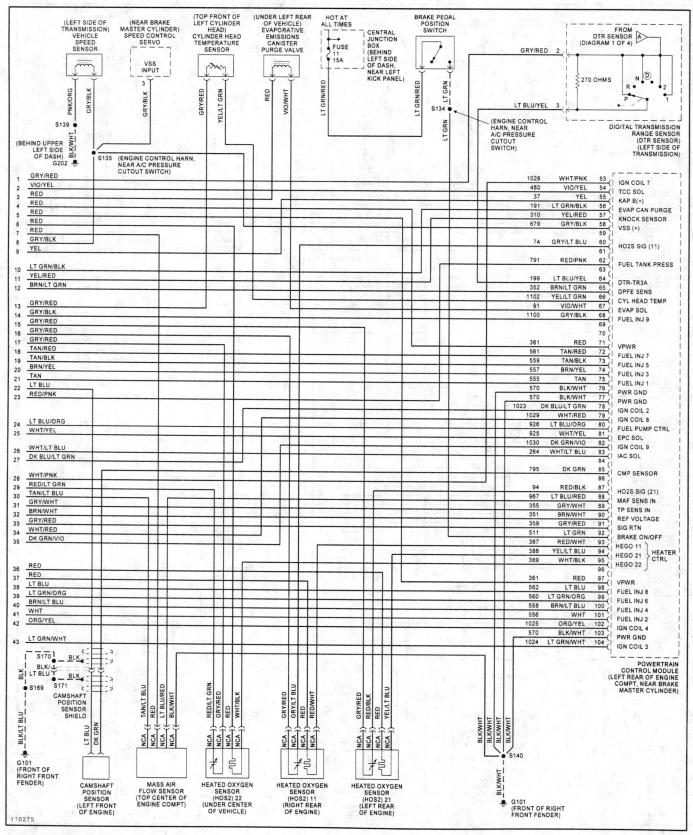

Fig. 46: *Econoline – E250 & E350 Super Duty (6.8L – 4 Of 4)*

110275

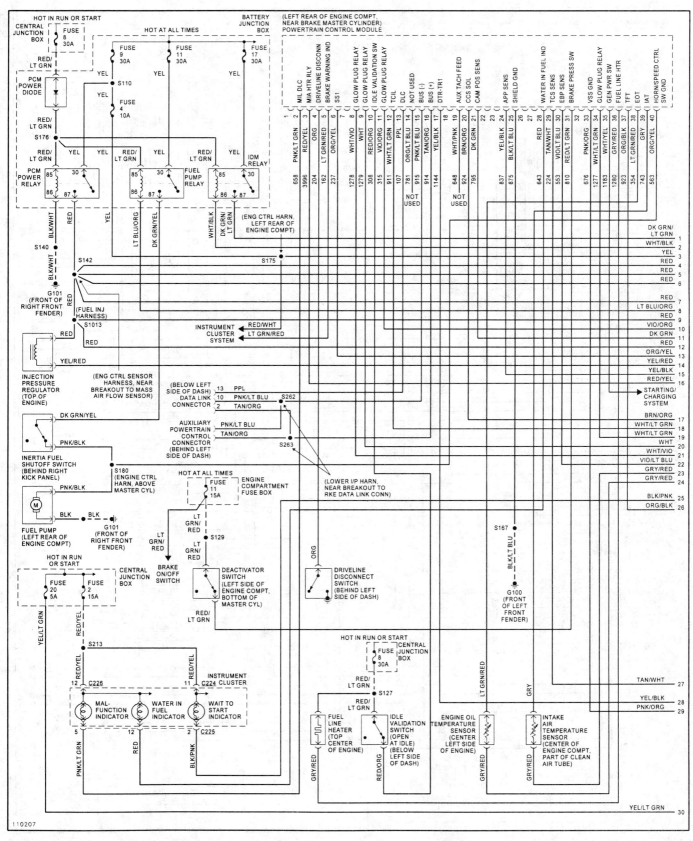

Fig. 47: Econoline – E250 & E350 Super Duty (7.3L Turbo Diesel – 1 Of 3)

110207

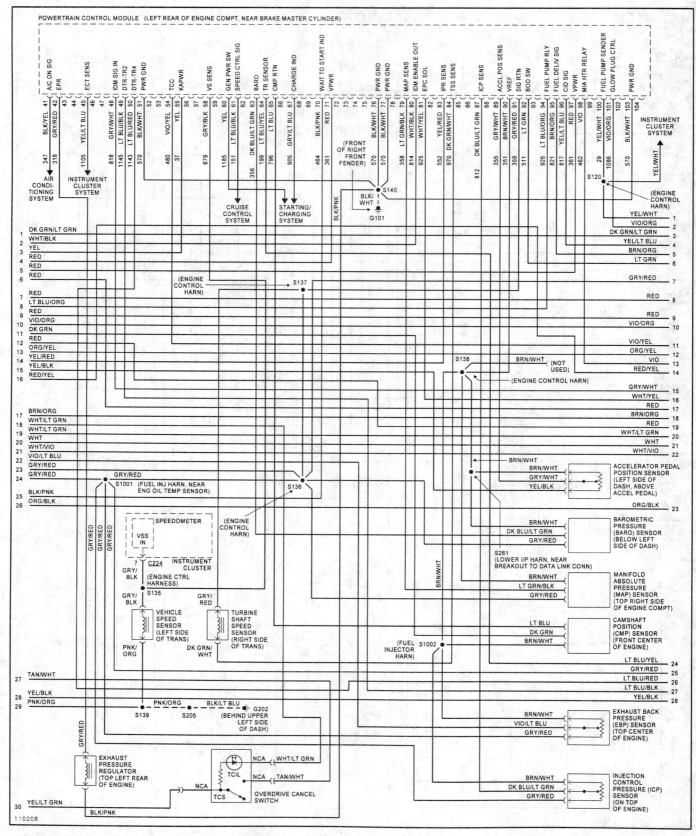

Fig. 48: Econoline – E250 & E350 Super Duty (7.3L Turbo Diesel – 2 Of 3)

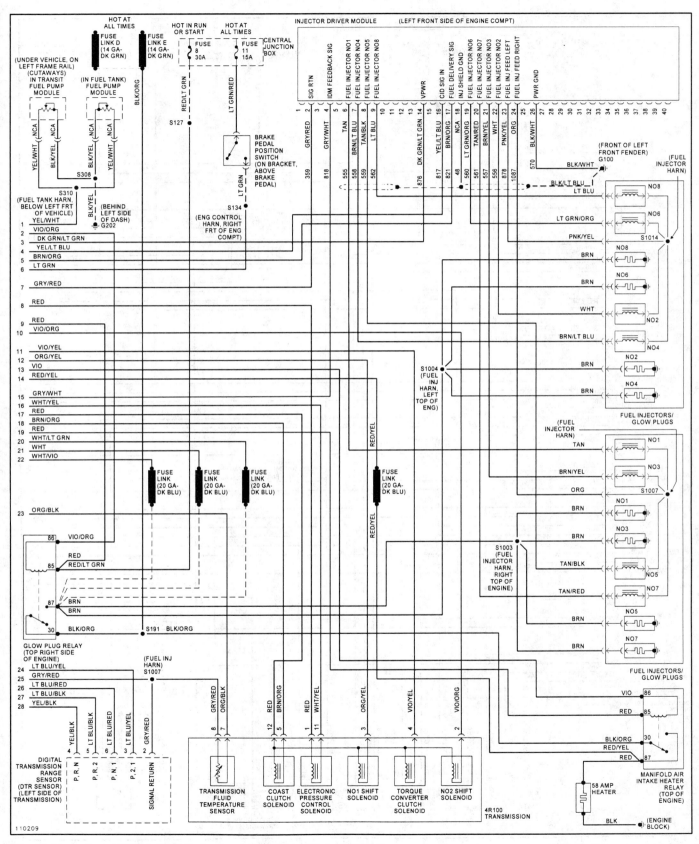

Fig. 49: Econoline – E250 & E350 Super Duty (7.3L Turbo Diesel – 3 Of 3)

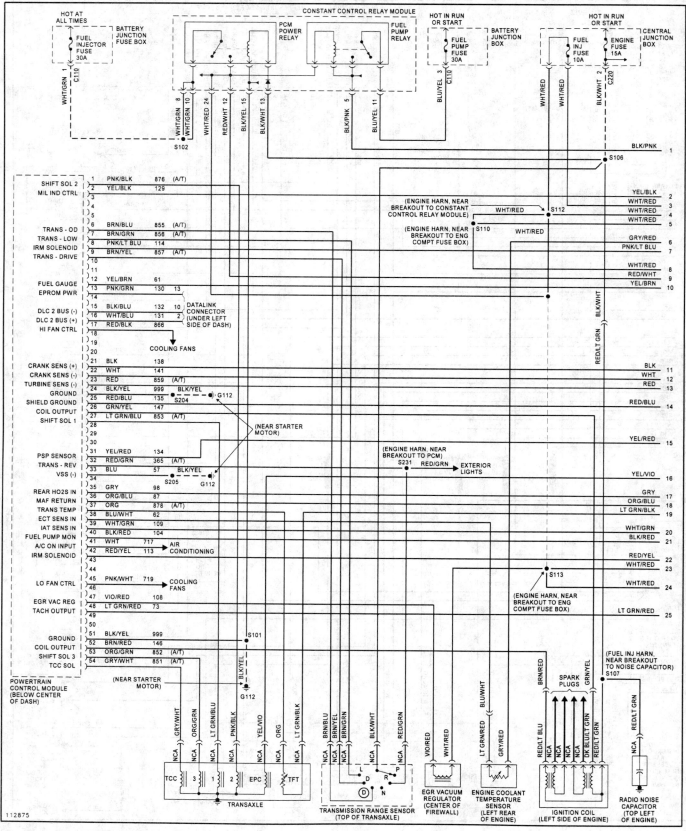

Fig. 50: Escort & Tracer (2.0L – 1 Of 3)

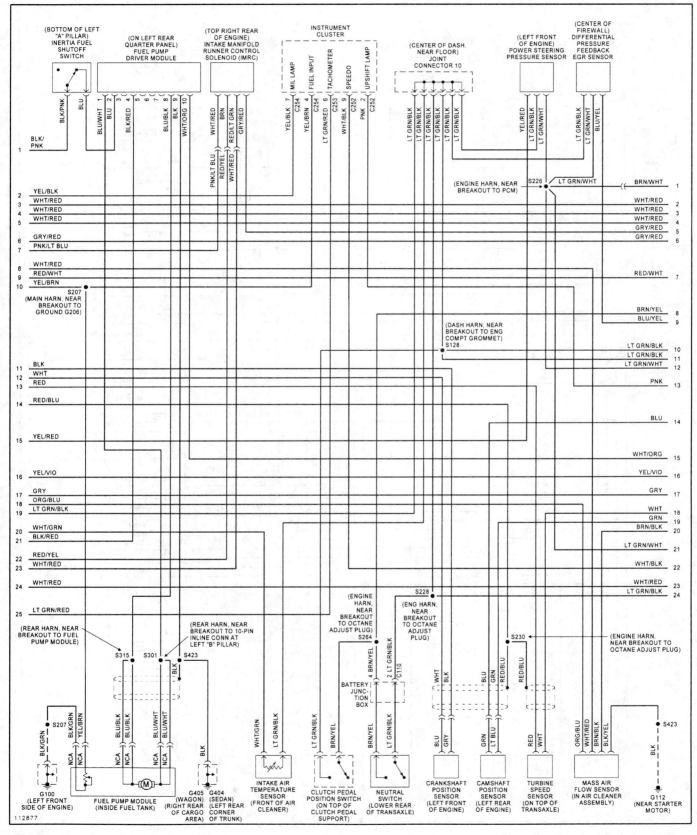

Fig. 51: Escort & Tracer (2.0L – 2 Of 3)

112877

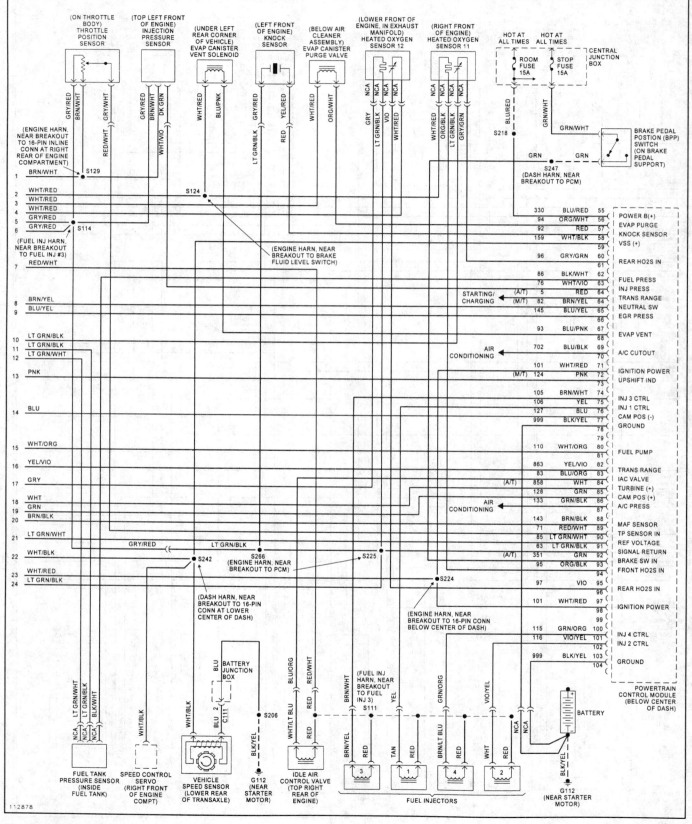

Fig. 52: Escort & Tracer (2.0L – 3 Of 3)

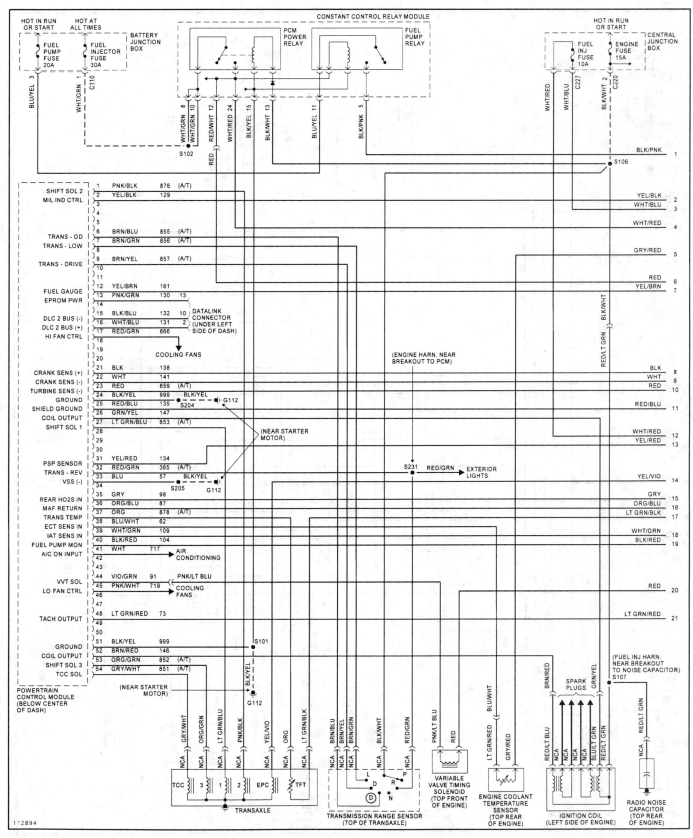

Fig. 53: Escort ZX2 (2.0L – 1 Of 3)

112894

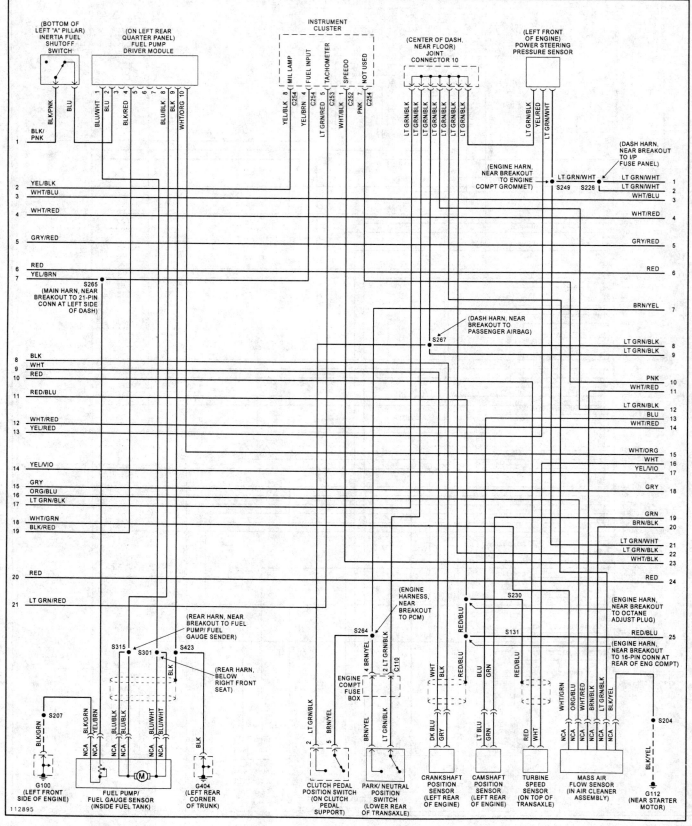

Fig. 54: Escort ZX2 (2.0L – 2 Of 3)

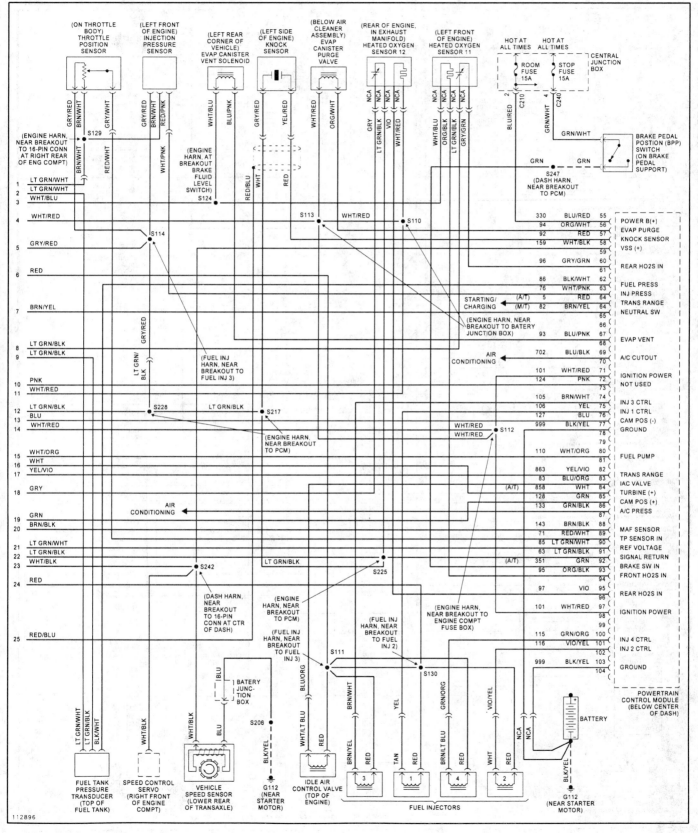

Fig. 55: Escort ZX2 (2.0L – 3 Of 3)

112896

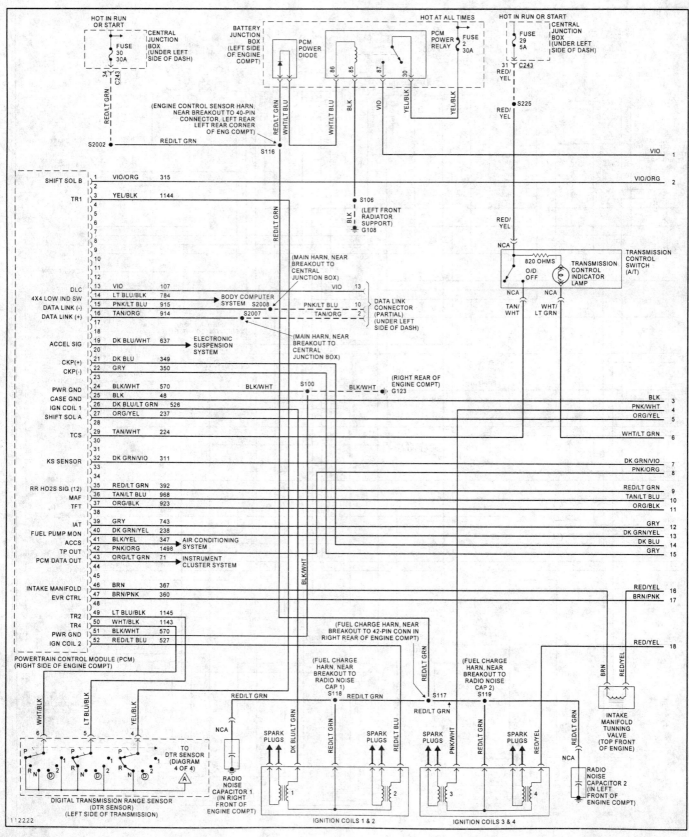

Fig. 56: Expedition (4.6L – 1 Of 4)

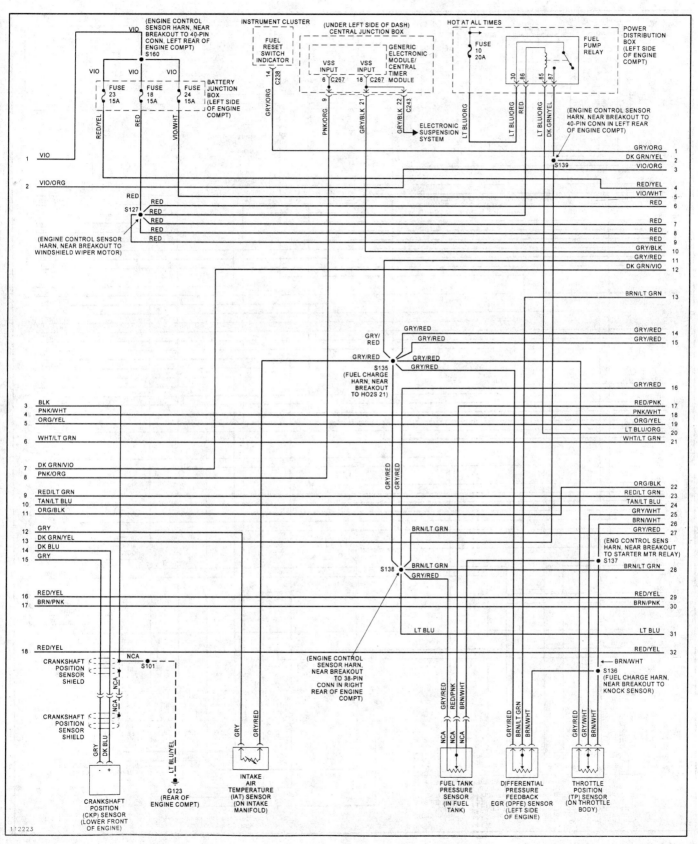

Fig. 57: Expedition (4.6L – 2 Of 4)

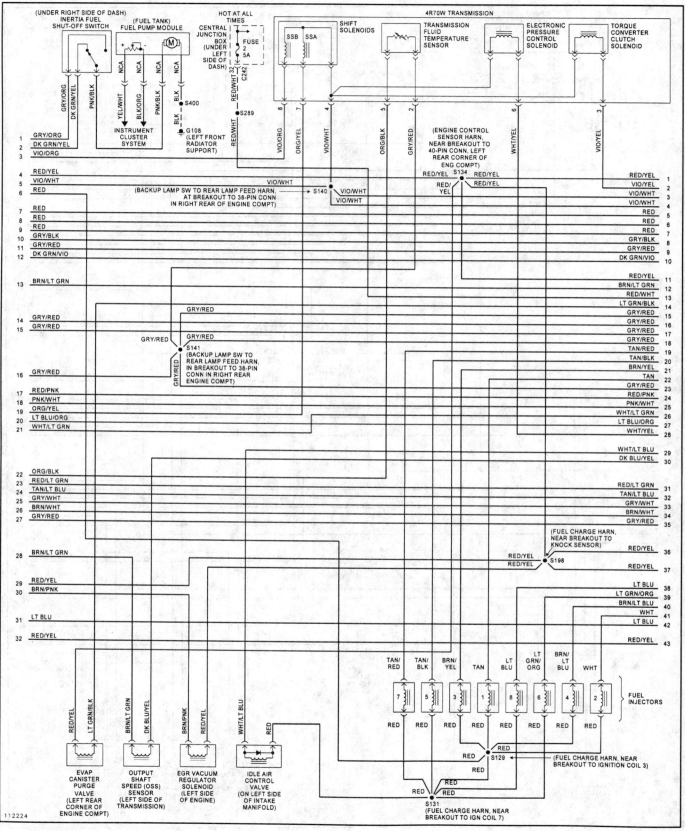

Fig. 58: Expedition (4.6L – 3 Of 4)

112224

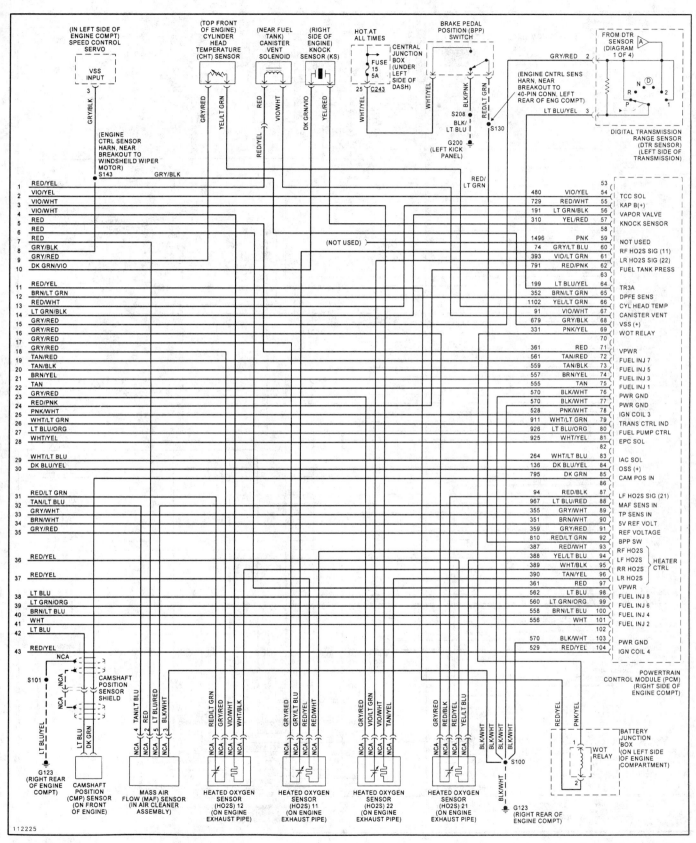

Fig. 59: Expedition (4.6L – 4 Of 4)

112225

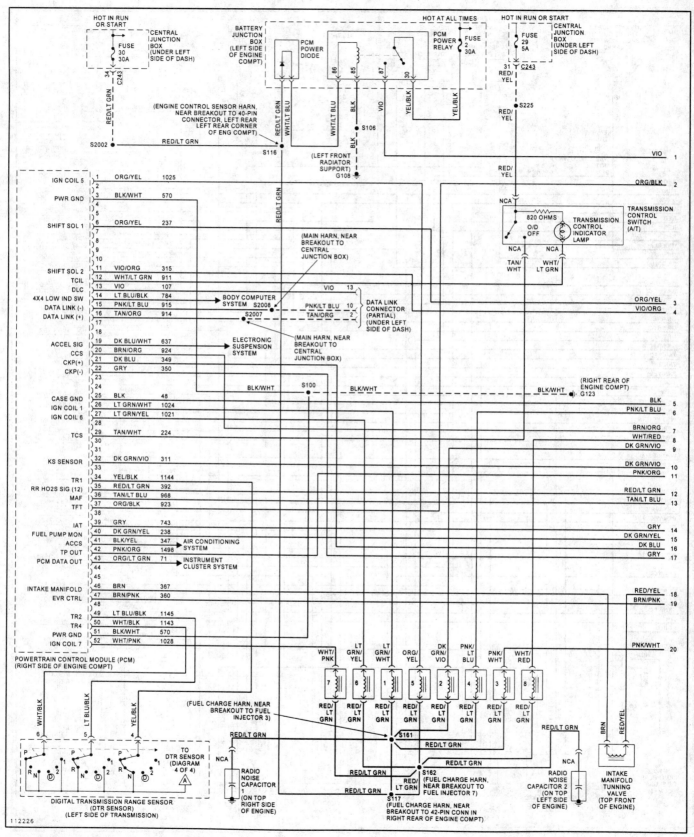

Fig. 60: Expedition & Navigator (5.4L – 1 Of 4)

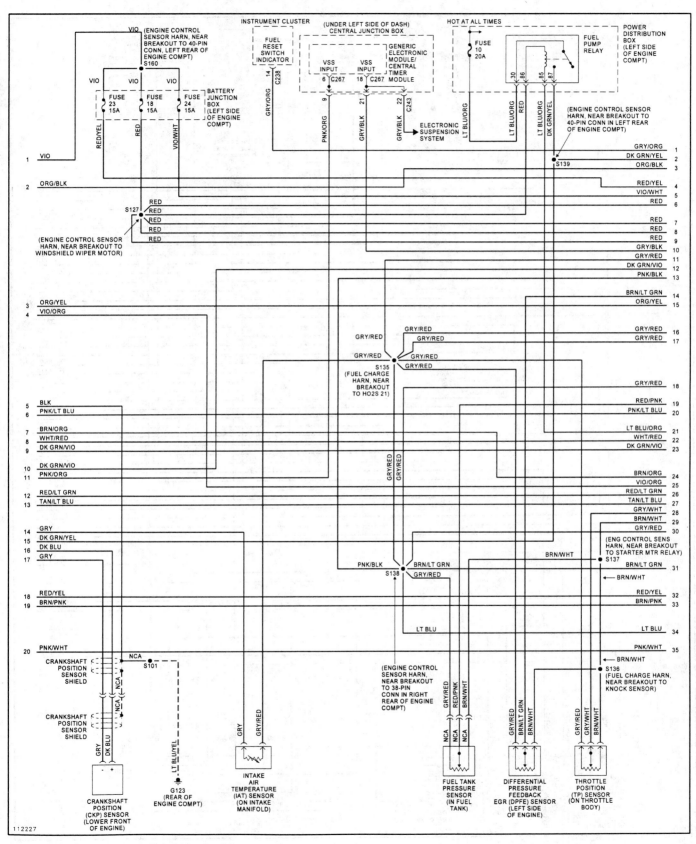

Fig. 61: Expedition & Navigator (5.4L – 2 Of 4)

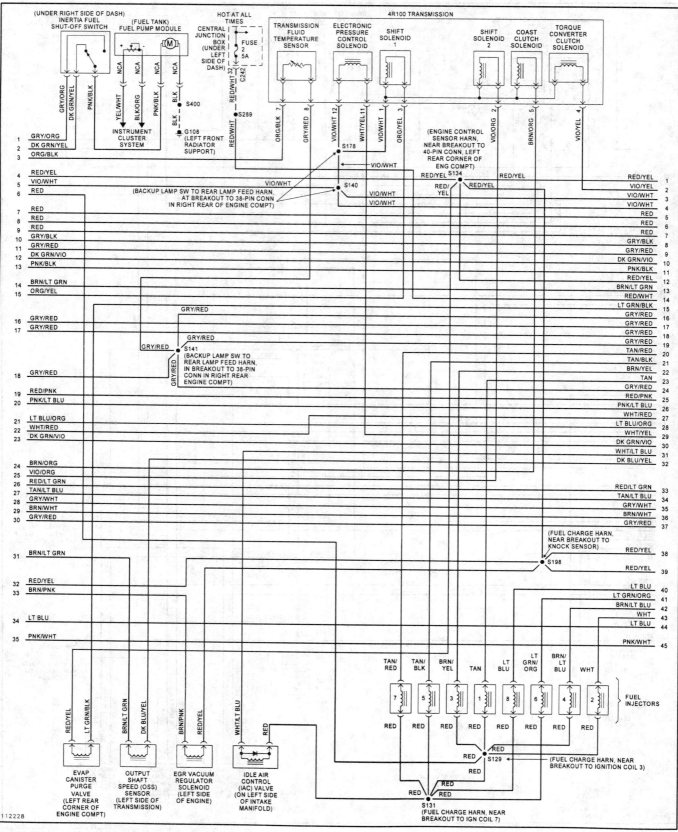

Fig. 62: Expedition & Navigator (5.4L – 3 Of 4)

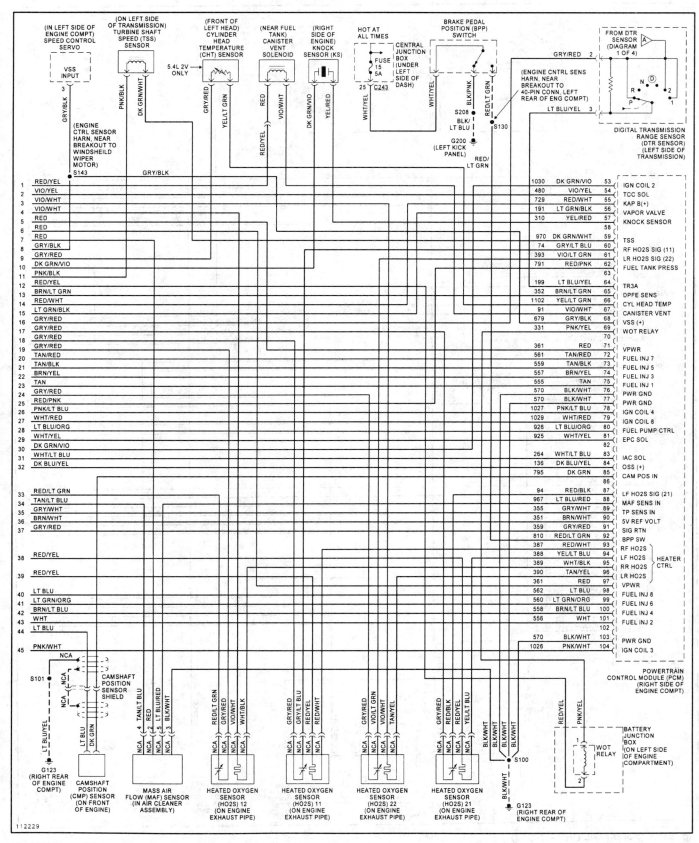

Fig. 63: Expedition & Navigator (5.4L – 4 Of 4)

112229

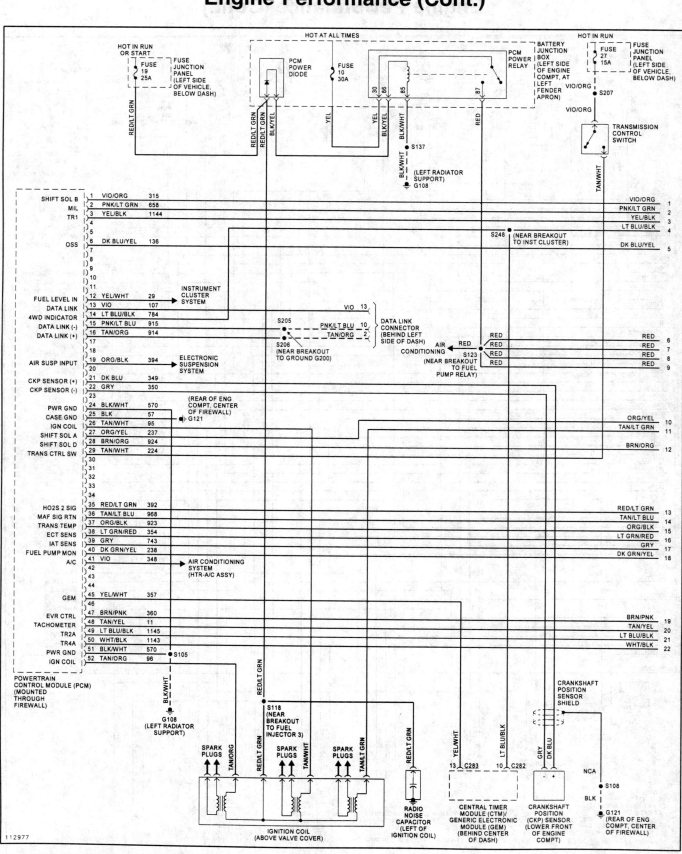

Fig. 64: Explorer (4.0L OHV – 1 Of 4)

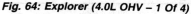

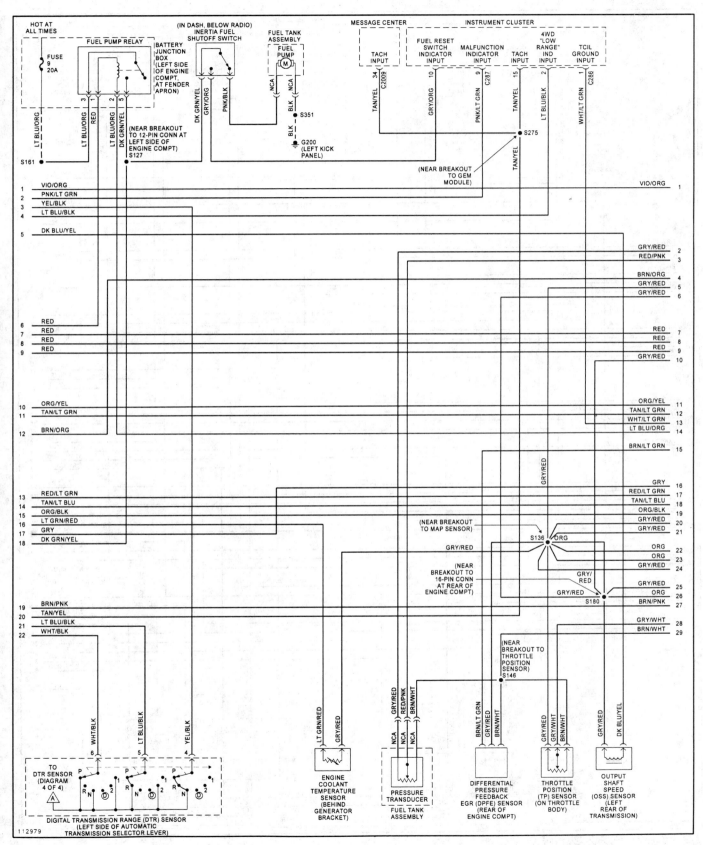

Fig. 65: Explorer (4.0L OHV – 2 Of 4)

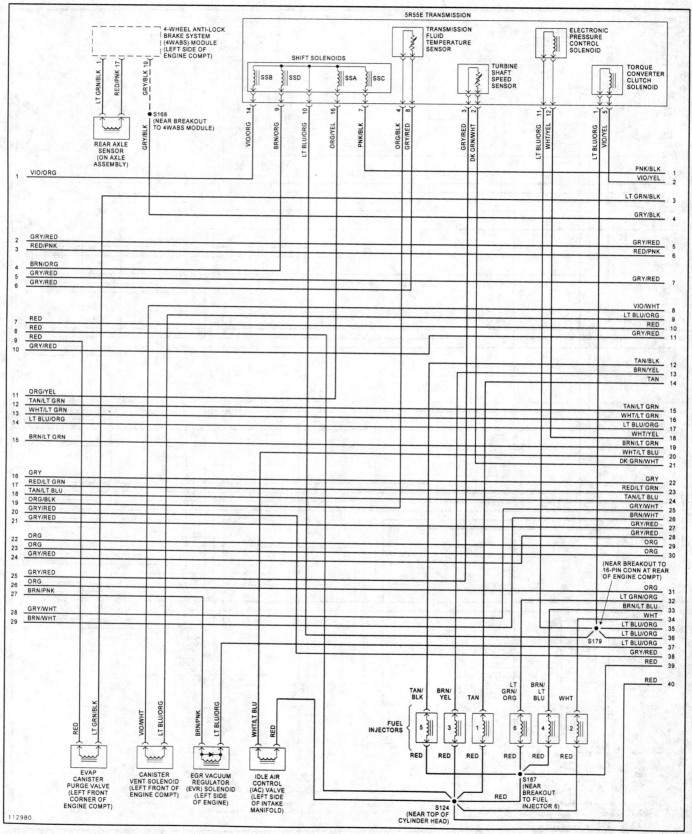

Fig. 66: Explorer (4.0L OHV – 3 Of 4)

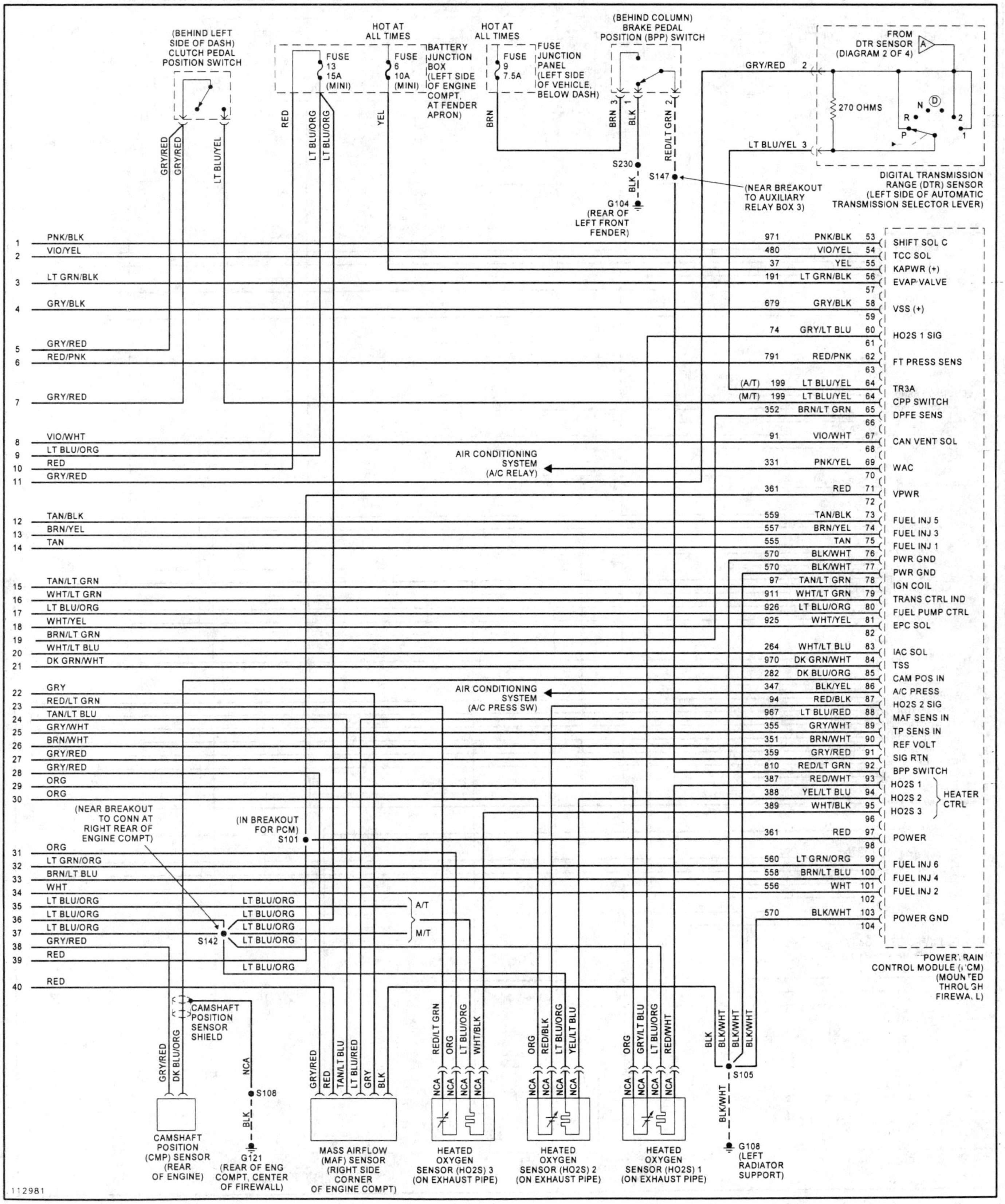

(BEHIND LEFT SIDE OF DASH) CLUTCH PEDAL POSITION SWITCH

HOT AT ALL TIMES

HOT AT ALL TIMES

(BEHIND COLUMN) BRAKE PEDAL POSITION (BPP) SWITCH

FROM DTR SENSOR (DIAGRAM 2 OF 4)

FUSE 13 15A (MINI)
FUSE 6 10A (MINI)
BATTERY JUNCTION BOX (LEFT SIDE OF ENGINE COMPT, AT FENDER APRON)
FUSE 9 7.5A
FUSE JUNCTION PANEL (LEFT SIDE OF VEHICLE, BELOW DASH)

270 OHMS

GRY/RED 2

LT BLU/YEL 3

DIGITAL TRANSMISSION RANGE (DTR) SENSOR (LEFT SIDE OF AUTOMATIC TRANSMISSION SELECTOR LEVER)

S230
S147
BLK
G104 (REAR OF LEFT FRONT FENDER)
(NEAR BREAKOUT TO AUXILIARY RELAY BOX 3)

Pin	Color		No	Color	Pin	Signal
1	PNK/BLK		971	PNK/BLK	53	SHIFT SOL C
2	VIO/YEL		480	VIO/YEL	54	TCC SOL
			37	YEL	55	KAPWR (+)
3	LT GRN/BLK		191	LT GRN/BLK	56	EVAP VALVE
					57	
4	GRY/BLK		679	GRY/BLK	58	VSS (+)
					59	
5	GRY/RED		74	GRY/LT BLU	60	HO2S 1 SIG
6	RED/PNK				61	
			791	RED/PNK	62	FT PRESS SENS
					63	
7	GRY/RED		(A/T) 199	LT BLU/YEL	64	TR3A
			(M/T) 199	LT BLU/YEL	64	CPP SWITCH
			352	BRN/LT GRN	65	DPFE SENS
					66	
8	VIO/WHT		91	VIO/WHT	67	CAN VENT SOL
9	LT BLU/ORG				68	
10	RED		331	PNK/YEL	69	WAC
11	GRY/RED				70	
			361	RED	71	VPWR
					72	
12	TAN/BLK		559	TAN/BLK	73	FUEL INJ 5
13	BRN/YEL		557	BRN/YEL	74	FUEL INJ 3
14	TAN		555	TAN	75	FUEL INJ 1
			570	BLK/WHT	76	PWR GND
			570	BLK/WHT	77	PWR GND
15	TAN/LT GRN		97	TAN/LT GRN	78	IGN COIL
16	WHT/LT GRN		911	WHT/LT GRN	79	TRANS CTRL IND
17	LT BLU/ORG		926	LT BLU/ORG	80	FUEL PUMP CTRL
18	WHT/YEL		925	WHT/YEL	81	EPC SOL
19	BRN/LT GRN				82	
20	WHT/LT BLU		264	WHT/LT BLU	83	IAC SOL
21	DK GRN/WHT		970	DK GRN/WHT	84	TSS
			282	DK BLU/ORG	85	CAM POS IN
22	GRY		347	BLK/YEL	86	A/C PRESS
23	RED/LT GRN		94	RED/BLK	87	HO2S 2 SIG
24	TAN/LT BLU		967	LT BLU/RED	88	MAF SENS IN
25	GRY/WHT		355	GRY/WHT	89	TP SENS IN
26	BRN/WHT		351	BRN/WHT	90	REF VOLT
27	GRY/RED		359	GRY/RED	91	SIG RTN
28	GRY/RED		810	RED/LT GRN	92	BPP SWITCH
29	ORG		387	RED/WHT	93	HO2S 1
30	ORG		388	YEL/LT BLU	94	HO2S 2
			389	WHT/BLK	95	HO2S 3
					96	
31	ORG		361	RED	97	POWER
					98	
32	LT GRN/ORG		560	LT GRN/ORG	99	FUEL INJ 6
33	BRN/LT BLU		558	BRN/LT BLU	100	FUEL INJ 4
34	WHT		556	WHT	101	FUEL INJ 2
35	LT BLU/ORG				102	
36	LT BLU/ORG		570	BLK/WHT	103	POWER GND
37	LT BLU/ORG				104	
38	GRY/RED					
39	RED					
40	RED					

HEATER CTRL (HO2S 1, HO2S 2, HO2S 3)

AIR CONDITIONING SYSTEM (A/C RELAY)

AIR CONDITIONING SYSTEM (A/C PRESS SW)

(NEAR BREAKOUT TO CONN AT RIGHT REAR OF ENGINE COMPT)
(IN BREAKOUT FOR PCM) S101
S142
S108
A/T
M/T

POWERTRAIN CONTROL MODULE (PCM) (MOUNTED THROUGH FIREWALL)

CAMSHAFT POSITION SENSOR SHIELD

G121 (REAR OF ENG COMPT, CENTER OF FIREWALL)

S105
G108 (LEFT RADIATOR SUPPORT)

CAMSHAFT POSITION (CMP) SENSOR (REAR OF ENGINE)

MASS AIRFLOW (MAF) SENSOR (RIGHT SIDE CORNER OF ENGINE COMPT)

HEATED OXYGEN SENSOR (HO2S) 3 (ON EXHAUST PIPE)

HEATED OXYGEN SENSOR (HO2S) 2 (ON EXHAUST PIPE)

HEATED OXYGEN SENSOR (HO2S) 1 (ON EXHAUST PIPE)

112981

Fig. 67: Explorer (4.0L OHV – 4 Of 4)

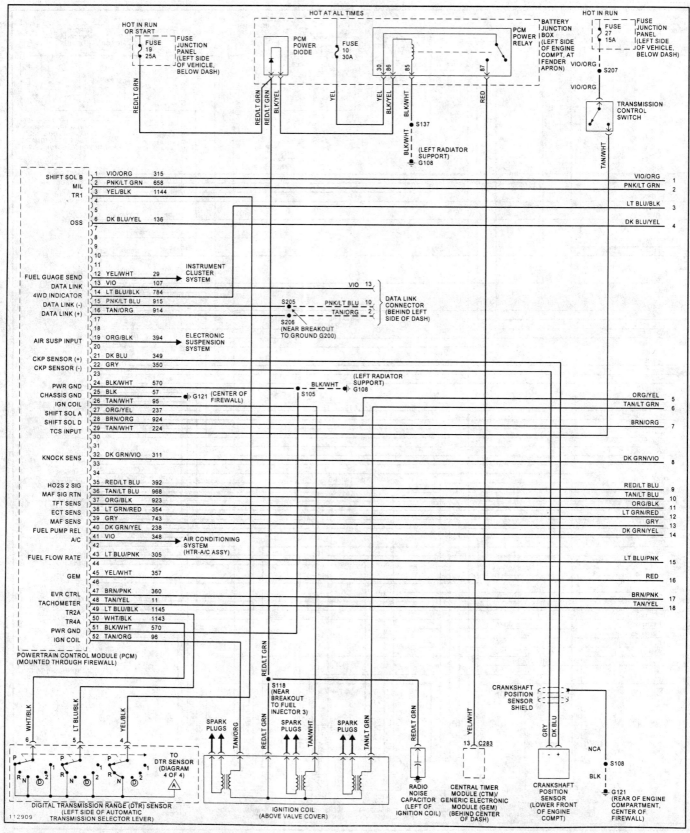

Fig. 68: Explorer & Mountaineer (4.0L SOHC – 1 Of 4)

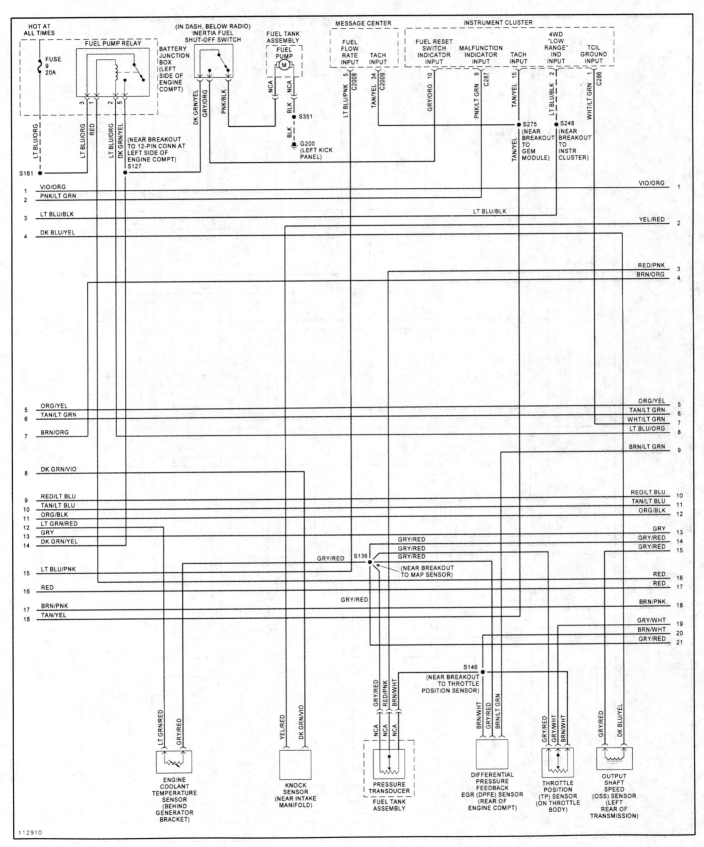

Fig. 69: Explorer & Mountaineer (4.0L SOHC – 2 Of 4)

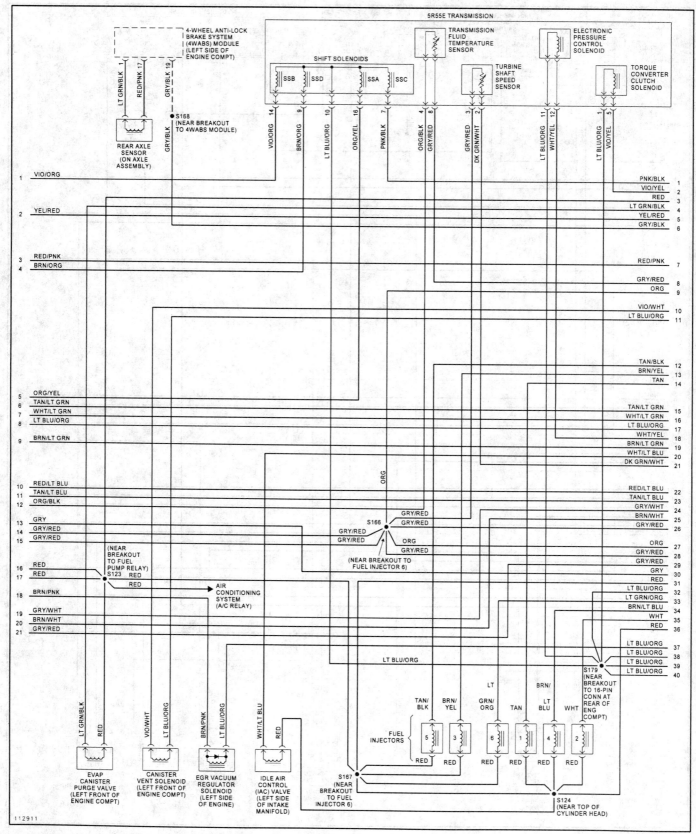

Fig. 70: Explorer & Mountaineer (4.0L SOHC – 3 Of 4)

HOT AT ALL TIMES

FUSE 13 15A (MINI)

FUSE 6 10A (MINI)

BATTERY JUNCTION BOX (LEFT SIDE OF ENGINE COMPT, AT FENDER APRON)

HOT AT ALL TIMES

FUSE 9 7.5A

FUSE JUNCTION PANEL (LEFT SIDE OF VEHICLE, BELOW DASH)

(BEHIND COLUMN) BRAKE PEDAL POSITION SWITCH

FROM DTR SENSOR (DIAGRAM 1 OF 4) A

GRY/RED 2

270 OHMS

N D
R 2
P 1

DIGITAL TRANSMISSION RANGE (DTR) SENSOR (LEFT SIDE OF AUTOMATIC TRANSMISSION SELECTOR LEVER)

RED

LT BLU/ORG

LT BLU/ORG

YEL

BRN

BRN 3

BLK 1

RED/LT GRN 2

S230

S147

LT BLU/YEL 3

BLK

RED/LT GRN

G104 (REAR OF LEFT FRONT FENDER)

(NEAR BREAKOUT TO AUXILIARY RELAY BOX 3)

#	wire		971	PNK/BLK	53	SHIFT SOL C
1	PNK/BLK		480	VIO/YEL	54	TCC SOL
2	VIO/YEL		37	YEL	55	KAPWR (+)
3	RED		191	LT GRN/BLK	56	EVAP
4	LT GRN/BLK		310	YEL/RED	57	KNOCK SENS
5	YEL/RED		679	GRY/BLK	58	VSS (+)
6	GRY/BLK				59	
			74	GRY/LT BLU	60	HO2S 1 SIG
			393	VIO/LT GRN	61	HO2S 4 SIG
7	RED/PNK		791	RED/PNK	62	FT PRESS SENS
					63	
8	GRY/RED		199	LT BLU/YEL	64	TR3A
9	ORG		352	BRN/LT GRN	65	DPFE SENS
					66	
10	VIO/WHT		91	VIO/WHT	67	CAN VENT SOL
11	LT BLU/ORG				68	
			331	PNK/YEL	69	WAC
					70	
			361	RED	71	VPWR
					72	
12	TAN/BLK		559	TAN/BLK	73	FUEL INJ 5
13	BRN/YEL		557	BRN/YEL	74	FUEL INJ 3
14	TAN		555	TAN	75	FUEL INJ 1
			570	BLK/WHT	76	PWR GND
			570	BLK/WHT	77	PWR GND
15	TAN/LT GRN		97	TAN/LT GRN	78	IGN COIL
16	WHT/LT GRN		911	WHT/LT GRN	79	TRANS CTRL IND
17	LT BLU/ORG		926	LT BLU/ORG	80	FUEL PUMP REL
18	WHT/YEL		925	WHT/YEL	81	EPC SOL
19	BRN/LT GRN				82	
20	WHT/LT BLU		264	WHT/LT BLU	83	IAC SOL
21	DK GRN/WHT		970	DK GRN/WHT	84	TSS
			282	DK BLU/ORG	85	CMP SENS
			347	BLK/YEL	86	A/C PRESS
22	RED/LT BLU		94	RED/BLK	87	HO2S 2 SIG
23	TAN/LT BLU		967	LT BLU/RED	88	MAF SENS IN
24	GRY/WHT		355	GRY/WHT	89	TP SENS IN
25	BRN/WHT		351	BRN/WHT	90	REF VOLT
26	GRY/RED		359	GRY/RED	91	SIG RTN
			810	RED/LT GRN	92	BPP SWITCH
27	ORG		387	RED/WHT	93	HO2S 1
28	GRY/RED		388	YEL/LT BLU	94	HO2S 2
29	GRY/RED		389	WHT/BLK	95	HO2S 3
30	GRY		390	TAN/YEL	96	HO2S 4
31	RED		361	RED	97	POWER
32	LT BLU/ORG				98	
33	LT GRN/ORG		560	LT GRN/ORG	99	FUEL INJ 6
34	BRN/LT BLU		558	BRN/LT BLU	100	FUEL INJ 4
35	WHT		556	WHT	101	FUEL INJ 2
36	RED				102	
			570	BLK/WHT	103	POWER GND
37	LT BLU/ORG				104	
38	LT BLU/ORG					
39	LT BLU/ORG					
40	LT BLU/ORG					

HEATER CTRL

(NEAR BREAKOUT TO 16-PIN CONN AT REAR OF ENGINE COMPT)

GRY/RED

S180

GRY/RED

ORG ORG
ORG ORG

ORG

AIR CONDITIONING SYSTEM (A/C RELAY)

AIR CONDITIONING SYSTEM (A/C PRESS SW)

(IN BREAKOUT FOR PCM)

S101

S142

(NEAR BREAKOUT TO CONN AT RIGHT REAR OF ENGINE COMPT)

POWERTRAIN CONTROL MODULE (PCM) (MOUNTED THROUGH FIREWALL)

DK BLU/ORG
GRY/RED

CAMSHAFT POSITION (CMP) SENSOR (REAR OF ENGINE)

GRY
TAN/LT BLU
RED
LT BLU/RED
GRY/RED
BLK

MASS AIRFLOW (MAF) SENSOR (RIGHT SIDE OF ENGINE COMPT)

RED/LT BLU
ORG
LT BLU/ORG
WHT/BLK

NCA NCA NCA NCA

HEATED OXYGEN SENSOR (HO2S) 3 (ON EXHAUST PIPE)

ORG
GRY/LT BLU
LT BLU/ORG
RED/WHT

NCA NCA NCA NCA

HEATED OXYGEN SENSOR (HO2S) 1 (ON EXHAUST PIPE)

ORG
VIO/LT GRN
LT BLU/ORG
TAN/YEL

NCA NCA NCA NCA

HEATED OXYGEN SENSOR (HO2S) 4 (ON EXHAUST PIPE)

ORG
RED/BLK
LT BLU/ORG
YEL/LT BLU

NCA NCA NCA NCA

HEATED OXYGEN SENSOR (HO2S) 2 (ON EXHAUST PIPE)

BLK
BLK/WHT
BLK/WHT
BLK/WHT

S105

BLK/WHT

G108 (LEFT RADIATOR SUPPORT)

112912

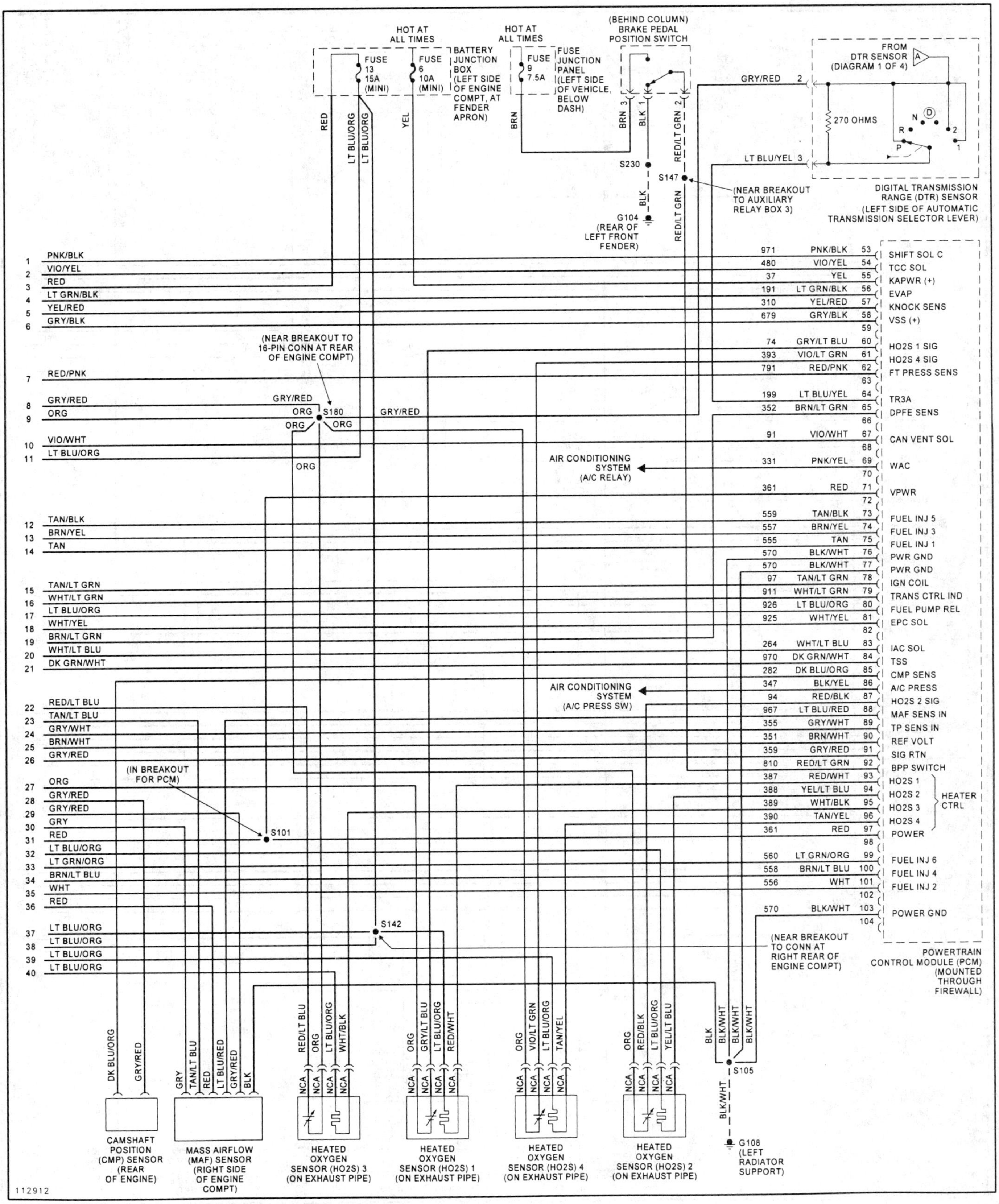

Fig. 71: Explorer & Mountaineer (4.0L SOHC – 4 Of 4)

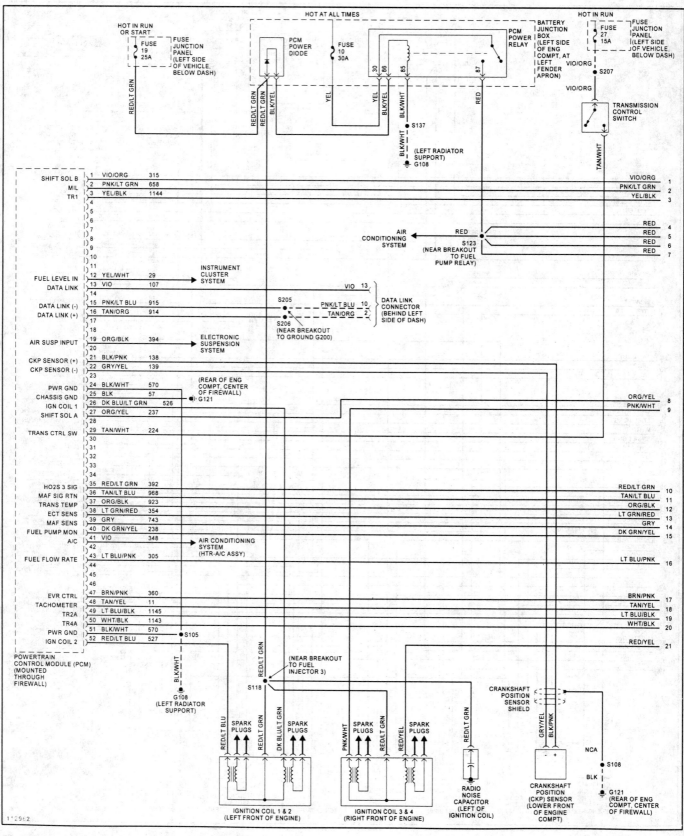

Fig. 72: Explorer & Mountaineer (5.0L – 1 Of 4)

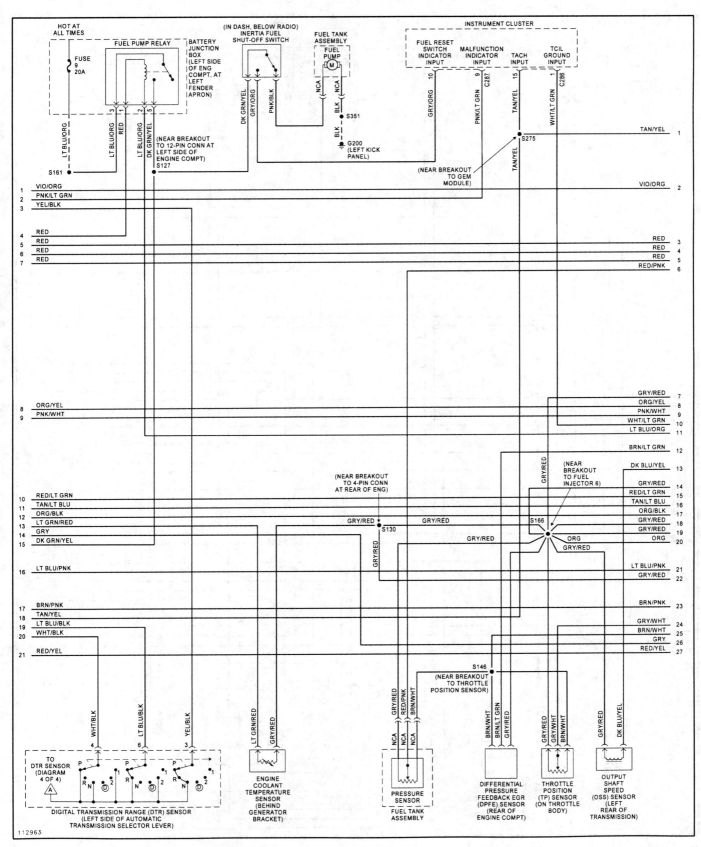

Fig. 73: Explorer & Mountaineer (5.0L – 2 Of 4)

112963

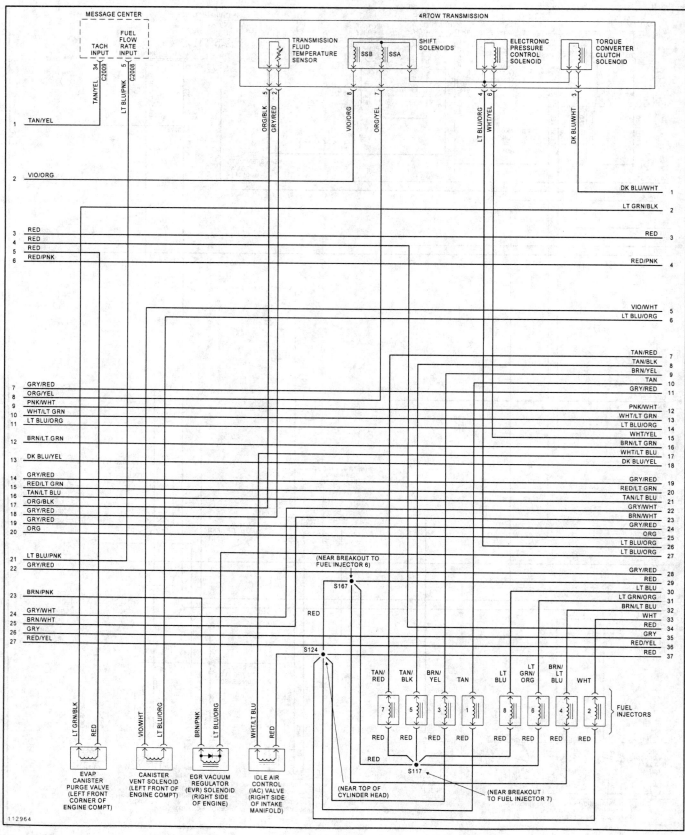

Fig. 74: Explorer & Mountaineer (5.0L – 3 Of 4)

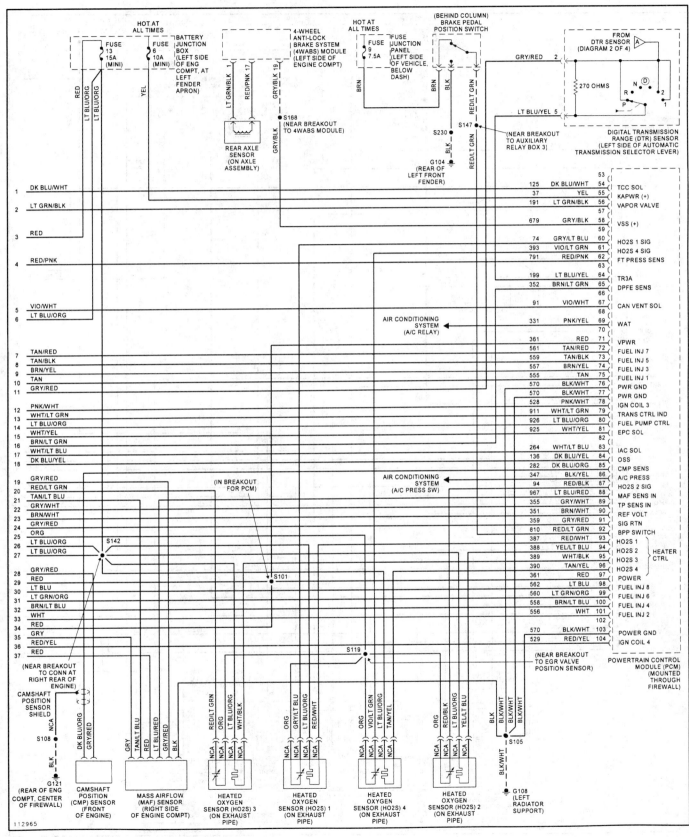

Fig. 75: Explorer & Mountaineer (5.0L – 4 Of 4)

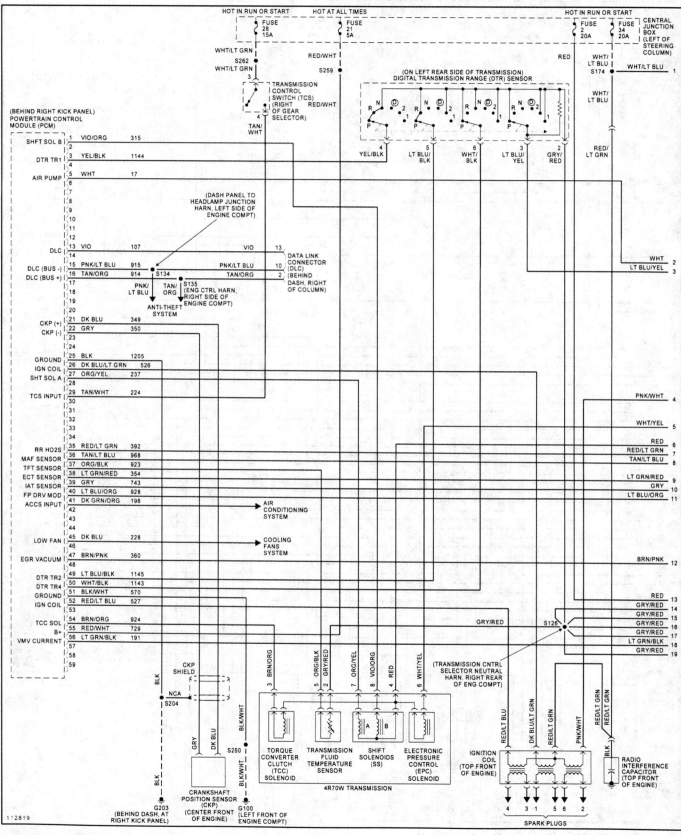

Fig. 76: Mustang (3.8L – 1 Of 3)

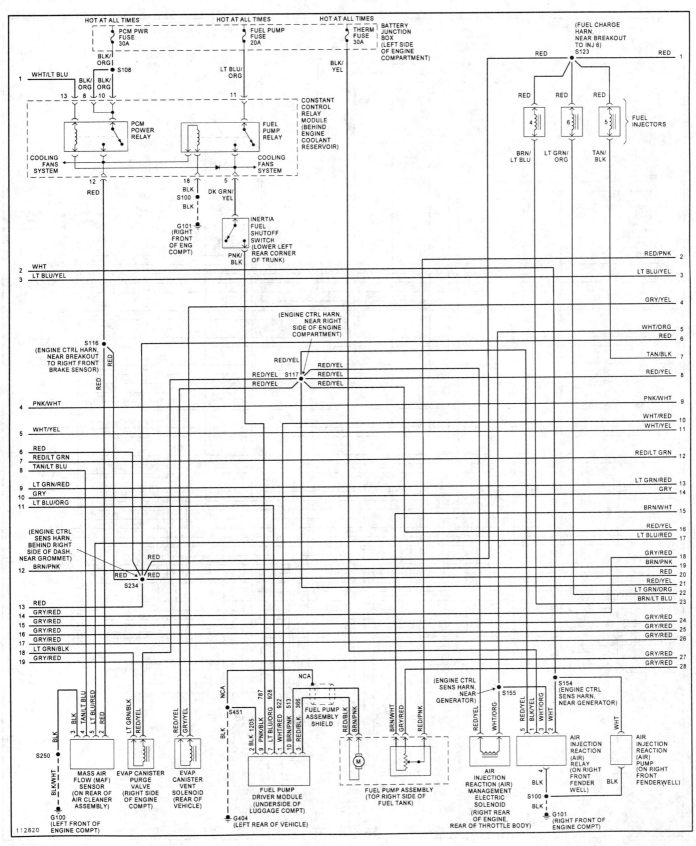

Fig. 77: Mustang (3.8L – 2 Of 3)

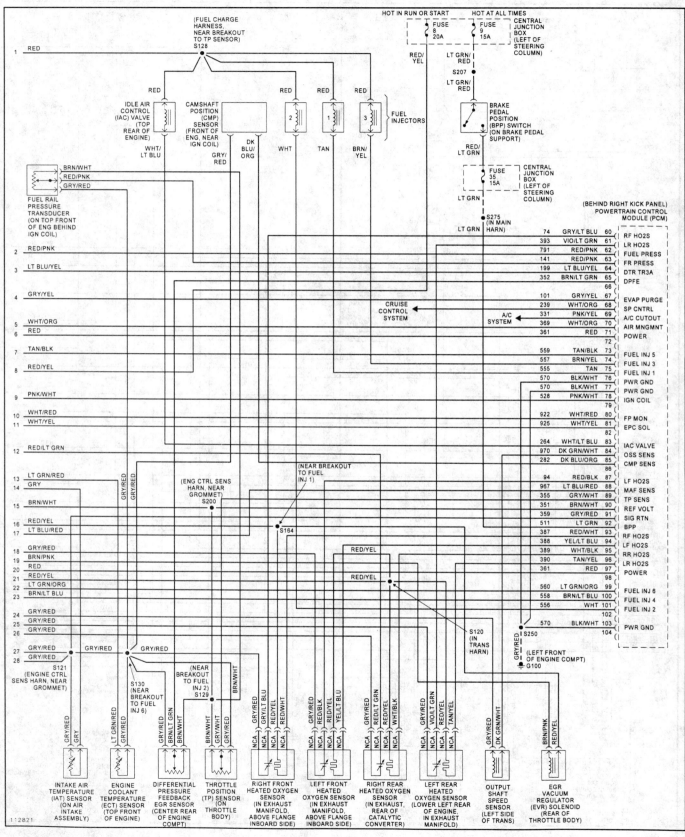

Fig. 78: Mustang (3.8L – 3 Of 3)

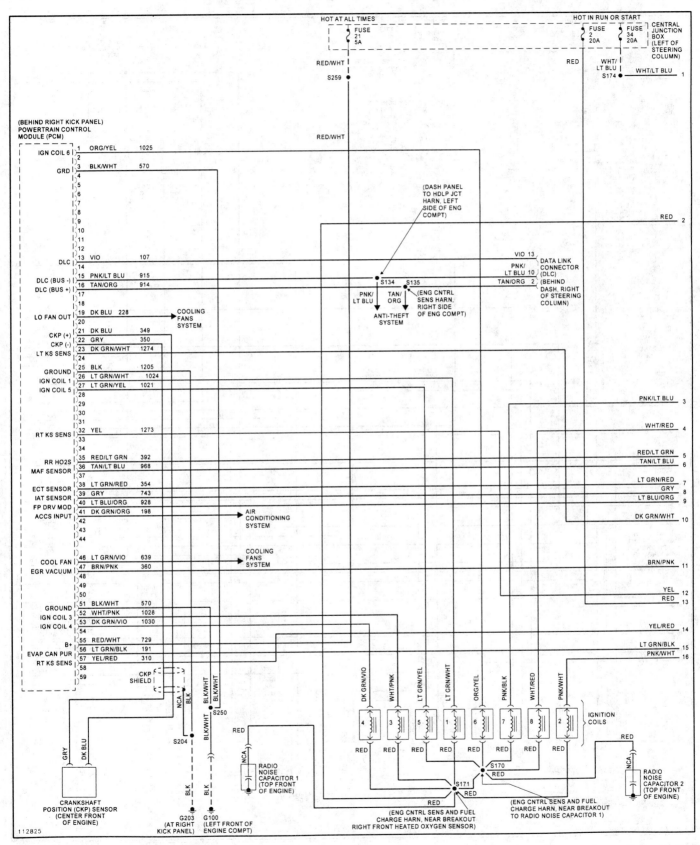

Fig. 79: Mustang (4.6L DOHC – 1 Of 3)

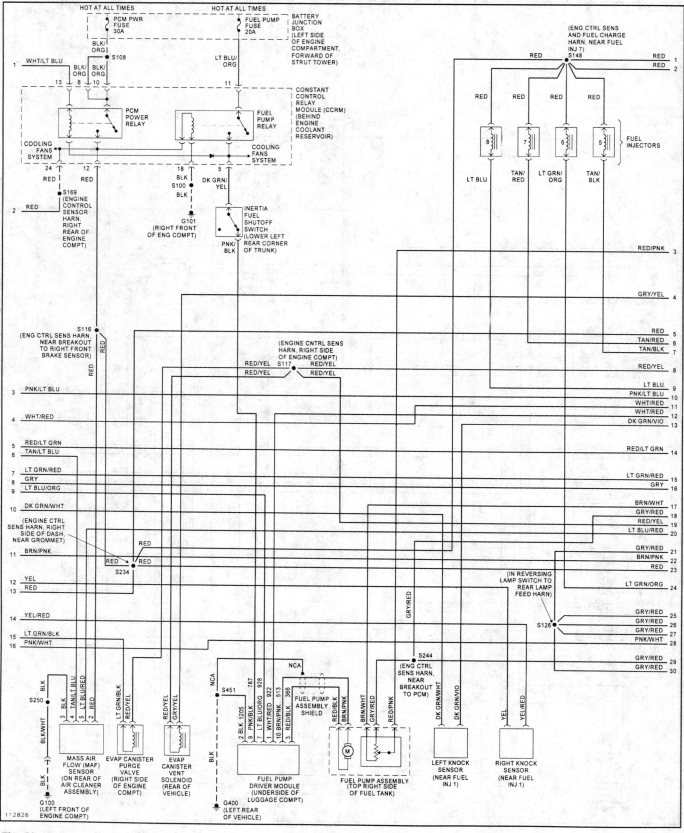

Fig. 80: Mustang (4.6L DOHC – 2 Of 3)

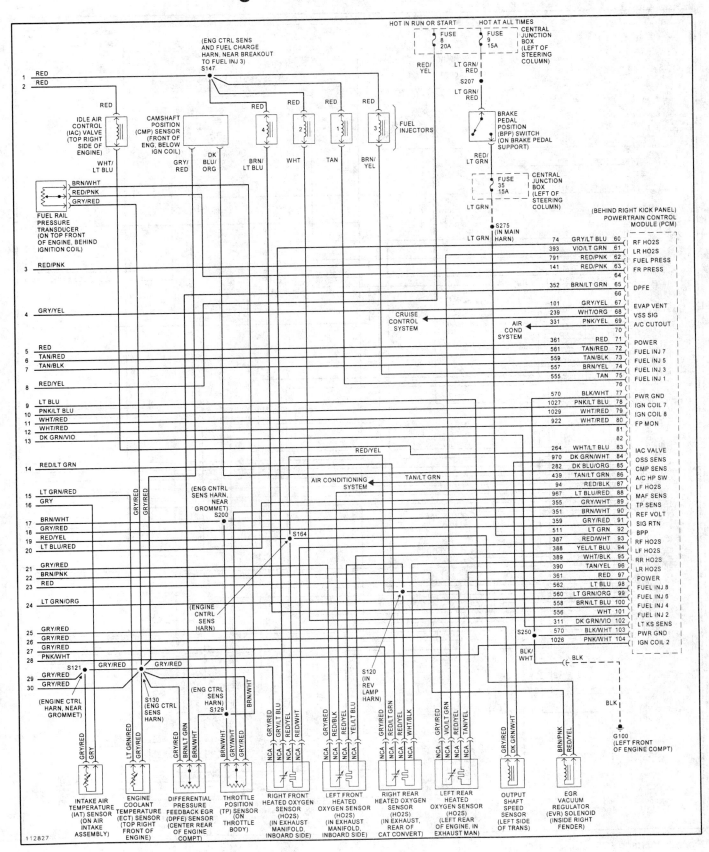

Fig. 81: Mustang (4.6L DOHC – 3 Of 3)

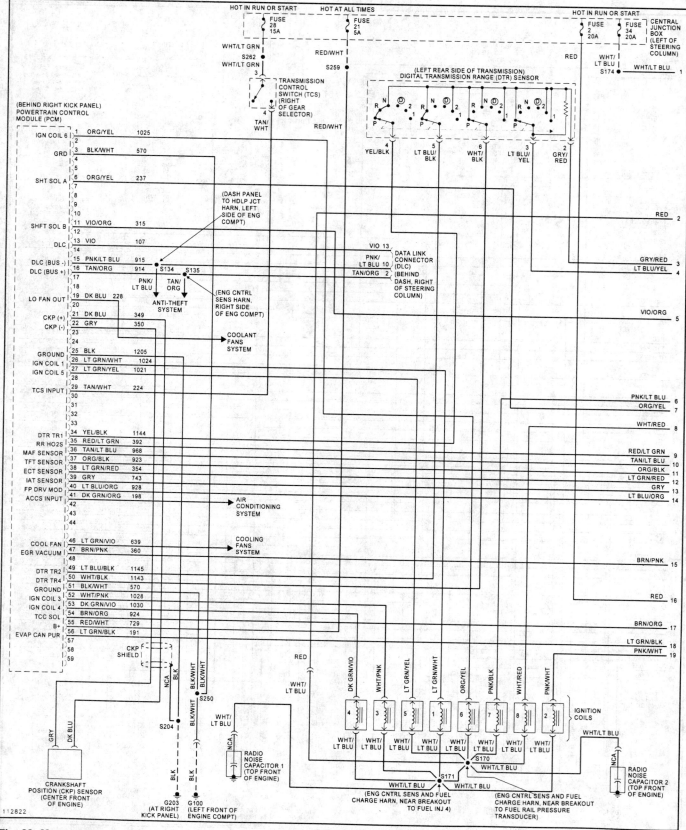

Fig. 82: Mustang (4.6L SOHC – 1 Of 3)

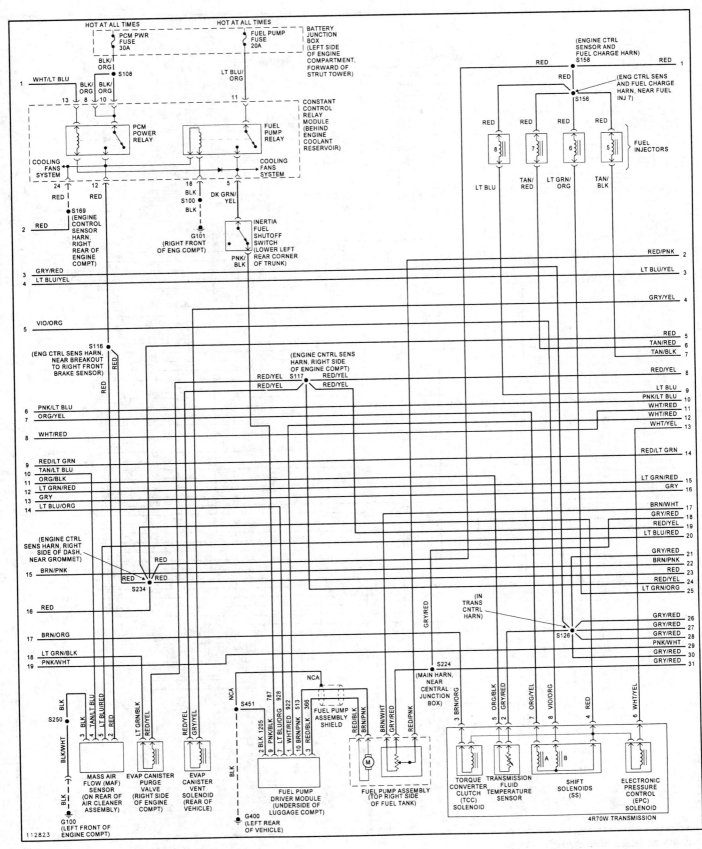

Fig. 83: Mustang (4.6L SOHC – 2 Of 3)

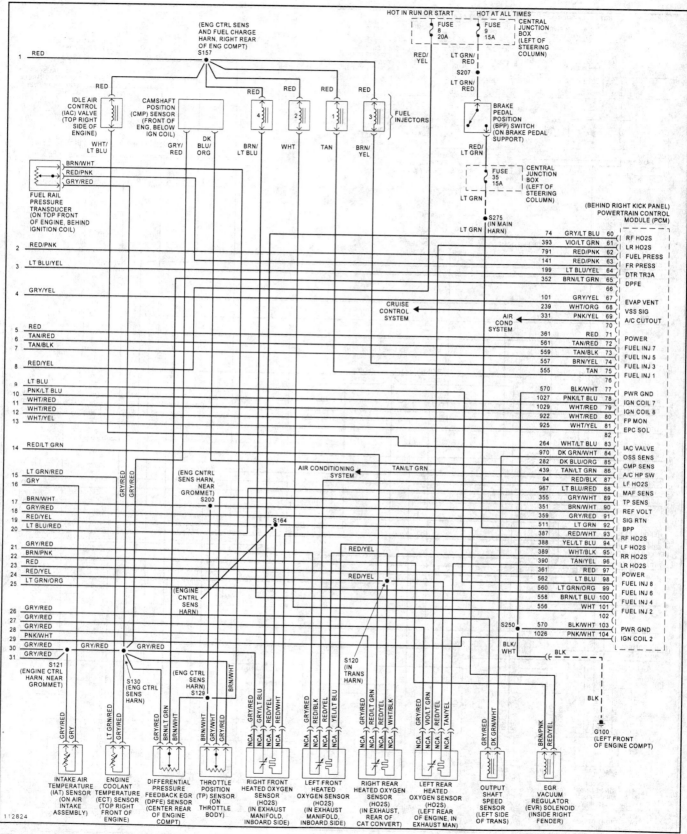

Fig. 84: Mustang (4.6L SOHC – 3 Of 3)

112824

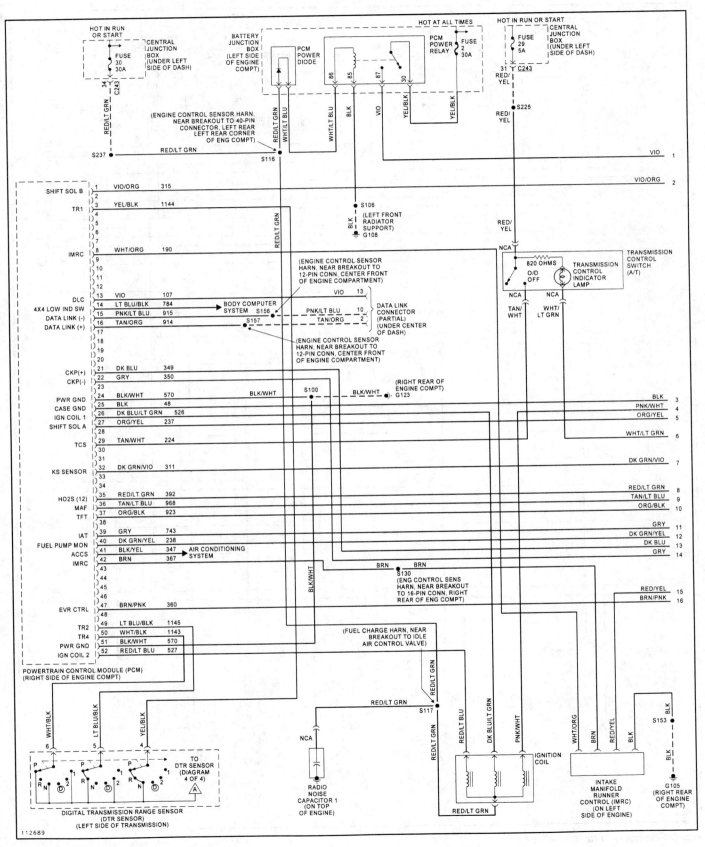

Fig. 85: Pickup – F150 (4.2L – 1 Of 4)

112689

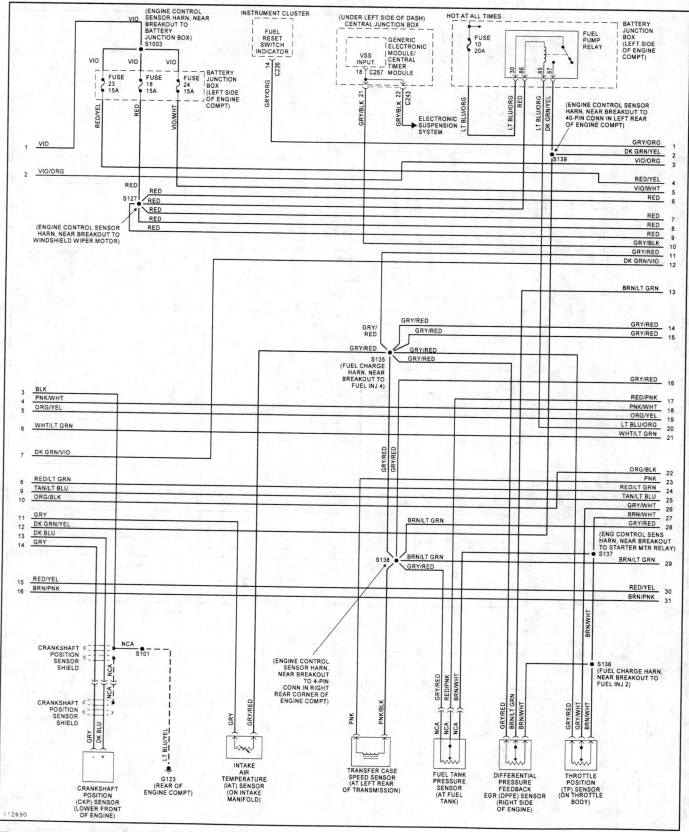

Fig. 86: Pickup – F150 (4.2L – 2 Of 4)

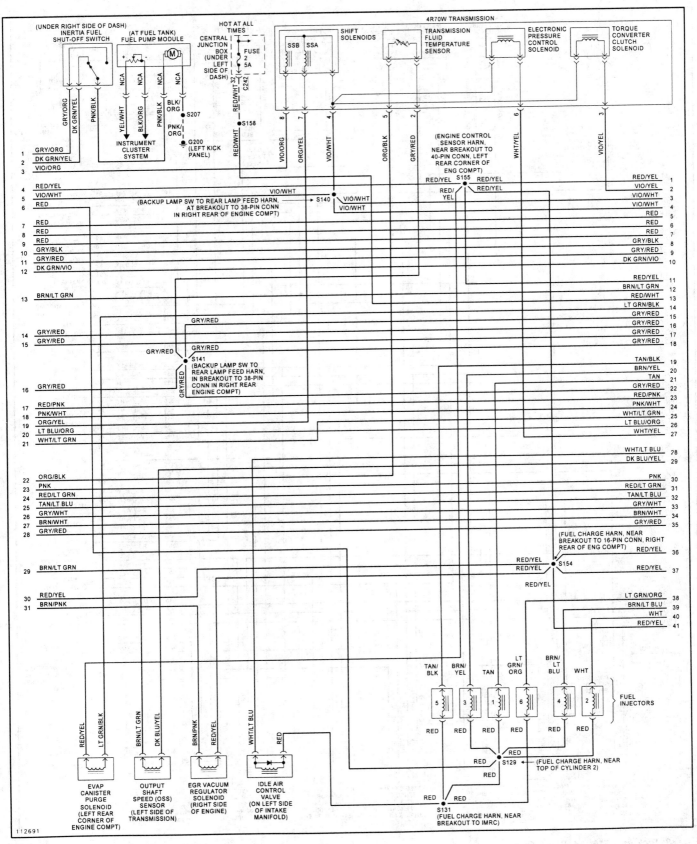

Fig. 87: Pickup – F150 (4.2L – 3 Of 4)

112691

(IN LEFT SIDE OF ENGINE COMPT) SPEED CONTROL SERVO

(ON LEFT SIDE OF ENGINE) CYLINDER HEAD TEMPERATURE SENSOR

(NEAR FUEL TANK) CANISTER VENT SOLENOID

(RIGHT SIDE OF ENGINE) KNOCK SENSOR (KS)

HOT IN START

HOT AT ALL TIMES

CENTRAL JUNCTION BOX (UNDER LEFT SIDE OF DASH)

BRAKE PEDAL POSITION (BPP) SWITCH

FROM DTR SENSOR (DIAGRAM 1 OF 4)

VSS INPUT

3

GRY/BLK

(ENGINE CTRL SENSOR HARN, NEAR BREAKOUT TO WINDSHIELD WIPER MOTOR)

GRY/RED   YEL/LT GRN

RED   VIO/WHT

DK GRN/VIO   YEL/RED

FUSE 20 5A   FUSE 15 5A

4   25   C243   RED/BLK   WHT/YEL   WHT/YEL   BLK/PNK   RED/LT GRN

GRY/RED   2

S208   BLK/LT BLU   S297   LT BLU/YEL   3

(MAIN HARN, NEAR BREAKOUT TO INSTRUMENT CLUSTER)

RED/YEL   LT BLU/YEL

G200 (LEFT KICK PANEL)

M/T   A/T

RED/LT GRN

DIGITAL TRANSMISSION RANGE SENSOR (DTR SENSOR) (LEFT SIDE OF TRANSMISSION)

S143   GRY/BLK

#	Wire		#	Wire	Signal
1	RED/YEL		53		
2	VIO/YEL		54	VIO/YEL 480	TCC SOL
3	VIO/WHT		55	RED/WHT 729	KAP B(+)
4	VIO/WHT		56	LT GRN/BLK 191	VAPOR VALVE
5	RED		57	YEL/RED 310	KNOCK SENSOR
6	RED		58		
7	RED		59	PNK 1496	SPEED SENSOR
8	GRY/BLK		60	GRY/LT BLU 74	RF HO2S SIG (11)
9	GRY/RED		61	VIO/LT GRN 393	LR HO2S SIG (22)
10	DK GRN/VIO		62	RED/PNK 791	FUEL TANK PRESS
11	RED/YEL		63		
12	BRN/LT GRN		64	LT BLU/YEL 199	TR3A (A/T) BPP (M/T)
13	RED/WHT		65	BRN/LT GRN 352	DPFE SENS
14	LT GRN/BLK		66	YEL/LT GRN 1102	CYL HEAD TEMP
15	GRY/RED		67	VIO/WHT 91	CANISTER VENT
16	GRY/RED		68	GRY/BLK 679	VSS (+)
17	GRY/RED		69	PNK/YEL 331	WOT RELAY
18	GRY/RED		70		
19	TAN/BLK		71	RED 361	VPWR
20	BRN/YEL		72		
21	TAN		73	TAN/BLK 559	FUEL INJ 5
22	GRY/RED		74	BRN/YEL 557	FUEL INJ 3
23	RED/PNK		75	TAN 555	FUEL INJ 1
24	PNK/WHT		76	BLK/WHT 570	PWR GND
25	WHT/LT GRN		77	BLK/WHT 570	PWR GND
26	LT BLU/ORG		78	PNK/WHT 528	IGN COIL 3
27	WHT/YEL		79	WHT/LT GRN 911	TRANS CTRL IND
28	WHT/LT BLU		80	LT BLU/ORG 926	FUEL PUMP CTRL
29	DK BLU/YEL		81	WHT/YEL 925	EPC SOL
30	PNK		82		
31	RED/LT GRN		83	WHT/LT BLU 264	IAC SOL
32	TAN/LT BLU		84	DK BLU/YEL 136	OSS (+)
33	GRY/WHT		85	DK GRN 795	CAM POS IN
34	BRN/WHT		86		
35	GRY/RED		87	RED/BLK 94	LF HO2S SIG (21)
			88	LT BLU/RED 967	MAF SENS IN
			89	GRY/WHT 355	TP SENS IN
			90	BRN/WHT 351	5V REF VOLT
			91	GRY/RED 359	REF VOLTAGE
36	RED/YEL		92	RED/LT GRN 810	BPP SW
			93	RED/WHT 387	RF HO2S
37	RED/YEL		94	YEL/LT BLU 388	LF HO2S
			95	WHT/BLK 389	RR HO2S
			96	TAN/YEL 390	LR HO2S
			97	RED 361	VPWR
38	LT GRN/ORG		98		
39	BRN/LT BLU		99	LT GRN/ORG 560	FUEL INJ 6
40	WHT		100	BRN/LT BLU 558	FUEL INJ 4
41	RED/YEL		101	WHT 556	FUEL INJ 2
			102		
			103	BLK/WHT 570	PWR GND
			104	RED/YEL 529	NOT USED

HEATER CTRL

(NOT USED)

POWERTRAIN CONTROL MODULE (PCM) (RIGHT SIDE OF ENGINE COMPT)

S101   NCA   NCA   NCA

CAMSHAFT POSITION SENSOR SHIELD

S100

LT BLU/YEL   RED/YEL   BLK/WHT

G123 (RIGHT REAR OF ENGINE COMPT)

BLK/WHT   RED/YEL   DK GRN

CAMSHAFT POSITION (CMP) SENSOR (ON FRONT OF ENGINE)

4 TAN/LT BLU   2 RED   5 LT BLU/RED   3 BLK/WHT
NCA NCA NCA NCA

MASS AIR FLOW (MAF) SENSOR (IN AIR CLEANER ASSEMBLY)

RED/LT GRN   GRY/RED   VIO/WHT   WHT/BLK
NCA NCA NCA NCA

HEATED OXYGEN SENSOR (HO2S) 12 (ON ENGINE EXHAUST PIPE)

GRY/RED   GRY/LT BLU   RED/YEL   RED/WHT
NCA NCA NCA NCA

HEATED OXYGEN SENSOR (HO2S) 11 (ON ENGINE EXHAUST PIPE)

GRY/RED   VIO/LT GRN   VIO/WHT   TAN/YEL
NCA NCA NCA NCA

HEATED OXYGEN SENSOR (HO2S) 22 (ON ENGINE EXHAUST PIPE)

GRY/RED   RED/BLK   RED/YEL   YEL/LT BLU
NCA NCA NCA NCA

HEATED OXYGEN SENSOR (HO2S) 21 (ON ENGINE EXHAUST PIPE)

BLK/WHT   BLK/WHT   BLK/WHT   S100

BLK/WHT   G123 (RIGHT REAR OF ENGINE COMPT)

RED/YEL   PNK/YEL

1   WOT RELAY   2

BATTERY JUNCTION BOX (ON LEFT SIDE OF ENGINE COMPARTMENT)

112692

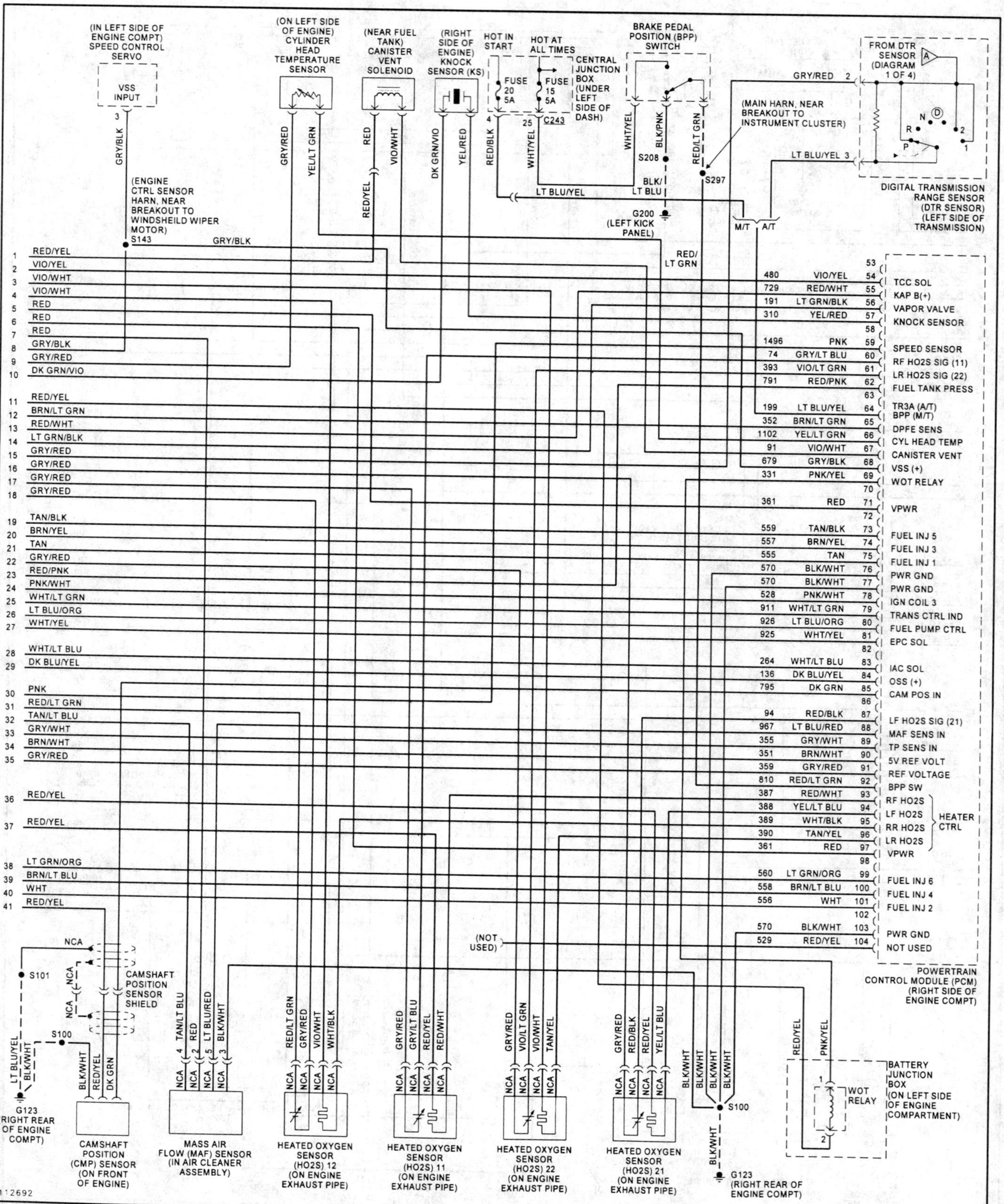

Fig. 88: Pickup – F150 (4.2L – 4 Of 4)

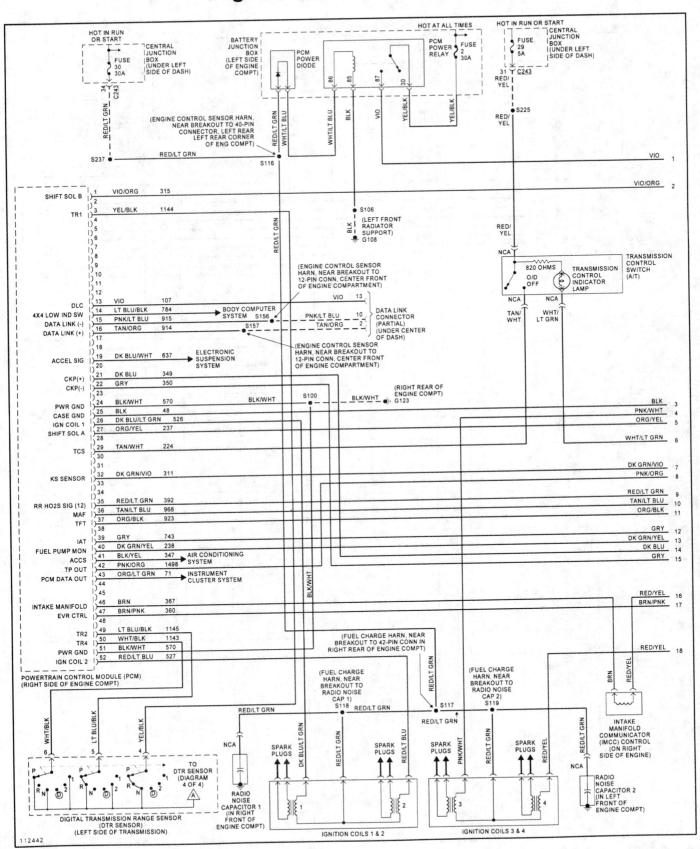

Fig. 89: Pickup – F150 & F250 (4.6L – 1 Of 4)

112442

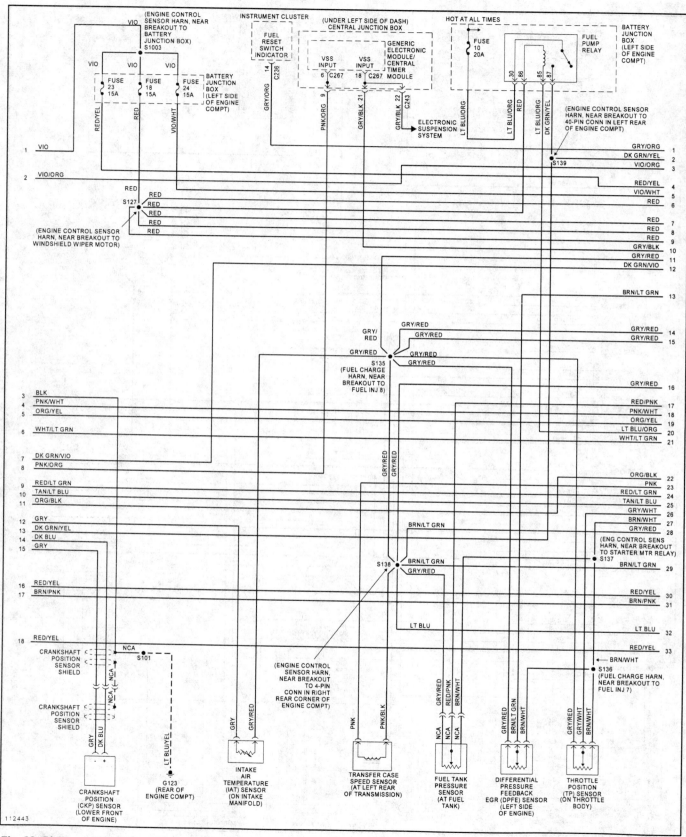

Fig. 90: Pickup – F150 & F250 (4.6L – 2 Of 4)

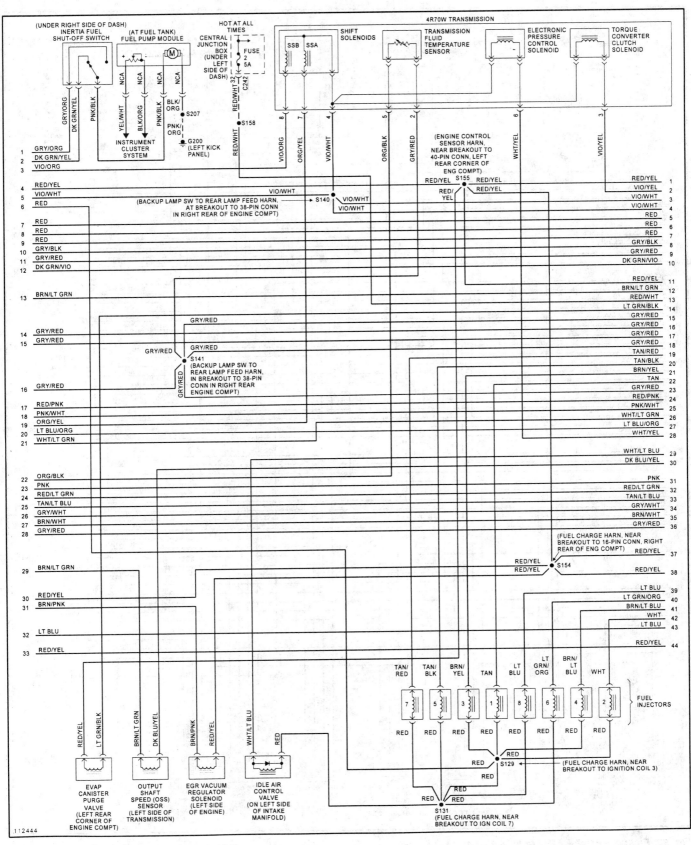

Fig. 91: Pickup – F150 & F250 (4.6L – 3 Of 4)

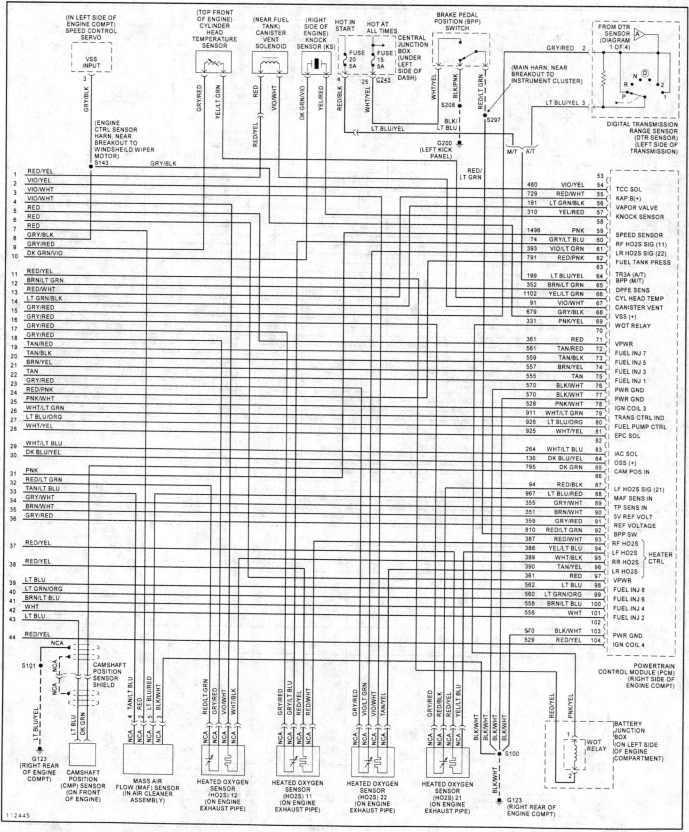

Fig. 92: Pickup – F150 & F250 (4.6L – 4 Of 4)

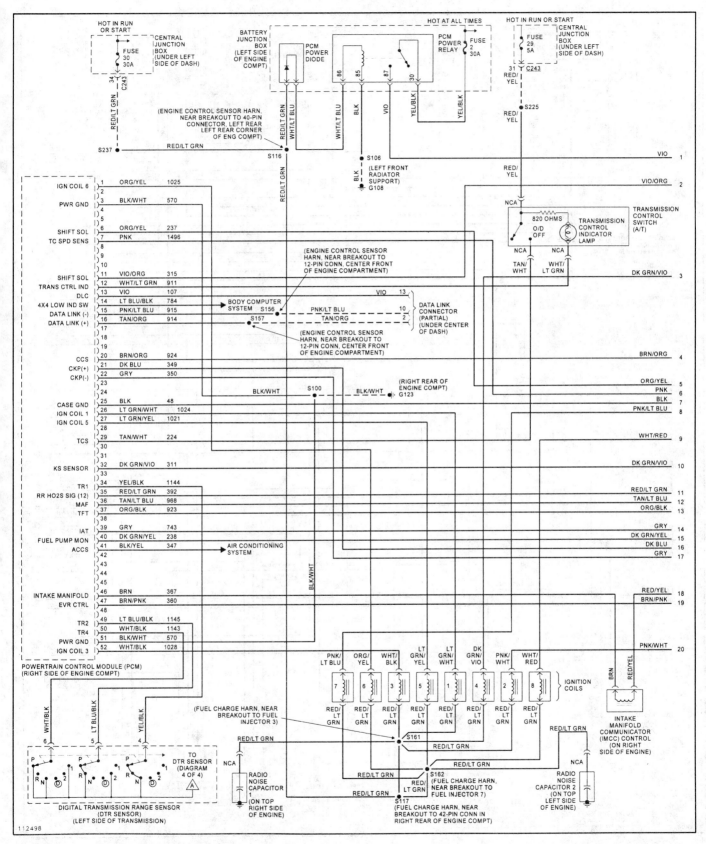

Fig. 93: Pickup – F150 & F250 (5.4L Gasoline – 1 Of 4)

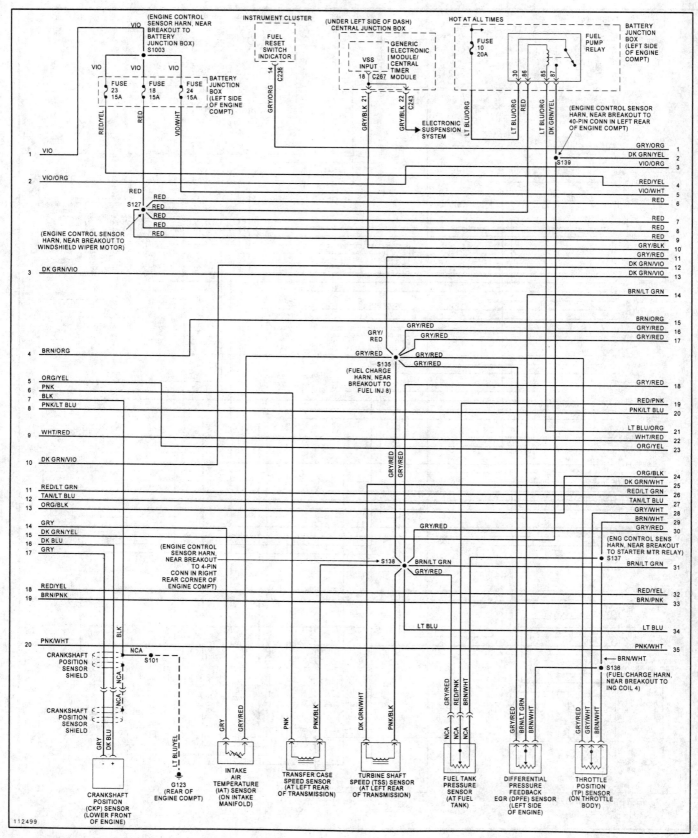

Fig. 94: Pickup – F150 & F250 (5.4L Gasoline – 2 Of 4)

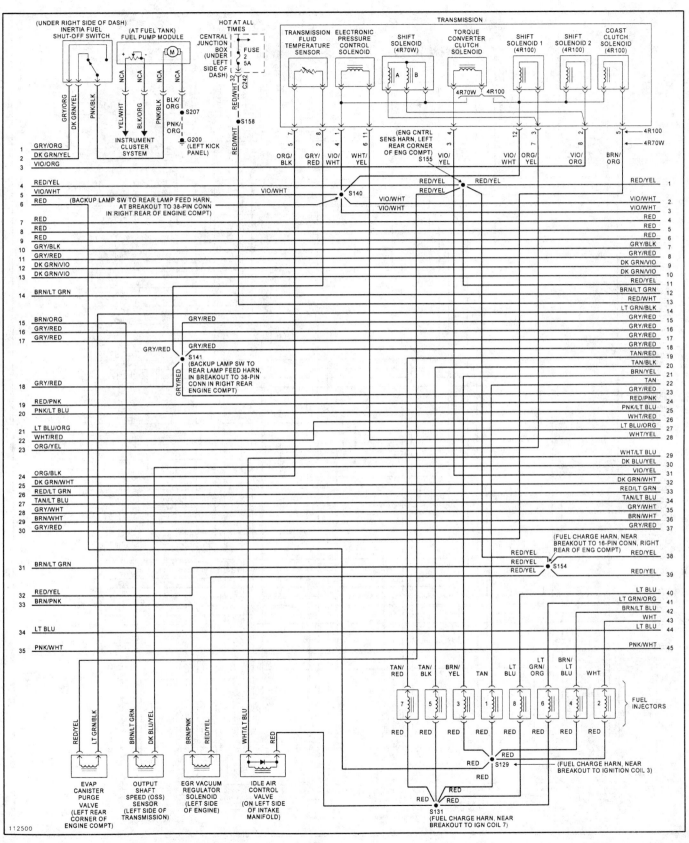

Fig. 95: Pickup – F150 & F250 (5.4L Gasoline – 3 Of 4)

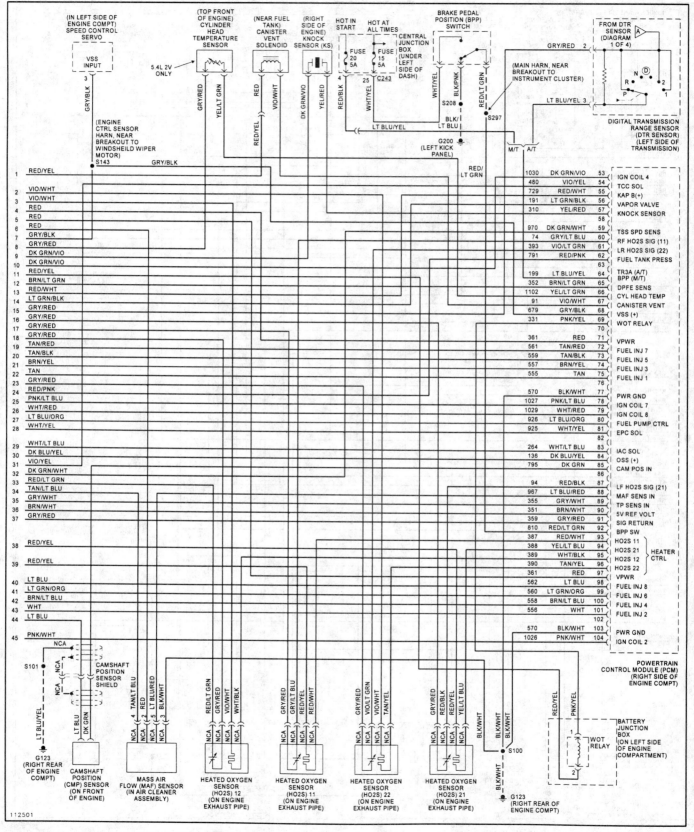

Fig. 96: Pickup – F150 & F250 (5.4L Gasoline – 4 Of 4)

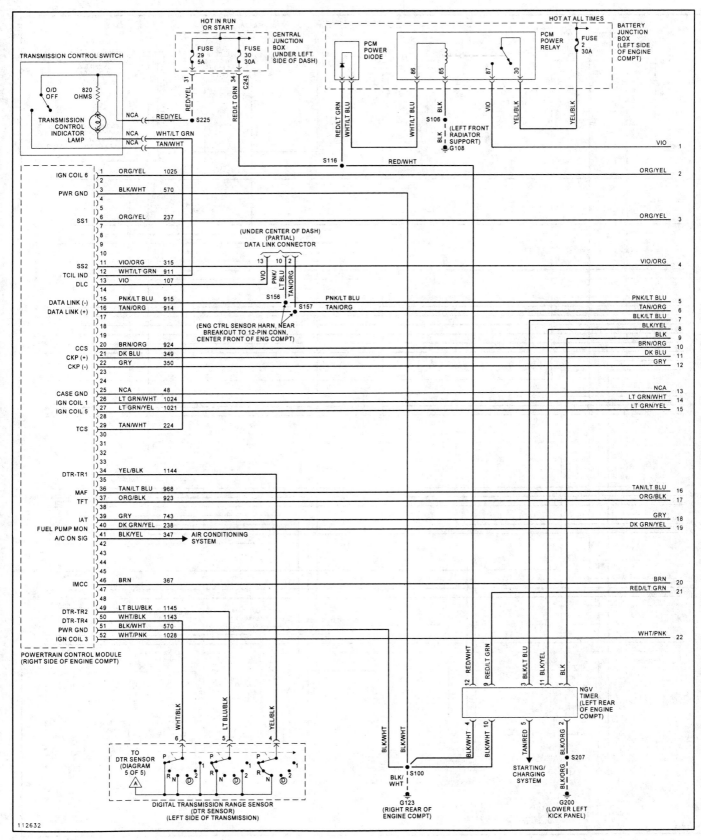

Fig. 97: Pickup – F150 & F250 (5.4L CNG – 1 Of 5)

112632

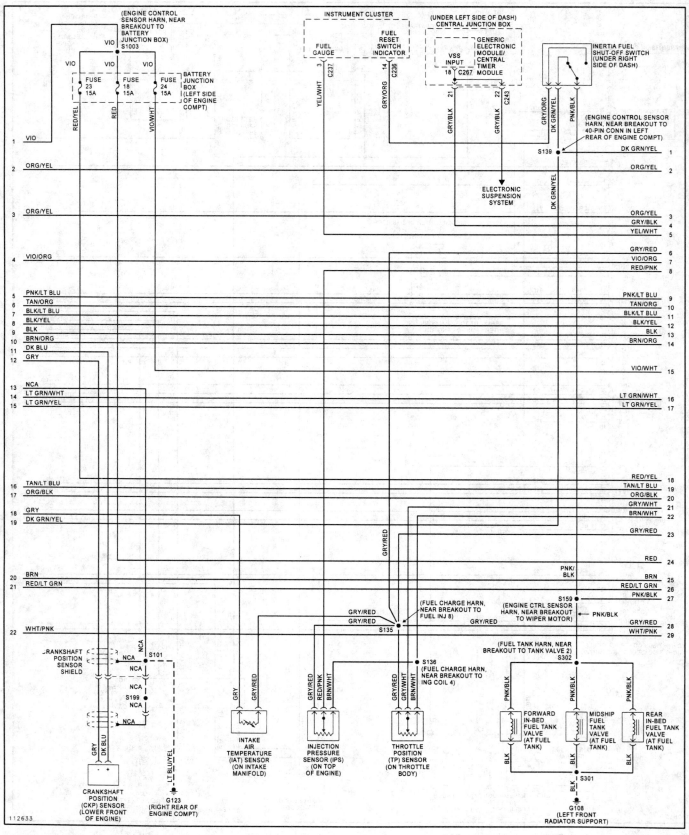

Fig. 98: Pickup – F150 & F250 (5.4L CNG – 2 Of 5)

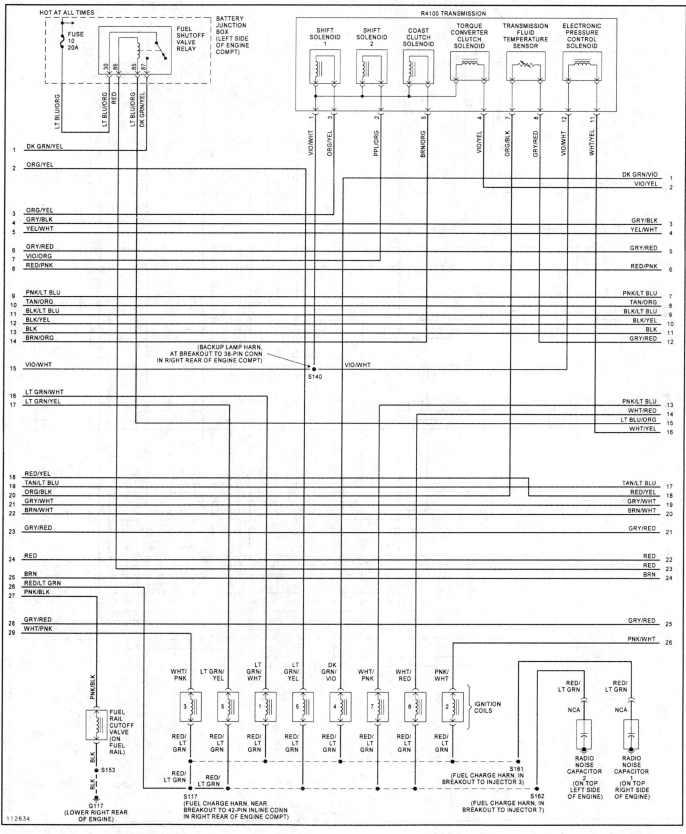

Fig. 99: Pickup – F150 & F250 (5.4L CNG – 3 Of 5)

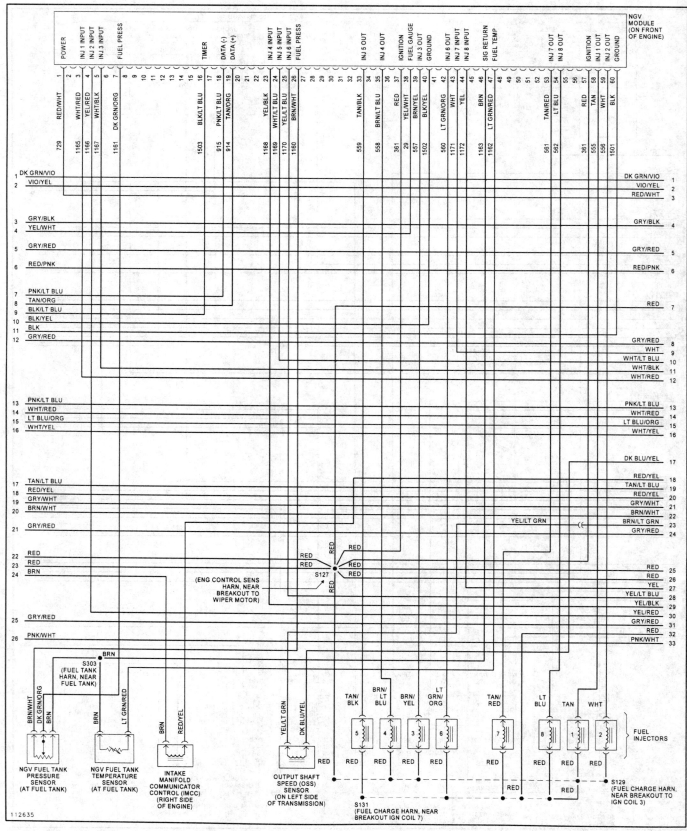

Fig. 100: Pickup – F150 & F250 (5.4L CNG – 4 Of 5)

112635

(LEFT SIDE OF ENGINE COMPT) SPEED CONTROL SERVO

(TOP FRONT OF LEFT HEAD) CYLINDER HEAD TEMPERATURE SENSOR

(LEFT REAR OF TRANS) TURBINE SHAFT SPEED SENSOR

HOT AT ALL TIMES

HOT AT ALL TIMES

CENTRAL JUNCTION BOX (UNDER LEFT SIDE OF DASH)

BRAKE PEDAL POSITION (BPP) SWITCH

FROM DTR SENSOR (DIAGRAM 1 OF 5)

VSS INPUT

FUSE 2 5A

FUSE 15 5A

32 C242   25 C243

GRY/RED 2

270 OHMS

LT BLU/YEL 3

DIGITAL TRANSMISSION RANGE SENSOR (DTR SENSOR-A/T) (LEFT SIDE OF TRANSMISSION)

GRY/BLK

GRY/RED

YEL/LT GRN

PNK/BLK

DK GRN/WHT

RED/WHT

WHT/YEL

WHT/YEL

BLK/PNK

RED/LT GRN

S208

BLK/LT BLU

S297

(MAIN HARN, NEAR BREAKOUT TO INSTRUMENT CLUSTER)

RED/LT GRN

G200 (LOWER LEFT KICK PANEL)

#			POWERTRAIN CONTROL MODULE
1	DK GRN/VIO	1030 DK GRN/VIO 53	IGN COIL 4
2	VIO/YEL	480 VIO/YEL 54	TCC SOL
3	RED/WHT	729 RED/WHT 55	KAP B(+)
		56	
		57	
		58	
4	GRY/BLK S143 GRY/BLK	970 DK GRN/WHT 59	TSS SENSOR
		74 GRY/LT BLU 60	HO2S SIG (#11)
5	GRY/RED	61	
		1164 LT BLU 62	EFT SENSOR
6	RED/PNK	141 RED/PNK 63	INJ PRESSURE
		199 LT BLU/YEL 64	DTR-TR3A
		48 NCA 65	NOT USED
7	RED	1102 YEL/LT GRN 66	CYL HEAD TEMP
		67	
		679 GRY/BLK 68	VSS (+)
		331 PNK/YEL 69	WOT RELAY
		70	
8	GRY/RED	361 RED 71	VPWR
9	WHT	1171 WHT 72	NGV MODULE
10	WHT/LT BLU	1169 WHT/LT BLU 73	NGV MODULE
11	WHT/BLK	1167 WHT/BLK 74	NGV MODULE
12	WHT/RED	1165 WHT/RED 75	NGV MODULE
		76	
		570 BLK/WHT 77	PWR GND
13	PNK/LT BLU	1027 PNK/LT BLU 78	IGN COIL 7
14	WHT/RED	1029 WHT/RED 79	IGN COIL 8
15	LT BLU/ORG	926 LT BLU/ORG 80	FUEL CTRL
16	WHT/YEL	925 WHT/YEL 81	EPC SOL
		82	
17	DK BLU/YEL	264 WHT/LT BLU 83	IDLE AIR CTRL
		136 DK BLU/YEL 84	OSS SENSOR
		795 DK GRN 85	CMP SENSOR
18	RED/YEL	86	
19	TAN/LT BLU	94 RED/BLK 87	HO2S SIG (21)
20	RED/YEL	967 LT BLU/RED 88	MAF SENS IN
21	GRY/WHT	355 GRY/WHT 89	TP SENS IN
22	BRN/WHT	351 BRN/WHT 90	5V REF
23	BRN/LT GRN	359 GRY/RED 91	SIG RTN
24	GRY/RED	810 RED/LT GRN 92	BPP SWITCH
		387 RED/WHT 93	HO2S (11)
		388 YEL/LT BLU 94	HO2S (21)
		95	
		96	
25	RED	361 RED 97	VPWR
26	RED	1172 YEL 98	NGV MODULE
27	YEL	1170 YEL/LT BLU 99	NGV MODULE
28	YEL/LT BLU	1168 YEL/BLK 100	NGV MODULE
29	YEL/BLK	1166 YEL/RED 101	NGV MODULE
30	YEL/RED	102	
31	GRY/RED	570 BLK/WHT 103	PWR GND
32	RED	1026 PNK/WHT 104	IGN COIL 2
33	PNK/WHT		

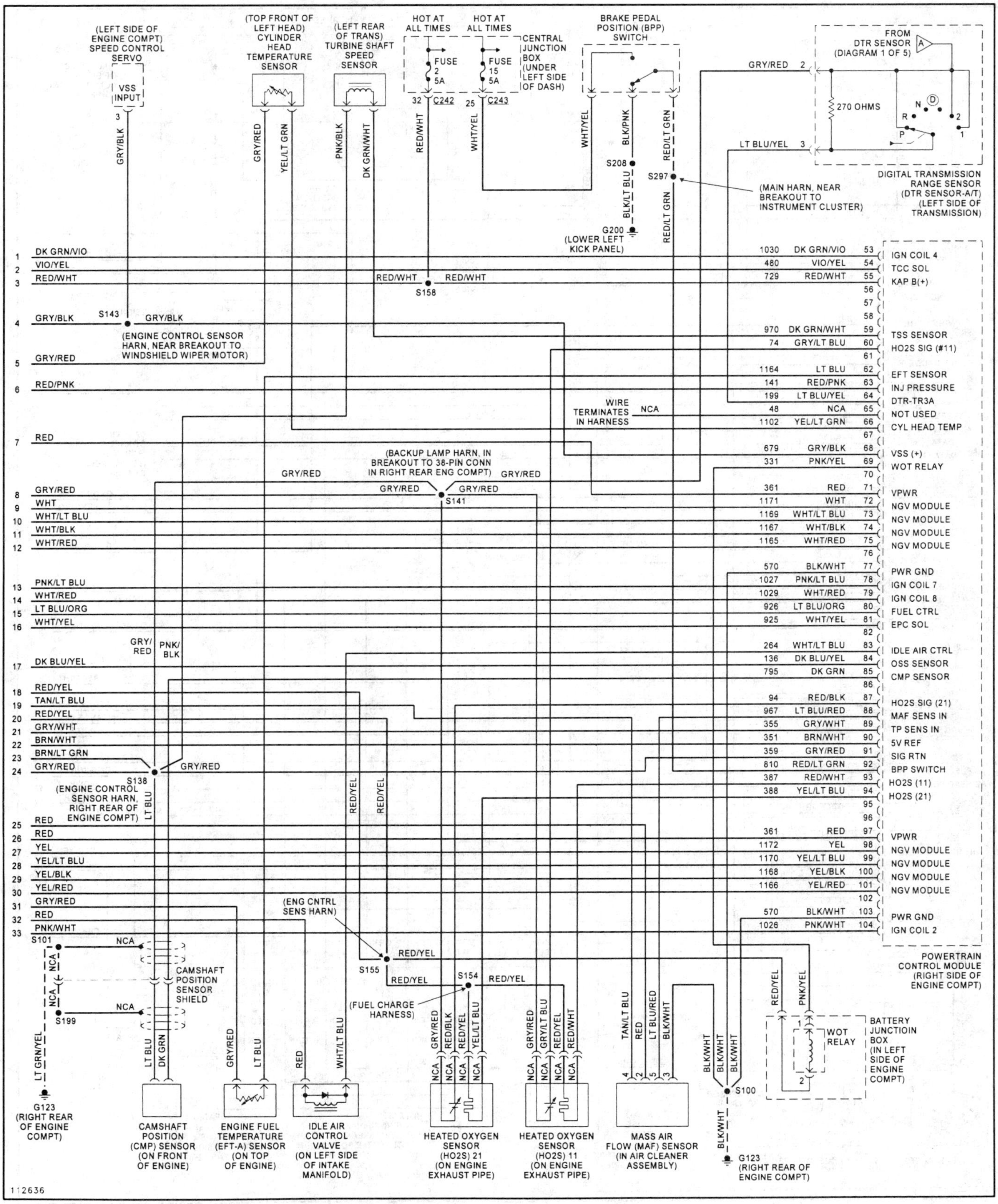

S158

S141 GRY/RED

S138 (ENGINE CONTROL SENSOR HARN, RIGHT REAR OF ENGINE COMPT)

(ENGINE CONTROL SENSOR HARN, NEAR BREAKOUT TO WINDSHIELD WIPER MOTOR)

(BACKUP LAMP HARN, IN BREAKOUT TO 38-PIN CONN IN RIGHT REAR ENG COMPT)

WIRE TERMINATES IN HARNESS NCA

POWERTRAIN CONTROL MODULE (RIGHT SIDE OF ENGINE COMPT)

S101 NCA

CAMSHAFT POSITION SENSOR SHIELD

S199 NCA

(ENG CNTRL SENS HARN)

S155 RED/YEL

S154 RED/YEL

(FUEL CHARGE HARNESS)

WOT RELAY

BATTERY JUNCTION BOX (IN LEFT SIDE OF ENGINE COMPT)

S100

G123 (RIGHT REAR OF ENGINE COMPT)

G123 (RIGHT REAR OF ENGINE COMPT)

CAMSHAFT POSITION (CMP) SENSOR (ON FRONT OF ENGINE)

ENGINE FUEL TEMPERATURE (EFT-A) SENSOR (ON TOP OF ENGINE)

IDLE AIR CONTROL VALVE (ON LEFT SIDE OF INTAKE MANIFOLD)

HEATED OXYGEN SENSOR (HO2S) 21 (ON ENGINE EXHAUST PIPE)

HEATED OXYGEN SENSOR (HO2S) 11 (ON ENGINE EXHAUST PIPE)

MASS AIR FLOW (MAF) SENSOR (IN AIR CLEANER ASSEMBLY)

112636

PCM Pin	Function	Color	Circuit
1	IGN COIL 6	ORG/YEL	1025
2	MIL IND	PNK/LT GRN	658
3	PWR GND	BLK/WHT	570
4	NOT USED	LT BLU/YEL	322
5			
6	SHIFT SOL 1	ORG/YEL	237
7			
8			
9	FUEL GAUGE IN	YEL/WHT	29
10			
11	SHIFT SOL 2	PPL/ORG	315
12	TRANS CTRL IND	WHT/LT GRN	911
13	REPROG PWR	PPL	107
14	4X4 LOW IND SW	LT BLU/BLK	784
15	DATA LINK (-)	PNK/LT BLU	915
16	DATA LINK (+)	TAN/ORG	914
17			
18			
19	FPSR CNTRL	ORG/LT GRN	27
20	CCS	BRN/ORG	924
21	CKP(+)	DK BLU	349
22	CKP(-)	GRY	350
23	PWR GND	BLK/WHT	570
24	PWR GND	BLK/WHT	570
25	DIAG GRD	LT BLU/YEL	567
26	IGN COIL 1	LT GRN/WHT	1024
27	IGN COIL 5	LT GRN/YEL	1021
28			
29	TCS	TAN/WHT	224
30			
31			
32			
33	VSS (-)	PNK/ORG	676
34	TR1	YEL/BLK	1144
35	HEGO 12	RED/LT GRN	392
36	MAF	TAN/LT BLU	968
37	TFT	ORG/BLK	923
38			
39	IAT	GRY	743
40	FUEL PUMP MON	DK GRN/YEL	238
41	AC HEAD PRESS SW	TAN/LT GRN	439
42	NOT USED	GRY/RED	1101
43	DATA OUTPUT	ORG/LT GRN	71
44			
45	TEMP OUTPUT	RED/WHT	39
46	INTAKE MANIFOLD	BRN	367
47	EGR SOL	BRN/PNK	360
48	TACH	WHT/PNK	648
49	TR2	LT BLU/BLK	1145
50	TR4	WHT/BLK	1143
51	PWR GND	BLK/WHT	570
52	IGN COIL 3	WHT/PNK	1028

POWERTRAIN CONTROL MODULE (PCM)
(ON LEFT SIDE OF FIREWALL)

112637

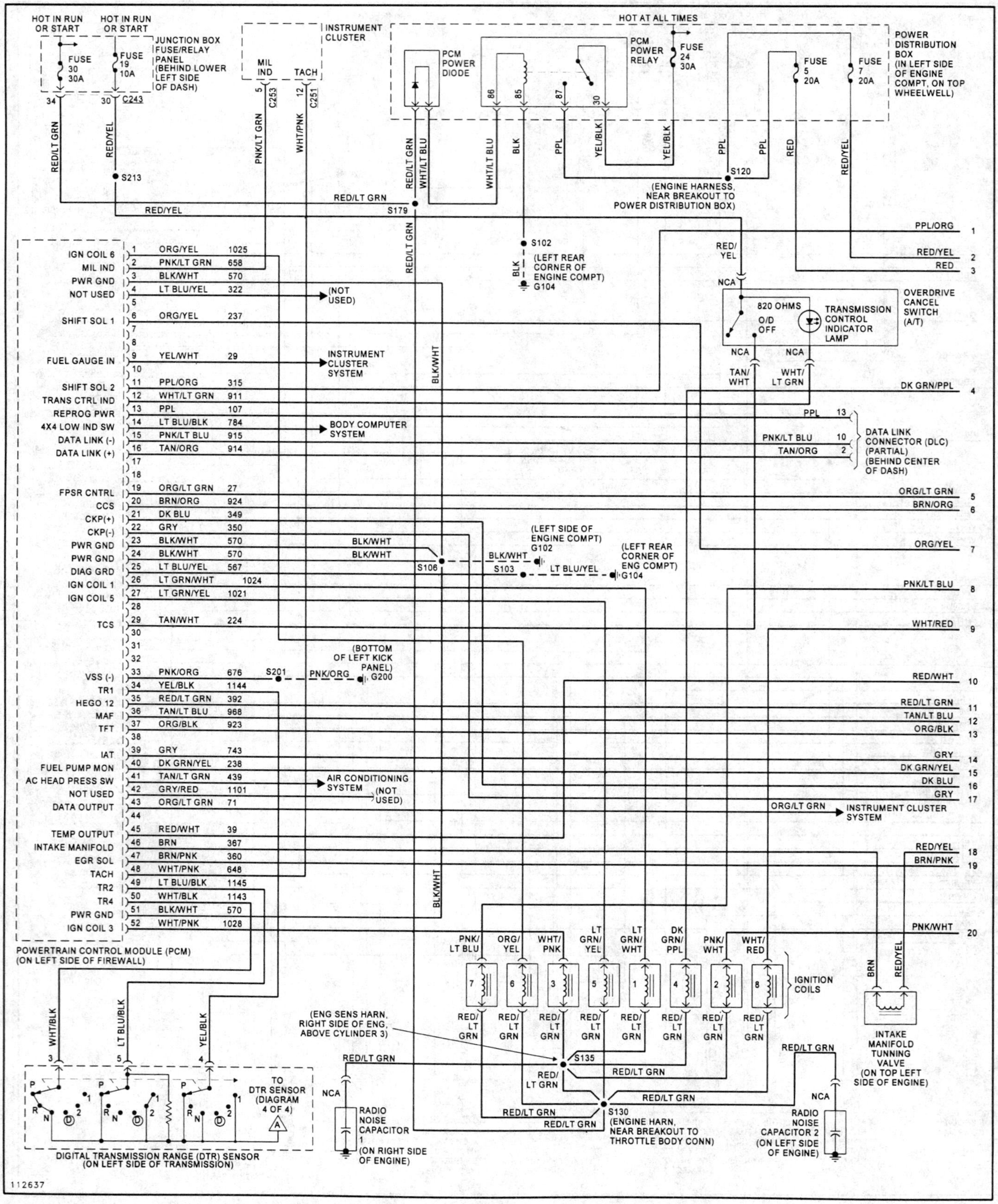

Fig. 102: Pickup – F250 Super Duty & F350 Super Duty (5.4L – 1 Of 4)

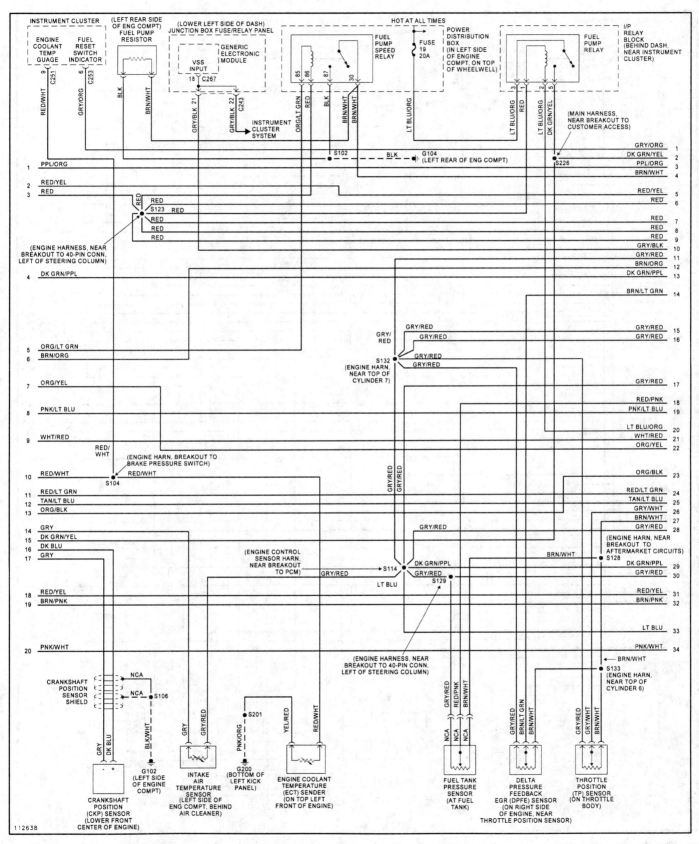

Fig. 103: Pickup – F250 Super Duty & F350 Super Duty (5.4L – 2 Of 4)

1999 WIRING DIAGRAMS

Engine Performance (Cont.)

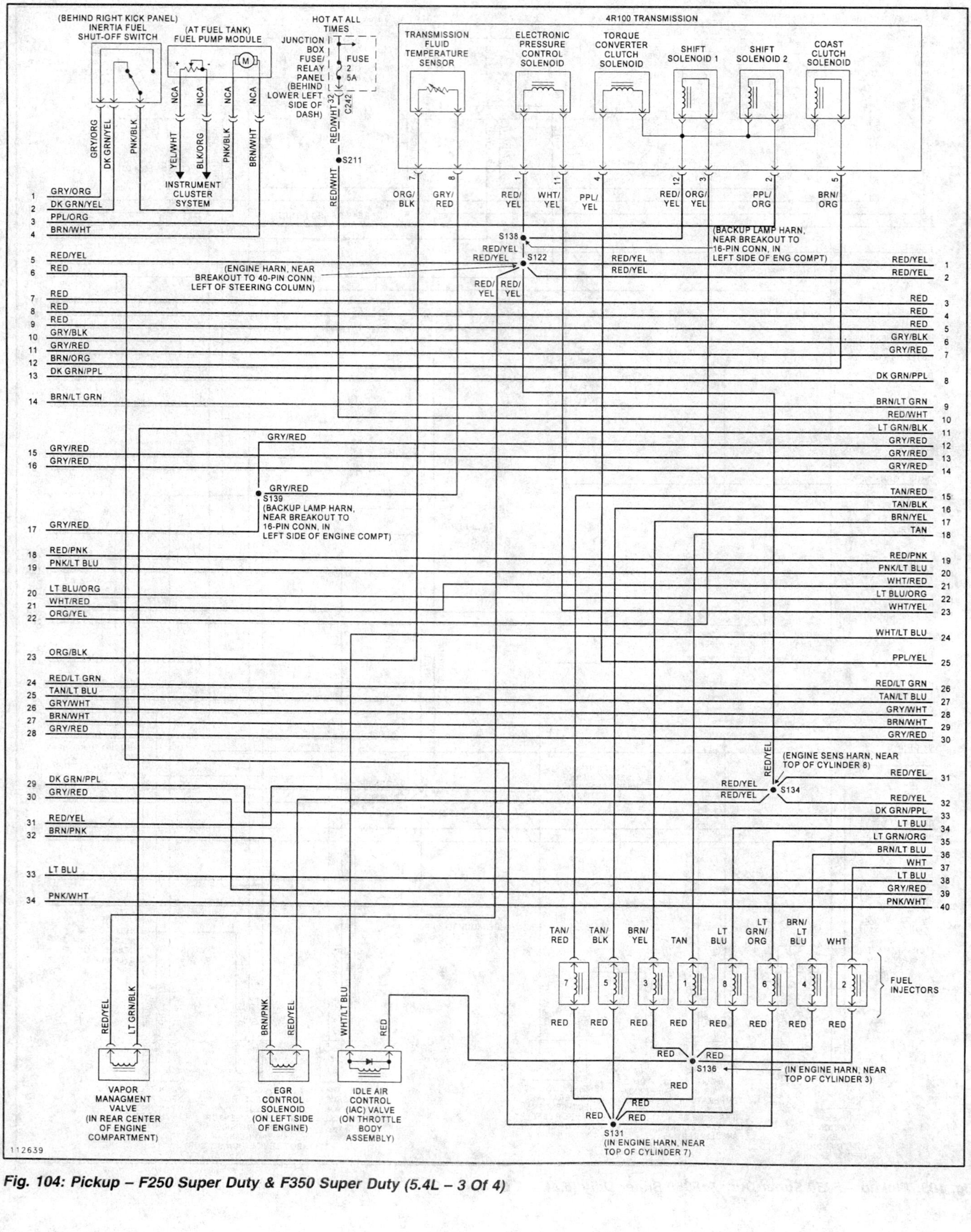

Fig. 104: Pickup – F250 Super Duty & F350 Super Duty (5.4L – 3 Of 4)

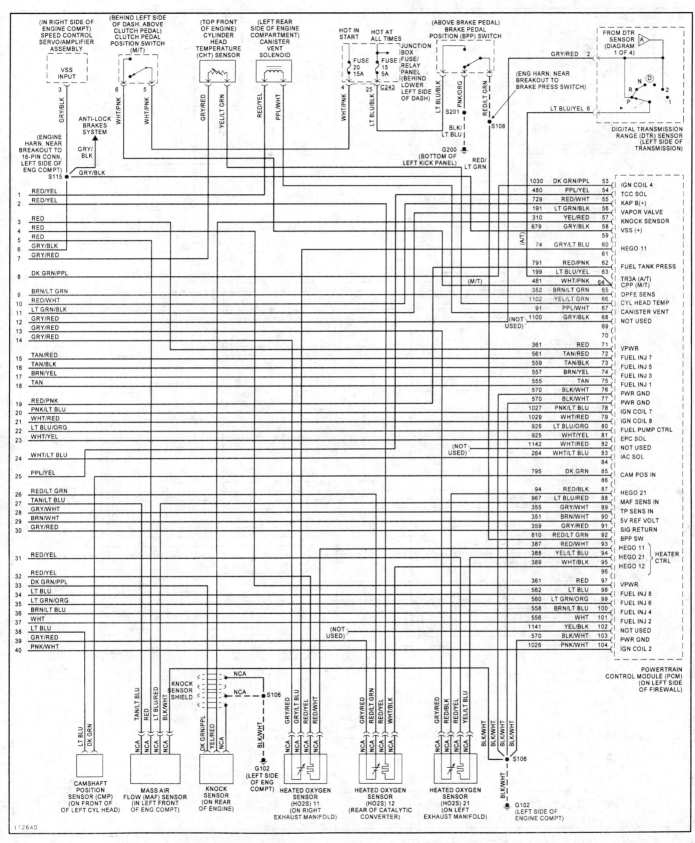

Fig. 105: Pickup – F250 Super Duty & F350 Super Duty (5.4L – 4 Of 4)

112640

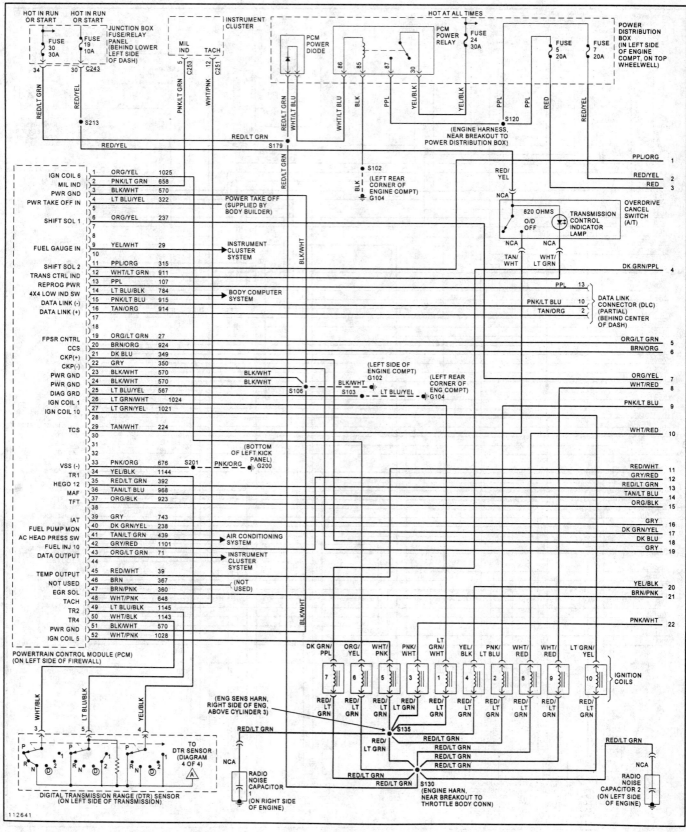

Fig. 106: Pickup – F250 Super Duty & F350 Super Duty (6.8L – 1 Of 4)

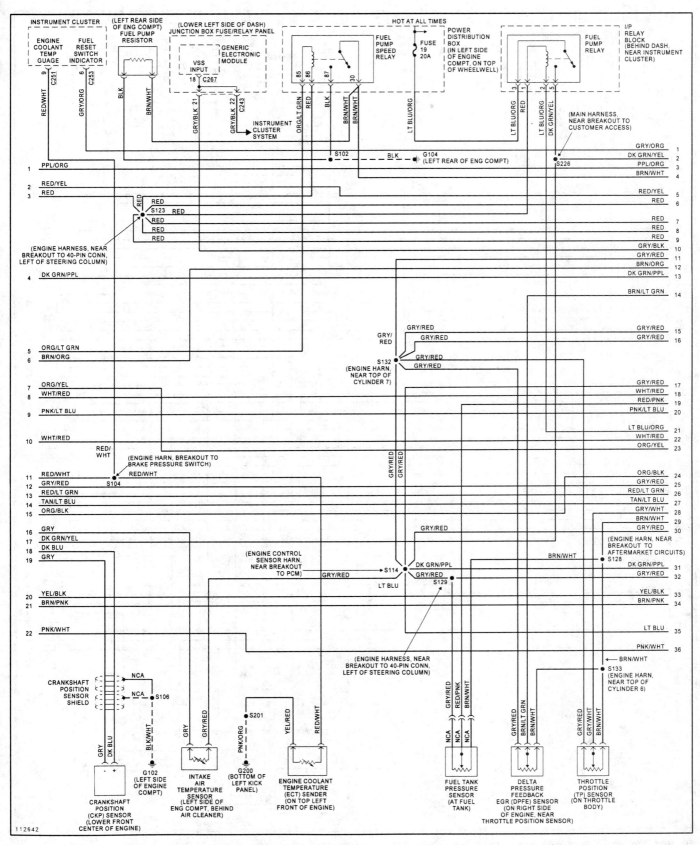

Fig. 107: Pickup – F250 Super Duty & F350 Super Duty (6.8L – 2 Of 4)

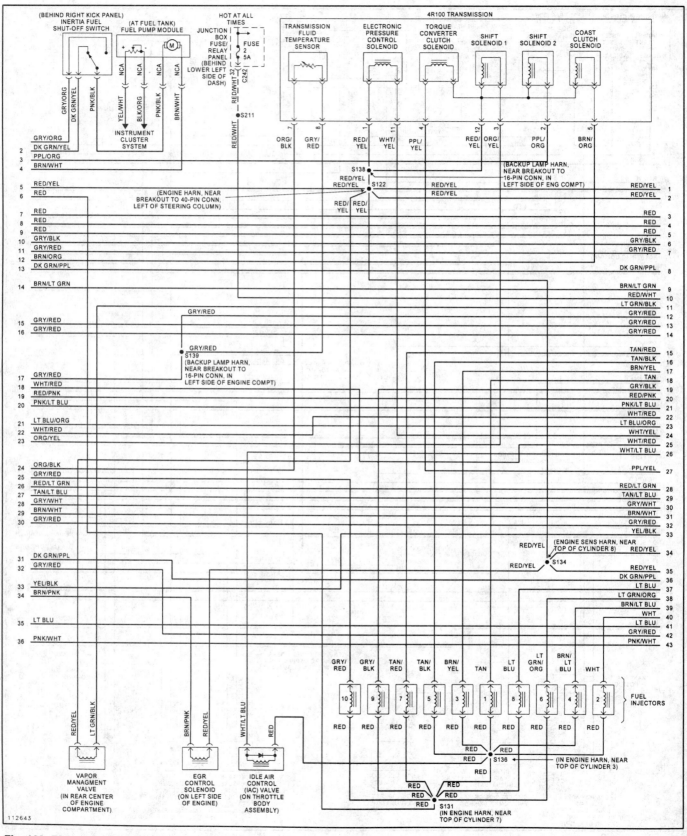

Fig. 108: Pickup – F250 Super Duty & F350 Super Duty (6.8L – 3 Of 4)

112643

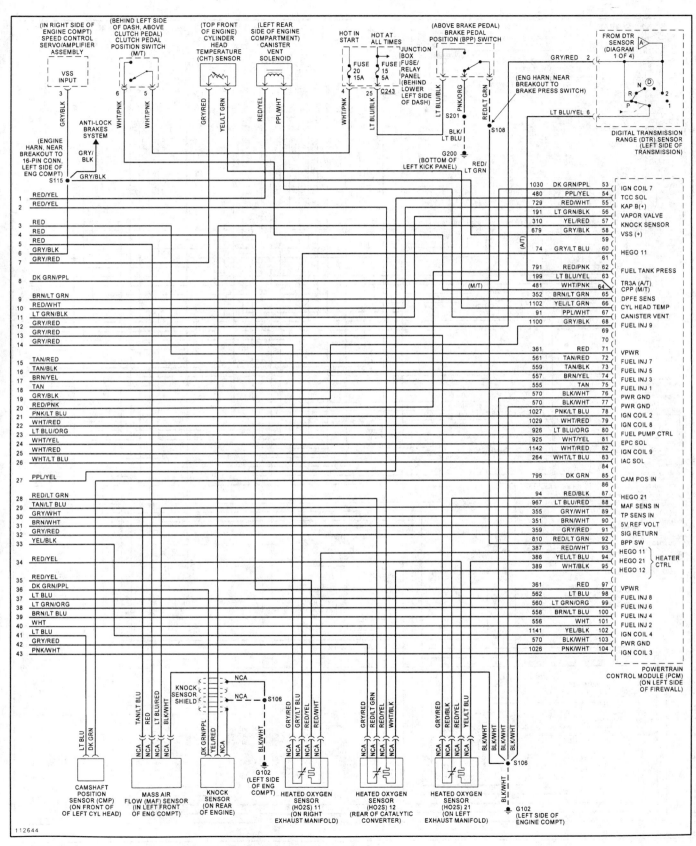

Fig. 109: Pickup – F250 Super Duty & F350 Super Duty (6.8L – 4 Of 4)

112644

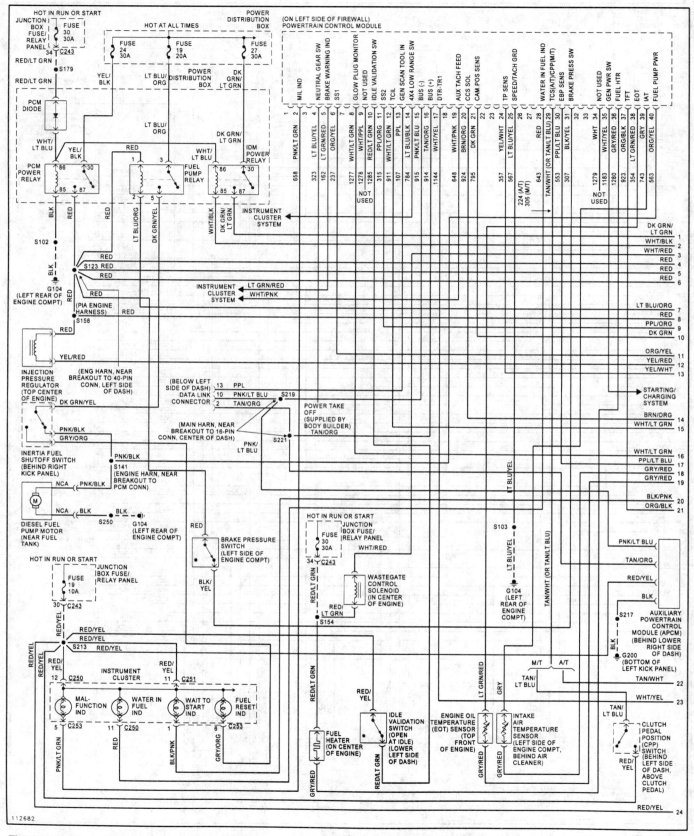

Fig. 110: Pickup – F250 Super Duty & F350 Super Duty (7.3L Turbo Diesel – 1 Of 3)

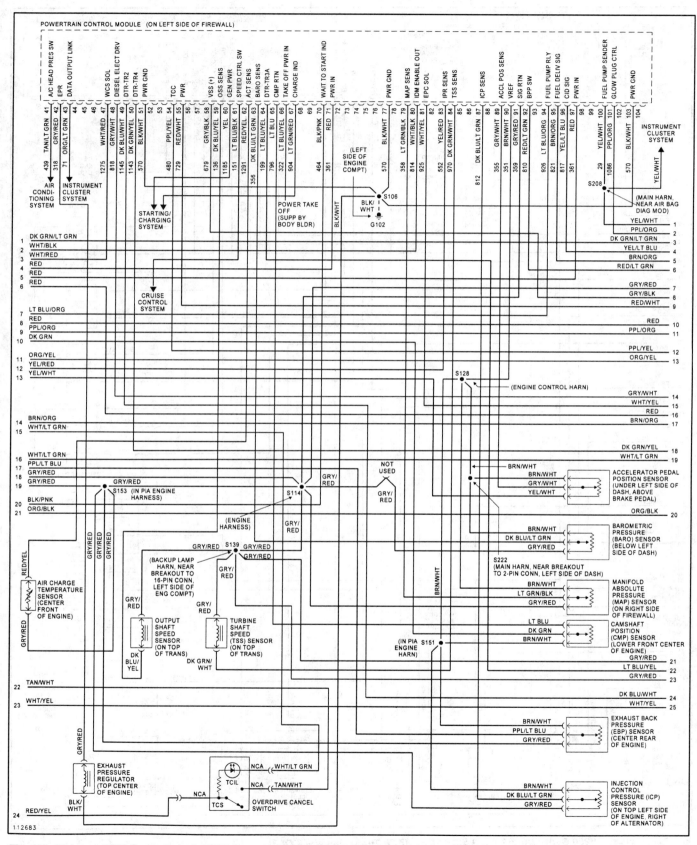

Fig. 111: Pickup – F250 Super Duty & F350 Super Duty (7.3L Turbo Diesel – 2 Of 3)

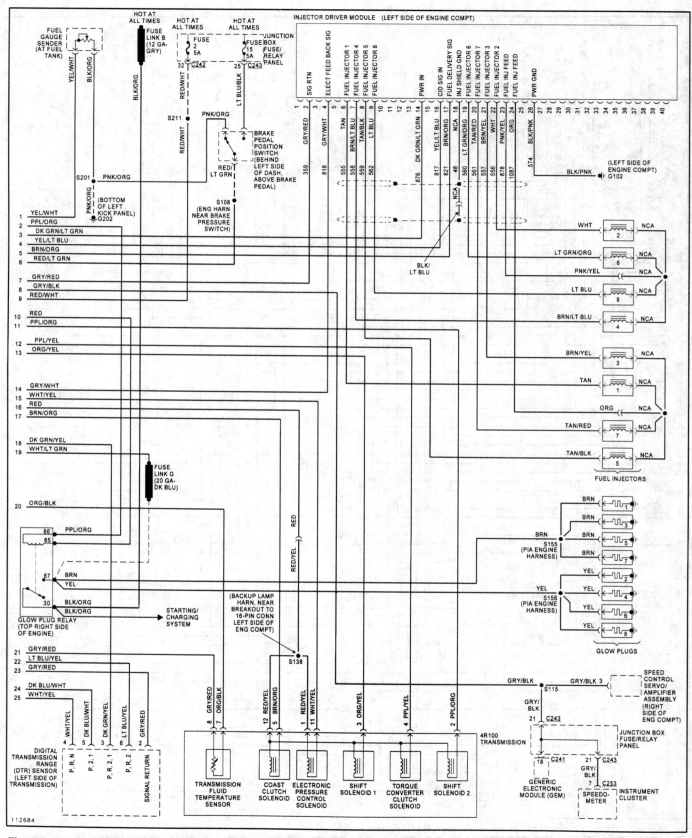

Fig. 112: Pickup – F250 Super Duty & F350 Super Duty (7.3L Turbo Diesel – 3 Of 3)

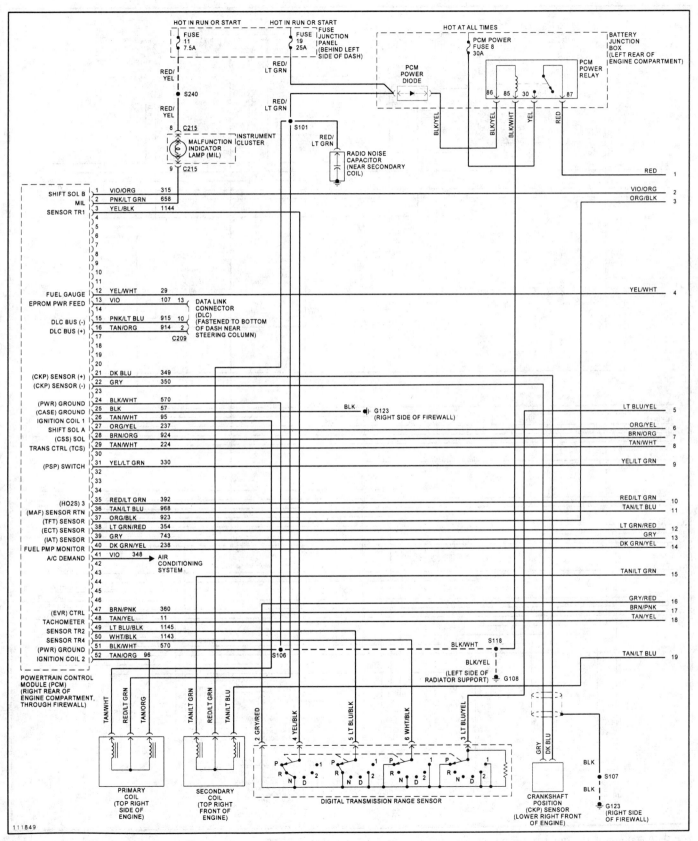

Fig. 113: Ranger (2.5L – 1 Of 4)

111849

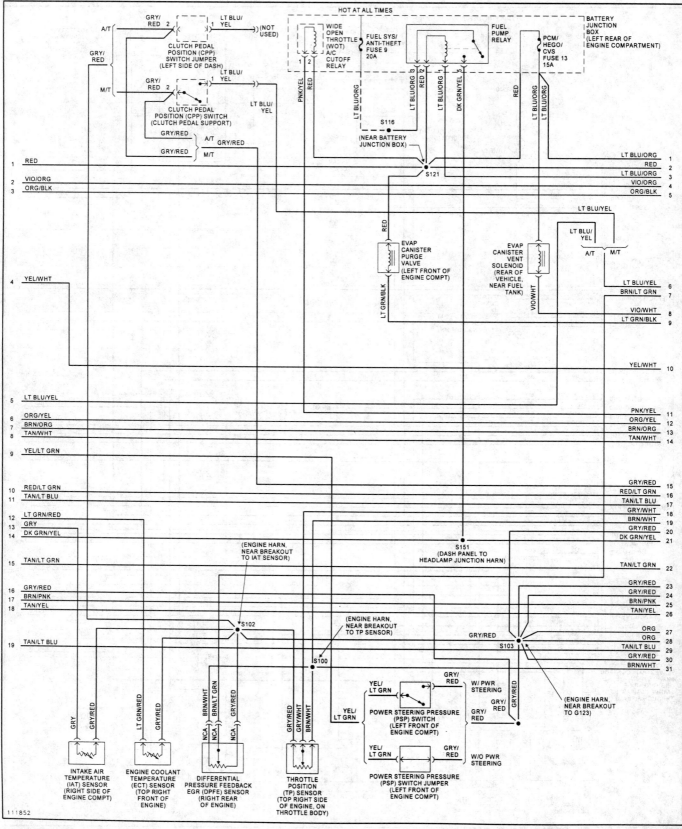

Fig. 114: Ranger (2.5L – 2 Of 4)

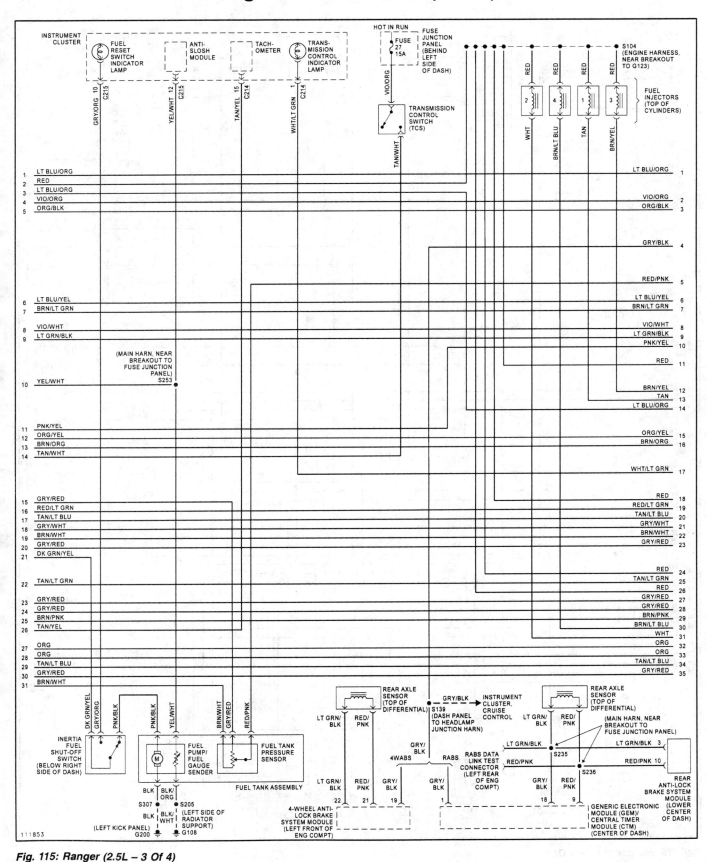

Fig. 115: Ranger (2.5L – 3 Of 4)

111853

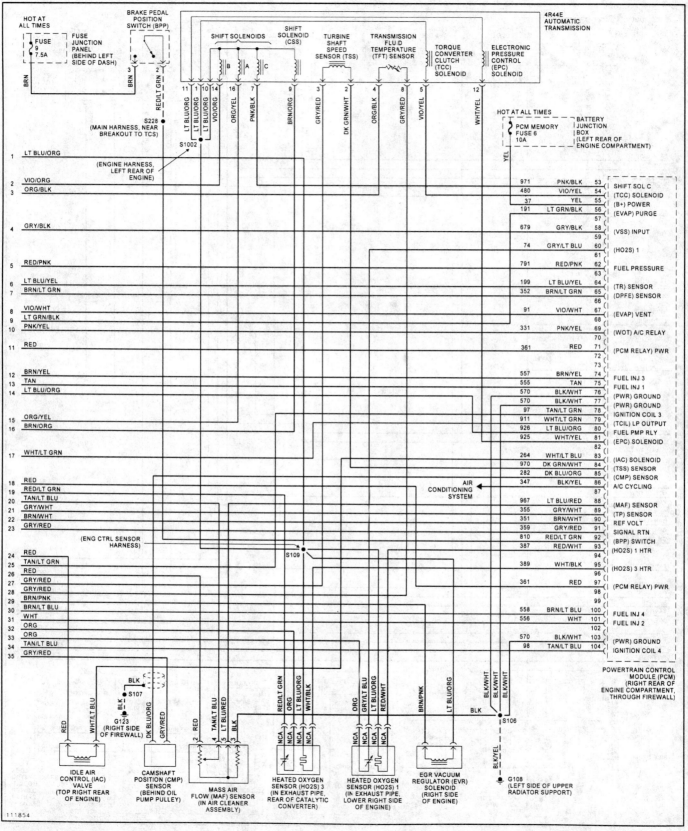

Fig. 116: Ranger (2.5L – 4 Of 4)

111854

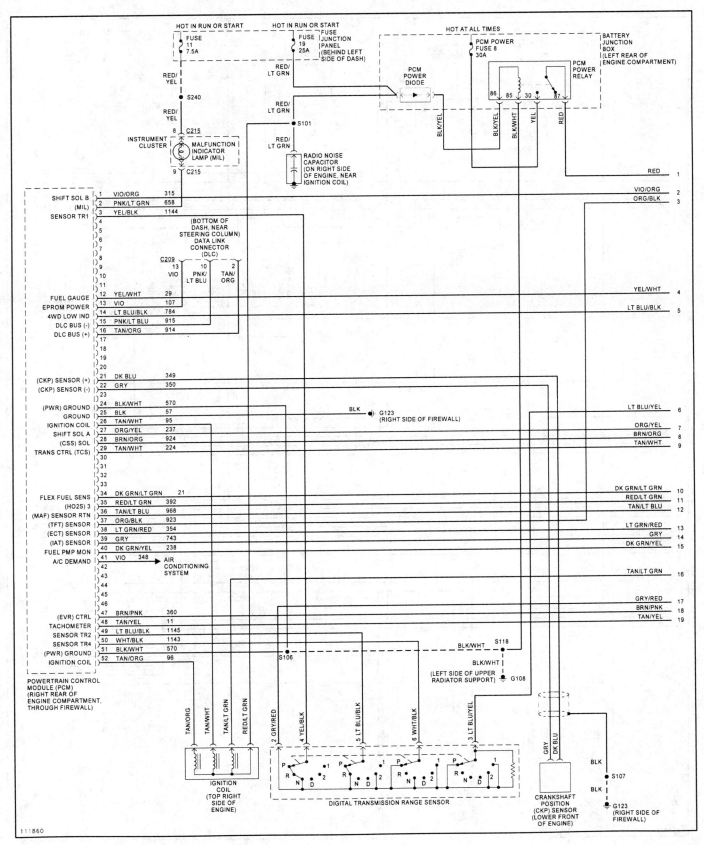

Fig. 117: Ranger (3.0L – 1 Of 4)

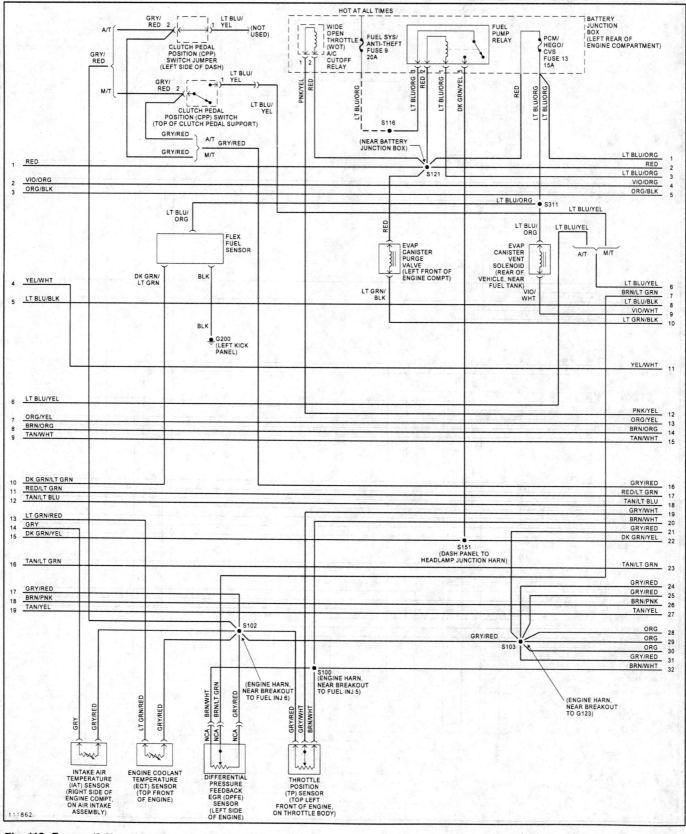

Fig. 118: Ranger (3.0L – 2 Of 4)

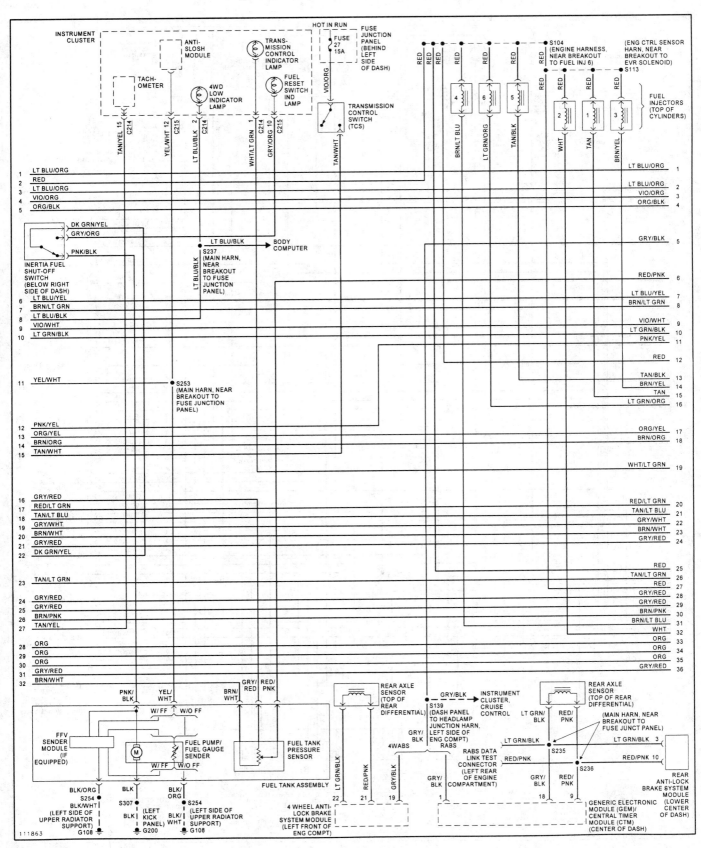

Fig. 119: Ranger (3.0L – 3 Of 4)

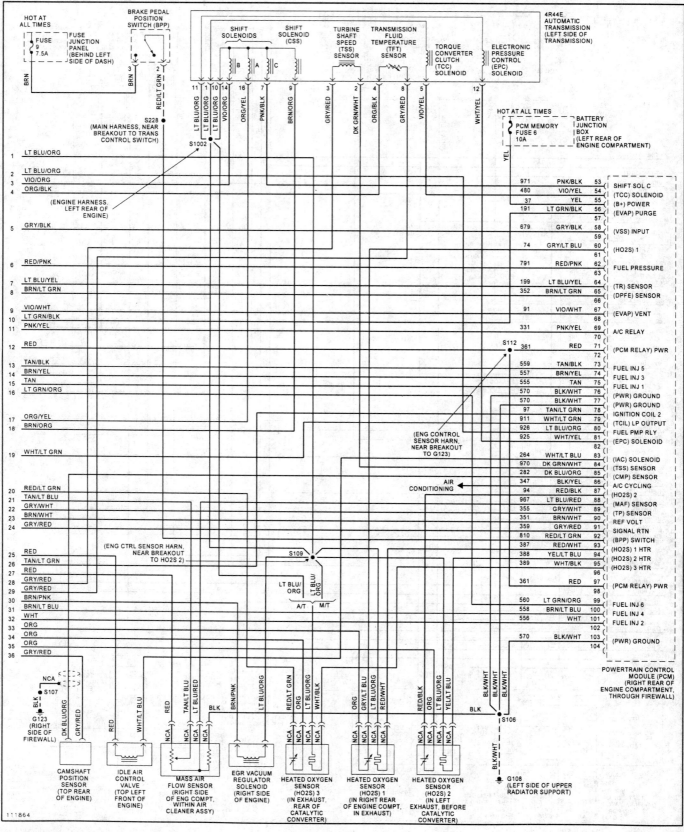

Fig. 120: Ranger (3.0L – 4 Of 4)

111864

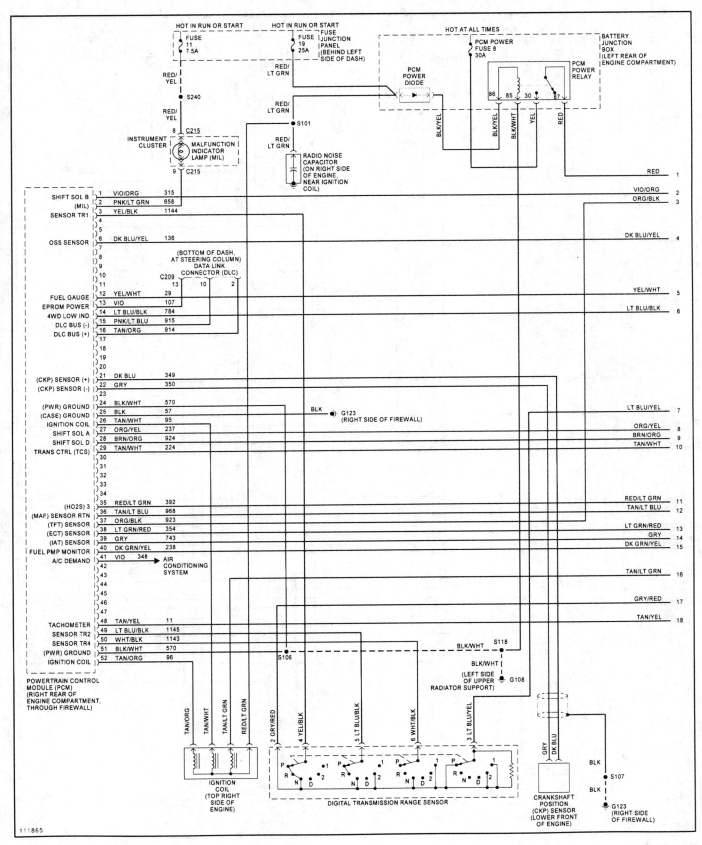

Fig. 121: Ranger (4.0L – 1 Of 4)

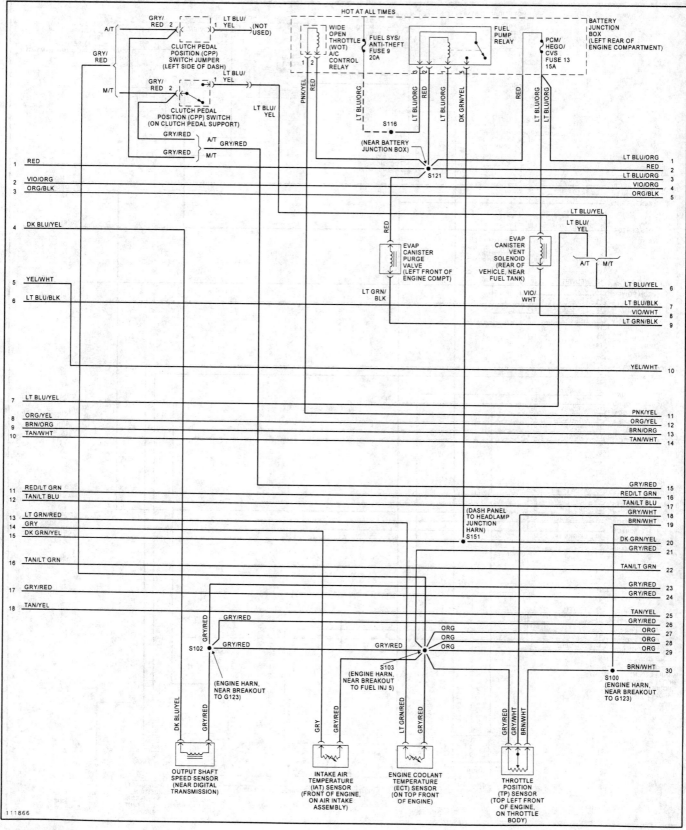

Fig. 122: Ranger (4.0L – 2 Of 4)

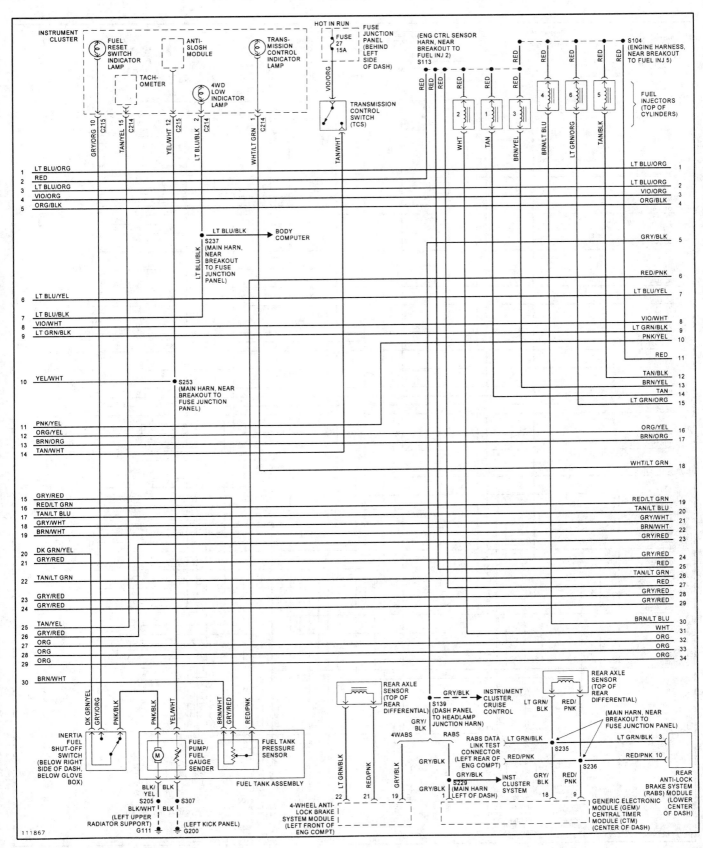

Fig. 123: Ranger (4.0L – 3 Of 4)

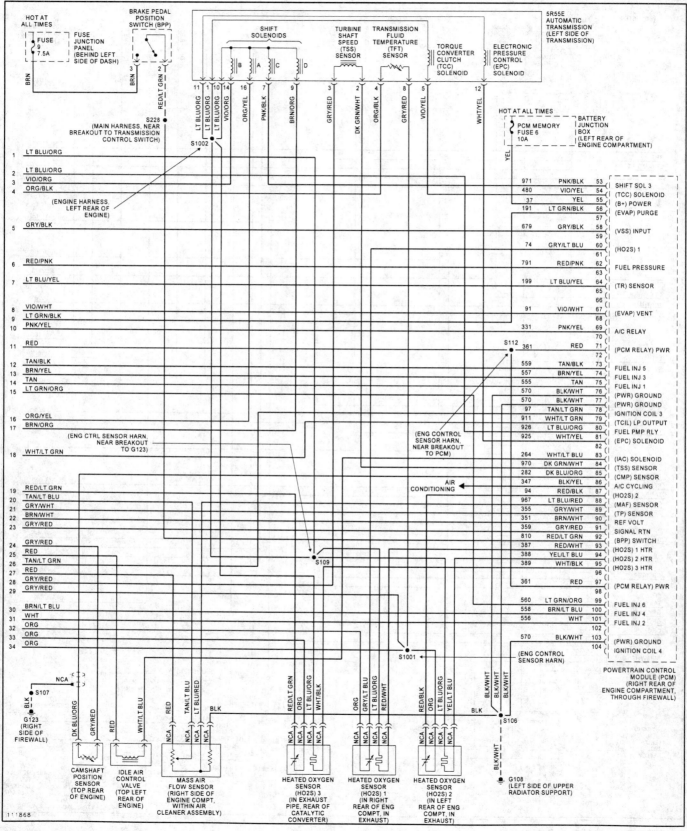

Fig. 124: Ranger (4.0L – 4 Of 4)

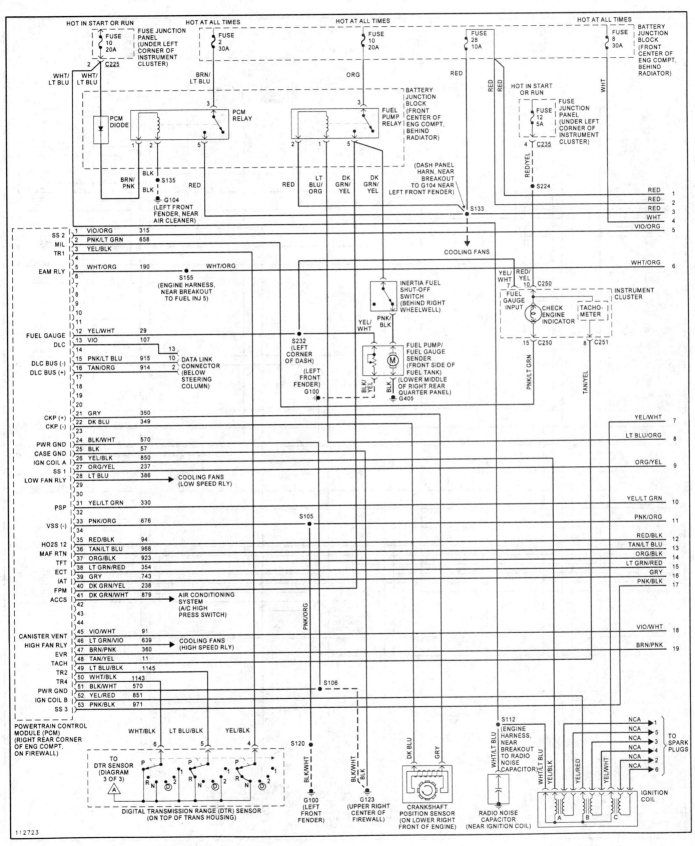

Fig. 125: Sable & Taurus (3.0L 12-Valve – 1 Of 3)

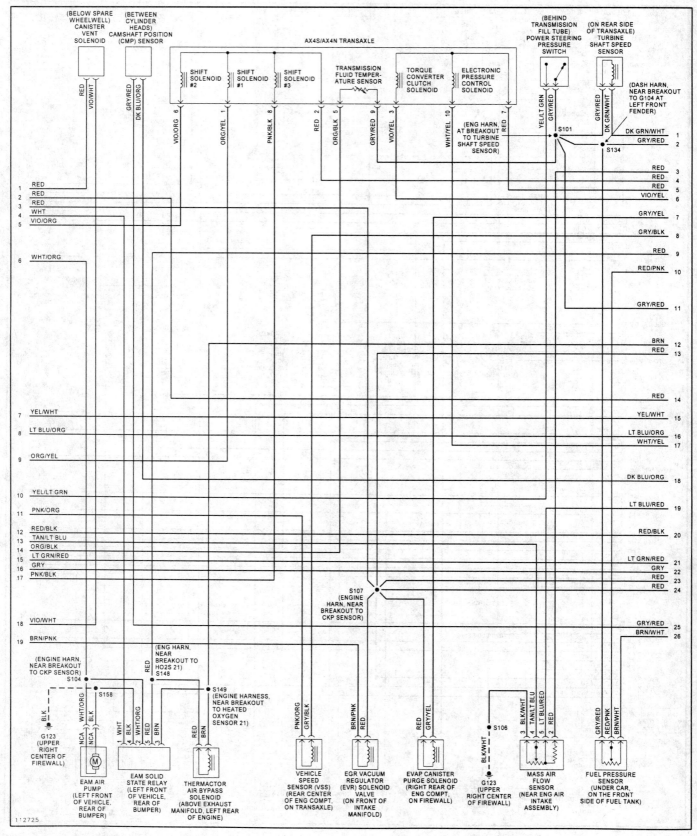

Fig. 126: Sable & Taurus (3.0L 12-Valve – 2 Of 3)

FUSE JUNCTION PANEL (UNDER LEFT CORNER OF INSTRUMENT CLUSTER)

HOT AT ALL TIMES

FUSE 28 15A

C247

(UPPER FRONT SIDE OF BRAKE PEDAL) BRAKE PEDAL POSITION (BPP) SWITCH

FUEL INJECTOR 2

FUEL INJECTOR 4

FUEL INJECTOR 6

(REAR CENTER OF ENG COMPT) IDLE AIR CONTROL VALVE

FUEL INJECTOR 1

FUEL INJECTOR 3

FUEL INJECTOR 5

HOT AT ALL TIMES

FUSE 19 15A

BATTERY JUNCTION BOX (FRONT CENTER OF ENG COMPT, BEHIND BATTERY)

(ON TOP OF TRANS HOUSING) DIGITAL TRANSMISSION (DTR) RANGE SENSOR

FROM DTR SENSOR (DIAGRAM 1 OF 3)

LT GRN/RED
LT GRN/RED
RED/LT GRN
RED
WHT
RED
BRN/LT BLU
RED
LT GRN/ORG
RED
WHT/LT BLU
(ENGINE HARN, NEAR FUEL INJ 5)
TAN
RED
RED
BRN/YEL
RED
TAN/BLK
(ENGINE HARNESS, NEAR BREAKOUT TO ENGINE OIL PRESSURE SWITCH)
DK GRN/ORG
S144
(ENG HARN, NEAR BREAKOUT TO CKP SENSOR)

1 DK GRN/WHT
2 GRY/RED
(MAIN HARN, NEAR BREAKOUT TO G200 AT LEFT KICK PANEL)
S308
S111
RED
3 RED
4 RED
5 RED
S103
6 VIO/YEL
7 GRY/YEL
8 GRY/BLK
S104
9 RED
10 RED/PNK

GRY/RED 2
LT BLU/YEL (OR PNK/BLK) 3
270 OHMS

11 GRY/RED
INSTRUMENT CLUSTER
12 BRN
13 RED
AIR CONDITIONING SYSTEM
14 RED
15 YEL/WHT
16 LT BLU/ORG
17 WHT/YEL
(ENG HARN, NEAR BREAKOUT TO ENG OIL PRESS SWITCH)
18 DK BLU/ORG
AIR CONDITIONING SYSTEM
19 LT BLU/RED
20 RED/BLK
21 LT GRN/RED
22 GRY
23 RED
24 RED
25 GRY/RED
26 BRN/WHT
S102

480	VIO/YEL	54 TCC
1076	DK GRN/ORG	55 KAPWR
101	GRY/YEL	56 EVAP CANP SOL
		57
679	GRY/BLK	58 VSS (+)
		59
74	GRY/LT BLU	60 HO2S 11
393	VIO/LT GRN	61 HO2S 22
791	RED/PNK	62 FTP SENS
		63
199	LT BLU/YEL	64 TR3A
352	BRN/LT GRN	65 DPFE SENS
		66
		67
		68
331	PNK/YEL	69 AC RLY OUT
200	BRN	70 EAM RELAY
361	RED	71 VPWR
		72
559	TAN/BLK	73 FUEL INJ 5
557	BRN/YEL	74 FUEL INJ 3
555	TAN	75 FUEL INJ 1
570	BLK/WHT	76 PWR GND
570	BLK/WHT	77 PWR GND
852	YEL/WHT	78 IGN COIL C
		79
926	LT BLU/ORG	80 FPM
925	WHT/YEL	81 EPC SOL
		82
264	WHT/LT BLU	83 IAC
970	DK GRN/WHT	84 TSS SENS
282	DK BLU/ORG	85 CMP SENS
347	BLK/YEL	86 A/C PRES
392	RED/LT GRN	87 HO2S 21
967	LT BLU/RED	88 MAF SENS
355	GRY/WHT	89 TP SENS
351	BRN/WHT	90 REF VOLT
359	GRY/RED	91 SIG RTN
810	RED/LT GRN	92 BPP
387	RED/WHT	93 HO2S 11
389	WHT/BLK	94 HO2S 21
388	YEL/LT BLU	95 HO2S 12
390	TAN/YEL	96 HO2S 22
361	RED	97 VPWR
		98
560	LT GRN/ORG	99 FUEL INJ 6
558	BRN/LT BLU	100 FUEL INJ 4
556	WHT	101 FUEL INJ 2
		102
570	BLK/WHT	103 PWR GND
		104

HEATER CTRL

S100
S110

POWERTRAIN CONTROL MODULE (PCM) (RIGHT REAR CORNER OF ENG COMPT, ON FIREWALL)

(ENGINE HARNESS, NEAR BREAKOUT TO TURBINE SHAFT SPEED SENSOR)

(ENGINE HARNESS, NEAR BREAKOUT TO FUEL INJ 6)

GRY/RED
GRY
GRY/RED
LT GRN/RED
GRY/RED
BRN/LT GRN
BRN/WHT
GRY/RED
GRY/WHT
BRN/WHT
RED/BLK
GRY/RED
RED
YEL/LT BLU
GRY/RED
GRY/LT BLU
RED
RED/WHT
GRY/RED
VIO/LT GRN
RED
TAN/YEL
GRY/RED
RED/LT GRN
RED
WHT/BLK
BLK/WHT
S106

NCA

INTAKE AIR TEMPERATURE SENSOR (ON AIR INTAKE ASSEMBLY)

ENGINE COOLANT TEMPERATURE SENSOR (REAR OF ENGINE BLOCK, NEAR THERMOSTAT)

DELTA PRESSURE FEEDBACK EGR (DPFE) SENSOR (ON INTAKE MANIFOLD)

THROTTLE POSITION SENSOR (BEHIND INTAKE MANIFOLD)

HEATED OXYGEN SENSOR 12 (DOWNSTREAM FROM CATALITIC CONV 1)

HEATED OXYGEN SENSOR 11 (REAR OF ENG COMPT, ON EXHST MANIFOLD)

HEATED OXYGEN SENSOR 22 (DOWNSTREAM FROM CATALITIC CONV 2)

HEATED OXYGEN SENSOR 21 (FRONT OF ENG COMPT, ON EXHST MANIFOLD)

G123 (UPPER RIGHT CENTER OF FIREWALL)

112726

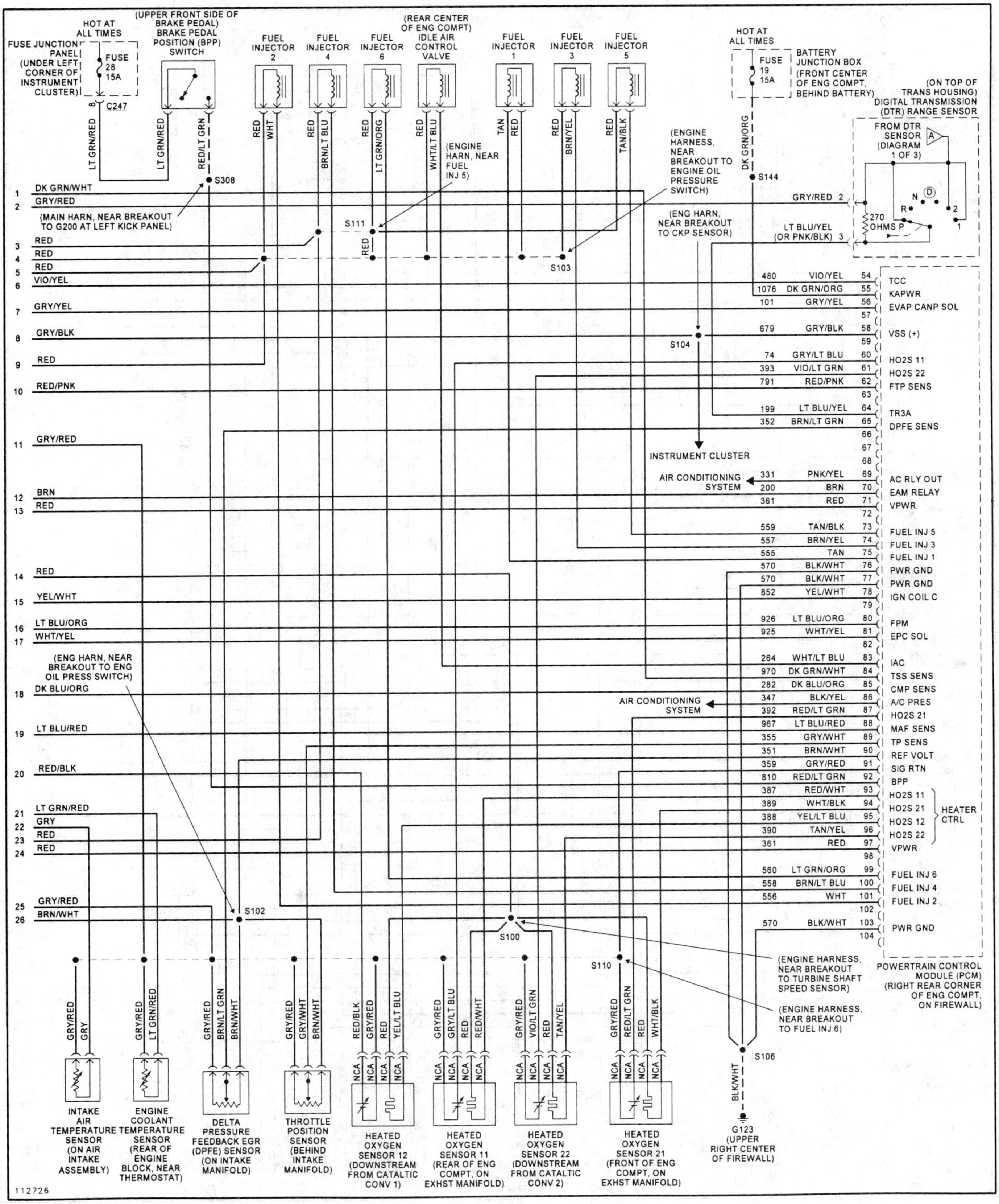

Fig. 127: Sable & Taurus (3.0L 12-Valve – 3 Of 3)

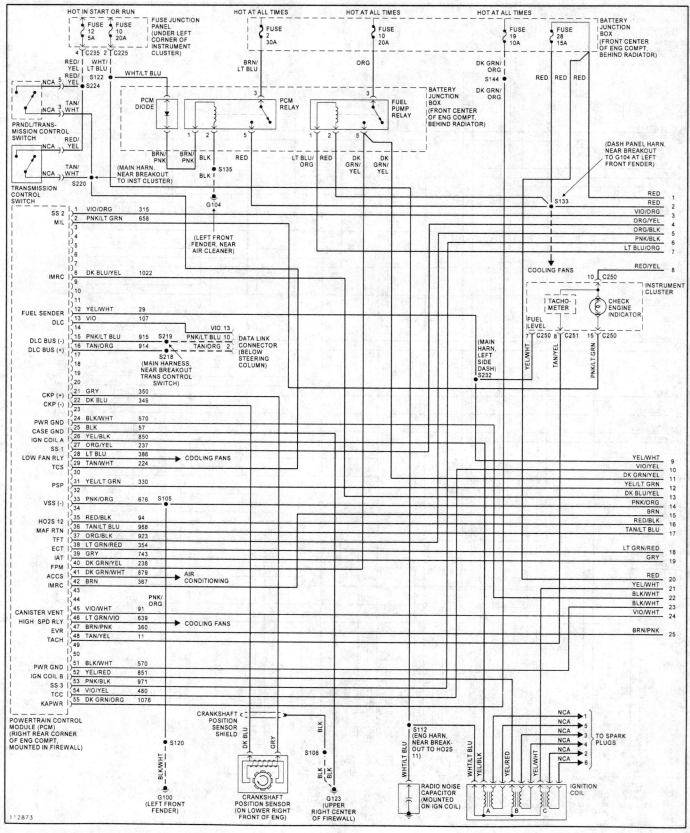

Fig. 128: Sable & Taurus (3.0L 24-Valve – 1 Of 3)

112873

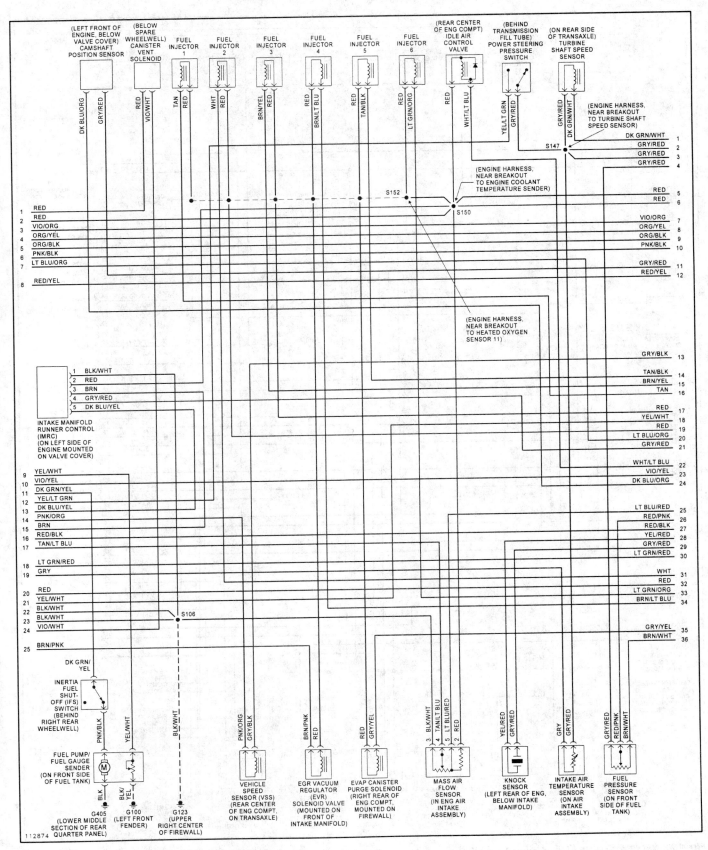

Fig. 129: Sable & Taurus (3.0L 24-Valve – 2 Of 3)

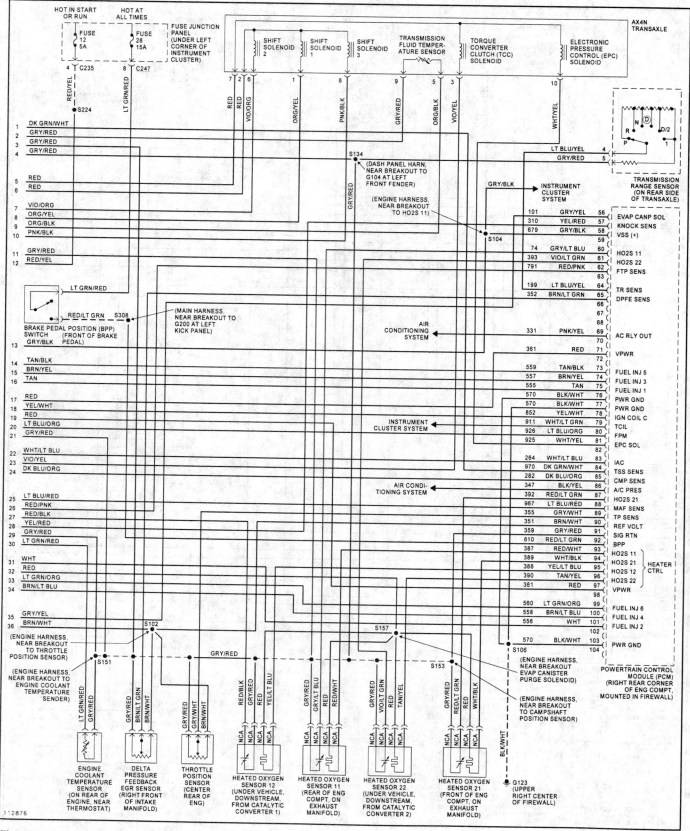

Fig. 130: Sable & Taurus (3.0L 24-Valve – 3 Of 3)

112876

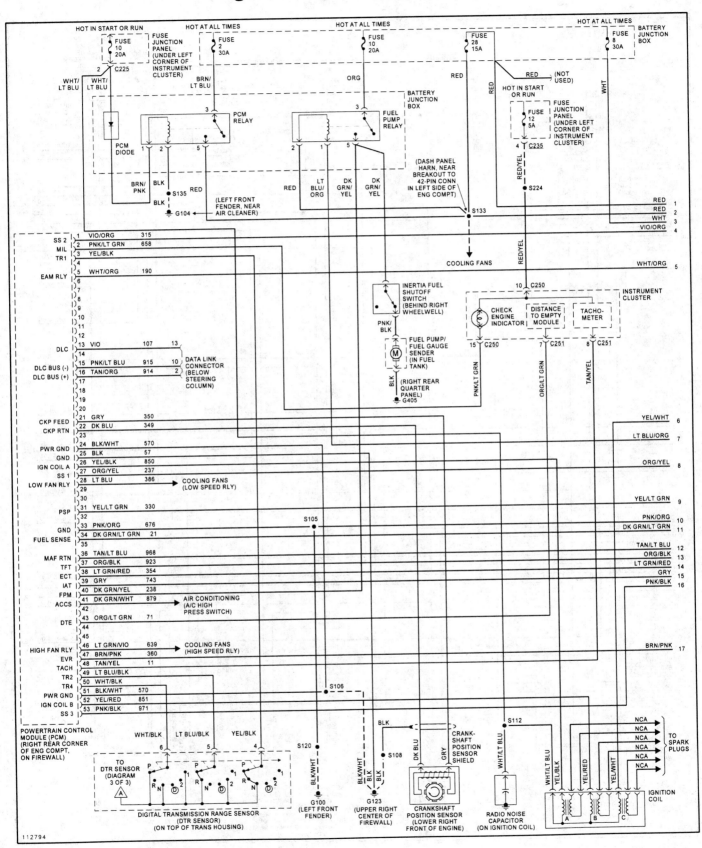

Fig. 131: Taurus (3.0L Flexible Fuel – 1 Of 3)

112794

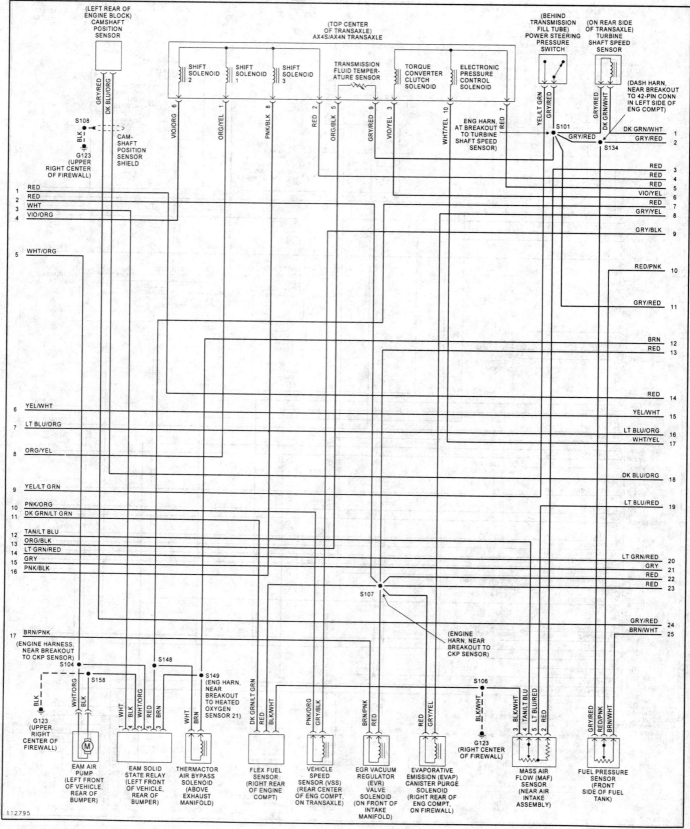

Fig. 132: Taurus (3.0L Flexible Fuel – 2 Of 3)

1999 WIRING DIAGRAMS
Engine Performance (Cont.)

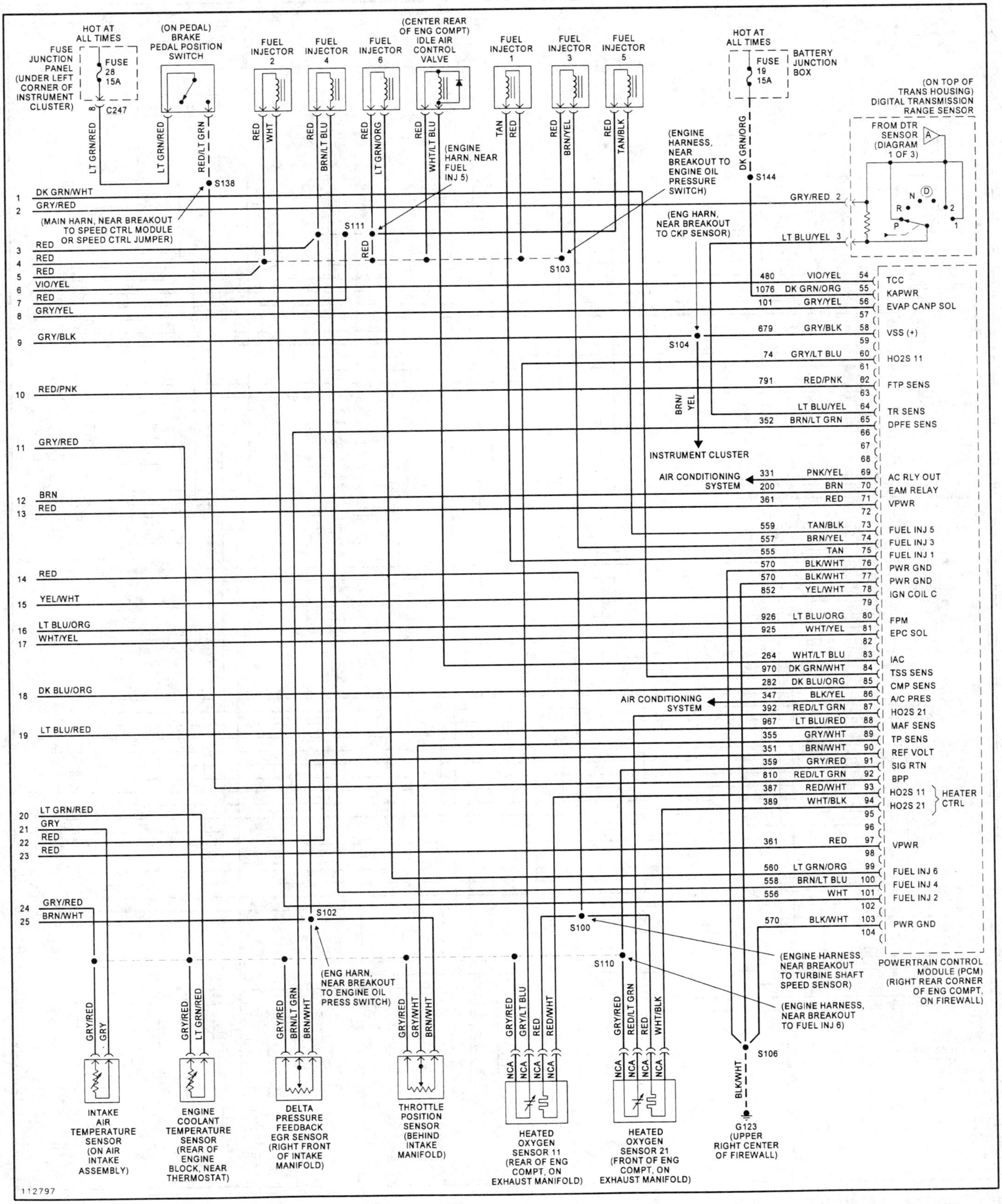

Fig. 133: Taurus (3.0L Flexible Fuel – 3 Of 3)

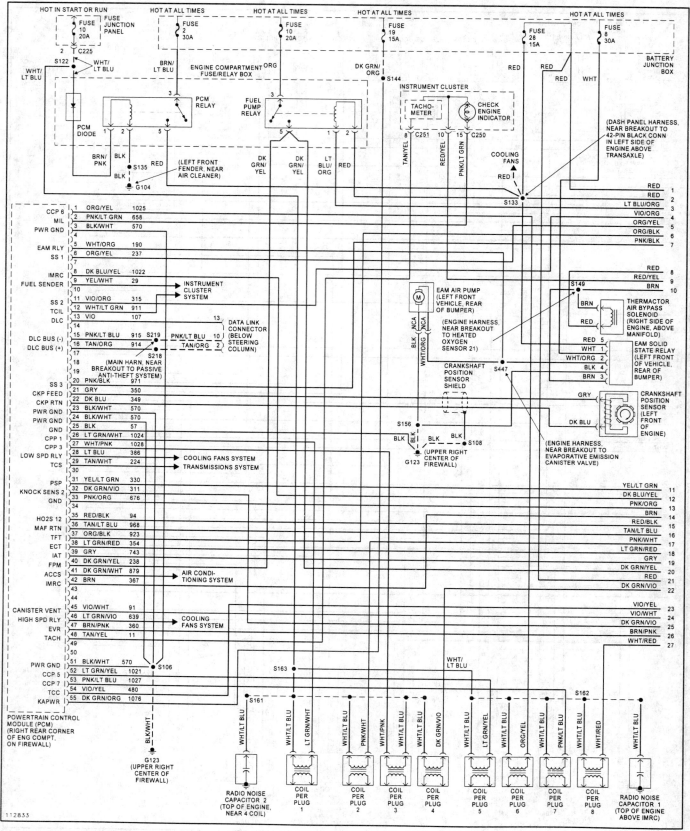

Fig. 134: Taurus (3.4L SHO – 1 Of 3)

112833

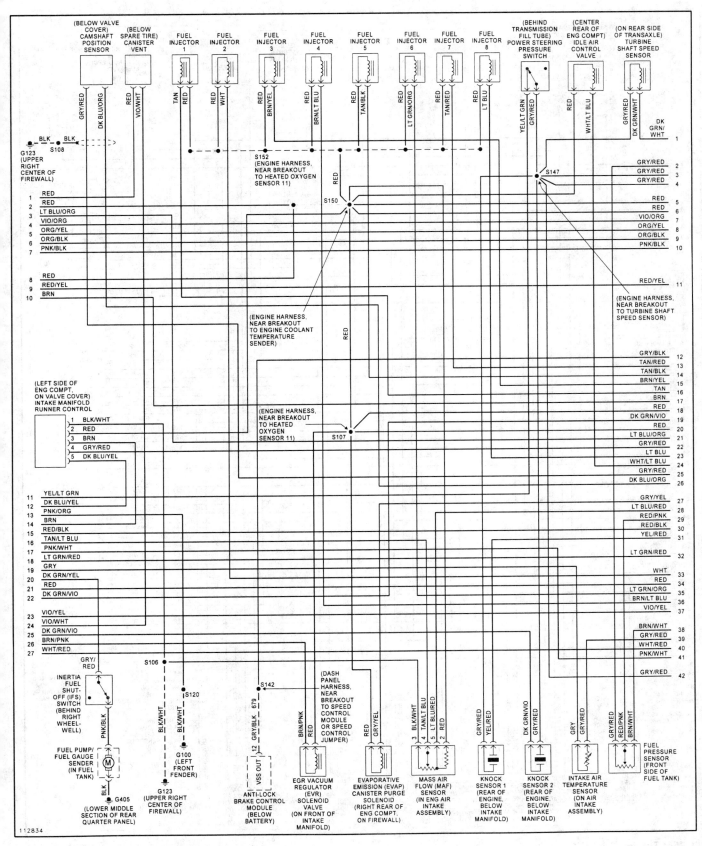

Fig. 135: Taurus (3.4L SHO – 2 Of 3)

112834

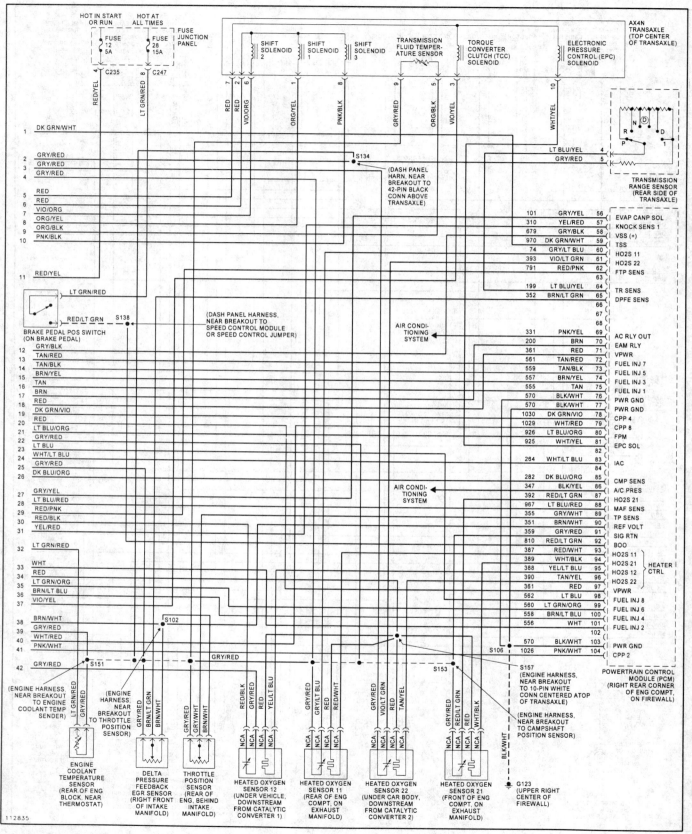

Fig. 136: Taurus (3.4L SHO – 3 Of 3)

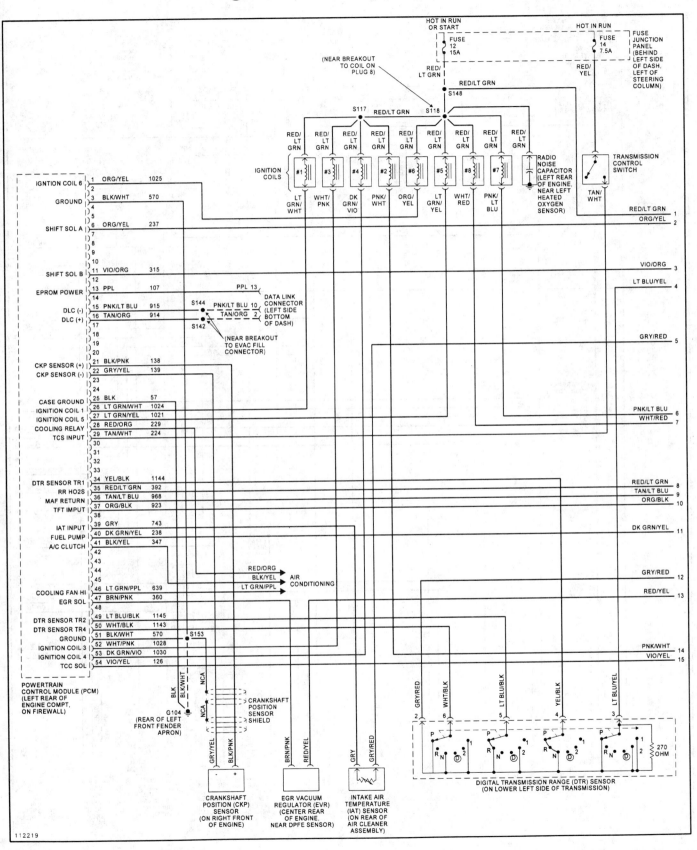

Fig. 137: Town Car (4.6L – 1 Of 3)

112219

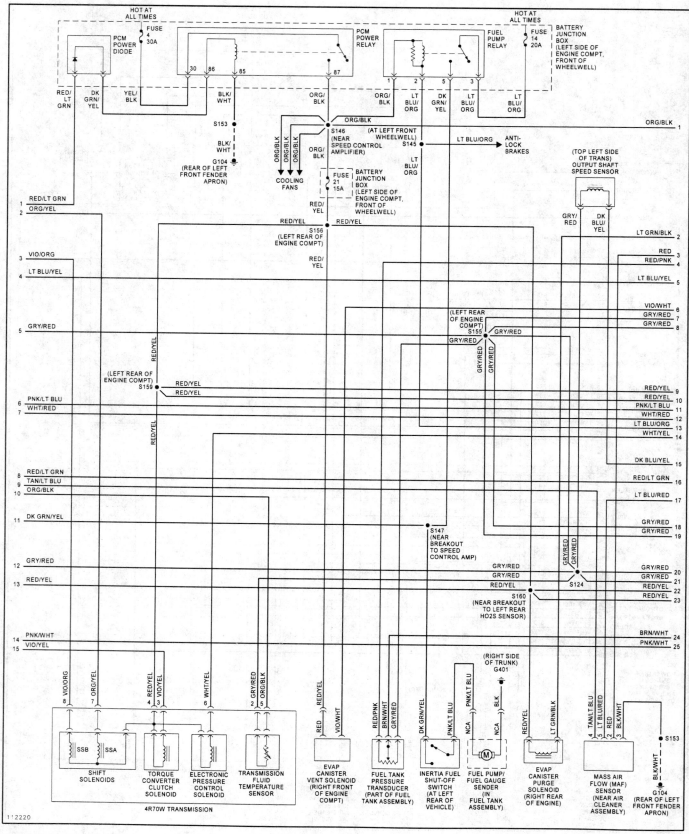

Fig. 138: Town Car (4.6L – 2 Of 3)

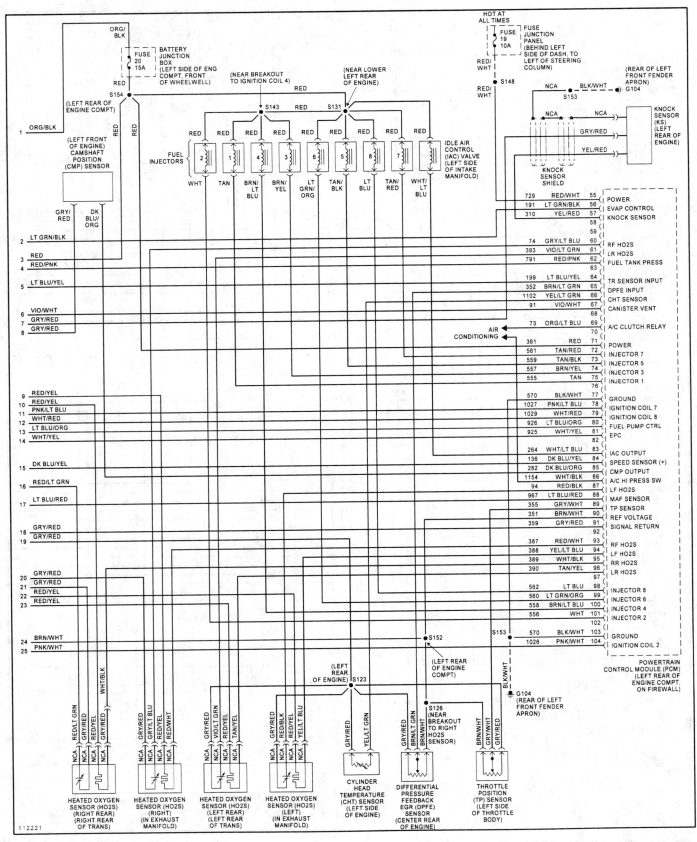

Fig. 139: Town Car (4.6L – 3 Of 3)

EVAP CANISTER PURGE VALVE (ON RIGHT SIDE OF ENGINE)

BATTERY JUNCTION BOX (LEFT FRONT OF ENG COMPT)

HOT AT ALL TIMES

FUSE 6 10A

POWERTRAIN CONTROL MODULE (PCM) POWER RELAY (BEHIND RIGHT SIDE OF DASH)

HOT IN START

FUSE 38 7.5A

HOT IN START OR RUN

FUSE 54 10A

FUSE JUNCTION PANEL (BEHIND DASH, LEFT OF STEERING COLUMN)

(CENTER REAR OF ENGINE) MANIFOLD ABSOLUTE PRESSURE (MAP)/ BAROMETRIC PRESSURE (BARO) SOLENOID

GRN/BLK
BLK/WHT
RED
RED
WHT/GRN
RED
BLK/WHT
BLU/BLK
BLU/YEL

S112

S238 (WITH DRL)

SPEED SIGNAL OUTPUT

INSTRUMENT CLUSTER

PNK
BLU/YEL

6 C267A (ELECTRONIC)
4 C266B (ANALOG)

Pin	Name	Wire	Code
1	PWR TRANS	BLU	AV01
2	RES INPUT	WHT	AV98
3	RPM	GRN/WHT	AV02
4	PCMR	WHT/GRN	AV04
5	EVAP VALVE	GRN/BLK	AW18
6			
7	TCM	GRN/BLK	AV56
8	I/P MP	ORG/BLK	AV05
9	ACDPS	BLU/BLK	HX01
10	GND	BLK	EP06
11	FPR	BLU/RED	AV54
12	A/C RELAY	LT GRN	HA41
13			
14			
15			
16			
17	DIAG CONN	BLU/WHT	AV23
18	MIL	VIO	NR01
19	GND	BLK	EP13
20	ST SIG	BLU/BLK	AV34
21	ACDPS	WHT/RED	HA45
22	TCM	GRY/RED	ZY13
23	TP	RED	AV20
24	TCM	GRN/WHT	AV57
25	TCM	WHT	AV58
26	TP SWITCH	BRN/YEL	AV33
27	VSS	GRN/YEL	AV32
28			
29	HFAN 2 RLY	WHT	AV58
30	HFAN 1 RLY	GRN/YEL	AV61
31	TCM	PNK/BLK	AV61
32	HFAN1/FAN2 RY	PNK/BLK	AV61
33	TCM (TP)	RED/GRN	AV34
34	HFAN 1 RLY	BLU/RED	AW17
35	PSP	PNK	AV12
36			
37			
38	IGN	BLU/YEL	AV36
39	GND	BLK/RED	ES39
40	CMP SENSOR	WHT	AV22
41	MAP/BARO	PNK	AW25
42			
43	CKP	LT GRN	AV09
44			
45	GND	BLK/RED	ES48
46	CMP SENSOR	WHT	AV30
47	CMP SENSOR	ORG	AV31
48	HO2S	LT GRN	AV19 (OR AW30)
49			
50			
51			

W/ ELECTRONIC CLUSTER

INSTRUMENT CLUSTER

GRN/WHT

BLU/BLK
WHT/RED

AIR CONDITIONING SYSTEM

LT GRN

S219

BLK

GRN/YEL
GRN/YEL
S255 (BEHIND CENTER OF DASH)

TRANSMISSION SYSTEM

(BEHIND TOP CENTER OF DASH)

GRN/YEL
S254

CRUISE CONTROL SYSTEM

GRN/YEL

BLU 1
WHT 2
BLU/RED 3
BLK/YEL 4

BLK/YEL 5
BLU/WHT 6
VIO 7

BLK/WHT 8
BLK/WHT 9

BLK/YEL 10

WHT COOLING FANS SYSTEM
GRN/YEL
PNK/BLK
BLU/RED

WHT/PNK 11
BLU/YEL 12
BLU/YEL 13

S242
BLU/YEL (BEHIND TOP CENTER OF DASH)

NCA

(BEHIND TOP CENTER OF DASH)
BLU/YEL S241
BLU/YEL

NCA

BLK/YEL 14
PNK 15
LT GRN 16
PNK 17

WHT

S108

BLK/RED
WHT
S222

WHT WHT
S265

PNK 18
WHT 19
ORG 20

BLU/YEL
BLU/YEL
S1002 (TOP LEFT SIDE OF ENG COMPT)

BLU/YEL 21
BLU/YEL 22
BRN 23

POWERTRAIN CONTROL MODULE (PCM) (BEHIND RIGHT SIDE OF DASH, BEHIND GLOVE BOX)

TRANSMISSION SYSTEM

(NEAR TRANS)

(BEHIND TOP RIGHT SIDE OF DASH)

S110

BLK/RED

G134 (TOP OF ENGINE)

LT GRN/RED 24

Pin	Name	Wire	Code
17	TP IN	RED/GRN	AV34
18	PSG	BLK/YEL	ZY35
8	TP REF	BRN	ZY31

C277B

Pin	Name	Wire	Code
16	TP SWITCH	BRN/YEL	AV33
7	PCM	PNK/BLK	AV61
17	WOT IN	RED/WHT	ZY21
6	PCM	WHT	AV58
5	PCM	GRN/WHT	AV57
15	PCM	GRN/BLK	AV56
14	PCM	GRY/RED	ZY13

C277A

TRANSAXLE CONTROL MODULE (TCM) (BEHIND INSTRUMENT PANEL)

BLK/RED
BLK/RED
S278

BRN/YEL

BRN/YEL S134
(CENTER REAR OF ENG COMPT)

BRN
S2036 (BEHIND LEFT SIDE OF DASH)

BRN 25

BRN

BRN
BRN
S277 (RIGHT SIDE OF ENG COMPT)

BRN 26

BLK/YEL
WHT/PNK
BLK/YEL
LT GRN/RED
BLK/YEL
RED
BRN
S2037 (LEFT REAR SIDE OF ENG COMPT)

BRN/YEL
BLK/RED
S108
NCA
BLK/RED
BLK/RED
LT GRN
BRN/YEL
BLU/YEL
RED/WHT

BLK

G134 (TOP OF ENGINE)

CRANKSHAFT POSITION (CKP) SENSOR (BELOW DISTRIBUTOR)

THROTTLE POSITION SWITCH (ON THROTTLE BODY)

EGR TEMPERATURE SENSOR (ON UNDERSIDE OF THROTTLE BODY)

ENGINE COOLANT TEMPERATURE (ECT) SENSOR (ON LEFT REAR OF ENGINE)

THROTTLE POSITION (TP) SENSOR (ON THROTTLE BODY ASSEMBLY)

112215

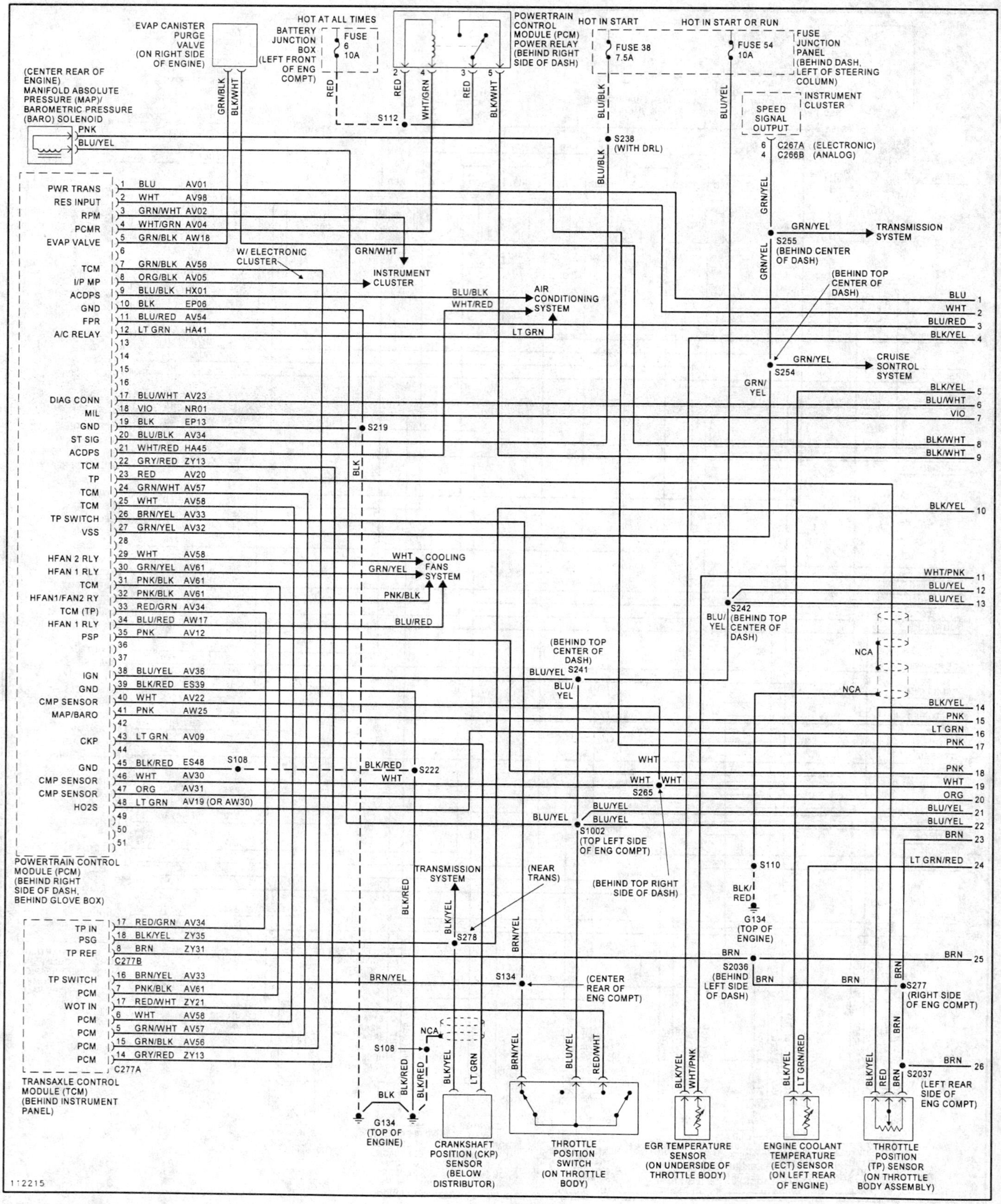

Fig. 140: Villager (3.3L – 1 Of 3)

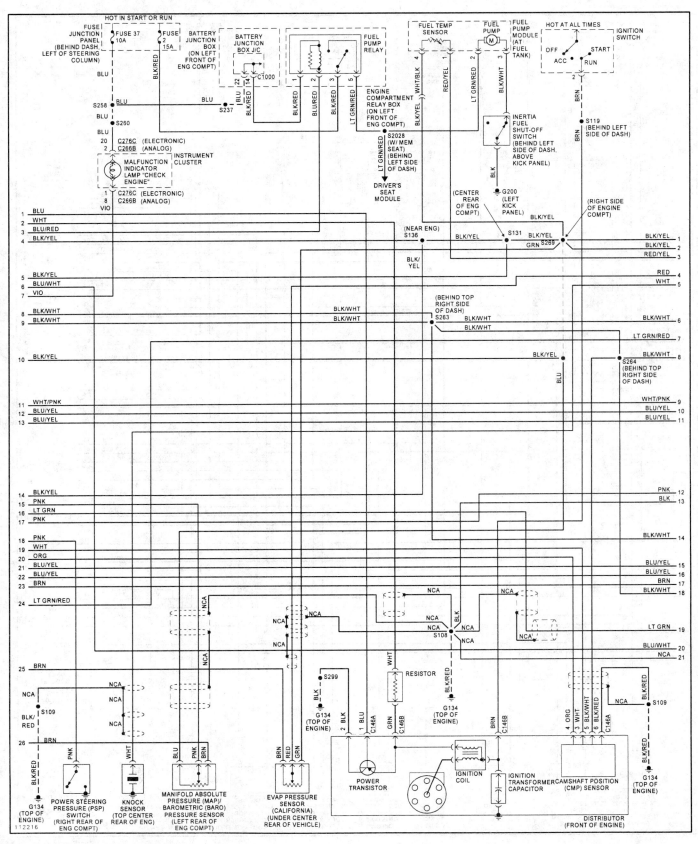

Fig. 141: Villager (3.3L – 2 Of 3)

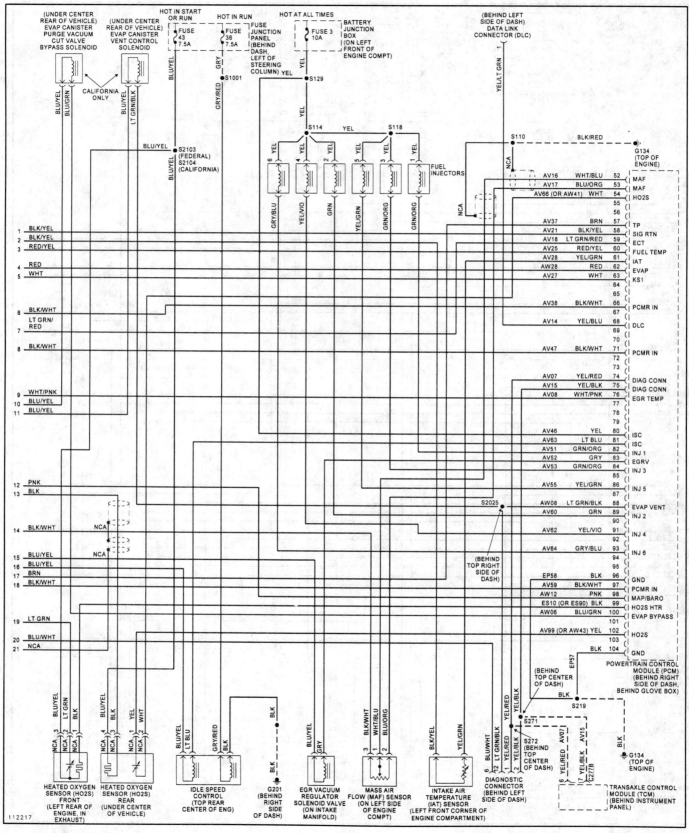

Fig. 142: Villager (3.3L – 3 Of 3)

112217

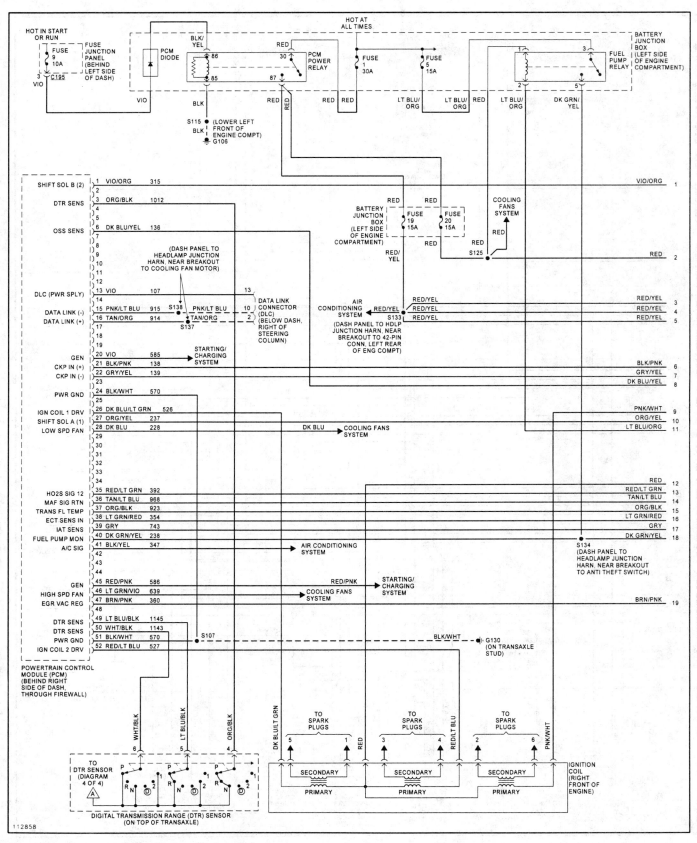

Fig. 143: Windstar (3.0L – 1 Of 4)

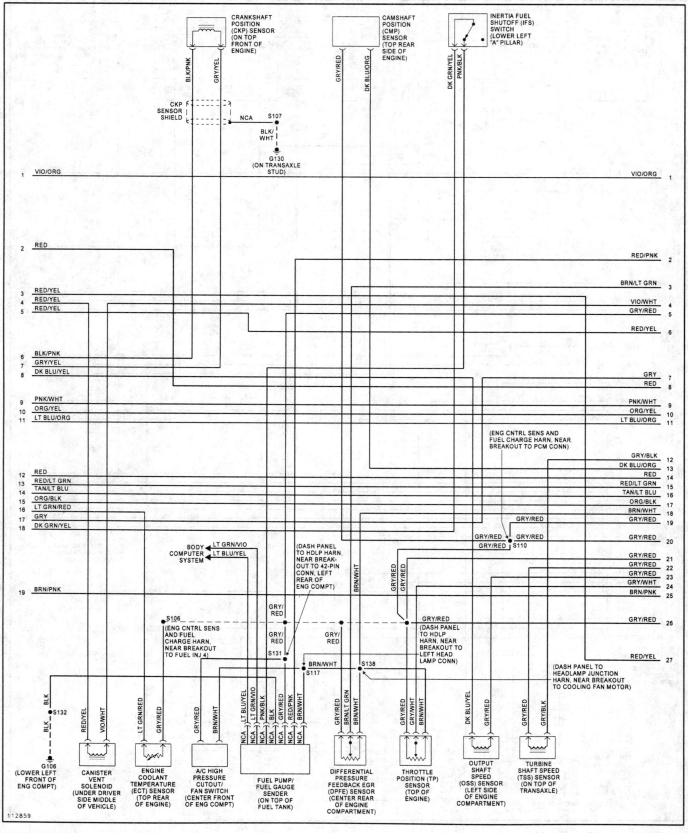

Fig. 144: Windstar (3.0L – 2 Of 4)

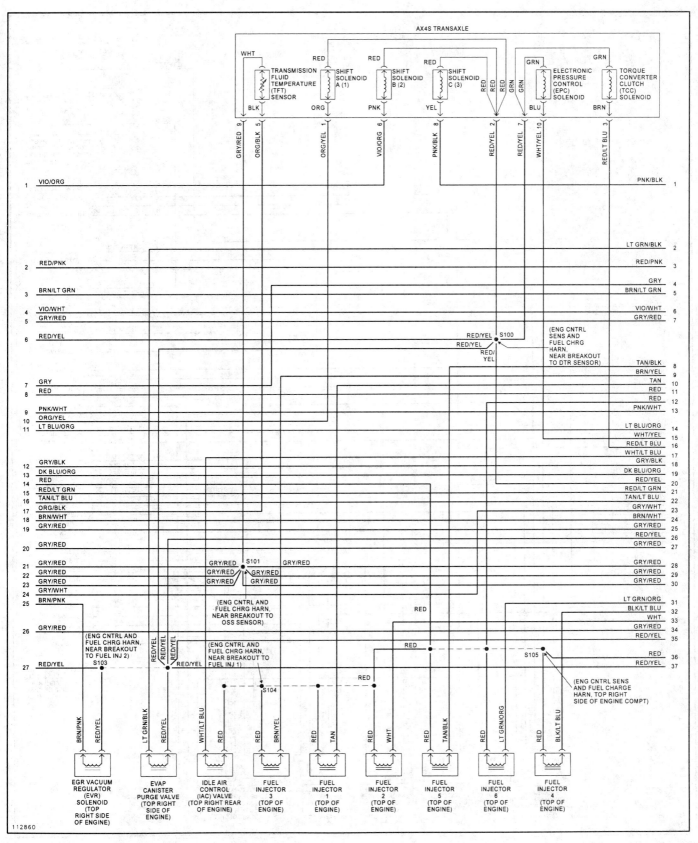

Fig. 145: Windstar (3.0L – 3 Of 4)

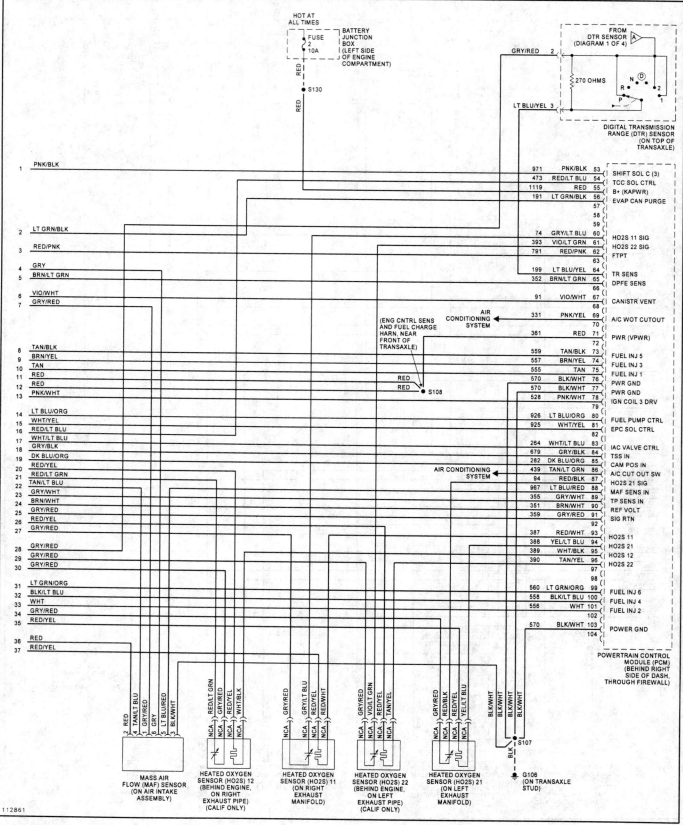

Fig. 146: Windstar (3.0L – 4 Of 4)

112861

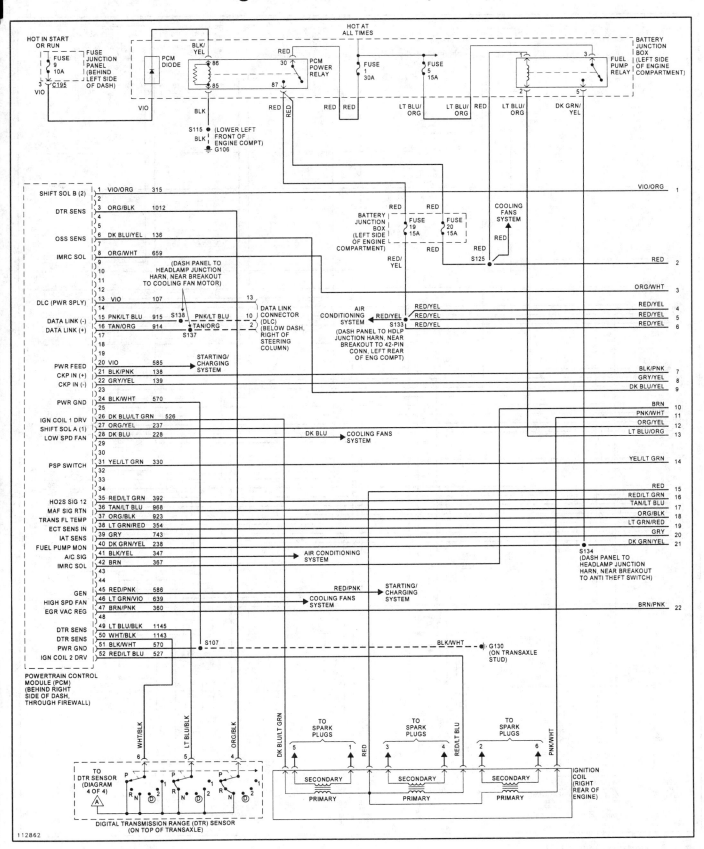

Fig. 147: Windstar (3.8L – 1 Of 4)

112862

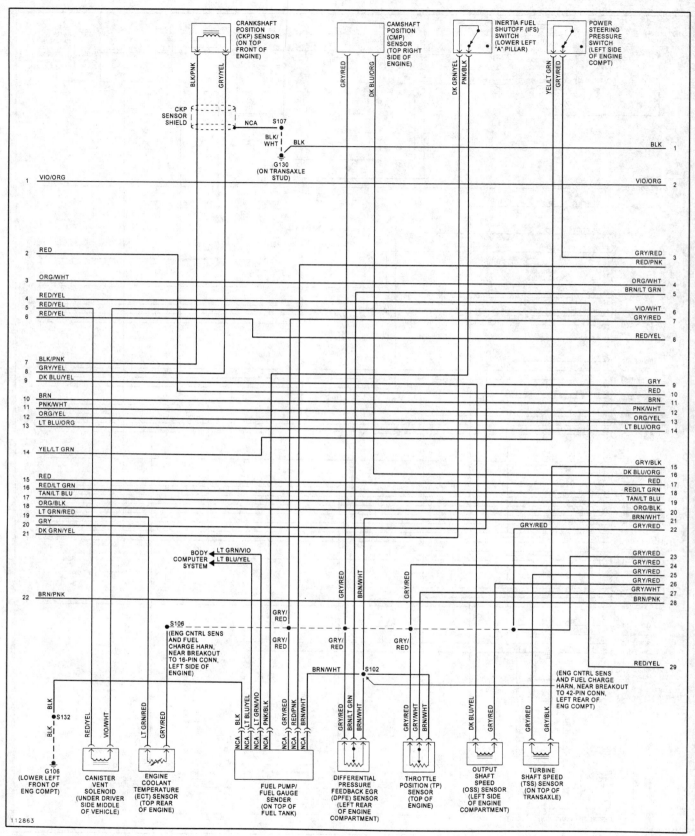

Fig. 148: Windstar (3.8L – 2 Of 4)

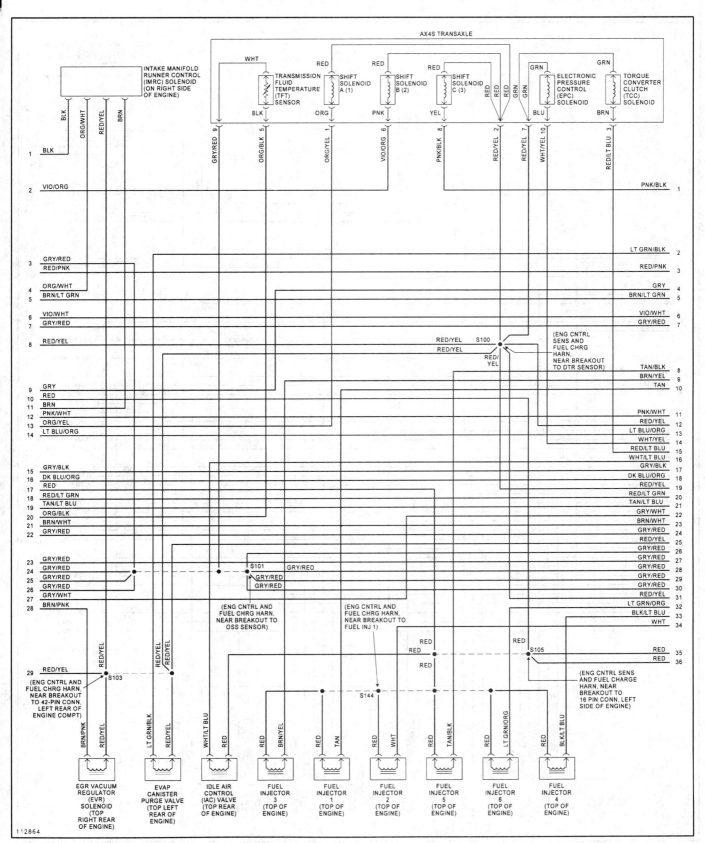

Fig. 149: Windstar (3.8L – 3 Of 4)

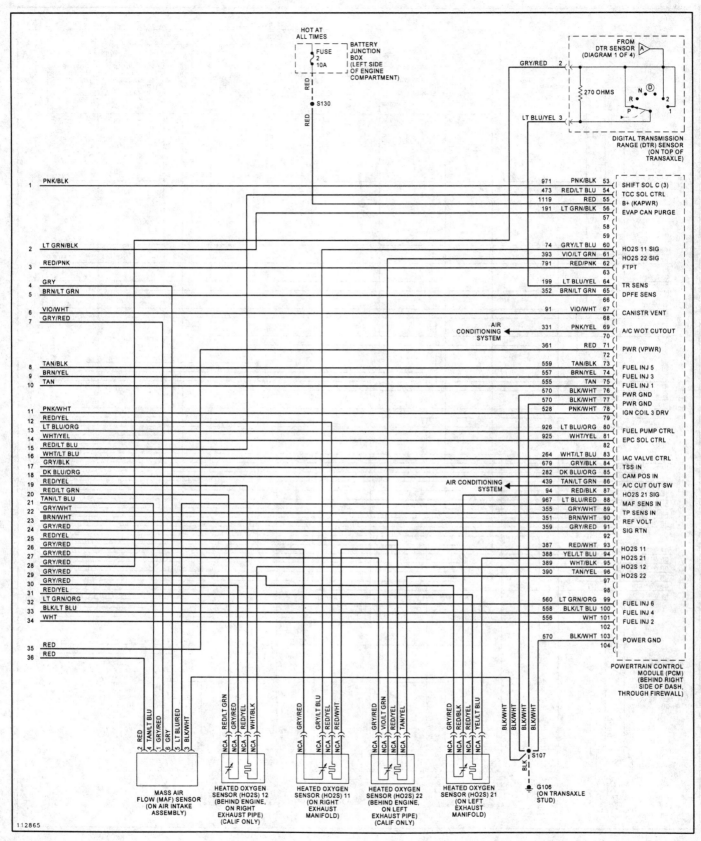

Fig. 150: Windstar (3.8L – 4 Of 4)